Jazz-Rock

Jazz-Rock

A History

Stuart Nicholson

Discography by Jon Newey

CANONGATE

First published in Great Britain in 1998 by
Canongate Books Ltd
14, High Street
Edinburgh EH1 1TE

British Library Cataloguing-in-Publication Data
A catalogue record for this book is available
upon request from the British Library

ISBN 0 86241 817 8

Printed in the United States of America
Bound in Great Britain by The Cromwell Press

To the beautiful Irene and Jim

Contents

Inamorata

... tomorrow's unknown, known life ... I love tomorrow!
—*Conrad Roberts, from Miles Davis's* Live-Evil

At the end of the 1960s, everything was a struggle, whether it was political or economic, social or individual, armed or unarmed. The common thread that ran through it all was the struggle to redefine and reimage your existence—to reject the stereotypes and distortions of the oppressors (the usual government thugs, racists, religious fanatics, bloated critics, and the like) in favor of literally changing reality. Change on this radical a scale could only be realized through the struggle to describe the past and present in a new, inventive, creative, and totally uncompromising language.

With music, and especially with what up until this point had been called "jazz," change is inevitable, and always *necessary*. "Jazz," as a word, can only really hurt creative musicians, and it will only protect musicians who aren't feeling so bad about representing the past in the restricted image of the jazz tradition, or about being supported by the shadow system of commercial and critical acclaim that the music "industry" perpetuates. Ultimately, for anyone creative, or inspired, or forward-thinking, or politically conscious, or just fed up, there is no satisfaction in being labeled and conveniently categorized and maintained by an oppressive apparatus like a record company. Artists like Miles Davis and Tony Williams (with his own group Lifetime, which he formed during his tenure with Miles) understood this. Beginning around 1968, they began moving away from points known within their spheres of musical subsistence—in the sense that at the time playing "jazz" allowed you to *subsist* and barely more than that—and into the unknown, into a space that had never before been occupied by the kind of energy, information, and music they were preparing to deliver.

Miles was turning his full attention to popular black music—especially Sly Stone's acid funk and Jimi Hendrix's psychedelic blues-rock—and while blending these influences with the mode and meter of other styles like African and Indian music, he was transposing the energy of rock and funk into electrified jazz. Miles gave a lot of freedom to his musicians once they were past a certain point; in terms of pitch, rhythm, and harmonics, everything evolved as sound because most of it wasn't fixed, because it came from different areas—all of which already constitutes an originality. Tony Williams was after a similar structure, but Lifetime was more of a playing experience on equal terms—a small group, a trio in which everyone had a kind of independence that allowed an adventurous exploration of extreme creativity. It was the music, not merely its packaging and technology, that was new.

These were artists who wanted to expand, to travel, to collaborate, to experience. To do that, they had to get out of the trap of representing the tradition of what was then called "jazz." The result was given the name of "fusion," which has its own bad connotations today, but back in the 1960s roads were opening up. Free jazz of the early 1960s had been an agent of evolution, and new directions were arising from different forms of music and cultural pressures. The real question was about the value of technique—free jazz players often felt this was an obstacle to feeling, and they favored pure improvisation and unbridled expression over technical virtuosity (though certainly innovators like John Coltrane and Ornette Coleman are masters of both). The new musicians, on the other hand, embraced technique, and along with it jazz widened its landscape to include influences it encountered around the world—rock, classical, and other traditional forms of music.

Unfortunately it was the growing obsession with technique, along with the efforts of record companies to co-opt, colonize, and control, that helped to assassinate the promise of fusion. By the mid-1970s the music had lost most of its spirit of presence, integrity, and commitment (with some exceptions, like John McLaughlin's group Shakti, among others). It seemed as though the initial surge of energy attached to the work of Miles and others at the time had overwhelmed people's perceptions; they couldn't imagine music like this, with all of it happening so very quickly and all at once. When something messes up your head, one reaction is to seek out what's more pragmatic and more thought-out—more technique-oriented, more rule-oriented, more grounded, more careful. This made fusion less psychedelic and less energized, and the music soon lost the mystery that had been at the center of what made it interesting. Fusion had started as a music of revolt—just as all movements in black music have started—until eventually it was transformed by indulgent and strictly outside forces into a repetitive commodity.

But energy doesn't operate under the laws of time. Fusion may appear to have surfaced for an instant and then just as quickly disappeared, but in reality everything is always a fusion of something. That energy still exists and is not only being absorbed and maintained but is constantly evolving—all that's necessary is the desire to look for it. There are records being created or even reconstructed today that strive for and successfully capture this intensity; I've been fortunate enough to experience it firsthand with Tony Williams in a group project called Arcana, and for a remix project focusing on Miles Davis's studio work from the early 1970s. Artists like Ornette Coleman, Graham Haynes, Talvin Singh, Jah

Wobble, James Blood Ulmer, Henry Threadgill, Trilok Gurtu, Carlinhos Brown, and others have also taken the original ideas of fusion into even further sonic territory, suggesting infinite paths for musical exploration of the future.

Up to now, it seems the later generations of musicians and listeners may have grown steadily disappointed by the crumbling of revolutionary ideologies and the apparent exhaustion of the avant-garde. But great tools take much time to be manufactured; the great tone is the tone that goes beyond all usual imagination. Recovering what we can from the ruins of the original hybrid of funky rhythms, psychedelic electronics, and jazz musicianship, we can help the next generation to learn from past mistakes. This is our legacy, and we have no choice but to see it put into action.

—Bill Laswell
mixed and mastered by Bill Murphy, Axiom Records
September 1997, New York City

Preface

With a new chic based on old brand names, jazz by the end of the 1980s had become self-satisfied. By the end of the 1990s it had become cocooned in establishment paranoia, disguised, as are many elements in our society, as tradition. Definitions of what jazz was and what it was not had begun to fill the air—if it had this, this, and this, it was jazz, but if it had that, it wasn't. Usually, whoever was doing the defining put themselves at the center of the action. It was all beginning to sound a little like Humpty Dumpty in *Alice through the Looking Glass*: "When I use a word," he said, "It means just what I choose it to mean." The problem was that the people doing the defining wanted jazz to be what it used to be, not what it is.

This book is one voice raised in protest, although it didn't start out that way. For some time I had been thinking about writing an overview of the main developments in jazz during the 1970s, a companion, in fact, to my first book, *Jazz: The 1980s Resurgence*. When I finally got to putting some ideas on paper about what I wanted to do, I realized that no serious study of jazz-rock had been written. The more I thought about it, the more jazz-rock seemed to be crying out to be documented, not only during the 1970s, but during the 1960s and, in terms of both its influence and its various configurations, into the 1980s and 1990s as well.

Given that definitions are always limiting, (I had wanted to call the book *Running the Voodoo Down*, but was assured nobody would know what I was talking about), I have stuck to the old-fashioned term jazz-rock because first of all I liked it, and secondly I wanted to make a distinction between it and fusion (and its latter-day equivalents, variously marketed as smooth jazz, quiet storm, lite-jazz, hot tub jazz, or yuppie jazz). Also, since there isn't a term that sensibly describes contemporary jazz empowered by the spirit of the early jazz-rock experimenters such as Tony Williams, Miles Davis, Jimi Hendrix, Mike Nock, Joe Zawinul, and Wayne Shorter, music that Jack DeJohnette once called "multi-dimensional," jazz-rock seemed as good a generic catch-all as any. I hope the musicians I have scooped up in the later chapters of this book illustrate this and how, without the legacy of jazz-rock, their music might not have had certain characteristics that made them stand out as the 1980s and 1990s progressed.

As this book is completed, jazz-rock has been with us for a period roughly equivalent to that between Louis Armstrong's solo on "Weather Bird" to Ornette Coleman's album *The Shape of Jazz to Come*. Thirty years is a long time in the history of jazz, yet jazz-rock still remains an enormously controversial sub-ject, not least because it has become increasingly perceived in terms of the com-mercial excesses of fusion. Indeed, the specter of fusion has grown so large, pri-marily through commercial FM radio, that today it fills the viewfinder, blotting out jazz-rock and distorting its achievements. In responding to commercial logic, fusion all but turned an art form back into a commodity by allowing itself to be shaped by the requirements of the marketplace. And as we all know, commercial radio gravitates to where the money is and the money is generated by whatever sells advertising. Fusion happened to click with the right money demographic, the 25 to 52-year-olds, and now there are almost two hundred New Adult Contemporary radio stations across the country specializing in formatting fusion with high rotation playlists often put together by market research firms specializ-ing in "audience testing" to ensure recordings are "selected on the basis of the broadest possible appeal" (i.e., the lowest common denominator).

Consequently jazz-rock has fallen into critical disfavor over the last decade to the extent that it has become fashionable to write off the whole genre because of fusion—a classic case of throwing the baby out with the bath water. Yet no-one would consider evaluating the Swing Era (which raises many similar issues posed by jazz-rock) in terms of Guy Lombardo, Glenn Miller, Kay Kyser, Blue Barron, Jan Garber, Art Kassel, Tommy Tucker, Gus Arnheim, Abe Lyman, Fred Waring, or Anson Weeks. Yet this is precisely the situation in jazz-rock; too often it is perceived in terms of artists like Kenny G, Najee, The Yellow Jackets, Spyro Gyra, the Rippingtons, Dave Sanborn, Kirk Whalum, Grover Washington, and George Benson at the expense of performances that matter.

The other impediment to a more widespread acceptance of jazz-rock has been the emergence in recent years of a "jazz canon" and the argument that denies the "jazz tradition" is a tradition of change. Yet the whole culture of jazz is based on change because that is the culture of the United States. If a product or enterprise does not keep reinventing itself, it is swept aside by something newer, bigger, and better. And if you doubt the speed of change, take a look around you: half of all the offices and malls standing in America have been built since 1980. The speed of change in the United States is dazzling, and that has been reflected in jazz—as any cursory listening to recordings from the Original Dixieland Jazzband's "Darktown Strutter's Ball," cut in January 1917, to the pre-sent day will reveal. To stop the clock in the 1990s and reinvent jazz as a para-digm of the 1950s and early 1960s runs counter to the culture from which it has emerged.

To me, jazz is an inclusive music that not only allows, but demands individu-ality and new concepts. To define jazz in terms of its past is dangerous for the future of the music. It was attempted in the 1940s when swing, and later bebop, commanded the ire of the moldy figs. But despite their claims of authenticity, that the only true jazz was New Orleans jazz, the ship of jazz continued to sail serenely on, disregarding dissenting voices and taking what it wanted from popu-lar culture, most notably Broadway standards, but from other sources as well. For example, both W. C. Handy and Jelly Roll Morton made use of the "Spanish tinge," Dizzy Gillespie borrowed from the popular Latin band of Machito (through the influence of his former mentor Mario Bauza), John Coltrane used exotic scales from India and devices related to Indian music, Stan Getz subpoenaed the Brazilian bossa-nova and Gunther Schuller even combined jazz and classical music. Today we accept the results of these influences on their own terms. Thus when rock became such a powerful force in the 1960s, threatening the very future of jazz, why shouldn't jazz, with its usual pragmatism, fashion a rapprochement here as well?

As Bill Laswell points out in his foreword, change is not only inevitable, it is necessary. Jazz-rock renewed the cycle of change in jazz at the end of the 1960s, and it has continued to evolve during the 1980s and 1990s in a way that other areas of jazz, with just a couple of notable exceptions in free jazz, have not. What I hope to show is why jazz-rock was a logical step for jazz to have taken in the context of its time and then trace the music's main developments, for good or bad, into the 1990s, taking time off for an occasional detour here and there that I hope will interest open-eared jazz fans. The 1960s were the twentieth century's most famous era after the 1920s and if you were young, the pop star became even more seductive than the film stars idolized by previous generations. Their impact on jazz was traumatic. Almost a whole generation haemorrhaged to pop and rock and in the social context of the time, jazz-rock was not only inevitable, it was necessary for the music's survival. This was widely acknowledged and anticipated at the time, not least by sages such as Dan Morgenstern, Leonard Feather, Ralph J. Gleason, Michael Cuscuna and Richard Seidel. To understand this, it is necessary to understand something of the social and economic factors that prevailed in the late 1960s.

When jazz-rock emerged at the end of the 1960s it was the last coherent radical jazz movement (and the only movement in jazz where European jazz musicians played a major inceptive role). Some may be surprised, in the face of fusion, with my choice of the word "radical." However, while Max Harrison has pointed out that free jazz almost succeeded in creating a wholly independent musical language of its own, I would go a stage further and argue that jazz-rock was also on the verge of doing the same with albums such as Miles Davis's *Agharta*, but had its ambitions stifled through commercialism. But at least jazz-rock broadened the tonal palette of jazz using new electronic technology, swept asymmetrical time signatures from the margins into the mainstream, set in hand a widespread use of exotic scales and asymmetrical rhythms from other cultures to an extent that had not been common in jazz before and reaffirmed the importance of composition following free jazz.

In the text I cite examples of corporate advertising, since once the major recording companies got behind the jazz-rock concept, the marketing push they gave the music was influential in speeding its acceptance into the jazz mainstream. However, with the first wave of jazz-rock bands, the record industry was marketing authenticity. But as the jazz-rock bandwagon gained momentum, the majors seemed unaware that authenticity could not be manufactured. Artists had to have authenticity for themselves. But by the mid-1970s there were no more Miles Davises, Mahavishnu Orchestras, Weather Reports, or Tony Williams Lifetimes on the horizon and the initial impact of jazz-rock became undone by cynical exploitation, which, of course, is what the music business is about.

Taking a music from the margins, marketing and mainstreaming it for wide popular acceptance is a continuous cycle enacted in pop and rock. Once jazz-rock entered this marketing cycle it was inevitable that its early promise would quickly become a distant memory as the music was bleached and sanitized for the widest possible consumption. But if by the mid-1970s jazz-rock had become undone by the sirens of commerce, its early promise had by no means been exhausted. My point is that once the Rubicon was crossed, good old rock music of the 1960s was never enough. It inspired a search for new rhythms and electronic tone colors which mixed with combinations of existing knowledge became the legacy of jazz-rock that was with us in the 1990s and which I attempt to deal with in the final chapters.

Of course, there will be artists some may think should have included in a study such as this, while others may think X or Y should *never* have been included. Equally there will be those who think I should have given more space to A and less on B and so on—such are the perils of an undertaking such as this. All I would say is that this is a personal history of jazz-rock, and I have addressed issues which seem important to me to present a balanced overview of the music and its subsequent developments. The problem in such an undertaking as this is, of course, space. Even in this form the book has been edited down from my original manuscripts, so some harsh choices have been made on the way about who to include, who to leave out and the amount of space to devote to various participants as the story unfolds. Jon Newey's discography includes a diversity of records that range further than space considerations in the main text allows. Between the two, readers should get a good idea of what jazz-rock is all about, as well as a context in which to situate it in its times.

I hope this book will prompt interest in and discussion about an area of jazz that for too long has avoided serious study. Clearly it is impossible not to acknowledge how the commercial potential of a jazz-rock union was exploited, first by bands in the Blood, Sweat & Tears nexus and later by fusion, but then a history of big bands would have to grapple with a Glenn Miller or a Harry James, or a history of bebop a Charlie Ventura or a George Shearing. Jazz is seldom without those who remove its rough edges and serve it with sugar. However, my prime concern is with the jazz part of the jazz-rock equation, and the developments I chart are united by the common thread of the jazz improviser's impulse and electricity.

The book concludes mid-1997, after a period of uncertainty in jazz following its optimistic renewal in the 1980s. I think it is worth emphasizing that just because some major figure has not arrived of the sort that providentially provided a rallying point for the diatonic, chromatic, free and jazz-rock eras does not mean jazz stopped evolving in the mid-1970s. Jazz has always been inexorably linked to the social fabric from which it emerged and this is central to understanding jazz-rock as it is any other era of jazz. By the 1980s and 1990s the task of moving the music forward passed to a diversity of individual contributors, many of whom have found their way into the final chapter of this book. It was no coincidence that the socio-political changes wrought during the 1980s in Reagan's America and Thatcher's Britain moved significantly towards decentralisation and a society that extolled individuals taking on responsibility for their own destiny. "It seems to me there is a very profound reason why there are no great leaders anymore," wrote Laurens Van De Post, "It is because they are no longer needed. The message is clear . . . every man must be his own leader."

Jazz has finally became too broad and diverse to be changed by the revelations of one man, and this is something it has not yet come to terms with, both from a musical and marketing perspective. And because it has become so broad and diverse, it takes a courageous man to define it. For if history has taught us anything, it is that no sooner do you find a definition that suits jazz today than someone comes along tomorrow and makes nonsense of it.

Thankfully, many of the musicians in the 1980s and 1990s are marching to the sound of their individual drums, fashioning their own highly personal take on jazz. Taking what is available to them from the acoustic and electronic heritage of jazz and, in many cases, looking beyond jazz for inspiration (as all the greats have done in the past, the Ellingtons, the Gillespies, the Coltranes and the Colemans) they are producing music that is new, fresh, and vital that reflects its own time and not the values of previous generations, no matter how appealing it may be to bask in the reflected glory of one of jazz's great posthumous heros. This music is as valuable in its own way as the music the has gone before, simply because it has grown out of the music that has gone before it. Suddenly jazz is sounding dangerous and subversive again, a sure sign that it is alive and well.

During the preparation of the book, I was delighted to discover how many people thought an undertaking such as this was long overdue, and was flattered by the willing assistance of so many people to make it a reality. Several musicians who were around when the first rumblings of a jazz and rock union were beginning to be felt read through various versions of my manuscripts and commented accordingly, adding their own reminiscences, including Mike Nock, Gary Burton, Warren Bernhardt and Mike Mainieri. Other musicians who allowed me to interview them at length for the book included Keith Jarrett, Joe Zawinul, Charles Lloyd, and Ian Carr. To them all my sincere thanks for their generosity with the precious gift of time, good humor and patience in fielding my innumerable questions.

I am especially grateful to the enthusiasm of Bill Laswell for reading through the text and making suggestions and several timely corrections, for his foreword and for accommodating my requests for interviews into his busy schedule in airport lounges and from hotels as he traversed the globe. Thanks also to Janet for helping make this possible. Bill also introduced me to Alan Douglas, who subsequently read, corrected and provided much background information regarding the chapter on Jimi Hendrix and in particular, Hendrix's relationship with Miles Davis. For this my sincere thanks.

It was not only musicians who were so kind with their time and knowledge. Jon Newey, who in contributing his discography made several welcome suggestions and spotted several errors in various versions of the text that passed through his hands. I am grateful to Paul Wilson at the National Sound Archive of the British Museum for his enormous help, time, and trouble and for reading through various manuscripts and for his suggestions. Thanks also to Andrew Simon, Head of the Jazz Section at the National Sound Archive for his generous response to my last-minute plea for help, to Ken Jones at the National Jazz Archive at Loughton Library, and to the Institute of Jazz Studies, Rutgers. Steve Sanderson and Kerstan Mackness of New Note Records were unstinting in their help and enthusiasm, often going beyond the call of duty, for which my sincere thanks. Adam Sieff and Sharon Kelly of Sony Jazz afforded me every possible assistance with stunning speed and enthusiasm for which I will always be grateful. Also thanks to Richard Cook and Becky Stevenson of Verve, my good friends Marsha and Bob Dennis for all those cuttings, etc., Max Harrison, Charles Alexander, Loren Schoenberg and Jed Williams. I am very grateful to my editor, Richard Carlin, who made this project possible, for a wonderful job in editing my original manuscript—from which I learned much about the craft of writing. Thanks also to James Hatch, my production editor, for calmly pulling all the pieces together. Thanks to my Mother for her encouragement and to my brother Malcolm, a source of suggestions before, after, and during reading the manuscripts, for his work in putting together the entry on Frank Zappa and for his unfailing good humor, particularly when my inspiration was flagging. My wife Kath somehow put up with the long hours I had to put in to get the project completed and to her my love. Finally sincere thanks to my in-laws, Jim and Eileen, to whom this book is dedicated (who neither know nor care anything about jazz-rock) for a fund of vulgar—but extremely funny—jokes (Jim), videoing sundry events on the hapless Welsh rugby scene, nights at Earls and a zillion other kindnesses along the way. Finally, a very special thank you to my agent Mandy Little for her faith in me and for her hard work on my behalf. We'll get there in the end, Mandy, you'll see!

Stuart Nicholson
Woodlands St Mary
Berkshire, England

Jazz-Rock

A History

CHAPTER 1

Ticket to Ride

On February 1, 1964, the Beatles reached the top of the United States singles charts. The success of "I Want to Hold Your Hand" was the culmination of an energetic promotional campaign by Capitol records, who had finally convinced themselves they could reproduce British "Beatlemania" in the United States. Although no one knew it at the time, it was a curtain-raiser to a remarkable period in popular music history that would transform the music industry, a period that began with what became known as "the British Invasion." Only twice before had British singles topped *Billboard*'s sales charts; this time, however, something different was in the air.

Traditionally British acts had found it almost impossible to register any meaningful chart success in America while, in contrast, Britain was just one more territory where U.S. record stars were routinely expected to score. Britain's top pop artist of the early 1960s, Cliff Richard, had flopped in the U.S. despite several promotional tours, finding himself second or third on the bill to one-hit wonders like Frankie Avalon or Fabian. Just how poorly British artists were regarded in the U.S. is best illustrated by Capitol Records' refusal to handle the Beatles' first three singles, despite the fact that Capitol was a *subsidiary* of EMI, the British conglomerate for whom the Beatles recorded.[1]

Yet eight weeks after "I Want to Hold Your Hand" had topped the *Billboard* chart, the Beatles had claimed the top *five* spots, with a further seven singles poised to follow. In their slipstream, other British artists began to find their way onto the U.S. charts. Out of the blue, the American music business found itself watching its top acts knocked off the radio and out of the charts by British acts. And with the Beatles responsible for 60 percent of all singles sales between late February and early March in the U.S., a *Billboard* editorial quipped "Britain hasn't been as influential in America since 1775."

Musically, the Beatles were both a shock and a breath of fresh air to America. When they arrived on February 7, 1964, they were already selling records worldwide at a monthly rate of $1.2 million.[2] Greeted by mob scenes, their two performances at New York's Carnegie Hall had sold out well in advance, and when they appeared on *The Ed Sullivan Show* on February 9 they drew the largest viewing audience in the history of American television. When their first album was released, *Meet the Beatles,* it outsold their number-one single 3.6 million to 3.4 million, the first time ever an album had outsold its single counterpart.[3]

The Beatles' music, wildly eclectic, was uniquely their own. From American rock and roll they had absorbed the styles of Elvis Presley, Eddie Cochran, Jerry Lee Lewis, Buddy Holly, and Chuck Berry. Yet while big popular acts like Presley had been built around the cult of the individual—a "star" singer with backing musicians—the Beatles took their inspiration from groups like the Drifters, the Dominoes, and the Coasters, whose "group" concept meant that every member was an essential and equal part of the whole. Their love of black rhythm and blues, which they first heard as youngsters in Liverpool, was immediately apparent in their music, and a whole generation began to ask why it had ignored this music for so long. With a flair for writing great songs, a stage presentation that had its roots in the British musical hall tradition, plenty of style, and a certain rebel charm, they were without precedent in popular music.

With their arrival in the States, the headline writers had a field day: "NYC Crawling with Beatlemania," "Beatle Binge in LA," and "Chicago Flips Wig" were typical. Two weeks later, the story was "Beatle Business Booming But Blessings Mixed" when orders for Beatles merchandise ran at $50,000,000, briefly outstripping the supply of their Capitol recordings. By early April, *Billboard* had decided, "Just about everyone is tired of the Beatles—except the listening and buying public." Overnight, every British chart contender was rushing to cash in on the Beatles' American success. Bands like the Dave Clark Five, the Searchers, Peter and Gordon, and—after several flops—Gerry and the Pacemakers all had important U.S. hits during 1964. Other British acts, like the Yardbirds, the Animals, and the Hollies, and the one-hit wonders Billy J. Kramer and Freddie and the Dreamers took a little longer but eventually broke in the U.S. later in the year. The Rolling Stones, with an image of rebelliousness that parents loved to hate, gradually developed an enormous following.[4]

Although legend has it that the British Invasion changed pop history forever, the full force of the Invasion lasted only a few months. By 1965, the top-selling group was The Supremes, even though U.K. bands had occupied the charts for seven months of the year. In fact, the magic of the British accent had long passed by the end of 1964, when groups could no longer hint they might have once visited Liverpool. America's response was spearheaded by the Byrds and Bob Dylan, whose "protest" songs broke record company taboos about dealing with controversial subjects, countering the Beatles' "Yeh, yeh, yeh" with "No, no, no." By then, rock and roll, that straightforward, unambitious consumer product of the 1950s, had metamorphosed into something more experimental, less categorizable, called rock.

With a billion-dollar gross for the industry looming in 1966, NBC TV took the unprecedented step of building a comedy series around a Beatles-like group called The Monkees, targeting it at an audience that could no longer be ignored, girls between nine and twelve. Although they only represented 6 percent of the U.S. population, they had spent 56.3 percent of the entire $650 million paid for recorded music in 1963 alone.[5] Initially, The Monkees existed only on the film set. Two of them could not play musical instruments, while Mike Nesmith and Peter Tork, the two "musicians" in the group, were not even *allowed to* play. Their first single, "Last Train from Clarksville," was released to coincide with their initial telecast and immediately hit the number-one spot with sales of over a million, selling a further two million units by the end of the year.

Meanwhile, in California the new music scene was about to explode. One weekend in June 1967 in a field near Monterey, California, eleven hundred of the world's media people gathered to witness the greatest rock extravaganza ever. A hundred thousand orchids were flown in from Hawaii and scattered among the huge crowds, while on-stage, banks of loudspeakers roared the new, revolutionary sound that would echo around the world. Clive Davis, the newly appointed chief executive of Columbia Records, was overwhelmed with what he saw. "It was the first time artists could just come on-stage and play for thousands of young people," he said. "I realized that this was a time for me to step forward and make my creative mark and sign up some of these wonderful new artists."[6] Among those he signed that year were Janis Joplin, Spirit, and Blood, Sweat & Tears, which represented something of an about-face for a label that had relied on a strict middle-of-the-road philosophy dictated since the early 1950s by the ubiquitous Mitch Miller.

Columbia were not alone in reacting to prevailing market forces. The hunt was on by all record companies to sign up new rock talent. As the music business found itself riding a huge boom, there was an excitement in the air that was not entirely driven by financial considerations. New areas of popular music were opening up to a young generation that was the most prosperous and uninhibited ever, receptive to the electronic sounds, thrusting rhythms, and flamboyant stars of rock. Around the music grew a media machine that created its own aristocracy for audiences measured in the millions. New entrepreneurs were entering the music business and surrounding themselves with young people doing a multitude of chores, including record production. The whole culture of the music industry was being transformed, and fast.

Although several older forms of American music had combined in its gestation, rock's origins lay primarily in the musical culture of black America. But while it drew heavily on the blues, it also drew on the white tradition of country music. Its early history was a confluence of these idioms: of white guitar players from Kentucky listening to records of the Delta bluesmen; of gospel and bluegrass; of western swing bands combining country music with jazz and blues; of Big Bill Broonzy, T-Bone Walker, and Chuck Berry; of the boogie-woogie craze of the 1940s; of big bands like Lionel Hampton—"I think I was the first to bring all that music from the Holiness Church, the beat, the hand clapping, the shouting, into the band business, when rock and roll came in they took a lot of things from us"[7]—and of jump bands like those led by Louis Jordan, one of Decca's best-selling "Race" artists between the late 1940s and early 1950s. When Jordan's "Blue Light Boogie" was topping the rhythm and blues charts in 1950, Tennessee Ernie Ford was hitting number one in the country charts with "Shotgun Boogie."

In 1951, cowboy-styled Bill Haley and his Saddlemen began covering black R&B numbers; by 1952, his renamed "Comets" were doing numbers like "Rock the Joint." Despite lingering western swing touches, rock and roll was on its way when Haley covered Joe Turner's "Shake Rattle and Roll." Although this was a second-rate cover version of Turner's hit, to white teenage audiences fed on sentimental trivia by artists like Eddie Fisher, Patti Page (of the ghastly "How Much Is that Doggie in the Window?" fame), the Four Aces, Rosemary Clooney, and Teresa Brewer, Haley was new, raw, and exciting, and his use of "hip" asides like "Crazy, man, crazy" clicked with white urban youth.

In the wake of the storm caused by the film *The Blackboard Jungle,* which used rock to symbolize adolescent rebellion, and Haley's hit number from it, "Rock Around the Clock," record companies began the search for new rock and roll signings. In January 1956 Elvis Presley cut his first recordings for RCA. Within a month "Heartbreak Hotel" had gone to the top of the charts, and the singer who began his career billed as a "Hill Billy Cat" was set to gross a hundred million dollars over the next two years. Haley and Presley, the acceptable white face of rock and roll, helped make it possible for black artists like Chuck Berry and Little Richard to move closer to the entertainment mainstream and white consumerism. "The first record I ever bought was by Little Richard and, at one throw, it taught me everything I needed to know about pop," enthused one white music journalist: "the message went 'tuttie fruttie all rootie, tuttie frutti all rootie, awopbopaloobop alopbamboom.' As a summation of what rock and roll was really about, this observation was nothing short of masterly."[8]

Yet by 1960, rock and roll, on the face of it, appeared to have run its course. Several of the early rock stars were dead, like Buddy Holly (killed in a plane crash) and Eddie Cochrane (killed in a car crash); in forced retirement due to legal problems, like Chuck Berry; had found religion, like Little Richard; or, like Elvis Presley, were singing like prerock crooners. In Britain, after the initial excitement created by the tours of Bill Haley and Eddie Cochrane, pop music gradually returned to emulating U.S. models, including stars who were groomed to look like their U.S. equivalent, exemplified in 1956 by Britain's lone Elvis imitator, Tommy Steele. But this was popular music without any teeth, since any vestige of a "tough" or "rebellious" image was soon dropped in favor of all-round family appeal, a fate that befell Cliff Richards, the next Elvis look-alike, after his hit "Move It" in 1958.

However, the arrival of rock and roll had set in place a chain of events that would transform popular music. Aspiring young British musicians had begun buying guitars and amps and drum kits made possible by a novel new American device, the installment plan (British "hire purchase"). They could now purchase instruments over time, so that a small monthly payment could finance big rock dreams. More particularly, the music they sought to emulate was by the original rock and rollers of the 1950s as much as their musical forerunners, the Chicago and Delta bluesmen.

Quite why British youth took the music of black American bluesmen to their hearts is unclear. Certainly it was a rebellion against the values of their parents, but it was also because the vernacular origins of the blues appealed to the primitive fantasies of white audiences from Memphis to Merseyside. Here was the real thing, a perfect antidote to the sugar-coated stereotypes of 1950s pop. In white romantic imagination, the tough, knowing sexuality of the blues was expressive of personal not social identity, sensual not cultural need. The blues was a music of escapism for teenagers in the suburban Southeast of England as much as for those in the industrial north. In ports such as Liverpool, Glasgow, and Newcastle, black American blues and R&B records were being brought ashore by seamen and devoured by budding young guitarists, singers, bass players, and drummers. But just listening hard to inspirational music is no guarantee you will be able to produce anything particularly exciting yourself.

At some point between 1960 and 1963, these young copyists decided that plausible imitation was not enough. They began writing their own songs, songs that unselfconsciously mingled black American sounds with parochial influences. By 1961 in Liverpool alone there were 273 garage bands playing some 300 clubs in the city. The majority of these groups had one thing in common, a basic umbrella style rooted in rhythm and blues. But in the stodgy British music scene, these provincial groups were initially ignored by the London-based music industry, giving them a chance to grow at their own pace without being rushed prematurely into recording studios. When one of these bands, the Beatles, broke through to mainstream recognition, there were countless others able to follow through with their own distinctive sounds, and a new chapter in the history of popular music opened. Who would have predicted that a British-ified version of black rhythm and blues could be sold back to America and result in a tidal wave of beat combos that, by the end of 1964, had swept through the Western world (and large parts of the non-Western world) as well?

Popular music has always been about youth, and a taste for its briefly fashionable sounds usually erodes with passing years. As we age, the number of recognizable names in the top ten usually reduces to zero, and the truth of the old maxim that pop music is only interesting to the generation that experiences it appears to hold true. Yet the 1960s have always been different. It was the decade that defined contemporary popular culture, when the ideology of adolescence became the ideology of youth, an ideology in which age was not a part. "I hope I die before I get old," sang The Who.

The post-World-War-II baby boom was central to this rearticulation of culture. By 1964, 40 percent of the population of the United States was under twenty.[9] These teenagers enjoyed an unprecedented level of affluence and thus enormous purchasing power, making them a desirable target for cultural industries. How they spent their money highlighted a rejection, conscious or not, of the values of their parents, with their conservative ideals and romanticized picture of family and national life that was rooted in the culture of the 1930s, 1940s, and early 1950s.

Gradually it seemed to many that a major division in society was opening up with the emergence of a so-called "generation gap" as young people began to search for alternative explanations of American life away from the mainstream.

The film star James Dean did much to embody this perceived breakdown in relationships between adolescents and adults in his films *Rebel Without a Cause* and *East of Eden* that for two generations of teenagers, at least, articulated a sense of being "misunderstood." This strong current of social nonconformity and rebelliousness among the young, their rejection of authority and their hostility towards "adult" institutions and conventional moral and social customs found expression in fashion, drugs, "free love," and rock music.

The 1960s was the "We Decade," a decade in which "we" would overcome, a decade when the rich and the poor, the leftists and the diehard capitalists, individualists and collectivists, consumerists and antimaterialists, hippies and rockers, civil rights activists and even plain old anarchists found common cause against the Bomb, the Vietnam War, imperialism, and a whole lot else. This loose coalition of protesters represented a counterculture that was united in its adoption of antiestablishment rhetoric and the questioning of society's basic values. A whole generation was emerging with new ideals and a shared belief that they could change the corporate state without violence. For a while it seemed enough. But in May 1968 student rioting in Paris almost succeeded in toppling De Gaulle's government as the Gaullist dream of a unifying culture was shattered by *le droit à la différence* extolled by the *soixante-huitards*. It sent a chill down the back of the establishment, who acted accordingly; in the U.S. later that year, police brutality caused riots at the Democratic Convention in Chicago, and in 1969 an oppressive police presence in several U.S. cities marked demonstrations by hundreds of thousands of people against the war in Vietnam. The Kent State massacre in 1970, in which four protesters were killed, was the culmination of a period of paranoid reaction to the counterculture movement.

Rock was the music that filled the void between life and art. In 1967 a broader perspective was offered with the Beatles' *Sgt. Pepper's Lonely Hearts Club Band,* in which rock and roll rubbed shoulders with instrumentation from European classical traditions and melodies that looked back to the English music hall. Rock was extending its boundaries. "The closest Western Civilization has come to unity since the Congress in Vienna in 1815 was the week *Sgt. Pepper* was released," said *Rolling Stone.* "In every city in Europe and America the stereo systems and the radio played [it]."[10] "Lucy in the Sky with Diamonds," a song title that could be reduced to the acronym LSD, described a world seen through "kaleidoscope eyes," institutionalizing a hallucinogenic drug in 1960s pop culture. Clearly deserting the spirit of early rock and roll, *Sgt. Pepper* had an authenticity of its own, but it was not the authenticity of the big beat. It stirred new ambitions and the notion that rock could be something bigger and better than the seemingly unambiguous consumer product it once had appeared to be.

The question no one seemed able to answer as the 1960s drew to a close, however, was how much bigger and better? Popular music appeared in crisis, which, like all crises in pop, was a universal confession that no one could see where the market was going or what it wanted. "The end of the Beatles as a group is now irreversible," said *Rolling Stone* in 1970; "Even the Stones have fallen into the ranks of the merely human unable to sustain the fantasies of a new generation. . . . There are no longer any super-humans to focus on."[11] This temporary respite gave jazz, sucked into in the undertow of popular culture for most of the 1960s, a chance to raise its voice in the unfolding scenario.

When Beatlemania broke, jazz musicians, promoters, club owners, and the jazz magazines were united in thinking that if they ignored the new rock music, it would go away. Early on it seemed as if it would be just another passing phase, a fad that would burn itself out like the twist or the locomotion. But it didn't. As Beatlemania gave way to rock and began swallowing up work opportunities for jazz musicians, animosity towards rock music grew. By the mid-1960s those inside the jazz camp viewed rock with suspicion and sometimes outright contempt, like a delinquent son who, by some fluke, had inherited the family silver. High on pain and joy, jazz was blowing its soul to heaven but no one seemed to be listening, while rock, with stubborn simplicity, was sweeping all before it.

By the early 1960s jazz could look back on almost fifty years of constant evolution and innovation that had frequently left both musicians and musicologists flat-footed. It had developed from a provincial Southern folk music to a sophisticated art form by the end of the 1920s, although such recognition would only be bestowed retrospectively. But if Duke Ellington could claim that music was his mistress, then jazz was often a very cruel mistress. Buddy Bolden, one of the original architects of New Orleans jazz, was admitted to a mental institution in a state of hopeless indigence in 1907; he finally died in 1931. Musicians who stepped forward to move the music on, such as Joe "King" Oliver, Jelly Roll Morton, Johnny Dodds, and Freddie Keppard, were all dead by 1941, and like Bolden, they died forgotten and penniless men.

They had been swept aside by the rise of the big band, whose increasingly sophisticated arrangements had largely replaced the ingenious polyphony of the New Orleans ensemble by the mid-1920s. Fate, however, was kinder to the big-band leaders, many of whom had made their fortunes by the time Charlie Parker and the bebop movement entered jazz. By 1948 bebop had sucked virtually all the young players entering jazz into its vortex, and a new musical agenda had taken hold, setting in motion a flight from the status quo and a quest for ever more challenging musical forms. Even so, throughout the 1950s a vocal minority remained convinced that Parker's music was not jazz. Little did they know what was around the corner. In the fall of 1959, Ornette Coleman opened at the Five Spot Café in New York and ushered free jazz into the public domain to no little controversy.

Coleman was simultaneously hailed a messiah and branded a charlatan; on the one hand he was thought of as the man to take jazz forward in much the same way as Parker had done in the 1940s, and on the other he was accused of being a fake, someone who could not run the changes or play in tune. While this critical ambivalence was to dog Coleman and many free jazz musicians throughout the 1960s, it added to the mystique of the music, which from the outset sought to be "outside" in both the literal and metaphorical sense. The seemingly random and abstract nature of the music inevitably posed problems of objective interpretation, and almost immediately lines of subjective critical demarcation were drawn. In 1961 Gunther Schuller praised Coleman for making "[a] unique contribution to contemporary music,"[12] while *Downbeat* editor Don DeMichael accused him of creating musical "chaos" that was "an insult to the listening intelligence."[13]

This situation was further complicated by a strong ideological undercurrent that began to spring up around free jazz that came into sharp focus in the hands of musicians such as Archie Shepp, whose controversial statements rather more than his music thrust him to the forefront of the debate. "We are not angry men. We are outraged," he proclaimed. "I can't see any separation between my music and my life. I play pretty much race music."[14] A growing political awareness and rejection of racial injustice within the black community had found focus with the passage of the Civil Rights Act of 1957 and, throughout the 1960s, white America struggled to come to terms with a problem in their midst that had been fermenting for generations.

The civil rights movement reached a climax in 1963. Beatings by white police and the arrest of Dr. Martin Luther King, Jr. marked a civil rights demonstration in Birmingham, Alabama culminating in President Kennedy's dispatch of 3,000 troops to maintain order. As a result, 200,000 "Freedom Marchers" descended on Washington, D.C. on August 28, 1963 where King galvanized the nation with his "I Have a Dream" speech at the Lincoln Memorial. So profound was his address that it helped pave the way for landmark legislation, the Civil Rights Act of 1964 and the Voting Rights Act the following year. Yet the problems between the races continued to fester, with the black population divided between peaceful confrontation in the mode of King and angrier political voices, such as Malcolm X and Bobby Seale.

In this tense climate, many black jazz musicians, who had for years felt exploited by the white entertainment infrastructure, were swept up by the rising tide of black nationalism. Although black protest had surfaced before in jazz,[15] the changing mood of the country, with black issues being forced to the forefront of the political agenda, lent greater force to musical protest. Sonny Rollins recorded his *Freedom Suite* in 1958; Charles Mingus recorded "Fables of Faubus" in 1959, openly contemptuous of the segregationist governor of Arkansas, Orval Faubus; and Max Roach recorded an album-length political statement with *We Insist! Freedom Now Suite* in 1960. Yet, while these messages were in tune with the times, it was not enough for many younger radicals who, rather than wanting to reform society, wanted to overturn it entirely.

A significant minority were bored by this music, which, despite its implicit political and social message, was as an extension of bebop. These musicians were impatient; they wanted change. The older order, their musical fathers, had not achieved it, so now, they reasoned, was the time for the young generation to try something new. Many held the view that the only true jazz musician was a black jazz musician and that, first and foremost, jazz was black protest music. To some extent the idea was abroad that the message was more important than the medium, that an indigenous music of social protest was more important than musical merit. Free jazz, or as it became known, "the New Thing," became an anthem that screamed rejection of inequality, a rallying cry with revolutionary connotations of a new order sweeping away the old. "Today's avant-garde movement in jazz," wrote Frank Kofsky, "is a musical representation of the ghetto's vote of 'no confidence' in the American dream—that Negro avant-garde intransigents, in other words, are saying through their horns . . . 'Up your ass, feeble-minded ofays!'"[16] Archie Shepp submitted a piece to *Downbeat* declaring his support for Ho Chi Minh and Fidel Castro—and received a phone call from editor Dan Morgenstern, who responded: "This article frightens me!" Later Shepp would declare his saxophone was like a machine gun in the hands of the Viet Cong, "We are only an extension of that entire civil rights–black Muslims–black nationalist movement that is taking place in America."[17]

But however much free jazz was politicized and intellectualized, the oblique nature of the music meant that a popular audience for it, even within the black community, was never a possibility. It was songs like Sam Cooke's "A Change Is Gonna Come," widely adopted as a black anthem, Curtis Mayfield's "People Get Ready," and, in 1968, James Brown's "Say It Loud—I'm Black and Proud" that captured the spirit of the times. In the face of what George Russell called free jazz's "war on chords," audiences, particularly the large white following jazz had enjoyed in the 1950s, began to drift away. Faced with seemingly random notes against an abstract background they found a disorder that was alien to their previous listening experiences. "The new jazz," critic Stanley Dance observed ruefully, "seems to be as unpalatable to most teenagers as to most adults and unquestionably has had an adverse affect on the jazz image."[18]

This situation was further exacerbated by many established musicians, conscious that free jazz appeared to be costing them more than a pound of artistic flesh, excoriating the music in public. "There are a whole bunch of cats who can't run the changes," complained pianist Hampton Hawes, "but they play a lot of that far out stuff. When you ask them 'What was that?' they say, 'Well I'm out there.' Now what is that crap. . . . Man, I don't care for 'out there.'"[19] Others, such as saxophonist Eddie "Lockjaw" Davis, who worked for a booking office in the 1960s between stints with the Count Basie Orchestra, blamed free jazz for the virtual collapse of the jazz club scene in the 1960s. "If a person comes into a club and does not understand or enjoy what the musicians are playing, he's not coming back. Therefore there's no business . . . [which] is why there's no clubs to speak of today [1970]. . . . Freedom has done more harm to the industry than any form of music."[20] Such outbursts had the effect of dividing the jazz world still further, with "the New Thing" held responsible for shooting jazz in the foot.

Free jazz, however, only served to exacerbate the downswing in the popularity of jazz as a whole. The real culprit was rock, which while not exactly casting jazz into exterior darkness, did at least relegate it to the commercial twilight. With sales of rock recordings exceeding the wildest expectations of even the most optimistic executive, record companies were becoming less and less interested in artists who could promise only small initial sales. Where previously a company like Columbia might take an inexpensive few chances recording a Buck Clayton jam session or a Charles Mingus imbroglio, hoping for a small profit on their initial outlay, jazz, when set against the potential returns to be made from rock music, suddenly found itself running a very poor second. "The villains behind the scenes," wrote the jazz critic Leonard Feather, "were the recording company heads, such as the vice-president of a major label who . . . was quoted as having sworn, 'If an artist cannot sell 100,000 records, I am not interested in that artist.'"[21]

Jazz, traditionally more of a catalogue seller, looks to slow but steady sales so that a nonchart album may eventually earn as much as a hit over a long period of time. Even avante-garde releases have, over a twenty-year period, proved to be lucrative propositions. Few jazz recordings *initially* sell in large numbers. Prior to the rock explosion, record company executives had broadly, if sometimes reluctantly, accepted this sales pattern, because a similar precedent existed in the sales of classical music recordings. But while many jazz and classical recordings eventually achieve respectable sales, the music business markets jazz under the umbrella of "popular music," for which the sole arbiter of success is measured in terms of units sold in the short rather than the medium or longer term. Now, with rock music claiming an ever greater share of the market, young audiences were no longer buying jazz records; they were buying pop, rock, and R&B records, everything, it seemed, *but* jazz recordings. "All of a sudden jazz became passé," reflected Miles Davis in 1989, "something dead you put under a glass in the museum and study. All of a sudden rock 'n' roll was in the forefront in the media. . . . Because of what people now thought jazz was—nonmelodic, not hummable—a lot of serious musicians had a hard time from then on. A lot of jazz clubs were closing down. . . . People were dancing."[22]

The writing had been on the wall for some time. When Elvis Presley encountered jazz lovers at a faculty party in the 1957 movie *Jailhouse Rock,* for example, they were depicted as pretentious and elitist. Rock and roll was portrayed as the music of adolescent rebelliousness and independence, while jazz was seen as hopelessly "square," the music of a previous generation. As the rock explosion took hold, there was unprecedented economic pressure on all those engaged in the jazz business. Promoters and club owners were quick to realize that rock acts, often seeking exposure in an attempt to break into the big time, would frequently appear at a fraction of the cost of an established jazz group *and* almost invariably do better business. "One treacherous night John Coltrane played in Chicago's 'Birdhouse,'" wrote Gordon Kopulous, "he played to an audience that numbered ten at its height. I counted. As if to underscore the whole thing in living theater, another group appeared that night on the South West side: Kenny Klope Fantastics—a rock group. And Jimmy Loundsberry, then a popular emcee. They packed 600 kids paying two dollars apiece and turned away 300."[23]

By the end of the 1960s, rock, both musically and socially, seemed as if it was about to overwhelm jazz. For jazz musicians, the balancing act between musical integrity and survival was becoming increasingly difficult to reconcile. An increasing number were finding their sight-reading and improvisational skills being called on for rock recording sessions. "They take this work," observed Leonard Feather, "because jazz records have a very small sale, while calls for performances in the rock field . . . have been growing daily."[24] But it was not just session work; younger jazz musicians were finding work in rock groups while many established jazz musicians made, in varying degrees, concessions to the changing musical landscape. Gerry Mulligan recorded an album called *If You Can't Beat Them, Join Them* that featured a photograph of him shrugging his shoulders, as if to indicate a mood of futility and abandonment of principles. In 1966, guitarist Gabor Szabo included a couple of Beatles' tunes on his album *Gypsy '66,* and his subsequent albums—such as *The Sorcerer, More Sorcery, Wind Sky and Diamond,* and *Light My Fire*—all contained current pop tunes as vehicles for improvisation over straight-ahead or light pop rhythms.

Eddie Harris, Sonny Stitt, Lee Konitz, and Clark Terry were among several musicians who began experimenting with a "Varitone," an electronic device that permitted over sixty "effects" such as octaves, echo, and tremolo on brass and reed instruments. The bastions of chamber jazz, the Modern Jazz Quartet, signed with the Beatles' production company, Apple, while Ella Fitzgerald, an interpreter of the American popular song *par excellence,* began giving prominence in her repertoire to so-so pop numbers like The Carpenters' "Close to You," Del Shannon's "Put a Little Love in Your Heart," the Beatles' "Something," and Carole King's "You've Got a Friend." To her pianist Tommy Flanagan's acute embarrassment, Fitzgerald even went as far as to call her trio "Ella Fitzgerald's New Sound," to appear "with it," explaining "I don't want to be considered, as the song goes, 'as cold as yesterday's mashed potatoes.'"[25]

More significantly, Duke Ellington, a pillar of jazz society since the 1920s and seemingly immune from the successive shocks announcing the new that had periodically swept through jazz and popular music, found himself forced to acknowledge that things were not what they used to be in January 1965, when he recorded cover versions of "All My Loving" and "I Want to Hold Your Hand" for his album *Ellington '66.* The following year, Count Basie went the full distance and recorded *Basie's Beatle Bag,* a Beatle songbook album arranged by Chico O'Farrill. And at the 1967 Monterey Jazz Festival, Woody Herman performed a proto-jazz-rock piece called "Woody's Boogaloo." By 1968 virtually all his repertoire revolved around a series of arrangements by Richard Evans of pop and rock songs that had been featured on his *Light My Fire* album. The same year the pseudo-psychedelic album jacket of Buddy Rich's *Mercy, Mercy, Mercy* announced another big band adapting to the changing times with performances of numbers such as "Big Mamma Cass," Bobby Gentry's "Ode to Billy Joe," and originals meant to be "in tune with the kids," such as "Acid Truth." Even free-jazz exponents were sucked up in the pressure to sell; "new thing" saxophonist Albert Ayler made extensive use of rock rhythm section patterns and "soul" singers on his album *New Grass.* The sight of jazz casting around the periphery of rock, apparently in an attempt to raise its profile, was the signal that many music commentators needed to advance the prognosis that the end of jazz was in sight. *Melody Maker* contained a "Requiem for a jazz we loved and knew so well."[26] *Rouge* magazine headlined "Jazz Is Dead . . . Folk Is Dead . . . Long Live Rock!"[27] while *Downbeat* pronounced "Jazz As We Know It Is Dead!" on its front cover.[28]

With jazz clubs closing and work opportunities drying up, musicians found themselves forced into non-jazz work, such as backing up singers (like Lou Levy accompanying Peggy Lee), playing in society bands (pianist Steve Kuhn), accompanying cabaret (pianist Jaki Byard at New York's 82 Club, where female impersonators put on musicals), playing in pit bands (bassist Aaron Bell in the Schubert Theater on Broadway), working in Las Vegas hotel bands (saxophonist James Moody), or taking day jobs (drummer Pete LaRocca and pianist McCoy Tyner, who were forced to drive taxicabs to make ends meet). Others, disenchanted with what was happening, moved to Europe, including Phil Woods, Ben Webster, Art Farmer, Benny Bailey, Johnny Griffin, Art Taylor, Carmell Jones, Leo Wright, Herb Geller, Kenny Drew, Stuff Smith, Jimmy Woode, Mal Waldron, Steve Lacy, Anthony Braxton, and several key members of Chicago's AACM. "The morale of the jazz community is rotten," said a gloomy *Village Voice* feature in 1967.[29]

The audience shift from jazz to rock was significant. Even *Downbeat* magazine, a solid and reliable chronicler of the winds of change that had blown through jazz since July 1934, saw its advertising space increasingly given over to advertisements for guitars and amplifiers as the rock boom took hold. Pictures of neatly groomed groups using Fender guitars while surrounded by adoring girls or endorsements from groups such as the Beatles for Vox amplifiers were sharply at odds with the editorial content, which remained steadfastly true to jazz until June 1967, when this curious paradox was finally resolved. A solemn half-page "Message To Our Readers" proclaimed, "Rock-and-roll has come of age . . . without reducing its coverage of jazz, [*Downbeat*] will expand its editorial perspective to include musically valid aspects of the rock scene."[30] Five months later, the Beatles made the front cover.

So large had the spectre of rock become that the idea of some sort of musical hybrid began to be floated. "Jazz is going to have to make some adjustments, I think, with the electronic world of rock and roll if it is to retain its validity," wrote Mike Zwerin in December 1966.[31] He was not alone. Concern was mounting that jazz had become an endangered species. "My complaint," wrote Jim Morrissey in the *Louisville Times* in 1967, "is that too many of the jazz greats are producing non-communicating music. They get deeper and deeper into their own bag where fewer of their fans hang-out. There must be some kind of wedding between jazz and the solid contemporary sounds evolving out of the early rock 'n' roll garbage."[32] Even *Time* magazine was drawn into the controversy with a feature entitled "A Way Out of the Muddle." Full of optimism and hope that a marriage between jazz and rock might happen, it even went as far as to wish the newlyweds "bon voyage."[33] But quite how any sort of rapprochement was going to be achieved was by no means clear during the summer of 1967.

Notes

1. Their first two releases, "Please Please Me" and "From Me to You," had to be franchised to Vee Jay Records of Chicago, and the third, "She Loves You," to Swan Records.
2. *American Popular Music Business in the 20th Century,* by Russell Sanjek and David Sanjek (Oxford University Press, New York, 1991), p. 148.

3. Ibid., p. 149.

4. Initially charting with "Not Fade Away," "Tell Me," and "It's All Over Now," it was not until "Time Is On My Side" and "The Last Time" that they finally reached *Billboard*'s Top 10. Even so, the number-one spot eluded them until "(I Can't Get No) Satisfaction" made it in 1965, leaving the way clear for "Get Off Of My Cloud" later in the year and a succession of hits until 1967, when they began to falter.

5. *American Popular Music Business in the 20th Century*, p. 148.

6. *All You Need Is Love*, by Tony Palmer (Weidenfeld & Nicolson and Chappell, London, 1978), pp. 232–233.

7. *Dancing in the Street*, by Rober Palmer (BBC Books, London, 1996) pp. 48–49.

8. *Ball the Wall*, by Nik Cohn (Picador, London, 1989), p. 73.

9. L. Grossberg, "Teaching the Popular," in C. Nelson (ed.), *Theory in the Classroom* (University of Illinois Press, Urbana, 1986), p. 172.

10. Quoted in *The Rolling Stone Illustrated History of Rock and Roll*, edited by Jim Miller (Picador, London, 1981), p. 185.

11. *Rolling Stone*, December 2, 1970, p. 33.

12. Forward to ten Coleman compositions by Gunther Schuller, published in 1961 by MJQ Music, Inc. Republished in *Musings*, by Gunther Schuller (Oxford University Press, New York, 1986), p. 81.

13. *Downbeat*, May 1961.

14. This is an often quoted remark of Shepp's—for example, in *Cats of Any Color*, by Gene Lees (Oxford University Press, New York, 1995), pp. 196–197.

15. Overtly in the case of Billie Holiday's "Strange Fruit" in 1939, obliquely in the work of Duke Ellington, such as his 1941 musical *Jump for Joy*, which included "Uncle Tom's Cabin Is a Drive-In Now."

16. *Black Nationalism and the Revolution in Music*, by Frank Kofsky (Pathfinder Press, New York, 1970), p. 131.

17. *Wire*, May 1993, p. 38.

18. *Downbeat Yearbook 1968*, p. 23.

19. *Downbeat*, October 17, 1968, p. 17.

20. *Downbeat*, from 1970 but no date or month, courtesy Institute of Jazz Studies, Rutgers University.

21. *Downbeat Yearbook 1971*, p. 10.

22. *Miles: The Autobiography of Miles Davis*, with Quincy Troupe (Simon & Schuster, New York, 1989), p. 262.

23. *Downbeat Yearbook 1973*, p. 18.

24. Ibid., p. 18.

25. *Houston Post*, January 7, 1968.

26. *Melody Maker*, September 2, 1967.

27. *Rouge*, October 1967.

28. *Downbeat*, October 5, 1967.

29. *Village Voice*, March 30, 1967.

30. *Downbeat*, June 29, 1967, p. 13.

31. Ibid., December 15, 1966, p. 13.

32. *Louisville Times*, December 9, 1967.

33. *Time*, August 1967.

CHAPTER 2

Wheels of Fire

Signs that the two hermetically sealed worlds of jazz and rock were about to collide were there, had anybody bothered to look, even as the Beatlemania craze exploded. Although it appeared as if London followed and then took over from the Liverpool-Merseyside sound, it had in fact developed its own quite independent underground music scene before the Beatles emerged, a scene that would shortly launch the Rolling Stones hard on the heels of the Fab Four. Particularly after the Stones' chart-breaking success in 1964, London became a major influence in the shift from Liverpool "beat" to blues-influenced "rock." Clubs like London's Marquee, where the blues purists gathered, or the Flamingo, home of the rhythm and blues fans, became the focal points of this scene.

Interest in the blues had grown since revivalist jazz band leaders (playing Dixieland-style jazz, known in Britain as trad jazz) such as Ken Colyer, Humphrey Lyttelton, and Chris Barber, had brought several seminal blues artists from America to tour with their bands in the 1950s. Barber's role was perhaps the most influential. He arranged visits by Muddy Waters, Otis Spann, Big Bill Broonzy, and Sonny Terry and Brownie McGhee. However, when Muddy Waters first visited Britain in 1958, jazz club audiences loudly protested over his use of a small amplifier; they were expecting acoustic blues-as-folk-music like that of Huddie Ledbetter (Leadbelly) or Big Bill Broonzy. Considering Waters arrived at the tail end of the rock and roll craze, the outrage he generated is hard to explain, but his visit is now regarded as a foundation stone of the British blues boom of the early 1960s. Four years later, tastes had caught up with contemporary blues sounds. On a return visit, Waters played acoustic guitar and was criticized for being too conservative!

By 1962, an active blues scene in London had taken root. Central to this scene was a trad jazz musician of Greek heritage named Alexis Korner. Korner had begun as a jazz pianist and guitarist in Chris Barber's band where his interest in blues grew. In 1955, he opened the Blues and Barrelhouse Club in London's Tottenham Court Road with fellow blues musician and enthusiast Cyril Davies, but when the club folded three years later he returned to playing with Barber. In February 1962, Korner and Davies formed their own band, Blues

Alexis Korner: The comings and goings of many of London's top jazz musicians in Korner's bands pointed to a confluence of jazz and rock in the early 1960's. *Left to right:* unknown pianist, Dick Heckstall-Smith, Korner, Jack Bruce, Mick Jagger, Cyril Davies. Drummer Charlie Watts, then playing revivalist jazz, is obscured.

Incorporated, opening on March 17, 1962 at their new club, which quickly became a Mecca for British blues fans, underneath the ABC Teashop in the London suburb of Ealing.

What is interesting about Korner's bands was his use, from the very beginning, of jazz musicians. The comings and goings of most of London's top jazz musicians in his bands over the next decade was instrumental in breaking down the artificial barriers between jazz and rock in Britain. The first edition of the band included, aside from Korner and Davies, a young drummer who had been playing revivalist jazz, Charlie Watts (who later went with the Rolling Stones), jazz bassists Spike Heatley and Jack Bruce (John Mayall/Cream), and from time to time the tenor saxophonist Dick Heckstall-Smith, who had come from a straight-ahead hard-bop gig with the Johnny Burch Octet and would continue playing jazz with the Bert Courtley Sextet into the summer of 1962 alongside the saxophonist Kathy Stobart.

Blues Incorporated regularly played London's Marquee Club, building a following who considered revivalist jazz too tame and the current British and American pop scene too boring and who saw the Korner-Davies mix of blues

marquee

90 Wardour Street | London W.1

Thursday, December 1st (7.30-11.0)

★ **GRAHAM BOND**
ORGAN-ISATION
★ **THE BUNCH**

Friday, December 2nd (7.30-11.0)
★ **"LET'S GO SURFIN' " — MARQUEE**
"BEACH PARTY"
★ **THE FENMEN**
★ **THE MAJORITY**

Saturday, December 3rd (2.30-5.30)
★ **THE SATURDAY SHOW**
Top of the Pops, both live and on disc,
introduced by guest D.J.s and
featuring star personalities

Saturday, December 3rd (8.0-11.30)
★ **THE HERD**
★ **JOHN'S CHILDREN**

Sunday, December 4th (8.0-10.30)
★ FROM THE U.S.A.
ROY ELDRIDGE
with **PHIL SEAMEN QUARTET**
(Tickets: Members 10/-. Non-members 12/6
available in advance or on the evening)

Monday, December 5th (7.30-11.0)

★ **ARTWOODS**
★ **THE NITE PEOPLE**

Tuesday, December 6th (7.30-11.0)
★ **JIMMY JAMES**
and the **VAGABONDS**
★ **SYN**

Wednesday, December 7th (7.30-11.0)

★ **GERRY LOCKRAN**
★ **THE SOUTHERN RAMBLERS**
★ **GOOCH** (The Great Blues Pianist)

Sunday, December 11th (8.0-10.30)
★ TED HEATH'S 21st ANNIVERSARY
★ **TED HEATH**
AND HIS MUSIC
AND GUESTS
(Members: 7/6. Non-members: 10/-
available in advance)

Graham Bond: An early precursor of jazz-rock, for many. His hard-edged pop music built around his Hammond organ cut loose with jazz improvisations, reflecting how close rock and jazz cultures coexisted in the mid-1960s London scene, as this lineup for the Marquee Club in 1966 shows.

and R&B an exciting alternative. Mick Jagger, Brian Jones, and Keith Richards often sat in with Korner, and their nascent group, the Rolling Stones, substituted for Blues Incorporated at the Marquee on July 21, 1962. Tensions, however, were growing within Blues Incorporated; Davies, an uncompromising Chicago blues fan, clashed with Korner, who was keen to keep his jazz roots in sight. After recording *R and B from the Marquee,* the two went their separate ways.

Korner reformed Blues Incorporated in June 1962, retaining Jack Bruce and Heckstall-Smith but adding two more musicians with backgrounds in jazz, Graham Bond on organ and alto sax—voted "Britain's New Jazz Star" in 1961 while a member of the Don Rendell sextet—and Peter "Ginger" Baker on drums. "I decided the only way I was going to make some money was to 'go commercial,'" recalled Baker, who had previously played revivalist jazz with the Bob Wallis, Terry Lightfoot, and Acker Bilk bands, and hard bop with the Johnny

Burch Octet and the Ronnie Scott, Bert Courtley, and Joe Harriott bands. "So I made a deliberate plan to . . . start playing R&B as opposed to jazz and it just took off. Half the band were straight blues players and half the band were straight jazz players and when we played together the effect we had on each other was amazing."[1]

This version of Blues Incorporated is generally regarded as Korner's classic lineup, and although it recorded for British Decca the results were not released and the master tapes have apparently been mislaid. Many musicians claim that at the very least this band pointed very strongly to a confluence between jazz and rock as early as 1962. They cite Baker's strong "rock" backbeat and long jazz improvisations from Bond and Heckstall-Smith as evidence for this claim, but with only one track surviving, an instrumental version of "Rockin'" from 1963,[2] it is difficult to verify. "Rockin'" was a good, old-fashioned boogie blues closer to the jump bands of the 1940s than jazz-rock.

Throughout the 1960s and into the '70s, Korner was a central figure on the London music scene, the "Father of Us All," as a feature in *Rolling Stone*[3] proclaimed in 1971, around whom jazz players as much as blues musicians gathered. "When I first played in London, Ginger Baker was very prominent as a *jazz* player," recalled the jazz trumpeter Ian Carr. "Then, when I replaced Graham Bond in the Don Rendell quintet, Jack Bruce used to come along and sit in; Jack was steeped in the blues but also a very fine jazz bassist. We used to do the all-night session at the Flamingo on a Saturday. We used to alternate with Georgie Fame and the Blue Flames and John McLaughlin was the guitar player so you got from McLaughlin his incredible jazz virtuosity from a guy who knew the blues inside out. The whole scene was like a soup, all things intermingling. The link between all these different factions of music was Alexis Korner; he was the catalyst who involved jazz musicians in what was going on in the blues scene."[4] A good example of this is Korner's album *Blues Incorporated* from 1963, which includes the jazz musicians Dick Heckstall-Smith and Art Theman on saxes, and the drummer Phil Seaman, illustrating the jazz spin that Korner liked to put on his rocking version of the blues.

"Alexis had everybody in his band at some point . . ." recalled the guitarist John McLaughlin. "I started with Alexis Korner. . . . In those days there were two clubs: The Marquee and the Flamingo. They were great. Everybody met everybody there and the attitude was that everybody could play with everybody. . . . I kept playing rhythm and blues and it was great because we were playing real jazz solos. It was blues but at the same time it was much more than the blues."[5] By February 1963, Jack Bruce, Ginger Baker, and Graham Bond had left Korner's Blues Incorporated to form a band of their own. For a while they worked as a trio, playing jazz gigs with the poet Pete Brown and working the rhythm and blues circuit in London and the provinces. They were soon joined by John McLaughlin who had just left Korner.

Solid Bond, a double album retrospective, includes tracks from June 1963 that feature the new lineup. A live session, it displays their jazz credentials. "The Grass is Greener" and "Ho Ho Country Kicking Blues" evoke the work of

Charles Mingus with their intensity and abandon and compare very favorably to the best British jazz of this period. Bond is extensively featured on alto sax and is an intense, fiery, and excitable player. Bruce on acoustic bass and Baker on drums emerge as very capable players more than able to hold their own in a contemporary jazz environment with a very fluid feel for time. McLaughlin, perhaps surprisingly in the light of his subsequent development as an artist, is overshadowed by the individual contributions of the rest of the group. Baker, who took over the running of the band because of Bond's unpredictability, was responsible for firing McLaughlin. "He was a moaner," he later claimed,[6] and turned to saxophonist Dick Heckstall-Smith to replace him.

By the time of *The Sound of '65*, and a further name change to the Graham Bond Organisation, the group had mutated into a commercial, blues-oriented, pop band, which could rather disconcertingly veer into trite ephemera, as a "B" movie appearance in *Gonks Go Beat* revealed only too clearly. The subsequent *There's a Bond Between Us* (1965) and some previously unissued tracks on *Solid Bond* from a 1966 session that included Jon Hiseman on drums do nothing to dispel this image, despite subsequent claims that they were an early precursor of jazz-rock. Rather, this is a somewhat hard-edged pop music built around Bond's Hammond organ. On just a few numbers, Bond cuts loose with jazz-based improvisations, particularly on "Wade in the Water" (a number that British audiences came to associate with him) that might be construed as pointing to a merger between jazz and popular culture. Nonetheless, "Graham was a crusader, a path finder," said Hiseman. "He was playing music with an improvisatory element in it, an element we take for granted in jazz, but which of course had never existed in pop music. And the blues was the public's link between improvised music and pop music."[7]

However, by October 1965, Bruce was out of the Graham Bond Organisation; his flamboyant bass playing did not fit in with Baker's musical vision. After a series of legendary on-stage spats between them, Bruce was unceremoniously dispatched when Baker pulled a knife on him. Bruce moved briefly to John Mayall's Bluesbreakers, which at the time featured Eric Clapton on guitar. There was an immediate personal empathy, and on *Primal Solos*, which was not released until 1985, the Bluesbreakers caught fire. "Eric and Jack really got off on each other," recalled the Bluesbreaker drummer Hughie Flint. "That was the beginning of Cream really."[8]

Clapton had been briefly with the Yardbirds, who had accompanied Sonny Boy Williamson on his U.K. tours. They wanted to move away from rhythm-and-blues-derived rock to something more commercial. When they recorded "For Your Love" it was too much for the avowed blues purist Clapton, whose solo on the B-side of the disc, "Got to Hurry," was by any standards an impressive blues performance in the Chicago style. Clapton joined Mayall's Bluesbreakers and during his short tenure with the group made sure that *Blues Breakers* from 1966 was one of the great British R&B albums of this period. Recorded shortly after Bruce had left the group, it drew heavily on black source material: Otis Rush, Little Walter, Ray Charles, and a version of "Ramblin' on my Mind" by the leg-

Cream: As early as 1966, they provided a working model of what a fusion between jazz and rock might actually sound like. *Left to right:* Eric Clapton, Ginger Baker, Jack Bruce. (Photograph by David Redfern/Redferns.)

endary Delta Bluesman Robert Johnson. On three tracks, jazzmen Alan Skidmore and Dennis Healy provide horn backgrounds. Skidmore's tenor solo on "Have You Heard" turned a lot of heads, including a young student named Michael Brecker at Indiana University, who remembers being knocked out by it. However, it was Clapton's playing on numbers such as "All Your Love" and "Steppin' Out" that suggested an important voice on guitar was poised to move onto center stage. That move was achieved with the group Cream, formed in July 1966.

Cream came into being when Ginger Baker sat in with Mayall's Bluebreakers and was greatly impressed with Clapton's playing. He approached the guitarist with the idea of forming a group, and Clapton agreed, suggesting Jack Bruce as bassist. Baker swallowed his pride, recognizing that, whatever personal difficulties he had experienced with Bruce in the past, he was nevertheless a fine bass player. "He came around to see me," recalled Bruce, "without a knife, and said he wanted to form this group with Eric and Eric was agreeable if I would be in it too."[9] Rehearsals began in Baker's front room, and from the outset the group clicked. "It was a similar thing to the Alexis Korner thing, in a way," said Baker. "Eric was a straight blues player and Jack and I were both jazz players . . . there weren't three musicians like us around, that's how the name Cream came about. We considered we *were* the cream."[10] What is significant is that Baker identified himself as a jazz drummer and Bruce identified himself as a jazz bassist, in the context of what would become one of the major rock bands of the 1960s.

Their hurried debut album, *Fresh Cream,* released in late 1966, drew heavily from black blues artists, including two songs by Delta bluesmen, Robert Johnson's "Four Until Late" and Skip James's "I'm So Glad." Also included was a version of "Spoonful," credited to Willie Dixon but owing much to Charlie Patton's "A Spoonful of Blues" from 1929. The result, with the exception of "I'm So Glad," was rather stilted, as the group clearly sought commercial success. Although vocals are prominent, bootleg CDs reveal that in live performance they gave way to lengthy improvisations in a way that had more in common with modern jazz than the blues in their disregard for the temporal limits of the popular song.

In 1967, Cream toured America and quickly became one of the biggest names on the rock circuit, *Life* magazine observing that "the healthiest development in popular music these days is the extraordinary convergence of jazz and rock."[11] Audiences were fascinated with Cream's extended improvisations and in particular Clapton's guitar playing. "I can only say that for the two minutes or twelve hours (I have no idea exactly how long the solo was) that Clapton soloed, I got as high up and as far out as I ever had on jazz," related one mind-blown *Downbeat* reviewer.[12]

Their second album, *Disraeli Gears,* was released in November that year and reflects the then-fashionable "psychedelia" craze with one of the most memorable album covers of the period, designed by the "underground" artist Martin Sharp, with whom Clapton was rooming at the time on Kings Road in Chelsea. With the single exception of "Outside Woman Blues," written by Blind Joe Reynolds, the album comprises original, blues-based compositions greatly influenced by the bluesman Albert King's album *Born Under a Bad Sign* and King's other Stax recordings. Also included was Bruce and poet Pete Brown's "Sunshine of Your Love" and Clapton's collaboration with Sharp that provided the album's highlight, "Tales of Brave Ulysses."

In 1968 came *Wheels of Fire,* a double album set that comprised one studio and one live album that reached number one on the American and British album charts. The live numbers, recorded at the Fillmore in San Francisco, clearly demonstrated the group's preoccupation with instrumental skill as an end in itself, with extended versions of "Spoonful" and "Toad" each about sixteen minutes in length. But it was Clapton's solo on "Crossroads" that is the album's focal point, some four minutes of flat-out blues playing that by any standards is impressive. "Clapton's virtuosity is so advanced and his uncanny knack of building effective, shattering climaxes unfailing," said *Downbeat.*[13]

As Ginger Baker has pointed out, Cream spent most of its existence touring, primarily in the U.S., where their album sales totalled some fifteen million.[14] When it all got to be too much they disbanded, making their last appearance at London's Albert Hall on October 26, 1968. Despite their relatively short existence, Cream was a highly influential band. While their role as a forerunner of hard rock, later evolving into heavy metal, and their influence on bands such as Led Zeppelin and Black Sabbath have been widely recognized, their impact on jazz has not. Yet Clapton, Bruce, and to a lesser extent Baker were among the finest instrumentalists in rock at this time. Certainly Clapton's dynamic and occasionally stunning guitar playing and Bruce's imaginative bass lines could not be dismissed by jazz musicians as mere commercial pop. Equally, Baker's drumming exhibited a degree of complexity inspired by Elvin Jones that brought polyrhythms into the forum of rock, and was in advance of practically every drummer on the rock circuit for most of the period the band was in existence. "The last time we were in the States," said Clapton in early 1968, "a lot of people in New York, you know, jazzers, were amazed that a pop group was doing such things and that we could get away with it." [15]

At best, Cream's performances transcended simple pigeon-holing; indeed, *Rolling Stone* magazine pointed out in 1968 that they had "been called a jazz group," [16] revealing the extent to which their extended improvisations impinged on jazz and the critical confusion this caused. Today we regard Cream as a rock band, but it is clear as early as 1966 that they were providing a working model of what a fusion between elements of jazz and rock might actually sound like.

It is significant to note that jazz history has traditionally relied on canon formation and a chronological "masterpieces only" approach in reconstructing the past. This exclusionary reading of history has its roots in the decades-old struggle to establish the validity of jazz alongside the Eurocentric tradition of Western classical music, and to establish jazz as a genuine "art" music in its own right. This approach identifies and exalts favored artists to support this argument while bypassing musicians or events that do not support the theory.

The emergence of jazz-rock has been largely divorced from the social and cultural changes of the period that were instrumental in prompting both jazz and rock musicians to think along similar lines. Rock bands who contributed to the growth of jazz-rock tend to be ignored as falling outside the scope of "jazz" history. Cream is a good case in point, demonstrating a merging of rock with elements of jazz. Against Clapton's blues-based improvisations, Bruce and Baker spun elastic variations of tempo and meter unheard of in rock. They explored polytonality, a sophisticated concept even in jazz, on their hit "I Feel Free." On "Spoonful," from the album *Wheels of Fire*, the chord sequence is quickly abandoned in favor of an extended vamp which initially is a feature for Clapton's guitar. As his improvisation progresses, Bruce's bass guitar takes a prominent role in accompaniment, contributing imaginative contrapuntal lines and interacting with Clapton's playing to the extent their performance gradually assumes the proportions of a duet. Meanwhile, Baker's drumming, built around a specific rhythmic figure carried mainly by the snare drum, is developed and expanded, appropriately coloring and commenting on the guitar and bass dialogue. Here was group improvisation that drew heavily on both Bruce's and Baker's jazz sensibilities. "[Ginger Baker was] really a leader," Eric Clapton told *Rolling Stone* in 1970. "I always felt . . . I [had] to fit into whatever concept he wanted to lay down . . . because he's much more of a jazz-based musician; the Cream was really a jazz group, a jazz-rock group." [17]

Certainly, Cream brought the technical and creative impulses of jazz musicians to the task at hand to produce something that was both exciting and unpredictable in a way that "pop" music quite simply was not. They had no great talent for, and did not rely on, singing or songwriting. The core of their live performance material was based on the blues. "Improvisation and performances which constantly renew themselves, that's our goal," asserted Jack Bruce, and there is no shortage of examples in Cream's discography to bear this out. [18] As the group developed, they decided the only restrictions to what they played would be imposed by their technical skills—no limitations harmonically, rhythmically, or melodically. More than any other group, they established the importance of improvisation and instrumental facility in rock. Their high profile on the American scene brought them to the attention of many forward-looking jazz musicians who recognized in their extensive and effective use of improvisation a real possibility in a union between jazz and rock. When pianist Chick Corea was a member of the Miles Davis Quintet in 1969, he told a *Downbeat* interviewer, "I've heard the Beatles records, which I like, but there's one album that Dave [Holland] has, an in-concert record of Cream. The fact that it's in concert enables them to stretch out, put in a middle section where they improvise. They're really good musicians and the tunes are extraordinary. It's [a] helluva record." [19]

When Ginger Baker left the Graham Bond Organisation to form Cream, he was replaced by Jon Hiseman, who had built up a considerable reputation with the London-based New Jazz Orchestra. Playing with Bond enabled him to turn pro. "I quit the jazz scene not because I didn't like jazz, but because the only way for me to get good was to play six nights a week," he reflected later. [20] From Bond he moved to Georgie Fame and his Blue Flames, and then to John Mayall's Bluesbreakers, appearing on the acclaimed album *Bare Wires,* which featured an influential, jazz-based horn section—including the trumpeter Henry Lowther and the saxophonist Dick Heckstall-Smith—predating American bands such as Blood, Sweat & Tears and Electric Flag. Hiseman took these various gigs with one aim in view: to form his own band. Colosseum burst on the world on October 13, 1968 at a discotheque in Scarborough. "I tried to form a band that was an improvisatory group . . . to do all the things that a rock group does," said Hiseman, "but also to play music that was as complex as anybody was playing." [21]

The nucleus of the band came from Mayall's Bluesbreakers. Heckstall-Smith and the bassist Tony Reeves joined Hiseman, with James Litherland on guitar and Dave Greenslade on keyboards filling out the group. The band's debut album from 1969, *Those Who Are About to Die Salute You,* kept one foot very firmly in the rock camp by liberally spicing the compositions with vocals, to connect with the broadest constituency. Counterbalancing these obvious commercial trappings was an experimental zeal that brought elements of jazz within a rock framework. On release in the U.S., *Downbeat* gave it a four and one-half star rating, saying "Colosseum are out of sight . . . the power and drive of traditional rock, the ensemble tightness, group empathy and . . . innovative soloing associated with jazz."[22] Their second album, *Valentyne Suite,* was more direct in its allusions to jazz. "Butty's Blues" is augmented by a big band with booting, straight ahead solos, "Valentyne Sweet" reveals Heckstall-Smith's mastery of Roland Kirk's two-horns-at-once technique, while "The Kettle" and sections of the "Valentyne Sweet" contain moments of rhythmic complexity that betrayed the band's jazz sensibilities.

Colosseum subsequently toured America, but its greatest impact was on the the European continent and in Britain. For some reason, the band did not break into the big time widely predicted for it, and it folded in 1971, although it subsequently reformed in the 1970s and toured Europe in 1994. As Hiseman has made clear, a merger of jazz and rock was clearly on the musical agenda of the times and Colosseum were a part of this. While the central thrust of the band was slanted towards rock audiences, it was nevertheless a part of an emerging consensus. "I think British musicians were ahead of the Americans in bringing rock into jazz," said Hiseman, "But I don't think we influenced the trend. I think it would have happened anyway."[23]

While Colosseum comprised musicians versed in jazz applying themselves to rock, by the end of the 1960s rock groups were emerging with musicians whose improvisational aspirations drew from their classical background. Both Pink Floyd and Soft Machine dallied with a variety of concepts that evoked twentieth-century composers such as Stockhausen, Boulez, and Terry Riley while making extended improvisation a feature of their performances. Pink Floyd, for example, refused to play their chart successes such as "See Emily Play" or "Arnold Layne" live. Instead, as *The Live Pink Floyd at Oude-Ahoy Hallen* (1967) and other bootleg albums reveal, they launched out on long freeform improvisations such as "Pow R Toc H." While this was by no means jazz improvisation, it was nevertheless a new and exciting concept and illustrates how the idea of extended electronic extemporization within a rock format was now very much in the air. Prompted in part by a drug-hazed audience who demanded a none-too-frantic music as accompaniment to the chemical substances they were popping, their mind-bending effects were accentuated by the often elaborate light and slide shows that served as a visual accompaniment to the music.

Soft Machine, who moved into the psychedelic underground from the burgeoning "Canterbury" music scene, were respectfully received as an opening act for Jimi Hendrix's 1968 American tour, just as their first album made the U.S. album charts. Their music was raw, sometimes intricate, and sometimes weird. Comprising Kevin Ayers on guitar, Mike Ratledge on keyboards, and Robert Wyatt on drums, they were, for a blink of an eye, an avant-garde jazz group before turning to experimental rock. Taking their name from a book by William Burroughs, which uses "soft machine" as a generic term for the human race, they initially attracted attention in 1967 by playing on the French Riviera for a production of Picasso's outrageous, erotic play *Desire Caught by the Tail,* which was reviewed by *Downbeat's* Mike Zwerin. "In between the vocals Soft Machine improvises and they swing," he said, adding "There is no doubt that the music they play is jazz."[24] This was by no means clear, however, on the strength of their first two albums, "the first of which was rather dull, the second not much better," noted *Rolling Stone*.[25] *Soft Machine,* recorded in 1968 and reaching the lower regions of the U.S. charts, today sounds rather self-consciously arty, particularly the opening of "Why Are We Sleeping." While "Priscilla" had the drummer Wyatt playing straight-ahead jazz rhythms at one point, their use of improvisation, such as in "Lullaby Letter," sounds rather immature. *Volume Two,* with an expanded lineup from later in the year, continued their somewhat precious-sounding originals, which were not helped by their weak melodic construction. While both albums seemed distant from anything that could be remotely construed as jazz-rock, their next album, *Third,* was among the first albums to present an aesthetically satisfying fusion of the two genres. "Certainly someone who'd been following their career at a distance could not have been prepared for this," said *Rolling Stone*.[26]

At the end of 1969 Soft Machine had reformed, following a visit to a London jazz club where their drummer Robert Wyatt had seen Keith Tippett's band. He virtually enrolled Tippett's whole front line for an expanded eight-piece lineup. Tippett, a jazz pianist in tune with the changing times, was also into jazz-rock. "I should imagine [it wouldn't] sound like jazz-rock now," he reflected some ten years later, "but anybody playing then with an eight [beat] feel was on the rocky side of jazz."[27] His recording of *I Am There . . . You Are Here* (1968), an original suite that hovers on the fringes of jazz and rock, is presumably the sort of style that attracted Wyatt. "I saw Keith Tippett's band and was struck . . . by his tough front line of horn players," Wyatt recalled. "We asked if we could borrow them to add spice to our distinctive but inflexible 'bees in a bottle' sound and they generously agreed to help out."[28] Interestingly, Tippett's sextet was also raided by Robert Fripp's experimental art-rock band King Crimson on albums such as *In the Wake of Poseidon, Lizard,* and *Islands.*

The lineup for Soft Machine's *Third* comprised Elton Dean on alto, Lyn Dobson on flute and soprano, Nick Evans on trombone, Jimmy Hastings on flute and bass clarinet, Hugh Hopper on bass, and Rab Spall on violin, together with the founding members Ratledge and Wyatt. Recorded in January 1970, every track exceeds seventeen minutes, and only one vocal, "Moon in June," which is instantly forgettable, is included. "Facelift," "Out-Bloody-Rageous"—showing a distinct Terry Riley "Rainbow in Curved Air" influence—and "Slightly All the Time" present interesting ensemble textures. If the results were somewhat primitive—Dean occasionally wanders out of tune, Rateledge's classically oriented keyboardisms often amount to empty noodlings, and Wyatt's execution was not as good as his imagination—there was no doubt that the band forecast an integrated version of jazz and rock. "The Soft Machine have made here the first successful exploration of one direction rock can go," said David Reitman in *Rock* magazine, ". . . the long improvised instrumental direction."[29]

The problem, however, was that if Soft Machine now appeared on the airstrip, it never truly got airborne. Subsequent albums showed no significant advance on a concept that proved to be bigger than the group, something that appeared clear on *Fourth.* "Soft Machine has yet to transcend its inspirations," observed Robert Palmer in *Rolling Stone*.[30] Without a major improviser or any innovative figurehead with drive, vision, and more especially direction to match their idealism, the band floundered. Band members came and went with increasing velocity as Soft Machine reinvented itself in various guises throughout the 1970s and into the 1980s. Although jazz musicians such as John Marshall on drums and John Ethridge on guitar passed through its ranks—and, in 1975, the guitarist Allan Holdsworth, who appeared on the album *Bundles*—there was never any suggestion, as there was fleetingly on *Third,* that they might ever get ahead of the game.

Like Soft Machine, many other British rock bands were content to draw on jazz for ideas, and in many cases inspiration, but they did not move towards a wholehearted fusion between jazz and rock. Countless examples abound of how jazz was permeating British rock in the late 1960s, before more exotic mutations flooded the market in the '70s, such as "glam" and "glitter" rock and a rampant tendency as the decade progressed towards "sophistication" in bands like Yes, Genesis, Pink Floyd, and Queen. Yet in 1968, for example, the blues-rock group Ten Years After included the old Woody Herman hit "Woodchoppers Ball" on their 1968 *Undead* album, their post-Clapton, axe-hero Alvin Lee's solo jazz in all but name only. The flautist Ian Anderson based his whole style on Roland Kirk's approach to the instrument, from grunts and groans to voice-flute unisons and octaves. His group Jethro Tull even worked out on Roland Kirk's "Serenade to a Cuckoo" on their debut album from 1968, *This Was.* No sooner was the album recorded than Tull lead guitarist Mick Abrahams left to form his own group, Blodwyn Pig; tenor saxophonist Jack Lancaster's solid workout on "Ahead Rings Out" on *Blodwyn Pig,* again from 1968, is a solid, jumping blues straight out of the Big Jay McNeely rulebook.

As the 1960s gave way to the 1970s, Robert Fripp's King Crimson made an impression on young American jazz musicians experimenting with jazz-rock, not least Gary Burton and Chick Corea.[31] Beginning as an art-rock band in 1969 with *In the Court of King Crimson,* the band evolved through many changes of personnel, with the guitarist Fripp the constant factor. The classic lineup formed in late 1972 with Fripp on guitar, David Cross on violin and mellotron, John Wetton on bass, Bill Bruford on drums, and Jamie Muir on percussion, cutting three albums in an eighteen-month span, *Lark's Tongue in Aspic, Starless and Bible Black,* and *Red.* They played with intensity and dark fury, all captured on *The Great Deceiver (Live 1973–4),* which delivers freeform improvisation, extended blowing, and crunching ominous grooves based on the quantity and quality of Fripp's guitar and Bruford's (who had left Yes to join Crimson) hyperactive drumming. While the group's soloing stands up today far better than their songs, *Deceiver* presents evidence of the band's maturity into a high-energy, improvising ensemble that made extensive use of rock rhythms. Other strong improvisational talents at work within the rock forum that owed much to the methodology of jazz included the former John Mayall drummer Keef Hartley with his ensembles of varying sizes, the guitarist Fred Frith and the saxophonist Tim Hodgkinson with Henry Cow, and the guitarist Allan Holdsworth with Gong.

However, British jazz musicians were on the whole rather more cautious about incorporating rock elements into jazz. Despite the forays of several musicians into the rock and R&B scene, jazz audiences, as distinct from rock audiences, were less receptive to the notion of combining jazz with elements of rock music. Dick Heckstall-Smith felt that the British jazz scene at this time took itself all too seriously and that musicians and audience had seemed to have forgotten how to enjoy themselves; "I began to feel there was altogether too much good taste in the British jazz scene," he said later.[32] Yet the rock revolution was something musicians could hardly ignore. In December 1967 the pianist Gordon Beck confronted the repertoire of popular culture using as his accompanists John McLaughlin on guitar, Jeff Clyne on bass, and Tony Oxley on drums. The resulting album, *Experiments with Pops,* prefigured the pianist Herbie Hancock's approach to popular tunes in *The New Standard* (1996) by some thirty years by reshaping pop songs through meter and rhythmic changes and often drastic reharmonization, making the outline of the original tunes appear like some distant signpost glimpsed in the fog.

Beck, a virtuoso pianist, created a fine jazz album in *Experiments with Pops,* working in the post-bop idiom. The record deserves recognition today for its resourceful adaptation of pop hits such as "These Boots Are Made for Walking"—treated modally à la "Milestones"—"Up, Up and Away," "Good Vibrations," and "Monday, Monday." These songs were treated as vehicles for improvisation without drawing on rock elements *per se.* Once the barrier had been breached by importing the repertoire of rock and pop into jazz without a sacrifice of musical integrity, the next challenge—importing the *sounds* of rock, in terms of its rhythms and electronic tone colors—had to be confronted. Here John McLaughlin uses a harsher, rock-influenced tone rather than the round, precise, hornlike tone favored by jazz guitarists within the Charlie Christian–Tal Farlow–Wes Montgomery school. Nevertheless, his fluency and imagination within the post-bop idiom appears complete.

In 1968, the trumpeter Ian Carr began considering capitalizing on his experiences working in the 1960s London scene. Carr had made a small but secure reputation as a member of his brother Mike's group, the Emcee Five, in the Newcastle area. A lyrical and undemonstrative player, he contributed two imaginative solos in "The One that Got Away" and "Stephenson's Rocket" collected on *Bebop from the East Coast.* On moving to London, he joined Don Rendell to form the Rendell-Carr Quintet, making five albums that were broadly in the hard-bop mainstream before deciding to go it alone. He secured gigs with Alexis Korner and directed a big band behind Eric Burdon's Animals, and then experimented with free jazz. "After free jazz, there seemed nothing else to do," he recalled. "The Beatles were attractive, and suddenly you think there is a way forward. And there was Miles Davis who had already done a lot of things with a rock-ish feel by then. But when I decided to move into jazz-rock it was because I was fed up with free jazz. I'd done it, but where do you go from there?"[33]

In mid-1969, Carr formed Nucleus to explore a jazz-rock fusion, and in January 1970 they recorded *Elastic Rock.* "When I recorded *Elastic Rock,* Miles's recording of *In A Silent Way* was yet to appear in Britain," he recalled. "It didn't reach us until after *Elastic Rock* was actually out, and then we knew! There *was* a way forward, there was a way of renewing yourself, doing new things. But we weren't working on the same sort of things as Miles. We were looking at the blues, for example, and how it could be metrically subdivided into different sections and time signatures."[34] The best example of this, and the most memorable track on the album, was "1916."

In the early months of 1970, Nucleus was chosen to represent Britain at the International Jazz Festival at Montreux, where the European Broadcasting Union sponsored a jazz "competition" between the European nations. Nucleus won the prize, an appearance at the Newport Jazz Festival. "The American musicians were extremely friendly and showed a lot of curiosity and interest in what we were playing," said Carr. "However, our problem was that we never got our records out in America until too late; John Hammond wanted to do a deal as soon as we came offstage, but I was badly advised, sticking out for too much money because of the rock thing."[35] After Newport, Carr played the Village Gate in Greenwich Village. "*Bitches Brew* was out when we went to New York in 1970, they had a track from it on the juke-boxes, 'Miles Runs the Voodoo Down' that was a fantastic," Carr said. "But what surprised me was that musicians were coming up to us and saying, 'What do you call this music, what is it?'"[36]

Nucleus recorded a series of albums for the British market that were never heard in the States. Taken together they represent a solid body of achievement that thoughtfully experimented with structure, meter, and texture. *We'll Talk About It Later* and *Solar Plexus* followed hard on the heels of *Elastic Rock*, all recorded in 1970. "Another key thing was that in England we were familiar with Indian music, ragas, which is mostly symmetrical," continued Carr. "McLaughlin knew Indian music too incidentally, and Miles was not into that; unusual time signatures; 'Snake Hips' on *Solar Plexus* is out of Indian music; I grew up with Indians, went to college with them and shared a house in college, ate their food heard their music, so my music came from a different standpoint to the direction Miles went in."[37] Carr's subsequent albums included *Belladonna* (1972), which brought together a strong lineup that included Allan Holdsworth on guitar and Gordon Beck on piano. *Labyrinth* (1973), used a double quartet augmented by Gordon Beck on piano, Tony Coe on saxophones, and Kenny Wheeler on trumpet mixing free jazz and rock, and it stands with Carr's later albums *Inflagrante Delicto* and *Out of the Long Dark* as among the best representations of his work.

Today, Nucleus's first recordings genuinely suggest artistic potential in a jazz-rock fusion. However, by the late 1960s, developments in America had been gathering momentum to an extent that would overshadow Carr's work in Britain. Although Joachim Berendt has observed that "with a bit of exaggeration one could say in Great Britain, the 1960s was already a decade of fusion music,"[38] this is only partly true. The result was less a creation of fusion *per se* than one of jazz musicians crossing over into rock. Certainly they brought their jazz sensibilities to bear on matters such as improvisation and rhythmic complexity, but, for the most part, these bands performed mainly to rock audiences, who provided the biggest paycheck, rather than the jazz constituency, who did not, and their music was framed accordingly. However, by the end of the 1960s a fusion between jazz and rock was also on the musical agenda of a number of young American jazz musicians who were influenced, both musically and socially, by the sudden and unexpected rise of rock music. What was going on around them in their own music scene had begun to make them think that if jazz was to progress, then a marriage with rock in some way, shape, or form was the way forward.

Notes

1. Ginger Baker interview, BBC TV documentary.
2. On the CD *Bootleg Him!* by Alexis Korner, track 7 (Castle Classics CLACD 291).
3. *Rolling Stone*, July 8, 1971, pp. 16–17.
4. Interview with the author, December 14, 1995.
5. "John McLaughlin," by Joachim Berendt, *Jazz Forum*, pp. 31–32.
6. Ginger Baker interview, BBC TV documentary.
7. *Music Outside*, by Ian Carr (Latimer, London, 1973), pp. 59–60.
8. *Blues in Britain*, by Bob Brunning (Blandford, London, 1995), p. 46.
9. *Zig Zag* 22, p. 4.
10. Ginger Baker interview, BBC TV documentary.
11. *Life*, January 1968.
12. *Downbeat*, July 25, 1968, p. 16.
13. Ibid., February 6, 1969, p. 23.
14. *Atlantic and the Godfathers of Rock and Roll*, by Justine Picardie and Dorothy Wade (Fourth Estate, London, 1993) p. 136.
15. *Rolling Stone*, February 24, 1968, p. 22.
16. Ibid., May 11, 1968, p. 14.
17. Ibid., October 15, 1970, p. 22.
18. *All You Need Is Love*, by Tony Palmer (Weidenfeld & Nicolson and Chappell, London, 1976) p. 275.
19. *Downbeat*, April 3, 1969, p. 22.
20. *Music Outside*, by Ian Carr (Latimer, London, 1973), pp. 59–60.
21. Ibid., p. 63.
22. *Downbeat*, November 13, 1969, p. 19.
23. Interview with the author, December 19, 1995.
24. *Downbeat*, October 5, 1967, p. 16.
25. *Rolling Stone*, January 7, 1971, p. 40.
26. Ibid.
27. *Blues Music and Jazz Review*, July 1979, p. 29.
28. Liner notes by Robert Wyatt, *The Soft Machine: Third* (BGO Records, BGOCD 180).
29. Quoted in *Downbeat*, January 7, 1971, p. 22.
30. *Rolling Stone*, September 2, 1971, p. 33.
31. Interview with the author, November 29, 1994.
32. *The Safest Place in the World*, by Dick Heckstall-Smith (Quartet, London, 1989), p. 45.
33. Interview with the author, December 14, 1995.
34. Ibid.
35. Ibid.
36. Ibid.
37. Ibid.
38. *The Jazz Book*, by Joachim E. Berendt (Paladin, London, 1984), p. 41.

CHAPTER 3

Free Spirits

For aspiring young jazz musicians growing up in the 1960s, the social revolution was happening all around them. Whether their politics were of the New Left, the Love Generation, or the rising tide of black militancy, they were at least united in antiwar rhetoric and a hatred of racism and petty bourgeois propriety. Turning up at demonstrations was as much an excuse to get stoned, to find a new date, or to fight the police, as to protest, yet a basic underlying demand for change was always in the air.

Tripping on acid had made thinking the unthinkable commonplace. And, as a not entirely unconnected phenomenon, popular culture was swept with unusual connections and new ideas. LSD, capable of "transforming the mundane into the sensational,"[1] arguably led to a greater sensibility towards color and design, and certainly had an important influence on pop culture, media style, and advertising. Traditional taboos were being broken at every level of society, from dress codes to sexual inhibitions. "One discovers how far one can go only by travelling in a straight line until one is stopped," wrote Norman Mailer in 1965.[2]

In this new climate of enquiry, integrating jazz and rock seemed like the most logical connection to make in the world, a new idea in a decade where new ideas were being tried out every day. "Everybody was dropping acid and the prevailing attitude was 'Let's do something different,'" said guitarist Larry Coryell, who in 1965 was just twenty-two years old. "We were saying, We love Wes [Montgomery], but we also love Bob Dylan. We love Coltrane but we also love the Beatles. We love Miles but we also love the Rolling Stones. We wanted people to know we are very much part of the contemporary scene, but at the same time we had worked our butts off to learn this other music [called jazz]. It was a very sincere thing."[3]

Combining jazz and rock was seen not as a commercial proposition but as a way of expanding the music in a new direction, as bebop and free jazz had done before. It was a concept that was enthusiastically received by the underground press. "Psychedelic rock and avante garde jazz are being fused into an orgasm of emotion and integral art-life totality," said a feature in the alternative New York paper, the *East Village Other*. "This music shouts with the rage of social order and burns with love."[4] Here was a way for young jazz musicians to find a voice in jazz that did not cut them off from the culture of *their* generation. There was an excitement in the air of being caught up in something that was bigger than their own private tastes. "Whether you can dig it or not," said *Rolling Stone* in 1968, "There is little doubt that this is going to be the young jazz of the future and it is refreshing and hopeful for the world of music to discover just how few barriers there can be between two musical forms that are usually fiercely repelling each other."[5]

Larry Coryell arrived in New York on September 3, 1965 from the University of Washington in Seattle and moved into an apartment at 19 Eldridge Street, near New York's Bowery district. On his block lived the West Coast tenor and flute player Jim Pepper, who in turn introduced him to the eighteen-year-old drummer Bobby Moses, to guitarist Columbus "Chip" Baker, and to bassist Chris Hills. Together they roamed the jazz spots of Manhattan, sitting in with whomever they could, including Charles Lloyd, Chico Hamilton, and Don Cherry. They gathered every Thursday at a local club called L'Intrigue to jam with a group of like-minded musicians including the guitarist Joe Beck—who got the gig since he knew the owner—Randy Brecker on trumpet, Mike Mainieri on vibes, Warren Bernhardt on piano, and Donald MacDonald on drums; they were among the first jazz musicians to attempt combining jazz and rock.

"This went on for about a year," said Warren Bernhardt, "certainly until well into 1966. To me that was the beginnings of jazz-rock; to my knowledge there was no one else combining rock and jazz improvisation at that time, combining styles like that. It was a whole different spirit, very much the spirit of the sixties. We started growing our hair long and all that kind of thing. LSD was part of the scene. The music was adventurous and maybe a little chaotic—there was some free [jazz] mixed in there too—they were exciting times!"[6]

While jamming with Herbie Mann, Coryell impressed Clark Terry, who introduced him to the record producer Bob Thiele. He was soon in the recording studios with Pepper, Baker, Hills, and Moses, now calling themselves Free Spirits. Their eponymous 1966 album for ABC-Paramount reveals a rather self-conscious band using rock rhythms and jazz improvisation. Coryell's awkward vocals, perhaps a nod to the rock audience who expected lyrics along with their music, were less than convincing. "I was disappointed in the record we did together," observed Moses. "It was recorded before we had worked together very much."[7] Nevertheless, the group had made their mark as one of the very first jazz-rock groups, with Coryell clearly a man to watch. The band did not make much money and so had a relatively short life, gigging in discotheques and finally landing an extended run at The Scene before it broke up. Coryell then joined the trumpeter Randy Brecker for a short run before moving to a quartet led by the vibist Gary Burton in early 1967.

Born in 1943, Burton was a teenage prodigy on vibes who was signed by RCA in 1960, making his recording debut as a seventeen year old before enrolling at Berklee College of Music, where he studied until 1962. *New Vibe Man in Town*, recorded in 1961 while he was still a Berklee student, places him in a challenging trio lineup with Gene Cherico on bass and Joe Morello on drums. "Vibes have never been exploited very much because no-one has developed enough tech-

ABC RECORDS PRESENTS

the "now" group—
with the "now" sound...

THE FREE SPIRITS

Free Spirits: A rather self-conscious mix of rock rhythms and jazz improvisation in which some awkward vocals were less than convincing, Free Spirits were among the first bands to place jazz-rock on the musical agenda. (Courtesy of the Institute of Jazz Studies, Rutgers University.)

nique," he said, "I'd like to try and do it."[8] Far from youthful bluster, Burton was already among the finest vibists in jazz, and during the next few years he set about proving it to the rest of the world. In 1963 he recorded *Something's Coming* with the guitarist Jim Hall, Chuck Israels on bass, and Larry Bunker on drums; this album revealed a Bill Evans influence on his playing. In 1966 he cut another trio album, *The Time Machine,* with Steve Swallow on bass and Larry Bunker on drums, but the album highlight was a "conversations with myself" version of the Beatles' composition "Norwegian Wood" with Burton multitracking vibes, bass marimba, and piano.

These albums were recorded while Burton served successive stints as a sideman with the George Shearing Quintet (1963) and the Stan Getz Quartet (January 1964 to December 1966). Burton shone in both bands; his 1963 tracks on *The Complete Live Recordings of George Shearing,* for example, reveal how he was given his head, responding with a high level of creativity, while his work with Getz on *Nobody Else But Me*—recorded in 1964 but not released until 1994—shows the saxophonist according him equal solo space, the ultimate accolade from a prickly perfectionist. By 1965 Burton was topping the

Downbeat Critic's Poll as "New Star" on vibes, and great things were expected from the twenty-two year old.

Burton perfected the use of a four-mallet technique, and the speed of his execution allied to a fluent use of chord substitutions made the vibraphone sound like a new instrument in his hands. Gone was the horn-like single note approach of a Lionel Hampton, Milt Jackson, or Bobby Hutcherson; in its place were shimmering textures and fast-moving chorded lines that established him as an important individual voice on an instrument that could so easily swallow a player's identity. *Tennessee Firebird,* from September 1966, came towards the end of his three-year stay with Getz and saw him turning from bluegrass to Bob Dylan's "I Want You" and "Just Like a Woman." Produced by the veteran Nashville guitarist and studio hand Chet Atkins, the album was an attempt to connect jazz with country. "Stan had taken Brazilian music and played with it," he recalled. "That's what made me think of country music. On *Tennessee Firebird* I tried everything I could think of, different styles of country music. It wasn't that successful, but I enjoyed it. . . . I'd asked Roy Haynes to be on it. I told him what I was going to do and he said he'd try anything once!"[9] Indeed, on the album cover there is a photo of a bemused Haynes watching the session unfold.

Burton left Getz to form his own group and, with representation by George Wein, organizer of the Newport Jazz Festival, he was quickly overwhelmed with work. "The first booking with my new quartet was in January 1967 at Lennie's-on-the-Turnpike near Boston," recalled Burton. "I had met Larry Coryell a few months earlier in New York at a jam session that saxophonist Steve Marcus had taken me to, and I had already been booked into Lennie's for early January as a trio. I was going to use Eddie Gomez and Joe Hunt, Bill Evans's rhythm section, since he was on a break at that time. After getting acquainted with Larry, I decided to ask him to join me for the week in Boston and make it a quartet and that became the group for the first three months of gigs in the New York area, mostly working at the Café au Go Go. When the first out-of-town gig came up, Gomez and Hunt returned to Bill's trio and I hired bassist Steve Swallow, who I had played with in Stan Getz's group, and Stu Martin on drums."[10]

In April 1967, Burton was scheduled for a record date, but with Hunt just leaving and Martin just starting, he was not sure how things would go. He turned again to the drummer Roy Haynes, his former colleague in the Getz quartet, replacing Martin for the recording of *Duster* on April 18–20. Awarded five stars by *Downbeat,* its contemporary tone and feeling of freshness is still apparent today. This was due in part to Burton's careful choice of strikingly original compositions, most notably from Swallow and from outside the group by Mike Gibbs and Carla Bley, whose fourteen-bar non-blues "Sing Me Softly of the Blues" was an album highlight. Of the Gibbs compositions, "Sweet Rain" was also recorded around the same time by Stan Getz on one of his most memorable albums,[11] while on "Liturgy" and the waltz time "Ballet," the full, chorded sound of Burton's vibes was set off by Coryell's acid tone on guitar. It was a sound associated with a "rock" guitar, but Coryell's technical facility, melodic construction, and harmonic savvy were beyond the ken of any rock musician. His fast, single-note lines were a perfect contrast to Burton's clusters of sound. On Steve Swallow's "General Mojo's Well Laid Plan," the unmistakable sound of rock's square rhythm section patterns are suborned by Haynes into a jazz context.

Together with Coryell's *Free Spirits*, Burton's *Duster* was among the first recordings that suggested an artistically and aesthetically satisfying synthesis of jazz and rock was possible. "When I started the group it was very unusual to be away from jazz into pop rhythms," Burton recalled in 1971. "Our motivation was to give us something else to play. Steve Swallow and I were very worried when we started that it might hurt our popularity because our audience then was right into jazz—and there was some resentment when we changed."[12]

Burton's role in giving the sound of the rock guitar a vital and intrinsic role within the ensemble, plus the group's youthful appearance, allowed them to work in distinctly non-jazz venues, such as Manhattan's The Scene. However, he refused to surrender the jazz identity of his group, working towards a specific jazz-rock synthesis. "One shouldn't play rock tunes in a jazz setting," he asserted, "that isn't what it's all about."[13] On one memorable occasion in the summer of 1967, Burton's group played Bill Graham's Fillmore in San Francisco, sharing the bill with The Electric Flag and Cream. The Flag and Cream both used huge stacks of Marshall speakers, while in contrast Coryell used a small suitcase-sized Fender amp and speaker and Burton played acoustically. With only a fraction of the other groups' volume they nevertheless won the crowd over.

From the start Burton made a conscious effort to touch base with a younger audience; he and Coryell grew their hair to the then-fashionable shoulder length and wore casual but contemporary clothes on stand. Often, his group ended their concerts by dismantling the vibes and drums, making a pile of them center stage, and adding the guitar and bass to them before all four walked off. As a finale it made an effective contemporary climax, a subtle parody on Jimi Hendrix setting fire to his guitar or Pete Townsend of The Who smashing his Fender Stratocaster to smithereens. All this was in stark contrast to the neat suit-and-tie and crew-cut look that Burton sported during his tenure with Shearing and Getz, and it was not initially without controversy. "People said I was doing it to attract attention and go commercial," he said in 1968, "but that soon died away as others started doing it . . . one reason why jazz isn't more popular with young audiences is that it's hard for them to identify with forty-ish musicians in tailored suits. They could loosen up some."[14]

Stu Martin's last major date with the group was at the Newport Jazz Festival on Saturday evening, July 1, 1967. His replacement was Bob Moses, whose presence added to the controversy among jazz critics as to whether the quartet was or was not playing jazz-rock. In fact their rhythmic approach was very fluid, and square rhythm section patterns came and went at the need of the moment. After jazz-rock had become absorbed into the jazz mainstream by the late 1980s, this sort of thing was commonplace in post-bop ensembles, but in the late 1960s it was far from the accepted norm. Burton himself was anything but enigmatic about the influence of rock on his music. "It's the most alive and timely music around today—jazz seems to me one of the most slack and dated," he told the *Village Voice*.[15]

The Gary Burton Quartet in 1969: *Left to right:* Jerry Hahn, Burton, Steve Swallow, Bill Goodwin. Burton's pioneering jazz-rock experimentation from 1967–1972 represents a much-overlooked body of work that suggested the possibility of an aesthetically satisfying union of jazz and rock. (Courtesy of the Institute of Jazz Studies, Rutgers University.)

Moses, the former Free Spirits drummer, was at the time living in the same building as Coryell at 19 Eldridge Street. Something of a musician's community, the building also housed bassist Arthur Harper, Charles and JoAnne Brackeen (Charles was the building supervisor), the Free Spirits bassist Chris Hills, and the New Zealand–born pianist Mike Nock. Jesse Colin Young and the Youngbloods lived across the street. During the daytime an informal quartet comprising Coryell, Nock, Hill, and Moses regularly jammed together, joined by saxophonist Steve Marcus, a former Berklee graduate and Stan Kenton–Woody Herman alumnus. "Our music was inspired by the Beatles, the Byrds, the Stones, and Coltrane's 'free style,'" recalled Nock. "It was also a protest against a lot of the conservatism that was so prevalent in jazz even then. I remember a night when Steve Marcus played me a choice selection of Beatles music, it had a profound affect on both of us. I was playing all this musicians' music, not really getting off on it. Then I heard a James Brown record and it floored me. I'd been in the jazz syndrome and you can't find jazz musicians to play that kind of time. They think it's beneath them, yet they can't play it. I wanted to play a simple kind of music that grooved me, in those days we didn't think of it as 'jazz-rock,' it was just the music we wanted to play."[16]

Marcus assumed leadership of this informal gathering, calling it Count's Rock Band, and financed a record date with Gary Burton acting as producer.

Burton and Marcus shopped the tapes around for about six months before Herbie Mann's new record label Vortex took them. *Tomorrow Never Knows* was released in 1968 under Marcus's name and included an uncredited appearance by Burton sitting in on tambourine—Marcus had earlier appeared on Burton's album *Tennessee Firebird*—"Gary was a school mate from Berklee where we all used to play together," said Nock.[17] Burton's behind-the-scenes role underscores the exchange of ideas that was occurring among this new generation of jazz musicians on the New York scene, and shows how a consensus was emerging that a jazz-rock synthesis represented an exciting new way forward for jazz. "The healthy abrasiveness of Marcus's music reminds me of the function which Norman Mailer fulfils so well on the literary scene: shake them up—wake them up," said Mike Zwerin in *Downbeat*.[18] "I find this the most interesting development in American music in a long time—we are beginning to have pop influenced jazz. Pop music has finally got something to give back [to jazz]; rock, electronic music with a beat. It's nice to hear somebody taking advantage of it." The album received a five-star award.

"Our idea was to play free contemporary jazz over modal rock grooves," said Nock,[19] and on numbers such as "Eight Miles High" the group succeeded in their objectives, paying only lip service to the Byrds' theme before launching into some ferocious blowing featuring Marcus, who plays in a middle-to-late period Coltrane bag. This was uncompromising jazz played over a rock beat and stands up well today. Clearly of its time—the recorded sound, the addition of Dominic Cortese's accordion, and the rhythm section's "feel" for rock are clearly very "sixties"—this music was nevertheless a genuine attempt to extend the language of jazz. The melody of Donovan's hit "Mellow Yellow" was played more or less straight throughout, but with overdubbing Marcus, Coryell, and Nock launched into some feral free blowing in surreal counterpoint to their "straight" statement of the theme. However, the title track was the album's most successful cut, the Beatles' tune no more than a head to provide a vehicle for some strong, uncompromising improvisation for Coryell (clearly under the spell of Jimi Hendrix), Nock, and Marcus.

Marcus's second album, *Count's Rock Band*, came a year later but surprisingly did not fare so well at the hands of reviewers. Despite a memorable "Ooh Baby" with Marcus demonstrating what a fine saxophonist he was, *Downbeat* awarded it three stars, noting that "Nock is a first-rate pianist with enormous versatility."[20] Their final album, *The Lord's Prayer*, was recorded in the summer of 1969, by which time Nock had departed for the West Coast, so Herbie Hancock substituted on both acoustic and electric pianos. However, Nock did return for an appearance at the Newport Jazz Festival with the group on the evening of July 4, 1969. Shortly afterwards the band wound up when Marcus went out on the road with Woody Herman in the late summer. "When we started it was before I'd heard any rock bands like the Cream stretching out," observed Nock. "Looking back I always think that it was one of the first *true* jazz-rock groups, at least on records."[21]

Meanwhile, Gary Burton's first album with Bob Moses was recorded in August 1967. *Lofty Fake Anagram* was a calmer affair than *Duster*, less concerned

Steve Marcus: By 1967 his group Count's Rock Band were
mixing powerful Coltrane modal grooves with rock rhythms.
(Photograph by Stuart Nicholson.)

with exploiting technique than with exposing meaning, particularly in their interpretation of Duke Ellington's "Fleurette Africaine." Steve Swallow's composition "General Mojo Cuts Up" is a freeform-jazz-rock piece similar in concept to
the Count Rock Band's "Back Street Girl" on that band's eponymously titled
second album. Burton and Coryell's playing often blurred the distinction
between accompaniment and counterpoint, particularly on Paul Bley's "Mother
of the Dead Men" and "I'm Your Pal," although on "Lines" they sounded a little
baroque. "The musicianship here is of a very high level—as one would expect,"
said *Rolling Stone.*[22] A measure of how the progress of Burton's group was being
followed by other jazz musicians is revealed in a private recording made in early
1968 at the home of the London pianist and composer Bob Cornford. In a
rehearsal tape made with guitarist John McLaughlin, they recreate the final cut

on the album, "Good Citizen Swallow," in which McLaughlin consciously emulates Coryell's style.[23]

The Burton Quartet also had a profound effect in Germany following their appearance at the Berlin Jazz Days festival on November 5, 1967. The notoriously fickle Berlin audience gave Burton what Leonard Feather described as "The culminating ovation of the entire festival." He continued, "Rarely have I witnessed such a wild reaction to any group at any jazz festival."[24] That such a fusion between jazz and rock was even being contemplated by U.S. musicians came as a shock to German audiences and musicians. The German writer Alexander Schmitz has pointed out that Burton's concert turned the German jazz scene around "more or less overnight,"[25] while the guitarist Volker Kriegal later wrote, "The filigree beauty of Gary Burton's music was miles away from the crudity of noisy rock 'n' roll bands. Gary's floating sounds conveyed a liberating, free and easy sense of living. What a difference to our jazz scene, which had keyed itself in between bitterly serious free jazz and conventional stiffness."[26]

Also appearing at the Berlin Jazz Days was the Detroit-born vibist Dave Pike, whose resume included work with Paul Bley, Harold Land, Dexter Gordon, Bobby Timmons, and Jaki Byard and recordings with Attila Zoller, Clark Terry, Bill Evans, and Kenny Burrell. After the concert he decided to settle in Europe, moving to Düsseldorf with his wife and child. In 1968 he was taken to the Jazzkeller there by the bassist Anton Rettenbacher to hear Volker Kriegal play. Their subsequent meeting resulted in the formation of the Dave Pike Set in the autumn of that year, comprising Pike on vibes, Kriegal on guitar, Rettenbacher on acoustic and electric basses, and Peter Baumeister on drums. Their model was the Burton quartet, but from the start the Set intentionally avoided standards from the Great American Songbook, which Pike, "a bebopper through and through," appreciated most. The band favored rhythm ostinati and odd meters, and mixed free jazz with rock rhythms. "The Dave Pike Set was no cheap imitation of the Gary Burton Quartet," asserted Kriegal, "even though it showed the same line-up . . . one reason being Dave Pike's and Gary Burton's different ways of playing the vibraphone. Already at that time Gary's specialties were cleverly woven harmony progressions and the polyphone splitting of chords with the help of the four-mallet technique. Dave, on the other hand, played very down-to-earth, very rhythmic . . . single line improvisations."[27] Between November 1968 and the end of 1972, the group toured extensively, including an appearance at the 1971 Newport Jazz Festival, and released six albums, *Noisy Silence–Gentle Noise, Four Reasons,* and *Live at the Philharmonie* (all 1969), *Infra Red* (1970), *Album* (1971), and finally *Salomão* (1972).[28]

There was a sense of innocent adventure with these albums that characterized the best of the early jazz-rock experiments. Although the level of musicianship was high, they did not exploit virtuosity as an end in itself, and in their eclecticism they saw beyond a marriage of jazz and rock to a more inclusive vision of jazz that was decades ahead of its time. In a sense, the Pike Set did not incorporate rock so much as the spirit of the 1960s. From their debut album it was clear indeed this was no imitation of Burton's group. Their extroverted stance saw to that. Conceptually, they were the logical continuum of what Burton had begun, moving the premise of jazz-rock on into other areas of music that few subsequent jazz-rock bands contemplated on either side of the Atlantic. Kriegal changed the tonal climate of the group by using acoustic and electric guitars, distortion—"Big Schlepp"—and on some cuts he uses a sitar. In January 1969 he was among the first jazz guitarists to make use of the wah-wah pedal, on "Walkin' Down the Highway in a Raw Red Egg." He also doubled on bass while Rettenbacher played cello on "Greater Kalesh No. 48," which again altered the texture of the group.

Rettenbacher and Baumeister had a spring quite uncharacteristic of European rhythm sections of the period and retained a fluid balance between rock and straight-ahead patterns, often within the same composition, such as on "Noisy Silence–Gentle Noise." In 1969, they employed Latin-American rhythms on "Rabbi Mogen's Hideout," while in 1972 they moved further into World rhythms when they combined with the Brazilian Grupo Baiafro De Bahia, for the album *Salomão*.

The overall tonal climates of Burton's and Pike's groups were set by the respective leaders' quite distinct approaches, with Pike's aggressive, single-note attack rooted in bebop quite different from Burton's chord blocks inspired by Bill Evans. It is difficult to imagine Burton's quartet recording anything as extroverted as "Regards from Freddie Horrowitz," as it is for the Pike set to have recorded anything as considered as Burton's "Liberty Bell." "We did not want deadly serious music, but something light and bright," said Kriegal. "[We] rather played for hedonistic high spirits, none of us was a 'hard-core ideologist.'"[29]

Subsequently Kriegel and the bassist Eberhard Weber (who joined the Pike Set in 1971) formed the group Spectrum in 1972 when Pike returned to the U.S. In 1969 the pianist Wolfgang Dauner began reflecting the influence of the Beatles and formed the jazz-rock band Et Cetera, while Klaus Doldinger's Passport embraced jazz, classical, and rock. In the Netherlands, Jasper Van 't Hof, who had recorded with Dauner, formed Pork Pie with Charlie Mariano and Philip Catherine. They became one of the most popular of the European jazz-rock groups, while in the mid-1970s Volker Kriegal was instrumental in forming the United Jazz and Rock Ensemble, an occasional band that continued to record and tour into the 1990s.

Perhaps Burton's most famous album with his quartet, *A Genuine Tong Funeral*, was recorded in November 1967 with the addition of Steve Lacy on soprano sax, Mike Mantler on trumpet, Gato Barbieri on tenor sax, Jimmy Knepper on trombone, and Howard Johnson on tuba and baritone sax. A series of tone poems composed and conducted by Carla Bley, who also played piano and organ, it was subsequently performed on WGBH, Boston's educational television channel, to considerable acclaim.

On February 23, 1968 Burton's quartet gave a concert at the Carnegie Hall Recital Room, producing *Gary Burton in Concert,* one of the few live recordings in Burton's discography. In person, Burton's playing could reach impressive levels of virtuosity, a side of him that he preferred to keep under wraps when in the studio making records. "All those notes flying everywhere. It's kind of like show-ing off," he once said. "I prefer my recorded work to be more considered, thoughtful statements."[30] This is one reason, perhaps, that Burton has never *quite* been given his due by the critics. Even so, *In Concert* is an excellent album and was awarded four and one-half stars by *Downbeat*. "Burton has deepened his mastery of his instrument . . . his convolute improvisations are brilliantly execut-ed and conceived," said fellow vibist and reviewer Don DeMicheal.[31]

Moses left the group shortly afterwards, with Roy Haynes moving into the group on a full-time basis; after their appearance at the Newport Jazz Festival on Thursday, July 4, 1968, Coryell left to join Herbie Mann's group. He was briefly replaced by Chick Corea before the southwestern guitarist Jerry Hahn joined the group. Hahn had made a name for himself with the John Handy Quintet on the West Coast with his playing on *Live at the Monterey Jazz Festival* from 1965 and *The 2nd John Handy Album* from 1966. On numbers such as "Dancy, Dancy" and "Blues for a Hamstrung Guitar," it was clear he had devel-oped an original style that had echoes, like the playing of Ornette Coleman and Dewey Redman, of the Texas-Oklahoma influence of country music and blues.

The rejigged group recorded *Country Roads and Other Places*, which contains "And on the Third Day," one of Mike Gibb's most memorable compositions, on September 25, 1968. Hahn's musical personality is so strong that the loss of Coryell is not missed; in fact his C&W origins seem to appeal to Burton, who duets engagingly with him on "Wichita Breakdown." This marked Burton's final, and best, album for RCA. The death of Steve Sholes, an RCA vice president who supported Burton's music, coupled with the insensitivity of the new manage-ment, led him to sign with Atlantic.

Burton's first album for his new label was *Throb,* recorded in June 1969 with Hahn on guitar, Swallow on bass, Bill Goodwin on drums, and guest Richard Greene on violin. Greene's presence allowed another peek at Burton's C&W roots—Burton's first recording had been in 1961 with Hank Garland—since Greene was a one-time bluegrass player who had turned to rock, leading the group Seatrain. The result was impressionistic hoedown, with Hahn losing none of the fluency of jazz, but adding a country "twang" to his playing that sat well with Burton's own use of pitch-bending. Overall, the down-home feel detracts from the gravitas of Burton's earlier work in what was destined to be an album that was more pleasing than profound. In April 1970, somewhat bemused by the lack of sales, Atlantic began a belated publicity campaign for the album, with the caption "If You Overlooked Gary Burton's New Album It's Our Fault":

When Gary Burton's first Atlantic album was released last fall we should have taken out ads extolling it. Because it happens to be pretty damn good. . . . We didn't because: 1. We didn't think we had to since Gary has a large following in both jazz and rock fields. 2. We were very busy at the time. . . . Unfor-tunately we did Gary a disservice which we hope this ad will correct. Gary is well and happy with Atlantic Records. . . . If you haven't heard Gary Burton's new album do it now. It doesn't matter whether you dig jazz, rock or underground. Gary's outstanding musicianship has won him fans in all fields.[32]

As an attempt to bolster sales, this ad was largely unsuccessful, but corporate advertising was designed not so much to sell a record as explain how it should be interpreted—and convey an attitude. The tongue-in-cheek tone of this ad and the pseudohip language ("It doesn't matter whether you dig jazz, rock or underground") were designed to appeal to young consumers. Atlantic was also trying to educate rock fans that there could be something in jazz for them to "dig"— and vice versa. Despite Burton's previous success with the RCA label, jazz-rock was still a new concept and the potential of his music to appeal to jazz *and* rock fans was a continuing theme in corporate adverts. When *Good Vibes* came out later in the year, Atlantic supported it with an advertising campaign announcing "A Jazzman Gone Rock." Ads such as this helped sell the concept of jazz-rock to a new listening audience.

In the fall of 1969, Burton toured Europe as a part of "Jazz Expo '69," now with David Pritchard on guitar. During the tour, he encountered the pianist Keith Jarrett in Europe. "I asked him about his music and about the possibility of working together," Burton recalled. "He was not yet with Miles Davis, but touring with a trio of his own. He returned to the States and we performed a half a dozen gigs together that summer since he didn't join Miles's band until some time later."[33] One of their most memorable performances together was their appearance on Saturday afternoon, July 11, 1970, at the Newport Jazz Festival. Twelve days later Jarrett was in the recording studio with Burton's regular quartet, now with Sam Brown on guitar.

Jarrett was an acoustic pianist who, when he had recorded with Miles Davis a matter of weeks before (in May), was persuaded to play electronic keyboards, apparently against his better judgement (post-Davis, Jarrett never played electronic instruments again). However, despite his protestations, it should be remembered that on his own debut album, *Restoration Ruin* (1968)—where he performs (dreadfully) in the singer-songwriter mode of Bob Dylan—Jarrett overdubbed any number of instruments including electric guitar, electric bass, and electronic keyboards. Equally, with Burton, Jarrett had no inhibitions, real or imagined, against playing both acoustic and electric instruments, something he does with audible joy, contributing to the palpable empathy between the two musicians. In fact, during their European meeting, Burton had asked Jarrett to join his band. "Gary was having trouble with his guitarist," said Jarrett. "He knew I was over there, so he asked me if I would be willing to play with them and I said no. But I did ask him if he needed some music and, when he said yes, I said, 'Maybe I'll write some.' A few months later I realized I had already written music suitable for Gary's group and we did the album."[34]

Gary Burton & Keith Jarrett was released on February 22, 1971 and was immediately hailed as a classic in the music press. "Grow Your Own" pleasingly confronts the "big beat" of rock that leads into a fascinating *a cappella* duet between Burton and Jarrett, while "The Raven Speaks" moves from rock to funk. These pieces were not a surrender to glossy artifice but a successful attempt to make a combination of jazz improvisation and rock rhythms work. "That was a good time for me, I liked the music on that album," said Jarrett. "Ensemble's a little ragged sometimes, but I enjoyed the session—we enjoyed the session—and it shows."[35] Today this album is now largely forgotten, but its impact on musicians at the time was considerable. For example, Woody Herman, whose band was always stocked with hip young players, soon picked up on it and in 1972 he recorded an album called *The Raven Speaks,* the title track one of the four originals Jarrett contributed to the session.

By 1972, however, Burton had returned to Berklee College of Music, where he had studied as a teenager, to join the teaching faculty. "I never have wanted to do anything other than my own music and at Berklee I can do that," he said. "I am able to work with people with whom I feel comfortable and creative in a professional sense. At the same time I am able to work with students from whom I get new ideas."[36] In 1984, he was appointed Berklee's Dean of Curriculum, and in 1995 he became its Executive Vice President. Today, Burton's pioneering jazz-rock experimentation represents a much overlooked body of work—not helped by the fact that, even by the late 1990s, none of it had been rereleased on CD.[37] Consequently, with the passage of time, Burton's quartet has become all but forgotten, a footnote in history, much like the highly original work of his fellow mallet man Red Norvo in the 1930s.

The abyss that gobbled up Gary Burton's work from the 1960s, however, is not half as deep as the one which claimed flautist Jeremy Steig. Along with Burton and Coryell, he was among the very first musicians to reach a synthesis of jazz and rock with his band Jeremy and the Satyrs. Steig had debuted as a leader on record with *Flute Fever* (1963), a blowing session with pianist Denny Zeitlin hastily assembled by producer John Hammond. Steig subsequently went with the Paul Winter Sextet, where he met pianist Warren Bernhardt. In 1967 he was asked by the singer-songwriter Tim Hardin—best known for his composition "If I Were a Carpenter"—to put together a band to back him at an engagement at The Scene. Steig assembled Bernhardt, Don Payne on electric bass, and Donald McDonald on drums, but Hardin failed to show. The band was a modest success, however, and decided to stay together as Jeremy and the Satyrs with either Glenn Moore or Eddie Gomez on bass, the addition of Adrian Guillery on guitar, plus, at various times, Mike Mainieri on vibes. Steig often used a tape loop to create ethereal duets with himself, Guillery incorporated Hendrix-inspired feedback into his solos, and Donald McDonald made frequent use of rock rhythms. "Jeremy was the consummate Village artist," said Mainieri. "He was one of the first jazz musicians I knew who was into the Beatles. He grew his hair long, and when he wasn't practising the flute, which was like ten hours a day, he was a painter, and very talented. His father Bill had been a cartoonist in the *New Yorker* for years."[38]

Working clubs like The Scene, the Village Vanguard, The Village Gate, and the Café au Go Go—where they stayed off and on for about a year—their brand of electronic jazz was often adventurous. "We all had tape recordings of random

Jeremy Steig: Although his group Jeremy and the Satyrs did not get to record until 1968, they were among the first wave of musicians who experimented with mixing jazz and rock. (Courtesy of the Institute of Jazz Studies, Rutgers University.)

sounds," said Bernhardt, "and at any point in our performance we would play them. Sometimes everybody's tape sounds were playing at once. It was crazy. I remember when we played the Village Vanguard opposite Freddie Hubbard, who was straight-ahead hard bop, we drove Max Gordon crazy—he hated us. It was because we were doing things jazz groups weren't supposed to do! The year before I'd been playing for Gerry Mulligan and when he heard the group he refused to speak to me!"[39]

The group began opening for Hardin and then acting as his backing band in venues that jazz musicians never played, such as the club Balloon Farm on St. Marks Place and the Electric Circus. In 1969, they played the Woodstock festival with Hardin, opening new young ears to the prospect of extended jazz improvisation. Hardin made two albums with the Satyrs, *Tim Hardin 3 Live in Concert* (without Steig) and *Bird on a Wire* with an augmented Satyrs lineup that included guitarist Ralph Towner and pianist Joe Zawinul. With their increasing underground popularity, the Satyrs acquired a management team, the famed rock entrepreneurs Albert Grossman and John Court of Grosscourt, and went out on tour, playing at the Fillmore opposite Cream and at Winterland opposite Janis Joplin.

In 1968 Grosscourt negotiated a record deal with Reprise, and later that year came *Jeremy & The Satyrs* with Gomez on bass. However, observers at the time felt it was not an accurate representation of the band since Mainieri didn't make the date and the group restricted themselves to mostly blues-based material. "It was commercial, straight-ahead stuff compared to what we did in person," said Bernhardt. "Something they thought would sell records; live we were far more adventurous."[40] Even so, a number like "Superbaby," a simple blues in F with Guillery doubling on harmonica, alternated straight-ahead and rock rhythms with Steig contributing a solo of striking vitality that made use of double-time passages and flute "effects" such as playing and singing simultaneously and harmonic double stops to produce two notes simultaneously. If several tracks now sound dated and of their time, such as "World of Glass Teardrops," the band had nevertheless integrated rock successfully into jazz, and a *Downbeat* review of just two and one half stars now seems rather harsh.[41]

The Satyrs succeeded in creating a viable fusion of jazz and rock—not one genre with hints of the other, not a song-by-song alternation of the two, but a new hybrid—and Steig's inventive playing on flute along with group members like Gomez on bass and Bernhardt on keyboards, who had previously distinguished themselves in a straight-ahead context, gave character to their less-inspired compositions. However, by 1969 Steig was back playing straight-ahead jazz gigs in a quartet format with Mainieri. In 1970 he was in the studios to cut *This Is Jeremy Steig,* a quartet date with Bernhardt, Moore on bass, and McDonald on drums. Somehow Steig could not quite get his act together on record or, occasionally, in person. However, a *Camera Three* appearance with the Bill Evans trio on CBS TV resulted in the celebrated *What's New* album with Evans from 1969. *Monium* (1974), with just Gomez and Marty Morell on drums, both from Evans's trio, plus Ray Mantilla on percussion, better essayed his talent, but his foray into jazz-rock, on record at least, was largely over. By 1974, despite being signed by Columbia, he was on the road with another talented player destined for obscurity, organist Larry Young.

Steig and members of The Satyrs were part of an informal group of musicians that gathered to rehearse, jam, hang out, and party in the general offices of Gnu Music, the headquarters of the vibist Mike Mainieri's music publishing and commercial TV music firms. "It began in 1965 with a small circle of members from the Jeremy Steig group The Satyrs," Mainieri recalled. "They included pianist Warren Bernhardt, acoustic bassist Hal Gaylor, drummer and resident guru Donald McDonald, guitarist Joe Beck, and myself."[42] This "small circle," together with Steig, Sam Brown on guitar, Chuck Rainey on electric bass, and Sally Waring's vocalizing, gathered for Mainieri's *Journey Thru an Electric Tube* (1967). On it, Mainieri put microphones on each resonator of his instrument.

"That was the first time anybody used fuzztones and wah-wahs on the vibes," he said. "In 1965 I had started working out how to mike the vibes. The Satyrs had begun to crank up the volume, everyone in the band seemed to have an amp except me and I couldn't hear myself. I started working with mikes, then Barcus-Berry came out with some pick-ups which I used. Volume was the way things were going after all the rock groups."[43] In essence the album was an extension of the ideas explored by Jeremy and the Satyrs and by a composers' forum in New York that Mainieri had been invited to join by Frank Zappa. "Zappa had this thing going in the Garrick Theater above the Café au Go Go," said Mainieri. "I started studying string arranging to participate, hence the string quartet on the album."[44]

By 1969 word had spread of Mainieri's informal jam sessions. "Some nights only a few stragglers would arrive, but there would be many nights twenty or thirty hippies would play, sing, and dance until we shook the 1950s out of our skins," Mainieri continued. "The musical ideas were launched from single sketches and vamps that would sometimes last for nearly an hour, changing shape, tempos, and soloists, depending on who suddenly fell by or split. It also gave Jay Messina, then an assistant recording engineer, a chance to practice his trade, so I accumulated hours of tape and often the results turned out pretty good."[45]

Michael Lang, one of the producers of Woodstock, "fell in love with the band" and decided to release some of this material. *White Elephant Vols 1 & 2* originally appeared on the Sunshine label and captured the spirit of the times with a remarkable roll call of players, including Randy and Michael Brecker, Ronnie Cuber, Steve Gadd, George Young, Frank Vicari, Tony Levin, and many more, that had swollen the "small circle" of friends to a tribal experience. *Vol 1* is perhaps the most valuable of the two-volume set because the vocals—which Mainieri concedes sound "naive and a little corny in these cold, grey 1990s"[46]—are not as prominent as they are on *Vol 2*. Vocals apart, the band lock into some grooving vamps, occasional psychedelic interludes, and some impassioned soloing from the likes of Cuber and Randy Brecker in "The Jones," Randy Brecker again in the ballad-vamp "Look in His Eyes," and the saxist Mike Brecker—who almost as soon as he arrived in New York was hailed as "one of the best young tenor saxophonists anywhere, jazz or rock or otherwise" by Don Heckman of the *Village Voice*[47]—in "White Elephant."

"Most of us had conservative family backgrounds and the social changes in the sixties really opened us up musically and emotionally," said Mainieri. "Everyone grew their hair long, everyone was into the Beatles and later, who didn't have a Stevie Wonder album—six Stevie Wonder albums! And Marvin Gaye and all those great artists. This was all something new, the social climate was in flux and it was a great time to be caught up in. We could all play straight-ahead stuff, I'd been with Buddy Rich for a couple of years, we could play free—we did a long track on *Journey Thru an Electric Tube* that was far out—but here was music I was involved in with my friends, my generation, it was what was happening and it was a new exciting direction."[48]

For these musicians, combining jazz and rock was not "selling out," but the most logical musical direction to pursue that was in touch with the social changes going on all around them. "We were just searching for ways to break down barri-

Mike Mainieri's White Elephant Band: By 1969, several of New York's finest young musicians were getting together for jazz-rock jams at Mainieri's studio. *Standing, left to right:* Annie Sutton, Barry Rodgers, Nick Holmes, Steve Gadd, Hugh McCraken, Frank Vicari. *Seated on chairs, left to right:* Jon Pierson, George Young, Mainieri, Nat Pavone, Donald MacDonald, Ronnie Cuber, Randy Brecker. *Seated on the floor, left to right:* Warren Bernhardt, Mike Brecker, Tony Levin. (Courtesy of Mike Mainieri.)

ers," recalled Mike Brecker. "It was a very fertile period. People were experimenting, trying different things. It was an exciting time to be in New York."[49] The White Elephant band, also known as Red Eye (slang for cheap wine), barely existed out of the rehearsal studios, the music they played and recorded during their "off-duty" hours was for the enjoyment and recreation of the participants themselves. They made a stir in 1970 with appearances at the Village Gate, and they had a week at the Village Vanguard, an appearance at the Alice Tully Hall in New York's Lincoln Center, and a few more minor gigs around New York. For all concerned, the band represented a labor of love. "There wasn't any work to speak of," said Mainieri. "If we made $50 a night when we did play, it was a lot. It was weird music, it wasn't commercial. Our last concert in Amherst University there were a thousand kids sitting around, they thought it was great."[50]

With an impossibly large head count, Red Eye was clearly not designed to fly, but instead it spawned several combinations of musicians all working to get their own version of a jazz-rock off the ground. One was Ars Nova, a vocally oriented group that included the guitarist Sam Brown. Another attempt was made by L'Image, a band that rehearsed and performed in upstate New York for six months. "I was living in Woodstock playing in a band with Mike Mainieri, Warren Bernhardt and Tony Levin," said the drummer Steve Gadd. "That's why I had moved to Woodstock. The idea was to get this band off the ground, so I was spending four days in Woodstock and three in the city. I'd come in and take as many sessions as I could in three days."[51] After playing about a couple of dozen gigs in upstate New York and backing Carly Simon, the band fell apart with Gadd's departure, despite record company interest.

Gadd had heard another group called the Encyclopedia of Soul that excited him. "[It was] at Mikell's and I told [drummer] Christopher [Parker] . . . if ever you can't do it every night, man, I'd be glad to alternate with you. So Christopher said yeah, because he was busy in the studios . . . so I started splitting the nights with Christopher, he'd work two nights and I'd work two nights."[52] The band was run by the bassist Gordon Edwards and had Charlie Gordon on saxophones, Cornell DuPree on guitar, and Richard Tee on organ, often with Jimmy Smith deputizing. When Gordon dropped out he was replaced by Eric Gale on guitar.

The band were approached by Warner Brothers and signed a deal in 1976. With a record contract in the offing, Gadd left L'Image entirely and enrolled in the band. Now with a two-drummer lineup in Gadd and Parker, the band changed their name to Stuff. The essence of Stuff was the grooves they set up. "There was something about the way they all played that I had never experienced," continued Gadd. "The groove, and just that feel . . . I felt I had so much to learn . . . as I had approached music on another level, like bebop . . . and these guys approached music just as intensively, but from a simpler way, a simpler song form. . . . It was done on a real simple level and a real groove level and it was a challenge."[53] The group recorded several albums through 1980, including two live sets. Stuff explored the groove from every conceivable angle and subjected it to varying degrees of intensity, the highlights being Gales's and DuPree's understated solos and Tee's jubilant piano and organ. Virtuosity was always masked in deference to the communal spirit of the groove, but such close examination of simple themes often didn't stand up to scrutiny, as *Live Stuff* (1978) demonstrates. However, *Live in New York* (1980), recorded at their regular haunt, Mikell's, remains a good representation of the what the band was all about.

While Stuff did not achieve any great commercial success, it spawned a legion of jazzy pop and funk groups before breaking up. "Stuff didn't get along too well," said Richard Tee. "There were technical things, management and personal things that broke it up."[54] The concept of Stuff was revived in May 1985 by Gadd, who formed the Gadd Gang with Ronnie Cuber on baritone, Cornell DuPree on guitar, Richard Tee on organ, and Eddie Gomez on bass. Their eponymous debut album was released first in Japan, immediately notching up sales of more than 100,000. Again the essence was the groove: finding it, sustaining it, and developing it. They showed what it was all about on "Watching the River Flow" but failed to sustain the mood throughout the album, thwarted in most cases by a poor choice of material. This proved to be a problem on the subsequent *Here & Now* (1988), which was frankly dreary. However, when they performed live, the band seemed capable of moving mountains.

Randy Brecker—at twenty-two already a veteran of Blood, Sweat & Tears and jazz ensembles such as Clark Terry's big band, the Duke Pearson band, and the Horace Silver quintet—made his debut as a leader on record with *Score* from January–February 1969. Together with his brother Michael, then a nineteen-year-old tenor saxophonist just in from Philadelphia and making his recording debut, they were joined by several like-minded young jazz musicians including the guitarist Larry Coryell, in whose group Randy had briefly appeared, Hal Galper on piano, Eddie Gomez on bass, and either Mickey Roker or Bernard Purdie on drums. Brecker mixes his ideas about incorporating rock into jazz with straight-ahead pieces, a hint of free playing and bossa nova. "Name Game" is very much influenced by the Miles Davis Quintet at this time; it features long melodic lines that allowed the rhythm section to lay down the sort of square rhythm section patterns used by Tony Williams on Davis's *E.S.P., Miles Smiles, Sorcerer,* and *Filles de Kilimanjaro.* The title track and "The Vamp," however, have a modified soul feel, presaging the Brecker's "heavy metal bebop" of the mid-1970s.

One frequent White Elephant collaborator was the trombonist Barry Rogers who had worked in several Latin bands and who first met the Brecker brothers in an R&B band called Birdsong, led by Edwin Birdsong. "[Barry] was like a father to me," recalled Mike Brecker. "I was eighteen, fresh on the scene and he took me under his wing."[55] Rogers persuaded both Breckers and the former Birdsong drummer Billy Cobham—who had earlier played with Joe Tex, the Sam and Dave Revue, and Horace Silver—to join the organist Jeff Kent and the bassist Doug Lubhan, a couple of aspiring singer-songwriters who wanted to put a band together to perform their original material. Lubahn had formerly been the leader of a group called Clear Light and had shown up on a number of albums by The Doors, while Kent had gigged around New York, primarily concentrating on writing. After a few college gigs and dates at New York's Electric Circus and Tarot Discaraunt, the band came together in earnest with the addition of the guitarist John Abercrombie, fresh from Berklee College, and the ex-Children of God lead singer Edward Vernon. Calling themselves Dreams, they felt confident enough to play a showcase at the Village Gate, which had just switched its music policy to rock. In the audience was Clive Davis, head of Columbia Records, who promptly signed them to his label.

Live, the group presented themselves more as a jazz band who consciously set about making themselves palatable to a wider (younger) audience. Their first album, recorded in autumn 1970, was, according to those who saw the band live, framed with commercial considerations in mind. "Dreams wasn't really a commercial band," said Mike Mainieri. "It didn't have a lead singer like Blood, Sweat & Tears or put on an obvious 'show' like they did. Dreams was much more interesting and challenging, the music was more complex and guys really got a chance to stretch out, and you've got to realize they had Billy Cobham, who was a sensation. The record company was fighting them, they wanted them to be heavy on vocals, but when they went out they were light on vocals and really stretched out. BS&T never got that far out."[56]

Cobham's remarkable drumming quickly established him as the band's major star at live performances, "Billy was incredible," said Jeff Kent. "We would just let him play and it was like fireworks. He could create this kind of pyrotechnic thing that people had never heard before. And then when Michael soloed, it was just so far ahead, so superior to the token amount of soloing that was going on in other [jazz-rock] bands of the time."[57]

Their first album features a number of interesting cuts. "Holli Be Home" features Randy Brecker's Harmon-muted trumpet and an out-of-tempo section, but it is only when he plays a brief open solo that the number takes off. "Try Me" is a little more interesting in that Cobham's drumming takes a more prominent role and Abercrombie contributes a "far-out" solo full of feedback and distortion. Michael Brecker opens "Dream Suite," an extended composition in three parts, and is also featured impressively in the final section of the suite, along with his brother and Abercrombie, before Cobham segues into "New York." This is the best cut of the album, with an impassioned Michael Brecker solo that makes extensive use of the interval of a fourth, a beautifully poised open horn solo from Randy, and a wonderfully raw Abercrombie who is faded out all too early in a "McArthur Park"-type ending. This track offers a better indication of what the band sought to achieve in live performance: powerful extended soloing and riffing combined with the extraordinary power generated by Cobham's presidential drumming. Here the band appear as a logical extension of the "White Elephant" sessions, with plenty of solo space and informal riffing over a solid, grooving rhythm section. For a moment we have an indication why this band was considered by musicians as perhaps the most important of the early jazz-rock bands, something the album as a whole did not succeed in conveying.

By 1971, despite commanding up to $5,000 a night on the college circuit, the band seemed to be going nowhere and lack of commercial success was causing frustrations within the group. "Doug Luban and Jeff Kent . . . [were] very gifted people but they didn't know how to lead a band," observed Billy Cobham. "They were misled by a fellow named Barry Rogers, who played trombone in the band. To make a long story short . . . the band fired them. Now I agree that Jeff and Doug were musically not up to par at the time, and I was part of it. If I hadn't wanted it to go down, I feel I would have done something not to let it go down. But I really had devoted a lot of time to Dreams and I had very little to show for it."[58]

Luban and Kent were replaced by Don Grolnick on keyboards and Will Lee on bass, and this revised lineup with Bob Mann on guitar journeyed down to Memphis to record their next album, *Imagine My Surprise,* which was released at the end of 1971. Produced by the guitarist Steve Cropper, resident session guru at Stax Records, the album went overboard to court the hit makers (the teenage audience). There were even fewer solos, although Randy plays muted trumpet in the title track, and Michael makes the most of his twenty-seven-bar solo in "Child of Wisdom."

Faced with a brief opportunity to shine in "Child," the younger Brecker makes the most of it. He gives his solo direction by dividing it into two parts, the first seventeen bars built from complex polytonal ideas with an occasional blues-derived phrase that touches on the dominant B minor tonality. Using considerable rhythmic variation, he introduces repeated phrases for emotional impact and leads into a contrasting second section of ten bars that comprise strong, simple blues-based ideas that had been hinted at in the early part of the first section. Even at this early stage of his career, Brecker had it together: an emotionally compelling and driving tone, superb technique (the solo covers three full octaves, from low B-flat to altissimo B-natural), plus the use of a number of devices, like alternate fingering and "bending" notes, to heighten the intensity of his solo that would become something of a signature.

Despite the overtly commercial stance of *Imagine My Surprise,* Dreams never hit the big time. Relegated to an opening act for Mother Earth and Canned Heat at New York's Beacon Theater on Broadway in late 1971, the end was in sight when Billy Cobham, one of the band's main spark plugs, left to join a group being assembled by the British guitarist John McLaughlin. "We never wrote anything down," said Randy Brecker. "We basically worked off cues that would allow the music to go from section to section with a lot of group improvising in between, kind of in a Mingus mode. . . . [Miles Davis] used to come down and hear us a lot. We'd play the Village Gate and he'd always be sitting in the back, listening intently."[59] The band limped on for a few months with Arthur Schwartzberg on drums before breaking up in early 1972.

If Dreams found the energy of rock rhythms seductive then, as *Imagine My Surprise* all too clearly showed, the possibility of reaching a mass audience was also seductive. As they moved closer to popular culture, integrity was now hostage to market forces. Although recorded evidence largely suggests otherwise, Dreams nevertheless provided a context for jazz musicians to demonstrate their talents by opening up the charts for periods of extended blowing as a matter of course.

"Doing that second record, under the influence of production, we tried to make everything like a single because we really wanted a hit," said Mike Brecker. "It ended screwing us up a lot because we devoted a considerable amount of energy to something we realized we weren't cut out to do."[60] With the collapse of Dreams, Mike and Randy Brecker joined the Horace Silver Quintet, featuring on *In Pursuit of the 27th Man,* and at the end of 1973 they appeared on Billy Cobham's second album as a leader, *Crosswinds.* Cobham went out on the road to promote the album in March 1974, and both Breckers toured with him, appearing on *Shabazz,* recorded live at the Montreux Jazz Festival and at London's Rainbow Theatre.

Throughout the 1970s both Breckers began an increasing involvement in studio work in tandem with performing with a variety of bands around New York. Mike became involved in keyboard-synthesizer player Bob Mason's group Stardrive, appearing on their "spacey," synth-oriented debut album from 1973, *Intergalactic Trot,* which included covers of Beatles and Sly and the Family Stone hits. Meanwhile Randy went on the road with Deodato, who had just scored a big hit with *2001,* before joining a group assembled by the guitarist Larry Coryell. He next went on the road with Stevie Wonder to support *Superstition* and recorded with James Brown. After recording one album with Coryell, Randy was reunited with his brother in another version of Billy Cobham's group in the spring of 1975, recording *A Funky Thide of Sings.* However, they left immediately afterwards to tour with their own band, the Brecker Brothers, to support the release of their first album.

Composed and produced by Randy Brecker, *The Brecker Brothers* included Dave Sanborn on alto, Harvey Mason on drums, the former Dreams sidemen Don Grolnick on keyboards, Bob Mann on guitar, Will Lee on bass, and the former White Elephant percussionist-drummer Ralph MacDonald. "It was the off-shoot of two things," said Mike Brecker. "Randy had been writing very prolifi-cally over a two year period, great songs, very unique and very creative. Also, just for fun, we'd been jamming once a week with Dave Sanborn, Chris Parker, Will Lee and Don Grolnick at Don's apartment in Manhattan. At that point Randy was approached by Arista to do an album. We put the two ideas together, the idea of just playing and these very complex, very dynamic compositions and came up with the first Brecker Brothers album."[61]

Strongly rooted in the soul-jazz–R&B idioms, the highly technical charts were executed with an ease and precision that belied their complexity. The album's only weakness was the decision to include vocals. Nonetheless, a cut from the album released as a single, "Sneakin' Up Behind You" crept onto the Top 40, ensuring a successful commercial debut for the band by selling over 200,000 copies. In 1976 came *Back to Back.* The background vocals remained, with the addition of the lat-est disco beats, which highlighted the band's commercial outlook. "The whole album seems to be an embarrassment," said *Downbeat,* awarding the album just two stars.[62] It was the group's last outing with a three horn front-line; subsequent albums reverted to the two brothers' trumpet-tenor lineup.[63] The Brecker Brothers group wound up in 1982, but during this period they continued to be active as in-demand session musicians and with a variety of other projects.

It is fair to say that commercial considerations meant that none of the group's albums were entirely satisfactory, but equally each album was not without absorbing solo work from both Michael and Randy and some well-written, angu-lar bebop-influenced horn lines.[64] Perhaps the best representations of the Brecker Brothers sound were their first and last albums. "We did not have any pressure from the record company telling us what to do [on the first album]," said Randy Brecker. "The music was spontaneous and not pre-conditioned. And the last one [*Heavy Metal Bebop*] because we really got back to our original con-cept. With the records in between, I felt too many people were trying to channel our directions, like the record company, band members, managers and so on. When we did the last we did it our way."[65]

Heavy Metal Be-Bop was recorded live in 1978 at My Father's Place, a popular folk-rock club in Roslyn, Long Island (except for the studio track "East River"). Randy, who by now had both recorded and performed with James Brown, took something of the rhythmic complexity of the J.B.s and merged it with intricate

The Brecker Brothers: Trumpeter Randy (left) and saxophonist Michael, two formidably talented young musicians, formed the Brecker Brothers band in 1975. (Courtesy of the Institute of Jazz Studies, Rutgers University.)

horn lines that became the model for countless fusion bands in the 1980s and 1990s. *Heavy Metal Be-Bop* is a commercial album, yet is free of the ingratiating compromises like "Finger Lickin' Good" and "Lovely Lady" on earlier albums that, presumably, were aimed at the teenage pop market. The fast-flowing, sixteenth-note lines in "Some Skunk Funk," zipping past at a rate of some eight notes per second, highlighted the slick technique on display, while Mike Brecker contributed an impressive solo on "Funky Sea, Funky Dew." Randy Brecker made creative use of wah-wah attachment and a harmonizer that duplicated his trumpet sound in other pitches and deserves to be acknowledged as Miles Davis's peer on electric trumpet. Yet, overall, while there were good solos and often well-constructed compositions with unexpected harmonic twists, there remained a slickness and a surface gloss that succumbed to the demands of commerce.

Both brothers pursued their own careers in the 1980s. Randy was involved in the Jaco Pastorius ensemble Word of Mouth and with his own hard-bop ensemble with the tenor saxophonist Bob Berg, the pianist Dave Kikowski, the bassist Dieter Ilg, and the drummer Joey Baron, recording *Live at Sweet Basil.* In 1987 Michael made his much-awaited debut as a leader on records with *Michael Brecker* and on the strength of it was named *Downbeat* "Jazz Artist of the Year." The success of the album and its follow-up, *Don't Try This at Home* (1988), brought him onto the touring circuits with a group comprising Mike Stern on guitar, Joey Calderazzo on keyboards, Jeff Andrews on bass, and Adam Nussbaum on drums. Brecker's playing reached impressive heights in concert, prompting hopes of a live album, but this did not materialize. Instead, two bootleg albums document this band from 1989, *The Michael Brecker Band Live* and *The Cost of Living,* the latter recorded live in Belgrade without Stern and with Jay Anderson on bass. Both feature extended versions of compositions from the two studio albums, including "Nothing Personal," "Original Rays," "Chime This," "The Cost of Living," and "Istbynne Reel," the latter a workout on his Electric Wind Instrument (EWI).

Although there had been a brief reunion of the Brecker Brothers in 1984, only an inner circle of friends and habitués of Seventh Avenue South, the Manhattan jazz club, were aware of the four-night engagement. However, in 1992 the Breckers reformed the band, Randy explaining, "We never intended for it to disperse for so long. The idea was just to take a temporary respite because we had played together for so long. But we just got busy with different things."[66] *The Return of the Brecker Brothers* presents slick compositions, brilliant recorded sound, and ideas inspired by Michael Brecker's work with African musicians on Paul Simon's *Graceland* and *The Rhythm of the Saints* albums, as well as the subsequent *Born at the Right Time Tour.* The African vibe is most clearly felt on "Wakaria (What's Up?)," a 12/8 groove based on *bikoutsi,* a rhythm from the Cameroons. The Breckers also touch base with hip-hop in "On the Backside," and reunite the band's original horn section with Dave Sanborn on "King of the Lobby." With this and the Grammy-winning *Out of the Loop* (1994) it was impossible not to acknowledge the impossibly tight ensembles, but the undeniable flights of virtuosity somehow could not overwhelm the commercial stance of the music. By then, the Breckers were among the foremost instrumentalists in jazz, widely respected by their peers, having distinguished themselves in a wide variety of performing situations.

The Breckers' success was in sharp contrast to the career of Larry Coryell, who when he left the Gary Burton Quartet was widely acknowledged as one of the most creative and accomplished guitarists of the young generation of jazz musicians. In 1968 he won the top guitar spot in the *Downbeat* Critic's Poll for "Talent Deserving of Wider Recognition," and after a short period with flautist Herbie Mann that produced the album *Memphis Underground* (1969), he secured a recording contract with Vanguard records. He also appeared on a Mike Mantler composition on a session that would form part of the first recording of the Jazz Composers Orchestra, which Coryell considered a career highpoint.[67]

However, after leaving Burton, Coryell underwent an intense reaction to the steadfast drive for perfection that characterized Burton's music. "It's just that I had to *rock out* more, play loud, go through a phase where I almost lost my hearing. . . . I mean, it was like the Jazz Age of the 1920s, a time of upheaval and hedonism, almost. Everybody was out there for the perfect kind of acid trip, the perfect orgasm, the perfect kind of rock music that would give you the perfect kind of 'Hey man, I was really out of it,'" he said.[68] His recordings reflect his lack of direction, such as *Lady Coryell* with its liner notes comparing him to Charlie Christian, but the vinyl included a performance of a Junior Walker soul tune washed with psychedelia; *Downbeat* refused to rate it.[69] *Coryell* was a better balanced effort in which he was more firmly in command of his ideas, yet the best cut of the album, "Jam with Albert," was not planned at all, taken from an impromptu session taped by an alert studio engineer.

In 1968, Coryell was reunited with longtime friend and musical associate Mike Mandel on keyboards—a graduate of Boston's Berklee College of Music and the New England Conservatory of Music—with whom he had played as a fifteen-year-old in a group called the Checkers, backing up performers such as Roy Orbison, Bobby Vee, and Gene Vincent. They formed a guitar-organ-drums trio and were hustling for work when they got a call from Jack Bruce, fresh out of Cream, for a whirlwind Stateside tour with a group known as Jack Bruce and Friends.

In 1969, Coryell cut *Spaces,* by far his best album to date and among the best in his discography. "This is one of the most beautiful, perfectly realized instrumental albums in a long while," said *Rolling Stone* when the album was released in 1971.[70] Coryell was equally enthusiastic: "It's one of the greatest records of our generation," he modestly exclaimed.[71] With a lineup that included John McLaughlin on guitar, Chick Corea on electric piano, Miroslav Vitous on bass, and Billy Cobham on drums, Coryell and McLaughlin swap blistering licks on "Spaces (Infinite)" and share moments of quiet introspection on "Rene's Theme." Yet just how variable Coryell could be was illustrated by *Larry Coryell at the Village Gate,* recorded January 21–22, 1971. With just a trio, Coryell went into his rock bag for an indifferent set that failed to impress.

Later in the year, Coryell began developing a band with saxophonist Steve Marcus that went under various names, the most lasting of which was Fourplay. "It was a joke," Coryell recalled. "Our whole attitude towards life at that time was a joke. Marcus and I drank a lot"—which led to the first of Coryell's bouts with alcoholism—"and we made all those albums, a series of search parties. It was terrible."[72] Three albums came out of this period with Marcus—*Barefoot Boy, The Offering,* and *The Real Great Escape.* Eventually Coryell realized he had to pull out of the personal situation in which he found himself. "I spent five days sitting by the phone trying to call Marcus, my best friend, and tell him we were through," he said.[73]

Coryell's next move was to form a new ensemble called Eleventh House in late 1973 with the trumpeter Randy Brecker, Mandel on keyboards, Danny Trifan on bass, and Alphonse Mouzon on drums. It was his first step to steer a perceivable career course. "This is a logical extension of Fourplay in as much as it is a quintet and it plays my material and other people's, and it falls within the music that's known as jazz-rock. The band is tighter, more disciplined and Mandel is more out of the shadows in this group, but then everybody's *playing,"* he explained.[74] Coryell put aside his hollow-body Super 400 and started using a solid-body guitar, seeking to compete with his friend and rival John McLaughlin's success with Mahavishnu.

Recorded at the end of September 1973 after a performance at My Father's Place in Roslyn, Long Island, *Introducing the Eleventh House* was released in 1974 to a four-star review from *Downbeat,*[75] and the portents for the group looked good. Album highlights included "Birdfingers," "Funky Waltz," and Wolfgang Dauner's "Yin." Technically Coryell seemed to be entering a new phase of his career. Brecker's mastery of the "electric" trumpet added unusual tonal colors to the group, using a Mu-tron, fuzztone, and wah-wah, stretching the instrument into new territory. The response of the music press was uniformly favorable, many openly expressing delight that Coryell had finally got his act together. Then, after six months Randy Brecker abruptly left to the join drummer Billy Cobham's group; Coryell was devastated. "I went into a big personal depression," he confessed later. "I had dug the cat so much, I didn't realize how much I depended on him. Mike Lawrence came into the band, he very quietly put up with all my shit. It's like I had to act out a final obnoxious drama: rolling on the floor at a Harry Nilsson session, broken bottles, falling over guitars, being asked to leave record dates. I guess it all had to work out."[76]

The new lineup appeared on *Larry Coryell and the Eleventh House at Montreux,* a somewhat self-indulgent live set recorded July 4, 1974. Coryell was clearly seeking to impress in terms of fast execution and a rather heavy-handed use of distortion, while the band were solid and workmanlike with Mouzon adopting a high-profile role similar to that of Billy Cobham in John McLaughlin's Mahavishnu Orchestra. Nonetheless, a European tour in early 1975 saw the band receive rave reviews. "Coryell . . . is amazing," said *Melody Maker* of their Paris concert.[77] The ups and downs continued with a change of record companies in 1975, which produced *Level One* on the Arista label and a sharp levelling off of the band's artistic aspirations. "What is so disappointing about this album . . . is the sheer anonymity of it all," said *Melody Maker.*[78] *Aspects* followed in 1976, by which time Terumasa Hino had come in on trumpet with John Lee on bass and Gerry Brown on drums. With production by Randy Brecker and guest appearances from the Brecker Brothers front line of Randy and Michael Brecker and Dave Sanborn, the record was calculatedly commercial in a disco-fun mode, Coryell again failing to make a definitive impression on disc. Later that year, he dissolved the band, going acoustic and performing duets with Philip Catherine and Steve Khan and in 1979 touring with John McLaughlin and Paco De Lucia in an acoustic trio setting.

With Eleventh House, Coryell had let business matters slip, recording for Arista while still under contract with Vanguard, and he became embroiled in expensive litigation. Frustrated by his management team, he turned his career over to his wife to manage. In 1978 another bout of alcoholism claimed him, and

Larry Coryell: A brilliant young musician who never realized his full potential. (Courtesy of the Institute of Jazz Studies, Rutgers University.)

yet another followed in 1981 during a period of self-imposed exile. "Early on Larry was trapped by his talents," said friend and keyboard player Mike Mandel. "People saw his talent and energy. Everyone wanted to use him for all his versatility. . . . Working on the road can be very lonely. People can seduce you with love, flattery, with drugs. . . . So with a push towards drugs and the identity problem as a guitarist Larry became confused. This push and shove, this turbulence got to him, distorted his artistic focus and his personality. My problem was more speed, his more alcohol."[79] Sadly, the man who helped found jazz-rock never managed to capitalize on it.

Yet clearly there existed a commercial potential for jazz-rock, and it only seemed a matter of time before the major recording companies became involved

in what was being talked about as "the new music." When in 1967 the industry
leader Columbia Records had begun showing interest in jazz-rock, it seemed the
music industry cycle of the emergence of a new style from the musical margins to
its mainstreaming to maximize profits would once again be enacted. For jazz and
rock, the tensions between art and commerce, which until the late 1960s had
been largely absent, were about to begin.

Notes

1. *On Record,* edited by Simon Frith and Andrew Goodwin (Routledge, London 1990), p. 435.
2. *The Presidential Papers,* by Norman Mailer (Corgi, London, 1965).
3. *Downbeat,* May 1984, p. 16.
4. Magazine article courtesy of Mike Nock, *East Village Other,* probably May 1968.
5. *Rolling Stone,* February 10, 1968, p. 19.
6. Interview with the author, February 28, 1997.
7. *Downbeat,* December 4, 1975, p. 18.
8. Liner notes, *Gary Burton: New Vibe Man in Town* (RCA/BMG 74321 21828 2).
9. *Downbeat,* August 8, 1968, p. 14.
10. Letter to the author, February 28, 1997. Grateful thanks to Gary Burton for checking through the text and advising me on several points.
11. *Sweet Rain* (Verve 815054–2), recorded by Stan Getz on March 30, 1967.
12. *Melody Maker,* July 3, 1971, p. 10.
13. *Downbeat,* January 11, 1968, p. 25.
14. Ibid., August 8, 1968, p. 14.
15. *Village Voice,* July 6, 1967.
16. Letter to the author, December 31, 1996.
17. Letter to the author, February 6, 1997.
18. *Downbeat,* April 18, 1968, p. 39.
19. Letter to the author, December 31, 1996.
20. *Downbeat,* May 15, 1969, p. 27.
21. Letter to the author, December 31, 1996.
22. *Rolling Stone,* March 9, 1968.
23. Courtesy of The National Sound Archive, British Museum; thanks to Paul Wilson.
24. *Downbeat,* January 11, 1968.
25. Liner notes, *The Dave Pike Set: Masterpieces* (MPS 531 848–2), p. 2.
26. "Jazz & Rock," by Volker Kriegal, in *Jazzrock—Tendencies of a New Kind of Music,* a collection of essays (rororo vol. 7766, Germany, 1983), p. 59.
27. Ibid.
28. These albums were anthologized on *Dave Pike Set: Masterpieces* (MPS 531 848–2) in 1996.
29. "Jazz & Rock," by Volker Kriegal, in *Jazzrock—Tendencies of a New Kind of Music,* a collection of essays (rororo vol. 7766, Germany, 1983), p. 59.
30. Interview with the author, December 17, 1993.
31. *Downbeat,* December 26, 1968, p. 26.
32. Trade advertisement for *Throb* (Atlantic 1531), April 1970.
33. Letter to the author, February 28, 1997.
34. *Downbeat,* January 20, 1972, p. 36.
35. Interview with the author, April 7, 1993.
36. *Downbeat,* February 17, 1972, p. 31.
37. Other than the anthology *Artist's Choice* (RCA ND 86280), as of mid-1997 Burton's pioneering work had not been reissued on CD.
38. Interview with the author, January 14, 1997.
39. Interview with the author, February 28, 1997.
40. Ibid.

41. *Downbeat,* May 2, 1968, p. 29.
42. Interview with the author, January 14, 1997.
43. Ibid.
44. Ibid.
45. Ibid.
46. Ibid.
47. Quoted in *Downbeat,* January 7, 1971, p. 23.
48. Interview with the author, January 14, 1997.
49. Quoted in liner notes by Bill Millkowski for *Dreams* (Columbia/Legacy CK 47906).
50. Interview with the author, January 14, 1997.
51. *Talking Jazz,* by Ben Sidran (Pomegranate Artbooks, San Francisco, 1992), p. 185.
52. Ibid.
53. Ibid.
54. *Downbeat,* October 1987, p. 18.
55. Quoted in liner notes by Bill Millkowski for *Dreams* (Columbia/Legacy CK 47906).
56. Interview with the author, January 14, 1997.
57. Quoted in liner notes by Bill Millkowski for *Dreams* (Columbia/Legacy CK 47906).
58. *Downbeat,* March 14, 1974, p. 15.
59. Quoted in liner notes by Bill Millkowski for *Dreams* (Columbia/Legacy CK 47906).
60. *Downbeat,* June 21, 1973, p. 32.
61. *Wire,* July 1991, pp. 36, 70.
62. *Downbeat,* June 17, 1976, p. 1976.
63. *Straphangin',* the disco-oriented *Don't Stop the Music, Détente,* produced by George Duke, and *Heavy Metal Be-Bop.*
64. Their work was anthologized in 1990 on *The Brecker Brothers Collection Vols. 1 & 2* (Novus ND 90442 and ND 83076), which gathered together their most enduring tracks.
65. *Cadence,* October 1986, p. 14.
66. *Downbeat,* October 1992, p. 17.
67. The association with Mantler would be renewed in 1977 on Mike Mantler's artistically successful album *Movies,* with an impressive lineup including Mantler on trumpet, Carla Bley on piano, Steve Swallow on bass, and Tony Williams on drums.
68. *Downbeat,* February 26, 1976, pp. 13, 14.
69. Ibid., September 18, 1969, p. 20: "There is no way to rate this album."
70. *Rolling Stone,* April 1, 1971, p. 40.
71. *Downbeat,* November 9, 1972, p. 18.
72. Ibid., February 26, 1976, p. 14.
73. Ibid.
74. *Melody Maker,* March 1, 1975, p. 26.
75. *Downbeat,* April 11, 1974, p. 18.
76. Ibid., February 26, 1976, p. 14.
77. *Melody Maker,* February 8, 1975, p. 22.
78. Ibid., August 9, 1975, p. 32.
79. *Downbeat,* June 1980, pp. 21, 64.

CHAPTER 4

Spinning Wheels

On August 13, 1967 the legendary Five Spot at the southeast corner of St. Marks Place and Third Avenue in New York City closed its doors for the last time. The most famous jazz club of the late fifties and early sixties that had seen Ornette Coleman launch free jazz onto an unsuspecting world and was once a home away from home for Thelonious Monk and Charles Mingus was no more. "Jazz just isn't profitable anymore," said the owner, Joe Termini. "Not enough people came in for me to pay the bills. For college kids, the place to go used to be a jazz club. Now they have other interests."[1] Termini had found he could make more money selling pizzas in his take-out next door.

That same year, Eddie Condon's club on East 56th Street failed to open after its annual summer layoff. After twenty-two years Condon's club, originally on West 3rd Street in Greenwich Village before it moved uptown in 1957, had become an institution. "My place wasn't like some of those clubs that opened then closed before you could get drunk in them," Condon had once quipped.[2] At the end of March 1968 another jazz club bit the dust. The Frammis, on Manhattan's East Side—where the guitar legend Tal Farlow had made one of his famous "returns" to the music business the previous October—became Discotheque Frammis. By 1969 there were only six jazz clubs left in New York; earlier in the decade there had been almost thirty.

Jazz was in crisis and it was not just a matter of fewer places for musicians to work. None of the surviving New York clubs were really prospering, and few were advertising enough (or even at all), claiming they could not afford to since audiences were not exactly beating down their doors to get in. "During the heavy rock years, from 1966 to 1969," wrote Albert Goldman in 1971, "we heard the same old stuff the guys had been playing for years. It was an embarrassing scene. Jazz had lost its audience and was talking to itself."[3] College kids, who during the 1950s provided jazz with a solid base of support, were now swept up by the rock craze. They looked down with disdain at the perceived shortcomings of a hopelessly square generation that preceded them. "Hey, you hipsters, dig that cat's craaazy beat," cries one rock fan as he passes a jazz club and his friends collapse to the pavement, crippled by mirth.

To make matters worse, recording opportunities for jazz with the major recording companies were now looking increasingly bleak. The labels' energies were now almost totally devoted to increasing their share of the rock market. Columbia Records' sales had jumped from 15 percent of the market in 1964 to 60 percent in 1969 after Clive Davis, their president, had signed a number of major new acts, including several at the 1967 Monterey Rock Festival. The Warner-Reprise-Atlantic group was equally aggressive, releasing well over 100 rock albums during the 1968–1970 period that sold more than a million copies, while their singles had shared a major portion of *Billboard*'s Hot 100.[4] On the nation's 2,000 FM stations, Top-40 programming dominated the airwaves. "It's a strange thing," observed saxophonist Julian "Cannonball" Adderley. "Here we have a generation of kids who are raised on a constant diet of music; they all buy records and have transistor radios and a radio in the ear. The only thing wrong is, they don't get to hear jazz."[5]

In 1967 the record industry's idea of a great jazz record was guitarist Wes Montgomery's *Goin' Out of My Head*. Jazz, however, was the last thing on Montgomery's mind when he cut the disc. Against a glossy orchestral backdrop, his cover versions of contemporary pop hits stuck pretty close to the melody and failed to suggest his stature as an improvising jazz musician. Even so, *Goin' Out of My Head* won a Grammy award for the "Best Instrumental Jazz Performance of 1966." Montgomery's warm, blues-influenced playing, his use of octaves and double octaves, and his "impossible" block chording were universally emulated by guitarists playing in many different styles. His influence directly or indirectly reached into easy-listening music, film scores, pop records, and rock musicians from Jimi Hendrix to Jerry Garcia of the Grateful Dead, as well as practically every post-1959 jazz guitarist. Montgomery repeated his successful formula on albums such as *California Dreamin'*, *Tequila*, and *A Day in the Life*, the best-selling jazz album of 1968.

Montgomery's success marked a small step along the road to where jazz and rock would eventually meet. In many ways he was the first "fusion" artist, a term dreamt up by record producer Orrin Keepnews when the guitarist first transcended the strictures of straight-ahead jazz to cross over into a popular vein in 1963. The resultant album, *Fusion!*, might have marked Montgomery's first meeting with strings, but it also coined a name that would enter the jazz lexicon in the 1970s.

Montgomery's booming sales were almost matched by a series of albums by Bud Shank. His 1966 *Michelle*, for example, was a series of flute-plus-orchestra covers of pop hits such as "Sounds of Silence," "Yesterday," and "Girl." The sales these pop-jazz albums were achieving was not something the record industry could ignore. The idea caught on, and a surprising number of soloists were importuned into alien territory to make albums they probably wanted to forget as soon as they had cut them. Stan Getz was among those convinced to try his hand at the pop repertoire. His album *What the World Needs Now* (1968) was an eminently forgettable collection of Burt Bacharach and Hal David hits, while mere mention of his 1970 album *Marrakesh Express*, produced by "Fifth Beatle" George Martin, would probably make Getz spin in his grave like a lathe. The sirens of commercialism even tempted Dizzy Gillespie out from the honorable estate of bebop; on the album *My Way* (1969), he covered horrors like "Galveston" and "This Girl's in Love with You."

Albums like these showed that while jazz musicians were quite prepared to take new compositions from popular culture, as they had traditionally and successfully done in the past with Broadway show tunes, they failed to realize that in the rock era, the days of covering a popular tune were all but over. In covering contemporary pop tunes, the jazz musician's instrumental versions obscured the dimensions of the original hit song that made them compelling and subversive in the first place. Bud Shank covering "Sounds of Silence" on flute sounds inauthentic because it is impossible to disentangle the memory of Simon and Garfunkel's original hit from the actual song itself. Singers and song had become bonded in a performance that exhausted the song's meaning.

Pop and rock succeed in spite of mediocre lyrics and simplistic chord progressions because it is the *performance* that achieves an autonomous character, not the song. This autonomy embraces musical as well as nonmusical factors such as style, fashion, and sex appeal, none of which were exactly a jazz musician's stock-in-trade. It took a good few turkeys for jazz musicians to realize that approaching rock through its repertoire by recording "jazz" versions of popular hits by everyone from the Beatles to Dionne Warwick was a futile exercise, winning them no new fans among either audience.[6]

Jazz musicians initially sought to control rock, attempting to get it to conform to their notion of primitivism. But control is incompatible with rock's energy, and to avoid its primitivism was to fail to acknowledge the source of its popularity, volume, and power, courtesy of Jim Marshall's monster hundred-watt stacks. "All that mattered was the noise it made," said rock critic Nik Cohn, "its drive, its aggression."[7] While rock's mega-decibel blasts were part of the natural selection that separated adults from youth, it was also a major hurdle jazz had to confront if there was going to be any rapprochement with its noisy second cousin. The standard rhythm section used in jazz—acoustic piano, *contra-bass,* and drums—sounded trite when trying to simulate rock. Jazz musicians found the concept of volume a denial of subtlety, failing completely to appreciate how it contributed to rock's authenticity. To them rock was a rhythmical thing, like a bossa nova, and initially they assumed it could be accommodated by simply playing the appropriate rhythmic patterns. But to younger audiences, this was missing the point by a mile.

If volume was one aspect of rock that jazz musicians had difficulty in coming to terms with, then rock's electronic instrumentation—the new technology that made it all possible—was another. The acoustic bass had long been dropped in popular music in favor of the electric Fender bass, first used in jazz by Monk Montgomery in Lionel Hampton's band in the early 1950s. In rock, guitarists tended to turn the volume up to distortion level and climax their solos with feedback at glass-shattering intensity, something of a contrast to the neat, well-rounded tone of the jazz guitar that had remained essentially unchanged since Charlie Christian plugged in with Benny Goodman in August 1939. And most rock groups carried any number of electronic keyboards from the awful, but once ubiquitous, Farfisa Compact Organ to the gutsy Hammond B-3, plus a liberal sprinkling of Wurlitzer and Fender Rhodes electric pianos, Hohner clavinets, and, later, Moog and string synthesizers. Clearly, if a distinct genre of jazz-rock was to come about, then in its quest for authenticity jazz was not only going to have to raise the decibel level but also embrace electronic instrumentation as well.

The honest brokerage of the blues provided some solutions to these problems, initially by co-opting elements of jazz into the blues-rock arena. The Paul Butterfield Blues Band, formed in 1963, was a white twenty-one-year-old vocalist's homage to the bluesmen he had jammed with on Chicago's South Side, including Muddy Waters, Howlin' Wolf, and Otis Rush. His band included Wolf's bassist Jerome Arnold and, originally, drummer Sam Lay and another white revivalist, guitarist Mike Bloomfield, whose guitar work showed the influences of straight blues, jazz, and even Indian music. Bloomfield stretched out impressively on the group's second album, *East-West* (1966), on the long, thirteen-minute title track, drawing as much from the influence of Indian classical music of Ravi Shankar and Ali Akbar Khan as from John Coltrane's handling of Eastern modes.

Bloomfield's significance was in his emphasis of instrumental prowess within Butterfield's authentic blues-rock band. Like Eric Clapton with Cream, his use of extended improvisation helped establish the cult of the lead guitarist and the importance in rock of the extended power solo. The fact was that aspiring young, white suburban guitarists of the period, frantically copping licks from Chuck Berry and Rolling Stones records, had never been exposed to the instrumental proficiency of a Bloomfield or a Clapton. And, for kids who were *really* into guitar playing, listening to these guitarists took on almost spiritual proportions, culminating in the "Clapton is God" graffiti in London clubs that gave kids an image they could relate to: a white version of the blues.

Unlike Cream, however, the Butterfield band was perhaps *too* concerned with an accurate reproduction of the blues idiom. Perhaps it was their closeness to the source that made them more reverential, at least in their covers of blues standards. There were no geographic constraints on Cream, whose lack of inhibition was a trademark. This is most apparent in a comparison of the two bands' versions of "Spoonful."[8] Clapton, in contrast to Bloomfield, moves beyond the bonds of authenticity to impose his own personality on the song.

However, Butterfield also had the capability to stretch out, as he showed when he moved from the blues to Nat Adderley's "Work Song," a staple of the 1960s jazz repertoire, also from *East-West*. What would be a small step in jazz turns out to be a giant step for a blues-rock band. Maybe the bassist Jerome Arnold was a bit stiff walking and the drummer Billy Davenport sounded bemused by jazz's straight-ahead rhythm patterns, unable to come to terms with the rolling 12/8 triplet feel essential to "swing," but Bloomfield's driving solo, his very intensity, and his clear tribute to Wes Montgomery in his use of octaves clearly shows how rock was peering over the fence and looking at jazz as early as 1965.[9] This hard-swinging, searingly intense conflation of jazz and rock laid down a marker for future trends.

Bloomfield left Butterfield in 1966 and formed a band that featured the drummer Buddy Miles—a youthful prodigy he had filched from Wilson Pickett's road group—the lead singer and conga player Nick "The Greek" Gravenites, Barry Goldberg on keyboards, and Harvey Brooks, an accomplished session musician, on bass, plus Marcus Doubleday on trumpet and Peter Strazza, Stemsie Hunter, or Herbie Rich on saxophone. The horn section essentially functioned in the same way as in a soul band, albeit with an occasional jazz-based solo. Calling themselves Electric Flag, "An American Music Band," to differentiate themselves from the bands of the British Invasion, they were signed in 1967 by Columbia for a $50,000 advance, a figure that even today many jazz musicians would gladly accept.[10] Their debut album, *A Long Time Coming,* was released in 1968 and peaked on the *Billboard* chart at thirty-one.

On tracks like "Goin' Down Slow" and "Texas," the band put together two powerful, and authentic, blues performances with impressive guitar work from Bloomfield in the latter. In contrast, "Killing Floor" with its superb send-up of Lyndon Johnson is pure can't-sit-down soul, "You Don't Realize" is soul balladry, while "Sittin' In Circles" is pure pop. At their best, with Bloomfield's powerful, searing solos, Brooks's mobile bass lines, and Miles's dramatic drumming, the band seemed capable of scaling the heights. "Flag was exciting," said *Rolling Stone,* "though they weren't half as good on wax as they were in person."[11] In early 1968, Leonard Feather played *A Long Time Coming* to Miles Davis for a *Downbeat* Blindfold Test. Davis, in his hotel room, was surrounded by James Brown, Dionne Warwick, Tony Bennett, the Byrds, Aretha Franklin, and the Fifth Dimension, but not a single jazz instrumental. Davis was impressed by the Flag cut, saying, "Who was that? Leave that record here, it's a nice record. . . . It's a pleasure to get a record like that, because you know they're serious no matter what they do. . . . I liked the rhythm on that. I mean, if you're going to do something like that, man, you've got to *do* it."[12]

Electric Flag did not last long, victims of that well-worn euphemism "personal problems." They debuted at the Monterey Rock Festival on June 17, 1967, and although they are missing from D. A. Pennebaker's movie of the occasion, two tracks from the concert were eventually released, "Drinkin' Wine" and "The Night Time Is the Right Time."[13] Subsequently Flag became regulars at Bill Graham's Fillmore, where they once shared the bill with Cream, with Bloomfield and Clapton squaring off for a delighted audience.

In 1968, Bloomfield abruptly abandoned his creation, linking up with the producer and keyboard player Al Kooper and Stephen Stills for the one-off album *Super Session,* which produced one of rock's more elegant tribute's to John Coltrane, "His Holy Modal Highness." Meanwhile, Electric Flag managed just one more album, with Hoshal Wright substituting for Bloomfield—*The Electric Flag: An American Music Band*—before finally collapsing. An attempt to rejuvenate the band in 1975, *The Band Kept Playing,* failed to match the energetic diversity of their still largely startling debut. Electric Flag's significance is perhaps less in its music, something between "progressive" soul and the *lingua franca* of the blues (albeit with an occasional, depressing detour into pop), and more in its role in what is generally considered as the first wave of "jazz-rock" bands that grafted a horn section onto a rock rhythm section.

While the Electric Flag were playing the Bitter End in Greenwich Village, another group was getting itself together just across Bleecker Street in the Café au Go Go. These musicians had come together after the breakup of Al Kooper's Blues Project, a band that incorporated jazz elements in its extended jams on numbers like "Electric Flute Thing," an Al Kooper composition that featured the flautist Andy Kullberg. The Blues Project had acquired a tremendous underground reputation and even briefly broke nationwide when "Flute Thing" became a hit. When the Project split up in 1967, Kooper and the guitarist Steve Katz were joined by the jazz drummer Bobby Colomby, and together they began thinking of forming a new band. "Jazz has become stagnant," asserted the twenty-four-year-old Colomby in 1968. "It just seems too depressing at this stage. There is so little glory or real happiness around jazz."[14] Colomby's contention was that jazz musicians either had to gain the respect of the public by assuming the dignity of concert artists or had to go underground and create unorthodox sounds that defied all ground rules so that only a few would understand them. The former, he felt, was boring and the latter was doomed to remain underground, virtually unheard by the public at large. For an ambitious young jazz drummer it seemed only natural to find another route out of this perceived impasse.

Along with Kooper, he was attracted to the idea of mixing jazz improvisation with rock using a modified big band lineup. Kooper was particularly inspired by Maynard Ferguson's mid-band recordings for Roulette and the Don Ellis big band.[15] When he heard some horn arrangements that James Guercio had penned for a pop group called the Buckinghams on the album *Time and Changes,* Kooper, along with Colomby and Katz, decided to go with an experiment giving equal prominence to a horn section within a rock band. Colomby began rounding up suitable musicians, including the alto saxophonist Fred Lipsius, who began arranging Kooper's original compositions. "We spent a month and a half period looking for the right horn thing," said Kooper. "We rehearsed about two months, got fourteen tunes together and opened for Moby Grape at the [Café] au Go Go. Three different labels came around. Columbia seemed the most understanding, above and beyond the business aspect, so we signed."[16]

In December 1967, Columbia threw a party for 450 members of the media at Steve Paul's club The Scene in Manhattan to introduce Blood, Sweat and Tears to the world. Celebrations went on into the small hours and the result was write-ups for the as-yet unrecorded group in *Cashbox, Newsweek,* and a host of other national publications. Meanwhile, Kooper, mindful of the Buckinghams' use of brass, had approached Guercio to produce the new album. Guercio declined, so Blood, Sweat & Tears went into the studios in November 1967 with the producer John Simon, who had produced The Band. Despite a Grammy nomination and some good reviews, including one from *Rolling Stone,* who said "Blood, Sweat & Tears is the best thing to happen in rock and roll so far in 1968,"[17] their debut album, *Child Is Father for The Man,* struggled to make forty-seven in the chart.

Today it is difficult not to conclude that the *Rolling Stone* reviewer must have heard this album very early on in 1968.[18] It sounds more a product of the pop world, and any connections with jazz-rock appear tenuous. Weighted heavily in favor of Kooper's vocals, the horns were not asked to undertake anything remotely complex. Certainly there is a brass presence, sometimes a pretentious one such as on "Morning Glory" and sometimes a seemingly gratitutious one, such as on "I Love You More Than You'll Ever Know," but overall the emphasis was on catchy hooks and hummable riffs. Many of the compositions were by Kooper, who was wildly eclectic, kowtowing in the direction of the Beatles in "The Modern Adventures of Plato, Diogenes and Freud," The Animals in "I Love You More Than You'll Ever Know," and Gary Puckett and the Union Gap. And in "Without Her" they sounded as far as way from rock in one direction as they were from jazz in another. In a last-ditch effort to stir public interest, a single was released of two tunes from the album, "I Can't Quit Her" and "House in the Country." It failed to chart.

Inevitably, straining in several directions at once for commercial success and not finding it caused tensions within the group. After playing the Garrick Theater in New York, there was a falling out between Kooper, Colomby, and Katz. Kooper left, and the trumpeter Randy Brecker also departed; it seemed like the end of the group. However, a new singer, the Canadian David Clayton-Thomas, was brought in, after overtures were made to everyone from Laura Nyro to Stevie Wonder, and Lew Soloff took over Brecker's chair. James Guercio was again approached to take on production duties and this time he accepted. "I knew that Blood, Sweat and Tears was a direct step from the energies I had created with the Buckinghams," he recalled. "By the time of the second album they were in a paranoid state, their first album hadn't been a success and they felt Kooper was doing them in."[19]

On the eponymously titled *Blood, Sweat & Tears,* released in December 1968, the elements of pop, rock, and jazz coalesce in a way that they did not in *Child is Father to the Man.*[20] Even so there are some tracks that are practically unlistenable today, such as Laura Nyro's "And When I Die," but on the strength of two singles that went gold, the Gary Puckett-like "You Made Me So Very Happy" followed by an exuberant "More and More"—"Spinning Wheel," the group was made. In April 1969 the album itself went gold.

Blood, Sweat & Tears tended to present jazz and rock as two separate species, rather than an integrated hybrid, so that the two styles emerged as separate elements within an overall composition. The best-known number from the album, the hit "Spinning Wheel," subsequently covered by several jazz groups including the Maynard Ferguson Orchestra on *MF Horn II,* serves as a good example. A staccato fanfare leads into Clayton's vocal against a powerful "rock" backbeat. Interestingly, although his vocal uses a simple AABA format, its unusual thirty-nine-bar length features "A" sections of the standard eight-bar length but a fifteen-bar "B" section. The "jazz" element is represented by a straight-ahead twenty-seven-bar open trumpet solo by Lew Soloff[21] following a fifteen-bar transition after the vocal chorus. The rhythm then returns to the "rock" backbeat before a wearying *ach du lieber Augustin* ending.

Equally, the Billie Holiday–Arthur Herzog, Jr. standard "God Bless the Child," revived the year before by a group called Loading Zone with a young keyboard player called Tom Coster, moves from the ballad treatment of the Holiday original, albeit now a slow rock ballad, to—somewhat incongruously—a bright Latin instrumental section featuring Jerry Hyman on trombone. As if this were not enough, it is further contrasted by bright, straight-ahead solos by Lew Soloff on trumpet and Fred Lipsius on alto before seguing back to the original ballad tempo. The message was plain: *this* was rock and *this* was jazz. However, the performance, beyond its novelty value of moving from rock to jazz and back to rock, is ultimately unsuccessful because the ear is drawn to the subsequent instrumental elements of the jazz interlude rather than Clayton-Thomas's vocal. For those seeking to identify with the ballad performance, the instrumental section is an intrusion. Similarly, a perfectly valid instrumental section is undermined by distancing it from the audience in the middle of a sentimental ballad performance. Equally puzzling was the inclusion on the album of the Erik Satie theme from "Trois Gymnopédies," in essence a third-stream performance.

Musical considerations aside, BS&T was ultimately a commercially produced group whose product was intended for consumption by a mass market, and their music was shaped accordingly. In their quest for profit, record companies like to offer the promise of innovation or change with their new signings. In using their corporate clout to get behind a mixture of jazz and rock, Columbia were simply reflecting the industry's constant drive to expand their market share by the creation and marketing of "new" products.

Columbia's timing in moving into jazz-rock with Blood, Sweat and Tears was just about perfect. There had been no shortage of speculation in the press about a jazz-rock hybrid, and now corporate advertising was reinforcing the concept by attempting to deliberately stimulate a potential mass market. In early 1969 the notion of what jazz-rock might sound like was something of an unknown quantity for mass audiences, so the potential of *Blood, Sweat & Tears* for crossover appeal to both jazz and rock audiences was spelled out by Columbia. Under the headline "Pretend It's Jazz," Columbia gave what were, in essence, directions on how to interpret the music as much for the music press as the public in its glossy ads:

> Don't think about the fact that [*Blood, Sweat & Tears*] is currently the hottest rock album in the country. Pretend it's jazz. (Undoubtedly, one of your fellow jazz freaks has already mentioned the album. So now, instead of just dismissing it, pretend it's a jazz album. And buy it.) Listen to the album, and enjoy it as jazz. . . . Then listen to it again. And enjoy it for what it is. Rock. Drenched with jazz, but powerful, rock, nonetheless. Then if it disturbs you that you've come to love an album that's, after all, rock, you know what you can do. . . . Pretend it's jazz.[22]

Record companies do not produce records and simply lay them out in the marketplace, leaving the rest to fate. They try to persuade potential customers to buy their product by highlighting why they think their product is valuable. This is done by trying to define the evaluative grounds of the product in the hope that the music press will continue and elaborate their theme, and here corporate advertising was designed not so much to sell the recording as to explain how it should be interpreted. It was framed to persuade critics and journalists to write about the recording in the right way and within the right discursive framework to lubricate the public's desire to make a purchase.

The early reviews of BS&T followed Columbia's lead, such as a 1969 *Time* review, which stated, "The group is also the most successful yet to combine jazz-flavored brass and reeds with rock guitar and rhythm,"[23] and a review in the *Los Angeles Times* a couple of months later, commenting that "BS&T is bringing into rock an orchestral sound, warm harmonic concepts and improvised jazz solos."[24] When *Downbeat* magazine presented their first feature on the group in 1969, discussion centered on the appeal of the group to jazz and rock audiences: "Blood, Sweat & Tears is helping more people get attuned to jazz textures . . . like rock, jazz is communal music and can have a broad appeal. I think a healthy trend right now is to regard basic blues, rock and what we call jazz as forms of one encompassing music." Equally, *Melody Maker* took up the theme, prompted by Columbia's advertising, of a bilateral affinity to both jazz and rock fans: "They have been labelled a 'jazz-rock' band because they are wide enough to swing as well as rock."[25]

By the end of 1969, Columbia's promotion had paid off handsomely. *Blood, Sweat & Tears* had gone from gold to platinum (a million sales) to triple platinum and fans, hungry for more BS&T, started buying *Child Is Father to the Man*. Later in the year this too went gold. However, success on such a massive scale subsequently led to confused musical directions and writing that was often pretentious and overbearing. "After we got successful we also got stagnant," said Lew Soloff. "All of a sudden from being a band that played and had some degree of success, we were the hottest thing in the United States—overnight . . . [we] became prisoners of our hit tunes."[26] In 1971 Clayton-Thomas was the first in a series of defections until eventually only the drummer Colomby remained of the original members. Even so, several jazz musicians subsequently passed through the band, including trumpeter Tony Klatka from Woody Herman's Swingin' Young Herd, saxophonist Joe Henderson, bassists Ron McClure and Jaco Pastorius, pianist Larry Willis, guitarist Mike Stern, and trombonist Dave Bargeron. Artistically, however, the group's output continued to be very uneven, many numbers no more than so-so pop songs. Solid tunes like "Go Down Gamblin'" on *BS&T4* (1971) were rare, while dogs like "Mama Gets High" or "Cowboys and Indians" lay in wait. When *New Blood* appeared in 1972, a resurgence seemed possible thanks to a more artistically rounded performance, but by then the group's popularity was on the wane.

BS&T's emergence in the late 1960s was virtually parallel with another band signed to Columbia that mixed horns with rock, Chicago, or as they were known

Blood, Sweat & Tears: Vocalist David Clayton-Thomas singing the band's biggest hit, "Spinning Wheel." (Photograph by Stuart Nicholson.)

initially, Chicago Transit Authority. They were formed in 1967 by a group of De Paul University graduates, including trombonist James Pankow, trumpeter Lee Loughnane, drummer Danny Seraphine, and reedsman Walter Parazaider. After several changes in the rhythm section, the group coalesced with the addition of Terry Kath on guitar, Peter Cetera on bass, and Robert Lamm on keyboards. James Guercio was a fellow student of the founding members at De Paul. He majored in composition and studied bass. He produced five hit singles for the Buckinghams while at the same time trying to help his former college buddies.

"Chicago at the time were a lounge band playing in Chicago and were known as the Big Thing," he recalled. "I knew them and I used to give them charts from the Buckinghams' first album so that they could stretch out from the soul stuff they were doing."[27] Guercio helped get them a contract with Columbia and produced their albums until 1977. Their first album, a two-disc set called *Chicago Transit Authority* (1968), went platinum and was still on the *Billboard* album charts in 1975. "There's 77:43 of music on these two records," said *Downbeat*. "70:50 of it is at least good and some is very heavy indeed."[28]

Initially, Chicago was less circumspect than BS&T in its use of rock. The ambitious "Free Form Guitar," a six-minute new thing/heavy metal freak-out by Kath, sounds more dangerous than anything BS&T ever attempted, and could explain why Chicago became one of Jimi Hendrix's favorite groups. Indeed, in a 1971 interview trumpeter Lee Loughnane disagreed with the "jazz-rock" label which was hung on the group, saying he thought Chicago was "a rock and roll band."[29]

The group recorded two more double-album sets in 1970 and a triple-album set the following year, *Live at Carnegie Hall*. Unfortunately their laudable productivity exposed all they had to say fairly early on in their existence; thereafter they settled for a role in the easy-listening market. By the mid-1970s they were turning out bland, but nevertheless best-selling, ballads such as "If You Leave Me Now" from 1976.

Chicago, a seven-piece group with a three-man horn section, and BS&T, a nine-piece group with a five-man horn section, were essentially similar bands. However much they disliked comparisons—Chicago claimed they were a rock group that did jazz-influenced numbers while BS&T claimed they were a jazz outfit that did rock-influenced numbers—they did have at least one thing in common, and that was the ability to make each succeeding album appear incrementally worse than the one before.

Flock, formed in 1968, succeeded in synthesizing varied musical perspectives while BS&T and Chicago tended to separate one from another. Flock flared brightly but disappeared with hardly a trace, yet their musical ideas were fluid rather than sequential, constructing vast sprawling epics that were full of interesting touches and clever flourishes. Often they sounded as if they were trying to cram too many ideas in a composition, but their energy and ideas, such as their use of collective improvisation that was reminiscent of free jazz and of Charles Mingus, were irresistible.

After considerable success with a number of single records on a local Chicago label, the Flock added their former roadie and occasional guitarist Jerry Goodman on violin and started concentrating on new, original material written by the sax player Rick Canoff and the guitarist Fred Glickstein; the remainder of the lineup was Jerry Smith on bass, Ron Karpman on drums, and, filling out the horn section, Tom Webb (sax) and Frank Posa (trumpet). When the local club owner Aaron Russo heard the band at his Kinetic Playground, a converted theater, he told the band he wanted to manage them and arranged a showcase with Columbia, Atlantic, and several other big labels; Columbia won the auction to sign them.

Their debut album, *Flock*, from 1969, says more in one disc than Chicago were able to do in *XVIII*, or BS&T, who spent most of the early 1970s denying that they were over-precise and clinical, in all theirs. "Clown" explodes from the beginning; here there is the impact and drive of rock, with the horn section functioning within the ensemble rather than sounding like an appendage grafted onto a rock band. Goodman emerges as a highly capable soloist, "the important event on the album," observed *Rolling Stone*.[30] The opener also featured a close-harmony vocal quartet, a somewhat bizarre but, if nothing else, attention-grabbing feature, their "Yeah, yeahs," a parody of the Beatles' "She Loves You." Today Glickstein's acid-rock guitar sounds dated, but it nevertheless adds to the period charm of the piece, as does Karpman's pre-high-compression drum sound.

The band liked tempo changes and interludes based on chords quite remote from the original composition, unconsciously echoing the concept behind Connie Boswell's brilliant arrangements like "Whad'ja Do to Me?" for the Boswell Sisters in the early 1930s. On "Truth," a fifteen-minute fantasia on a twelve-bar blues, for example, Flock make good use of tempo changes to move to a logical climax with Goodman's electric violin the main showpiece. Stretched out so much it sags in the middle, its laudable ambition is thwarted by lack of gravitas.

All in all, this first album was greeted with much enthusiasm in the rock and jazz press, as much for its promise as its achievements. "Flock is not, as John Mayall contends [in the liner notes] the best band in America," asserted *Rolling Stone,* "but it is good enough to merit a close listening now and a considerable degree of hope for the future."[31]

While their 1969 single aimed at the charts, "What Would You Do If the Sun Died," is best forgotten, Flock's second album, *Dinosaur Swamps,* recorded between May and October 1970, has more focus than their debut album without sacrificing their eclectically episodic *brio;* "Hornschmeyer's Island" is a journey from the Hard Rock Café to tea-dance politeness via a swinging jazz waltz, with Jerry Goodman's solo the highlight. Equally, "Big Bird" channel-zaps from country into a creditable straight-ahead jazz section featuring Frank Posa on trumpet and Goodman's violin. "Lighthouse" showcases the drummer Karpman; a solid technician, he slips in a flam paradiddle some two years before it became one of drummer Billy Cobham's most imitated licks. As with their debut album, Flock continued to display a "considerable degree of hope for the future," despite dallying with self-indulgence. Inspired neither by big bands or nor by soul music, they had a capacity to surprise and a grittiness and awkwardness that could not quite be swallowed up by commercialism.

The band broke up before they completed their third album, *Flock Rock,* on which they were working in December 1970, but in 1993 four previously unreleased tracks that reflected something the band loved dearly, collective and creative jamming, appeared on *The Best of Flock.* When the band split they had a reputation for being ahead of their time, and certainly their recorded legacy suggests an innovative and artistically diverse band that successfully integrated rock, jazz, blues, and country, and even a dash of folksy humor. "What a group," enthused *Billboard,* "remarkable musicianship . . . truly unusual."[32]

By the end of 1969, bands and albums modelled on the BS&T–Chicago concept were breeding like mayflies in permanent hatch.[33] Some, like Illustration and Ides of March, were somewhat shameless in their attempt to ape the BS&T formula, even hiring (horrible) David Clayton-Thomas soundalikes as their lead vocalists. Ten Wheel Drive had a showy lead singer in the Janis Joplin mode,

Genya Raven; while Cold Blood, a soul-influenced, eight-piece band from the Bay Area, had a three-man front line and had a powerful lead singer in Lydia Pense. From Oakland came Tower of Power, with a rugged horn section that was hired intact for any number of albums where, er, a "rugged horn section" was required.

Meanwhile, some mainstream jazzers were jumping on the horns-with-a-beat bandwagon. Herbie Mann, darling of bourgeois jazz fans and anxious not to miss out on anything that might extend his commercial appeal, added a BS&T-style horn section on his *Muscle Shoals Nitty Gritty* album from 1970. That same year, Chet Baker, the once-hip trumpeter from the cool school of the 1950s, began his long journey back from drug-induced obscurity with *Blood, Chet and Tears,* an album so awful it probably postponed any progress on his comeback trail for the duration of its availability. It included, you've guessed it, covers of several BS&T hits.

In 1971 Epic records signed Chase, a nine-piece band that took the horn-plus-rock formula of BS&T-Chicago to a logical, albeit *extremus absurdus* conclusion with a four-man trumpet section so powerful that it made even Kenton's halls of brass sound effete, something the Epic marketing department quickly latched onto:

LISTEN TO A NEW GROUP BLOW THEIR BRAINS OUT. Chase: The first rock horn band with a chorus of trumpets. . . . Music that builds and climaxes in screaming songs arranged out of four trumpets on top of a powerful rhythm section. Chase: If they're going to blow their brains out, they'd like it to be in your home.[34]

Led by one of the outstanding big-band lead trumpeters of his generation, Bill Chase, the front line was backed by keyboards, guitar, bass, and drums, plus the vocalist Terry Richards. All, with the exception of the bassist Dennis Johnson and the guitarist Angel South, had a solid background in jazz. Chase had made his name in the bands of Maynard Ferguson, Stan Kenton, and, most impressively, Woody Herman before becoming a musical director, arranger, and lead trumpet at large in Las Vegas. Disaffected with the Vegas scene, Chase craved the excitement of big bands and sought to create this within a jazz-rock context. His band was nothing if not distinctive, the trumpet quartet performing gymnastically challenging charts paced by the leader's brilliant upper-register playing.

Explosive live performances at the Kansas City and Newport Jazz Festivals and showcase features on the *Tonight* and *Smothers Brothers* TV shows helped their debut album, *Chase,* to achieve sales of almost 400,000 in 1971. From the trumpet-laden tour de force "Open Up Wide" to somewhat bizarrely titled originals like "Hello Groceries," Chase had worked the novelty of their agile trumpet front line to death by the end of the album. It was one-dimensional stuff, relying on power and stamina to bludgeon the listener into submission. The compositions, after the trumpet flash was stripped away, were functional and not much else. Yet band and album leapt to the top of the 1971 *Downbeat* Reader's Poll and was earmarked for a bright future. However, their second album, $\Sigma NN\Sigma A$ (1972), proved to be a bitter disappointment both for fans of the band and for Bill Chase himself. His attempt to compose a symphonic trumpet suite failed to impress, and the group went on an extended hiatus. They reformed in 1974 and recorded a new album, *Pure Music,* to mixed reviews. Even so, a comeback seemed within their grasp until, while en route to play the Jackson County Fair, an air crash killed the leader and three sidemen, Wallace Wohn, Walter Clark, and John Emma, on August 9, 1974.

By then the game was up for bands based on the BS&T-Chicago formula. After the initial enthusiasm for "big band rock," the concept quickly ran its course. The idiom was exhausted, Chase's empty virtuosity summing up how imitative instrumentation rather than musical innovation was used to cash in on a fundamentally simple concept. Rock critics—such as Greil Marcus, Dave Marsh, and Robert Christgau—saw in BS&T, Chicago, and groups like them an ongoing tension between musical aspiration and the pull of commerce, with the latter coming out on top. For them, "big band rock" did not rock enough and the jazz was not jazzy enough. Even worse, there was no real "star" with whom audiences could identify. Even when the singers sang, the most personal and communicative link between bandstand and dance floor, they often showed little empathy with their audiences, their problems, or their aspirations. These bands were scarcely a charismatic package and posed an "image" problem that rock critics were quick to identify.

Rock's appeal to teenage audiences was bound up in social as well as musical phenomena, but it was its importance as a social phenomenon that rock critics wrote about. Musicological explanation alone could not begin to demonstrate its significance. Yet in contrast, the very essence of jazz-rock was that it was a musicological phenomenon, something that from the outset set it apart from the rock mainstream. While jazz criticism tended to be musicologically based, placing emphasis on musical qualities, rock criticism embraced non-musical factors whose significance could not be reduced to considering its formal musical qualities. From early on a musicological approach to rock criticism was largely discredited by rock writers since it reduced the music to a disembodied presence lacking any social referents, the very things with which rock audiences identified. In the rock world, groups like BS&T and Chicago were put, to use Al Quaglieri's term, "on hipness probation."[35]

What these bands lacked was sex appeal, and despite their commercial success, jazz-rock was unable to provide the answer to the problems that ailed rock at the end of the 1960s. By 1971 rock's attention was being turned elsewhere, leaving the position of the BS&T-style bands as equivocal to rock fans as jazz fans, who felt they were musical "sellouts" that smacked of a commercial marriage of convenience, producing a music that was packed with compromise. Their concept was simple and thus easy to reproduce and held out the promise of commercial success, as Bobby Colomby observed in 1969: "As soon as we make a lot of money, a lot of kids are going to say, 'Hey, that's the secret, get a lot of guys together, get some horns, and we can make some money too.'"[36]

Indeed, for the most part these bands surrendered artistic aspiration for the pursuit of commercial gain and, with the possible exception of Flock, represented an amalgam of existing styles rather than a fresh concept. But somehow that was not the point; it was how the public at large saw these "horns and rock" groups that counted, and they saw them as jazz-rock bands, and this, ultimately, was their contribution. It was not so much in combining elements of jazz with rock as the enormous publicity and popularity they gained for trying to do so. More importantly, it made a financially beleaguered jazz world sit up and think seriously about the prospect of jazz-rock, if only because of the rock-style capital gains that flowed from commercial success. With the RIAA certifying a third million-selling single from the album *Blood, Sweat & Tears*—the first time in the history of the association that three singles had gone gold from one LP[37]—the record industry saw a way of turning around their unprofitable jazz sales by giving the music a contemporary spin. "Clive Davis was the President of Columbia Records and he signed Blood, Sweat and Tears in 1968 and a group called Chicago in 1969," recalled Miles Davis. "He was trying to take Columbia into the future and pull in those young record buyers. . . . He started talking to me about trying to reach this younger market and about changing."[38]

Notes

1. *Downbeat,* 5 October 1967, p. 15.
2. Ibid., 16 November 1967, p. 13.
3. *Sound Bites,* by Albert Goldman (Abacus, London 1992), p. 236.
4. Statistics from *American Popular Music Business in the 20th Century,* by Russell and David Sanjek (Oxford University Press, New York, 1991), pp. 206–210.
5. *Melody Maker,* September 2, 1967.
6. This problem of authenticity was not confined to jazz. When Hollywood first tried to reproduce the sound of rock, the ersatz compromise they came up with kidded no one. The former Dizzy Gillespie pianist Lalo Schifrin concentrated on writing music from the mid-1960s and soon became a prolific composer of film scores. Yet as soon as he tried to provide suitable rock accompaniment for the sundry bikers, hippies, and drug addicts that inhabited the B-movie scripts of his early films, the results sounded like a Holiday Inn lounge band on a bad night. To make matters worse, he institutionalized his failure to grasp what rock was all about on his 1971 album, *Rock Requiem,* which is still recalled with a shudder by many of the hardened West Coast session musicians who participated in it.
7. *Ball the Wall,* by Nik Cohn (Picador, London 1989), p. 72.
8. Butterfield's version can be heard on *East-West* and Cream's on *Wheels of Fire* from 1968. Cream also recorded a studio version of *Spoonful* on *Fresh Cream* from 1966. The song seems derived from Howlin' Wolf's 1960 recording, itself a combination of two Charley Patton songs, "A Spoonful of Blues" and "Jesus is a Dying-Bedmaker" from 1929.
9. By March 1971, Bloomfield was sitting in with the Woody Herman big band on the album *Brand New.*
10. Columbia wrote off half towards the cost of their first recording, which was deducted from the artist's royalties. With a profit of over 75 cents from each recording sold, the entire $50,000 was more than recouped from the sale of 70,000 albums (*American Popular Music Business in the 20th Century,* by Russell and David Sanjek [Oxford University Press, New York, 1991], p. 212).
11. *Rolling Stone,* February 15, 1969, p. 28.
12. *Downbeat,* June 27, 1968, p. 33.

13. On the 1995 release *Old Glory: The Best of Electric Flag* (Columbia/Legacy CK 57629).
14. Ibid., March 21, 1968, p. 25.
15. Al Kooper to Leonard Feather, *Downbeat,* November 11, 1971, p. 23.
16. *Rolling Stone,* April 27, 1968, p. 16. Originally the band had seemed set to go with Atlantic, but Clive Davis, the newly appointed head of Columbia, increased his offer.
17. Quoted in liner notes for *The Best of Blood, Sweat & Tears: What Goes Up!* (Columbia/Legacy 481019 2).
18. *Rolling Stone,* April 27, 1968.
19. *Melody Maker,* February 7, 1970.
20. *New York Times,* Mike Jahn's review of *Blood, Sweat & Tears* album, December 25, 1968.
21. Actually it ends on a *rallentando* on bars 26–27 leading into a drum pickup at what would presumably be bar 28. The final section of the solo divides itself neatly into three sections of four bars of chromatically descending augmented ninth chords, although the final four bars appear of ambiguous length because of the *rallentando.*
22. Columbia advertisement for *Blood, Sweat & Tears* (Columbia CS 9720), which appeared in the music press in early 1969.
23. *Time,* May 9, 1969.
24. *Los Angeles Times,* December 20, 1969.
25. *Downbeat,* July 24, 1969, and *Melody Maker,* in late 1969 and 1970, both used the Columbia advertising as an underlying theme.
26. *Downbeat,* February 15, 1973, p. 18.
27. *Melody Maker,* March 7, 1970.
28. *Downbeat,* October 2, 1969, p. 17.
29. *Melody Maker,* June 12, 1971, p. 11.
30. *Rolling Stone,* October 18, 1969.
31. Ibid.
32. Quoted in liner notes, *The Best of Flock* (Columbia/Legacy CK53440).
33. These included Paul Hoffert's thirteen-piece, self-styled "rock orchestra" Lighthouse; Gas Mask, produced by the Miles Davis studio whizz Teo Macero and featuring the trumpeter Enrico Rava; Dallas County; Sons; Stardrive; Symphonic Metamorphosis; Hardin/York; Jellyroll; Little John; the British group If; John D'Andrea and the Young Gyants; Ambergris, produced by Steve Cropper; and the Second Coming.
34. Trade advertisement for *Chase* (Epic E 30472), summer 1971.
35. Liner notes, *The Best of Blood, Sweat & Tears: What Goes Up!,* p. 7 (Columbia/Legacy 481019 2).
36. *Downbeat,* July 24, 1969.
37. *Cashbox,* January 24, 1970.
38. *Miles: The Autobiography,* by Miles Davis with Quincy Troupe (Simon & Schuster, New York, 1989), pp. 287–288.

CHAPTER 5

Sorcerer

M iles Davis signed with the Columbia record label on October 26, 1955 for a
$4,000 advance against royalties, then a sizeable sum for any recording
artist and unheard of for a jazz musician. At the time he was already under contract to the Prestige label, the only recording company to sign him while he had
been a junkie. Now he was clean. The hit of the 1955 Newport Jazz Festival,
where as a last-minute addition to the program he received a standing ovation
that put him back on the map after a period of drug-induced semi-obscurity, the
subsequent publicity enabled him to form a regular working group of his own.
With John Coltrane on tenor sax, Red Garland on piano, bassist Paul Chambers,
and "Philly" Joe Jones on drums, he debuted at the Anchors Inn in Baltimore on
Monday September 28, 1955. The quintet was at once recognized as the boss
group in jazz even though Davis disbanded and reformed it four times during the
following twenty-seven months because of drug problems with his key sidemen,
Coltrane and Jones. When, in the spring of 1958, the pianist Bill Evans replaced
Garland, Jimmy Cobb replaced Jones, and Julian "Cannonball" Adderley was
added on alto saxophone, Davis had a sextet that would become recognized as
one of the greatest small groups in the history of jazz.

By the early 1960s, Davis's group had undergone several more changes but
hadn't relinquished its reputation as jazz's preeminent group, even though the
vanguard had been claimed by free jazz, ushered in by Ornette Coleman in 1959.
Davis went his own way, dismissing Coleman's music, saying "No matter how
long you listen to it, it doesn't sound any good."[1] By 1963, Davis had gathered
around him a new rhythm section that comprised pianist Herbie Hancock,
bassist Ron Carter, and the seventeen-year-old drummer Tony Williams. Along
with the 1961–1965 John Coltrane rhythm section (pianist McCoy Tyner, bassist
Jimmy Garrison, and drummer Elvin Jones), it would become the most important and influential rhythm section in contemporary jazz. On albums such as *My
Funny Valentine, Four and More,* and *In Europe,* their startlingly high levels of
musicianship, interaction, and rapport set a standard in jazz in the same way the
Basie rhythm section had done in the late 1930s. Unfazed by the fastest or slow-
est tempos of jazz, they also used a variety of non-timekeeping techniques that
added significantly to the drama of their performances, such as avoiding stating
the tempo in certain sections, the use of silence for dramatic effect, the use of

out-of-tempo coloration, and, as if conducted by some unseen hand, gradual accelerations and decelerations of tempo.

In 1964, the tenor saxophonist Wayne Shorter joined Davis. Not only was he an extremely original and inventive soloist, he was also one of the most accomplished composers in jazz who combined unusual combinations of chords[2] with subtle, undramatic melodic themes that were far from the norm in jazz at that time. Shorter's compositions seldom used bridges or turnarounds, thus avoiding the regular series of cadences that customarily cropped up in traditional popular song forms such as the thirty-two-bar AABA structure. Instead, he used simpler forms, such as "E.S.P." on Davis's *E.S.P.* (1965), with an all-"A," sixteen-bar melody that repeatedly went up and down an interval of a fourth;[3] "Iris," a 16-bar waltz, again all-"A" or "AB" forms, such as the 24-bar composition "Witch Hunt" from his own album *Speak No Evil.* Shorter's curve-ball compositions quickly changed the sound of Davis's quintet, moving it away from a repertoire centered on standards, the blues, and originals from the likes of Thelonious Monk, Victor Feldman, and Jimmy Heath to originals from within the quintet, largely Shorter's own but also from Hancock, Carter, Williams, and Davis himself that took their lead from Shorter's approach.

Shorter brought something new to jazz, melodies that broadly favored a slow-moving line, often characterized by a "dreamy" feel. Such compositions allowed considerable latitude to the rhythm section, who were no longer required to explicitly state the beat in the old straight-ahead "hard-bop" style with the pianist comping like a Bud Powell, a walking four-to-the-bar bass line, and the drummer using ride cymbal patterns with the high hat closing on the two and four. Instead, Shorter's compositions allowed a far more flexible and interactive role in accompaniment. From 1965, this style gradually came to characterize Davis's quintet. Shorter's "Eighty-One" from *E.S.P.* (1965) had Williams using square drum patterns that would increasingly creep into his playing over the next couple of years. Another Shorter piece, "Dolores" from *Miles Smiles* (1966), was a thirty-eight-bar piece with the front line's phrases divided into two, two and one-half, three, and three and one-half bars. The spaces between these simple theme fragments allowed the rhythm section to come to the fore, assuming the center of interest along with the front line. "The seed was planted with 'Dolores,'" explained Shorter.[4] By 1967, Shorter's "Nefertiti" from the album of the same name had a simple yet haunting, sixteen-bar "A" theme that was repeated over and over for the duration of the performance—about ten minutes—that gave great freedom to Tony Williams, for whom it was virtually a feature. This exchange of roles—by giving the burden of complexity to the rhythm section rather than the front line—would later become a feature of 1970s jazz-rock.

The distinctive flavor of Shorter's compositions greatly emancipated the role of the drummer Tony Williams. His playing was a sourcebook of new ideas for drummers; rarely settling into one specific meter for the duration of a tune, he used imaginative and audacious polyrhythms that displayed remarkable independent coordination of hands and feet while his solos might blur into a compendium of percussive effects free from meter. As early as 1964 he was playing pieces without consistently closing his high hat on the second and fourth beats of the bar, instead using them in ringing bursts to provide eruptions of color. By 1966 he reversed this process, closing the high hat on every beat of the bar, such as on "Freedom Jazz Dance" from *Miles Smiles* (1966), a device that would become widely adopted by jazz-rock drummers in the 1970s. In "Stuff" from *Miles in the Sky* (1968) and "Vonetta" from *Sorcerer* (1967), he used unmistakably square drum patterns, something he had been gradually introducing since using them for a short interlude on "My Funny Valentine" from the 1964 Davis live album of the same name. Equally radically, Ron Carter had perfected the use of repeated ostinato figures that were far removed from the traditional walking bass line.

In 1967, Davis was searching for richer sounding, contemporary textures, altering the sound of his acoustic quintet in December 1967 with the inclusion of the electric guitarist Joe Beck—although the results weren't issued until 1979. "At the time Miles didn't have the faintest idea of what I should play," said Beck. "I just flailed around like a drowning man. Later . . . he got to where he really knew what he wanted from the instrument, but what I did with him was pretty useless from a musical standpoint."[5]

Davis continued to feel his way forward into 1968; that year's *Miles in the Sky* featured Herbie Hancock using a Fender Rhodes electric piano on "Stuff," while Williams's square rhythm patterns clearly suggest rock. The guitarist George Benson made a guest appearance on the Wayne Shorter composition "Paraphernalia," although the rhythmic climate on this and the remaining tracks, "Black Comedy" and "Country Son," was post-bop. By *Filles de Kilimanjaro*, Miles's overlooked album from 1968 that numbers among his finest achievements, Williams's use of square rhythm patterns was now quite pronounced, clearly resembling rock drumming. "Mademoiselle Mabry (Miss Mabry)," a subtle abstraction of "soft soul," gives the clearest evidence yet of how closely Davis was following events in black popular culture. With Carter's use of ostinato figures it was clear that Davis had now moved some considerable distance from the harmonic complexity of the standard repertoire of the 1950s.

Filles de Kilimanjaro was subtitled "Directions in Music," playing down the jazz connection in the hope of improving sales. The head of Columbia, Clive Davis, recalled that, "Miles called me to complain about record sales. He was tired of low sales and angry about it. Blood, Sweat and Tears had borrowed enormously from him and sold millions . . . while he was struggling from advance to advance. 'If you stop calling me *jazz*, man,' he said at one point, 'and just sell me alongside these other people, I'll sell more.' In part I agreed with him."[6]

Davis's music was now in delicate balance. It had evolved in incremental stages through the 1960s, employing a variety of advanced methods of improvisation that continue to be explored in contemporary jazz today. While several pieces relied on specific chord changes, others used modes and ostinatos, while others utilized the "time, no changes" principle, where the choice of chords was at the discretion of the improviser. Some compositions even mixed "time, no changes" with specific chords, such as "Prince of Darkness," a sixteen-bar composition with just a few prearranged harmonies occurring at regular points throughout the tune. Davis's music was highly sophisticated; time and meter mutated at the rhythm section's will while improvisations often veered into abstraction and fragmentation, as in the 1965 *Live at the Plugged Nickel* set. In 1967 Davis had also begun the practice of segueing the tunes he played in nightclub sets into one continuous performance. The only problem was that Davis's music was now popular with everyone except the general public. His albums weren't selling in sufficient numbers to please Columbia and audiences weren't turning up at personal appearances in big enough numbers to justify the kind of money he charged, then the highest in jazz.

In 1967–1968 it was not Miles Davis whom jazz audiences were flocking to see, but the tenor saxophonist Charles Lloyd, whose group bloomed brightly in the jazz garden, artificially nourished and force-fed by nimble promotion and publicity. Lloyd had joined the drummer Chico Hamilton's group as a twenty-three year old, becoming the group's manager and principal arranger during his three-year stay and contributing all the compositions on Hamilton's *Drumfusion* album. In 1964 Lloyd replaced Yusef Lateef in the Cannonball Adderley Sextet, and a TV broadcast of the band in England later that year[7] reveals him to be an interesting soloist in a Coltrane-lite mold.

In August 1965, Lloyd formed his own group with the help of George Avakian, who became his de facto manager. Avakian, who had worked with names such as Louis Armstrong and Duke Ellington, was the record producer largely responsible for signing Miles Davis to Columbia. He was convinced Lloyd was a coming star and arranged a half-hour syndicated television show, "Jazz Discovery: Charles Lloyd," that was the first example of TV helping introduce and promote a new jazz personality. Avakian also bankrolled Lloyd's first album *Discovery!* with Don Friedman on piano, Eddie Khan or Richard Davis on bass, and Roy Haynes or J. C. Moses on drums, intended to capitalize on the telecast, and bankrolled part of Lloyd's second album, *Of Course Of Course.* There were few sales, however, and Lloyd decided to reform his group and sign with Atlantic.

In early 1966 Lloyd had gathered around him some of the most adventurous young musicians of their generation in Keith Jarrett on piano, Cecil McBee on bass, and Jack DeJohnette on drums, revealing his new group on *Dream Weaver.* Avakian decided to build the group up in Europe before launching them on the American circuit. The group picked up rave reviews in a spring European tour and returned in the summer; they were the hit of Antibes Jazz Festival. "Their set was one of the most exciting experiences I have had in a long time. . . . [The quartet] has now established itself as one of the major new arrivals in jazz," said *Melody Maker.*[8] Their third trip to Europe that year produced two albums, both recorded in Aulaen Concert Hall, Oslo, on October 29, 1966. *In Europe* and *The Flowering* capture the group's free-flowing, freeform approach to improvisation in numbers like "Gypsy 66" and "Manhattan Carousel."

On home ground, however, Lloyd was still to make a breakthrough. In New York there was a skepticism concerning a musician whose career had been large-

ly West Coast based, and several critics had not bothered to check Lloyd out
when he had performed there. However, on September 18, 1966, Lloyd played
the Monterey Jazz Festival to enthusiastic reviews. The band's performance was
later released as *Forest Flower* to encouraging sales and a review of four and one-
half stars from *Downbeat:* "Lloyd's quartet and its quick rise to international
recognition provides an antidote to the disparaging commentary floating around
about the current state of jazz."[9]

The favorable publicity from Monterey resulted in a profile in *Harper's* magazine that focused on the plight of a young musician searching for an audience

The Charles Lloyd Quartet: *Left to right:* Ron McLure,
Jack DeJohnette, Lloyd, Keith Jarrett. Lloyd suggested
that it was possible rock could provide jazz with a
genuine source of energy and inspiration and revealed a
large, young audience open to new ideas. By playing
rock venues like the Fillmore West, Lloyd surprised
everyone in jazz by clicking with the "love and peace"
generation and by 1967–1968 was the most popular act
in jazz. (Courtesy of the Institute of Jazz Studies, Rutgers University.)

when times were tough in jazz. Lloyd's name was spreading. With both Jarrett and DeJohnette younger than Lennon and McCartney, it seemed only natural that the group should adopt the casual, colorful clothing of the prevailing Californian flower-power climate instead of the lounge suits and ties that they had worn during their first European tours. Their new, colorful visual signature with caftans and beads and long, sometimes ecstatic versions of tunes with hip titles like "Love Ship" resulted in an approach from Bill Graham to play the Fillmore in San Francisco, the top rock emporium in the world. To the surprise of everyone, they clicked with the crowds and were called back for several encores. "The audience back then weren't sure how to be hip," said Keith Jarrett. "There wasn't any word coming down from the media on how you became 'hip,' at any particular moment. So they were forced to have their own feelings about things when they listened to music. So I think that at this point in time people were more open to things and Charles was a beneficiary of that."[10]

Avakian made sure the novelty of Lloyd's breakthrough with rock audiences made headline news in the music press and the popular dailies, with *Billboard* hailing them as "the first psychedelic jazz group."[11] Lloyd was suddenly news and commanding four-figure sums for personal appearances. "A nice thing about the 1960s was the radio was more free form," reflected Lloyd. "They would play my music alongside Jimi Hendrix or the Grateful Dead, or Ravi Shankar, Otis Redding and all that. It was a time of idealism and there were not these lines of demarcation, kids were listening to all kinds of music. So when we played for them at the Fillmore, we were very lovingly and warmly received and it opened a door, because things were kind of depressed in the jazz scene, jazz clubs were struggling for their existence. All the San Francisco groups loved our music— Grateful Dead, the Airplane, Janis Joplin rallied around us. The Dead's favorite album at this point was *Dreamweaver* and when they heard it they wanted to improvise more. Jerry [Garcia] was always talking about us recording together. There was exchange of ideas among musicians. Bob Dylan and Robbie Robertson were friends and they played a song called 'Memphis Blues Again' so I came up with 'Memphis Dues Again.' We were all youthful, we didn't have lines of demarcation that exist today—I thought, and still think, Dylan was an enormously important musician."[12]

In early 1967 a live album was recorded at the Fillmore. Now with Ron McClure on bass, *Love-In* became something of a hit record, its psychedelic cover in shocking pink with a huge heart framing a picture of the band appealing to the "love-and-peace" generation who otherwise never bought a jazz album. Lloyd was a jazz musician in the right place at the right time. "Who else is there?" said his booking agent. "Either you get someone old enough to be their father or a bunch of angry guys pouring frustration, protest and hate messages out of their horns. That's not the message these kids want to hear."[13]

Despite a so-so review in *Downbeat, Love-In* was described as "a healthy example of how rock and jazz can coexist while swinging."[14] Yet there were moments in "Tribal Dance," for example, where Lloyd and DeJohnette duet like Coltrane and Elvin Jones, and in the down-home "Is It Really the Same?"

Charles Lloyd became a big hit with the crowds at the Fillmore.

Jarrett makes use of dissonance and abstraction that must have scared rock audiences stiff. It's remarkable what uncompromising jazz Lloyd and his musicians actually played in a rock venue, albeit carefully balanced with numbers like the title track employing a "rock" beat, and Jarrett's own calypso-styled "Sunday Morning." Here too was an early example of Jarrett's stream-of-consciousness soloing that freely associated a myriad of influences that made the word "eclectic" sound narrow and limiting. DeJohnette's approach to rhythm was fluid, mutating patterns that implied rock, but with the flexibility of jazz drumming. A good example of his imaginative and creative approach is on "Memphis Dues Again/Island Blues." Although Lloyd is slightly sharp, the track is nevertheless an excellent example of the group's appeal; an *a cappella* introduction by Lloyd is followed by the blues section and a strong backbeat from DeJohnette, with

Lloyd making much of the plagal cadences. Yet on Jarrett's solo the backbeat is mutated into something far more subtle, allowing greater rhythmic freedom for Jarrett's imagination to take flight. From the same sessions came the subsequent album, *Journey Within;* although it tried to cover too many bases—Jarrett's soprano saxophone playing, "new-thing" collective improvisation, and exotic extended "peace and love" compositions—the album documents a jazz group's unusual rapport with a rock audience.

In 1967 Avakian arranged a high-profile tour of Russia for the group, the first jazz group to tour there since Benny Goodman's State Department visit in 1962, which Avakian had also accompanied. It meant high-profile cover in the world's media, and on his return Lloyd found himself the most publicized figure in jazz for years, ensuring good sales for *Charles Lloyd in the Soviet Union,* recorded during his tour there. At the end of the year *Downbeat* readers voted him "Jazzman of the Year," capping a year of startling success in reaching an audience that jazz musicians had, until now, thought impossible to tap. "I play love vibrations," explained Lloyd in the argot of the times: "Love, totality, like bringing everyone together in a joyous dance."[15]

Nonetheless, it's fair to say Lloyd's group never achieved their full potential. Lloyd was a capable player, not as bad as the critics would have us believe but not so good as to deserve all the brouhaha heaped upon him, which possibly accounts for a sudden crisis of confidence in his playing. It deteriorated so massively that Jarrett and DeJohnette felt compelled to confront him about it. "Jack said to me 'We have to tell him, we have to do something,'" recalled Jarrett. "So then Jack and I said 'Listen Charles,' I think it was Jack who was the one who spoke most on this. He said: 'I don't know what is the word to call it, but you've been playing flat, it's like there's nothing happening, it almost sounds debauched.' And Charles said, 'Well maybe I want to play debauched.' And Jack and I looked at each other and said, 'OK, it's the beginning of the end of the band.'"[16]

The group's final album together was *Soundtrack,* recorded live at New York's Town Hall on November 15, 1968. After confronting Lloyd about his playing, DeJohnette was the first to leave, replaced by Paul Motian. In early 1969 the *San Francisco Examiner* noted, "Lloyd is writhing and jerking more on stage these days, to the detriment of his instrumental offerings."[17] Shortly afterwards the band was put on an extended hiatus, only to learn that Lloyd had omitted to tell them he had formed a new group. Without his gifted rhythm section, however, Lloyd wasn't going anywhere. "We were in a situation we weren't all that comfortable with, being accepted as a, you know, rock-type act," said Jarrett. "Charles set himself up as a guru of jazz, or a guru of pop, and that wasn't comfortable for Jack or myself, because we knew it wasn't really 'real.' . . . The real part of it was when we played, when we just hoped we could make good music."[18]

After *Moon Man,* a poetry-and-neo-hip-jazzy-rock album from 1970, he signed with A&M records, producing albums such as *Waves* and *Geeta* in 1973–1974. Taking up transcendental meditation, Lloyd withdrew from music until 1982, when he was tempted out of retirement by the talented young French pianist Michel Petrucciani. Taken together, the main attraction today of Lloyd's albums from his 1966–1968 period is in the playing of the young Keith Jarrett and Jack DeJohnette. Their fluid approach to rock's rigid rhythmic structures— in which both McBee and McClure played a key, but largely unacknowledged role—and their remarkable empathy still communicates now as does their unmistakable joy of playing. Performances such as "Forest Flower" and "East of the Sun" from *Forest Flower,* for example, still sound remarkably fresh today.

Surprisingly, Lloyd didn't try very hard to reach a fusion of jazz and rock. Instead he hired young baby-boomers who were in tune with the changing times. Their approach to rock's rhythms made it clear their talents were far from exhausted in exploring the style, and while the band didn't betray a single, exclusive commitment to integrating rock and jazz, they always worked with great poetic license in whatever particular style they explored. The group's significance was more in its time rather than in leaving any lasting impression on jazz. Lloyd suggested that it was possible rock could provide jazz with a genuine source of energy and inspiration, and he revealed a large, young audience open to new ideas. As Keith Jarrett observed in 1974, "There are lots of records of that band and it was an 'obvious' band. Not as mysterious as Miles's band. We were too young to be mysterious."[19]

Lloyd's emergence as leader of a "psychedelic" jazz group in West Coast rock circles was against the backdrop of the "San Francisco sound," which had begun in a little-known neighborhood called Haight-Ashbury (the city's hippie epicenter), in the bohemian houseboats of Sausalito, and in the purlieus of the University of California at Berkeley. It was a tight-knit scene; many of the musicians knew each other from playing the folk circuit, and among the early San Francisco bands was a great sense of community. They shared the same houses and apartments, the same roadies, and often the same women and drug dealers. A particular feature of these bands was their extensive use of improvisation that initially emerged from jamming together for their own pleasure. When the San Francisco rock bands began to emerge around 1965, most shared a fascination with modal forms and long, jam-session versions of rock numbers both in performance and on record. Seen in this context, Lloyd's music was tailor-made for the San Francisco existentialists, with long haunting flute solos and extended piano or tenor improvisations using rock-oriented rhythms. Equally, the leader's great interest in transcendental meditation found its way into his stage patter and into song titles like "Meditation," "Karma," and "Journey Within" that connected with a generation in search of a closer rapport with the infinite.

The innovative concept of having a jazz group open for bands like the Paul Butterfield Blues Band or the Grateful Dead was pioneered by Fillmore owner Bill Graham, who led a personal crusade to educate public taste by booking a wide variety of artists on one bill. A typically egalitarian Fillmore lineup, like the one from September 11, 1966, had Elvin Jones, the Joe Henderson Quartet, Jimi Hendrix, Big Mama Thornton, Great Society, and Jefferson Airplane all in one evening! Soon Fillmore's only real rival, the Avalon Ballroom, began a similar mix 'n' match policy. In such circumstances jazz began to bleed into rock and vice versa through the genuine curiosity of the musicians. On the one hand rock groups were exploring extended improvisation, while on the other jazz musicians were experimenting with rock rhythms and the new electronic technology—electric pianos, phase shifters, flangers, wah-wah effects, and so on—creating a more honest artistic union than the obviousness of the East Coast bands such as Blood, Sweat & Tears and Chicago.

Long a center of bohemian culture, San Francisco had attracted Beat Generation writers and jazz musicians in the 1950s; one holdover from this period was the author Ken Kesey, famed for his antiestablishment novel *One Flew Over the Cuckoo's Nest.* Kesey began sponsoring famous all-night parties, known as "acid tests" because they involved feeding his guests doses of LSD through spiked drinks. (At the time, the drug was still legal.) To accompany the mass mayhem, Kesey took on as his houseband a group of ex-folkies who lived together in the Haight-Ashbury neighborhood. Originally known as the Warlocks, they would soon metamorphose into the trippiest of all San Francisco bands, the Grateful Dead. In their own way, the Dead would parallel 1960s jazz musicians in their exploration of the mystic sounds of the East, the free improvisation of Ornette Coleman, and the modal approach to improvisation of the Miles Davis and John Coltrane combos.

It was no good playing three-minute pop songs or even blues numbers for the acid test devotees. The Dead, with their unfathomable sense of mission, played long sets because their pot-smoking, LSD-eating hippie audience wanted them to, allowing them to trip out to the incredible volume and the fantastic light and slide shows that were a part of the acid-rock experience. Music was for dancing and free expression, and a key factor was the strong improvisatory element introduced by breaking open songs for extended jams that went on forever for the hallucinating dancers. The Dead had a considerable reputation for playing while stoned, and while they could be frustratingly erratic they were capable of awe-inspiring rock during their performances, which could go on for upwards of five or six hours. "We were playing to people who were taking LSD and dancing their hearts out," explained the lead guitarist and group guru Jerry Garcia, "and it was easy, because we were playing from that flow."[20]

When the band was first approached about recording, Garcia and the others felt that the Dead was not a recording group. "I don't believe the live sound, the live excitement can be recorded," they told *Newsweek,*[21] believing the impact of their incredible volume would be dissipated by domestic hi-fi. And they were probably right—in performance the Dead were fanatical about the sound of the band, using walls of speakers and banks of amplifiers that amounted to almost thirty tons of equipment, and no recording could get anywhere near reproducing the sheer visceral power of the Dead, live.

In spite of their doubts, their debut album, *Grateful Dead* from 1967, and *Live Dead* from 1970 are good examples of the band's style during this period. The freeform "Dark Star" from the latter, with Garcia's spidery yet individual lead lines and Phil Lesh's fluid bass work, was clearly an attempt to create a major work and on its own terms succeeds as a controlled piece of improvisation that showed just how narrow the gap between rock and jazz could be in the hands of an accomplished rock guitarist. Garcia, a perennial jammer, used to sit in with keyboard man Howard Wales (who appeared on the Dead's *American Beauty* album) at San Francisco's Matrix Club in the early 1970s, which quickly became a Monday night event. Their association produced *Hooteroll?* and with it an insight into Garcia's improvisatory style away from the Dead. Garcia, who never made any secret of his love for jazz and had Ornette Coleman open for the Dead in the 1980s, later got to record with Coleman on *Virgin Beauty* (1988).[22]

Like the Grateful Dead, Jefferson Airplane jammed often and at length in live performance, although as *Rolling Stone* pointed out, "their jams seldom centered around the blues but instead displayed a more intellectual and complex approach that was loud but not hard."[23] However, their open-ended jamming rarely appeared on record, which tended to emphasize their hits and folk-rock background. There are a few pieces that evidence the influence of jazz on the band. *After Bathing at Baxter's* included the number "Chaynge" with an episode of free-tempo collective improvisation, for example. Brief solo appearances on many of the group's albums by lead guitarist Jorma Kaukonen, ably supported by bassists Jack Casady and the jazz-based drumming of Spencer Dryden, hint at what the band must have sounded like live. The strong folk bias of Kaukonen's playing on the early albums gave way to the influence of other rock players including Jerry Garcia and Eric Clapton as the band evolved and, like Garcia and many of the acid-rock guitarists, he began to look to jazz for inspiration.[24] Jefferson Airplane was one of the many bands at the time exploring how jazz musicians approached modal, or perhaps more accurately "one-chord" improvising, and how they managed to sustain interest over long periods of static harmony, the basis for much of acid rock's long "psychedelic" jams.

When the Cream arrived at Fillmore West, their long jazz-influenced sets made a considerable impact on the San Francisco bands. "They were the first power trio," said Bill Graham, "blues-based but with that powerful rock and roll guitar. . . . They destroyed everyone at the Fillmore."[25] Eric Clapton recalls that Cream just came out and did their thing: "We went out there and took on San Francisco and we didn't even know what we were up against. Even though there were the Grateful Dead and Jefferson Airplane and Big Brother, they were kind of playing pop music. There weren't relating to their roots too well. They were trying to get away from it all. . . . The first show we did at the Fillmore . . . we found we were doing long, sort of jazz-based solos with everybody jamming."[26]

Rock's new preoccupation with improvisation did not go unnoticed in the jazz press. No doubt to their surprise, Country Joe and the Fish were the subject of a *Downbeat* feature that described them playing a whole hour-and-a-half set of total improvisation, under the caption "Country Joe and the Fish-Improvisers."[27] Around this time—maybe coincidentally—just like the San Francisco bands, Miles Davis began playing nightclub sets as one continuous piece of music. A kind of cross-pollination—with rock musicians listening to jazz and jazz musicians listening to rock—was beginning to create a climate in which some sort of jazz-rock union seemed inevitable and was widely anticipated in the press, if only to restore the failing commercial fortune of jazz. "A particularist, exclusive and non-proselytizing attitude ill behooves jazz in its present predicament, which briefly stated is the crying need of a bigger audience. If rock offers jazz a bridge, jazz would be foolish not to cross it," wrote Dan Morgenstern in 1968.[28] Even if some reports of the arrival of jazz-rock were premature—Michael Cuscuna hailing The Doors' eponymously titled debut album as "the first successful synthesis of jazz and rock," for example[29]—a general sense of expectation that the improvisational practices of jazz might help renew rock was in the air. More particularly, with a trade story in *Billboard* announcing that jazz had hit rock bottom in 1969,[30] rock was widely seen as the catalyst that might well revitalize an ailing jazz.

With 1968 turning into 1969, amid hip listeners' album collections of the Beatles, Grateful Dead, Jefferson Airplane, Country Joe and the Fish, Quicksilver Messenger Service, the Last Poets, and the mandatory Ravi Shankar LP, you were just as likely to stumble across a John Coltrane or Pharoah Sanders album. Although jazz was thought of as distinctly un-hip, there were several ingredients in the music of Coltrane and Sanders that contributed to their assimilation by the spiritually inclined members of the counter-culture. Sanders's albums such as *Tauhid* and *Karma,* with their lack of artifice and their simple plea for universal peace and harmony, were in matchless synchronicity with the prevailing atmosphere and aspirations of the alternative society of the late 1960s. The spirituality and nonliteralist global inspiration of Sander's music—often trance inducing with wordless Sufic chants, African drums, and rock-like rhythms—ideally suited the Afghani vibe of 1969 as it did the acid jazz of the 1990s.

These concerns with mysticism and spirituality equally led many rock musicians into the music of John Coltrane. An enormously charismatic figure, Coltrane's personal philosophy embraced alternative religions while his music betrayed his fascination with the mystic East, an infatuation shared by many in the counterculture movement. In the early 1960s Coltrane had had a minor hit with "My Favorite Things," in which he abandoned the chord structure after the exposition of the melody and opened up the song with an extended major-minor vamp. Over this simple, uncluttered harmonic base he devised a way of imposing sequential patterns by adding and altering the basic harmonies using chord stacking or substituting nonstandard modes—those of Spain and India were particular favorites. The result was a solo that appeared to possess the sort of direction normally derived from a preset chord progression, despite the simple harmonic base. By the middle to late 1960s, the way Coltrane dealt with modal forms had begun creeping into the playing of rock guitarists who were exploring modes as a basis for their long, psychedelic jams.

Especially influential was Coltrane's 1962 album *Impressions* and the famous title song that borrowed the chord structure of Miles Davis's "So What" from *Kind of Blue:*

A (8 bars "D" Dorian mode) + A (8 bars "D" Dorian mode) + B (8 bars "E-flat" Dorian mode) + A (8 bars "D" Dorian mode)

As the piano and bass drop out, Coltrane's duet with the drummer Elvin Jones reaches a climax. Within Coltrane's extroverted shrieks, he retains little motifs within his solo that also relate to the techniques employed by Indian musicians. Coltrane had been listening to the music of Ravi Shankar for at least two years prior to the recording, probably because of Yusef Lateef's influence. He was seized by the spareness and abstraction of Indian music, with its emphasis on melody and rhythm rather than harmony, and began corresponding with Shankar in 1961, finally meeting him in 1965.[31] This interest is also reflected in "India,"[32] the opening track of *Impressions,* which incorporates the general feeling and color of Indian music.

Coincidentally, another influential musician fell under the spell of Ravi Shankar's sitar playing. The floodgates opened when George Harrison, the lead guitarist of the Beatles, drawn to the teachings of Eastern religionist Maharishi Mahesh Yogi, used a sitar in "Norwegian Wood" on *Rubber Soul* (1965). This fascination with the East dovetailed neatly with Coltrane's explorations, and Eric Clapton, Duane Allman, and Jimi Hendrix were among several rock guitarists who carefully studied Coltrane's music. Allman, in particular, was an avid fan of Coltrane and Miles Davis, and his exceptionally creative solos with the Allman Brothers Band suggested the possibility of rock becoming an improvising soloist's idiom. "You know," Allman once explained to Robert Palmer, "[my] kind of playing comes from Miles and Coltrane and particularly *Kind of Blue.* I've listened to that album so many times for the past couple of years, I haven't hardly listened to anything else."[33]

The Allman Brothers' double-album set *The Fillmore Concerts* (1971) ranks as one of the finest concert rock albums ever recorded, and Duane Allman's soloing lent great credibility to jazz-length improvisations in rock, an idea initially advanced by the San Francisco bands. James Gurley, for example, of Big Brother and the Holding Company, spent hours and hours between gigs sitting alone in his Pine Street apartment off Haight-Ashbury attempting to transcribe the ecstatic frenzy of Coltrane's improvisations for guitar. His long solo in "Ball and Chain" from the 1968 Janis Joplin album *Cheap Thrills* was almost entirely inspired by Coltrane. Even the first "psychedelic" rock hit "Eight Miles High," by the Byrds, used a four-note motif from the beginning of Coltrane's "India" to lead from the opening vamp into the song proper; this was later repeated at intervals throughout the composition. The Byrds guitarist Roger McGuinn has spoken at some length about how he was trying to emulate Coltrane's soprano saxophone style on his twelve-string guitar, right down to "the sound of the valves [on the saxophone] opening and closing."[34] The guitarist Carlos Santana, who also emerged from San Francisco's psychedelic scene shortly before its eventual collapse, was another important rock musician who studied Coltrane's methods extensively.[35]

Coltrane had once dreamt of a beautiful drone, a single tone produced by a tamboura that underpins much Eastern music, and began introducing a drone in his own music by using two acoustic basses in numbers like "India." His deepening religious fervor was reflected on his 1964 album *A Love Supreme,* which was almost entirely modally based and included an eponymous incantationary four-note chant that became a familiar sound on college campuses where the album's message was tailor-made for the peace-and-love generation. Coltrane in effect crossed over into the counterculture with this album, both spiritually and musically, and his improvisational methods provided a way out of the diatonic jams in which San Francisco rock was becoming increasingly marooned. By the end of the 1960s, several spiritually inclined rock bands were actually including Coltrane pieces in their repertoire; "India," for example, appeared on albums by The Corporation and the London-based Mighty Baby.

However, for young jazz musicians on the West Coast, work opportunities in what was, for a while at least, the epicenter of the rock world were few and far between. "There was no work playing jazz at that time," said the pianist Mike Nock. "We were trying to survive in a world that didn't relate to bebop. We were looking for a way to play that audiences could understand, but not play down to them. Fortunately the rock scene was very open to new bands and sounds.

John Handy became the first jazz group to benefit from Bill Graham's egalitarian booking policy that mixed jazz, folk, blues, rock, and pop artists on the same bill.

Freeform radio had a lot to do with this openness. Everybody listened to KSAN, which played a wide variety of music, dependent on DJs' tastes."[36]

Nock had moved to the West Coast to join a band led by the former Charles Mingus alto saxophonist John Handy, who had built a considerable following among the college crowds in San Francisco. Handy had performed in Bill Graham's first promotion in San Francisco, a benefit for the San Francisco Mime Troupe, with whom Graham was then performing, at the Calliope Warehouse on November 6, 1965. Also on the bill were The Fugs and Jefferson Airplane, plus a poetry reading from Lawrence Ferlinghetti. To Graham's surprise, the benefit was a sellout. "People lined up in the street for the party," he said. "Huge hoards of people, thousands of them. Legally the loft held maybe six or seven hundred. I'd say we had fifteen hundred in there at one time."[37] The benefit raised $4,200 and Graham realized he had tapped into a vast audience. After the huge success of a second benefit concert, Graham left the mime troupe to concentrate on promotion, and Handy was frequently the jazz artist he called up to fill out the bill. By 1967 Handy, because of his exposure to young audiences, was speaking glowingly of the Beatles and asserting his group was "doing the same kind of thing in jazz," saying, "The kids who dig rock music and my music . . . [are] concerned about Viet Nam and Civil Rights."[38]

Handy made a considerable impact at the Monterey Jazz Festival in 1965, playing in a style influenced by the classic John Coltrane quartet, with modal pieces played in the hypnotic, swaying "three" feel characteristic of Elvin Jones's timekeeping, albeit without Coltrane's emotional intensity. Handy's group gradually built up a dedicated following, becoming a regular at Delano Dean's Both/And Club in San Francisco. The guitarist Jerry Hahn combined the flavor of both jazz and rock in his playing, while the former Sun Ra violinist Michael White provided an effective contrast to Handy's Coltrane-influenced alto, enabling them to communicate with young audiences open to new musical ideas on the burgeoning Frisco music scene. "If Only We Knew," on *John Handy Recorded Live at the Monterey Jazz Festival,* reveals this post-Coltrane feel, while "Spanish Lady" was derived from the Gregorian chants he sang as a youth and based on a single minor chord. "We played like it was a matter of life and death," recalled Hahn of their Monterey appearance. "I was scared to death and had the shakes, but we all survived!"[39]

By 1966 the Handy quintet had launched themselves into West Coast eminence, their regular appearances leaning into rock with their strong yet flexible rhythmical approach generated by Hahn, bassist Don Thompson, and drummer Terry Clarke. The band earned admirers from the Rolling Stones to the entire Woody Herman band. "Dancy Dancy," a modified fast bossa nova from *The 2nd John Handy Album* revealed a well-integrated group cohesion and compelling lyricism from Handy, Hahn, and White that balanced the often opposing poles of communication and artistic integrity. "Blues for a Hamstrung Guitar," a feature for Hahn, made use of square, rock-influenced rhythm section patterns without being boxed in by the ubiquitous backbeat and gave a free rein to Handy's natural tendency toward uncomplicated lyrical improvisation.

John Handy: With his extroverted quartet including guitarist Jerry Hahn, violinist Michael White, bassist Don Thompson, and drummer Terry Clarke, he communicated with young audiences open to new musical ideas on the burgeoning San Francisco music scene. (Courtesy of the Institute of Jazz Studies, Rutgers University.)

This unique, congenial group played their last date together at Sacramento State University in November 1966, ending a five-week tour of the western states. By then Hahn had recorded his debut album as a leader, *Ara-Be-In*, with Mike White on violin and the Charles Lloyd rhythm men Ron McLure on bass and Jack DeJohnette on drums, plus Noel Jewkes on tenor sax. Mostly inspired by the then-fashionable mysticism associated with the Far East, it reflects the open-eared climate of experimentation that included an Ornette Coleman hoedown.

Handy reformed his group with Mike Nock on piano, Albert Stinson on bass, and Doug Sides on drums, debuting it at the Antibes Jazz Festival in July 1967. Stinson and Sides were later replaced by Larry Hancock and Bruce Cale on bass and drums, respectively, and this new lineup, with White back on violin, appeared at San Francisco's Both/And early in January 1968 playing opposite the Bill Evans trio, who later praised Nock as a "creative pianist."[40] Later in the year the group cut *Projections,* continuing the saxophonist's mixture of good-natured high spirits and Coltrane-influenced playing, with Nock emerging as the group's new star. "It might be interesting to hear his ideas in a self determined context," said John Litweiler in *Downbeat.* "Despite his usefulness in Handy's peculiar music, Nock's approach indicates that he has other things to say."[41]

Those other things Nock had to say included a greater use of rock rhythms, finding a ready accomplice in the violinist White. When one night Handy failed to turn up because of illness, Nock and White covered the gig using their own material. Things went well and they continued rehearsing by day and playing for Handy by night, joined by the former Stan Getz and Roland Kirk drummer Eddie Marshall and a variety of bass players including James Leary. By the summer the prospect of just a handful of gigs with Handy prompted them to try their luck on their own.[42]

Nock called his new group Fourth Way, inspired by Ouspensky's delineation of the fourth dimension as "a spatial sensation of time" that ultimately transcends "to cosmic consciousness." A professional musician since the age of fourteen, Nock had moved to Auckland as a sixteen-year-old, then to Sydney, before ending up in London as house pianist at Ronnie Scott's for six months in 1960. After studying at Berklee, during which time he played in Herb Pomeroy's group and in a quartet with Sam Rivers and a young Tony Williams, he became the house pianist at Lennie's in Boston between 1962–1963, playing with the likes of Coleman Hawkins, Pee Wee Russell, and Benny Carter. In early 1964 he played a gig with Yusef Lateef in Connelly's Stardust Room in Boston that led to an invitation to join the saxophonist on a regular basis on June 29. His first regular gig with Lateef yielded three albums, *Live at Pep's, Club Date,* and *Live Session.* After staying with Lateef for about a year, recording *1984* in 1965, Nock decided to freelance on the New York scene to experience a wider spectrum of music.

Between early 1965 and 1967, Nock worked with Art Blakey, Sonny Stitt, Elvin Jones, Freddie Hubbard, Booker Ervin, Stanley Turrentine, Jim Pepper, Barre Phillips, and The New York Improvisation Ensemble, and for six months in late 1965 as pianist for Dionne Warwick. He then formed his own group with Cecil McBee and Eddie Marshall to open at New York's Dom (a cavernous social club owned by a Polish-American cultural society and leased to Andy Warhol for his famous Exploding Plastic Inevitable happenings as well as for other hip events), and recorded *Almanac* in early 1967. His first involvement with jazz-rock came with Steve Marcus and the Count's Rock Band (see chapter 4), his attitude towards jazz changing after working with Warwick. "We'd play the same notes every night, very little change," he recalled. "I'd never done that before. But you really get into feelings, like pulling back the beat here or you speed it up—all those subtle rhythmic things—shit I never even knew about as a jazz musician!"[43] In July 1967 he had a call from John Handy, who had heard him with Lateef in San Francisco a couple of years earlier, and accepted an offer to join a new band the saxophonist was putting together.

Nock was among the first musicians to specialize on the electric piano. "It was a revelation to me to be able to play with a volume equal to a front-line horn by using the Fender Rhodes," he said.[44] Fourth Way debuted in San Francisco's Jazz Workshop on 14 August 1968 with White, Marshall, and John Wilmeth on bass and were an immediate success. "An uncanny meeting of musical minds . . . Fourth Way's sounds come as a most profound experience," said the *San Francisco Examiner.*[45] When later playing opposite the Charles Lloyd quartet, Nock persuaded Lloyd's bassist Ron McLure to join the group on a permanent basis. Quickly establishing a cohesive group identity, the group impressed David Rubinson of Fillmore West, who began booking them regularly. In West Coast terms at least, Fourth Way had arrived. "Live they are phosphorescent, almost more than one can absorb," enthused the *San Francisco Examiner.*[46]

"It was a very exciting period musically," Nock recalled. "At the time there were no role models so we were free to shape the music how we wanted, plus we had a growing audience interested in anything we did. I always wanted to hear the *jazz* thing, especially from the rhythm section. Without drummer Eddie Marshall, for example, there wouldn't have been a Fourth Way. The band, like all the San Francisco bands, was very much the result of shared communal effort from the management right through to the way we rehearsed and played the music. It was this quality that really differentiated us from the East Coast bands, it was laid back, not so technically oriented, unlike the bands I heard coming out of New York."[47]

After an impressive performance in the 1968 DeYoung Museum Concert Series,[48] the group were signed by Capitol, recording on their subsidiary label Harvest. They recorded three albums during their three-year existence, *The Fourth Way, The Sun and The Moon Have Come Together,* and *Werewolf.* A good example of how the band sounded comes from the live *The Sun and The Moon Have Come Together,* a broadcast the band played at The New Orleans House, Berkeley, in 1968. On the album, Nock emerges as an accomplished pianist whose arrangements for the group made use of adventurous bass lines and offered fluid and imaginative rock rhythm patterns; soloist Michael White is also a standout performer. "Blues My Mind" shows how Nock had quickly discovered how muddy chords voiced in thirds sounded on an electric piano, adapting to the "new" style of voicings in fourths for a cleaner, contemporary feel. When White makes his entry, he picks up on this interval, the beginning of his solo effectively a fantasia built around the interval of a fourth.

After a successful appearance at the Monterey Jazz Festival in 1969, they appeared the following year at the Montreux and the Newport jazz festivals. Their set at the Montreux festival was recorded and released as *Werewolf,* which turned out to be their final album together. At the time it was considered a controversial performance, but today it stands as one of the classic recordings of jazz-rock. By then Nock was using one of the most complete, and impressive, electronic keyboard setups in jazz, a stunning array of synthesizers, ring modulators, flanges, Fender Rhodes piano, and wah-wah pedals, using them to their fullest capabilities from far-in to the far-out reaches of white noise. Combined with McLure's bass guitar and White's electrified violin—which also used distortion as an effective extension of the instrument's sound—he finally realized the

Mike Nock and Fourth Way *Left to right:* Michael White, Nock, Ron McLure, Eddie Marshall. "When a history of electronic music is written, the pioneering work of Fourth Way should neatly eclipse the influence of many other more highly publicized groups," said *Rolling Stone.* (Courtesy of Mike Nock.)

fluidity of expression inspired by Coltrane's free style that he had been reaching for with Count's Rock Band. Here, the harmonic-melodic concepts of Coltrane's classic quartet were realized within an electric—and electrifying—jazz-rock context. "The Fourth Way demonstrate, in their most eclectic album to date, that we are still only beginning to discover the *musical* ramifications of amplification, ring modulators and other effects," said *Rolling Stone.* "When a history of electronic music is written, the pioneering work of Fourth Way should neatly eclipse the influence of many other more highly publicized groups."[49]

However, the band were experiencing some internal problems. Ron McLure returned east and was replaced by Seward McCain on electric bass, but when Michael White left after playing his final gig with the band at Ventura College, California, on April 30, 1970, it spelled the end of Fourth Way. White had signed a recording contract with the Impulse label, deciding to pursue what turned out to be an ill-advised solo career. "[That] was a particular shame," reflected Nock in 1977. "The band was tailor-made for him to do his thing. Now he's driving a bus. After he split everything fell apart. If only I'd tried harder to keep it together. But lots of musicians . . . come up to me in New York and they say ours was the first music like [jazz-rock] that they ever heard. I'm amazed they remember, they even know the tunes. It makes me feel good. We felt special back then."[50] Nock reformed the group as a trio with the bassist Steve Swallow and the drummer Elliot Zigmund, playing both electric and acoustic pianos, and in 1970 was one of the first jazz musicians to adopt the Arp synthesizer. The group held on to its loyal following but failed to record, and within a couple of years Nock returned to New York.

Fourth Way's approach to jazz-rock was achieved with integrity and poise. In 1968, it was among the first bands to wholeheartedly *combine* elements of both jazz and rock as well as to harness the new electronic technology to produce something fresh and new. "It wasn't commercially based music," Nock points out. "That came later and that's when jazz-rock lost its appeal for me, when it became known as fusion. In the early days it was a much more innocent music. It seemed to me at that time jazz music had a chance to regain some of the broad-based appeal it had back in the 1930s."[51]

Yet none of the Fourth Way albums were reviewed in *Downbeat* magazine, then as now one of the main opinion formers in jazz. The band's existence was acted out almost wholly on the West Coast, the wrong side of the continent to get press notices that matter in the music business. The sense that a new page was being turned when jazz entered the new age of rock-influenced music came, ironically, as Fourth Way broke up. It was to be enacted almost entirely on the East Coast under the eyes of a music press who had widely predicted such a move, and were looking for a player around whom they could construct history.

Notes

1. *Downbeat,* June 13, 1968, p. 34.
2. Shorter was among the few musicians in the 1960s to use suspended ♭9 chords, then a relatively new sound in jazz harmony.
3. Played x2 as 12 bars + 4-bar turnaround, 12 bars + 4-bar conclusion.
4. *Downbeat,* July 14, 1977, p. 58.
5. *Guitar Player,* April 1996, p. 32.
6. *Clive: Inside the Record Business,* by Clive Davis (William Morrow, New York, 1975).
7. BBC TV's *Jazz 625.*
8. Quoted in *Downbeat,* March 23, 1967, p. 15.
9. *Downbeat,* June 1, 1967, p. 35.
10. Interview with the author, April 7, 1997.
11. Quoted in liner notes, *Love-In* (Atlantic 588077).
12. Interview with the author, July 31, 1997.
13. Quoted in liner notes, *Love-In* (Atlantic 588077).
14. *Downbeat,* September 21, 1967, p. 32.
15. Quoted in liner notes, *Love-In* (Atlantic 588077).
16. *Keith Jarrett,* by Ian Carr (Paladin, London, 1992), p. 39.
17. *San Francisco Examiner,* February 10, 1969.
18. Interview with the author, April 7, 1997.
19. *Downbeat,* October 24, 1974, p. 16.
20. *Dancing in the Street: A Rock and Roll History,* by Rober Palmer (BBC Books, London, 1996), p. 160.
21. Quoted in *Downbeat,* September 21, 1967, p. 32.
22. Over the years, the Dead have been the favorite rock band of many jazz musicians, not least Branford Marsalis who, at the expense of sounding out of his depth, sat in on *Infrared Roses.* In January 1996, Joe Gallant, a downtown New York bassist, mounted a big-band reworking of the Dead's 1975 album *Blues for Allah* at the Knitting Factory, while keyboard experimenter and Knitting Factory regular (and Seattle resident) Wayne Horvitz

called one of his outré jazz quartets Pigpen, after the Dead's "Pigpen" McKernan. In 1993, saxophonist David Murray appeared as a special guest of both the Dead and the Jerry Garcia Band, electrifying three sold-out concerts. As a result, Murray featured the music of the Dead on *Dark Star* from 1996 that even had a guest appearance by guitarist Bob Weir. "Improvisation: that relates to my whole purpose as a jazz musician, about being in the moment," said Murray. "When the Dead got into those long improvisations, that's what I would live for. . . . Having played with them three times, one thing about Jerry [Garcia] that really stood out was his dedication to improvisation. He was always ready to improvise. He missed his calling: he really should have been a jazz musician, but then he wouldn't have made any money!"

23. *Rolling Stone,* December 2, 1970, p. 33.
24. Even their hits claimed jazz inspiration. Grace Slick described their 1967 hit "White Rabbit" in this way: "The music is a cross between [Ravel's] *Bolero* and Miles Davis's *Sketches of Spain,* the words from *Alice in Wonderland.*" *Sketches of Spain,* of course, contained the first famous modal tune "Pan Piper" that preceded *Kind of Blue* by one year. The Miles Davis connection crops again on "Rejoyce" from *After Bathing at Baxter's* where the arranged instrumental passages are distinctly reminiscent of Gil Evans's writing on *Miles Ahead* and *Porgy and Bess.*
25. *Bill Graham Presents: My Life Inside Rock and Out,* by Bill Graham and Robert Greenfield (Delta, New York, 1993), pp. 214, 217.
26. *Downbeat,* June 11, 1970, p. 14.
27. Ibid., September 5, 1968, p. 21.
28. *Downbeat Yearbook 1968,* p. 13.
29. *Downbeat,* May 28, 1970, p. 13.
30. Quoted in *Downbeat,* April 30, 1970, p. 12.
31. *Chasin' the Trane,* by J. C. Thomas (Elm Tree Books, London 1976), pp. 90–91.
32. An adaptation of his composition "Mr. Knight" from *Coltrane Plays the Blues,* recorded on October 24, 1960.
33. Liner notes, Miles Davis's *Kind of Blue* (Columbia Legacy CK 64935), p. 9.
34. *Dancing in the Street: A Rock and Roll History,* p. 165.
35. Santana's career and his jazz influences are examined in chapter 13.
36. Conversation with the author, July 12, 1996.
37. *Bill Graham Presents: My Life inside Rock and Out,* p. 123.
38. *Downbeat,* May 4, 1967, p. 17.
39. Ibid., October 1996, p. 34.
40. Ibid., May 28, 1970, p. 26.
41. Ibid., January 9, 1969, p. 22.
42. Handy, whose flirtation with rock rhythms was among the earliest in jazz, promptly returned to the mainstream, forming an easy listening "New Thing" group with the vibist Bobby Hutcherson that failed to impress. By 1968, Handy was becoming increasingly involved in music education on the West Coast, which progressively removed him from regular performance, although he did resurface briefly in the 1970s when he decided to cut some awful disco-oriented albums. Subsequently Handy never quite succeeded in capturing the genial creativity of his groups with Hahn or Nock, nor was he able to reproduce the kind of national success enjoyed by Charles Lloyd. Although the three albums from this period suggest that he never fully exploited the group's potential, they do represent a solid body of work that today stands in the first row of the second rank of jazz during this period. In August 1994 Handy reconvened the original band with White, Hahn, Thompson, and Clarke for a rapturously received appearance at Yoshi's Nitespot in Oakland that had crowds queuing outside three hours before opening: *Live at Yoshi's Nitespot* (Boulevard BLD 531 DCD).
43. Conversation with the author, July 12, 1996.
44. Letter to the author, December 31, 1996.
45. *San Francisco Examiner,* September 10, 1968.

46. Ibid., September 9, 1969, p. 28.

47. Letter to the author, December 31, 1996.

48. "Fourth Way had a big supporter in Kitty Griffin of the New Orleans House," said Nock. "She gave us a regular place to play which was tremendously helpful to the band's development, playing to rock audiences, Hells Angels, hippies and even the occasional jazz fan!" Letter to author, December 31, 1996.

49. *Rolling Stone,* April 15, 1971.

50. *Downbeat,* April 7, 1977, p. 36.

51. Letter to the author, December 31, 1996.

CHAPTER 6

Voodoo Child

Charles Lloyd's success had set the jazz world talking. Few considered him to be a "great" saxophonist, in a league with a Charlie Parker or a John Coltrane, yet by moving closer to popular culture he was enjoying remarkable popularity while the rest of the jazz world was in the doldrums. Certainly, as far as Miles Davis was concerned, there was a matter of pride at stake as Lloyd shot to jazz stardom. "[Miles] wants to be rich, he wants to be powerful and the only way to do that is to be on top in the profession," observed the bassist Dave Holland,[1] who had joined Davis's group in time to appear in two numbers on *Filles de Kilimanjaro*. And there was no doubt that Davis enjoyed the most flamboyant lifestyle in jazz, living in penthouse apartments and driving Ferrari sports cars.

However, Davis's position as the pacesetter in jazz was under threat, and musicians were looking to see what his response would be. He was aware that his music needed to change and added a guitar to his lineup on a couple of record dates in late 1967 and early 1968, but his public would not hear these experiments for some while. On March 8–9, 1968, Miles shared the bill at New York's Village Gate with Charles Lloyd. "They were playing a cross between jazz and rock, very rhythmic music," said Davis,[2] who was now under no illusions as to the basis of Lloyd's appeal. Davis was also being exposed to rock in his personal life. In September 1968 he married Betty Mabry, who introduced him to black rock and musicians such as Jimi Hendrix and Sly Stone. "[Mabry] was a big influence on my personal life as well as my musical life," he later confessed.[3]

Meanwhile, Clive Davis, the head of Columbia Records, was putting increasing pressure on Miles to produce albums that would sell in the quantities his rock signings were delivering. "It eventually got to be a problem," said Clive Davis; "50,000 albums barely takes you out of the red ink. We began to give Miles additional money each time he recorded an album; we weren't making any money at all."[4] Miles Davis was soon acquainted with the commercial facts of life. "I'm more interested in how we're going to get youth to really listen to jazz," the Columbia boss explained in 1971:

> Use your genius and start communicating, get into exciting areas, use other instrumentation, bring your musical ideas to new people. If the artist is not interested in doing that, then I'm not interested in having that artist record

for us. . . . For instance Miles Davis. I encouraged Miles to go in a new direction. It seemed that Miles . . . could have a separate career as the music was evolving, and I urged him to change . . . so after an initial blowing-up, where he asked for his release . . . which was just a short-lived burst of feeling and marvellously Miles in nature, he called me and said he was prepared to embark on this route.[5]

Davis's last album, *Filles de Kilimanjaro* from 1968, took his music up to the doors of rock by modifying and redefining the classic hard-bop ensemble, but it was obvious he would have to go further to reach an accomodation with his record boss. Also, his quintet was beginning to break up, forcing him to rethink his approach completely. Ron Carter was the first to leave, triggering a similar expression of intent from Williams, and when Hancock failed to return on time from a holiday in South America, he was replaced by Chick Corea. Such wholesale changes meant either trying to get different musicians to re-establish the status quo or using the combined experiences of new musicians to strike out in fresh directions. Never one to look back, Davis chose the latter option, although he appeared far from sure how to reposition his music. He dropped in at a Laura Nyro recording session and was almost persuaded to sit in, and he occasionally turned up at James Brown gigs. "The music I was really listening to in 1968 was James Brown, the great guitar player Jimi Hendrix and a new group . . . Sly and the Family Stone," recalled Davis. "But it was Jimi Hendrix that I first got into when Betty Mabry turned me on to him."[6]

Hendrix's seminal *Electric Ladyland* was released in 1968, hitting the U.S. charts at ninety-eight on October 19 and shooting to number nine the following week; by mid-November it had made number one. On it were two extended jams, captured in the studio when the tape machines were left to run: "Rainy Day Dream Away," with guests Freddie Smith on saxophone, Mike Finnigan on organ, and Buddy Miles on drums, and "Voodoo Chile," with guests Stevie Winwood on organ and Jefferson Airplane's Jack Casady on bass. In both of them Hendrix arrives at a distinct jazz-rock synthesis, creating a smokey jazz-club ambience "that is closer to Grant Green and Charles Earland than to the frenzy of a rock concert."[7] "Voodoo Chile" is the great primeval jazz-rock jam, taking up most of side one of the vinyl release. Totally unplanned, Hendrix simply dictated the mood and let the musicians improvise. On "Rainy Day, Dream Away" he told everyone, "We're gonna shuffle in D, real mellow with one change, very laid back," and to the organist Mike Finnigan he said, "You be like Jimmy Smith and I'll be like Kenny Burrell, that's what I'm looking for."[8] Although not recognized at the time, perhaps not even by Hendrix himself, this was music that spilled out of rock and into jazz, blurring the distinction between the two; who can say which style predominates?

What seemed to interest Davis was the manner in which Hendrix had achieved this. By the time *Electric Ladyland* had hit number one, Davis had also begun a practice of augmenting his basic group with "guests" in the recording studios, creating a loose, jam-session environment as a way to move his music forward, "like them old-time jam sessions we used to have in Minton's back in the old bebop days,"[9] he rationalized later, conscious of how the language of bebop had evolved.

Although Herbie Hancock had been replaced by Chick Corea in September, both pianists appeared on a session from November 1968. In a somewhat bizarre pairing of his new and old rhythm section—Hancock and Carter lining up alongside Corea and Holland—the group recorded somewhat inconclusive versions of "Two Faced" and "Dual Mr. Tillman Anthony," with Williams on drums. Davis was again in the studios later that same month, this time with *three* electric pianos—Corea, Hancock, and Joe Zawinul—plus Shorter, Holland and Williams. "Splash," was a modified blues in 5/4 that sounded more like a Blue Note boogaloo of the period. On "Directions" the former Charles Lloyd drummer Jack DeJohnette made his recording debut with Davis. All of these transitional takes were held over for release for more than ten years.[10] The next time Davis was in the recording studios, however, was to have a profound effect on the world of jazz.

In A Silent Way was recorded on February 18 and 20, 1969. "This one will scare the shit out of them," Davis told the music journalist Don Heckman.[11] On it, he made an unambiguous move to combine jazz and rock. Yet for all the album's notoriety among jazz purists, the results were hardly what Grateful Dead or Rolling Stones fans would have recognized as rock. Instead, Davis aligned himself alongside recent developments in soul music with a deep, dark hypnotic rhythmic groove.

As the 1970s approached, soul musicians were extending the music's boundaries in a way that had little to do with James Brown or Aretha Franklin. Hip new sounds, exemplified in 1969 by Isaac Hayes's lengthy ballads on *Hot Buttered Soul,* Donny Hathaway's *Everything Is Everything* from 1970, and Marvin Gaye's *What's Goin' On* from 1971, were favoring a less aggressive, "softer" approach. A good example of this new breed of soul musician was the Howard University graduate Donny Hathaway. After playing a little jazz piano around the local night spots to help subsidize his studies, he was introduced to Curtis Mayfield, leading to recording sessions in Chicago and New York. After his arrangements for the Staple Singers, Carla Thomas, and a few others impressed the bandleader King Curtis, Hathaway landed a contract with Atlantic records. His 1970 debut album, *Everything Is Everything,* included "The Ghetto," which reflected a soft soul "groove." Using jazz licks played by Hathaway on a Fender Rhodes piano over a repeated two-bar minor vamp, he established a hypnotic but ominous mood. In place of the brash soul backbeat was a more subtle rhythmic pulse, the vocals were no more than a chant, and the piece was long (for pop music), running almost seven minutes.

It was against this backdrop of musical change sweeping through popular black music that *In a Silent Way* (1969) should be viewed. However, the manner in which Davis achieved his new style, through informal *Electric Ladyland*–style studio jamming, marked a departure from the careful preparation of his previous albums. "This is the kind of album that gives you faith in the future of music," said Lester Bangs in *Rolling Stone.* "It's not rock and roll but it's nothing stereo-typed as jazz either. . . . It's part of a transcendental new music which flushes categories away."[12]

In the space of the five months that separated *Filles de Kilimanjaro* and *In a Silent Way,* the sound of Davis's group had undergone a radical transformation. For recording purposes the English guitarist John McLaughlin was co-opted into the studio ensemble along with the pianists Joe Zawinul and Herbie Hancock, who, with the regular pianist Chick Corea, completed an unusual three-keyboard setup. Holdover Wayne Shorter now favored the brighter-sounding soprano sax to cut through Davis's new electric ensemble. "Miles was hardly ever in the studio," said Zawinul. "He was in the control room. On 'In a Silent Way' I played organ and Chick and Herbie a little keyboards. Miles let me do the session, more or less, and then he come out when it was right and boom! When he played, the groove was there. We were all careful, not *too* careful, but everybody had so much respect for the next guy. I was not knocked out, frankly speaking. For me it was swimming too much, but there was something good about it. You bring a lot of people together and we made something out of it because you had such great musical performers."[13] Davis reduced the changes on Zawinul's composition "In a Silent Way" to a simple pedal point, heightening a feeling of suspended animation that permeates the album.

While the *sound* of Davis's ensemble was truly different from anything that had gone before, another striking deviation was a concerted application of post-production techniques by the producer Teo Macero. Davis had previously utilized such techniques during the recording of *Miles Ahead* in 1957, which featured a large number of edited or spliced takes, overdubs, and postproduction work to produce a classic; equally, *Porgy and Bess* and *Sketches of Spain* contain much after-the-fact rationalization.

In popular music, the notion that an album should sound like a "captured" live performance had increasingly given way to elaborate production techniques in the studio.[14] By the mid-1960s, the development of multitrack recording made it possible to store different instruments on separate tracks and, in the final mixdown, add, re-record, or alter the relationship of these tracks. Producers could now work on a tape to create a performance comprising several events recorded on quite separate occasions, working raw ideas into attention-grabbing musical events. Gradually, five- to ten-minute performances that never existed in real time emerged through multitracking, overdubbing, tape splicing, and other sonic legerdemain. Such studio creations demand to be heard on their own terms, for what they are rather than what they are patently not—"captured" live performances—since the important thing about art is not the means used to achieve an end, but the end it achieves. Pop and rock artists no longer tried to capture the sound of a live performance in the studio, but now tried to figure out how to reproduce on-stage the sounds they conjured up in the studio.

Miles Davis was one of the first jazz musicians to recognize the fast-developing studio technology—and here Jimi Hendrix also deserves credit; his *Axis: Bold as Love* from 1967 was received as "a miracle of four-track recording." Without many preconceived notions, Davis was nudging his talented sidemen towards finding a route into jazz-rock by allowing the tapes to run during long and often rambling jam sessions, and handing the results over to producer Teo Macero to edit and reassemble into a coherent performance. Despite the fact that, from *In a Silent Way* on, Davis's albums were undoubtedly fashioned by Macero, the trumpeter himself was notoriously emphatic that all hosannas should accrue to himself.[15] "Miles always wanted to take credit for everything," explained Macero. "You know, he'd walk into the session, play, then walk out. In the 26 or 28 years we worked together he maybe came to the editing room five or six times. He never saw the work that had to be done on those tapes. I'd have to work on those tapes for four to five weeks to make them sound right."[16]

The music for *In a Silent Way* was selected from a three-hour session and reduced to two performances of around twenty minutes each that in their original form took one side each of a vinyl LP. "In a Silent Way/It's About That Time" actually uses the same splice of "In a Silent Way" to open and close the number with a second mood sandwiched between. On "SHHH/Peaceful," a simple vamp continues throughout, with Davis directing the instrumental traffic and ensemble density. In terms of the rhythmic feel he was unequivocal: "I wanted to make the sound more like rock," he said.[17] This music was no gesture at past glories, but instead it was a promise of new ones to come. While it was not the commercial success usually claimed for it, reaching only 134 on *Billboard*'s chart, it nevertheless demonstrated the artistic feasibility, if not quite yet the commercial viability, of jazz-rock.

Yet the calm, ordered sound that characterizes *In a Silent Way* was the antithesis of what Davis's regular quintet of Shorter, Corea, Holland, and DeJohnette were playing when it went out on tour that spring. Described by *Downbeat* as "on the edge,"[18] there was nothing to suggest that their studio experiments had been moving closer to rock. "I wish this band had been recorded live because it was a really bad motherfucker," asserted Davis, ". . . Columbia missed out on the whole . . . thing."[19] In fact the band was recorded, in Europe in early 1969; *Double Image,* a well-recorded, live bootleg album, contains just two compositions, the title cut and "Gemini." Here any move towards rock had been abandoned in favor of free jazz, which Davis had earlier dismissed at the hands of Ornette Coleman. It was the end of Davis's association with the bop and post-bop tradition; here was energetic playing, full of dense textures, sustained turbulence, and periods free from any specific pulse. "He put a cap on a certain style of acoustic jazz music with Herbie and Ron and Wayne and Tony," explained Corea, "and then he let the world of changing harmonies go, started going into vamps and jungle music, primitive rhythms and abstracted melodies. The years *we* were on tour, the sets I played would be one improvisation from beginning to end with a few little cues from Miles to change the tempo or key. Every tune we played was in this incredible abstract form; the meat of the rendition was free improvisation."[20]

Davis was now concerned with areas of musical color and enforced spontaneity; solos, especially those of Corea and Shorter, avoided the streams of 8th notes that were the essence of bop orthodoxy and instead employed fragmentation. A walking bass line had gone completely; instead, motifs used for coloration added spice to the instrumental stew while Corea avoided comping in the traditional bop sense, splashing abstract electronic colors behind the soloists. Drum patterns sporadically implied abstract rock rhythms, DeJohnette mainly presenting an undercurrent of activity that was more concerned with texture than with rhythmic drive. Davis himself was polarized between lyricism and "outside" playing. It was an approach that could not have been in greater contrast to *In a Silent Way*. In September Miles appeared at the Monterey Jazz Festival, and the organizer Jimmy Lyons noted, "Davis [was] groping for a new sound. He'd eventually find it but the audience was impatient with his long, anxious noodlings."[21]

But if Davis's music appeared in flux, so too did popular culture, which was undergoing a dramatic transformation as the certainties of the 1960s were being swept aside. Rock was losing its innocence, and the consequences of the decade's indulgences were seen for what they were. There had been widespread belief in the spiritually therapeutic value of psychedelic drugs, and rock's pharmacological eclecticism had led to the widespread use of practically anything that could be popped, smoked, or injected. Drugs had become part of the scene, and even those in the audience who didn't take them applauded the music that celebrated their use. "One pill makes you larger, one pill makes you small, and the pills that mother gives you don't do anything at all," sang Grace Slick in Jefferson Airplane's "White Rabbit." Yet by the end of the decade, Haight-Ashbury, like London's Carnaby Street before it, had turned to blatant commercialism. The Summer of Love ended in a series of celebrated drug burnouts, a chain of self-destruction that left the music in crisis. "The musicians did it to themselves," said the Fillmore entrepreneur Bill Graham. "It got to the point where the public would go to shows just to see if the musicians would turn up, and when they did turn up it was an event."[22]

The ethos of sex-and-drugs-and-rock-'n'-roll was beginning to take its toll on a generation of music makers. In July 1969 Brian Jones of the Stones was found dead in a swimming pool, the cause of death either asthma, drowning, a heart condition, or drugs. Worse was to come when the Stones played the Altamont Speedway near San Francisco in December. Mick Jagger looked on as Hell's Angels, who were supposed to be providing the "security," hacked and stomped to death Meredith Hunter, an eighteen-year-old black man who had foolishly brandished a pistol. The following month the bodies of Roman Polanski's wife Sharon Tate and four others were found at her Los Angeles home; Charles Manson, leader of a hippie commune nearby, was indicted for the crime, along with several others. In September 1970, Jimi Hendrix died from inhalation of vomit following barbiturate and alcohol intoxication, and the following month Janis Joplin died from a heroin overdose. In 1971, Duane Allman was killed in a motorcycle crash near Macon, and Jim Morrison died in his bathtub in a Paris hotel room, probably from a drug overdose. In New York and San Francisco, Bill Graham's two rock emporiums, Fillmore East and Fillmore West, closed their doors for the last time. "The scene has changed," said a disenchanted

Graham. "What exists now is not what we started with and does not seem to be a logical extension to the beginning."[23] As if to emphasize that a curtain was descending on an era, the Beatles broke up, the group that sang "All You Need Is Love" ending their career among bitter exchanges of betrayal, lawsuits, and acrimony.

Yet while Jim Morrison and Janis Joplin had functioned brilliantly as rock *stars,* only Hendrix stood as a serious musical force. In him rock had lost one of its most important and singular innovators and gained one of its most celebrated heroes of excess. Hendrix was a guitar genius whose playing revealed hitherto unglimpsed horizons. He possessed an emotional range far greater than any contemporary guitarist. He demonstrated that the electric guitar was first and foremost an *electronic* instrument rather than an amplified acoustic one, opening up a whole new world of musical possibilities that balanced energy and ingenuity, distortion, feedback, sustain, and new fretboard techniques (primarily hammering on the strings to play countermelodies) into vital and integral components of a style. In the same way Cecil Taylor redefined the piano and John Coltrane the tenor sax, Jimi Hendrix redefined the electric guitar. An innovator who reshaped sound, his playing had a profound effect on jazz, although this has scarcely been acknowledged. Under his fingertips was a vast spectrum of guitar-playing sounds—blues, jazz, R&B, soul, and rock—and from it he created a style so revolutionary it soared above arbitrary categorization. "Nobody could doubt that Hendrix was a rock and roll musician, yet, to jazz musicians . . . he was also a jazz performer," said a prescient *Rolling Stone* appreciation a month after his death. "When Jimi Hendrix took a solo it had everything."[24]

Like Louis Armstrong, Hendrix played out the role of the exotic black man to white audiences, acting out what Ted Gioia has called "The Primitivist Myth,"[25] a "noble savage" grappling with musical forces he seemed barely to understand. Hendrix's simultaneous status as stud and guitar hero was underlined by thrusting, grinding performances that were explicit, crude, and often aggressive expressions of male sexuality. He was the first rock star to truly exploit the guitar as a penis extension. This rather degrading image remains a troubling one, because it obscures his music at the expense of a freakishly flamboyant veneer that helped make him so popular. Yet even these performances were no more than an extension of the extravagant displays of guitar exhibitionism of the 1950s R&B scene by the likes of T-Bone Walker, doing the splits while soloing, or the crazy stunts of Johnny "Guitar" Watson, Guitar Slim, and Clarence "Gatemouth" Brown, all of whom played the guitar behind their heads or with their teeth.

Up to 1966, Hendrix's career had included spells with the Impressions, Sam Cooke and the Valentinos, Little Richard, Arthur Lee, the Isley Brothers, and the soul singers Lonnie Youngblood and Curtis Knight. In the mid-sixties, performing as "Jimmy James," Hendrix was playing a Greenwich Village coffee house for $3 a night. He also sat in with Jeremy and the Satyrs during their extended run at the Café au Go Go, among many others. "There was no doubt that Hendrix had a vibe, charisma, call it what you will," said Mike Mainieri, the Satyrs' vibist. "He would come in and sit in and it was like being around Miles.

You knew you where in the presence of greatness, someone doing something really original. No one had to tell you, you knew. Those days sitting-in was common, you went somewhere to hear music and you never knew who might turn up. We just played the blues, but Jimi played the shit out of them. And yes, he influenced young jazz musicians. I wanted that volume and I wanted to bend those notes like he did. So I got an echo-plex and worked out a way to do it on vibes. Those were exciting times."[26]

"Discovered" in Greenwich Village by the Animals bassist Chas Chandler, Hendrix moved to London and plunged into the bohemian lifestyle of the counterculture movement that was a million miles from the black consciousness of the sixties. For Hendrix, once buried anonymously in a succession of soul and blues bands doing endless one-night stands across America, to be suddenly idolized by the stars of British rock and blues must have been a heady experience. Likewise, his appearance on the London rock scene was a revelation to his British counterparts, who had learned their craft from records rather than through life's experiences. Here was the real thing, "the personification of Black music," said Alexis Korner.[27] Hendrix quickly attracted the attention of London's rock aristocracy, from the Beatles to the Stones to The Who. U.K. Top-10 successes with "Hey Joe" and "Purple Haze," the latter with the classic line "'Scuse me while I kiss the sky," completed Hendrix's ticket to superstardom. Although he only released three studio albums between his arrival in England on September 21, 1966 and his death on September 18, 1970—*Are You Experienced?, Axis: Bold as Love,* and *Electric Ladyland*—all were masterpieces, in spite of obvious "filler" tracks.[28]

Hendrix returned to the United States in June 1967; his appearance at the Monterey Pop Festival is now part of rock music's defining moments. He remained in America for the remainder of the year touring, returning to Britain for his second U.K. tour in November and December. On January 30, 1968 he embarked on another gruelling U.S. tour, this time encompassing fifty-four concerts in forty-seven days, enjoying reverential audiences wherever he played. "Hendrix is tops and 1968 was his year," observed *Rolling Stone.*[29] During a month in England in early 1969, he sat in with Roland Kirk at Ronnie Scott's jazz club on March 6. "He came off that jam feeling he had found a soul-mate," said Alan Douglas, Hendrix's friend and later his record producer. "Roland Kirk could go anyplace musically, you couldn't upset him, he would be playing three instruments at once and Jimi loved his madness and his inventiveness and his magic. He was non-conforming to the general rules of music and so was Jimi because he didn't know what the rules were anyway!"[30]

Seven days later Hendrix returned to the U.S. and spent some time jamming in the recording studios. At 2 A.M. on March 25, he was joined at the Record Plant studio by John McLaughlin and Dave Holland, participants in the *In a Silent Way* session with Miles Davis the previous month. Together with Buddy Miles on drums, they played into the night. The results, *Hell's Session,* a bootleg album released in 1988, are inconclusive. "It was just a jam," said McLaughlin. "It was four o'clock in the morning and everybody was a bit tired."[31]

However, personal problems—that well-known music press metaphor for drugs and alcohol abuse—loomed, and in May 1969 Hendrix was arrested in Toronto for possessing heroin, an event that would cloud the remainder of the year. Another meeting with jazz musicians occurred when Hendrix's long-time drummer Mitch Mitchell introduced him to Tony Williams. At the time, Williams was setting up his own group with McLaughlin and the organist Larry Young. Mitchell arranged for Hendrix to sit in with them; the meeting apparently didn't go too well. However, on May 14, Hendrix and the organist Larry Young reunited for some freeform improvising that subsequently appeared on the album *Nine to the Universe,* released in 1980. Compiled by Alan Douglas to illustrate the guitarist's affinity with jazz, it revealed a very different guitarist from the one who pumped out "Purple Haze" every night. "I like free-form jazz," Hendrix once said. "The groovy stuff instead of the old-time hits."[32] Alan Douglas explains what Hendrix meant: "Jimi didn't like jazz from the point of view of guys getting up and playing 16 choruses of 'How High The Moon,' that's exactly the way he described it to me. Jazz is many things, but it is not supposed to be boring and the one thing that was happening during that time was that it was getting very boring. Other than Coltrane and Miles and a couple of young guys on the scene, such as Charles Lloyd, jazz wasn't doing anything. Musicians were just redoing the masters and not as well, so consequently Jimi was into his own music. There was no category for it. It transcends all those categories. You could call it jazz if you were a jazz musician, you could call it blues if you were a blues musician, and you could call it pop if you were a pop musician. It falls into all those categories."[33] In "Young/Hendrix" the guitarist uses sustained feedback and wah-wah effects in an improvisatory context, juxtaposed against the riffs of Young's organ. On these sessions, the possibilities of rock-jazz fusion emerge as something real, tangible, and in places euphoric.

Hendrix was also a friend and particular favorite of Miles Davis's wife, Betty Mabry, but in March 1969 trumpeter and guitarist were yet to meet. Mabry threw a party for Hendrix in Davis's apartment to introduce them, but the inscrutable host didn't show, claiming he was delayed at a recording session. Davis left a piece of sheet music with a new composition for Hendrix to look over, and phoned to see what the guitarist thought of it. Hendrix had to confess he couldn't make head or tail of it since he didn't read music. When they finally did get to meet, however, Davis was impressed. "Jimi was a great natural musician," he said. "Once he heard it, he heard it, he really had it down. . . . He had a natural ear for hearing music. . . . It was great. He influenced me, I influenced him. . . . Jimi Hendrix came from the blues, like me. We understood each other right away because of that."[34] Subsequently, Davis and Hendrix used to hang out together when they were both in New York. "Jimi and Miles liked each other," said Airto Moreira, "[Miles] was asking Jimi all kinds of questions and they were exchanging ideas and things."[35]

The effect Hendrix had on open-eared jazz musicians was profound. "He was just running away with it," said Douglas. "Everyone in jazz, blues, and rock all felt lost. There were musicians in every genre who were very successful and took

Jimi Hendrix: Jazz has failed to acknowledge the debt it owes to Hendrix. (Photograph by David Redfern/ Redferns.)

their music seriously and who found themselves icons of popular interest. In jazz it's Miles Davis. They felt they were evolving, making progress with their art and all of a sudden here comes Hendrix and he jumps seven miles ahead of them. There was envy, jealousy and admiration, they all began to question themselves, readjust to what they were hearing. Jimi sounded like a new age. I remember I was with Miles Davis at Fillmore East and we were both watching Hendrix perform, all he kept saying was, 'What the fuck is he doing? What the fuck is he doing?' over and over again, just mumbling to himself."[36]

Such was Davis's regard for Hendrix's music that it seemed only a matter of time before idea was floated that they should record together. According to Douglas, Davis suggested it at a social gathering. Negotiations subsequently reached an advanced stage; Tony Williams was to be the drummer and a date was booked at the Hit Factory in New York. The agreement was for a share of the royalties only, no advances to any of the parties concerned. A matter of hours before the session, Davis demanded an advance of $50,000, and the date fell through. Nevertheless, Davis remained a fan of Hendrix's music, and from the start had shared his enthusiasm with close friend and collaborator Gil Evans, who in a classic case of opposites attracting, also became a fan. During a 1980 interview, Evans sat at the piano and pointed out in words and music how he and Davis had incorporated the chords of Hendrix's "The Wind Cries Mary" into Davis's recording of "Filles de Kilimanjaro."[37]

Although today the Evans-Hendrix connection is common knowledge, less well-known was arranger Quincy Jones's friendship with Hendrix. Both came from Seattle and both had attended Garfield High School. "He was dying to play jazz," said Jones. "He used to come over to the house and sit under the grapefruit tree and stuff. He was really a reflective person. I knew his daddy."[38] When Jones was planning his 1970 album *Gula Matari* it was agreed that Hendrix would play on one number, and Jones actually arranged the Nat Adderley composition "Hummin'" with Hendrix in mind. Despite promises to appear at Rudy Van Gelder's studio in March and May 1970 to record with Jones, Hendrix failed to show and the solo spot was given to Belgian guitarist Toots Thielemans.

Meanwhile, Hendrix continued to try to stretch the boundaries of his performances and recordings. On April 25, 1970 Hendrix began his "Cry of Love" tour of the United States at the Forum in Los Angeles. When he played Berkeley Community Center a month later, his music was in flux. During a break in the performance, Hendrix confided in Carlos Santana that he was thinking about a new Afro-jazz context for his playing. "He was getting into Gil Evans and Sun Ra," said Santana, himself a guitarist with a strong jazz bias. "He was hungry for the same thing we're all hungry for: multiplicity, but still retaining your individuality."[39]

It was around this time Alan Douglas began tentative moves to record Hendrix as a featured soloist with the Gil Evans Orchestra. "I had been with Jimi for enough time to realize he was getting frazzled and upset by the constant touring and the incredible pressure put on him by management to continue the pop-star game which he abhorred completely," said Douglas. "I thought it would be nice if he could get up in front of a band and play and not worry about having to write all the material and write all the lyrics, move away a little bit from the pop concept that everyone was demanding from him and just play his guitar, which he liked to do very much. I was always a great admirer of the Miles Davis and Gil Evans albums, and so I called Gil and asked him if he would be interested in doing an album with Jimi and he told me he would be thrilled, because he thought Jimi Hendrix was one of the great musicians he had ever heard, and that's how it began. Later I talked to Miles about it and he thought it was a good idea too and he was going to help when we got it together."[40] The plan was to record them performing Hendrix tunes arranged by Evans live at Carnegie Hall. "We were talking about doing a guitar album . . . all new material," Evans told *Guitar World.*[41] A meeting had been arranged for Monday, September 21, 1970 to finalize details. "We were waiting for Jimi to come when we found he died in London. Choked on his own vomit," said Davis, who subsequently flew out to Seattle with Betty Mabry to attend Hendrix's funeral.[42]

Hendrix died on September 18, 1970, but the Gil Evans concert featuring his music subsequently went ahead as part of the New York Jazz Repertory Company's 1974 season with the Japanese guitarist Ryo Kawasaki playing Hendrix's solos. Shortly afterwards they recorded *The Gil Evans Orchestra Plays the Music of Jimi Hendrix* at RCA's Studio B in New York City. "Stop and think about Hendrix's guitar work, about how difficult it was, and is, to play the guitar that way," said Evans, "the use, the *correct* use of electronics. And for him it was the natural way. What I do is try and keep Jimi in mind when arranging his music. A very, very great guitar player."[43] Evans continued to play Hendrix's music until his own death on March 20, 1988. Quite what would have come out of his meeting with Hendrix is impossible to speculate, but suffice it to say that the concept was a continuation of Evans's work using Miles Davis as a featured soloist against a backdrop of a big band on *Miles Ahead, Porgy and Bess,* and *Sketches of Spain,* three albums that number among the most important recordings of the twentieth century.

Even though Hendrix came within days of realizing his stated ambition to record with a jazz orchestra,[44] there is no shortage of examples in his discography of effortless dissolution of generic distinctions. "Hendrix was beyond all the categories," said the saxophonist Steve Lacy, "and that's the kind of stuff I like, stuff that transcends those earthly categories."[45] Sometimes that magic could sound like three guitars at once, achieved by inducing feedback on a couple of guitar strings while playing lead on others and hammering on answering phrases on the fretboard. Like any great jazz musician, Hendrix's sense of time was highly developed, and his improvisations seemed to have a floating quality, never appearing to be shackled to the ground beat. Often, like those of a Louis Armstrong or a Charlie Parker, his solos appeared as complete statements where nothing could be added or taken away without destroying the symmetry of the whole.

Part of Hendrix's significance to jazz musicians was how his recordings offered young guitarists a way out of the claustrophobic Charlie Christian–Tal Farlow–Jimmy Raney–Herb Ellis–Wes Montgomery role-model hierarchy, by offering a radical alternative to the ever-faster squalls of clean, single-note runs, by harnessing volume and feedback to corruscating effect. Jazz has always been about exploring new sounds as a basis for musical expression, from the plunger mutes of Bubber Miley to Lester Young's reversal of Coleman Hawkins's approach to the tenor saxophone. In 1974 the pianist Paul Bley formed the group Scorpio, saying "The implications of electric instruments cry out for freedom just initiated by Jimi Hendrix."[46]

Just how significant an alternative Hendrix posed for the jazz world was actually acted out at the old Scene Club in New York City on June 22, 1968. "I saw [Larry] Coryell once—he was one of the few people who ever got up and tried to cut Hendrix," said the drummer Robert Wyatt, then opening for Hendrix as a member of Soft Machine. "He was leaping backwards and forwards, his fingers flying, and Hendrix—when it came to his solo—just went 'ba-WO-O-O-

OWWWW' and it just *erased* the last ten minutes with one note. It was silly of Coryell to try. It was like walking into a blowtorch . . . the fool!"[47] It was a salutary lesson to Coryell, who later said, "Jimi Hendrix is the greatest musician who ever lived, as far as I'm concerned. The stuff I saw him do in person in jam sessions was some of the heaviest jazz music I ever heard."[48]

Hendrix forced jazz musicians to consider volume as an aspect of authenticity, something that initially came as a shock to a bebop-oriented virtuoso player like Coryell, for example. Hendrix also demonstrated to jazz musicians more credibly than any other rock guitarist that intensity in loud amplified sound could be created through the use of distortion. By the early 1970s, jazz keyboard players and guitarists were experimenting with overdriving their instruments and using distortion boxes—among the first to respond was Chick Corea with Miles Davis and Joe Zawinul on the Tokyo concert portion of *I Sing the Body Electric.* These jazz players in turn influenced other jazz musicians, albeit at one remove.

That Hendrix's compositions could move close to the orbit of jazz can be heard most clearly and obviously in "Third Stone from the Sun," from his debut album, *Are You Experienced?* Here amid Hendrix's imaginative sonic soundscapes, jazz and rock rhythms are contrasted during the long, six-minute-and-forty-second instrumental track where drummer Mitch Mitchell displays his love of Elvin Jones and Hendrix uses his long, trademark sustain. "Jimi was the cat," said Foley (Joseph McCreary), the Miles Davis bassist. "Wasn't out there trying to be heavy. He just did what he felt. Jimi was one of the greatest jazz cats ever lived—he invented fusion on his first record. 'Third Stone From the Sun'—the swing in that! Gil Evans heard it. After a while Miles heard it. A lot of jazz cats are hearing it now."[49]

Technically more impressive is "Machine Gun," from *Band of Gypsys,* an ill-fated group Hendrix briefly headed. After a sustained note that still manages to freak out listeners today, Hendrix plays some of the fastest guitar he ever recorded, complete with seemingly impossible hammer-ons. It produced a remarkable flowing solo that is melodically inventive and dramatically paced.

Hendrix made extensive use of pentatonic scales in rock at a time when they were considered more the province of jazz musicians, particularly in "The Wind Cries Mary," "Little Wing," and "This May Be Love." "Hear My Train A'Coming," "Hey Joe," and "Red House" combine minor and major pentatonic scales with a blues scale. He also habitually detuned his guitar down a half step for greater impact (E-flat–A-flat–D-flat–G-flat–B-flat–E-flat); for some tunes he detuned a whole step, and for "Hear My Train A'Coming" he tuned down *two* whole steps. Hendrix also employed octave work à la Wes Montgomery on numbers like "Third Stone from the Sun" and "Instrumental Solo" from *Woodstock.* He even used them on one of his most famous composition, "Purple Haze"—in which his solo is based on the Dorian mode—although they became more prevalent as a compositional device in his later music. Among the songs in the Hendrix discography that featured fairly complex chord progressions (in the jazz sense) were "Little Wing" (whose intro remains a rite of passage for all rock guitarists), "Crosstown Traffic," and "Bold As Love."

By 1968 Hendrix was using hours and hours of studio time, jamming for his own pleasure and working out new compositions and ideas. "Because he couldn't read or write music," said Alan Douglas, "he would spend all the time he could when he wasn't on the road in the studio or at home, working things out on tape. His problem was that he had so many ideas and if he didn't notate it in some manner it would be flooded by a hundred more ideas. It was very time-consuming for him and in the last days of his life we had a plan where he was going to go to Juilliard, I had arranged he would go three evenings a week, and he was going to learn to read and write music to alleviate himself of the constant pressure to have to record everything all the time."[50] Some of the structures he arrived at in this way were often quite sophisticated, such as the seven-part sonata-rondo structure of "1983 . . . (A Merman I Should Turn to Be)" from *Electric Ladyland,* effectively:

$$A + A^1 + A^1 + B + A + C + A + \text{coda (B–A)}$$

However, Hendrix clearly enjoyed simple, looser forms, something he revealed early on with "Are You Experienced?" based on a simple two-chord vamp, from the first studio album of the same name.

By the time of the two-album set *Electric Ladyland,* in essence cut during May and June 1968, alongside specific compositions like "Gypsy Eyes," Hendrix continued to experiment with looser forms. The extended studio jams on "Voodoo Chile" and "Rainy Day Dream Away," his visionary glimpse of fusion that so excited Miles Davis, combined the instrumental virtuosity associated with jazz and the electronic tone colors and big beat of rock. But for black audiences grooving to Sly Stone, James Brown, and the Stax and Motown labels, Jimi Hendrix must have sounded as if he came from another planet—how could you dance to a rock waltz like "Manic Depression" from *Are You Experienced?* He even recorded solos and rerecorded them backwards to form parts of his compositions; "Castles in the Sand," "Driftin'," and "Are You Experienced?" contain examples of this dramatic and arresting technique.

Even though Hendrix drew on the traditions of black music, his music was simultaneously singularly different from them. Ironically, Hendrix drew from a style the black community had already disposed of, the blues, having absorbed the music of Robert Johnson, Elmore James, B. B. King, and Albert King in his youth. "Spanish Castle Magic" from *Axis* was washed with an unmistakable blues feeling, while the live "Red House" displays some of the finest blues guitar soloing on record. However, Hendrix's electrification of the blues guitar showed more where he came from rather than where he was going.

Nevertheless, Hendrix was a true revolutionary—perhaps the only one to emerge from the 1960s rock explosion—but he also had the potential to go much further. "Hendrix's soloing was definitely in the jazz tradition and a lot of members of the jazz community picked up on it," said the guitarist Al DiMeola, who was born in 1954. "Not everyone, of course—there's a lot of players from the old school who couldn't stand to listen to Hendrix. But for my generation, most everyone will admit he was a leader."[51] Equally, Miles Davis has pointed out that there was a fairly general consensus among the leading jazz musicians he knew that had Hendrix moved into jazz, he would have been one of the greats.[52]

Notes

1. *Miles Davis,* by Ian Carr (Quartet, London, 1982), p. 161.
2. *Miles: The Autobiography,* by Miles Davis with Quincy Troupe (Simon & Schuster, New York, 1989), p. 281.
3. Ibid., p. 280.
4. *Clive: Inside the Record Business,* by Clive Davis (William Morrow, New York, 1975).
5. *Downbeat,* September 16, 1971, p. 18.
6. *Miles: The Autobiography,* by Miles Davis with Quincy Troupe (Simon & Schuster, New York, 1989), p. 282.
7. *Downbeat,* October 1982, p. 20.
8. Liner notes, Polydor 847 233-2.
9. *Miles: The Autobiography,* by Miles Davis with Quincy Troupe (Simon & Schuster, New York, 1989), p. 290.
10. On *Water Babies* in 1977.
11. *Stereo Review,* November 1974.
12. *Rolling Stone,* December 1969, p. 33.
13. Interview with the author, October 2, 1996.
14. Most famously, the pop producer Phil Spector's creation of a "wall of sound" for groups like the Ronettes was nothing like anything you ever heard in a concert hall. It was a source of inspiration to the Beach Boys' Brian Wilson, who produced *Pet Sounds* in 1966, revealing that the group's real potential lay in the recording studio. When Paul McCartney heard it, he was inspired to come up with the concept for *Sgt. Pepper's Lonely Hearts Club Band,* a recording that took nine months of careful editing to piece together in the studio, in 1967.
15. *Miles: The Autobiography,* by Miles Davis with Quincy Troupe (Simon & Schuster, New York, 1989), p. 290.
16. *Wire,* December 1994, p. 24.
17. *Miles: The Autobiography,* by Miles Davis with Quincy Troupe (Simon & Schuster, New York, 1989), p. 286.
18. *Downbeat,* August 7, 1969, p. 28.
19. *Miles: The Autobiography,* by Miles Davis with Quincy Troupe (Simon & Schuster, New York, 1989), p. 287.
20. *Downbeat,* December 1991, p. 17.
21. *Dizzy, Duke, the Count and Me,* by Jimmy Lyons with Ira Kamin (California Books, San Francisco, 1978), p. 111.
22. *All You Need Is Love,* by Tony Palmer (Weidenfeld, Nicolson & Chappell, London, 1976), p. 269.
23. *Downbeat,* June 10, 1971, p. 9.
24. *Rolling Stone,* October 15, 1970, p. 8.
25. *The Imperfect Art,* by Ted Gioia (Oxford University Press, New York, 1988), pp. 19–49.
26. Interview with the author, January 14, 1997.
27. *All You Need Is Love,* by Tony Palmer (Weidenfeld, Nicolson & Chappell, London, 1976), p. 267.
28. *Cry of Love* was released shortly after Hendrix's death.
29. *Rolling Stone,* February 1, 1969, p. 14.
30. Interview with the author, August 20, 1997.
31. *Downbeat,* October 1992, p. 20.

32. *Jimi Hendrix—Electric Gypsy,* by Harry Shapiro and Caesar Glebbeek (William Heine-mann Ltd., London, 1990), p. 178.
33. Interview with the author, August 20, 1997.
34. *Miles: The Autobiography,* by Miles Davis with Quincy Troupe (Simon & Schuster, New York, 1989), pp. 282–283. Although Hendrix only recorded one true twelve-bar original, "Red House," many of his compositions borrowed extensively from the blues progression.
35. *Wire,* March 1997, p. 40.
36. Interview with the author, August 20, 1997.
37. *Jazz Spoken Here,* edited by Wayne Enstice and Paul Rubin (Louisiana State University Press, Baton Rouge, 1992), p. 145.
38. *Downbeat,* January 1990, p. 20.
39. *Musician,* December 1990, p. 76.
40. Interview with the author, August 20, 1997.
41. *Guitar World,* March 1988.
42. *Miles: The Autobiography,* by Miles Davis with Quincy Troupe (Simon & Schuster, New York, 1989), p. 308.
43. Quoted on liner notes to *The Gil Evans Orchestra Plays the Music of Jimi Hendrix* (RCA LSA 3197).
44. Interview published in *Melody Maker,* September 13, 1970.
45. *Crosstown Traffic,* by Charles Shaar Murray (Faber and Faber, London, 1989), p. 204.
46. *Downbeat,* August 15, 1974, p. 9. In his group were Ross Traut on guitar, Jaco Pastorius on bass, and Bruce Ditmas on drums.
47. *Crosstown Traffic,* by Charles Shaar Murray (Faber and Faber, London, 1989), p. 198.
48. *Downbeat,* 9 November 1972.
49. Ibid., May 1991, p. 25.
50. Interview with the author, August 20, 1997.
51. *Downbeat,* October 1982, p. 17.
52. *Crosstown Traffic,* by Charles Shaar Murray (Faber and Faber, London 1989), p. 205.

CHAPTER 7

Dark Magus

At 8 A.M. on August 18, 1969, Jimi Hendrix closed the Woodstock Festival with a masterful deconstruction of "The Star Spangled Banner," the defining moment of the Woodstock festival and the subsequent film. Performed at a moment of unprecedented social and cultural upheaval being enacted out against a backdrop of the Vietnam War and black militancy, it was a performance that subsequently took on an almost supernatural resonance and remains one of the landmark recordings of rock.

The following day in New York, Miles Davis was in the recording studios to start work on *Bitches Brew*, a recording that would have equal resonance in the world of jazz. Sleeve-note writer Ralph J. Gleason called it "electric music," but this was electric music that had Hendrix's influence hovering over it, marking the beginning of Davis's odyssey into the vortex of the guitarist's electronic imagery. Once again Teo Macero let the tape machines run, and the album that emerged from the twenty or so reels captured between August 19 and 21, 1969 gave momentum to a new movement that resulted in the biggest audience for a jazz-based music since the Swing Era. Davis recorded *Bitches Brew* driven by a mixture of pressure from Clive Davis—"Clive felt I wasn't making enough money for the company"—and pride—"I wasn't prepared to be a memory."[1] In the past, Miles had proved time and again that where he led, others followed, so when *Bitches Brew* was released in spring 1970 the portents were clear: jazz-rock represented the way ahead because Miles Davis said so.

For at least two years prior to *Bitches Brew*, jazz-rock had been bubbling beneath the surface, but the style needed someone of sufficient stature to "sanction" the dawn of a new era. Just as Joe "King" Oliver, Louis Armstrong, Benny Goodman, Charlie Parker, John Coltrane, and Ornette Coleman had come to personify specific eras in jazz history, so Miles Davis would come to signify the era of jazz-rock fusion. Consequently Davis would be credited with "inventing" the genre, and, thanks to his standing within the jazz world, he would also be acknowledged as establishing the new music's "legitimacy."

While *Bitches Brew* has now come to represent a significant point in jazz history, it is often overlooked that this was the first major jazz album in which an artist's work was deconstructed in post-production, and it is only from its reconstructed form that we construe its meaning. "I had carte blanche to work with

112

Miles Davis and Fourth Way play Zellerbach Auditorium, Berkeley, California, 1970. (Courtesy of Mike Nock.)

the material," said Macero. "I could move anything around . . . and then add in all the effects—electronics, delays and overlays."[2] Macero's use of tape delay on Davis's trumpet, for example, is a subtle touch that helps make the acoustic instrument blend into the electronic soundscape. "A lot of the stuff we used on *Bitches Brew*," continued Macero, "was invented for us by CBS technicians and was widely imitated for years after. I don't think Miles ever made a complete take on any of the tracks on *Bitches Brew*. He would be working it out in the studio and take it back and re-edit it front to back, back to front and the middle somewhere else. . . . The construction of the pieces was really done in the editing room and not the recordings."[3]

There can be no mistaking how the deeply mysterious groove of Hendrix's "Voodoo Chile" was echoed on *Brew*'s "Miles Runs the Voodoo Down," both artists appropriating voodoo symbolism, a holdover from West African mystical practice, to make a statement about their black identity. Davis purposely avoids popular music's smooth corners with a grittiness that flies in the face of commercialism, using dissonant chords and angular, open-ended improvisation. There are no cadences, nothing resolves as the music defines its own process, solos rise out of the matrix of sound and sink back into the mix. Nonetheless, the title track uses a recognizable form, a simple alternation of two blocks of music. The first, comprising sections one, three, and five, is free-metered and rhapsodic; the second, sections two and four, is based on an ostinato.

The instrumentation included two keyboards (Zawinul with either Corea or Larry Young), two bassists (Holland or Harvey Brooks from the Electric Flag), three drummers (either DeJohnette, Lenny White, or Charles Alias), John McLaughlin on guitar, and a percussionist (Jim Riley), with Bennie Maupin on bass clarinet weaving in, out, and around a thick electronic ensemble topped by Shorter's soprano and Davis himself on open or wah-wah trumpet—a device first employed by Sun Ra a couple of years earlier on *When Angels Speak of Love*. "By now I was using the wah-wah on my trumpet all the time so I could get closer to that voice Jimi [Hendrix] had when he used wah-wah on the guitar," explained Davis.[4]

This mysterious brew extended over two vinyl albums that were presented wrapped in a gatefold pack with stunning art work by Mati Klarwein. Alchemically African, it marked a break with the hipster-literate tradition of album sleeves done in-house by Columbia in the fifties and early sixties. An Israeli-born artist, Klarwein also created the sleeve for Carlos Santana's *Abraxis,* and he was commissioned by Davis himself. Marketed heavily by Columbia in the spring of 1970, *Bitches Brew* was dubbed "A Novel by Miles Davis" in their promotional advertising: "*Bitches Brew* is an incredible journey of pain, joy, sorrow, hate, passion, and love. *Bitches Brew* is a new direction in music by Miles Davis. *Bitches Brew* is a novel without words."[5] As in the promotion of *Filles de Kilimanjaro* and *In a Silent Way,* at Davis's express wish, any reference to jazz was replaced by references to "a new direction in music," since the term "jazz" in 1970 was seen as pejorative and limiting, especially by the youth market. To reach younger fans, Columbia issued a single from the album, "Miles Runs the Voodoo Down," hoping for chart action.

Columbia clearly felt the music was sufficiently elusive in category for people to make of it whatever they wanted. This stylistic ambiguity was reinforced in their advertising, giving emphasis to a "new" product—a "new" direction in music—not only to distinguish the "old" acoustic Miles Davis from the electric "new," but also to represent a "new" musical fashion. This "always new" approach adopted by popular music marketing implies selling a "new" artist as a replacement for a previously "old" artist—who wants yesterday's "old" acts when you can have today's "new"? Here, although it's an "old" act—Miles Davis had been around since the late 1940s, after all—it's a "new direction" and an "incredible journey," a subtext picked up in the *Rolling Stone* review of the album: "The record is yet another step in the unceasing process of evolution Miles has undergone."[6]

With Columbia aggressively pushing *Bitches Brew,* radio stations began playing it, particularly "underground" stations like New York's WNEW-FM, helping it reach thirty-five on the *Billboard* chart. By the end of its first year, it had sold over 400,000 units and won the 1970 Grammy Award for Best Jazz Record, and it has remained a staple of Columbia's catalogue ever since. Clive Davis was vin-

Miles Davis: To distinguish the "old" acoustic Miles Davis from the "new" electric one, Miles changed his wardrobe to go with the new electric music. (Courtesy of the Institute of Jazz Studies, Rutgers University.)

dicated, and Miles was widely seen as having moved to the forefront of jazz. This astute change of musical backdrop, changing the setting in which Davis presented a trumpet style that remained quintessentially his own, was—although he did not know it at the time—the final act in a career of musical prestidigitation that had kept him ahead of the game since the famous Birth of the Cool sessions in 1949. Davis, neither prophet nor martyr, was trying to make sense of the fast-changing world around him. The extent of his success is proven by his compelling relevance to contemporary music today.

When Miles had completed *Bitches Brew,* Clive Davis persuaded him to play the two great rock emporiums owned by Bill Graham, Fillmore West in San Francisco and Fillmore East in New York. At first Miles resisted, but Clive Davis was a persuasive man. "From my point of view," he explained, "[Miles] was playing only before small audiences in small jazz clubs. . . . He didn't want to play places like the Fillmore."[7] Getting Miles in front of younger audiences, Clive Davis reasoned, would enable him to expand the base of his support. His first venture in front of rock crowds was as an opening act for Steve Miller and Neil Young and Crazy Horse at Fillmore East in March 1970. A month later he opened for Stone the Crows and the Grateful Dead at Fillmore West. "What got me more than anything else was that a good portion of the Dead fans really got into Miles," said Bill Graham. "Some of them even danced to his music."[8] It was a successful gambit, repeated in June and July, bringing Davis in front of large audiences who might otherwise never have heard him. Over the next couple of years he toured as an opening act for Laura Nyro, Blood, Sweat & Tears, Carlos Santana, The Band, and Crosby, Stills, Nash & Young. His association with the latter group resulted in his recording "Guinnevere" in early 1970, composed by David Crosby.

During the Christmas break in 1969, Wayne Shorter decided to leave Davis's group. His replacement was Steve Grossman, a nineteen year old from Brooklyn and, in the context of Davis's past groups, a somewhat lightweight stand-in. However, saxophone solos were no longer the raison d'être of his music as they were in the days of Coltrane, Adderley, and Shorter. Indeed, even Davis's own playing veered sharply in favor of fragmentation and coloration, his old narrative certainties reduced to fragments, distorted and electrified through a wah-wah attachment. "The electric instruments we've been using destroy a large number of subtleties in the music," said David Holland. "One of the things I'm disappointed about is that the potential of the band has never been fully explored. We've got Keith, Chick, Jack DeJohnette, and the new tenor player Steve Grossman and they're all really creative musicians . . . but Miles needs to control the band, he needs to mold us and give us roles to play so that all the music comes out as his conception. It's still very strong, but depersonalizing it in that way stops it reaching its real peak."[9] Holland was not alone in believing that Davis had no clear idea in what direction to take his music. "It was weird because of the disorganization of the group," said Chick Corea. "The only organization was Miles spearheading. He'd go out and play and you'd follow; whenever he'd stop playing, he never told the group what to do, so we all went and did whatever. . . . He'd stop playing and the whole thing would blow up."[10]

This lack of direction was reflected in the recording studios through November 1969 and into March 1970. Ideas were tried out or musicians simply thrown together in the hope that creative sparks might fly to provide some answers.[11] "Miles moves very slowly," said Dave Holland. "He's advancing all the time, of course, but he does it very cautiously."[12] In November 1969 the then-fashionable sitar appeared on "Great Expectations"; in January 1970, Billy Cobham, the drum star from Dreams, was paired with Jack DeJohnette on three tracks; in February 1970 "Willie Nelson," with its rather delicate country-rock beat, was cut as a tribute to the country star; while "Duran" flirted with a mobile bass line and stabbing chords à la James Brown's funk. Despite his interest in the music of James Brown—"I listen to James Brown and those little bands on the South Side. They swing their asses off," Miles said in 1969[13]—the bass lines in his music would, in the main, remain pedestrian in comparison. What he did seem to take from Brown was his on-the-spot method of composition, which would become a feature of Davis's live performances, achieved by minimalistic nods and gestures to alter the texture of the music or cue a key or tempo change—or even a new composition.

This somewhat indeterminate period of experimentation continued into March 1970 with Teo Macero trying to add a little interest to "Go Ahead John" by placing a tape loop halfway through the piece in the postproduction stage, making Davis's solo appear as if he is in dialogue with himself. "One thing about Miles and his music, about working with Miles," explained Macero, "you can experiment as much as you wish. You can take his music, you can cut it up, you can put filters in, you can do anything you want to."[14] But if his recordings post-*Bitches Brew* represented uncertainty, the confusion was resolved in April 1970 when he decided to confront the music of Jimi Hendrix head-on. When Miles boasted in *Rolling Stone* that he could "put together a better rock and roll band than Jimi Hendrix,"[15] it was as much a macho challenge as a statement of intent.

Jack Johnson, the soundtrack music from the producer Jim Jacob's film of the same name, was again "cut up" by Macero. As with Davis's other film soundtrack albums, *Ascenseur pour l'échafaud* from 1957 and *Siesta* from 1987, there were moments that were subservient to visual, rather than musical, logic. Nevertheless the Davis-McLaughlin jam during the first half of "Right Off" is arguably the trumpeter's most powerful and dramatic statement in his whole discography. Framed by the raw electronic energy inspired by Jimi Hendrix, Davis showed he had by no means abandoned the lyricism of his acoustic period, his solo as impressive as any in his long career.

"That's Miles's most favorite record," said John McLaughlin. "We were in the studio, Herbie Hancock, Michael Henderson, Billy Cobham, and me, and Miles was talking with Teo Macero in the control room for a long time. I got a little bored and I started to play this shuffle, a kind of boogie in E with some funny chords. The others picked it up and locked in. The next thing, the door opened and Miles runs in with his trumpet and we played for about 20 minutes. It was a large part of the record. It came out of nowhere."[16]

McLaughlin's guitar was recorded forward in the sound mix. His powerful opening chords announced a solo that, while being atypical of his style in that it is mainly chorded, threatens to dwarf anything that follows. Around bar 50, however, he begins to set the stage for Davis's entry, dropping in volume, and from around bar 60 he constructs a climactic buildup to frame Davis's entry at bar 75, a masterpiece of impromptu construction that presented the trumpet player with a perfect launching pad for his solo. Davis made the most of what he was given; indeed, his entry is one of the great moments of jazz-rock. As with all his finest solos, it has great structure and poise. But it is quite unlike his work with acoustic ensembles; instead of introspection and control, his playing was more outgoing and full of tension, often contrasting staccato passages with fast, sweeping runs that incorporated the high register of his instrument. The drama of Davis's entry had been enhanced by McLaughlin's modulation from E major to B-flat; however, bassist Michael Henderson, then playing with Stevie Wonder's group Wonderlove, missed the key change and stayed in the original key for a further twelve bars until he realized his error, creating a clash of tonalities that adds to drama of the moment. It is a reminder of the informality of these studio jam sessions and the extent to which Davis had become a one-take artist, convinced that the spontaneity could not subsequently be recaptured.

"Right Off" lasts for some twenty-six minutes, but it is McLaughlin and Davis who command our attention with their relentless and ultimately triumphant purpose. Davis's solo, full of power and aggression, insists uncompromisingly on his right to endure; indeed, the trumpeter later said he had a boxer's movements in mind during the recording.[17] After eleven minutes, the rhythm fades for an interlude of Davis's Harmon-muted trumpet, which in turn gives way to bass and drums and Grossman's soprano sax. The only dull patch is Hancock's keyboard solo at the fifteen-minute mark, but with McLaughlin's insistent guitar riffs, something of the original drama of the opening passages returns, with further solos by Hancock, Grossman, and McLaughlin leaning heavily on the wang-bar.

The remaining track, "Yesternow," with a bass-line derived from James Brown's "Say It Loud I'm Black and Proud," was heavily cut-and-pasted in the postproduction stage by producer Teo Macero to create a finished product. On what is a forlorn and pensive workout against a static harmonic backdrop, "Yesternow" comprises at least five separate episodes spliced together, including an extract from "Shhh/Peaceful" recorded the year before with totally different personnel! All are essentially freeform pieces with no preset chord changes, relying on a simple vamp and the musician's integrity to produce appropriate solos or simpatico background coloration. This method of on-the-spot composing often meant that many pieces sounded like works in progress rather than the finished article. "If you leave the room to answer a phone call and return ten minutes later you won't have missed much," quipped *Rolling Stone*.[18] As each section fades in and fades out, the actor Brock Peters's voice, representing that of Jack Johnson, comments on how the world would never forget he was black. It was a comment that had equal resonance in the instance of Davis's own life.

In live performance, however, the music of Miles Davis remained steadfastly inscrutable. On April 10, 1970, three days after recording *Jack Johnson,* he cut his first live album since the *Plugged Nickel* engagement in 1965. The result, *Black Beauty: Miles Davis at Fillmore West,* saw his ensemble moving towards textural density at the expense of melodic and harmonic exploration. Notes did not seem to matter except in their overall contribution to the background density; musicians played through the music, not on top of it. This music was not without controversy. Many traditionalists saw Davis sacrificing himself on the altar of progress, and for them this "new direction" was unbearable. The piquancy of hearing his trumpet briefly emerge from the thickets of electronically generated sound to allow the old pathos and poignancy to ring out was, for them, nothing short of a tragedy.

What Davis was playing was neither lowbrow nor highbrow but directed completely over the heads of his audiences, who, for the most part, accepted it with perplexed patience. Away from the recording studios, Davis was exploring free jazz with a vengeance, a music of random associations, fragmented ideas, and swirling textures where rock rhythms were bent in and out of shape like images glimpsed in a hall of mirrors. Many writers dubbed it "space jazz," a term that derived from the music of György Ligeti and the way he used bleeps, chirps, and oscillating sounds on the soundtrack of the motion picture *2001*. Less charitably, the term was also used to denote music to get "spaced-out" to. In any event, Davis was far from pandering to teenage tastes; this was hardly music for Adorno's "humming millions"[19] and was as remote from the expectations of jazz fans in one direction as it was from rock fans in another, resulting in a complete paradox with jazz fans thinking it was rock and rock fans imaging it was jazz.

While *Black Beauty* appeared only in Japan, *Miles Davis at Fillmore,* from two months later, was aimed at the American market. In their promotion, Columbia traded heavily on a subliminal connection with acid, reinforced by a "psychedelic" album cover and advertising in the music press that played on space-is-the-place metaphors, while at the same time alluding to Davis's widely acknowledged role as a musical pathfinder:

> The 10th Planet. The place where you now live is full of comfortable music and predictable sounds. It's full of feedback. It's full of fuzztones. It's full of songs that never go beyond an "E" progression. It doesn't have to be that way. Take a trip with Miles Davis on his latest album to a place where the clichés of today's music don't exist. Where the only limitation is yourself. Who knows, you might never come back.[20]

The references to space and tripping were unmistakable and in tune with the times. That the music might be not be readily understood by its potential audience was acknowledged by a preemptive challenge: "the only limitation is yourself." By going on "a trip" with a musical pathfinder to a place where "comfortable music and predictable sounds" do not exist, then how you cope is a measure of your hipness. If you're hip and up with his music then "who knows, you may never come back," the implication being that music this good may just take a while to understand.

Although this was a clever ploy designed to sell records, despite heavy marketing, this uncompromising album struggled to reach 123 on the *Billboard* chart. Making no concessions to commercialism, there was a wild freedom about these electronic jam sessions named after the night they were recorded; "Friday Miles" begins with a free improvisation that moves into a rehearsed theme with a slow pulse. After a percussion interlude, Davis enters and cues the funk groove of "Bitches Brew," which elides into a free exchange of electronic keyboards and back again to the theme, which continues to the end of the track. In its edited form, the whole set took twenty-seven minutes and fifty seconds and, like the other three sets that make up the album, contains moments that are good, bad, and indifferent.

Davis was slated to appear at the Randall's Island Festival in New York in July 1970, fronting a "supergroup" of Eric Clapton and John McLaughlin on guitars, Larry Young on organ, Jack Bruce on bass, and Tony Williams on drums.

This fascinating lineup never got on-stage, however, when, after considerable publicity, Davis announced he would only play the Festival with his own band. Jack Bruce, who had tried to organize the gig, told *Rolling Stone* that "Miles wants to be a pop star in the sense that he wants exposure in the pop world. [He] feels that he can turn on hip people if he has that exposure."[21] Davis had plenty of opportunity to test this theory in the coming months when he toured the U.S. as the opening act for Santana.

In August Davis appeared at the huge Isle of Wight Pop Festival with saxophonist Gary Bartz in for Grossman. Also on the bill were Sly and the Family Stone, Procol Harum, Ten Years After, and Kris Kristofferson. "Jimi Hendrix was there too," said Davis. "He and I were supposed to get together in London after the concert and talk about an album we had finally decided to do together. We had come close once to doing one with producer Alan Douglas, but the money wasn't right. . . . We had played a lot at my house, just jamming. We thought the time was right to do something on record."[22] Davis blamed transportation problems for their failure to meet up. Eight weeks later, Hendrix was dead.

When Davis returned from Europe, Corea and Holland left the group. Corea was not replaced, leaving Jarrett as the sole keyboard player, while the bassist Miroslav Vitous was tried out before the electric bassist Michael Henderson finally joined the band on a full-time basis, having recorded with Davis in the past. His background was not jazz but R&B.[23] "When Michael Henderson joined the band Miles actually called a rehearsal," said Keith Jarrett. "Michael didn't know jazz at all—he was from Motown. We had this little rehearsal and I was supposed to show him the songs. And I started to play what I had been thinking the songs were and Miles says, 'No, man, that's not the tune,' and I said, 'Well, show it to me.' And he showed it to me and it was nothing like what we were doing with the song in concert! Miles was just putting together colors he liked, he liked Motown bass players, he liked funky guitar players, but he wanted these musicians to know more than they were doing, because Miles knew more than he was doing. It was experimental music—if you said to Miles in the dressing room after the show, 'Let's hear some more of that jazz-rock,' he wouldn't have known what you were talking about. It was like gathering a bunch of people together and saying, 'I'm not going to tell you much, but you're all here for a reason,' and then letting the music find its level. So Miles might set up an idea, like a rhythmic motif, and give almost no information about anything else. And the piece would develop by itself. When I joined the band I didn't know any of the tunes, and when I left the band I didn't know the tunes!"[24]

Columbia recorded Davis's revamped lineup extensively in mid-December 1970 during a stint at the Cellar Door, a Washington jazz club. On an impulse, Davis called New York and asked John McLaughlin to fly down to beef up the band for recording purposes. Other than a so-so session recorded earlier in the year with Hermeto Pascoal, the majority of *Live-Evil* comes from the Cellar Club sessions. It dips into the *Bitches* pot with quasimysterious atmospheric pieces that in places suggest the influence of Tony Williams's new band, Lifetime, feeding into Davis's music. There is a powerful ebb and flow of dynamics and polyrhythmic activity while the band grope around hoping something—anything—might happen. Bartz was sharply at odds with this brand of electronic experimentation. His down-to-earth melodicism contrasted with Davis's esoteric jargon of wah-wah trumpet blats and the ferocious speed of McLaughlin. Boredom and interest are dancing partners on the twenty-three-minute-twenty-six-second "Funky Tonk," a to-and-fro between yawning monotony and fascinating detail. Jarrett's unaccompanied solo on electric piano emerges as the central point of interest, primarily because his work with Davis was, on record at least, mainly confined to ensembles. Davis himself, as on *At Fillmore,* was guilty of over-repeating coloristic wah-wah-isms, milking the effect long after it was dry. In the end, over thirty reels of tape were used to produce 100 minutes of music; a spark was clearly missing, and Davis turned to McLaughlin, asking if he would join the group. McLaughlin declined. It is a measure of Davis's dissatisfaction with his music at this point that he neither took the band into the recording studios during 1971 nor had Columbia record them live. When *Live-Evil* was released in early 1972, it reached 125 on the Billboard chart with *Downbeat* giving it just two and one-half stars. "Because it is a Miles Davis album one inevitably feels a keen sense of disappointment that's disproportionate to the music's dereliction."[25]

Davis's itinerary for 1971 began in Los Angeles in the early spring, where he opened for The Band at the Hollywood Bowl before moving to New York to play the Gaslight in May and the Newport Jazz Festival in July, and touring Europe in the fall. "I got a tour in Europe," he told Leonard Feather. "I'll make about $300,000 on it. Then I won't work again until the spring and I'll make a spring tour."[26] Around this time it was rumored he was thinking of retiring, banner headlines appearing in both *Jet* and *Melody Maker* enquiring "Is Miles Quitting?," giving tax problems with the I.R.S. as a possible reason.[27] Feather noted that Davis's schedule now amounted to a "policy of semi-retirement," predicting this this might become "almost total inactivity" before much longer.

On his return from Europe, Davis played New York's Philharmonic Hall on November 26, 1971 and appeared more determined than ever to reach young audiences, using half his fee to buy $2,000 worth of tickets and instructing them to be distributed to young people. Davis then put his band on hold—it was the final gig Keith Jarrett played—and ill health, first arthritis of the hip, and, in April 1972, gallstones, prolonged his layoff until June 1972. In August he cut *On the Corner.* Mixed like a rock record and heavily massaged in postproduction, the cover art by Corky McCoy was of cartoon characters "from the ghetto" that masked the static, funk-inspired groove of the music within. Some controversy surrounds the precise personnel on this album; Teo Macero gave one set of names to the press while the saxophonist Dave Liebman insisted it was incorrect and gave another.[28] Certainly the music gave the musicians little opportunity to stand out, making aural identification almost impossible; the distinctive guitar work of John McLaughlin, for example, was buried deep in the mix. Liebman, although not a member of the band, had been invited by Davis to participate in the session. "When I arrived in the studio, the recording was in progress," he recalled. "Miles motioned me to take out my horn and play. I had no idea of the key or where to start conceptually. . . . The music with Miles was very heavily influenced by Sly Stone and James Brown. To my mind, there was a Sun Ra influence also."[29]

On the Corner provoked an immediate rumpus. Davis later claimed that, with it, he had made a real effort to reach young black people. If black audiences were into funky grooves, he reasoned, that's what he would give them (notwithstanding the incongruous inclusion of Collin Walcott's sitar at some points). When the album didn't connect—it only reached 156 on *Billboard*'s listings—it was not the music he blamed but his record company for failing to promote it. In reality it is doubtful that outside of Bob Dylan any major artist had gone so far as Davis to distance himself from his fans. A clue to his thoughts behind *On the Corner* was in his refusal to allow the names of the participating musicians to appear on the album cover, suggesting that he was concerned only with textures, presenting a maximum of rhythmic density and a minimum of creative melodic exploration. Awarding it two stars, *Downbeat* inquired rhetorically, "Take some chunka-chun-ka-chunka rhythm . . . you've got your 'groovin'' formula and you stick with it interminably to create your 'magic.' But is it magic or just repetitious boredom?"[30]

This trend towards a collective identity was emphasized by Davis's choice of personnel, often drawn from a pool of players. Unlike the past, when Davis had become known as the "star-maker" in jazz, some of the current crop of musicians entered his band as unknowns and departed enjoying a similar status. He had discovered, it seemed, that textural density could be created by mediocre talent just as well as it could by high flyers like Jarrett, Corea, or Shorter. In July Miles was arrested for arguing with a tenant, and his subsequent failure to appear at the Newport Jazz Festival in New York prompted further speculation about retirement. But just a few days later he was in the studios to cut "Molester," a 45-rpm single for the pop market. During this period, Paul Buckmaster, who had acted as musical director for both Elton John and Leonard Cohen, stayed with Davis at his New York home, reportedly "contributing to the album Miles was doing, the contents said to be 'extremely lyrical.'"[31] The press report proved wide of the mark, however. But during his stay with Davis, Buckmaster apparently turned him on to the spacy electronic imaginings of the twentieth-century modernist Karlheinz Stockhausen.

Recorded at Philharmonic Hall on September 29, 1972, *In Concert* was in essence a live reproduction of the rhythmic collages of *On the Corner.* A fermenting electronic and rhythmic stew, the album was marked by large sections of musical temporizing with periods of coherence bracketed by arid stretches of minimalistic vamping against vigorous polyrhythms. Except for San Francisco critic Ralph J. Gleason, the critics gave it less-than-rave notices.[32] As a result Davis fired his manager of seventeen years and hired Neil Reshen, who specialized in artists deemed "difficult." This unsatisfactory phase in Davis's career was brought to an end at 8 A.M. on October 19 on Manhattan's West Side Highway when he fell asleep at the wheel of his Ferrari and crashed into the divider, breaking both his ankles and necessitating hospitalization for ten days. It was during his long period of recuperation that Miles returned to taking cocaine. "Everything started to blur after I had the car accident," he confessed.[33]

When he returned to the performing circuits at the Village East (formerly Fillmore East) on January 12, 1973, Miles was sporting a moustache and fronting a new group featuring Dave Liebman on soprano sax, Reggie Lucas on guitar, Cedric Lawson on organ, Michael Henderson on bass, Al Foster on drums, Badal Roy on tabla, and M'tume on congas. The group "sounded much more vital and together than when we last heard it at Philharmonic Hall," observed Dan Morgenstern in *Downbeat.*[34] When he took the band on tour, subsequent reviews were by no means as kind as Morgenstern's, but Davis, hobbling about stage on crutches, was apparently enjoying himself.

When Lonnie Liston Smith replaced Lawson, Davis became frustrated with his playing and, after a tour of the Midwest, dropped keyboards altogether from his lineup, replacing Smith with the dashiki-clad, former Chess Records session-musician Pete Cosey on guitar, who had appeared on albums by Billy Stewart, Etta James, Fontella Bass, and most notably Howlin' Wolf's *The Electric Album* and Muddy Waters's *Electric Mud.* His group was now dominated by guitars; slowly but inexorably Davis was moving towards the sound of his favorite guitarist, Jimi Hendrix. "From the time that Jimi Hendrix and I had gotten tight, I had wanted that kind of sound. . . . Pete gave me that Jimi Hendrix . . . sound I wanted," he said later.[35] Davis's personal troubles continued when, on February 23, he was arrested in front of his New York apartment on West 77th Street for possession of cocaine and a loaded pistol, and on March 1 he was fined $1,000 in a Manhattan criminal court after pleading guilty to the charges.

Despite these legal problems, in June Davis embarked on his first tour of Japan, covering ten cities, followed a month later by the first of two European tours he would undertake during 1973. His appearance at London's Rainbow Theatre in July was notable for the incredible volume level of the band. After four years on the rock circuits playing venues like the Fillmores, Davis had no option other than to conform to the expectations of his audiences to whom volume was an important part of the rock experience. However, rock is a melody-oriented music, with the drums and bass defining a metronomic rhythmic pulse and the electric guitar, rock's basic coloristic device, providing both rhythmic and melodic elements that gelled into a cohesive whole that could be readily interpreted throughout the whole dynamic range. In contrast, Davis's music was simultaneously polyrhythmic and polyphonic and was without any melodic line. At the low volumes of domestic stereo equipment, his music appeared muddy and diffuse; "It's a music that does not transpose easily to records," observed *Melody Maker.*[36] In live performance, amplified to high volume, the complexity of Davis's music was revealed in teeming coloristic detail. Volume had become an essential component of his music and seemed to give even the most ordinary sounds unimagined dimension and nuance. Yet this music was quite different from the big beat of rock since the individual role of each band member came into focus in a series of individual, yet interconnecting dramas enacted on a broad musical tapestry. "The sound just kept getting higher because when it's higher you can make people feel things better," explained Davis.[37]

Equally, the physical presence of Davis-as-star and the subtle interaction of his real-life history—as a man who had influenced the destiny of jazz more than once—with what he was playing provided extra meaning to his live performances. This mediation between image and audience was reinforced by his stage presence, a role which he had developed over many years and was designed to show elaborate disdain for his (predominantly white) audience. It was a role that was recognized by his fans as "true to life" and was interpreted as a reaction to incidents in which he had been victimized by racism, such as a white policeman assaulting him outside Birdland in 1959. Without playing a note, Davis's attitude communicated just as much as his instrumental technique. He projected an image that was appealing to the public and was the source of his so-called star quality. "His personality is magnetic," wrote *Melody Maker.* "[He] stands mostly with his back to the audience but sometimes wanders round the stage like a panther. He keeps lubricating his trumpet and drinking something that's kept on top of the organ. He spits forcefully on the floor about three times and does not utter a word. Arrogance is the keynote: nobody need argue with me. I'm Miles Davis. I'm RIGHT!"[38]

Davis's music during this period is documented by a recording of his appearance at the Olympia in Paris on July 11, 1973, released under the title *Miles Davis en Concert avec Europe 1.* Recorded by the French radio station Europe 1, it lacked, of course, Teo Macero's postproduction techniques—editing, splicing, double-tracking, echo, reverb, compression, and so on—that were used to enhance Davis's music. Nevertheless the recording clarity and mix was of a high professional standard and provided a window into Davis's music at this time—a sprawling, electronic miasma without resolution and occasionally without direction, but one that defined itself through complex interplay, like an African drum choir. Dave Liebman played with conviction and authority, while Davis's warpingly forlorn electric trumpet remained the focal point amid a multitude of sonic colors and metric accents. "There was no direct harmony present, meaning chord changes as such," observed Liebman. "Although the bass lines were key-centered, the way Miles and myself played over them gave the music a distinct polytonal flavor. Melodically there were no extended lines . . . in fact the few heads we played were basically two or four bar riffs and many of the tunes had no discernible melody at all. Concerning the elements of form, there were no intros, outros, codas, interludes, tags, etc. All the tunes segued into each other in live performance. . . . On the surface it was a mixture of funk/pop rhythms, riff-like vamps, electronic and percussive colors and in and out of key improvisations. But what it really came down to was the relentless screaming sound and energy of the music as well as the spontaneous direction of the leader. . . . He did what he wanted, when he wanted—never predicatable—and the sidemen had to be on the case all the time. We had no modus operandi—it went from night to night." [39]

In September 1973, Miles cut a couple of tracks that would subsequently appear on his 1974 album *Get Up with It.* Afterwards, he again toured Europe but was forced to get medical advice in Sweden because of his frail health. Even so he embarked on another exhausting round of concerts in January 1974, culminating in a concert at Carnegie Hall on March 30. Columbia were there to record the event, which was released in Japan as *Dark Magus*. So offhand had Miles become with his music that he told the tenor saxophonist Azar Lawrence to turn up at Carnegie Hall for an audition, in full view of his paying audience, while simultaneously being recorded by Columbia! A few months prior to the concert guitarist Dominique Gaumont had been added to the Reggie Lucas–Pete Cosey tandem. "[With the addition of Gaumont] the sheer wall of sound had reached critical mass. [Gaumont's] contribution was one of density (à la Hendrix) and you hear a lot of him on [the] recording," said Liebman.[40] Gaumont, a self-confessed Hendrix fan, later said, "I discovered Hendrix at fifteen [and] . . . spent a year in my basement practicing the guitar like a madman."[41]

In May and June 1974, Davis completed *Get Up With It*, marketed by Columbia as "Another bitch. A different brew. Get Up With It."[42] Once again Davis was being cleverly marketed by Columbia in the trade press. "Get Up With It" was a rallying call that again alludes to Davis's role as a musical pathfinder, suggesting that Davis's recordings are not for passive listening; they demand some sort of effort on the part of the listener to understand what's going on—you have to catch up with him, he has moved on again, a reiteration of the "always new" marketing ploy of pop music. Included was a number dedicated to Duke Ellington, who had died on May 24, 1974, "He Loved Him Madly." This tribute was featured, somewhat cynically, in the marketing of the album: "Less than a week after Duke Ellington's death Miles Davis entered the recording studio and recorded side one of this album—an exhausting and exhilarating tribute to one of America's greatest musicians. The side is called 'He Loved Him Madly' and it's a powerful, evocative listening experience."[43]

In fact, Davis is something of an absentee landlord on the Ellington tribute, making his entry halfway through the thirty-two-minute track. Neither exhausting or exhilarating, it is the epitome of Davis's wait-and-see-if-something-happens approach to recording. On this occasion nothing did, the Ellington connection appearing as tenuous as it was exploitative. Yet despite all the brouhaha from Columbia's marketing department, *Get Up With It* only reached 141 on Billboard's album listings. Even so, it is perhaps the widest-ranging of all Davis's electronic albums after *Bitches Brew*, and certainly some compositions were more coherent than the dense rhythmic stews he was creating in live performance, with "Calypso Frelimo" and "Maiysha," touching on World music. However, "Rated X" had Davis on organ in a bleak, Phantom-of-the-Opera mood and it was not until 1997 that producer Bill Laswell realized the potential of this number on *Panthalassa: The Music of Miles Davis (1969–1974)*. By using an alternate take and remixing it carefully, the transcendence and essence of the music in this piece and in "Billy Preston," recorded the same day, emerged with compelling relevance to contemporary times. "Red China Blues" is an oddity in the Davis discography, recorded when he was recovering from two broken ankles in early 1973 and when he did not have a regular band. Featuring Wally

Chambers on harmonica and the session drummer Bernard Purdie, it was a down-home blues with simulated electronic brass riffs that was clearly aimed at MOR airplay. Despite the uneven quality of the album, for the first time in a while Davis earned a five-star rating in *Downbeat:* "Miles is moving in sonic territories that we as yet can not hear," the review somewhat cryptically observed.[44]

Davis's finest collaborator from this period was Brooklyn-born guitarist Dave Liebman. He played with Charles Lloyd and Lennie Tristano in the late 1960s, subsequently achieving some prominence as a member of the rock group Ten Wheel Drive in 1970. After three and a half years with Elvin Jones, appearing on the drummer's legendary *Live at the Lighthouse* (1972), he joined Davis at Fillmore East on January 12, 1973, while still performing with Jones. Of his eighteen months with Davis he said, "To listen to Miles Davis so closely was among the greatest lessons I ever experienced."[45]

In June 1974 Liebman left Davis's group after a tour of Brazil.[46] Liebman had recorded an album with a group he called Lookout Farm the previous year, and the release of the record was timed to coincide with the group's public debut at the Village Vanguard on June 6, 1974. Their eponymously titled debut album, recorded in October 1973, is another overlooked classic of the period. Using a core group of Richie Beirach on piano, Frank Tusa on bass, and Jeff Williams on drums, Liebman augmented the group with John Abercrombie on acoustic and electric guitars and a large percussion section that included Don Alias and Badal Roy. It remains a significant album through its "inclusive" approach by blending jazz-rock and World music elements together in a lyrically convincing way that suggested, perhaps more than Davis or any other group of the time, an important new direction for the music. "*Lookout Farm* is a perfect album," said *Downbeat,*[47] while expressing misgivings at a perceived lack of focus—something that today is considered the album's strength. The group suggested great promise, which it quickly fulfilled. At New York's Bottom Line in the summer of 1975, they were described as "five strong individual egos producing a music unusually potent in its spirituality and intensity and in its textural and rhythmic design."[48] Their second album, *Drum Ode* (1974), from the same year, moves to cover more territory but fails to match the originality of the debut. Subsequent albums included *Sweet Hands* (1975), which fused jazz and Indian music, and a *Lookout Farm*-with-guests album, *Live from Onkel Po's Carnegie Hall* (1975).[49]

By 1974, Miles Davis was a physical wreck, taking drugs and painkillers just to get through each day. While in São Paolo, Brazil during a South American tour in the final two months of the year, he started to think seriously of retiring from music. By his own admission, he was drinking a lot of vodka, smoking marijuana, and doing a lot of cocaine, and his music was as bleak as the chemical transformations taking place in his mind. On Davis's first visit to Los Angeles in three years, Lee Underwood observed, "He may still be searching for the perfect musical means of expressing his diabolical vision, but I personally believe he is leading us into an area that has all of the subjectively frightening urgency, the angry darkness and the screaming jungle ferocity of . . . [a] broodingly primeval subconscious."[50]

Dave Liebman: An accomplished soloist who left Miles Davis to form the fine group Lookout Farm. (Photograph by Stuart Nicholson.)

In January 1975 Davis embarked on a tour of Japan, recording the music from successive concerts at the Osaka Festival Hall on February 1. However, the two resulting albums, *Agharta* and *Panagaea,* sound for all the world as if they were recorded on different days in different years at different locations. Davis's "Interlude" solo on *Agharta* was easily diminished by his past accomplishments, yet on "Prelude" he sounds disarmingly like his old, poetically vulnerable self. "I'm a firm believer that his playing didn't change but the setting he put himself in did," said guitarist Mike Stern. "If you take Miles and transcribe a couple of solos from early on and later, it's a lot of the same stuff. [There are a] few new ideas here and there but mainly what he put around him was his way of really changing."[51]

Agharta and *Panagaea* were Parthian shots that abstracted Hendrix's electronic maelstroms through Pete Cosey's incredible noise guitar, while Reggie Lucas's funky lyricism touched base with Hendrix's R&B roots. In a 1973 interview, Davis said, "I tell the guitar player that if he likes Hendrix . . . to play something like that, just to open it up."[52] Cosey and Lucas did just that, and the result was the rather austere vision that belied subsequent accusations of Davis having "sold out to commercialism."[53] This is hardly music designed for commercial application, such as FM airplay, dancing, or passive listening. In fact, it is quite the reverse, with Cosey's waves of overdriven guitar confronting the New Thing implications of Hendrix's flights of sonic fury. Indeed, there continues to be a fundamental misreading of Davis's music during the 1970–1975 period which was largely, but not exclusively, freeform collective improvisation whose mood and color were mediated and spontaneously ordered by Davis. While the electronic tone colors were those associated with rock music, the methodology behind achieving this dense sonic imagery had its roots in collective improvisation, the oldest form of jazz expressionism, which dated back to the ensembles of New Orleans.

On his return from Japan, Davis was taken ill in St. Louis and was hospitalized for three months. Back on the touring circuit in May, he served as an opening act for his former pianist Herbie Hancock and his electronic group. It was an irony that was not lost on him. Bitter, he vented his frustration on Hancock, subsequently having to make his peace after the tour. Tired and artistically drained, Davis felt he had "nothing else to say musically."[54] *Agharta* only reached 168 on the *Billboard* chart, while his poor health was making it increasingly difficult to contemplate further touring. After Davis's concert at New York's Lincoln Center in June, he disbanded his group to undergo hip surgery and was hospitalized for several weeks. After a lengthy period of convalescence, his desire to return to playing and the concert circuits was blunted. Instead, he turned his attention to playing the piano and composition. Still a sick man, he was frequently swept by boughts of depression and physical pain, which he sought to alleviate with cocaine. Although nothing would be heard from him until 1980, he was hospitalized several times for throat and gallstone surgery, a further hip operation, and treatment for a peptic ulcer.

In the 1950s and 1960s Davis had told his musicians he was paying them to practice on the music stand, a policy that had produced music that was fresh, dangerous, and on-the-edge, with jazz giants like Bill Evans, John Coltrane, Tony Williams, Herbie Hancock, and Wayne Shorter rising to the challenge. However, lesser mortals could hardly be expected to deliver at that sort of level, and several of Davis's albums after *Bitches Brew* attest to this fact. Between 1970 and 1975, Davis's personnel was not as stable as it had been for the preceding fifteen years. John Coltrane and Wayne Shorter had remained with him for five years apiece, but when Shorter left, Davis employed more than five different saxophonists in as many years. This coincided with a period when ensemble textures predominated and "jazz solos" per se became a secondary consideration. Now miles of tapes were edited down to album-length tracks and the results bore little resemblance to what the musicians had in mind when they were jamming in the studio or on-stage.

Miles Davis: In the past he had proved time and again that where he led others followed, so when *Bitches Brew* was released to great success in the spring of 1970, the portents seemed clear. Jazz-rock represented the way ahead because Miles Davis said so. (Photograph by David Redfern/Redferns.)

In addition to the acknowledged classic jazz-rock fusion albums, other albums by Davis from this period were often characterized by obfuscation or lack of direction. His music habitually centered on simple basic structures: a pedal point, a few repeated chords, a repeating bass figure, or a mode. Complexity was now centered in the rhythm section who provided a presence of often complex, spontaneously improvised, multilayered rhythmic interaction. Often Davis, playing electronic, wah-wah trumpet, contributed to this rhythmic turbulence. In live performance Davis often seemed to be improvising around specific textures, to create sound-on-sound pastiches. His 1969–1970 band featuring Chick Corea was characterized by a high level of abstraction that was by no means characteristic of jazz-rock—indeed this band has never been given its due recognition as a free-jazz ensemble. Yet, as Dave Holland has pointed out,[55] this band, later joined by Keith Jarrett, never realized its full potential. Davis also imported World influences into his music—colors of India and South America, for example—but did not exploit them to broaden the base of his music in the way that several musicians who followed in his wake did.

The vision most frequently glimpsed in Davis's music of this period was that of Jimi Hendrix, sometimes through the influence of Tony Williams's Lifetime (as on *Live-Evil*), while the ambient drones of *Agharta* were probably the closest approximation to how a Miles-meets-Hendrix session might have turned out. *Agharta* has become a key album whose influence continues to be felt today. In many ways, it was the way Davis harnessed Hendrix's waves of harmonic distortion that pointed the way for others, including those beyond the boundaries of jazz in the "amorphous spaces" of avant-rock. Jon Hassell has written about how he was "lost and found in the luxuriant jungle of *Bitches Brew*,"[56] while on the sleeve notes of his 1982 album *On Land* Brian Eno cited Teo Macero's "revolutionary production" on "He Loved Him Madly" from Davis's *Get Up With It* as a touchstone for his own explorations into recorded sound. Both Bill Laswell and his longtime associate guitarist Nicky Skopelitis drew heavily on "the tribal perspectives of *Bitches Brew*"[57] right down to cover art resembling Mati Klarwein's voodoo symbolism. In 1997 Laswell acted as producer in a modern-mix translation of extended themes from *In a Silent Way, On the Corner,* and *Get Up With It.* Sequenced as a continuous suite of music, *Panthalassa: The Music of Miles Davis (1969–1974)* included previously unheard outtakes and unissued original performances that were mixed using the wisdom of hindsight, with subtle refractions of ambient and other contemporary trends in electronic music. It not only revealed the relevance of Davis's legacy to younger ears who had found their way to his music through sampling, but for older ears it placed his early 1970s music in a new contemporary perspective that projected its relevance beyond the Millennium.

Ultimately, however, Davis's contribution to jazz-rock was less one of innovation and more one of validation. He gave momentum to a new musical genre and became its most charismatic figure, contributing at least three major albums—*In a Silent Way, Bitches Brew,* and *Jack Johnson*—in the process. Yet considering the number of occasions he recorded between 1970 and 1975, taken as a whole the legacy of those years was a series of albums of variable quality. As

Gertrude Stein once said of Hemingway, "You do something first, then someone else comes along and does it prettier."

Notes

1. *Miles: The Autobiography,* by Miles Davis with Quincy Troupe (Simon & Schuster, New York, 1989), p. 288.
2. *Wire,* December 1994, p. 24.
3. Ibid.
4. *Miles: The Autobiography,* by Miles Davis with Quincy Troupe (Simon & Schuster, New York, 1989), p. 309.
5. Trade advertisement for *Bitches Brew,* Spring 1970.
6. *Rolling Stone,* May 28, 1970, p. 50.
7. *Downbeat,* September 16, 1971, p. 18.
8. *Bill Graham Presents: My Life Inside Rock and Out,* by Bill Graham and Robert Greenfield (Delta, New York, 1993), p. 310.
9. *Melody Maker,* June 13, 1970: Dave Holland interview.
10. *Downbeat,* March 28, 1974, p. 15.
11. The results weren't released at the time, appearing on composite albums released several years after the event: *Big Fun, Circle in the Round,* and *Directions.*
12. *Melody Maker,* June 13, 1970: Dave Holland interview.
13. *Rolling Stone,* December 13, 1969, p. 23.
14. *Downbeat,* July 18, 1974, p. 20. Much of this music would probably not have seen the light of day had Columbia not wanted to keep Davis on its roster during the period he withdrew from music making in the late 1970s. As Teo Macero, who selected what was to be issued on albums such as *Directions* and *Circle in the Round,* has pointed out, "When he was not playing, his career went on—thanks to me, working in the studio with tapes we'd amassed. Without that he would have been in the soup" (*Dancing in Your Head,* by Gene Santoro [Oxford University Press, New York, 1994], p. 154).
15. *Rolling Stone,* June 25, 1970, p. 10.
16. *Wire,* Issue 53, July 1988, p. 37.
17. Jack Johnson was World Heavyweight Boxing Champion in 1908.
18. *Rolling Stone,* July 8, 1970, p. 37.
19. *Introduction to the Sociology of Music,* by T. W. Adorno (Seabury, New York, 1976), pp. 61–62.
20. Columbia advertisement for *Miles Davis at Fillmore,* trade press, December 1970.
21. *Rolling Stone,* June 25, 1970, p. 10.
22. *Miles: The Autobiography,* by Miles Davis with Quincy Troupe (Simon & Schuster, New York, 1989), p. 308.
23. He later played for Norman Connors and discovered a knack of writing eerie ballads, such as "Valentine Love," "We Both Need Each Other," and "You Are My Starship," all of which enabled the drummer to figure in the R&B Top 10. Subsequently, Henderson's own album *Solid* was a top-10 soul entry in 1977.
24. Interview with the author, April 7, 1997.
25. *Downbeat,* April 13, 1972, pp. 22–26.
26. *From Satchmo to Miles,* by Leonard Feather (Stein & Day, New York, 1972), p. 247.
27. *Melody Maker,* July 31, 1971, p. 4; *Jet* printed a similar story the week before.
28. Liebman recalls the personnel as Liebman (soprano sax, 1st side only); Carlos Garnett (soprano and tenor sax, 2nd side only); Chick Corea, Herbie Hancock, and Harold Williams (keyboards); John McLaughlin (guitar); Colin Walcott (sitar); Michael Henderson (bass); Jack DeJohnette and Billy Hart (drums); Don Alias and M'Tume (percussion); and Badal Roy (tabla) (*Downbeat,* April 26, 1973). To complicate things even further, drummer Al Foster also claims to have played on some of the sessions

included in the album (*Downbeat,* July 17, 1975, p. 12) and while confirming the presence of Hancock and Hart, he also adds saxophonist Bennie Maupin.

29. *Self-Portrtait of a Jazz Artist,* by Dave Liebman (Advance Music, Rottenburg 1988), p. 50.
30. *Downbeat,* March 29, 1973, p. 22.
31. *Melody Maker,* June 17, 1972, p. 6.
32. *In Concert* struggled to reach 156 on the *Billboard* chart.
33. *Miles: The Autobiography,* by Miles Davis with Quincy Troupe (Simon & Schuster, New York, 1989), p. 318.
34. *Downbeat,* March 1, 1973, p. 10.
35. *Miles: The Autobiography,* by Miles Davis with Quincy Troupe (Simon & Schuster, New York, 1989), pp. 319–320.
36. *Melody Maker,* July 21, 1973, p. 48.
37. *Miles: The Autobiography,* by Miles Davis with Quincy Troupe (Simon & Schuster, New York, 1989), p. 313.
38. *Melody Maker,* July 21, 1973, p. 48.
39. Liner notes to *Dark Magus* (Columbia/Legacy C2K 65137), by Dave Liebman.
40. Ibid.
41. *Milestones II,* by Jack Chambers (University of Toronto Press, Toronto, 1985), p. 267.
42. Columbia advertisement for *Get Up With It,* trade press, January 1975.
43. Ibid.
44. *Downbeat,* February 27, 1975, p. 19.
45. *Self-Portrait of a Jazz Artist,* by Dave Liebman (Advance Music, Rottenburg, 1988), p. 51.
46. He was replaced by saxophonist Sonny Fortune, who remained until May 1975, when Sam Morrison took over. "When I was playing I was totally involved in what was going on," Fortune said later. "It's just that there wasn't very much of me needed. I was confined to very little participation in the music. . . . It wasn't very rewarding" (*Downbeat,* 12 February 1976, p. 16–17).
47. *Downbeat,* December 19, 1974, p. 22.
48. Ibid., October 23, 1975, p. 40.
49. In 1976, Liebman ventured into a more commercially oriented version of jazz-rock with the Liebman-Ellis band, a collaboration with the former James Brown sideman Pee Wee Ellis. "The combination was interesting, but neither commercial enough nor serious enough to be popular one way or the other," said Liebman later. In 1979 he recorded *What It Is,* a highly successful "fusion" album with the up-and-coming greats John Scofield on guitar, Kenny Kirkland on piano, Marcus Miller on bass, and Steve Gadd on drums. In 1981 he formed Quest, a superb acoustic, post-bop quartet that became his main vehicle for expression, but he returned to jazz-rock in 1994 with *Miles Away,* a tribute to Miles Davis. Revisiting Davis's repertoire from "Boplicity" to "Code M.D.," it numbered among the most valuable albums of the early 1990s with vivid electronic imagery and accomplished solos by the leader, who sadly still remained one of the great under-recognized instrumentalists in jazz.
50. *Downbeat,* March 13, 1975, p. 36.
51. *Jazz Times,* January–February 1992, p. 22.
52. Stephen Davis, "My Ego Only Needs A Good Rhythm Section," reprinted in *The Miles Davis Companion,* edited by Gary Carner (Schirmer Books, New York, 1996), p. 153.
53. Perhaps the most emphatic accusation was stated in Stanley Crouch's article "On the Corner: The Sellout of Miles Davis," republished in *Reading Jazz: A Gathering of Autobiography, Reportage, and Criticism from 1919 to Now,* edited by Robert Gottlieb (Pantheon Books, New York, 1996), pp. 898–914.
54. *Milestones II,* by Jack Chambers (University of Toronto Press, Toronto, 1985), p. 322.
55. *Melody Maker,* June 13, 1970.
56. *The Wire,* December 1994, p. 28.
57. Ibid., p. 79.

CHAPTER 8

The Inner Mounting Flame

W hen Lester Bangs reviewed Miles Davis's *In a Silent Way* in *Rolling Stone* magazine,[1] it was followed by his critique of *Emergency!* by Tony Williams's Lifetime, so closely were the two records released. If Davis's album was characterized by an absence of significant musical events, favoring pastoral tone colors and delicate shading, then Williams's vision of an amalgam of jazz and rock was its complete antithesis. "Here is where we take a giant step into the future," said Bangs. "Williams and his associates stand at the frontier."[2]

On the Davis date, Williams's drumming had been the very model of discretion, reduced to keeping basic time in deference to the subdued mood of the session. Twelve weeks later with his own group, he was bursting with things to say and new ways to say them. Manic and desperate, Lifetime gave apodictic testimony that they had discovered a new and exciting way of combining jazz and elements of rock. Where Davis was tentative, unsure even, Williams appeared to have glimpsed the future and, for a moment at least, it seemed as if it was to him, rather than to Davis, that destiny was beckoning, "[Lifetime] are jazz musicians who have seen through the pop artifice and picked up on the very best rock has to offer, making their music a totally unique entity, the kind of super-inspired workmanship that promises to set styles for years to come," continued Bangs.[3]

Davis, however, had two things that Williams did not: good management in Jack Whittemore and a major-label record deal with Columbia. It was to prove crucial; Lifetime would burn brightly and suddenly extinguish itself, the victim of poor management, poor promotion, and poor record sales. Yet in 1969 all of that was ahead of them. While the mood of *In a Silent Way* seemed to be mediated by its album title—and echoed in the names of the numbers within, "Shhh/Peaceful" on side one and the eponymously titled flip side—Williams produced a roar the like of which had never been encountered in jazz. *Emergency!* was the first jazz record to confront rock's raw energy, its drive, its aggression, and its volume. The passage of time has done nothing to lessen its impact.

Williams had been with Miles Davis for five years when he left to form his own band in early 1969. A child prodigy, the first time he played drums in front of an audience was when he was eight years old. His father, a weekend saxophonist, began taking him to local Boston jazz clubs, and by the time he was twelve Williams was well enough known to sit in with Art Blakey's Jazz Messengers and with Max Roach's group. Around this time, the saxophonist Sam Rivers became his mentor, giving the youngster a regular gig. "Even at thirteen Tony knew where he was all of the time," Rivers said in 1964. "As he matured, what impresses me about him is the emotional content of his playing. No matter how technically fascinating he becomes, you are always aware of his sensitivity and the emotional power behind all his technique."[4]

After working with Rivers, Williams became a member of the house rhythm section of the Boston club Connelly's, where he backed countless visiting name jazz musicians, including the saxophonist Jackie McLean. Amazed by the youngster's prowess, McLean brought him to New York in December 1962 to play with his group in the off-Broadway production, *The Connection.* In February 1963 Williams made his first recording, for a McLean album called *Vertigo.*[5] In May of that year he moved straight to the top spot in jazz when Miles Davis phoned from California to invite him to join his quintet. He was just seventeen.

While with Davis, Williams cut some of the first free-jazz albums on the Blue Note label, with Eric Dolphy, Andrew Hill, and as a leader himself, on *Lifetime* (1964) and *Spring* (1965). Williams left Miles Davis in March 1969. "The reason I left when I did—which was right after *In a Silent Way*—was . . . specifically to put a band together," he said. "I thought it was best to do it then when I was still young."[6] But Williams did not have in mind forming a conventional jazz group; he wanted something in tune with the changing times that reflected *his* generation's musical tastes. After all, he was still only twenty-four. "The Beatles influenced me a lot," he said. "I was the only musician in 1964 to have a Beatles poster on my wall in the apartment I lived in. Miles lived upstairs from me and . . . I remember I told Miles in '64 or '65 that we ought to play a concert opposite the Beatles, but he didn't understand it then. . . . I remember hearing Gary Burton's band . . . and then I would listen to Charles Lloyd's group and I would say that if they could do it, then I could."[7]

The first person Williams turned to for his new group was master deconstructionist and guitarist Sonny Sharrock, but he didn't want to play "rock and roll." Instead, Williams turned to the British guitarist John McLaughlin. Then twenty-six, McLaughlin had a background in music that was as diverse as any jazz musician of his age. Born in Yorkshire in 1942, his first interest was the piano, which he studied at the age of nine, taking up the guitar and getting into country blues, flamenco, and finally jazz through Django Reinhardt records.[8] His first professional job was with Pete Deuchar's Professors of Ragtime in 1958, which eventually took him to London where he gradually established himself on the flourishing R&B scene. The comings and goings of musicians among the vast number of ad hoc bands during this period make documentation difficult, but among the first groups McLaughlin played with in 1961 were the Marzipan Twisters, the Al Watson band, and a first stint with organist Georgie Fame and the Blue Flames in the summer and fall of 1962.

McLaughlin spent most of 1963 with Graham Bond before joining the Tony Meehan Combo in October, and then the Brian Auger Quintet (playing alongside an Irish bass player called Rick Laird) in early 1964. That year he also worked with trumpeter Ian Carr while beginning to pick up regular session work, most notably with the "Ready Steady Go" TV orchestra, and appearing on the Rolling Stones album *Metamorphosis* (1964) alongside fellow session guitarist Jimmy Page, to whom he apparently gave lessons. After a year with Herbie Goins and the Night-Timers from spring 1965 to spring 1966—including a remarkably uncharacteristic crack at penning a soul number, "Cruising," for the B-side of a Goins single—he began an association with the vocalist Duffy Powers. "I knew instinctively that he would be an international star," said Powers in 1992, "and against his protests I told him it would be on his own. . . . Musically he was fantastic."[9] Powers, a blues-based singer who had begun with Alexis Korner, used some of the top British jazz musicians of the period, including Phil Seaman, Danny Thompson, Jack Bruce, and Terry Cox. McLaughlin appeared on his album *Innovations* (1965–6; later rereleased as *Little Boy Blue*) and contributed some strong, authentic blues playing and a particularly sensitive backing to the Billie Holiday number "God Bless the Child."

In 1967 McLaughlin worked with the organist Mike Carr's trio and can be heard swinging in "grits and gravy" style on "Bell's Blues" from *Bebop from the East Coast*. He also became involved with a strange jazz and poetry band called The Huge Local Sun with the likes of Pete Brown, Dick Heckstall-Smith, and Danny Thompson that eventually became Pete Brown's First Real Poetry Band. He also played in bassist Thompson's trio, appearing on BBC's "Jazz Club" twice in 1967, the recordings revealing his tone to be in the Tal Farlow–Jimmy Raney–Herb Ellis school while revealing tantalizing glimpses of his phenomenally fast execution. "I think it is a wonderful thing for the British jazz scene that there are young musicians coming up doing this sort of thing and doing it so superbly," said compere Humphrey Lyttelton. However, most of the recordings from this period reveal McLaughlin more as an accompanist of imagination and resource happy to adapt to the needs of the moment than as a soloist destined for great things. He returned to Georgie Fame and the Blue Flames in the fall of 1967 and through 1968, appearing on Fame's "Knock on Wood/Road Runner" single and Fame's hit album *The Ballad of Bonnie and Clyde*. By now he was getting session work with the likes of Tom Jones, Engelbert Humperdinck, Petula Clark, and David Bowie, appearing on *The World of David Bowie,* which was recorded in 1967. "After some time this session thing was driving me completely crazy," he recalled. "I had to do it in order to survive and yet more things were happening musically that I wanted to do. Finally one day I woke up and I said to myself I cannot do this anymore."[10]

Moving to Germany, he joined the composer-vibist and multi-instrumentalist Gunter Hampel's group Time Is Now and immersed himself in free jazz. "While I was with Gunter I lived in Antwerp so I could go back to England every now and then," continued McLaughlin. "We had a little band with bass player Dave Holland and drummer Tony Oxley and it was fantastic. I did a

record called *Extrapolation* with Tony Oxley and John Surman on baritone."[11]
By the time of this recording, on January 16, 1969, Holland had already left for
New York the previous July to join Miles Davis, so Brian Odges came in on
bass. Included was a McLaughlin–Duffy Power co-composition "It's Funny"
(Power was credited as "Dussy Downer") and a tribute to Pete Brown, "Pete
the Poet." *Extrapolation* remains an overlooked classic of the period[12] that
evolved out of the ideas and concepts McLaughlin had been working on with
the Gordon Beck Quartet, an association that produced *Experiments with Pops*
in December 1967. Rhythmically and harmonically fluid, *Extrapolation* made
use both of modal harmonies and of the "time, no changes" principle as a basis
for improvisation in which the composition provides tempo, key, and mood,
leaving the choice of chord changes to the spontaneous interaction of improviser and accompanists. It was the last port of call before abandoning harmony
entirely and striking out into free jazz.

What is immediately striking is McLaughlin's technical facility and his tone,
which was hard, cutting, and metallic in a way favored by rock guitarists. He also
accented his notes evenly, rather than employing a "jazz-swing" feel, using relatively little syncopation in the construction of his phrases. In short, McLaughlin
had devised an approach to the electric guitar that was wholly his own and quite
unlike that of any other player in jazz; along with Larry Coryell he was responsible for bringing the sound of the rock guitar to the jazz mainstream. "A few
months later," continued McLaughlin, "in November 1968, I got a call from
Dave [Holland]. He was in Baltimore, and guess who he was with? I said Miles.
'No,' he said, 'Tony Williams and he wants to talk to you.' Tony said he would
like to form a band and he would like to have me. Jack DeJohnette had played
him a tape he had done with me a few months before while he was in London
with Bill Evans. So I said: 'When you are ready, just call me.'"[13]

That tape, if the provenance is correct, was recorded on October 28, 1968
with Dave Holland, Jack DeJohnette, and an unknown pianist, and is still in existence.[14] Two tracks are with an acoustic piano and are subdued, post-bop compositions using a tonal center or "time, no changes" as a basis for improvisation,
creating moods of fluid introspection. Rhythmically and harmonically,
McLaughlin is at home in this challenging climate, responding to the ebb and
flow of creative impulse yet subtly mediating the mood of the music through the
strength of his own musical personality. His virtuosity is masked except for sudden technicolor flashes that suggest a musician with much in reserve. The final
track is constructed around a two-bar rock vamp, derived from the first two bars
of "Money." Here, out of the gaze of the public, was a glimpse of the future, a
recording that demonstrates more than any other of the period a union between
jazz and rock that confronts volume—electricity—as an important element in
constructing a new dynamic. While this is fiercely interactive music making—
every player listening and responding to each other—the climate is governed by
DeJohnette's refraction of rock rhythm patterns and the insistent bass line.
Power and volume were central to group's expressionism. As the music swirls
and eddies around the collective energy of the moment, it leaps free of the tradi-

Tony Williams: One of the greatest drummers in jazz, Williams formed Lifetime in 1969, a daring trio who explored the sonic space opened up by Jimi Hendrix and free jazz. Although it only lasted until April 1971, its effects are still being digested today. (Photograph by Stuart Nicholson.)

tional song forms associated with rock into open form, enabling the musicians to take the music wherever they want. What is particularly interesting is the extent to which this music—and McLaughlin's central role within it—closely prefigured what was about to follow.

The call from Tony Williams to join his new band came at the end of January 1969, and McLaughlin left London for New York on Saturday February 3. On his arrival, he was taken up to Harlem to jam. "I first heard John at Count Basie's," said Larry Coryell. "After 30 seconds of his first solo, I turned to my wife and said: 'This is the best guitar player I've ever heard in my life.' That night everybody was there, everybody from Cannonball's group; Miles was there, Dave Holland and we were all knocked out by that fantastic debut of John."[15] Miles Davis immediately invited McLaughlin to participate on his upcoming record date on February 18, which produced *In a Silent Way*. "I was very nervous simply

John McLaughlin: His staggering virtuosity radically changed the sound and style of the jazz guitar. When he formed the Mahavishnu Orchestra, he set new levels of ensemble cohesion and group interaction. (Photograph by Stuart Nicholson.)

because this man had lived inside of my imagination, inside my record player for so many years," said McLaughlin. "Suddenly to be confronted with the actual reality, it was quite disturbing emotionally, but not in an unpleasant way."[16] At the session Davis sensed his nervousness: "I told him, 'Just relax and play like you did up at Count Basie's and everything will be all right.' And he did."[17]

Davis saw great potential in McLaughlin and immediately asked him to join his own group, somewhat to the guitarist's embarrassment. "It was unbelievable for me," said McLaughlin. "Imagine, I had to turn down Miles because it was more important for me to go with Tony Williams. I had compositions and I realized with Tony I would have more of a chance to play them than with Miles."[18] Even though he declined the offer to join Davis's working band, McLaughlin emerged as a key sideman on Davis's recordings over the next two years, appearing on *Bitches Brew, Circle in the Round, Directions, Jack Johnson, Get Up With It, On the Corner,* and *Live-Evil.* After appearing on the latter album, recorded live at the Cellar Door, Washington, D.C., in December 1970, Davis again asked McLaughlin if he would consider leaving Lifetime to join him. Again McLaughlin declined; "I had too much invested in Lifetime," he explained. "I had freedom there that was irreplaceable."[19]

One of Lifetime's first gigs was at the Village Vanguard, where the band was reviewed by Ira Gitler: "There has been a lot of talk about 'energy' music in the past few years. Williams's trio has energy to spare—and the creativity to give it direction."[20] Al Kooper, still with Blood, Sweat & Tears, also went along to see them in an A&R capacity for Columbia records, but to the band's amazement he turned them down. "We couldn't believe it," said McLaughlin. "I lost all my respect for him immediately because we were burning."[21] It was the first of several disappointments the band had to endure. They were eventually signed with Polydor, then a new and unestablished company in America. Their first album was recorded in New York City's Olmstead Sound Studios on May 26 and 28, 1969, but it was not without problems, as Phil Schaap discovered when he attempted to remaster the tape for CD reissue. "For a start the reissue is nowhere near the standards of 1990s audio, or even those of 1969 when it was originally recorded," Schapp said. "There were problems with McLaughlin's guitar attachments, a broken studio organ and then we discovered distortion in each of the eight channels, the worst offender being the track isolating Williams's bass drum. But if this was not enough, the tape machine used at the recording session was woefully out of spec. That we could correct, but of course sonic problems still remained, but at least the CD reissue is an improvement on the analog issue."[22] When McLaughlin got to hear Polydor's original mix he was shocked. "I realised they had no respect for musicians," he said.[23]

Despite the recording problems, *Emergency!* remains one of the most important jazz-rock albums of all time. While early experiments such as those by John Handy, Mike Nock, Jeremy Steig, Larry Coryell, Gary Burton, Charles Lloyd, and, just a few weeks earlier, Miles Davis had incorporated rock's rhythms and, in some bands, the electronic sounds of rock, none had used the dynamics of electricity to such coruscating effect as Lifetime. Widely influential, it was Lifetime, rather than Miles Davis, to whom several key bands of the 1970s looked for inspiration. It is interesting to note that prior to the *Emergency!* sessions, all the band members had jammed with Jimi Hendrix, and it is impossible not to think of this music being touched by his musical conception. "I loved Jimi and I met him in New York," said McLaughlin. "I played with him. . . . I was playing this hollow-bodied Hummingbird and it was feeding back all the time, it was so loud in there. But I didn't care. . . . Jimi was killing."[24] Their meeting, taped on March 25, 1969 with Dave Holland on bass and Buddy Miles on drums, was extensively bootlegged as *Hell's Session,* but apparently a subsequent Hendrix–Tony Williams jam, also held at the Electric Ladyland studios, was not recorded. "Unfortunately it didn't work out too well," said Williams.[25]

The third member of Lifetime, the organist Larry Young, had sat in on a rehearsal session May 14 with Hendrix that was posthumously released on the album *Nine to the Universe.* Young had studied piano as a child but switched to organ at fourteen when his father opened a hometown club with an organ on its bandstand. At the time the instrument was enjoying great popularity through hit recordings by the likes of Bill Doggett, and Jimmy Smith, and later Brother Jack McDuff, Baby Face Willette, and Johnny "Hammond" Smith. Young did not follow the blues-preaching route of his predecessors, instead applying the harmonic ideas and improvisational techniques of John Coltrane to the organ, as a result of hanging around Coltrane's house for hours on end playing and experimenting with the saxophonist. His light, fluent touch was widely admired, both on a series of albums under his own name for the New Jazz and Prestige labels and, in the mid-1960s, with some adventurous albums for the Blue Note label that defined his approach as quite different from that of the Jimmy Smith school. Beginning with *Into Something* and extending over a further five albums, Young established himself as the most influential organist of his generation. When Young joined Lifetime, it gathered together some of the most advanced young musicians in jazz, but with a difference. They were all inspired by the electronic sounds of rock, and on *Emergency!* they inhabited the same terrifying electronic spaces Jimi Hendrix had opened up. "I was heavily influenced by Jimi Hendrix," confirmed Williams.[26]

The impressive title cut moves from a fast, repeated four-bar riff to a slow, spacey half-tempo improvisation by McLaughlin, and it is unmistakably colored by rock's sound (guitar tone) and volume (both guitar and organ are overdriven to distortion point), but not rock's rhythms—in fact, Williams's drumming is straight-ahead, post-bop. With the reprise of the opening four-bar riff after McLaughlin's solo, Williams's drumming adopts squarer rhythmic patterns, but reverts to post-bop as the tempo halves again for Young's solo, which is climaxed on a note of free jazz. Again the four-bar motif returns and Williams adopts a more rock-oriented approach to his drumming, to cries of exhortation from the band. "Via the Spectrum Road" reveals rock's rhythms more specifically, but "Spectrum," a McLaughlin composition that had earlier appeared on *Extrapolation,* again uses post-bop rhythms. It is worth noting that tracks like "Emergency!" and "Spectrum" were an extension of the free-flowing approach of *Extrapolation,* but reinforced by the volume and energy associated with rock. However, the album *Emergency!* was not an unqualified success; the main culprit, Williams's vocals on "Where" and the group vocal on "Via the Spectrum Road," probably accounted for a four-star rating from *Downbeat,* who nevertheless cited the band as creating "the freshest and most original sounds being made today."[27]

Booked into clubs like the Village Gate in New York, the Both/And in San Francisco, and Shelly's Manne Hole in Los Angeles and into rock venues like Fillmore East, Ungano's, and the Electric Circus in New York, and the Boston Tea Party—opposite the Who—in Boston, Lifetime experienced difficulty clicking with "the Woodstock nation." Although open-eared jazz fans and progressive rock fans were knocked out, a wider base for the audience remained beyond the band's grasp, and it is not difficult to guess why when listening to broadcast tapes of the band from the period.[28] Lifetime made no concessions to commercial expediency except for an occasional half-spoken vocal from Williams that today repels rather than attracts. Often Williams made no reference to rock rhythms at all. Here was bold uncompromising jazz, full of complex instrumental interaction and sophisticated soloing that often dispensed with prewritten harmony and sometimes ventured into abstraction.

It is hardly any wonder that Polydor's advertising for *Emergency!* warned listeners they might be "shaken up" by what they heard:

> If it shook up Ralph Gleason imagine what it'll do to you. Critic Ralph Gleason gets our nomination for the man most likely to have heard everything. That's why we're pleased to tell you that he called Tony Williams' music: "Absolutely unlike any other instrumental sound I ever heard."[29]

Gleason at the time was the jazz and rock critic for the *San Francisco Examiner* and one of the founders of *Rolling Stone* magazine.

In many ways, Lifetime were an abstraction of Cream, with their "power trio" approach to improvisation, albeit closer to the edge than the blues-based improvisations of the earlier band, a group which Williams is on record as having admired. Williams, however, saw his failure to break through to a wider audience as less a musical problem, more a logistical one: "The main problem was the management. They believed in us, but they didn't have the capability to keep the band working. There was interest in the group in certain areas of the country, but we just couldn't get the gigs. The record company was the other problem. Polydor had just opened up in America and they didn't have any distribution."[30]

In September 1969, Lifetime appeared at the Monterey Jazz Festival, where Gleason reported that they "played exceptionally well. It is a completely new sound in jazz, an amalgam of electronic volume and percussion that is dissonant and sinewy and can be overwhelming."[31] Despite such high-profile gigs, however, the band were barely getting enough work. Nevertheless, they were continuing to grow and develop. Interviewed in January 1970, Larry Young observed, "It's much more of a unit now. It's like everybody's more interested in the unit than playing personalities."[32]

The following month they entered the recording studios again. Their second album, *Turn It Over,* saw the band moving closer to rock on some tracks and offering a broader range of compositions. "Play loud!" said the sleeve, inviting the listener to try to reproduce the sound of the band live. This time there were fewer compositions from Williams and more from McLaughlin and Young, with numbers by Chick Corea ("To Whom It May Concern"), Carlos Jobim ("Once I Loved"), and John Coltrane ("Big Nick"). The former Cream bassist Jack Bruce sat in with the band, appearing on three tracks; he was in the States touring with his group called Jack Bruce and Friends. "One night," he recalled, "we had just finished a set and someone came up and said 'Hello, I'm Tony Williams, would you like to play on my album?'"[33]

As his playing with Eric Clapton and Ginger Baker suggested, Bruce was one of the few electric bass players of the period capable of responding to the free-flowing creative impulses of the band with imaginative and spontaneously conceived rock-inspired bass lines, but initially even he found it difficult to create a role for himself within the group, as *Turn It Over* reveals. "Ever since I heard Tony's *Emergency!* album I thought that's the band I'd like to play with," he said.

"It was a tremendous honor to be asked to appear on the album."[34] *Turn It Over* got a rating of four and one-half stars in *Downbeat,* again not helped by Williams's vocalizing. "An album with a lot of good music, but whose overall effect is lessened by some less-than-good vocals," opined *Rolling Stone.*[35] On the more uncompromising numbers, however, exemplified by their scorched-earth version of "To Whom It May Concern," *Turn It Over* appeared more focused than its predecessor. "Recording that album wasn't a pleasant experience," said Williams. "There was a lot going on socially at the time and it was a reaction to that. There was a lot of tension and anxiety. The title was about turning over society. The album was black, the liner notes were very hard to read—it was aggressively antagonistic."[36]

Bruce returned to the U.K. after his "Friends" tour, rejoining Lifetime in time for their one-and-only single, "One Word." It represented an attempt to raise the group's profile in the U.K., released to coincide with a three-month tour of Britain at the end of 1970. It flopped. Playing every gig they could get, from drunken audiences to super-hip, after-hours clubs, the group refused to perform encores because they considered the practice "showbiz." Although Lifetime seemed poised to establish themselves as the major force in the jazz-rock revolution, they were still not making much money. "Tony was driving the gig wagon," said Bruce. "John McLaughlin's an incredible musician yet he's never made the bread he should."[37] Gradually problems with Bruce's manager Robert Stigwood began to manifest themselves: Bruce's name had to follow Williams in the billing and had to be printed the same size as Williams's; sometimes Bruce was required elsewhere, so the group was reduced to a trio; and so on. Lifetime were scheduled to record during the British tour and do a live album, but nothing happened. On their return to New York the band were once again slated to record, but once again did not. "Everything except the music was incredibly bad," said McLaughlin. "Management, economics, administration, organization . . . incredibly bad."[38]

The writing was on the wall, and in April 1971 the band broke up with much mumbling about conflicting egos but with the general consent of all concerned that their best was still unrecorded. "Lifetime was, without a doubt, the best band there ever was in the world," asserted Jack Bruce. "I really believe that, and anybody who listened to the band with an open mind, let the music wash over him, would have realized that. The fact that racial differences could unite and to form a gestalt that worked, I've never experienced energy like that in a band."[39] Sadly, Williams's career in the 1970s, either musically or philosophically, never seemed to recover from the musical high of the original Lifetime. As *Emergency!* revealed, Lifetime was a logical extension of the ideas worked out in England by McLaughlin on *Extrapolation.* Without McLaughlin, Williams struggled to position his music within the jazz-rock idiom. While personal tensions within the band discharged themselves in long, exciting collective improvisations, Williams's problem appeared to be his inability to impose a decisive shape to his music, something that was more clearly revealed in his subsequent bands during the 1970s. In 1971 came *Ego,* a somewhat bizarre record where the leader was joined by two percussionists, Ted Dunbar on guitar, Young on organ, and the bassist Ron Carter, who also doubled on cello. Once again Williams was ill-advised to sing, which he does on three tracks, while the climate of the album was biased towards R&B. It was followed by *The Old Bum's Rush,* another puzzling affair with William's father on tenor saxophone and vocals by a former member of the girl-group the Ronettes, Tequila. "Sadly, the album is another flawed Lifetime effort," said *Rolling Stone.*[40]

With neither album a success, either critically or financially, Williams withdrew from the scene. He resurfaced briefly to record and tour with Stan Getz in a straight-ahead jazz context, opening in New York's Rainbow Room at Radio City in February 1972 to instant acclaim with a group that also included Chick Corea on piano, Stanley Clarke on bass, and Airto Moreira on percussion. After the engagement they went immediately into the recording studios to cut *Captain Marvel,* which not only numbers among Getz's finest albums but also had an important impact on Corea's subsequent career moves. During the summer they toured the European festival circuits without Airto and were the hit of the Montreux Festival; their performance was captured on the live album *The Stan Getz Quartet at Montreux.* In 1974 Williams appeared again, this time on Stanley Clarke's eponymously titled second album.

In 1975, Williams reactivated Lifetime, employing Tequila on vocals, Webster Lewis on keyboards, Allan Holdsworth, formerly of the Soft Machine and Gong, on guitar, and Jack Bruce on bass; however, this group only recorded in Sweden. When they returned to the States, Williams tried a new lineup—at one point trying out a young bass player named Jaco Pastorius—and ended up with a revamped combo comprising Holdsworth, Alan Pasqua on keyboards (whose playing credits included Don Ellis, Stan Kenton, and Frank Foster), and the former Motown bassist Tony Newton. They began gigging in New York and within weeks were signed by Columbia. The resulting album, *Believe It,* recorded in July 1975, was a disappointment; it was significantly less ambitious than *Emergency!* The man who helped redefine the role of the drummer in contemporary jazz now appeared content to keep time behind a competent but dispassionate ensemble, less interested in blazing new trails than in ingratiating themselves with record buyers. His predicament was that his adventurous past was writ so large that it tended to diminish anything new that he attempted. On this and the more commercial *Million Dollar Legs,* which followed a year later, there was none of the dynamic edge or variety in his playing that had set him apart earlier in the decade, and with the emergence of drummers such as Billy Cobham and Alphonse Mouzon, events elsewhere in jazz-rock were moving ahead of him.

In the 1980s and 1990s, Williams returned to an acoustic quintet and produced a series of critically acclaimed albums for the reconstituted Blue Note label. Williams died in a Los Angeles hospital following what should have been a routine gallstone operation on February 23, 1997. One of his last professional acts was his participation in the second part of a recording project called Arcana, which was directly inspired by the original Lifetime. The first Arcana project, a trio comprising Williams, bassist Bill Laswell, and guitarist Derek Bailey, produced *The Last Wave* in 1996, described by *Wire* magazine as "one of the year's most sensational moments."[41] Bassist and producer Laswell had first worked with Williams on the now (in)famous Public Image Ltd. *Album* in the mid-1980s. "Derek had always wanted to play with Tony," explained Laswell. "I had been talking to Tony about new projects and when I mentioned this, Tony was very keen on the idea. Derek's total improvisation side-steps any notion of fusion; it continues in the tradition Williams defined with Lifetime—a progressive and multi-textural jazz-rock fusion."[42] *The Last Wave* was followed by *Arc of Testimony* (1997), again with Laswell on bass and production duties, this time with Pharoah Sanders on tenor saxophone, Byard Lancaster on alto, Graham Haynes on cornet, and Nicky Skopelitis and Buckethead on guitars.

"*Testimony* incorporates the spirit of the original Lifetime along with electronic ambient sweeps, free improvisation and the latest studio technology," said Laswell. "It's spontaneous improvising and composing and it's visceral."[43] These important valedictory statements reveal Williams's music turning full circle, returning to the ranks of the crusading avant-garde that was a feature of his early career on his own albums *Lifetime* and *Spring* and on those of others, such as Eric Dolphy's *Out to Lunch*. In the wake of his unexpected passing, they stand as important testaments not only to his creativity, but as a final vindication of his original dream realized with Lifetime in 1969 of taking music to the limits and moving beyond arbitrary categories.

In contrast to the Orson-Wellesian career path of Williams, John McLaughlin's experience with Miles Davis and with Lifetime gave him the confidence to launch his own career as a bandleader and establish himself as one of the most highly regarded guitarists in jazz. In London during the 1960s he had a reputation for being a bit wild; the bassist Jack Bruce recalled that while he was with The Graham Bond Organisation, for example, "John was really playing great, but he was getting very stoned, which was really saying something in those days. He actually fell off the stage at one gig in Coventry in an extremely stoned state and played this death chord as he landed . . . kkkkrrruuugggggg!"[44] By the time he reached America he had put all that behind him. "Just before I went to America I started to do yoga exercises in the morning," McLaughlin said. "I arrived in Manhattan, I thought I had to get myself more together, so I did more exercises. I was doing an hour and a half in the morning and an hour and a half in the evening. Just yoga. So after a year of doing this I felt great physically, but I thought I was missing the interior thing, so I went to meditate with different teachers and suddenly one day Larry Coryell's manager introduced me to Sri Chinmoy, immediately I felt good about him, he said some important things to me."[45] In his quest for spiritual enlightenment, McLaughlin took Chinmoy as his guru, and thereafter a certain mystic idealism overpowered interviews he gave to the music press during this period as he aspired to become "the cosmic instrument of God."

In his musical life, McLaughlin recorded two key albums in 1969 away from the aegis of Miles Davis and Tony Williams: *Super Nova*, with Wayne Shorter, and *Infinite Search*, with Miroslav Vitous. He also signed a record contract with

Alan Douglas of Douglas Records for just over $2,000 for two albums. The first, *Devotion,* the album whose title reflects his spiritual quests, was recorded in February 1970 with Larry Young plus two musicians from Hendrix's Band of Gypsies, Billy Rich on bass and Buddy Miles on drums. Strongly influenced by the density and complexity of Lifetime and Hendrix's psychedelic flamboyance, it lacked the inspirational turmoil that Williams's drumming brought to the music. McLaughlin went out on the road with Lifetime right after it was record-ed and when he returned discovered, somewhat to his chagrin, that the album had been mixed, edited, and sent for production without his input.

In May 1970, McLaughlin recorded *Where Fortune Smiles* for the Pye label, an album that explored further the precepts of *Extrapolation.* Joined in New York by John Surman and with Dave Holland on bass, the group was filled out with Stu Martin on drums and Karl Berger on vibes. Released in the U.S. for the first time in 1975, its pioneering impact was lost through the passage of time, but for once the recording-company hyperbole was close to the truth when it claimed it was "one of the most significant recordings of the jazz-rock fusion."[46] Like *Extrapolation,* it was a minor classic and, once again, has been overlooked.

During the balance of 1970, McLaughlin worked sessions for tenor saxophon-ist Joe Farrell for his *Song of the Wind* album, and for fellow guitarist Larry Coryell, appearing on *Spaces* and *Planet End.* On the former, he contributed an acoustic solo on "Rene's Theme" that many consider among his most lyrical work. However, on "Spaces (Infinite)" and "Wrong Is Right," McLaughlin plays electric guitar—pitted against friend and rival Coryell—and serves notice of just what fast playing is all about.

After being encouraged by Miles Davis to form his own band, McLaughlin brought two musicians together for his second album for Alan Douglas—*My Goals Beyond* from 1971—whom he thought might be interested in joining him at some point in the future. He had seen drummer Bill Cobham playing with Horace Silver in Ronnie Scott's club in London and had subsequently got to know him through Davis, with whom they had both recorded. "Billy was the first man I talked to about coming into my new band," said McLaughlin. "He impressed me so much, I was very happy when he said he would join me."[47] Jerry Goodman was in fact his second choice as a violinist; McLaughlin had originally wanted Jean-Luc Ponty, who declined, and Goodman was chosen after McLaughlin listened to contemporary albums with violin players. "When I heard Jerry Goodman with The Flock I knew the search was over," he said. "After a lit-tle detective work I discovered he was living on a farm in Wisconsin. I contacted him about doing . . . *My Goals Beyond* then talked to him about a permanent thing."[48] However, *My Goals Beyond* became known less for the ethno-fusion tracks—with the addition of bassist Charlie Haden, saxophonist Dave Liebman, drummer/percussionist Airto Moreira, and Indian musicians Mahalakshmi and Badal Roy—than for a side of solo acoustic guitar which became the forerunner of countless similar albums.

Gradually McLaughlin gathered around him like-minded sidemen, musi-cians who, as he put it, were "excited about playing music beyond category."

Miroslav Vitous recommended keyboard player Jan Hammer, who at the time was accompanying Sarah Vaughan. McLaughlin recruited Rick Laird on bass, with whom he had played in England. By then Laird had studied for two and a half years at Berklee and put in road time with the Buddy Rich Orchestra. The band started rehearsing in July 1971. "Right from the beginning we had a beautiful rapport," said McLaughlin. "One evening I was telling Sri Chinmoy that I got a band together and I wanted to give it a name, and he said 'We'll call it the Mahavishnu Orchestra.' I said, 'Mahavishnu Orchestra? This is going to take everybody out!'"[49]

The Mahavishnu Orchestra opened at Greenwich Village's Gaslight Café in July 1971 and so mesmerized audiences there that it was immediately held over. McLaughlin, dressed in white, was a striking figure using a double-necked guitar, at the time a great novelty. "It was because I always liked the 12-string," he explained. "I played 12-string with the Gordon Beck Quartet in England on *Experiments with Pops*. Twelve-string is great for arpeggios; I like arpeggios on guitar and the 12-string is perfect. Then I had a six-string for solos."[50]

McLaughlin's aim was to rehearse the band to the point where their performances became increasingly intuitive, with the goal of making each member capable of responding to the other's next move without thinking, reaching a kind of freedom within form. From the start, both rock and jazz critics expressed admiration for the Mahavishnu Orchestra and it is easy to see why. The group exhibited an astonishing degree of ensemble cohesion at blisteringly fast tempos and were unconstrained by unusual time signatures or abrupt changes of meter. Here was a band of virtuosos, and often, through tonal manipulation, it was difficult to discern who was playing what at a given moment: an electrified violin, a synthesizer, a guitar?

While there had been plenty of long, loud guitar solos in rock after the emergence of Cream and the San Francisco bands, McLaughlin brought a stunning technique allied to melodic invention and harmonic substance that left his fellow guitarists gasping. He was soon acknowledged as the most influential guitarist in jazz since Wes Montgomery. His virtuosity also provided inspiration to rock guitarists, helping contribute to a rise in instrumental proficiency in rock during the first half of the 1970s. While Mahavishnu represented virtuosity, it was virtuosity reinforced by intensity. Volume played an important role in the music. "By this time I'd been getting louder and louder with Tony [Williams]," said McLaughlin. "I was into loud music, I wanted to play loud. [Mahavishnu] was a powerful band."[51] But, as he has pointed out, without his experiences with Miles Davis and Lifetime, there would have been no Mahavishnu. "I was conscious of what I wanted to do, the way I wanted to play, nobody was doing," said McLaughlin. "But it took the years I spent with Tony and Miles to give me the possibility of giving birth to the form that I wanted to use, which was primarily expressed in the first Mahavishnu Orchestra."[52]

While at the Gaslight, Mahavishnu went into the recording studios to cut *The Inner Mounting Flame* in early August 1971. McLaughlin regarded the band as a

Billy Cobham: Swept to international recognition with the Mahavishnu Orchestra, Cobham became *the* drummer of the 1970s. (Courtesy of the Institute of Jazz Studies, Rutgers University.)

focus for his compositions, which were often as complex as any bebop lines, but merging a wide range of influences from rock to the Eastern cultures.[53] While the band had not quite shaken down into the unit it subsequently became in terms of ensemble cohesion and control at fast tempos, the album nevertheless remains an impressive statement that turned out to be more influential in its time than *Bitches Brew.* For all its innovative importance, *Brew* had often been turgid and congested with discursive melodies and soloing. *Inner Mounting Flame* represents the next decisive step in the evolution of jazz-rock fusion. The music was more focused in structure and rhythm, and the much-debated twilight zone between jazz and rock was filled with electronic energy suggested by Jimi Hendrix. Collective ensemble interplay was reinforced with an intensity that belied its spontaneity; in the setting of the Mahavishnu Orchestra, Cobham's role was elevated to that of an equal voice. McLaughlin realized that the new electronic technology demanded an update of old musical devices to produce a fresh instrumental approach. Mahavishnu's closely woven ensemble style was braced by well-rehearsed riffs and dramatic counterpoint that was given momentum by returning to an earlier jazz device of trading two- and four-bar statements. The result of this aerodynamic engineering was a ensemble modelled for speed and precision.

Nothing like the sound of "Meetings of the Spirit" or "The Noonward Race" had ever been heard in jazz or rock. The newness was in virtuosity itself. With the Mahavishnu Orchestra, McLaughlin conceptualized an effective context in which to focus his playing that was wholly unique. Here fast tempos and varied thematic lines were reinforced by a rhythmic complexity provided by the drumming of Cobham, which was quite new. Where Tony Williams assumed that audiences played the ground beat in their heads, leaving him free to create a rhythmic counterpoint to a pulse implied as much as explicitly stated, Cobham superimposed interesting meters beneath a composition and then gloried in subdividing the beat, cramming it with unusual grouping of notes played around the full range of his kit that set the standard for a new generation of stick-men in jazz and rock. If Tony Williams was a key drummer of the 1960s, then Cobham took over this mantle for the 1970s with performances such as "Vital Transformation" and "The Awakening."

The Inner Mounting Flame, to McLaughlin's surprise, reached 89 on the *Billboard* chart and, in jazz terms at least, became a major hit. "I didn't expect the success of Mahavishnu Orchestra," said McLaughlin. "No one was more surprised than me."[54] Even today, the album conveys the feeling of something new, that here was a significant technical advance in the music. "Its coherence and control comes as a shaft of light on the muddied and confused," said *Melody Maker;* "the effects of this remarkable album will be far reaching."[55] From its use of unusual time signatures, such as in "Dawn," which contains a shift in meter from 7/4 to 14/8, or in the polymetric and polytonal "The Dance of Maya," which contrasts 20/4 against 17/8, to the speed and dexterity of the unison phrasing of keyboards, violin, and guitar, new standards were being set in jazz. Even an old Lifetime number, "One with the Sun," originally with a Jack Bruce vocal, gets a facelift and appears as the instrumental "One Word." Thanks to the album's success, Mahavishnu moved onto the rock circuit, a move that distanced it from jazz audiences but placed it before younger fans raised on rock to whom such virtuosity was completely new.

The follow-up, *Birds of Fire,* recorded in September and October 1972, was released in 1973 and reached 15 on the *Billboard* chart, an incredible achievement for a jazz album. The title track is one of the band's most memorable pieces; in the unusual time signature of 18/8, it opens with an ominous crashing of a gong that leads into McLaughlin's dramatic theme statement on his overdriven guitar against a violin and bass ostinato before the guitar and violin state a theme that leads into passages of free-flowing improvisation.[56] All the compositions on *Birds of Fire* were by McLaughlin except Miles Davis's "Miles Beyond"; however, the inclusion of a tranquil numbers such as "Hope"—like "Lotus" on *Inner Mounting Flame*—could be somewhat disconcerting from a band of such unrelenting power and exuberance, sounding for all the world as if a different group entirely had wandered into the studio. The album also produced the only single released by the original Mahavishnu Orchestra, "Open Country Joy," which came out in Spain.

In 1973 Mahavishnu toured Europe. Videos of the band in concert[57] reveal that numbers they had performed on the debut album, which were already performed at very brisk tempos, had been speeded up further in what had become breathtaking displays of ensemble work and solo virtuosity. "Speed had become all important," observed *Melody Maker*. "[There] were many, many moments of punishing pace, abrupt gear changes and the acceleration almost crushed the breath from your lungs."[58] As he had in the group Dreams, Cobham emerged as a star. "His astounding dexterity makes one squint at the stage trying to peer through the perspex kit to see if there's not someone there with him," continued *Melody Maker*. "Two hands and two feet just AREN'T enough to play that way."[59]

On August 17–18, 1973, the band performed in Central Park and the concert was recorded by Columbia, from which three tracks were used for *Between Nothingness and Eternity—Live*. Live albums are always risky undertakings, but they do provide music's most vital life studies. Unlike the previous albums that contained eight and nine compositions, respectively, here perhaps is the most discursive of the early Mahavishnu albums, exposing McLaughlin's limitations as a writer. The twenty-one-minute "Dreams" filled one side of the original vinyl release, and is a series of fragmented episodes reminiscent of the long flights of fantasy undertaken by Flock. From the deliberate, suspended prelude it builds, via a series of accelerandos, to faster tempos, returning occasionally to the major-triad figure that ties the "visions" together. However, "Trilogy," three McLaughlin compositions segued into one long performance, opened the set with typical brio, imperiously announcing the premier jazz-rock band of the early 1970s. When the album was released at the end of 1973 its five-star rating from *Downbeat* was claimed as a matter of course; however, its showing on the *Billboard* chart at 41 was a disappointment, "McLaughlin's music does not so much progress as repeat itself," said *Rolling Stone*. "Even the most incandescent licks lose a great deal of firepower the third time around."[60]

However, for all the on-stage demonstrations of mutual love, fault lines had begun to form in the band. Mahavishnu was a microcosm of the sixties' preoccupation with alternative religions and philosophies. Often bad experiences with drugs were behind a search for alternative paths towards spiritual enlightenment—which in many instances became a case of substituting one habit (drugs) for another (Eastern religion). McLaughlin had thrown himself into the teachings of his Indian guru Sri Chinmoy with all the fervor of a born-again evangelist, often beginning concerts dedicating his music "to the Supreme Lord, the Supreme Musician." During the band's tour through Germany, one television interview with McLaughlin saw him talking less about music, more about the wonders of spiritual enlightenment. "[John had] talked about the fact he used to be into smoking and drugs and stuff," said Billy Cobham, "and he did something bold in a way, because he went from there completely over to the other side—no smoking, no drugs whatsoever—totally vegetarian, cleansing his system, and to me that's an indication of someone trying to find peace of mind."[61] Other members of the band were not so philosophical about McLaughlin's spiritual quest and all that it implied: meditation, diet, India, and religion. "The real problem was with Jan Hammer and Jerry Goodman," said McLaughlin. "They were really heavily against it. Finally it became a big psychosis."[62]

While in London in 1973, an attempt to paper over the cracks was made by recording originals from the rest of the band; it was a failure. "That recording date was a disaster," said Rick Laird. "We salvaged nothing from it. After five days I remember John leaving the date crying."[63] Meanwhile, McLaughlin went on tour with Carlos Santana—who had also become a convert to Sri Chinmoy's teachings—in the fall of 1973, promoting their joint album *Love Devotion Surrender,* which had been released in July. Eventually going gold (half a million sales), the album drew on a mix of Lifetime, Mahavishnu, and Santana members including Larry Young, Billy Cobham, Jan Hammer, bassist Doug Rauch, and Armando Peraza among sundry percussionists. A series of ecstatic jams on Coltrane and Coltrane-influenced material, a distinct Mahavishnu Orchestra influence pervades "The Love Divine," while Coltrane's "A Love Supreme" reflects the Santana band's approach, with both guitarists able to inhabit each other's world without any stylistic incongruity. The extended "Let Us Go Into the House of the Lord" works well—which McLaughlin's equally elongated "Dreams" did not—while Coltrane's "Naima" is an ecstatic acoustic guitar duet. "McLaughlin . . . introduced me to Coltrane's 'Naima,'" said Santana. "He taught me the chord changes, the melody and everything. We thought it was a very spiritual and meditative mood."[64] With two large color photos of Sri Chinmoy adorning the gatefold album and an essay on peace and love by Chinmoy himself, the accent was unmistakably on matters mystagogic.

McLaughlin's piety and the Santana tour served only to exacerbate the feelings that were coming to a head in the Mahavishnu Orchestra. "We went to Japan and it didn't get better. It got worse. . . . It also had to do with success. You know, success is hard to take," continued McLaughlin.[65] When the tour was over, the pressure of some 200 one-nighters in the U.S. in 1972 and 250 days on the road in 1973 came to a head with an interview Jan Hammer gave to *Crawdaddy* magazine. "Jan Hammer sort of put John down," said Cobham. "[John] really took it hard and that started everything off again. That was the beginning of the end."[66] The band's last concert was given on December 29, 1973 in Detroit, and the members went their separate ways; "The Inner Mounting Flame Goes Out" noted *Downbeat.*[67] Even in the mid-1980s, when McLaughlin proposed a reunion concert of the original Mahavishnu Orchestra with the proceeds going to charity, old enmities remained.

The first three albums by the Mahavishnu Orchestra dramatically altered the musical landscape of the burgeoning jazz-rock movement. Today they remain benchmarks of ensemble cohesion and inspired improvisation, and they sparked off a host of imitators who exploited speed of execution and flashy unison riffs, using them as an end to themselves, as did an album by Goodman and Hammer, *Like Children,* made after Mahavishnu broke up. In contrast, Billy Cobham, whose playing was such an integral part of the Mahavishnu sound and who once said the band's super-intensity had forced him to "compete physically" in terms of stamina and speed,[68] consciously avoided creating a similarly super-intense context to feature his playing. His first recording under his own name had been made several months before Mahavishnu split, during a week's break from touring in May 1973, fuelling speculation that he was about to leave. Leaving, however, was not on his mind. The date had come about through the frustration of not having his own material played by the Mahavishnu Orchestra. Released on October 1, 1973, *Spectrum* was eclectic, loose, and funky, something Mahavishnu was not. It was well received, remaining on *Billboard*'s album chart for over five months, and today is regarded as something of a jazz-rock classic thanks to the presence of the late Tommy Bolin, a rock guitarist of great promise, who played in all but two numbers.

At the end of 1973 Cobham—still technically a member of the Mahavishnu Orchestra—cut *Crosswinds,* a concept album, and was pondering the possibilities of putting together a band to promote it with Mahavishnu manager Nat Weiss. Recorded with Randy Brecker on trumpet, Garnett Brown on trombone, Mike Brecker on tenor sax, John Abercrombie on guitar, George Duke on keyboards, and John Williams on bass, the album's centerpiece was the four-piece suite "Spanish Moss: A Sound Portrait," intended to be a representation of where Cobham saw his music at that point in his career. In the fourth movement, "Flash Flood," Duke plays in a meter of five and Cobham and the horns in four under Abercrombie's solo, changing to a meter of 17/4 for Randy Brecker's solo. The piece evoked the Dreams' "New York Suite."

When Mahavishnu split up, Cobham hastily went ahead with his own band, called modestly "Billy Cobham." Using the *Crosswinds* personnel, the road band substituted Milcho Leviev in on keyboards, Alex Blake on bass, and Glenn Ferris on trombone. "Billy Cobham" opened at My Father's Place on Long Island in New York at the end of March 1974 and then embarked on a short tour as an opening act for the Doobie Brothers, returning to New York at Easter.

However, in July a disastrous European tour followed—eight gigs in one month—and Cobham struggled to keep the band together. The live album *Shabazz* documented their concerts at the Montreux Jazz Festival and at London's Rainbow Theatre but offered little in imaginative ensemble writing, relying on the old hard-bop formula of head-solos-head. The Breckers, Ferris, Abercrombie, and Leviev grappled manfully with long tracts of solo space goaded by Cobham's inspirational drumming. A virtually unchanged personnel cut *Total Eclipse,* which saw Cobham increasingly intent on the maximization of his commercial potential. In spring 1975 the band were on the West Coast, where they cut *A Funky Thide of Sings,* but immediately afterwards the Breckers left to tour with their own band, leaving Cobham searching for replacements for an upcoming European tour.

Frustrated with his lack of commercial success on the touring circuits, Cobham consciously attempted to frame his music for the widest possible appeal. "I have to put something out that is going to be saleable," he said, "and not just to a select jazz audience either. I mean mass appeal. . . . Some may call it prostitution; I still call it music."[69] The trade advertising for *A Funky Thide of Sings* took up this theme: "Yes! It's the Funkiest Billy Cobham album since *Spectrum.* It's an album you can dance to as well as listen! You know—Funky."[70]

Still using the Brecker Brothers, but now with Tom Malone on trombone and John Scofield on guitar, Cobham's writing did little justice to his drumming skills. Live, however, his incendiary stickwork could still pull the crowds, irrespective of his musical surroundings, although he had now slid onto second-rate tour circuits. Even so, in early 1976 he set an attendance record at New York's Bottom Line, with a new group. Through the late 1970s, with varying personnel and on various records, Cobham continued to struggle to define both the context and content of his music.

Newly signed to Columbia in 1977, he was invited to appear as part of a "supergroup" that CBS presented at the Montreux Jazz Festival in July. A slimmed-down version of the group was assembled in November–December for a four-week tour. Comprising Cobham, Tom Scott on reeds, Steve Khan on guitar, Mark Soskin on keyboards, and Alphonso Johnson on bass, the group produced a live memento of the tour, *Alivemutherforya*, with each artist doing a party piece from his latest Columbia offering. Disenchanted after playing in the *Saturday Night Live* TV showband during 1978–1979, Cobham moved to Zurich in 1980. Although he was asked to join a Mahavishnu tour/reunion in 1984, Cobham discovered soon after that the tour was already underway with another drummer taking his place. He returned to the United States to work and record with the rock band Bobby and the Midnights, featuring Bob Weir from the Grateful Dead, and then signed with the GRP label, garnering a Grammy nomination for "Zanzibar Breeze" from his 1986 album *Power Play*. Ultimately, Cobham's solo career never lived up to his initial reputation. Virtuosity as an end in itself was not enough—his artistic choices, often dictated by commercial rather than aesthetic motives, appeared to stand in the way of him becoming anything more than "the great drummer who used to play with Mahavishnu."

Meanwhile, by early 1974 McLaughlin had drawn together a new Mahavishnu ensemble with violinist Jean-Luc Ponty, Gayle Moran on keyboards and occasional vocals, Ralphe Armstrong on bass, and Michael Walden on drums,[71] plus a string trio and two horns. The grandiosity of Mahavishnu Mark II seems a reflection of the times, particularly in the context of what was happening in art and progressive rock, where groups were filling stadiums with theatrical pomp—lights, costumes, and elaborate stage sets. The group's album *Apocalypse,* recorded in London in March 1974 with the London Symphony Orchestra, conducted by Michael Tilson Thomas, and produced by George Martin—whom McLaughlin had got to know from his London session-musician days—remains a somewhat overblown experiment. "Once you're past the terrible poetry of Sri Chinmoy—which doesn't, unfortunately, stay on the cover as usual . . . there are the usual amounts of good music and fine playing, but I'm not about to filter off the noise of eighty gents in evening dress or ignore the painfully banal mantras of the Chinmoy brood just to get next to Johnny Mac's real business," quipped the *New Musical Express*.[72] What McLaughlin had created was not so much an evolution into something greater but into something that was not as great; his playing, though impressive, did not come across as inspiring within the larger context.

Later in 1974, perhaps realizing that the symphony experiment was not totally successful, McLaughlin cut *Visions of the Emerald Beyond* with a drastically pared-down string section. Originally conceived as a double album—with the second album planned to be a series of acoustic duets with his wife Eve McLaughlin—the concept was shelved in favor of the group's high-octane stuff. But even this was not wholly successful. Jean-Luc Ponty demonstrates a greater degree of virtuosity than Goodman, but by now there was a feeling among McLaughlin's fans that the band were coasting on their reputation, substituting speed for substance. Nonetheless, the powerful "Eternity's Breath (Parts I and II)"—despite incorporating a somewhat disconcerting use of voices that was one of the album's distracting features—uses subtle rhythmic devices such as two bars of five punctuating a line of four, while on "Part II" the five figure reappears in the bass line. "Can't Stand Your Funk," released as a single in the U.K. in 1975, uses a 10/8 meter and includes moments of free blowing humor in their bow to soul music, while "Lila's Dance" seemed reminiscent of Flock.

In the spring of 1975, Gayle Moran left, replaced by Stu Goldberg, and just as the band were about to embark on an extensive tour, Jean-Luc Ponty pulled out.[73] Barely six months before, Ponty had declared that he had found a soul mate in John McLaughlin and that their working relationship would be a lasting one. But after just two albums and barely a year together their relationship ended on a sour note. "I left earlier than I thought I would," Ponty admitted at the time, "mostly because of an incident which occurred over a copyright matter which upset me. McLaughlin asked me to perform a solo with Echoplex which was quite personal and I didn't realize it would become a separate track ['Opus 1,' fifteen seconds] credited to McLaughlin's composition. This has become a big matter between me, his management and his record company, and this is what finally made me decide to leave, although I had other personal grievances. . . . If I could have found a space within his band to make my own personal statements, then I think I might of [sic] stayed a long time. . . . From the very first note it was whooosh! So fast, no room for any dynamics. I kept wanting to stop the music and say 'Hey, what's happening?' Mahavishnu was sometimes like a car that could only function at 100 miles an hour. Crazy."[74]

Also hastening Ponty's departure was the release in May 1975 of his solo album *Upon the Wings of Music,* featuring the keyboard prodigy Patrice Rushen, the Mahavishnu bassist Ralph Armstrong, the guitarists Dan Sawyer and Ray Parker, and the drummer Ndugu Chancler. It turned out to be a surprisingly gentle fusion album for the former Frank Zappa violinist who had appeared on seminal Zappa classics like *Hot Rats* and *Apostrophe (')* and who in 1970 impressed on *King Kong,* an album-length exploration of Zappa compositions. Prior to joining Zappa, he and the pianist George Duke made *The Jean-Luc Ponty Experience* in September 1969. A live album recorded at The Experience in San Francisco, it was an early example of jazz-rock that combined bebop-derived improvisation over a rock beat. During their stay at the club, Frank Zappa frequently sat in with the group (although he is not on the album): "A mixture occurred at The Experience and it could not have been more successful. . . . [The audience] didn't look on Ponty's music as jazz or jazz-rock or any other force-fed label; it had a good beat, was unusual and exciting and was done with taste. . . . The set closed with a jam with Frank Zappa on guitar. Avant garde to say the least," said *Cash Box*.[75] Subsequently, Duke and Ponty would emerge as important Zappa sidemen during the 1970s.

In 1976, Ponty's regular band—Daryl Stuermer on guitars, Allan Zavod on keyboards, Tom Fowler on bass, and Mark Craney on drums—cut *Aurora* and *Imaginary Voyage,* which established the musical terrain the band would continue to explore for almost twenty years. Ponty, classically trained at the Paris Conservatoire, where he won the "Premier Prix" at seventeen, was both a formidable technician and a resourceful composer. His rhythmically complex, virtuostic style remained solidly in a jazz-rock vein (as opposed to jazz-funk) that owed much to the Mahavishnu Orchestra by harnessing their energy and complexity and combining it with a romantic, rhapsodic ingredient that added a soaring quality to his performances. Ponty's bands were remarkably consistent, and through constant touring, he picked up a considerable following, despite negligible airplay.

Album followed album—*Enigmatic Ocean* from 1976, *Cosmic Messenger* from 1977—but it was not until *Live,* from a December 1978 concert in Los Angeles, that the band's mechanical precision was matched by a certain flamboyance that more readily communicated the sense of drama they could convey in live performance. Containing some of Ponty's best compositions—"Aurora" from his second album, "Imaginary Voyage Parts III and IV" from his third album, "Egocentric Molecules" from *Cosmic Messenger,* plus "No Strings Attached" and "Mirage"—the band had shaken down into a cohesive, authoritative unit, if somewhat derivative. Even so, Ponty took the best of his previous mentors—Zappa and McLaughlin—to produce a band that seemed to be hitting its prime just as the jazz-rock era was coming to a close. Although much of this excitement began to wear thin as the 1980s progressed, Ponty's musicianship was never less than excellent even if the band became increasingly laden with electronic technology.

With Ponty's depature in 1975, the Mahavishnu Orchestra seemed to run out of steam. McLaughlin's interest in things Eastern culminated in his acoustic group Shakti, with whom he had begun performing in mid-1974. Their first album, *Shakti with John McLaughlin,* was recorded live at Southampton College, Long Island, New York, on July 5, 1975.[76] Meanwhile, the Mahavishnu Orchestra cut their final album of the 1970s during July and August 1975 in Herouville, France. *Inner Worlds* is almost unrecognizable from the group's earlier triumphs. It struggled to get one star in *Downbeat,* and the group was wound up shortly afterwards, McLaughlin claiming it did not have "enough cohesion."[77]

But if Mahavishnu was finished, McLaughlin was not. Having all but defined jazz-rock in the early 1970s, his career went in countless directions, with Shakti, the One Truth Band, and the best-selling acoustic-guitar trio with Al DiMeola and Paco de Lucia. McLaughlin headed a surprisingly lackluster 1980s version of Mahavishnu, in which he used a synthesized guitar interfaced with the Synclavier

Digital Music System. He also recorded again with Miles Davis in the 1980s on *You're Under Arrest* and *Aura*, and he appeared with him at La Grande Hall de la Vilette in Paris, in July 1985 and July 1991. The eighties saw a dazzling array of recordings in many styles, including a return to hard-bop for the soundtrack of the film *Round Midnight;* session work on albums by Stanley Clarke, the saxophonist Bill Evans, Danny Gottlieb, and Zakir Hussain; an appearance with the Gil Evans Orchestra at the Ravenna Festival in Italy in 1986; a return to symphonic aspirations with his *Mediterranean Concerto;* working as a producer for his second wife, the pianist Katia Labeque; in a trio with percussionist Trilok Gurtu on *Qué Alegria;* and performing a tribute to the pianist Bill Evans with a string quartet on *Time Remembered.*

In 1996, McLaughlin recorded *The Promise,* which featured a variety of performing situations including a return to authentic jazz-rock fusion. "I wanted that fusion feel on *The Promise,*" he said. "I love fusion; it's part of me. It's degenerated, but I don't care."[78] His flat-out playing on "Jazz Jungle" alongside Mike Brecker is an album highlight and a reminder of how powerful the idiom could be in the hands of musicians of integrity. However, perhaps the most enduring of all the albums, private tapes, and videos that document the latter part of McLaughlin's career are his recordings with Free Spirits (his "power trio," with organist Joey DeFrancesco and drummer Dennis Chambers)—*Tokyo Live* (1993) and *After the Rain* (1994), with Elvin Jones on drums. Since the demise of Shakti in 1978, McLaughlin seemed like a player in search of a context. But in returning to the Hammond organ, an instrument that played such an important part of his early career—with Georgie Fame and Graham Bond in 1960s London and with Larry Young in Lifetime—the wheel seemed to have turned full circle.

Many musicians, having made their mark early on, seldom dared to expose themselves to new challenges on such a scale as McLaughlin did, with all the attendant risk of failure. Yet he has remained faithful to his creative muse, despite periods of critical opprobrium, and unlike many of his contemporaries he has addressed himself to new ideas and new technology as willingly as he did at the outset of his career. "You gotta go that extra mile," he said in 1996. "However much you put into music, you get paid back manyfold, but only if you go the extra mile. You sleep less, work harder otherwise it stays superficial."[79]

Notes

1. *Rolling Stone,* December 13, 1969, p. 33.
2. Ibid.
3. Ibid.
4. Liner notes by Sam Rivers from his 1964 album *Fuchsia Swing Song* (Blue Note BN BLP4184).
5. It was not released for seventeen years, during which time it was always assumed that his second date with the saxophonist, *One Step Beyond* from April that year, was his debut on vinyl.
6. *Downbeat,* January 29, 1976, pp. 16–17.
7. Ibid.

8. McLaughlin's love of Reinhardt's partner, Stephane Grappelli, formed the basis of his lifelong affinity with the sound of the violin in jazz.
9. Liner notes, *Little Boy Blue* (Edsel EDCD 356).
10. Interview in *Jazz Forum,* unprovenanced. Courtesy National Sound Archive, London, p. 32.
11. Ibid.
12. For example, *Extrapolation* is not mentioned in *The New Grove Dictionary of Jazz* (Macmillan Press, London, 1988).
13. Interview in *Jazz Forum,* unprovenanced. Courtesy National Sound Archive, London, p. 32.
14. National Sound Archive, London, whose files give the October 1968 date. However, in a report in *Melody Maker* (April 19, 1969, p. 4), McLaughlin says, "It's possible that I'll be recording some tracks with Chick Corea, probably with Dave Holland and Jack DeJohnette." It is possible that these recordings could be of a later provenance, but they are nonetheless advanced in their conceptualization of a true jazz-rock fusion.
15. *Downbeat,* July 18, 1974, p. 35.
16. *Jazz-Rock Fusion,* by Julie Coryell and Laura Friedman (Marion Boyars, Boston, 1978), pp. 128–129.
17. *Miles: The Autobiography,* by Miles Davis and Quincy Troupe (Macmillan, London, 1990), p. 286.
18. Interview in *Jazz Forum,* unprovenanced. Courtesy National Sound Archive, London, p. 32.
19. *Milestones II: The Music and Times of Miles Davis since 1960,* by Jack Chambers (University of Toronto Press, Toronto, 1985), p. 224.
20. *Downbeat,* May 29, 1969, p. 29.
21. Interview in *Jazz Forum,* unprovenanced. Courtesy National Sound Archive, London, p. 32.
22. Interview with the author, October 20, 1996.
23. Interview in *Jazz Forum,* unprovenanced. Courtesy National Sound Archive, London.
24. *Record Collector,* unprovenanced. Courtesy National Sound Archive, London, p. 107.
25. *Jimi Hendrix: Electric Gypsy,* by Harry Shapiro and Caesar Glebbeek (Mandarin, London, 1992), p. 364.
26. *Downbeat,* January 29, 1976, p. 17.
27. Ibid., February 5, 1970, p. 22.
28. Unissued live tapes of Lifetime, probably broadcast from Slug's, New York City, middle to late 1969. Two source tapes of the same session. Courtesy National Sound Archive, London.
29. Advertisement in the trade press, October 1969.
30. *Downbeat,* January 29, 1976, p. 16.
31. Gleason's review of the 1969 Monterey Jazz Festival for the *San Francisco Chronicle,* reproduced in *Dizzy, Duke, The Count and Me,* by Jimmy Lyons with Irma Kamin (California Living Books, California), p. 167.
32. *Melody Maker,* January 17, 1970, p. 30.
33. Ibid., April 4, 1970, p. 16.
34. Ibid.
35. *Rolling Stone,* September 17, 1970, p. 44.
36. *Wire,* April 1997, p. 4.
37. *Rolling Stone,* January 7, 1971, p. 14.
38. *Melody Maker,* January 15, 1972, p. 28.
39. *Zig Zag,* issue no. 22 (unprovenanced). Courtesy National Sound Archive, London, p. 29.
40. *Rolling Stone,* March 29, 1973, p. 43.
41. *Wire,* January 1997, p. 37.
42. Conversation with the author, August 5, 1997.
43. Ibid.
44. *Zig Zag,* issue no. 22 (unprovenanced). Courtesy National Sound Archive, London, p. 4.

45. Interview in *Jazz Forum*, unprovenanced. Courtesy National Sound Archive, London, p. 33.
46. Pye Records trade advertisement, Spring 1975.
47. *Downbeat,* June 7, 1973, p. 46.
48. Ibid.
49. Interview in *Jazz Forum*, unprovenanced. Courtesy National Sound Archive, London, p. 34.
50. Interview in *Record Collector,* unprovenanced. Courtesy National Sound Archive, London, p. 108.
51. Ibid.
52. *Jazz-Rock Fusion,* by Julie Coryell and Laura Friedman (Marion Boyars, Boston, 1978), p. 129.
53. Prompted by an interest in Eastern religions stimulated several years earlier by Graham Bond. In fact, the riff of "Vital Transformation" has a distinct resemblance to an old Graham Bond number that McLaughlin used to play, "Baby Be Good to Me," while he was a member of The Organisation.
54. *Black Music & Jazz Review,* December 1978, p. 12.
55. *Melody Maker,* April 1, 1972, p. 28.
56. In April 1973, Don Sebesky scored the number for full orchestra for his *Giant Box* (Epic 450564-2) album, combining it with an extract from Stravinsky's "Firebird Suite." It was an interesting idea that might have worked better had the ensemble performed with more authority and sensitivity.
57. Courtesy National Sound Archive, London.
58. *Melody Maker,* July 7, 1973, p. 46.
59. Ibid.
60. *Rolling Stone,* February 28, 1974, p. 41.
61. *Melody Maker,* February 2, 1974, p. 15.
62. Interview in *Jazz Forum*, unprovenanced. Courtesy National Sound Archive, London, p. 34.
63. *Rolling Stone,* February 28, 1974, p. 11.
64. Liner notes, *Santana: Dance of the Rainbow Serpent* (Columbia Legacy CK64605), p. 20.
65. Interview in *Jazz Forum*, unprovenanced. Courtesy National Sound Archive, London, p. 34.
66. *Melody Maker,* February 2, 1974, p. 67.
67. *Downbeat,* February 14, 1974, p. 9.
68. Ibid., October 12, 1972, p. 15.
69. Ibid., December 4, 1975, p. 40.
70. Trade advertisement, February 1976.
71. Walden would later become one of pop music's top producers, for Whitney Houston, Kenny G, and others.
72. *New Musical Express,* June 1, 1974, p. 21.
73. McLaughlin was forced to embark on the tour without a replacement, and a truncated version of the band formed part of a double-header with the Jeff Beck Group, at that time enjoying chart success with *Blow by Blow,* the ex-Yardbird's unexpected diversion into fusion. "If you can only get to one concert this season," said the national publicity campaign, "this is the one."
74. *Melody Maker,* August 30, 1975, p. 18.
75. *Cash Box,* September 27, 1969.
76. McLaughlin's interest in Indian music dated back to his days on the British jazz scene, when Joe Harriott and John Mayer caused a stir with an album called *Indo-Jazz Suite* in 1966 that combined a five-piece jazz unit and four Indian musicians. On "Raga Megha," for example, Harriott improvised impressively over an authentic raga format.
77. *Downbeat,* June 15, 1978, p. 48.
78. Ibid., June 1996, p. 23.
79. *Guitar Player,* April 1996, p. 102.

CHAPTER 9

The Mysterious Travellers

In September 1959 Miles Davis made a final but unsuccessful attempt to dissuade alto saxophonist Julian "Cannonball" Adderley from leaving his sextet. Despite offering him a guaranteed annual salary of $20,000, far more than he could reasonably expect to make on his own, Adderley declined, choosing to re-form a quintet with his brother Nat on cornet. He was confident that this new group—with Bobby Timmons on piano, Sam Jones on bass, and Louis Hayes on drums—would succeed after his two years as a featured sideman with Davis.

Opening on September 21 in Philadelphia, at a salary of $1,500 a week, Adderley's new group was recorded live the following month at San Francisco's Jazz Workshop and the results released as *Cannonball Adderley in San Francisco.* One original tune by Timmons, "Dis Here," became a minor hit, and the band was on its way. Full of gospel hues, it set the tone of the group which, although rooted in bop, soon established a niche in what had become known as "soul-jazz," a back-to-the-roots style that was blues-and-gospel oriented and often enlivened with a strong backbeat.[1]

Timmons's "Dis Here" immediately struck a chord with both black and white audiences and was soon followed by "Dat Dere." Brother Nat contributed two more hits with "Work Song" and "Jive Samba," helping the Adderley quintet become one of the most popular jazz attractions of the 1960s. From January 1962 to July 1965 the group became a sextet, with the addition of a tenor player, first Yusef Lateef and later Charles Lloyd. However, after that, Adderley returned to a quintet setup because of economics and, as he noted wryly, "It's almost a rule of thumb that tenor players are long-winded types, and even when we would restrict the number of choruses ahead of time, tenor players would seem to run over. No brevity!"[2]

However, the most significant new player in Adderley's group was the Austrian pianist Joe Zawinul.[3] Beginning on accordion as a child, Zawinul had studied piano for several years with Valerie Zschorney, a pupil of Professor Weingartner who had in turn been taught by Franz Liszt. Zawinul subsequently worked on Austrian radio, as house pianist for Polydor records, and for several European jazz groups including that of Friedrich Gulda, with whom he was

158

Cannonball Adderley: The alto saxophone virtuoso came to personify "soul jazz." (Courtesy of the Institute of Jazz Studies, Rutgers University.)

closely associated, in which he played trumpet, bass trumpet, trombone, and clarinet. However, Zawinul realized that to really make it in jazz he had to move to America. He obtained a Berklee scholarship in 1959, but had only attended a few classes when he was offered the piano chair in Maynard Ferguson's big band, then regarded as one of the hippest ensembles in jazz, with a concentration of young talent and a fresh new book of arrangements by Willie Maiden, Slide Hampton, and Don Sebesky. Zawinul's fluent style was featured on Ferguson's *A Message from Birdland,* recorded live at Birdland on June 17, 1959.[4] By then he had already recorded his first album in the U.S., *To You With Love,* for the cut-price Strand label, sold at supermarket checkouts.

While with Ferguson, the trombonist Slide Hampton introduced Zawinul to an up-and-coming young tenor player named Wayne Shorter at the Ham 'n' Eggs, a small coffee shop near Birdland. Together they persuaded him to audition for the band. Beating out Eddie Harris and George Coleman, Shorter won the seat, albeit only staying for four weeks before departing to join Art Blakey's Jazz Messengers. Zawinul left a few months later after a clash with Ferguson and spent almost two years accompanying Dinah Washington, appearing on her hit record "What a Difference a Day Makes." Leaving Washington in March 1961, he worked briefly with the Joe Williams–Harry Edison group and saxophonist Yusef Lateef. In June, he accepted Cannonball Adderley's offer to join his quintet.

Zawinul brought thoughtfully constructed solos and restraint to a band that was often explicitly exuberant. His long, fast, sixteenth-note lines appear derived from Bud Powell through George Shearing, and his phrase construction was often extremely melodic. His use of bluesy figures seemed inspired by the pianist Red Garland, but already these aspects of his playing were being drawn into a very personal style. By the mid-1960s, key elements in Zawinul's playing were coalescing, most notably an aversion to cliché, an avoidance of the obvious, both rhythmically and harmonically, and a greater restraint in his playing inspired by Ahmad Jamal. "I tried to leave enough room for the players *and* for the audience," he explained.[5]

In early 1964 the band toured Europe, including several dates in Britain. Since the 1930s the British Musicians' Union had succeeded in securing a ludicrous ban on visiting American musicians unless British musicians enjoyed reciprocity of employment in the United States. Adderley's group was able to appear in Britain because an exchange group had been booked on a nationwide tour of the States. At the time, Adderley scarcely gave a thought to the group who made his appearance in Britain possible, but when he returned home he would never forget them. The Beatles transformed the music business in the United States almost overnight, and by 1967 the explosion of popular culture they triggered was sufficient to cause him to diversify an already extensive repertoire that ranged from uncompromising bop numbers such as "Dizzy's Business," "Bohemia After Dark," and "Gemini" to gospel-influenced numbers like "Work Song," "Trouble in Mind," and "Sack O' Woe." But any concessions to current musical fashion were achieved on Adderley's terms. "We don't take a hit rock and roll tune and play a jazz version of it," he asserted. "We create our music from within our group."[6]

Adderley had in mind the remarkable success of the Ramsey Lewis trio, whose version of "The 'In' Crowd" had recently earned a gold disc. Recorded live in the Bohemian Caverns, Washington, D.C., in May 1965, it became one of the biggest instrumental hits of the 1960s, triggering a string of similar "funky" covers of current pop songs. Lewis, the son of a gospel choirmaster, had signed to Phil Chess's Argo label in 1955 at the instigation of the Chicago DJ Daddy-O Daylie. A graduate of Chicago Music College and DePaul University, Lewis projected a funky, earthy feeling in his playing that reflected his gospel roots.

The Lewis trio's debut album, *Ramsey Lewis and his Gentlemen of Swing,* recorded in December 1956, included a jazzed-up version of Bizet's "Carmen" garnering them their first airplay. Thereafter, the group made a point of always including a "fun song" in their repertoire. In 1961 their single "Blues for the Night Owl" revealed their rapport with the blues. Like Avery Parrish's "After

Hours" from 1940, it comprised a string of public-domain blues riffs that were made effective through the group's conviction and soul. The first sign of a break-through came with *At the Bohemian Caverns,* recorded in June of 1964. Their "fun song" from that set, Chris Kenner's "Something You Got," generated R&B and pop airplay and was responsible for the album reaching number 63 on the pop charts.

Within a year, the group was back at the Caverns for a follow-up. This time, however, they had not yet selected their customary "fun song" for the set. While they were discussing possible alternatives over a coffee, their waitress Nettie Grey suggested a then-popular vocal hit by Dobie Gray called "The 'In' Crowd," written by the Los Angeles composer Billy Page. The crowd reaction when they played it that night was extraordinary. "As soon as we began playing it," recalled Lewis, "people started clapping, singing along, stomping. The feeling was incred-ibly infectious. We knew right away we had something special."[7] After nine years of moderate achievement, most of it in their native Chicago, the group were an overnight success, going from $2,500 a week to $6,500. The eponymously titled album reached number two on the charts and the single reached number five, earning the group a bucketful of music industry awards including a Grammy for "Best Instrumental of 1965."

"The 'In' Crowd" was a showcase for Lewis's simple, direct playing over a funky backbeat. "It's an interesting thing," he reflected in 1965, "the Bohemian Caverns is the kind of room where Monk and Coltrane play—representatives of what you'd call the real hard jazz in the purest sense. Yet when we play a thing like this, those audiences would react in what some people would call a square manner—clapping hands and singing along, the whole bit."[8] Those square rhythm patterns—gospel-like clapping on the second and fourth beats that accentuated the backbeat—and crowd atmosphere all contributed to what still remains an undeniably engaging performance. The whole point of the record is not its technical accomplishment, but the projection of a mood with its good-time feel. It remains, however, a jazz performance by a jazz group, and its pres-ence on the charts towering over the likes of Bob Dylan, the Beach Boys, and the Dave Clark Five came as a surprise to everyone in 1965, including Lewis himself. It reflected the changing climate of the sixties; audiences did not want to be bat-tered and tested by free jazz, they wanted to have a good time, and this is what Lewis gave them. "The most intricate chord in the whole thing, I think, is a sev-enth," he quipped.[9]

This simple, catchy formula was repeated with Lewis's covers of "Hang On Sloopy," which went to number 11 four months later, and "A Hard Days Night," which peaked at 29. This new-found fame and fortune was too much for the group to handle, however, and they split up.[10] Lewis formed a new group with the bassist Cleveland Eaton and the Chess house drummer Maurice White.[11] This new trio's first venture was an orchestral album recorded in May 1966 with arrangements by Richard Evans that included a reworking of the gospel stan-dard "Wade in Water." Released as a single, it immediately hit the big time, reaching number 19 on the charts. The single featured an over-recorded backbeat and Lewis's funky, blues-drenched piano. Fifteen years later Dizzy Gillespie made a comment that Lewis was playing "fusion" years ahead of its time. In Britain, where it reached 31 on the record charts, "Wade In Water" was immediately picked up by the Graham Bond Organisation, for whom the number became a signature tune.

Ramsey's high-profile hits, combining jazz improvisation with a solid backbeat associated with rock rhythms, represented an important marker along the way that pointed towards a confluence between jazz and popular culture. Jazz had ventured onto the Top 20 before in the 1960s, when Dave Brubeck's "Take Five" became an unexpected hit, but this was on its own terms. Soul-jazz was something different, and several earlier hits in the genre had already begun to cross over into the pop charts, including numbers such as "Comin' Home Baby," "Gravy Waltz," and "Watermelon Man." And while jazz artists like Horace Silver had played funky and bluesy-styled tunes before, soul-jazz exploited the sound of flatted thirds and sevenths and plagal cadences as an integral part of a music whose direction could be heard at its most explicit in the 1950s recordings of Ray Charles—dubbed the High Priest of Soul—and later in soul artists such as Aretha Franklin and James Brown. Soul-jazz went that extra mile towards an accommodation with popular culture to establish its rhythmic point of view as an important element in the jazz lexicon of the 1960s.[12]

However, the only jazz artist in the 1960s to get into the Top 20 after Ramsey Lewis's successes was Cannonball Adderley, who for many had come to personify the soul-jazz trend. "Let's say soul-jazz has developed along the lines of old things [the blues] utilizing elements of contemporary beats," he once explained.[13] On *Mercy, Mercy, Mercy: Live at "The Club,"* released in March 1967, Adderley mixed bop and blues with soul-jazz. On the title track, an original composition by Joe Zawinul, Zawinul plays the electric piano. While it might not have been the first time the instrument was used in jazz, it certainly became the most famous.[14] It immediately changed the tonal climate of the group; here was a contemporary sound, even though the style of Adderley's quintet remained unaltered. The song provided him with his biggest hit, which won a Grammy award for "Best Instrumental Performance of 1967," and national attention. "We were so popular that Bill Graham had us open for the Who," said Zawinul. "It might seem funny now, but people liked it! We played with Zappa, all kinds of people. Cannonball crossed over, that's a good word, he crossed over into something else where you bring people into your music."[15]

Adderley's next album, *74 Miles Away,* was also recorded live. In "Walk Tall," Zawinul uses the new Fender-Rhodes piano, which had been recommended to him by Victor Feldman. His attack is percussive and he makes use of distortion, something he also does in the title track on acoustic piano. During the front-line solos on "74 Miles Away," Cannonball and Nat used a tambourine to reinforce the highly rhythmical nature of the performance. When the tambourine was not in use, Zawinul placed it inside the grand piano, over the piano strings around the area of middle-C, constructing his solo using a mixture of tones distorted by the tambourine and "open" tones. By alternating the percussive sound of the strings covered by the tambourine with the rest of the piano, his solo becomes an object lesson in tension and release. When the tambourine is finally removed, his solo builds expansively to a climax. "'74 Miles Away' was in 7/4, but with a feeling like you didn't know it was," Zawinul explained. "I always like a strong approach to jazz, so I wrote it with a great rhythmic feel, it was not just a tiss-tikka-tiss cymbal beat. I don't like lightweight stuff, even the stuff I did with Miles, I didn't like so much. Too light!"[16]

This use of distortion was no accident. Zawinul regarded musical instruments as tools, vehicles with which to express a personal sound. "Even when I was a little kid I stole felt from a billiard table," he said. "I grabbed it and went home and glued it in my accordion soundboard on the left and on the right and on the base. The sound I got was incredible, yet I was only eight or nine—already I worked with things like that."[17] As soon as he took delivery of his Fender-Rhodes piano, he set about customizing the sound by removing the piano top and screwing down the tone bars to restrict their response, creating a more percussive, less ringing, but nevertheless pleasing variation of the Fender-Rhodes sound. On his final album with Adderley, *Country Preacher,* recorded in Chicago in October 1969, he used the Fender-Rhodes exclusively; in the title track, his own composition, it is clear he had developed an individual approach to the electric instrument. So meticulous was his construction of both his accompaniment and his solos that they actually sound like part of the song's construction.

"Country Preacher," a Zawinul composition dedicated to the Reverend Jesse Jackson, is a good example of how Zawinul's writing style had evolved and provides a valuable pointer to his approach in future years. The key was that the composition should appear to unfold spontaneously. The eight-bar piano introduction was a textbook example of concealing where the "one" was—so subtle was its displacement that a member of the audience is heard to exclaim, "What?"—and this continued through Cannonball's statement of it on soprano sax. The tension is resolved as the band explode with a brief, contrasting secondary theme on the one, then silence. The cat-and-mouse game begins all over again, to the audience's delight, as Zawinul returns with the original, elusive motif. It all appears to unfold naturally, like an improvisation, and relies for its effect not on technique, but on toying with the audience's expectation. "I had that little funky thing going on in there," smiled Zawinul.[18]

Also included on this album is another version of "Walk Tall," albeit a more resolute version than the one that appeared on *74 Miles Away,* with the backbeat stated in the manner of rock. Here Adderley succeeded in narrowing the stylistic gulf between jazz and rock on his own terms, without sacrificing his own distinctive musical personality. By subtly altering the spin of his music, a gospel-influenced backbeat becomes a rock-influenced one, yet the musical climate remained resolutely soulful and unmistakably Cannonball Adderley.

One of the highlights of the album was Nat Adderley's "Hummin'." Here the elements that contributed to the success of Ramsey Lewis's "The 'In' Crowd" are present—the backbeat reinforced by the handclaps of an eager, participatory crowd and an atmospheric "live" ambience. Roy McCurdy accentuated the off-beat, Walter Booker laid down a funky bass line, and Zawinul's accompaniment was a model of discretion. It combined to inspire Nat to produce an energetic solo that was subsequently transcribed note-for-note by Quincy Jones—tactfully avoiding the intonational lapses—for an all-star, five-man trumpet section on his 1970 big-band album, *Gula Matari.*

Two months after *Country Preacher* was recorded, on December 15, 1970, Zawinul left Adderley's quintet after almost ten years. "Needless to say," he pointed out at the time, "the parting with Cannon is friendly. . . . I'll love him forever, it's been a beautiful association."[19] Zawinul had decided to leave Adderley during the summer of 1970. While appearing at Shelly's Manne Hole in Los Angeles, he received a telephone call from Miles Davis, who had by then hired him for *In a Silent Way* in February 1969, *Bitches Brew* the following August, and *Big Fun* nine months later. Yet Zawinul had never appeared in public with Davis's band. "Miles called me one morning and said that Miroslav [Vitous] had joined his band and it would be nice if I joined too," he recalled.[20] However, while Zawinul had decided the time had come to leave Adderley, it was not to join Davis but to go out on his own. "As it happened, Miroslav and Miles couldn't get it together and then all of a sudden we were in New York calling each other one afternoon. My album had just come out and he suggested that he and I get together. He called Wayne and Wayne called me, we had a meeting and said, 'Shit, let's have a band,' you know?"[21]

By then, Zawinul, Vitous, and Shorter had each made albums that were at the cutting edge of jazz, and each, in its own way, was a significant precursor to what was about to flow from their new collaboration. During his Adderley years, Zawinul had recorded three albums as a leader, *Money in the Pocket, The Rise and Fall of the Third Stream,* and *Zawinul.* The last had both Vitous and Shorter in the lineup on what was a series of impressionistic tone poems that included "In a Silent Way" (performed as he intended the piece to go, rather than the truncated Miles Davis interpretation that remained on the tonic) and the impressive "Doctor Honoris Causa."[22] Vitous's *Infinite Search* (later re-released as *Mountain in the Clouds*) from November 1969 saw the leader constructing his compositions around his bass playing, but it was memorable for a coruscating version of Eddie Harris's "Freedom Jazz Dance" with inspired solos from John McLaughlin and saxophonist Joe Henderson. Vitous's compositions relied on rhythmic energy rather than harmonic complexity—as did Shorter's on *Super Nova,* recorded two months earlier—with drummer Jack DeJohnette and McLaughlin common to both sessions. Using modality and "time, no changes," they were models of integrated group interaction. Shorter's *Super Nova* was especially impressive—indeed Miles Davis had previously used three of its compositions, "Swee-Pea," "Water Babies," and "Capricorn," on his *Water Babies* album recorded in June 1967, although the results were shelved until 1976.

The as-yet unnamed group first tried the drummer Billy Cobham and the trumpeter David Lee from New Orleans before deciding to drop the trumpet altogether and opt for Alphonse Mouzon in place of Cobham. During this period of flux, John McLaughlin was approached to join the band but declined as he

Weather Report: The lineup for the band's second and third albums, *I Sing the Body Electric* and *Sweetnighter.* Clockwise from upper left: Josef Zawinul, Miroslav Vitous, Dom Um Ramao, Wayne Shorter, and Eric Gravatt. (Courtesy of the Institute of Jazz Studies, Rutgers University.)

was forming his own group.[23] After much discussion they decided to call themselves Weather Report. "It's Weather Report because that would allow us to change, just like the Weather so the scope is limitless, as the title suggests," explained Zawinul.[24] However, he now admits that when the band came together they were not at all organized, with, effectively, three leaders; there was no game plan, no master strategy other than to rehearse. "We had a rehearsal and we did an album right after we were formed," said Mouzon. "Then we had more rehearsals, and some more rehearsals—all we ever did was rehearse! We didn't do very many gigs."[25] Zawinul also approached the percussionist Airto Moreira to join the band. "While I was playing with Miles [Davis], Joe Zawinul asked me to become his partner with Wayne and Miroslav Vitous," he said. "I don't know why, I didn't like his approach. I was going to make it, the music the group was making was so beautiful. I said to Joe that I was going to make it. . . . I took two or three more days and decided not to make it. We had already taken the album cover shots and recorded the first Weather Report album. It caused real bad vibrations."[26] His replacement was Dom Un Romao, another outstanding South American percussionist, but by then Airto had overdubbed the percussion parts without ever appearing with the band live.

Recorded in three days in March 1971, *Weather Report* was released in mid-May accompanied by a certain amount of show-biz brouhaha from the Columbia press department and a lengthy encomium on the album sleeve by the label's chief, Clive Davis. Yet the lineup of the group was remarkably unsensational—tenor saxophone, piano, acoustic bass, drums, and percussion—no different from countless other groups in jazz. The music they produced, however, utilized this conventional lineup in highly unconventional ways. A point of departure from the approach of the standard saxophone quartet was signalled on "Eurydice," a piece that was freed from conventional metric and harmonic structure with a meter that was either intentionally vague or constantly shifting. Although Vitous played walking bass, he often abandoned this role to contribute embellishments and commentary to the ensemble. And while Mouzon played ride rhythm patterns and closed the high hat on the two and four, he also played the high hat on every beat and occasionally abandoned timekeeping in favor of coloration. Zawinul did not always comp for Shorter in the usual way; he commented on Shorter's solo and set up countermelodies. During his own solo, he made use of side-slipping and often played with just his right hand, increasing the effectiveness of the two- and three-note chords he introduced into his line. Airto's role was that of a colorist, interjecting speech-like sounds with a *cuica*. All in all this was a highly individual performance, a step on the way to the new directions the band would pursue on subsequent albums. Other highlights included "Milky Way," a tone poem that used the resonance of an acoustic piano in an arresting and imaginative way, "Seventh Arrow" and "Umbrella," which employed collective improvisation to achieve their effect, and the pastoral, undulating tone poem "Orange Lady," which evoked the impressionist composers Claude Debussy and Maurice Ravel. *Weather Report* was described by Zawinul as "a soundtrack for the imagination," a highly apt metaphor.

Awarded a five-star rating by *Downbeat* magazine, it won the "Jazz Album of the Year" in the magazine's annual end-of-year poll. Although it only reached 191 on the *Billboard* chart, Weather Report was earmarked as a band of the future. Looking back on the album, Zawinul said: "To me, the first album was three guys meet each other, and everybody is careful, make sure they don't step on no one—three good musicians with a talent for improvising play together—but to me that was searching, and I am not a searcher. Because when I improvise I've found it!"[27] During their first year together, Weather Report did not work much in the U.S., instead touring Europe and, in January 1972, Japan, where they had won the "Album of the Year" and "Band of the Year" awards from *Swing Journal.* By then Mouzan had departed, and his replacement was Eric

Gravatt, an erudite and intellectual drummer from Philadelphia. They sold out concerts in Tokyo, Osaka, and Sapporo, surprising Zawinul with the strength of enthusiasm that greeted them. "Our first album wasn't out but for four months and when we arrived at Tokyo airport there were hundreds of people waiting to greet us," he said.[28]

On January 13, Columbia recorded their concert at the Shibuya Philharmonic Hall in Tokyo, which produced two albums. The first, a double set, *Live in Tokyo*, was restricted to Japanese release. Here the emancipation of the ensemble from the predetermined roles of bop and hard bop that had begun on "Eurydice" was completed; a player might carry the melody briefly and those around him would respond in highly interactive ways. "On the second album there was more structure," said Zawinul. "Melodies had shorter motifs, a lot of it sounded improvised, but it was written to sound that way."[29] Fragments of melody might come from either Shorter, Zawinul, or Vitous—the soloist-accompanist roles of bop were abandoned completely—and in some pieces there was little distinction between the melody carrier and the accompanist.

This is music in which the elements of storytelling (the soloist), architecture (chord sequence), and resolution (form and structure) are largely replaced by a field of intensity built up through collective interaction. Zawinul's ethos was "no one solos, everyone solos." Sounds took their meaning from their relationship one to another rather than from their place in the musical whole, a linear rela-

Joe Zawinul: The driving force behind Weather Report. (Photograph by Stuart Nicholson.)

tionship of interconnecting events that expand and contract to fill the moment, gestures in time that do not have to satisfy form and structure with their systems of cadences, climaxes, transitions, modulations, and resolutions. The form was open ended, the structure was what it was at any given moment, an ever-changing succession of events. Rhythm, unlike its function within the popular song, was not bound up in the harmonic narrative; it remained apart, creating its own tensions and coloration. Every member had to be capable of playing melodically or creating sounds that added to the overall concept suggested by the composition. Elevated to an equal role to keyboards and saxophone, Vitous was well able to function in this environment, an outstanding bass virtuoso in a class with the likes of Scott LaFaro; an improviser first and a bass player second, Vitous's role with Weather Report demanded he constantly alternate between these roles.

While *Weather Report* had been an entirely acoustic album, *Live in Tokyo* used electric tone colors. In addition to an acoustic piano, Zawinul used his Fender-Rhodes with a ring modulator and a wah-wah attachment usually used by guitarists. The difference is striking; "Orange Lady," "Tears," "Seventh Arrow," and "Eurydice" from *Weather Report* are transformed. Live the band was aggressive and abrasive; for example, ten minutes into the opening medley comprising "Vertical Invader"–"Seventh Arrow"–"T.H."–"Doctor Honoris Causa," there was an episode of interaction that is free jazz in all but name. Another episode in the same medley had Zawinul using the acoustic piano with a metallic device over the strings, producing a sound similar to the tonal distortion he had produced on "74 Miles Away" with Cannonball Adderley. He also plucked the piano strings like a harp, adding to an ever-growing repertoire of tonal variety that would become a hallmark of the group.

An edited version of the opening medley,[30] together with "Surucucú" and "Directions," themselves part of a longer medley that originally included "Lost" and "Early Minor," formed side two of the vinyl issue of *I Sing the Body Electric*, the group's next U.S. release. Side one, a series of ambitious studio recordings made prior to the Japanese tour, opens with "Unknown Soldier" with Zawinul on acoustic piano, and the group augmented by Andrew White on English horn, Wilmer Wise on trumpet, Hubert Laws on flute, and haunting, wordless vocals by Yolande Bavan, Joshie Armstrong, and Chapman Roberts.[31] It said much for the experimental climate of the early 1970s that a major recording company released a recording such as this—which featured contrasting meters, improvisation, abstraction, and programmatic episodes—that was totally unique in jazz. Indeed, it is difficult to imagine any major recording company actively marketing such bold, serious, contemporary experimentation in today's heavily formatted musical culture. Remarkably, this uncompromising music actually reached 147 on the *Billboard* pop album chart.

Prior to Weather Report, there had been very few recordings in which individual improvisation was of secondary importance to collective improvisation. Examples that readily spring to mind include Lennie Tristano's "Digression" and "Intuition" (1949), *Free Jazz* by Ornette Coleman (1960), and *Ascension* by John Coltrane (1965). Yet none of these albums equalled the overall quality of work produced by these artists in noncollective contexts. In contrast, Weather Report stood out as highly successful exponents of this approach; to all intents and purposes this was electrified avant-garde. But this is not how Zawinul envisaged a future for the group, realizing that, if they continued to rely on spontaneity and creative impulse, the group would be hostages to fortune. "Sometimes we were very creative," asserted Zawinul, "but often it would happen that if we were not totally on, absolutely nothing! I didn't want that. I didn't want to search, the composition's got to be there. On the second album there was more structure. In the beginning let's say Weather Report was a joint thing. Then, after the second album there's no question about it, it became more and more my group. Wayne wanted it like that, but we were always 'partners in crime.' No Wayne, no Weather Report."[32]

Sweetnighter, recorded in early February 1973, saw Zawinul asserting a greater control over the band. His tunes began to predominate—half the compositions are his, including the first track on the album, crucial for airplay. He also arranged compositions from other members of the band, including Shorter. This new balance to its internal dynamics gave a stronger direction for the band. "*Sweetnighter* was a kind of getting down," Shorter explained. "We sort of half-intentionally wanted to stay away from the ethereal."[33] In two Zawinul compositions, "Boogie Woogie Waltz" and "125th Street Congress," the rhythm is quite

Wayne Shorter: His relationship with Joe Zawinul for almost fifteen years produced fifteen albums and one of the most diverse and impressive bodies of work in jazz outside Duke Ellington. (Photograph by Stuart Nicholson.)

specific, owing something to the complex "layering" of rhythms in the music of post-"Cold Sweat" James Brown. "I wanted the band to get stronger rhythmically," said Zawinul, "even stronger than Cannonball and Miles and all those. But there was just one thing, I just didn't like the backbeat, that two and four backbeat, it destroys and sensibility of rhythm because it is not rhythm, it is time, and time and rhythm in music are two different things. A groove is a groove, but time doesn't give you a groove, time gives you a certain exactness. '125th Street Congress' is a groove and that is what I wanted—I come from Cannonball, I come from Dinah Washington, everything I ever grew up with and liked about jazz is in there. That beat we use there, and on 'Boogie Woogie Waltz,' I taught the two drummers, sitting with them for hours and taught them how to play it and those very recordings are sampled on rap and hip-hop records now—it was the first hip-hop beat ever recorded!"[34]

To get the "groove" that set *Sweetnighter* apart from the two previous albums, Zawinul augmented the group for the recording date with the drummer Heschel Dwellingham and Andrew N. White III, who had contributed the haunting English Horn solos on *I Sing the Body Electric*. This time, however, White contributed broken or "funky" bass lines on electric bass, representing a significant departure from the more orthodox, acoustic sounds of Vitous and establishing a new rhythmic direction for the band.[35] Clearly the new direction Zawinul envisaged for the group was exposing limitations in the rhythm section. Gravatt was the first to go, replaced by the former Sly and the Family Stone drummer Gregg Errico. Disillusioned at having to play alongside Dwellingham, Gravatt would later leave jazz altogether, ending up working as a security guard in a maximum security prison in Minneapolis.

Sweetnighter is the first album on which Zawinul used a synthesizer. Unlike in many albums from the early 1970s when the synthesizer began to be used widely, Zawinul avoided obvious "electronic" effects. Instead, he sought "natural" sounds, sounds that had an acoustic resonance. "I'm not using the synthesizer because it's there," he explained. "I am a musician, I have studied the violin, and clarinet and trumpet and I only use what I need. For me it is a tool. The reason why synthesizers have such a bad reputation is because musicians don't know how to play them; they play everything instead of letting their personality express through the instrument."[36]

As the group's dynamic range expanded through the development of new electronic technology, the writing skills of Zawinul and Shorter encompassed the orchestral possibilites presented to them. There was still room for haunting, impressionistic tone poems evoking classical composers such as Debussy, Ravel, and Vaughan Williams, as in Zawinul's "Adios" or Shorter's "Manolete," but they were no longer centerpieces. Instead, the album's key numbers were "Boogie Woogie Waltz" and "125th Street Congress," both of which used prewritten figures that popped up at the beginning of the composition and at the end and occasionally in variation or abbreviated form within the pieces' improvised, closely woven textures of interchanging soloing and accompaniment.

Described as "The Third Stop On Weather Report's Fantastic Journey" in Columbia's trade advertisements, the album was promoted as experimental popular music rather than "jazz." During the early 1970s it was widely agreed within the industry that mention of the word was a major impediment to sales:

> Three years ago, a remarkable group of musicians embarked upon a musical journey. They visited musical places that had never been seen or imagined before. At live performances audiences were stunned; mesmerized by the beauty and impossibility of what they were hearing. Every so often the group would stop and record a glimpse of the vision. . . . Weather Report's latest point of departure is called "Sweetnighter," and it's easier to get to than you think. Travel light, just bring your ears, your mind and your soul. Don't be left behind. Catch Weather Report at "Sweetnighter."[37]

As with the Miles Davis advertising campaign, Columbia appealed to the record buyer's vanity in not wanting to be left behind, using the "incredible journey" theme they had previously incorporated into ads for *Bitches Brew.*

Weather Report's stature was such that the album was accorded two reviews in *Downbeat,* one awarding it five stars and other three, reflecting the controversy the band's change of direction caused. But as in 1972, they again won the "Jazz Combo" category of the magazine's Reader's Poll. Increasingly admired by the public, musicians, and critics alike, with each succeeding album, media interest was getting more and more intense. So when *Mysterious Traveller* came out in 1974, the absence of Miroslav Vitous, who the previous month had been quoted in *Downbeat* as predicting a great future for the band—"We're going to be playing together for quite a while unless something unexpected happens"[38]—was something of a cause célèbre. Clearly something unexpected had happened.

"*Mysterious Traveller* was the point where we had to let Miroslav go," explained Zawinul. "He was supposed to contribute music. He didn't, only an introduction which I used on 'American Tango,' which I shared with him. He didn't have anything and his playing—he insisted on playing with a bow, soloing, and his intonation was horrendous—I just couldn't take it on the bandstand. I wanted to leave, I said Wayne we gotta do something here, we gotta let him go or we're going to go down because it's not happening. Miroslav didn't have what we needed. We needed a fundamental bass player with imagination, a bass player who holds the band together. A band has to have bottom and he didn't have that—he should have been a guitar player. He could play, believe me, he's a helluva musician, but he didn't have what I call a bass concept."[39]

Vitous's replacement was Alphonso Johnson, who had played with Woody Herman (he appeared on Herman's 1972 album *The Raven Speaks*) and Chuck Mangione's group (on *The Land of Make Believe* from 1973). Zawinul had heard Johnson with Mangione when they played a date together in Philadelphia in October 1973. Later Zawinul called him up and asked if he'd like to audition for Weather Report. "Alphonso Johnson had a lot," said Zawinul, "he was young, he was bright, he was disciplined and he could lay down a groove that hurt and that's what I wanted."[40] By the time of the recording of *Mysterious Traveller,* Errico had also gone, replaced by Ishmael Wilburn.

Zawinul's composition "Nubian Sundance" opened the album, a joyous celebration that signalled that Weather Report had redefined themselves once again. By now Zawinul was using two Arp 2600 synthesizers, a Moog synthesizer, and a Fender-Rhodes piano with a phase-shifter, Echoplex, and wah-wah pedal. He had also moved from New York to the more congenial climate of the West Coast, where he lived in a house overlooking the Rose Bowl. In musical terms this relocation meant the group would be working in a new recording studio, Devonshire Sound in North Hollywood, where, with sound engineer Ron Malo, Zawinul began exploring to a far greater extent than before the possibilities offered by the studio. "Nubian Sundance" contained complex layers of rhythmic patterns using two drummers, Ishmael Wilburn and Skip Hadden, and two percussionists, Don Um Romao and Zawinul himself. The piece began as a recording of a Zawinul improvisation based on an ostinato in F major. Motifs and orchestral effects were overdubbed to produce a constantly changing canvas of sounds that at one point had Zawinul's voice mixed into the synthesizer riffs for additional color.

Alphonso Johnson's funky bass line features on "Cucumber Slumber"—extensively sampled by rappers in the late 1980s and 1990s—underpinned a deceptively simple "groove" performance that explained why Zawinul wanted him as bassist. He laid down such a strong line that it dictated the mood of the piece, the instrumental figures seeming to breathe in time with every note he played. The ambitious "Jungle Book" was another example of a performance that began life as a Zawinul improvisation and was built up in the studio (this time at Zawinul's home) through overdubbing to create a subtle fabric of wordless vocal choirs and exotic programmatic interludes (including the voice of Zawinul's young son crying). As a whole, the album realized, perhaps more than its predecessors, the potential offered by using the studio-as-laboratory to explore the tonal possibilities offered by the synthesizer's wide dynamic range in combination with other electronic and acoustic instruments. Here was a seemingly limitless range of musical colors and textures, a theme that would be expanded on in future albums.

During 1975, the group continued to be unsettled. Since Gravatt left, the problems had primarily centered on the drum chair. Said Zawinul, "There are very few guys in the world I like playing drums. What I didn't like was that they didn't have form, their stuff moves around all the time and I never liked that."[41] When Wilburn left, he was replaced by twenty-one-year-old Darryl Brown, who later became a surgeon. For *Tale Spinnin'* (1975), Leon "Ndugu" Chancler was the drummer (although he never toured with the band), together with percussionist Alyrio Lima. It was an album that consciously moved towards sunny climes, a more cosmopolitan groove, and the celebratory atmosphere unveiled in "Nubian Sundance."

The opening cut, "Man in the Green Shirt," an impressionistic boogie named after an old man whom Zawinul had seen dancing in the Virgin Islands, incorporated the conventional concept of soloist-and-rhythm, with subtle layers of complexity interacting beneath a slowly moving melody line. Shorter, almost solely responsible for this reversal of roles between front line and rhythm section with his work in the 1960s Miles Davis quintet, contributed "Lusitanos." After the introduction, a transitionary passage of twelve bars led into the main theme of twenty-five bars followed by an F-sharp-minor vamp for solos. The main theme then returned in truncated form (nine bars) and led into the coda comprising a return of the F-sharp-minor vamp and, on cue, a reprise of the opening transitionary passage, albeit in variation. The piece concluded with a return to the vamp figure (now modulated up a tone to A-flat) and an eventual fade. Since *Sweetnighter,* this return to specific, quantifiable musical structures had gradually been gathering momentum. Yet today, *Tale Spinnin'* sounds uncharacteristically light, both in tone and texture. It appears more as a precursor to the artistically and aesthetically satisfying period that was about to follow, which consolidated the band's move towards bold new ad hoc forms and structures.

When the band went on the road in 1976, Chester Thompson replaced "Ndugu" Chancler and the rhythm section now appeared settled. "Chester had just left Frank Zappa," said Zawinul. "He was [a] helluva drummer for a certain kind of music and that suited us at that time and together with Al [Johnson]— Chester was from Baltimore and Al was from Philadelphia—they had a tight little thing going. Then we added Alex Acuna on percussion, who loosened that stuff up—Alex was also a great jazz drummer. I remember we were playing at the Bottom Line in New York and Miles Davis was sitting in the front row. When we finished Miles led a standing ovation, and that was really nice. Afterwards, all he was talking about was the band, it was really smokin'. Then Al decided to go. He was at that time over two years with us and it was time for a move. He decided to make a band with George Duke, Billy Cobham, and that left it open for Jaco."[42]

Jaco Pastorius was born in December 1951 and brought up in Fort Lauderdale. He began working the Florida nightclub circuit in the late 1960s and, on the strength of his local reputation, he landed a gig with Wayne Cochran and the C. C. Riders in the summer of 1972. In 1973 he played in the house band of Bachelors III, a Fort Lauderdale nightclub, along with drummer Danny Gottlieb, guitarist Pat Metheny, and trumpeter Ron Tooley, before putting in six months of road time with Lou Rawls. He then joined a group led by the bop multi-instrumentalist Ira Sullivan. "All he was looking to do at the time was create music and play his instrument better than anybody else in the world," said Sullivan.[43]

In the summer of 1975, Blood, Sweat & Tears drummer Bobby Colomby "discovered" Pastorius at Bachelors III and signed him to Epic Records. Colomby acted as producer for *Jaco Pastorius,* placing the bass player in a variety of settings to show off his phenomenal ability. But it was Pastorius's showcase solo on Charlie Parker's "Donna Lee," accompanied only by percussionist Don Alias, that turned the music world on its collective ear. "With that stunning two-and-a-half minute showcase, Jaco single-handedly ushered in a new era of electric bass," said Pastorius biographer Bill Milkowski.[44] The bare instrumentation allowed a close examination of Pastorius's warm, singing tone, his lightning execution and clear articulation that were on a level of the finest horn players, and his harmonic and rhythmic originality that was frequently startling. Pastorius played just four choruses of Parker's sixteen-bar tune, comprising an exposition of the theme, a solo for the second chorus, an embellishment of the theme and modulation in the third chorus, and a reiteration of the theme in the new key for the fourth. His solo began with a break on bar sixteen of the first chorus that led into a fluent use of sixteenth notes during the subsequent two choruses, often in complex, broken phrases. What is immediately striking is his attack and fluidity across the whole range of electric bass—just as Jimmy Blanton opened up a new world for the acoustic bass thirty-five years before, Pastorius was doing so now with the electric bass.

Yet when Pastorius recorded "Donna Lee" in 1975, many of his techniques were not unknown to electric bass players. Stanley Clarke, for one, was considered a premier electric bassist in jazz with his virtuoso approach to the instrument. What set Pastorius apart, however, was the way his technique took bass-playing into hitherto unexplored realms; he utilized octaves, which until then had only been used by guitarists, and most dramatically of all he incorporated chords into his bass lines with a fluency that no one had dared attempt. Another key ingredient of Pastorius's playing that separated him from his predecessors was the way he regarded the electric bass as an electronic instrument rather than an amplified acoustic one, in the way Jimi Hendrix revolutionized the electric guitar. He had a remarkable control of harmonic overtones and, Hendrix-like, he harnessed feedback to creative effect. Virtually a complete unknown, Pastorius arrived in jazz as a true innovator on his instrument, greeted at first with skepticism and then with awe.

Several months prior to signing with Epic, Pastorius had been gigging in a trio led by Pat Metheny with Bob Moses on drums. In December 1975 they travelled to Ludwigsburg, Germany to record Metheny's debut as a leader on record, *Bright Size Life*, which according to Moses was not a good reflection of the group. "For me it doesn't capture what we were doing," he said.[45] In late 1975, Colomby arranged for Pastorius to sub for bassist Ron McClure in Blood, Sweat & Tears for about three months, which was followed by a call to make a recording date with Weather Report.

Zawinul had first met Pastorius in Miami in 1975. While setting up for a Weather Report gig, he was confronted by a tall, lean, young man who introduced himself as "the greatest electric bass player in the world." Bemused by this ballsy stance, Zawinul gave Pastorius his address, telling him to keep in touch. Pastorius wrote regularly, often sending him gig tapes. When Johnson announced that he was leaving in January 1976, the group was in the middle of recording *Black Market*.

"Jaco used to write to me a lot," said Zawinul, "so it came time for that opening, so I called him up."[46] Initially Zawinul had in mind Pastorius playing on one cut, "Cannonball," dedicated to his friend and former bandleader, who had died on August 8, 1975. "We brought him in and that was more or less his audition,"

Jaco arrives: *Left to right:* Jaco Pastorius, Peter Erskine, Joe Zawinul, Wayne Shorter. Weather Report's most memorable lineup. (Courtesy of the Institute of Jazz Studies, Rutgers University.)

he continued. "Wayne and I talked it over and we both agreed this kid could play."[47] In addition to "Cannonball," Pastorius contributed an original called "Barbary Coast," which would become something of a signature piece for the group in live performance. He officially joined Weather Report on April 1, 1976, "but when we started playing, Jaco and Chester [Thompson] couldn't play together, just couldn't make it," said Zawinul. "There was a thing went in me, we listened to this and we knew Jaco was the guy because he had the flexibility to grow and Chester was Chester. But everything worked out because Chester started working with Genesis and Phil Collins, carved out a major career he would never had with us. Then Alex came in on drums, with Manolo Bodrena, and that's when we started making our most successful records."[48]

Black Market, from 1976, was recorded in the middle of all the personnel comings and goings yet remains a remarkably well-integrated statement. By now Zawinul had added an Oberheim Prophet to his arsenal of keyboard instruments, a sixteen-voice polyphonic synthesizer with forty programmable presets. The Oberheim allowed him to play chords, something the early Arp 2600 would not, broadening the range of the band even further. The title track numbers among the band's most memorable performances. A prerecorded prelude leads into a vamp of gathering intensity, a prologue to a fanfare that announces the entry of Shorter's saxophone. It was guaranteed to bring a huge roar from the crowd in live performance, a moment of drama that is caught on two subsequent albums, *8.30* and *Havana Jam,* in which the tempos are noticeably brighter. "Gibraltar," originally slated to open the album, equally sparkles with vigor, while the two Shorter contributions, "Elegant People" and "Three Clowns," are impressive in their spare, yet moving writing.

When Weather Report went out on the road, the band were galvanized by the presence of Pastorious in their midst. He was soon stopping the show during his feature piece, a solo medley comprising Hendix's "Purple Haze" and "Third Stone from the Sun," Charlie Parker's "Donna Lee," Wilson Pickett's "Funky Broadway," and the Beatles' "Blackbird." "Jaco was in a space of his own," said Zawinul. "He was so different to all the other bass players at that time. He had that magical thing about him, the same kind of thing Jimi Hendrix had. He was an electrifying performer and a great musician. . . . Before Jaco came along we were perceived as a kind of esoteric jazz group . . . but after Jaco joined the band we started selling-out concert halls everywhere."[49]

Pastorius's extroverted presence in a lineup that contained two forty-some-thing leaders added immeasurably to the drawing power of the band, extending its appeal beyond jazz fans to rock audiences. But despite Pastorius's show-biz grandstanding—tossing his bass into the air, Hendrix-like assaults on his speak-ers, back-flips off his amplifiers, and visually underscoring his playing with wild choreography—Pastorius was an enormously creative musician, sharing producer credit with Zawinul on the group's next album, *Heavy Weather* (1977). He con-tributed two originals, "Teen Town," named after an area in his home state of Florida, and "Havona," and in postproduction displayed a thoroughgoing knowl-edge of the mixing board, where the concept of the studio-as-instrument was employed as never before.

When the album was released in early 1977, Columbia's marketing was intense and hard-hitting:

> *"Heavy Weather."* You can dress for it, but you can't escape it. Weather Report. *"Heavy Weather."* It's an album of driving, hard hitting jazz-rock, the kind that only Weather Report knows how to make . . . *"Heavy Weather."* Weather Report's stormy new music for a sunshine day.[50]

Heavy Weather reached number 30 on the *Billboard* chart and, with initial sales approaching 500,000, the album subsequently went gold. Critically acclaimed, *Downbeat* awarded the album five stars and its readers voted it "Album of the Year," while Zawinul's "Birdland," released in an edited form as a single, received a Grammy nomination as "Best Instrumental Composition."[51] The composition's complexity helps prevent the song's meaning from being exhausted by repeated listening, and even today it remains a tour-de-force that retains the capacity to surprise with its unusual construction. It opens with a question-and-answer riff of four bars based on the chord of G6 played in unison by the synthesizer and bass and repeated three times:

Introduction (12 bars) + theme "A" (24 bars) + G pedal (4 bars) + theme
"B" (20 bars) + theme "C" (9 bars) + transition (9 bars) + main theme "D"
(24 bars) + transition (8 bars) + bass synth soli (12 bars) + sax solo (14 bars
over 2 bars repeat descending chromatic chords) + transition (4 bars) +
theme "A" (24 bars) + coda: theme "B" (8 bars) + main theme "D" (4 bars
repeated to fade)

From the freeform pieces of *Live in Tokyo,* with their emphasis almost
entirely on improvisation, to the sophisticated ad hoc songform of "Birdland,"
in which improvisation was framed by an ingenious and elaborate orchestration,
a significant realignment occurred in Weather Report's philosophy. This evolution has often been portrayed by commentators as a swing from one extreme to
the other, from artistic aspiration to commercial consideration. With the passage of time, some writers have even claimed "Birdland" had a "disco beat"[52] to
reinforce the claim that, because the album sold well, the band must have "sold
out" to commercial considerations. This is hardly the case; "Birdland" does not
employ a disco beat that any self-respecting Donna Summer fan would recognize—in fact it uses a variety of rhythmic devices; for example, the coda uses
hand clapping to reinforce the 2 and 4, but then quadruples the speed to continuous eighth notes to intensify the rhythmic excitement. Equally, *Heavy Weather*
represents the high point in a logical continuum of evolution that began with
Sweetnighter.

Weather Report did not abandon collective expressionism in favor of orchestral structure; rather, they broadened their range. Elements of their earlier
style—improvised textures and collective improvisation—frequently appear in
their "orchestral" albums; this was especially apparent away from the formality
of studio performance, as live recordings and videos of the band reveal. As form
and structure began to balance improvisation, a step that became more apparent
from *Mysterious Traveller,* an emphasis on a polished studio sound grew. Weather
Report was one of the first bands in jazz to make use of the new musical technology, both in terms of electronic keyboards—*Tale Spinnin'* utilized Malcolm
Cecil's TONTO (The Original New Timbral Orchestra), a synthesizer studio—
and the latest recording techniques, abandoning recording in real time and making extensive use of multitracking, which had become the norm in rock music
after *Pet Sounds* and *Sgt. Pepper.*

The important new ingredient in *Heavy Weather* is Pastorius's bass playing. A
convincing soloist, even when keeping time he had the virtuosity to insert melodic asides that added variety and interest to his line as well as contributing to the
overall group sound. He is featured on "Havona," contributing a concise, well-
constructed statement, beginning with a simple motif which climaxes at bars 17
and 39 of his solo. He even works in a quote from Stravinsky's "Rite of Spring"
in bar 5, going on to develop his ideas with a blend of bebop-like lines, chromat-
ics, intervallic playing, and pentatonic scales. An important factor of his playing
was the drive and élan he brought to the band, which altered its entire rhythmic
climate. "He was always on," said Zawinul, "always pushing the band. And that

really kept all of us on our toes. Every band needs what I call a warhead—the driving force, the motor. And in this band, Jaco was the warhead."[53]

With rave reviews of the band in live performance during the extensive tour to promote the album, much was expected of the band's next release. When *Mr. Gone* appeared in 1988 it quickly went gold, reaching 52 on the *Billboard* chart, but the positive reaction that had greeted *Heavy Weather* seemed to have evaporated. Only one star was awarded by *Downbeat*, who dismissed it as "pregnant with superfluous electronic gimmickry."[54] Certainly the restraint Zawinul exercised in the past, in choosing subtle, acoustic sounding synthesizer tones instead of jarring, synthetic-sounding electrical ones, his avoidance of an explicit back-beat, and his ability to pare melodic construction down to the very core all went out of the window. Again the drum chair was unsettled, Alex Acuna tiring of the road and opting for a career as a session musician, so Zawinul called on Tony Williams, Steve Gadd, and a young drummer who had been turning a lot of heads—first with Stan Kenton and latterly with Maynard Ferguson—named Peter Erskine to fill in and audition for the band.

Recorded at the height of the disco boom, this is the album that makes concessions to that very commercial beat; indeed, all Columbia artists were being urged to jump on the bandwagon during this period, with potential new jazz signings to the label being told it's disco or nothing. "River People" was issued as a single, complete with a repeated bass line and handclaps, while Wayne Shorter's "Pinocchio," which had originally appeared on Miles Davis's *Nefertiti,* got a bright and bouncy treatment. *Mr. Gone* remains something of an indulgence on Zawinul's part, intended as a followup to *Mysterious Traveller,* a voyage of discovery extending the boundaries of the still-limited synthesizer technology, yet to be revolutionized by the MIDI era of sound sampling. "I feel that *Mr. Gone* was my solo album with Weather Report," he explained. "I was after new sounds, discovering new sounds, so it was a different kind of album to the others."[55]

Live, however, the band continued to set standards of excellence. By then, drummer Peter Erskine had joined the group to tour Japan and was now a regular member. "Peter had the goods," said Zawinul, not noted for his love of the drumming fraternity. "He was a wild, crazy kid, but he had the goods! Peter was great!"[56] On March 2, 1979, Weather Report appeared at the Karl Marx Theater in Havana, opening a historic three-day festival that marked the first concert in Cuba for twenty years given by artists from the United States. Erskine's impact on Weather Report can be heard on "Black Market" from the live album, *Havana Jam,* where bass and keyboards drop out (there is no percussion) and Erskine joins Shorter in an absorbing jazz-rock update of the John Coltrane–Elvin Jones duets.

Later in 1979 came *8.30,* the group's first double album since the Japanese-only release *Live in Tokyo.* Most of the album (three LP sides) was recorded live. Its highlights included "Badia" (from *Tale Spinnin'*) and "Boogie Woogie Waltz" (from *Sweetnighter*) in medley form, an uptempo version of "Teen Town" (from *Heavy Weather*), another (absorbing) version of "Black Market," "In a Silent Way," and "Slang," a feature for Jaco Pastorius that demonstrated Jimi Hendrix's influence by segueing Charlie Parker's "Donna Lee," John Coltrane's "Giant Steps," and Hendrix's "Third Stone from the Sun." The balance of the album comprised interesting studio experiments including "Brown Street," a carnival romp that builds and builds, and "The Orphan," which included ten members of the West Los Angeles Christian Academy Children's Choir. However, the live version of "Birdland" failed to match the dimensions that made the original recording so compelling, principally through the substitution of a shuffle-rhythm in place of the straight eight-note rhythm.

Weather Report's *8:30* won a Grammy award for "Best Jazz-Rock Album" of 1979, and at the end of 1980 the band topped the "Jazz Group" category for the ninth successive year in the annual *Downbeat* reader's poll, with *8.30* in the runner-up slot for the "Album of the Year"—five of the group's previous eight albums had won this category. Critically and commercially, Weather Report were riding the crest of the wave, but tensions were being created within the group through Pastorius's increasingly eccentric behavior caused by his alcoholism and cocaine addiction. Even so, on the band's next album, *Night Passage,* he again shared producer credit and contributed "Three Views of a Secret," which many consider his finest composition. The ABC structure, with A and C sixteen bars and B twenty-four bars, reveals imaginative melodic construction and sophisticated harmonic craftsmanship. The album employed a variety of approaches: neoclassical ("Rockin' in Rhythm"), post-bop ("Fast City" and "Night Passage"), World music ("Port of Entry" and "Madagascar"), and tone poems ("Three Views of a Secret" and "Dream Clock"). It scripted the manifesto for the 1980s, a pace that was now being forced by past achievements. However, during the band's subsequent tour to support the album, Pastorius's drunkenness and outrageous behavior almost caused him to be jailed in Japan. By the time of *Weather Report* (1982), he no longer shared production credit and had not contributed any new compositions, while his agile bass lines were almost buried in the mix. When the band went out on tour in April 1982 it was without Pastorius. "The time had come for him to go," said Zawinul simply.[57]

Their eleventh U.S. release, *Weather Report* saw the onset of a certain critical ennui. The album was received politely rather than enthusiastically. "It must surely be recognized that at the group's inception they turned the jazz world around," said *Downbeat*. "[So] is it fair to compare [this] to, say, their first totally revolutionary recording?"[58] The group's new lineup in the spring of 1982 introduced Victor Bailey on bass, Omar Hakim on drums, and Jose Rossy on percussion. In June they played Hugh Hefner's Playboy Jazz Festival at the Hollywood Bowl. The year before at the same event, they had received what the promoter George Wein described as "one of the greatest ovations I have ever witnessed in my many years of presenting concerts";[59] the problem for 1982 was what to do for a follow-up. The answer was the unexpected entrance of Manhattan Transfer, whose own version of "Birdland" had turned the tune into a hit for a second time. But the real showstopper was the band's version of "Volcano for Hire," a major feature for Shorter which, unlike the version on *Weather Report,* showed that the group was still a force to be reckoned with; this version appeared on *In Performance at the Playboy Jazz Festival* (1982).

Procession (1983) was enacted against a backdrop of World music and had another guest appearance by Manhattan Transfer in "Where the Moon Goes," while *Domino Theory* (1984) charts the ascendance of the drum virtuoso Omar Hakim, whose playing fed Zawinul just as Pastorius had done in the 1970s. Hakim's influence was very much to the fore in the driving "D-flat Waltz." A brilliant technician, his flamboyance went some way to compensating for the mysterious humility of Shorter on record. *Sportin' Life* (1985), saw Shorter briefly emerging from the shadows to contribute two numbers and share production duties. Zawinul, who as early as 1974 had considered including a vocalist in the lineup,[60] now drafted in a small vocal contingent headed by Bobby McFerrin to supplement his own Martian-sounding efforts using a Vocoder. But the release of the album was not supported by the usual promotional tour; Zawinul and Shorter stayed off the road to prepare outside projects. *Atlantis,* Shorter's first album since *Native Dance,* (1974), was released in 1985, and during 1986 he was at work on *Phantom Navigator.* By now the Shorter-Zawinul partnership that had produced fifteen albums and lasted almost fifteen years had all but run its course. But Weather Report's contract with Columbia called for one more album. Because of schedule conflicts, Peter Erskine returned to replace Hakim and ended up coproducing *This Is This* (1986). On the album sleeve Shorter and Zawinul are locked in left-handed handshake, although Shorter is missing on the opening tracks, replaced by Carlos Santana. The track "Update," however, gives a taste of what was to follow—a preoccupation with keyboard effects for their own sake when Zawinul went into the circuits as a solo act.

Zawinul had recorded *Dia-a-lects* in 1985, again turning to a Bobby McFerrin vocal entourage, but the result was disappointing. Zawinul toured as a single in the summer of that year but formed Weather Update in 1986, a Weather Report-style band with guitarist Steve Khan in place of Shorter. "My experience with Weather Update . . . ended up being Maiden Voyage and Farewell Tour all at once," said Khan. "There was no new music, no Weather Update music. There was just whatever Joe selected, which was not the richest material from Weather Report."[61] In 1988 came The Zawinul Syndicate, with the formidable young guitarist Scott Henderson, then a faculty member of the Guitar Institute of Technology in Los Angeles. On their albums, including *The Immigrants, Black Water,* and *Lost Tribes,* the overall impression was of exotic jazz-rock tone poems in which Zawinul's keyboard ingenuity occasionally appeared more important than content. However, in 1996 Zawinul unveiled a new Syndicate that seemed capable of taking up where Weather Report had left off. On bass was Jimmy Garrison's son Matthew (later replaced by Richard Bona), Gary Poulson on guitar, Arto Tuncboyaciyan on percussion, and a stunning drummer from the Ivory Coast, Paco Sery. Several of these musicians can be heard on his 1996 album, *My People,* which was sadly weakened by an abundance of vocals.

Of all the bands to emerge in the jazz-rock explosion, Weather Report was the most individual. "We play our brand of music," Zawinul once asserted.

"Nobody plays tunes like we play"[62]—and he was right. Even today Weather Report's best albums do not sound dated because in the main they avoided electronic artifice and the commercially popular dance rhythms of the time. Even though they did not use a regular vocalist or surrender to commercial expediency, all their albums charted in the top 200 in the U.S.A., making them the most successful of all the fusion groups. Despite being routinely described as a "jazz-rock" band, their stylistic outlook was extremely broad, perhaps the most inclusive in jazz. Their range extended from classical influences such as the French impressionists to free jazz, from World music to bebop, from big-band music to chamber music, from collective improvisation to tightly written formal structures, from modal vamps to elaborately conceived harmonic forms, from structures with no apparent meter to straight-ahead swing. Clearly any success the band enjoyed was achieved on their own terms. Both Zawinul and Shorter created a large body of work that, outside of Duke Ellington, numbers among the most diverse and imaginative in jazz. They achieved a successful integration of improvised lines within prewritten parts and successfully adapted to the possibilities offered by the new electronic technology to create a fresh and vital context for improvisation. Today, the recorded legacy of Weather Report represents one of the most significant bodies of work in post-1960s jazz.

Notes

1. The term "soul" would, by the mid-sixties, become a metaphor for the essence of blackness—soul brother, soul sister, soul food—and permeate every aspect of life in black communities.
2. *Downbeat,* November 16, 1967, p. 19.
3. Victor Feldman had replaced original keyboardist Bobby Timmons in 1960, and was thereafter replaced by Zawinul.
4. See *The Complete Roulette Recordings of the Maynard Ferguson Orchestra* (Mosaic MD10–156).
5. Interview with the author, October 2, 1996.
6. *Downbeat,* November 16, 1967, p. 17.
7. Liner notes *The Greatest Hits of Ramsey Lewis* (MCA CHD 6021).
8. *Downbeat,* December 2, 1965, p. 11.
9. Ibid.
10. Bassist Eldee Young and drummer Red Holt went on to form Young-Holt Unlimited, who had hits with "Soulful Strut" and "Whack Whack."
11. White would later form the successful pop group Earth, Wind and Fire.
12. Among the many popular artists working in this genre were Jimmy Smith, Charles Earland, Richard "Groove" Homes, Les McCann, Brother Jack McDuff, Jimmy McGriff, Stanley Turrentine, Lou Donaldson, Donald Byrd, and Grant Green, many of whom were extensively sampled by rap and hip-hop acts in the 1990s.
13. *Downbeat,* January 8, 1970, p. 12.
14. Zawinul's interest in the electric piano had stemmed from the time he was a member of Dinah Washington's group. Touring as part of a package with Ray Charles, Zawinul had been drawn to Charles's use of a Wurlitzer electric piano, which he had used on occasion during the tour with Charles's blessing.
15. Interview with the author, October 2, 1996.
16. Ibid.
17. Ibid.

18. Ibid.
19. *Downbeat,* December 10, 1970, p. 11.
20. *Rolling Stone,* September 27, 1973, p. 20.
21. Ibid.
22. It was subsequently scored for symphony orchestra in 1995, appearing under the new name "Gypsy" on Zawinul's *Stories of the Danube* (Phillips 454143-2) with the Czech State Philharmonic Orchestra.
23. John McLaughlin interview in *Jazz Forum,* unprovenanced. Courtesy National Sound Archive, London, p. 34.
24. *Black Music & Jazz Review,* June 1978, p. 12.
25. Ibid., November 1975.
26. *Downbeat,* November 7, 1974, p. 19.
27. Interview with the author, October 2, 1996.
28. *Rolling Stone,* September 27, 1973, p. 20.
29. Interview with the author, October 2, 1996.
30. The original 26:11 medley was pared down to 10:10.
31. It would subsequently be expanded and orchestrated for symphony orchestra in Zawinul's 1995 symphony, *Stories of the Danube.*
32. Interview with the author, October 2, 1996.
33. *Downbeat,* June 20, 1974, p. 38.
34. Interview with the author, October 2, 1996.
35. Both White and Vitous played in "Boogie Woogie Waltz" and "Manolete," while in "125th Street Congress" and "Non-Stop Home" White took over completely. Only in "Will," with White now on English horn, and in "Adios" was Vitous heard in his regular role with the group.
36. Interview with the author, October 2, 1996.
37. Columbia trade advertisement, fall 1973.
38. *Downbeat,* February 14, 1974, p. 38.
39. Interview with the author, October 2, 1996.
40. Ibid.
41. Ibid.
42. Ibid.
43. *Jaco,* by Bill Milkowski (Miller Freeman Books, San Francisco, 1995), p. 54.
44. Ibid., p. 61.
45. Ibid., p. 67.
46. Interview with the author, October 2, 1996.
47. *Jaco,* by Bill Milkowski (Miller Freeman Books, San Francisco, 1995), p. 73.
48. Interview with the author, October 2, 1996.
49. *Jaco,* by Bill Milkowski (Miller Freeman Books, San Francisco, 1995), p. 74.
50. Columbia trade advertisement, spring 1977.
51. "Birdland" was extensively featured by the big bands of Buddy Rich and Maynard Ferguson, and two years later it was a pop hit for Manhattan Transfer, with lyrics added by Jon Hendricks. Among several subsequent versions, Quincy Jones recorded the composition on his 1989 album *Back on the Block,* where he was joined in the ensemble by Zawinul himself on keyboards.
52. Among many examples, *What to Listen for In Jazz,* by Barry Kernfield (Yale University Press, New Haven and London), p. 19.
53. *Jaco,* by Bill Milkowski (Miller Freeman Books, San Francisco, 1995), pp. 80–81.
54. *Downbeat,* January 11, 1979, p. 22.
55. Interview with the author, October 2, 1996.
56. Ibid.
57. Ibid.
58. *Downbeat,* June 1982, p. 42.

59. Liner notes *In Performance at the Playboy Jazz Festival* (Elektra Musician 60298–1).

60. *Downbeat,* December 5, 1974, p. 10. See "Weather Report Hunts Vocalist."

61. Quoted in *Jazz: The 1980s Resurgence,* by Stuart Nicholson, p. 161 (Da Capo, New York, 1995).

62. *Black Music & Jazz Review,* June 1978, p. 14.

CHAPTER 10

Light as a Feather

By the time pianist Herbie Hancock joined the Miles Davis quintet in May 1963, he had already composed one of the most popular successes of the soul-jazz idiom. Latin bandleader Mongo Santamaria's cover version of Hancock's "Watermelon Man," from his 1962 album *Takin' Off*, made it onto *Billboard*'s "Hot Hundred." Subsequently the number was recorded by over 200 artists and established Hancock as one of Blue Note records' best-selling artists of the 1960s, a solo career that ran parallel to his six-year, fifteen-album stint with Davis.

Hancock's Blue Note albums included several important 1960s classics such as *Empyrean Isles, Maiden Voyage,* and *Speak Like a Child*. In contrast to the sophisticated interplay of his work with Davis, Hancock's own albums showed a preference for more straightforward forms. As early as 1966, the twenty-six year old was exploring the possibility of combining jazz with popular music. That year, he cut a rhythm and blues album with Eric Gale and Billy Butler on electric guitars and Bernard Purdie on drums, plus a four-piece front line that included Stanley Turrentine. "I wanted to explore my roots and pop music of today," he explained. "I wanted to see if I could make a record that was at the heart of rock."[1] However, Blue Note shelved the results. During this period, Hancock was also engaged in writing music for TV commercials (his famous composition "Maiden Voyage" started out as a cologne advertisement), film music (the score for Michelangelo Antonioni's film *Blow-Up,* one of the key films of the swinging sixties), and session work with Freddie Hubbard, Wes Montgomery, and Peter, Paul and Mary.

On August 31, 1968, Hancock got married and left for a honeymoon in Brazil. Food poisoning delayed his return, apparently annoying Miles Davis, who, in the interim, asked Chick Corea to leave Sarah Vaughan to join his group on keyboards. "I didn't leave Miles, I was asked to leave," said Hancock. "The timing wasn't great for me, but I also realized I'd probably need a push to leave no matter what happened."[2] He did not break away entirely from Davis, however, continuing to appear on his recordings for a while afterwards.

When Hancock told Davis's manager Jack Whittemore that he was going to form a band of his own, Whittemore asked him whom he was going to have in his trio. "When I told him I planned to lead a sextet, he told me it was impossi-

Herbie Hancock: After *Headhunters* his recordings neatly divide themselves into two categories—his electronic work, where he made a specific artistic choice to move into pop, and his acoustic work, which was confined to jazz. (Photograph by Stuart Nicholson.)

ble for a group of that size to survive," recalled Hancock.³ Given the slump of interest in jazz during the 1960s, Whittemore's remarks were hardly surprising, but Hancock was not deterred. His sextet debuted in November 1968 for an extended stay at New York's Village Vanguard with Hancock on acoustic and electric pianos, Johnny Coles on trumpet, Garnett Brown on trombone, Joe Henderson on tenor, Ron Carter on bass, and Albert Heath on drums. Much of the material they were playing at the time was characterized by the subdued tone colors and pastel shades of Hancock's 1968 solo album *Speak Like a Child.* "It's funny, when I did that record I knew that was the sound I wanted for my own band," said Hancock. "That's when I knew I was going to switch from Miles."⁴

Hancock's first album with his regular working group was *The Prisoner,* recorded in April 1969, and was close to the searching impressionism of *Speak Like a Child.* However, his next release, *Fat Albert Rotunda,* saw a much-enlarged group and a return to the rhythm and blues concept of his shelved

1966 experiment. Much of the music was derived from the soundtrack he had written for the Bill Cosby TV cartoon show *Fat Albert*. Solos were in short supply and the group sounded like a big band covering rock music, although when Woody Herman covered "Fat Mama" on his 1972 *The Raven Speaks* he made a better go of it. Where *The Prisoner* was awarded five stars by *Downbeat*, *Fat Albert* appeared lucky to collect two. The magazine said sharply, "Music is what Hancock produced until this LP. Therefore, let us hope that this album is a minor derailment."[5]

When the band went into the recording studios a year later, it was with a much-changed personnel that would stay together for the next four years, comprising Eddie Henderson on trumpet, Benny Maupin on tenor sax and bass clarinet, Julian Priester on trombone, Buster Williams on bass, and Billy Hart on drums. All the band affected Swahili names; Hancock's appellation was Mwandishi—meaning composer—from which his next album took its title. "My purpose in having this name is firstly I like the sound of it, and secondly I want to recognize my African ancestry," Hancock explained. "We're taking a look at ourselves and recognizing our heritage."[6] *Mwandishi* was primarily concerned with free forms and collective improvisation that often used unusual time signatures. "Ostinato (Suite for Angela)" is in 15/4, effectively a bar of 4/4 followed by a bar of 7/8, and features the rhythmic complexity brought to the recording session by Leon "Ndugu" Chancler, the Santana percussionist Jose "Cepito" Areas, and Ronnie Montrose. Most of the tunes appear to be "time, no changes" vehicles for improvisation, the structure of the melody providing the form and often guiding the improviser's destiny. Yet the result was sometimes shapeless, often rambling, and emotionally distant. Once again the critics were lukewarm. "Sub-par Miles Davis electric jazz," said *Downbeat*, who gave it three and one-half stars.

By now Hancock was using the Fender-Rhodes piano almost exclusively, plus a mellotron. "Miles Davis, Tony Williams, Cannonball Adderley and myself have gotten use to using electric instruments," he explained. "[We are] influenced by things that are happening in rock and we've found ways to use some of the things we've heard in more commercial aspects of black music to expand our horizons."[7] In February 1972, Hancock and his group entered the recording studios to make *Crossings*. At the suggestion of producer David Rubinson, Hancock allowed the synthesizer player (Dr.) Patrick Gleeson to overdub some effects on the completed takes with a view to giving the music broader appeal. "Electronics was associated with rock at the time—the synthesizers, just the sound of the stuff," said Hancock, "and so we felt like if we could do anything that could link us somehow to a wider audience, as weird as the music was, it could possibly help sales."[8] Hancock was quite taken with the synthesizer and invited Gleeson to join the group. Gleeson's work on *Crossings* today appears quite primitive, his synth effects sounding more like a Theremin, and was somewhat distracting in an album that struggled, like its two predecessors, to define itself. Even so, this neo-electronic experimentation was voted one of the ten best recordings of 1971 by *Time*, and interest in the group grew. One of the first jazz groups to take a synthesizer on the road, the band began to be booked into rock venues, including the Fillmores, the Winterlands, and San Francisco's Both/And.

For the next eighteen months, the enlarged band toured the circuits but failed to make the breakthrough to a larger audience that Hancock desired. "We had seven pieces and I couldn't support us all," he said. "We were playing two concerts a month—we weren't getting enough work, not enough to meet our expenses."[9] In 1973, hoping for better luck, the band signed with Columbia and, on *Sextant,* Hancock added a Hohner D-6 Clavinet with Fender fuzz, wah-wah, and Echoplex to his keyboard setup. However, the album did not make any great impact, only reaching 173 on the *Billboard* chart. Opening for Iron Butterfly and Canned Heat at Los Angeles' Inglewood Forum, Michael Ross of the *Los Angeles Times* observed, "It was an unfortunate case of being in the wrong place at the wrong time. Hancock's graceful masterly jazz was lost on the audience, as were his more easily accessible and rocking 'Wiggle Waggle' and 'Fat Albert Rotunda.' "[10]

Hancock's frustrations with a career that seemed to be headed nowhere came to a head while he was opening for the Pointer Sisters at the Troubador, also in Los Angeles. Finally he was forced to concede that his musical direction, long freeform "spacey" excursions, and episodes of recondite interaction were leaving his listeners confused. In comparison to the sort of crowd reaction the Pointers got, he realized that any possibility of his music crossing over into popular culture was remote. Within a month he had dissolved his band, his manager David Rubinson explaining to the press that he was in search of "a more solid direction for his music." Denying that Hancock was about to "go commercial," Rubinson said his client was going to "try and communicate more directly with his audience—build intensity through his sets and try and turn the crowd on."[11]

By 1971–1972, popular music had once again been swept by change. As the optimism of the 1960s faded, black music reflecting the changing dynamics of the inner cities gradually came to dominate the music scene. In 1971 Sly and the Family Stone's *There's a Riot Going On* broke through, and Marvin Gaye returned with *What's Going On,* an album of protest songs that produced an eponymously titled single and his biggest hit. A year later, Stevie Wonder's coming of age put *Music of My Mind* and *Talking Book* into the lists of million sellers. By then, three out of every ten records on Top 40 radio were from the Atlantic, Motown, and the Memphis-based Stax labels. The year 1972 also saw the rise of the Philadelphia Sound and a string of hits by producers Kenneth Gamble and Leon Huff for the likes of Harold Melvin, the O'Jays, the Three Degrees, and MFSB; that same year the Stylistics, the Jackson Five, Barry White's Love Unlimited, Al Green, and Earth Wind and Fire all made impressive showings on *Billboard*'s Hot Hundred.

But the man who had come to personify black music was the "Godfather of Soul," James Brown, dubbed the "hardest working man in show business." Brown's band performed with the discipline of the Count Basie orchestra. From the mid-sixties to the mid-seventies his soul revue played 300 nights a year across America. Brown revolutionized the foundation of soul music. The melody line to his songs had become progressively simplified while the rhythmic base was a

James Brown revolutionized the foundation of black music. (Photograph by Stuart Nicholson.)

maze of polyrhythmic complexity.[12] Chord progressions were increasingly reduced to an ostinato or vamp. The horn section was all but stripped of its melodic role; trumpets and saxes were now used to accent the beat over the chattering choke-rhythm guitar of Jimmy Nolen and staccato, broken bass patterns. Indeed, every band member's role was now percussive rather than melodic as parts moved around and jumped off each other behind Brown's stream-of-consciousness sermons. "Papa's Got a Brand New Bag" from 1965 reflected these changes in Brown's music, fashioned out of a vamp from an on-stage improvisation. In 1967 came another important hit, "Cold Sweat," which finally pulled together the key ingredients of earlier numbers like "Let Yourself Go," "Out of Sight," and, of course, "Bag." This pulsating, polyrhythmic music of great vitality was highly disciplined, and Brown himself demanded the highest standards from his band members. Tardiness was not accepted, and a missed note in performance often resulted in a fine.

Brown's autocratic style was causing friction in his band, which came to a head in 1969 when a faction within the band walked out, protesting against discipline, poor pay, and Brown's unwillingness to credit his sidemen on recordings. The dissenters formed a group of their own, Maceo & the Macks, but were no comparison to the Godfather of Soul, who carried on as if nothing happened. Brown recruited the Collins brothers from Cincinnati—William "Bootsy" on bass and Phelps "Catfish" on guitar. Bootsy, barely out of high school, was a revelation with his highly mobile bass lines, and Brown virtually rebuilt the band around his new star. Interacting with Bernie Worrell on keyboards and with drummers Clyde Stubblefield and Jabo Starks, the focus was almost entirely on the rhythm section. Guided by the increased compositional output of the legendary Bobby Byrd, they were now no longer the James Brown Orchestra but the JBs. Numbers such as "Get Up, Get Into It, Get Involved," "Sex Machine," "Give It Up or Turnit a Loose," "Soul Power," "Talking Loud and Saying Nothing," and "Super Bad" showed off the funky, syncopated bass lines Bootsy brought to the band that focused almost entirely on "the one," a series of complex figures that always turned on the "one," as in 1–2–3–4.

The highly percussive and polyrhythmic roles assigned to the horn and the rhythm sections in Brown's music had a strong corollary with African music in the way the rhythms were established to create what John Miller Chernoff has described as a "tension in time." In African polyrhythmic music, performers "resist the tendency to fuse the parts," while the "tension of the rhythms works to make time speed up or slow down." In effect, "African music is both slow and fast" in that it does not have one inner time but many, and the listener's attention may shift from one pattern of repetition to the other. "The duration of the style is important in terms of the crucial decision of when to change to get maximum effect. In the timing of the change the drummer . . . demonstrates his involvement with the social situation in a dramatic gesture that will play on the minds and bodies of his fellow performers and audience. . . . A change at just the appropriate moment will pace people's exposure to the deeper relationship of the rhythms."[13]

These aspects of African music had specific resonance in Brown's music, as in "Soul Power" (1971), a piece comprising an A section which is a vamp of indeterminate length and a B section of sixteen bars in a contrasting key. Brown engages people to participate in the rhythmic energy of the music during the A section, calling for the B section at appropriate moments during the performance with the cry "Hit me," or more specifically "Take the bridge." The effect is electric as Brown, in essence the metaphorical African lead drummer, "demonstrates his own awareness of the rhythmic potential of the music and his own personal control of its inherent power."[14]

Brown's revolutionary approach was being echoed on the West Coast, where former disc jockey Sylvester Stewart's group Sly and the Family Stone took funk onto the *Billboard* record charts and into mainstream America in a way that James Brown could not.[15] Stone's previous experience in San Francisco as a DJ meant he had contact with major acid rock groups like Jefferson Airplane—and he knew what appealed to a white, rock audience. Sly and the Family Stone were one of rock's first truly integrated bands, both racially and sexually. There was no slick choreography or mohair suits as in the Brown band—Sly's band looked and played as if they had just wandered in from Haight-Ashbury. Taking psychedelic rock's guitar sound, Sly Stone gave it a complex R&B bottom. Crucially, he gave his bass player Larry Graham a central role in his band's sound. Eighteen months after Stone's debut hit "Dance to the Music" from 1968, white America knew what funk was all about, and Stone's influence had coursed into both white and black pop music.

Larry Graham's innovative electric bass was unmistakable as he thumped the low strings with his thumb and plucked the top strings—known as "slapping and popping"—to get a sharp, percussive sound. Graham had developed the technique when playing duos with his organist mother to compensate for the lack of a drummer. His signature sound was a feature of Sly's music, such as his number one hit, "Thank You (Falettinme Be Mice Elf Agin)." Graham was one of the most influential bass players in the history of rock, but his importance did not stop there. By the mid-1970s every electric bass player in jazz had been forced to take on board Graham's new technique, particularly when Jaco Pastorius adopted thumbing and plucking as a feature of his playing. "Everybody started trying to take credit for it," said Bootsy Collins, "but it was Larry Graham, definitely Larry Graham. He was doin' with a bass what nobody was even thinking about."[16]

Larry Graham: The most influential bass player in rock, whose signature style of "slapping" and "popping" spilled over into jazz-rock and jazz. (Photograph by Stuart Nicholson.)

Meanwhile, Bootsy and Catfish Collins and Bernie Worrell had jumped ship from Brown's band to join George Clinton's Parliament/Funkadelic. Clinton's loosely formed bands were a gathering of talent influenced on the one hand by the music of Sly Stone and James Brown, and on the other by the theatricality of the British glam-rock scene. His goal was to create an over-the-top dance music that weaved humor, parody, and an ongoing socio-musical commentary from the ghetto with pure, unadulterated funk, which was achieved on albums like *Maggot Brain* (1971) and *America Eats Its Young* (1972). The impact of Brown, Sly Stone, and P-Funk was as profound on the world of pop as it was in jazz-rock fusion. It was no coincidence that Miles Davis's *On the Corner*—"I got a place for SSSlllyy," he confessed in 1973[17]—and Weather Report's *Sweetnighter* were both characterized by long, funky, polygrooves, and, by 1974, even Mahavishnu moved with the times in "Can't Stand Your Funk" on *Visions of the Emerald Beyond*.

By the time Herbie Hancock reformed his band in the summer of 1973, funk was now the new standard in black music and was the route he chose for his music. He had been listening to James Brown, Stevie Wonder, and especially Sly Stone, and had done some unreleased session work with Marvin Gaye. "I always had a secret desire . . . to play on some of Sly Stone's records. I really wanted to do that for two years," he said. "I was always amazed at every record he came up with. Then it came to me, why not do that kind of music? Not with him but with my own kind of group. It was music I believed in. It was honest music."[18]

Hancock's new unit was assembled with the specific intention of capturing the authentic sounds of funk, with only Benny Maupin remaining from his previous band. "I knew that I never heard any jazz players really play funk like the funk I had been listening to. Instead of getting jazz cats who knew how to play funk, I got funk cats who knew how to play jazz," he explained.[19] On bass was Paul Jackson, on drums Harvey Mason, and Bill Summers on percussion. By the time they went into the recording studios in the fall of 1973, Hancock had expanded his keyboard setup further with the addition of ARP Odessey and ARP Pro-Soloist synthesizers. The resulting album, *Headhunters,* was unmistakably funky, abandoning inference and allusion in favor of inculcation. "Chameleon" and Hancock's nod of approbation in the direction of Sly Stone, titled simply "Sly," were wholly inspired by Stone. "*Headhunters* was supposed to be a funk album," confirmed Hancock. "As it started to evolve, I heard it wasn't a funk album; but, whatever it was becoming, I liked the way it was headed. So I said, 'Whatever this is, let's do it.' So we did."[20]

Headhunters was an instant hit, with the single "Chameleon" appearing on DJ playlists alongside Stevie Wonder's "Living for the City" and Marvin Gaye's "Let's Get It On." The album rocketed to 13 on the *Billboard* pop chart, and by the end of the year it had sold 750,000 units, making it one of the biggest-selling jazz albums of all time and the first to be certified gold, later going on to platinum status.[21] *Headhunters* also included a harmonically modified version of "Watermelon Man" with Bill Summers playing a rhythm that related to Pygmy music from Africa on a beer bottle. Overnight Hancock became a major attraction on the rock and jazz circuits, perhaps explaining his subsequent reluctance

Herbie Hancock and the Headhunters Band: Their 1973 album *Headhunters* became one of the biggest-selling jazz albums of all time. (Courtesy of the Institute of Jazz Studies, Rutgers University.)

to stray far from the funk field, despite occasional acoustic excursions, until the mid-1990s. "One of the first concerts we did after Headhunters we were working opposite a couple of other groups, I think in Philly," recalled Hancock. "I walked in there, and one of the opening acts was on and I looked at the audience. I said, 'Wow, that's a lot of people in here tonight, who's the headliner?' And David Rubinson says, 'Don't you know what's happening here. You're heading the show!'"[22]

The follow-up album, *Thrust,* appeared in 1975, and Hancock further expanded his electronic keyboard setup with the addition of an Arp 2600 and an Arp

String Synthesizer. Mason had left, replaced by the metrically sturdy but less imaginative Mike Clark. Hancock contributed an excellent solo on electric piano on "Butterfly," a medium-tempo minor-7th vamp over which Hancock's polytonal approach made use of triads and fourths. However, the jazz-funk concept introduced with *Headhunters* produced a formula that could be exploited, and exploit it he did, over the ensuing years.

Later in 1975 came *Manchild,* aimed at Hancock's new dance-floor audience. "After *Thrust* I felt I had to meet the challenge of going towards the simple," he said.[23] Columbia's advertising was framed accordingly: "If you can listen to Herbie Hancock's 'Man-Child' and keep your feet still at the same time, see your doctor. Feel good music from one of the great musicians of all time. Herbie Hancock."[24] "*Man Child* falls short of expectations," was *Downbeat*'s response.[25] If an element of jazz improvisation was present in "Heartbeat," for example, it was locked into a rhythmic straitjacket that could not help but diminish its emotional force, and was inferior to the standards Hancock had set for himself with his acoustic work. Improvisation, in any event, was no longer the essence of these recordings, appearing less by design, more by accident. "As much as I kept trying to make it funk, it kept integrating with these jazz elements," Hancock explained.[26]

In 1975 Hancock wrote the music for the Charles Bronson feature film *Death Wish,* which featured his group, although Jerry Peters arranged and conducted the more heavily orchestrated numbers. Hancock's subsequent soundtrack album described as "banal" in one review,[27] and, among jazz fans at least, the feeling was that Hancock had crossed so far over into pop music he had almost disappeared without a trace. Such cavils were partly redressed on June 29, 1976 by a special concert at New York's Town Hall mounted by George Wein as part of the Newport Jazz Festival. Called "A Retrospective of the Music of Herbie Hancock," the concert almost failed to come off because, at this stage of his career, Hancock's manager David Rubinson was reluctant for his name to be associated with jazz since it might affect his pop sales. "I was still riding the charts with a hit pop record, which *Headhunters* was considered to be," said Hancock. "[My manager] asked George for something he thought he would never do. He said, 'Yeah, Herbie'll do it if you do like a retrospective of Herbie's music,' thinking 'George ain't gonna do that, he hasn't done a retrospective on Miles's music yet.' . . . So George came back and said, 'I think it's a great idea, let's do it.'"[28]

Featuring three bands, the first comprised Hancock's former colleagues from the Miles Davis quintet of the 1960s with Freddie Hubbard taking the place of Davis, the second reassembled the sextet Hancock led from 1969 through to 1973, while the final portion of the concert was given over to his then-current Headhunter band that included the Motown guitarist Melvin "Wah-Wah Watson" Ragin and Ray Parker, Bennie Maupin on sax and woodwinds, Paul Jackson on bass, James Levi on drums, and Kenneth Nash on percussion. The concert, subsequently released as *V.S.O.P.,* highlighted Hancock's ability in a challenging acoustic context only to show how he submerged it in the blatantly commercial surrounds of his then-current band, confirming the impression of a master musician content to let his talent languish in pursuit of commercial ends.

Later in the year *Secrets* continued Hancock's odyssey into artistic limbo, exemplified by "Doin' It," the extended opening track that even by Hancock's admission went on too long. "It's seven minutes and it should have been four," he said later. "It repeats itself too often. . . . We thought it would be hypnotic rather than monotonous."[29] Hancock's synthesized funk fantasyland was, in comparison to the real thing—Parliament/Funkadelic, for example—ersatz, while its relationship with jazz was tenuous. "Only the most ingratiating of folk would see merit here," said *Downbeat,*[30] awarding the album just two stars. Hancock continued to issue a steady stream of albums through into the 1980s, laden with vocoders and other gimmickry that echoed trends in popular music from turntable scratching to the robotic digital percussion of House. His greatest success came in 1983 with *Future Shock,* produced by Bill Laswell, which contained the Grammy-award-winning hit "Rockit," one of the biggest instrumental dance singles and video hits of the 1980s. "I've been trying to take the pop stuff more into the pop area and leave out the jazz," he explained in 1986. "I think I've pretty much succeeded at that because the last few records I don't consider jazz at all. . . . 'Rockit' has nothing to do with jazz."[31] He was right.

In contrast to his pop persona, Hancock continued a bilateral affinity with jazz, centering on an acoustic ensemble he led called VSOP (Very Special One-Time Performance) with former Miles Davis colleagues Wayne Shorter, Ron Carter, and Tony Williams and, at various times, guests Freddie Hubbard, Wynton and Branford Marsalis, and Mike Brecker, as a trio with Ron Carter and Tony Williams, and with various ad hoc groups. In 1992 he showed that his jazz chops were still intact when he toured with the VSOP group, with Wallace Roney taking Miles's role on trumpet, although the subsequent *A Tribute to Miles* with both live and studio cuts was a disappointment. In contrast, his playing reached impressive levels on *The New Standards* (1996), where he created jazz versions of contemporary pop hits. It served to emphasize that Hancock's recordings, by his own admission, neatly divide themselves into two categories, his electronic work, where he made a specific artistic choice to move into pop music, and his acoustic work, which he confined to jazz.

From *Headhunters,* Hancock's subsequent electronic albums saw him consciously distancing himself from jazz. His main frustration was with critics who judged these albums not as pop, as they were intended, but as jazz. "The very fact I come from the jazz tradition means there are certain expectations built into anyone who knows my history. So when I do the more commercial side of me, they use those expectations, which don't apply, and I wind up getting unfairly treated."[32] This situation was further confused by Columbia, who continued to market his electronic output under their "Columbia Jazz—Contemporary Masters" label. "Lots of musicians have instrumental solos and aren't associated with jazz," Hancock argued. "Because my name is associated with jazz, if I play two bars in the clear it's thought of as a jazz record."[33]

Hancock's decision to move away from jazz-rock per se towards an airplay-friendly instrumental pop music was paralleled in the work of the trumpeter Donald Byrd, who was responsible for introducing Hancock to the jazz world in 1961 when he invited the young pianist to move from Chicago to New York to join his group.[34] In the 1950s Byrd had been widely considered "a coming great" as a result of his work for Bob Weistock's Prestige label, where he was virtually the house trumpet-man. Between July 1955 and April 1958, he appeared on some sixty albums, performing with many of the era's greats before forming a regular working group with the baritone saxophonist Pepper Adams (1958–1961). Signing with the Blue Note label in 1958, he cut a string of widely admired albums for the label, many in a rigorous hard-bop-back-to-the-roots vein that in the 1980s and 1990s were extensively sampled, such as the infectious "Beale Street" from *Slow Drag* (1967).

In 1964, Byrd made an unabashed play for crossover popularity with *Up With Donald Byrd,* using female backup vocalists and a strong backbeat in numbers such as John Lee Hooker's "Boom, Boom" and Jimmy Reed's "My Babe" that had been reintroduced to mainstream U.S.A. by British beat groups such as the Animals, the Yardbirds, and the Rolling Stones. Also included in this proto-jazz-rock-pop album was the Animals' hit "House of the Rising Sun." At the time it represented but a small deviation in his jazz-oriented career path, but in 1969 he recorded *Fancy Free,* a modally based album that moved away from the soul-jazz/hard-bop rhythms of his previous albums to a light, gently swaying feel by using an electric piano and adding a two-man percussion section.[35] By *Electric Byrd,* recorded in May 1970, the emancipation from jazz's straight-ahead rhythms suggested on *Fancy Free* was now harnessed in favor of specific rock-rhythm section patterns. However, there was a feeling of following rather than leading about Byrd's new direction. "[This] album smacks of Miles Davis' current explorations," observed *Rolling Stone.* "It can be damn pleasant background music . . . [and] is getting quite a lot of airplay and isn't likely to offend anybody."[36] Less intense than Davis's *Bitches Brew,* despite the FM airplay the album did not produce the huge sales predicted for it.

By the early seventies, Byrd held a Ph.D. in college administration and was the chairman of the jazz studies department of Howard University. "My students turned me on to James Brown," he recalled in 1975, "and I knew this was it. I flipped when I heard it and said this is what I want to do. . . . I knew that if the jazz cats ever got hold of this . . . all they had to do was catch up with what the other cats were doing from the other side and turn it around. So I got my cue from Miles and people like that."[37]

In August 1971, Byrd got deeper into the soul-R&B feel by importing Joe Sample and Wilton Felder from the Crusaders on *Ethiopian Nights,* but it was not until *Black Byrd* from April 1972 that he made a significant commercial breakthrough. Produced, written, and arranged by a former student, Larry Mizell, the band included Larry's brother Fonce, another Byrd student, on trumpet along with Sample and Felder, the soul guitarist David T. Walker, and drummer Harvey Mason. Easily digestible, simple repetitive mood/dance music—"Get into the groove and move," intone the backup vocalists—this too was "pleasant background music," but it soared in the charts.

This sudden success allowed Byrd to purchase a private plane and a large collection of art and artifacts. In 1973, he began reinvesting his money in a sextet of Howard University students he called the Blackbyrds. While remaining full-time students, they took to the stage to test Byrd's theories of "applied music." Byrd negotiated a $100,000 contract with Fantasy records that initially resulted in three albums and two singles. Their first album, *The Blackbyrds,* broke on all the U.S. charts—jazz, soul and pop—while their vocal single "Walking in Rhythm," taken from their second album, *Flying Start,* went gold. With the aid of Byrd, the band mastered the art of touring while retaining their scholarly status. Their music, although selling at the time more albums than Miles Davis, is now long forgotten, a disposable mix of funk and pop.

Byrd himself continued to mine the formula that his album *Black Byrd,* Blue Note's most popular album in the history of the label, had opened up. *Street Lady* (1973) and *Stepping Into Tomorrow* (1974) continued the association with the Mizells, who added a full contingent of singers for the latter album. *Downbeat* took the unusual step of awarding it no stars, and by now it had been some while since Byrd had received a decent review in the music press. Blue Note, by then a division of United Artists records, responded to cries of "sell-out" when president Alvin Teller said, "I think Donald Byrd would be shocked at any accusations of 'commercial pandering,' because he's a man who takes his music very seriously."[38] However, in the real world, any pretense that Byrd's music was anything other than "commercial pandering" was answered by *Places and Spaces* from August 1975, his last collaboration with the Mizells.

Like Hancock, Byrd was producing pallid pop-funk, and, again like Hancock, Byrd made no pretension that what he was doing had anything to do with jazz. However, Byrd's Midas touch had deserted him after the success of his protégés the Blackbyrds, and although by the late 1970s he had made his fortune, musically he lost his way searching for another big hit. In his later career, he failed to successfully return to his earlier acoustic style or to continue his success in pop music, although he tried both.[39]

While Herbie Hancock and Donald Byrd stepped from the middle ground of jazz-rock and moved wholesale into pop music, pianist Chick Corea played the high-risk game of walking the boundary between the two. Initially, however, he was more interested in free jazz than jazz-rock, although while with Miles Davis he had recorded two albums with saxophonist Eric Kloss that suggested considerable affinity for the latter while deeply engaged in the former. A sightless person, Kloss was a musical prodigy who had recorded under his own name in a bop context since the age of sixteen. By the time he was twenty, in 1969, he had absorbed modal and free jazz and was turning to mixing jazz with rock, telling the producer Don Schlitten of his admiration for Frank Zappa's Mothers of Invention and how he was contemplating "some experimentation with serious rock . . . at least, the feeling that rock musicians are getting. . . . I'd like to combine jazz and rock. But it has to evolve, like everything."[40] He carried forward these experiments on *To Hear Is To See!* (1969) and *Consciousness* (1970), borrowing the complete Miles Davis rhythm section of Corea, Jack DeJohnette on drums, and Dave Holland on bass for these sessions. The second album, which included versions of Donovan's "Sunshine Superman" and Joni Mitchell's "Songs to Again Children," added the guitarist Pat Martino. The results were in the main successful and sincere, and quite different from Corea's approach with Holland and DeJohnette to jazz-rock with Miles Davis. Capturing the experimental spirit of the times, they reveal an honest mix of jazz and rock unencumbered by commercial aspirations.

When Corea finally left Miles Davis after a European tour in September 1970, he intended to continue exploring free jazz, which he had been playing with the trumpeter on albums like the live *Black Beauty* set from April 1970—albeit from an acoustic perspective. He was joined by Davis's bassist Dave Holland and drummer Barry Altschul, forming the group Circle. "During the time I was with [Miles's] band he became more of an abstractionist," said Corea. "I was very much into abstraction and wanted to do it even more than we were

Chick Corea: "Musically, my intentions were no longer to satisfy myself. I really wanted to connect with the world." (Courtesy of the Institute of Jazz Studies, Rutgers University.)

doing already. So near the end of the Miles thing Dave and I decided to form Circle to develop that way of playing."[41] Their first album, *The Song of Singing,* reflected this freeform approach to improvisation, although *Downbeat*'s observation contained a line that would return to haunt Corea in various guises time and again: "Everything is almost too sharp, too professional—almost mechanical."[42]

Shortly afterwards, the saxophonist Anthony Braxton joined them, and while the live *Paris Concert* (1971) was highly influential among the avant-garde, Corea himself perceived limitations in Braxtons's ability: "I felt I should have a real grounding in the basics of music, no matter what I played. That is, I should know rhythm, harmony, melody and be familiar with the great tradition of music to some extent. Anthony bypassed that grounding. . . . It's not possible to understand that very abstract stuff without understanding the basic blues. That's the kind of discrepancy that occurred with Anthony."[43] Corea's utopian dream of complete freedom of expression was doomed, it seemed, to stop a few blocks short of its destination.

Corea started yearning to return to melody, signalling this with his thoughtful playing on "Nefertiti" from *Paris Concert* and on his solo discs *Piano Improvisations Vol. 1 & 2* (1970). "That was when I discovered myself," he said. "I was beginning to put structure and melody and harmony back into my musical form."[44] Corea wound up Circle in the middle of a California tour in 1971. Around this time he had become a follower of L. Ron Hubbard's Scientology sect,[45] Hubbard's edicts leading him away from the traditional aspirations of artistic endeavor towards a somewhat less elevated goal of art-as-a-means-of-communication. This new pragmatism sought to provide a form of instant gratification for his audience, Corea explaining: "When I see an artist using his energies and techniques to create a music beyond the ability of people to connect with it, I see his abilities being wasted. . . . [I] take a look at people—at what will get across and be understandable to them—and then make something that 'happens now.'"[46]

While getting a band together to reflect this new outlook, Corea filled in by freelancing around New York. While playing with the Joe Henderson quartet, he met a young Philadelphian bass player called Stanley Clark. They struck up an immediate rapport and along with Airto Moreira, a Brazilian drummer-percussionist who was gigging with Miles Davis, the multireed man Joe Farrell, and Airto's wife Flora Purim on vocals, they began rehearsals. "The first piece I wrote was 'Return to Forever.' . . . I [had] totally reevaluated my past," said Corea. "Musically my intentions were no longer to satisfy myself. I really wanted to connect with the world."[47] The group took their name from the first composition Corea wrote for them, debuting at the Village Vanguard in November 1971. With only a few future bookings, Corea told the *Downbeat* reviewer Richard Seidel that they "planned to perform as a working unit whenever possible and would record soon."[48]

While playing at Ronnie Scott's in London in November, Corea bumped into Stan Getz, passing through after a two-year layoff in Spain. Corea had replaced Gary Burton in the Getz Quartet in 1966 and worked off-and-on for the saxophonist until 1968, when he joined Miles Davis. Corea had contributed "Litha" and "Windows" to the classic 1967 Getz album *Sweet Rain,* which took Getz into challenging new musical territory. Now on the verge of forming a new quartet, Getz commissioned a new book of compositions from Corea, asking him to put together a group for an important engagement he was scheduled to play at New York's Rainbow Room, opening on January 3, 1972.

With work still hard to come by, the Getz engagement provided an ideal opportunity for Corea to keep together key members of his band. Stanley Clarke, for example, was beginning to accept work from Pharaoh Sanders, Joe Henderson, and Art Blakey. In late December, Getz had Corea, Clarke, and Airto come to Shadowbrook, his twenty-three-room home in Irvington, a quiet suburb to the north of New York City, to rehearse. However, Getz was unhappy with Airto playing kit and moved him over to the percussion chair to make way for Tony Williams. Almost at once this new lineup clicked. Their opening was a huge hit, drawing large crowds for the duration of their stay. "The combination of Mr. Getz's highly experienced virtuosity with this remarkable rhythm section makes for jazz on an unusually sophisticated level," said the *New York Times.*[49]

Stanley Clarke: A formidable bass player who tried to reinvent himself as a pop-jazz star. (Photograph by Stuart Nicholson.)

While playing with Getz by night, Corea took his own band into the A&R Studios in New York by day to cut their first album together. *Return to Forever* remains one of Corea's most impressive works, an imaginative fusion of samba rhythms, jazz improvisation, and haunting compositions that balanced discursive melodicism—"Sometime Ago"—with succinct songwriting—"La Fiesta." Shortly after the conclusion of their record-breaking stay at the Rainbow Room, Corea was back in the A&R Studios on March 3, this time under Getz's leadership, to record *Captain Marvel.* Initially the whole album was given over to Corea's compositions "La Fiesta," "Five Hundred Miles High," "Captain Marvel," "Times Lie," "Crystal Silence," and "Day Waves." However, Getz didn't like "Crystal Silence" and replaced it with the Billy Strayhorn ballad "Lush Life." As with *Sweet Rain* from exactly five years earlier, it numbers among Getz's finest recordings.

Subsequently Getz assembled this highly contemporary group for occasional ad hoc performances in the spring of 1972. Although Hank Jones and Gary Burton replaced Corea for Getz's Newport–New York Jazz Festival appearance in July, the Rainbow Grill group without Airto was reassembled to play several summer festivals in Europe. The live set *Stan Getz at Montreux* contains memorable extended versions of "Lush Life" and Corea's "Times Lie" and "La Fiesta."[50]

Back in New York, Corea and Clarke left Getz to concentrate on Return to Forever full-time. In October 1972 they were in London to record their second album, *Light As a Feather.* Corea used more numbers written for Getz, "Five Hundred Miles High" and "Captain Marvel," plus four other originals—the title song, "You're Everything," "Children's Song," and "Spain." Comparing the numbers Getz recorded with the composer's versions is fascinating, particularly in how Getz played Corea's "singing" melodies while retaining his individuality, and how Getz projected a contemporary feel to his improvisations so as to mesh comfortably with Corea, Clarke, and Williams. In contrast, Corea's versions have a lighter, floating feel, often accented by Joe Farrell's use of flute or soprano in unison with Purim's sometimes wordless vocals backed by Airto's flowing, imaginative rhythms. Corea's "Spain" was specifically written with Airto's drumming in mind, and the fluid melodicism of Purim and Farrell is preceded by a freely interpreted extract from Joaquin Rodrigo's "Concierto de Aranjuez" to set the scene. This ebullient piece not only achieves its goal of communication, it does so without artifice.

However, the departure of Joe Farrell from the group in spring 1973 precipitated a change of musical direction. "I became intrigued with the modern way of playing the electric guitar, the sound of the guitar and also what a familiar language it creates in the world," said Corea. "The guitar seems like a very modern instrument of communication."[51] Farrell's replacement was the former Spiral Staircase guitarist Bill Connors, who had been consciously trying to move from rock into bebop and had been jamming with Mike Nock and Steve Swallow on the West Coast. By then, Airto and Flora Purim had left Corea to form their own group and had been replaced by drummer Steve Gadd and percussionist Mingo

Lewis. The band appeared at Paul Colby's Bitter End in April opposite Larry Coryell, by which time Corea had added further originals for the new guitar-based band, including "Captain Señor Mouse." A broadcast of the band[52] reveals them in transition, with "Spain" from the earlier repertoire not quite suiting the new configuration, and with two new Clarke originals, "After the Cosmic Rain" and "Bass Folk Song," suggesting an uneasy compromise between jazz-rock and Latin rock. The band went into the studios to cut *Hymn of the Seventh Galaxy*, but Gadd's refusal to tour meant he was replaced by Lenny White from the Latin-jazz-rock band Azteca—his previous musical associations included Joe Henderson, with whom he had played alongside Stanley Clarke. White gave the band an unmistakable rock underpinning, which prompted Corea to redo the whole album with White in August.

The rerecorded version of *Hymn of the Seventh Galaxy* was released in October 1973. Corea's decision to plug in, turn up the volume, and enter the jazz-rock ranks was largely inspired by the artistic and commercial success of the Mahavishnu Orchestra. "I feel the formation of the Mahavishnu Orchestra was equally important [as Miles Davis]. What John McLaughlin did with the electric guitar set the world on its ear," said Corea. "No-one ever heard an electric guitar played like that before, and it certainly inspired me. I wanted to express that emotion. John's band, more than my experience with Miles, led me to want to turn the volume up and write music that was more dramatic and made your hair move."[53] Taking McLaughlin's virtuosity as a license to demonstrate his own chops, Corea combined somewhat grandiose orchestral effects with stunningly fast passages of meticulous precision for guitar, bass, and keyboards. In particular, Corea's and Clarke's fast, complex octave unisons became widely imitated.

Yet for all their superficial gloss, the mechanical splendor of these workouts was emotionally distancing. Connors, a capable rock guitarist, was replaced in 1974 by a nineteen-year-old who had just six months of professional experience with Barry Miles and was still studying at Berklee College of Music. Al DiMeola's strength was his formidable technique, which better suited the disposition of the group. On *Where Have I Known You Before* (1974) Corea refined a technically demanding style of pomp and discourse that drew on his classical training, describing it to *Rolling Stone* as "combining all the most beautiful forms of music, classical, rock and jazz into a form that doesn't go over people's heads."[54] Dramatic orchestral effects abounded, boosted by Corea's Arp and Moog synths, and rubbed shoulders with virtuostic flourishes that made his audiences gasp, as indeed they were designed to do. "Chick's compositions were at the time the most challenging pieces written for electric guitar," said DiMeola. "RTF had a certain charisma and magic that translated on stage into something so powerful you could just sense it could eventually go over the top."[55]

Which it did, of course. After spending August to December 1974 on the road, climaxing their tour with a Carnegie Hall Concert, Corea took the band into the recording studios in January 1975 to cut *No Mystery*. "Celebration Suite (Part 1 & 2)"—a mini-symphony with a major theme, a subtheme, and an adagio—takes more than an over-the-shoulder glance at rock and the then-popular "symphonic" bands like Yes and Emerson, Lake & Palmer. Indeed, part of Corea's popularity should be seen in the broader context of "prog rock," which fostered a climate in which the flashy virtuosity of a Rick Wakeman or a Keith Emerson was widely applauded by rock audiences. Similarities were unmistakable: pompous themes, a preoccupation with speed of execution for its own sake, a reliance on the latest electronic hardware, and a shared spiritual and/or cosmic preoccupation, from Corea's *Hymn of the Seventh Galaxy* to Yes's *Tales from Topographic Oceans*. And it was not only Corea who was looking over his shoulder; Stanley Clarke professed an admiration for Yes bass player Chris Squire.

Corea, however, aware of his musical accomplishments, set out to prove he could build a bigger and better mousetrap. Retaining a solo contract with Polydor for projects under his own name, he signed Return to Forever with Columbia in 1976. Their debut album with the new label, *Romantic Warrior*, took fusion to new extremes of self-indulgence in what appeared to be a riposte to Rick Wakeman's *Myths and Legends of King Arthur and the Knights of the Round Table* from 1975. Opening with "Medieval Overture," Corea breezed through four programmatically styled pieces before climaxing with another mini-symphony, the "Duel of the Jester and the Tyrant (Part 1 & 2)," a wonderful example of what Charles Shaar Murray called "cornball monumentalism."[56]

Just as the symphonic rock bands eventually became discredited by rock critics for their empty virtuosity, Corea too was guilty of exploiting his technique at the expense of meaning, his music flowing between jazz improvisation and symphonic and commercial rock. He systematically set out to exploit his talent for commercial ends, creating a context for his playing that by his own admission was aimed at the broadest possible constituency. Obedient to the laws of homogeneity, there was a predictable gloss that readily succumbed to the temptations of grandiosity. Although Corea's high-tech MOR fusion became widely imitated, ultimately it was cute and pretentious.

Corea disbanded RTF in 1975 to form a bigger, orchestral version of the band, without a guitar this time, intended to feature his enormous keyboard setup. *Leprechaun*, recorded in 1975 but not released until the following year, won two Grammys and five stars from *Downbeat*. It had strings, horns, and voices and touched all bases, from classical suites to rock, from free form to the ethereal vocalizing of Corea's wife, Gayle Moran. *My Spanish Heart*, recorded in October 1976, contained moments when his talent shone relatively free from commercial artifice, but his remaining seventies albums moved Corea towards becoming one of the most popular jazz crossover artists of the day—albeit combining the worst of two worlds, a fusion of jazz's populist urge and rock's elitist ambitions.

With the breakup of RTF, DiMeola, Clarke, and White went their separate ways, each pursuing his own slant on fusion, but none escaping the shadow of Corea's ingratiating commercialism. DiMeola was initially filled with self-doubt as to how best to pursue his career when Corea announced he was disbanding. Despite his being named "Best New Talent of 1975" and garnering the "Best Jazz Guitar" prize from 1977 to 1981 from *Guitar Player* magazine, DiMeola's aesthetic aspirations did not run terribly deep. Such was the influence of players like John McLaughlin and Larry Coryell on DiMeola's playing that his goals at this stage of his career could be stated fairly simply. "I really wanted to become the fastest guitarist in the world," he recalled. "Just like the track stars want to become the fastest runner in the world."[57]

However, such ambitions are fine for track stars, but in fusion it triggered the guitar Olympics, where superficial flash was the only winner. Through the seventies and early eighties, DiMeola continued to churn out pyrotechnic albums, and in the early eighties he toured as part of a highly successful acoustic superstar trio with Paco de Lucia and John McLaughlin. On the whole, his solo outings were professional, predictable, and given to the exploitation of technique. By the mid-eighties, DiMeola was not so much running out of things to say as of new ways to say them. Facing this dilemma, he made an about-face to a largely acoustic style, revealing that having once played extremely fast, he could also play extremely slowly. *Tirami Su* (1987), engaged the spirit with "Beijing Demons," and while possessing DiMeola's customary professionalism, it also contained a realization that less can occasionally mean more.

Like DiMeola, Stanley Clarke had already begun a solo career on records while still with RTF. Clarke opted for the sort of pop-jazz that involved a lot of wide-eyed soloing, ear-to-ear grins, and announcements that proclaimed everyone in his band a genius. Clarke's debut as a leader, *Children of Forever* (1972), was among his best albums with the original Latin-style RTF. His next album from 1974 used Ken Scott, a British engineer who became his coproducer. This time, *Stanley Clarke* was in thrall to the electric RTF, using Bill Connors on guitar and Jan Hammer on keyboards, albeit with a degree of variation provided by Tony Williams on drums. It was not without its gruesome moments, however, such as Clarke's vocal on "Yesterday Princess" or the Third Stream fantasia "Spanish Phases for Strings & Bass." *Journey to Love* was an interesting date from 1975 that paired John McLaughlin with the guitarist Jeff Beck, at a time when the ex-Yardbird rock star had diverted temporarily into fusion. However, one of Clarke's best-remembered albums from this period is *School Days* (1976), with its cover art of the bassist engaged in the act of graffiti spraying. His fuzz bassline from the title track became de rigeur for garage-band bassists around the world. This was also the year RTF disbanded, but by then Clarke had put in extensive road-time with his own band when RTF was not on the road.

With each succeeding release, Clarke appeared to be trying to reinvent himself as a pop-rock star with jazz leanings, a new and novel species of musician who would eventually take up residence on FM radio. *Modern Man* (1978), for example, managed just two stars in *Downbeat*, who observed: "[This] is the kind of pop ephemera that will be disposed of quicker than used Kleenex."[58] By now it was a source of wonder as to exactly who it was who bought his records—or at least who would admit to owning copies of albums like *I Wanna Play for You* or *If Only This Bass Could Talk*. Clarke indulged his populist leanings with the Clarke-Duke Project, a band he coled with keyboardist George Duke that extended the boundaries of frothy "Look-Ma-No-Hands" instrumental pop on their 1981 debut album into frothy "Look-Ma-No-Hands" pop with the follow-up that had vocals, spawning the hit "Sweet Baby" that made the Top 20. The kind of self-serving grandstanding Clarke and Duke were capable of in live performance was documented on *Live in Montreux* from 1988.[59]

When Lenny White began his solo career in 1975, he too was still with RTF, but he had already served notice of his compositional style with "The Shadow of Lo," featured on Corea's *Where Have I Known You Before,* whose pretentious-ness was explained by inspiration from Gustav Holst, Jimi Hendrix, and Miles Davis. His solo debut, *Venusian Summer,* was muted because of commercial con-siderations, Patrick Gleeson's "spacey" synths giving way to trite funkisms. This lack of focus was apparent on his next three albums, which seemed to be attempts at creating the ultimate demo disc. Attempting a variety of approaches, there were some interesting moments, but never enough to fill an entire LP.

However, by this time, the game was almost up for the first wave of jazz-rock. "When fusion was first happening it was the most interesting music I had heard in my life," said George Duke. "It reached its peak with the Mahavishnu Orchestra . . . But it seemed like after that everybody was copying each other and getting too technically oriented, playing so many notes and scales that the feeling was going out of the music. Everybody was playing fast scales, and it just didn't interest me anymore."[60] A market had been identified and, in the process, jazz-rock's raw edges became smoothed over for commercial consumption.

Notes

1. *Downbeat,* May 1, 1969, p. 42.
2. *The Great Jazz Pianists,* by Len Lyons (Da Capo, New York, 1989), pp. 274–275.
3. Liner notes, *Herbie Hancock: The Complete Warner Bros. Recordings* (Warner Archives 9362–45732-2).
4. *Jazz-Rock Fusion,* by Julie Coryell and Laura Friedman (Marion Boyars, London, 1978), p. 162.
5. *Downbeat,* August 6, 1970, p. 23.
6. *Melody Maker,* August 7, 1971, p. 18.
7. *Downbeat,* August 21, 1971, p. 15.
8. *Talking Jazz,* by Ben Sidran (Pomegranate Artbooks, San Francisco, 1992), p. 112.
9. *Black Music,* January 1975, p. 30.
10. Quoted in *Music 71* (Maher Publications, Chicago, 1971), p. 10.
11. *Downbeat,* August 16, 1973, p. 12.
12. Changes that were being echoed in jazz through Wayne Shorter's compositions for the Miles Davis quintet with their smoothly contoured lines of sustained tones contrasted with highly active rhythm section interaction.
13. *African Rhythm and African Sensibility,* by John Miller Chernoff (University of Chicago Press, Chicago, 1979), pp. 112–114.
14. Ibid.
15. Brown's "Say It Loud, I'm Black and Proud" from the summer of 1968 did not find favor with white radio stations, and thereafter he found it almost impossible to get onto their playlists. He subsequently blamed them for his inability to enter the Top 20 until 1980.
16. *Dancing in the Street: A Rock 'n' Roll History,* Programme 9—Make It Funky (BBC TV).
17. "My Ego Only Needs a Good Rhythm Section," by Stephen Davis, in *The Miles Davis Companion,* edited by Gary Carner (Schirmer Books, New York, 1996), p. 164.

18. *Black Music,* January 1975, p.30.
19. *Jazz-Rock Fusion,* by Julie Coryell and Laura Friedman (Marion Boyars, London, 1978), p. 162.
20. *Downbeat,* January 1990, p. 19.
21. "Chameleon" provided the title track for a big-band album of chart covers by trumpeter Maynard Ferguson, who enjoyed considerable commercial success with the number, and in the 1990s it was extensively sampled by the hip-hoppers.
22. *Talking Jazz,* by Ben Sidran (Pomegranate Artbooks, San Francisco, 1992), p. 113.
23. *Downbeat,* September 8, 1977, p. 58.
24. Columbia trade advertisement, winter 1976.
25. *Downbeat,* January 15, 1976, p. 22.
26. Liner notes (Columbia 471235 2).
27. *Black Music,* July 1977, p. 37.
28. *Talking Jazz,* by Ben Sidran (Pomegranate Artbooks, San Francisco, 1992), p.113.
29. *Downbeat,* September 8, 1977, p. 58.
30. Ibid., November 18, 1976, p. 18.
31. Ibid., July 1986, p. 17.
32. Ibid., September 1982, p. 15.
33. Ibid., July 1986, p. 17.
34. Hancock appeared on Byrd's *Chant* in April 1961, and it was while recording *Royal Flush* with Byrd the following September that Alfred Lion of Blue Note offered Hancock a record contract in his own right.
35. This subtle refraction of rock's rhythmic pulse was sustained on *Kofi,* combining sessions from December 1969 and December 1970 that were not released until the 1990s.
36. *Rolling Stone,* February 4, 1971, p. 45.
37. *Melody Maker,* February 1, 1975, p. 39.
38. *Downbeat,* September 11, 1975, p. 45.
39. In 1988 he returned to acoustic jazz with *Harlem Blues* (Landmark Records LLP 1516) that added nothing new to the idiom and in 1993 he toured with rapper Guru, the talkative half of the chart duo Gang Star, to promote their album *Jazzamatazz,* which was subtitled "An experimental fusion of hip-hop and jazz." It was followed by *Jazzamatazz II.*
40. Liner notes, *To See Is To Hear!* (Prestige 7689), by Don Schlitten.
41. *Downbeat,* October 21, 1974, p. 14.
42. *Downbeat,* October 14, 1971, p. 20.
43. *The Great Jazz Pianists,* by Len Lyons (Da Capo, New York, 1989), p. 262.
44. *Downbeat,* October 21, 1976, p. 14.
45. It's interesting to note a parallel to Herbie Hancock's career here. Hancock was playing an esoteric kind of music but when he became involved in an alternative philosophy—in his case Nichiren Shoshu Buddhism—he suddenly began playing a more accessible, commercial type of music.
46. *Downbeat,* March 28, 1974, p. 15.
47. Ibid., October 21, 1976, p. 47.
48. Ibid., February 3, 1971, p. 28.
49. *New York Times,* January 8, 1972.
50. "La Fiesta" was also the high spot of Woody Herman's Grammy-winning album *Giant Steps,* one of his finest recorded performances since the 1940s.
51. *Jazz Forum,* unprovenanced. Jurg Solothurnmann talks to Chick Corea, p. 51. Courtesy of the National Sound Archive, British Museum.
52. For radio WLIR-FM, Quiet Village, Long Island.
53. *Downbeat,* September 1988, p. 19.
54. *Rolling Stone,* August 1, 1974.
55. Liner notes to *Chick Corea: Music Forever and Beyond* (GRP GRD–5–9819), p. 14.
56. *Crosstown Traffic,* by Charles Shaar Murray (Faber & Faber, London, 1989), p. 204.

57. Quoted in the liner notes to Al DiMeola's *Electric Rendevous* (Sony/Columbia 468216–2) by Bill Millkowski.

58. *Downbeat,* August 10, 1978, p. 30.

59. Clarke's *Live at the Greek* (Epic 4766022), released in 1994, with Najee on tenor, Larry Carlton on guitar, Deron Johnson on keyboards, and Billy Cobham on drums, was less pretentious but still aimed firmly at a following who appeared to value superficial flash at the expense of content.

60. *Downbeat,* November 1984, p. 17.

CHAPTER 11

Chain Reaction

In 1973, Columbia increased the advances against future sales to its top artists while at the same time increasing the amount spent on promoting them, to put pressure on its competitors. By 1974 all guarantees to artists had skyrocketed, and when MCA renewed Elton John's contract, they offered him the highest recording-artist guarantee to date—more than eight million dollars.[1] At the same time the cost of recording had leapt by 200 percent, while the energy crisis had created a shortage of vinyl (or polyvinyl chloride, a petroleum derivative used to make phonograph records). These factors combined to place unprecedented pressure on recording artists to attain sales targets, or be dropped from the label to whom they were signed.

In a marketplace where spiralling costs were reducing company profitability, margins were being squeezed all the way down the line. When it came to recording jazz, record producers convinced themselves that unless artists incorporated some sort of rock slant they wouldn't sell in sufficient numbers to turn a profit. Gone were the free and easy days of the 1960s when companies were more inclined to follow their instinct; now producers were less inclined to take chances, conscious of the marketing decisions behind every release. Many of the smaller, more experimental jazz labels had been gobbled up by the majors, and so they too were ruled by the new bottom-line thinking.

In such a climate, many jazz musicians were forced to reassess their artistic direction along the lines of socioeconomic reality. Those who had no affinity with what was going on in popular culture, but who felt pressured to respond in some way, found themselves being shoehorned into alien territory. Barney Kessel recorded "Hair is Beautiful," Ella Fitzgerald recorded "Sunshine of Your Love," Howard Roberts recorded "Spinning Wheel," and Paul Desmond recorded "Bridge Over Troubled Water." Never before had so many jazz musicians been importuned by the sirens of commerce into making something they neither understood nor cared for. But it didn't stop with jazz versions of pop hits. For a while, a rock-influenced version of soul-jazz, inspired by the success of Grover Washington's *Inner City Blues,* was eagerly adopted by even the most diehard jazz players.[2] Other musicians simply imported pop music effects to appear "with it." The Thad Jones and Mel Lewis Jazz Orchestra introduced rock rhythm patterns on albums like *Central Park North,* Charles Lloyd's *Moon Man* contained senseless and frustrating pop vocal effects, Benny Golson went disco with *I'm Always Dancin' to the Music,* and Bobby Hutcherson chose a pop-style rhythm section for *Linger Lane*, while Charlie Mariano went the whole hog and joined the rock group Osmosis. "It was impossible to hear any of the values he brought to his work in a long and distinguished career in jazz," wrote Leonard Feather.[3]

Coincidental with the harsh financial climate that record companies found themselves in during the early 1970s, Columbia *grand fromage* Clive Davis was dismissed, charged with improper use of company funds (he was later cleared of these charges). His uncanny instinct in responding to the sudden and unexpected rise of rock had turned around an important but conservative recording company into the most successful label of the era, with sales of rock records jumping from 15 percent to 60 percent for the five-year period ending in 1969. However, the cultural and musical changes he implemented were resented within the organization and, with a recession looming in 1973, he became the scapegoat for the company's perceived overextension.

Davis had played a significant behind-the-scenes role in giving the jazz-rock movement momentum, as much in persuading Miles Davis to change musical direction—thus in the eyes of many "sanctioning" the new music—as through the artists he brought to the label, such as the Mahavishnu Orchestra and Weather Report. The subsequent marketing push given to these artists through the resources available to a major recording company was considerable, giving jazz-rock a profile that it might not otherwise have enjoyed in the marketplace. When Herbie Hancock's *Headhunters* went gold, *Rolling Stone* announced that 1974 was "the year of jazz-rock." Hoping to repeat this success, the hunt was on for more artists who might have "crossover" appeal. Columbia consciously sought to establish themselves as the major force in jazz-rock fusion, heralding the trend as "the dawn of a new jazz age. Jazz has taken a long-overdue upbeat swing lately: the esoteric music of a relatively select few has become the music for just about everybody. . . . Jazz is entering a new age and we're very glad to hear it."[4]

But with Clive Davis's sharp ears and business instinct now replaced by accountants and "market strategies," the pioneering spirit of Columbia's early jazz-rock signings receded. Artists who ultimately failed to make their mark on the ledger in any significant way began to crowd Columbia's rosters, such as Dexter Wansel, Webster Lewis and the Post-Pop, Space-Rock, Be-Bop Gospel Tabernacle Orchestra and Chorus, Rodney Franklin, The Chris Hinze Combination, John Blair, Janne Schaffer, Hilary, Walt Bolden, and Jaroslav. Other majors followed Columbia's aggressive lead in signing up similar crossover artists, most of whom disappeared as their first albums hit the cut-out bins. With several musicians dedicating their not inconsiderable talents to middle-of-the-road blahs, including George Benson, Bob James, John Klemmer, and Hubert Laws, accusations became rife in the music press about "selling out." Unprecedented numbers of jazz musicians were making an attempt to get on what was now an accelerating bandwagon by producing "music in a style often more representative of what they hoped would sell than what they believed might endure,"[5] such as several horn players who "electrified" their instruments. Clark Terry, Sonny Stitt, and Eddie Harris were among several who experimented with a device known as the Varitone, something its manufacturer claimed would "extend your range a full octave by turning a knob. You play in perfect octaves . . . [plus] a built-in echo, a variable tremolo, all this is yours too . . . lets you cut through an electronic organ, a whole bedlam of amplified guitars."[6] Harris was the first of the acoustic hornmen to go electric, with albums such as *The In Sound* (1966), *The Tender Sound* (1967), *The Electrifying Eddie Harris* (1967), which featured the space-funk classic "Listen Here," and *Plug Me In* (1968). Harris always had good commercial instincts; his first album, *Exodus* (1961) sold over two million copies, and in 1972 he confronted jazz-rock literally by importing two rock musicians, guitarist Jeff Beck and keyboard player Stevie Winwood, on *Eddie Harris in the UK*.

Harris's large discography includes plenty of dogs, but at heart he was a down-to-earth soul jazzman, despite his commercial pretensions. An association with the pianist Les McCann produced what the *New York Times* called "a highly successful collaboration"[7] at the Montreux Jazz Festival in June 1969, documented on *Swiss Movement*. With McCann setting up some inspired grooves on "You Got It In Your Soulness," Harris and trumpeter Benny Bailey bring the crowd to their feet, with the pianist emerging as the star. The central exhibit was "Compared to What," an impassioned social commentary spelled out by McCann's vocals while he accompanied himself on acoustic piano, with Harris's electric sax solo sounding as if he was under water.

By 1971, an electrified version of soul-jazz was selling in large quantities, exemplified by the saxophonist Grover Washington Jr. on the CTI/Kudu record label. Washington had been signed to Kudu, a subsidiary of CTI Records, by CTI label head Creed Taylor, after he appeared on Johnny Hammond's album *Breakout* in 1971. Taylor was an experienced record company executive with a string of credits for the Verve and A&M labels. He left his position as staff producer at A&M Records in 1970 to launch his own label, Creed Taylor International, or CTI. He had a clear idea of what he wanted to achieve: sound and sleeve quality would be high, his roster of artists would appear on each others' albums, and Taylor would produce everything himself at Rudy Van Gelder's studios at Englewood Cliffs, New Jersey. Central to Taylor's production style was the role of house pianist-arranger Bob James, who himself later developed a separate career in listener-friendly "fuzak."[8] James became Taylor's right-hand man at CTI and eventually assumed production duties himself.

There was an intentional uniformity about CTI Records that served a specific purpose. Despite the adventurous histories of its artists, the CTI label was a guarantee of smooth, listener-friendly jazz. CTI signing, George Benson recorded just one perky album with an organ trio, *Beyond the Blue Horizon* (1971), before succumbing to the house style and becoming enveloped in strings on his best-selling *White Rabbit* from November 1971, where he was packaged by Taylor as the next Wes Montgomery. Notable jazzmen like Freddie Hubbard, Milt Jackson, Paul Desmond, and Stanley Turrentine all churned out well-performed, mellow jazz washed with gentle rock rhythms that could function as both foreground and background music. As safe for radio airplay as cocktail parties, Taylor had his artists record well-known melodies wherever possible to help sell their improvisational talents. Some CTI artists hit big using this formula: Eumir Deodato dominated the airwaves for almost six months in 1972 with his version of "Also Sprach Zarathustra." After hearing the classical version—as Richard Strauss intended it to be—on the soundtrack to Stanley Kubrick's *2001: A Space Odyssey,* Taylor suspected there was a hit in the making. He was right. A jazz-rock version with brass, woodwinds, and strings—with a rhythm section of Deodato on keyboards, John Tropea on guitar, Stanley Clarke on bass, Billy Cobham on drums, and Airto on percussion—won a Grammy, was nominated top instrumental by *Billboard, Cashbox,* and *Record World,* and was voted number one orchestral album by *Playboy* magazine.

Equally, Grover Washington's success on the CTI subsidiary Kudu owed much to the CTI formula, though Kudu artists were allowed a little "funky" latitude. In September 1971 Taylor asked Washington to deputize for Hank Crawford on a session and, to everyone's surprise including Washington's, the resulting album, *Inner City Blues,* was a huge success. "It happened so fast," recalled Washington in 1973. "One day people weren't listening to jazz . . . and the next thing jazz is selling."[9] In 1975 his album *Mister Magic* hit the number one spot on the album charts and was certified gold, followed in quick succession by more easy-listening albums. When CTI folded, *Winelight* on the Elektra label carried Washington's popularity into the 1980s, garnering a Grammy for "Best Fusion Album of 1981." In fact, Washington could be far more down-to-earth in live performance than his increasingly glossy albums suggested. During his appearance at the 1982 Playboy Jazz Festival, for example, he transformed his wispy Platinum-earning "Winelight" into something gutsy, a side of his playing the seldom surfaced on record.[10]

With the commercial success of Donald Byrd's *Blackbyrd* in 1972, Blue Note records, followed the lead of Kudu and moved into similar glossy, instrumental, fusion-styled territory. The famous independent jazz label was purchased in 1965 by Liberty Records, who in turn were purchased by media conglomerate United Artists. Original founder Alfred Lion stayed on until 1967 when ill health forced him to retire, while his partner Francis Wolff continued until his death in 1971. Fairly quickly thereafter, the label began specializing in "crossover" artists. "Blue Note was primarily a jazz label until not too long ago," said Alvin Teller, Liberty/United Artists president, "and I think a primary jazz attitude for a long time was to disdain commercial success. . . . There's nothing preventing a musician from following a legitimate course and becoming a commercial success. . . . Blue Note is no longer solely a jazz label, we are becoming much more of a contemporary/progressive label."[11] What Teller meant was that, like all the majors, Blue Note was recording commercial, funky pseudo-jazz with artists such as Noel Pointer, Earl Klugh, Bobbi Humphrey,

Eddie Henderson, and Ronnie Laws. Laws, whose *Pressure Sensitive* became the biggest selling Blue Note album, overtaking Donald Byrd's *Black Byrd*, was clearly a capable tenor saxophonist who hailed from the Houston jazz scene, but his big-toned Texas tenor was placed in formula funk surroundings, which on subsequent albums became tiresome and restricting.[12]

By now, fusion had become more and more frankly a commercial proposition. In many ways the career of the West Coast group the Jazz Crusaders became something of a metaphor for the commercialization of the music. At the beginning of their career they were a capable, well-organized hard-bop outfit. But with the haunting "Freedom Sound," from the 1961 album of the same name, the group not only had a title that resonated with the times but a more open, expansive, and less complicated sound that smoothed away the harsh contours of hard bop. Featuring founding members Wayne Henderson on trombone, Wilton Felder on tenor, Joe Sample's sprightly, bluesey piano that said just enough without being super clever, and "Stix" Hooper's tight drumming, the group's concept was quite different from that of the East Coast or Detroit jazz musicians. "We always had a factor of rhythm and blues under the music," said Sample, "and it was very, very appealing to listeners."[13] Yet there were few places for black jazz groups to play in Los Angeles; their only regular jazz gig was at the Lighthouse in Hermosa Beach. Between 1961 and 1969 they recorded seven albums for the local label Pacific Jazz, and while some had done well—*Freedom Sound* sold over 50,000 copies—they seemed to be going nowhere as a jazz group, never quite moving out of the first rank of the second tier of jazz groups of the period.

After a brief hiatus, they re-formed in 1969, and returning to their roots—they had begun as a dance outfit called The Nite Hawks—they added jazz licks to R&B rhythms and came up with *Old Socks, New Shoes*. In 1972 they dropped the word "Jazz" from their name and, with the addition of guitarist Larry Carlton, *Crusaders I* became their first big album, with sales of around 250,000, propelled by the hit single "Put It Where You Want It." A "groove" number, the piece is characterized by great restraint, with every musician subservient to the needs of the moment. The "groove" demands that you "listen with your body," its effectiveness almost entirely mediated by the physical effect the music has on its listeners—whether they feel compelled to snap their fingers or get up and dance. Engaging with the music in this way, rather than contemplating it, is quite different from "listening with the mind" and performances of, say, Beethoven, whose music often involves a denial of bodily repsonse as the mind absorbs its technical complexity. The groove is a rhythm-focused experience of African origin in which the body is engaged with the music in a way that it is not with European music, as John Miller Chernoff notes. "The African drummer concerns as much about the notes he does not play as the accents he delivers,"[14] and the groove shares this characteristic with its rhythmic economy in its concern with not overplaying to achieve its effect. This distinction is significant because The Crusaders' economical "grooves" became hugely influential. Tracks like "Sweet Revival" were widely imitated, inspiring a particular kind of jazz-influenced instrumental dance music that would come to dominate FM airplay.

Crusaders I was followed by the Grammy-nominated *The 2nd Crusade,* which again sold well, earning a four-star rating from *Downbeat,* who commented, "Crusader style music combines a brand of jazz that rocks, and rock that swings, along with some down-home funk that has gospel overtones."[15] From hole-in-the-wall jazz clubs the group moved into large popular clubs like the Roxy, the famous Hollywood night spot, and began selling out concert halls when they went out on the road on tour. "We proved that there was something in black instrumental music that could open doors," said Felder. "We play black influenced music that is very ethnic."[16]

The Crusaders had found a winning way with lightweight tunes based on solid rhythms and unpretentious solos that never reached beyond themselves. *Scratch,* a live concert at Los Angeles's Roxy Club recorded in 1973, epitomized this approach, with the band hitting their customary groove to the audible delight of their fans. When sales of *Southern Comfort* (1974) hit 500,000, the Crusaders had hit their creative peak. All that was left was more of the same, or the same with whistles and bells. That year Henderson left the band to become an independent producer, and in 1976 Carlton left to pursue a solo career. The band kept on into the 1980s, however, getting progressively more commercial.

The seventies-era Crusaders (prior to the departure of Wayne Henderson and Larry Carlton) virtually wrote the rulebook for simple, foot-tapping, electronic groove music, and the debt bands like Tom Scott and the LA Express, Stuff, Grover Washington, Jr., and Dave Sanborn owe the Crusaders is plain for everyone to hear. It is no exaggeration to say that subsequent generations of 1980s and 1990s pop-jazz fusion artists all took something of the Crusaders, either at first hand or at one remove through a whole host of Crusaders-influenced bands. Many artists hired Felder, Hooper, and Sample for their sessions just to get the "Crusaders groove," including Donald Byrd, Aretha Franklin, Johnny Mathis, Steely Dan, Joni Mitchell, David T. Walker, and Michael Franks. Never claiming to be among the jazz vanguard, their work was almost always mediated by good taste. While they could hardly be held responsible for what followed in their wake, it is instructive to listen to their early albums to hear the font of groove music that came to dominate FM fusion. "The challenges of the music are not always the complexities," Felder once observed. "The so-called simplicities can be very challenging."[17]

One of the first to adapt the Crusaders' style was their fellow West Coaster saxophonist Tom Scott. A child prodigy, he was an accomplished musician by the time he made his recording debut at seventeen in a group led by Roger Kellaway, *Spirit Feel.* Shortly afterwards he appeared on Oliver Nelson's *Live in Los Angeles* and was a featured soloist with the Don Ellis big band. He was soon a much in-demand session player, playing the Hollywood studios by day and jazz clubs by night. In the early 1970s he began playing every Tuesday night at a North Hollywood club called "The Baked Potato," a small jazz house that attracted some of L.A.'s finest jazz musicians, with a group that included pianist Mike Wofford, bassist Chuck Domanico, and drummer John Guerin. In 1973, Crusader Joe Sample came in on piano and Max Bennett—who would later appear on Crusader albums such as *Scratch* and *Unsung Heroes*—replaced

Tom Scott: A prolific composer for films and television whose use of electronic jazz-rock-influenced soundtrack music helped speed the popularization of a consumer-friendly mutation of jazz-rock known as fusion into the entertainment mainstream. (Photograph by Stuart Nicholson.)

Domanico on bass. Scott took this quartet to the International Song Competition in Caracas, Venezuela, and on their return the idea for a band called the LA Express was born when Sample and Bennett began playing Crusader-like grooves. "I have to credit Max Bennett with turning the band around from bebop to what is commonly known as fusion, though we didn't use the term at the time," recalled Scott. "He brought in a couple of tunes that were kind of rock-oriented. It was amazing to see what happened. First of all they were all real simple little tunes that were fun to play to kind of get a jazz-flavored groove happening. . . . Then it was suggested we add a guitar so we got Larry Carlton [then a Crusader regular] . . . and after a few months you couldn't get into the joint."[18]

In 1974 Scott was invited to appear on Joni Mitchell's album *For the Roses,* which led to his appearance with the LA Express on Mitchell's monster hit *Court and Spark,* for which he did all the arranging. Scott and the LA Express then went on tour backing Mitchell for seven months, recording the live *Miles of Aisle* (1974).[19] This exposure, together with his widely admired solo on Carole King's number-one single "Jazzman" (from *Wrap Around Joy*, 1974) helped Scott's career as a studio musician to take off.

However, Scott was having problems getting the LA Express recorded. He finally convinced friend and engineer Hank Cicalo to record them in his spare time during 1974. Lou Adler of Ode Records eventually bought the tapes but refused to sign the band, signing only Scott. The resulting album, *Tom Scott and the LA Express*, featured the group's "Baked Potato" lineup. It was a restrained affair, not far removed from the grooves of *Crusader II*. Only in "LA Expression" and "Vertigo" does Scott become animated, revealing a highly artic-ulate style rooted in hard-bop orthodoxy. "This album displays Scott's 'aware-ness' of the commercial market-place," observed *Downbeat* wryly.[20] When the Crusader members of the quartet went on tour, Larry Nash came in on key-boards and Robben Ford on guitar, and this revised lineup cut *Tom Cat* during the balance of 1974 and early 1975. Dealing with the jazz-rock idiom simply, using the tried and tested hard-bop methodology of head-solos-head, the results were, like hard bop, governed by the feel of the grooving rhythm section and the strength of the solos.

However, with Lou Adler set on developing Scott's career on record as a soloist, LA Express went their separate way, with David Luell replacing Scott on tenor and Victor Feldman replacing Nash on keyboards. Signing with Caribou Records, they recorded *LA Express* in 1976 and went on tour with Joni Mitchell. Later in the year they recorded *Shadow Play* but the results were a disappoint-ment. Sans LA Express, Scott linked up with the Stuff rhythm section of Steve Gadd, Eric Gale, and Richard Tee, plus Bob James on piano for a brief tour in 1975 to promote *New York Connection*. However, Scott's career on records appeared subservient to commercial rather than aesthetic considerations, con-sisting mainly of glossy ephemera. "I don't have a problem with this art versus commerciality debate," was Scott's masterful summation of the self-evident.[21] Far better were Scott's charts for Steely Dan on their *Aja* and *Gaucho* albums, although he initially was skeptical of the group's commercial potential. "I heard a test pressing that Walter [Becker] brought over," he said. "I put it on and thought, man, this is great. It's far too esoteric for the average pop buyer. It won't sell ten copies. Of course the thing went on the charts and stayed there about a year."[22] A telling statement indeed, since so much of Scott's recorded output acceded to H. L. Mencken's maxim that no one ever lost any money underestimating the taste of the American public. Artistically, however, Scott will probably never live down his stint as bandleader on *The Chevy Chase Show* or his decision in 1982 to work as Olivia Newton-John's musical director and flout the musician's boycott of South Africa by playing ten days at the exclusive Sun City resort.

Parallel with his performing career, Scott worked as a film and TV composer, perhaps exerting his greatest influence through his very popular scores. He wrote the music for numerous motion pictures, including *Uptown Saturday Night*,

Nine Lives of Fritz the Cat, Conquest of the Planet of the Apes, Mr. Culpepper's Cattle Company, and *The Sidecar Boys.* His specialty, however, was action-adventure television series, including *Canon, Dan August, Cade's Country, Barnaby Jones,* and *The Streets of San Francisco.* All these series commanded peak viewing spots and enormous audiences, particularly *San Francisco,* one of the best-loved police series of the 1970s. First broadcast by ABC in September 1972, it lasted through 120 hour-long episodes until June 1980. It was one of several major television series that were turning to slick, glossy, fusion-derived rhythm tracks with brief episodes of jazz improvisation to underscore the on-screen action. Originally, Patrick Williams provided the jazz-oriented scores for the series, performed by a full orchestra, but later episodes used electronically generated sounds. The reason for this may not initially have been a matter of public taste, but one of cost, since it is cheaper and easier to generate synthesized sounds than it is to use large orchestras. In the spring of 1975 Scott wrote the soundtrack music for *Starsky and Hutch,* an all-action cops-and-robbers show; the electronic jazz-rock-influenced background music for car chases, fight scenes, and shoot-outs was given considerable prominence over the eighty-eight episodes screened until late 1981. An overproduced version of Scott's theme music for the series, "Gotcha," appeared on *Blow It Out* (1977), which blurred the lines between his soundtrack and solo work (it could be argued that post–LA Express his albums were soundtracks for imaginary TV series). These shows, beamed in weekly to televisions across America at prime-time viewing slots, helped speed the popularization of a consumer-friendly mutation of jazz-rock that came to be known as "fusion" into the entertainment mainstream.[23]

The music industry's move towards a commercially popular jazz-influenced instrumental music was not all sellout, however. West Coast pianist Gene Russell made a sudden and initially very successful leap into entrepreneurship when he formed the Black Jazz label with Dick Schory in 1971. Recording a series of neglected artists from around the Los Angeles area, the company took off with remarkable vigor, achieving airplay and sales beyond anybody's expectations. Russell expanded his activities to include the "Black Jazz Festival" (a series of Sunday matinees at the Lighthouse on Hermosa Beach), showcases for Black Jazz artists at the Hollywood Palladium, and a short run of Black Jazz television shows.

One of Black Jazz's most popular acts was Doug Carn, who put out four albums on the label. An organist who was formerly with the Savoy label, Carn moved to the West Coast from Atlanta, where he was heard by Russell and signed to the label in 1971. With his wife Jean providing vocals, his debut, *Infant Eyes,* was a set of contemporary jazz classics which were provided with lyrics, such as Coltrane's "Acknowledgement," Wayne Shorter's title cut, and Horace Silver's "Peace." As with *Spirit of the New Land* (1972) and *Revelation* (1973), these tracks come out of the bebop tradition, Coltrane, and the electric fusion of jazz and rock. Although Carn was described as "one of the most creative new faces to emerge in the 1970s" who "is one of the very few to commercialize jazz without forsaking its substance,"[24] his music would be more interesting today if were not for the vocals; his wife's singing was a little inflexible and her phrasing stiff. Carn, who once recorded with Maurice White's popular Earth, Wind & Fire, was a strong soloist on organ and electric keyboards—he was among the first jazz keyboard players to use a Moog synthesizer—whose band included from time to time Ola Duru on trumpet, Rene McLean on saxes, Walter Booker on bass, Earl McIntyre on trumpet, Nathan Page and Calvin Keys on guitars, Ronnie Laws on tenor, and, in *Spirit of the New Land,* Alphonse Mouzon on drums.

Other Black Jazz signings included The Awakening, Calvin Keys, Roland Hayes, Walter Bishop Jr., Rudolph Johnson, Henry Franklin, Kellee Patterson, and Chester Thompson.[25] Their work represents a fascinating countercurrent to the major labels' tendency to commercialize and commodify jazz-rock into something bland and innocuous. These are unpretentious experiments in jazz-rock fusion without recourse to commercial artifice, and, although horns feature strongly, they do not come from the perspective of soul bands but from the hard-bop tradition. The Awakening, for example, was a direct meeting of hard-bop with electric keyboards and rock rhythms, while Calvin Keys used bop-derived heads over a relaxed rock rhythm setup by Ndugu Leon Chancelor on drums with bop-derived solos from the leader's guitar, Charles Owns on soprano, and Kirk Lightsey's electric piano. Despite the strong ties to a previous era of jazz, these bands, for the most part, sound invigorated by the new technology and rock rhythms, using them as a means to extend their expressionism, and in the main they avoid the jazz musician's tendency to overcomplicate rock rhythms. For five years the Black Jazz label released material by unknown artists defying the economic realities of the time, but in 1976 Gene Russell died and Dick Schory decided soon after to close the label after releasing twenty albums. However, despite the quiet popularity of the Black Jazz stable of artists, it was clear that there were no longer any groups emerging of the stature of a Miles Davis band, a Mahavishnu, or another Weather Report.

On the fringes, there was the godfather of rap, Gil Scott-Heron, who merged radical rants and heavily cadenced street poetry, influenced by the *Last Poets,* on albums like *Small Talk at 125th and Lenox;* later he would be acknowledged as a seminal influence by first-generation rappers like the Sugarhill Gang and Grandmaster Flash in the late 1970s. Lonnie Liston Smith and the Cosmic Echoes realized a space-is-the-place slant with *Reflections of a Golden Dream.* His first album, *Astral Travelling,* was made up of acoustic, texture-laden vamps, but by his fourth recording he had gone electric and was drawing on R&B influences on albums like *Cosmic Funk.* Cosmic jazz was the special province of astral traveller Sun Ra, whose mixture of outré big-band experimentation, space theater, and dalliance with black pop idioms appeared on over a hundred albums for his own self-produced label, Saturn Research, plus many for other labels that included voyages into avant-garde rock, among the many directions his band followed. Ra's *Space Is the Place* (October 1972), with its hypnotic chant on the title track, became popular with DJs in 1990. Indeed, the more abstract the soundtrack to club culture, the more people name-checked Sun Ra as an influence, as with the Mo' Wax/U.N.K.L.E. EP "Time Has Come."

David Sanborn: At pains to point out that he was not a jazz musician but he was almost always an engaging soloist, even if the context was often the pop end of R&B and funk. (Photograph by Stuart Nicholson.)

In general, however, by 1975 jazz-rock seemed to have surrendered to commercial homogenization, prompting critic Robert Palmer to observe that "electric jazz/rock fusion is a mutation that's beginning to show signs of adaptive strain. . . . Fusion bands have found that it's a good idea to . . . stick with fairly simple chord voicings. Otherwise the sound becomes muddy and overloaded. This means that the subtleties of jazz phrasing, the multi-layered textures of jazz drumming and the music's rich harmonic language are being abandoned."[26] A blandness was creeping into the music influenced by jazz-tinged, electronic instrumental music that flowed into the entertainment mainstream through television, films, FM radio, and recordings. The dominant non-jazz elements of the jazz-rock equation were no longer coming from the creative side of rock, but from pop music with simple melodic hooks and currently fashionable dance beats. Major record companies, catering to a perceived demand for this type of music, cranked out countless albums that were immaculately recorded concoctions of flawlessly executed but emotionally unengaging solos against bland supportive musicianship. Guitarists like Lee Ritenour—who worked on the soundtrack of *Saturday Night Fever* and *Grease*—and musicians such as Larry Carlton and Jeff Lorber became masters of electronic instrumental albums with pretty hooks and funky vamps out of the Crusaders nexus.

By the early 1980s, one of the most popular artists in crossover jazz was the alto saxophonist David Sanborn, influenced by Hank Crawford and with a background in R&B. "I came from the R&B side of the tree," he said. "I started out listening to Ray Charles and that really inspired me as a kid. That was a mixture of jazz, gospel, and rhythm and blues. That was my original inspiration."[27] After an illness he took up the alto and played alongside blues legends Albert King and Little Milton. After studying music at Northwestern University and the University of Iowa, he joined Paul Butterfield's Blues Band in 1967, going on to work with Stevie Wonder's entourage between 1970 and 1972, appearing on *Talking Book*. In 1973 he became a regular in Gil Evans's big band until the mid-1980s, and in 1976 he toured with the Brecker Brothers band. By the 1980s Sanborn had developed a highly personal tone on alto; intense, sometimes preaching, sometimes heartrending, he found himself in demand as a session player on albums such as *Undercover* by the Rolling Stones, *Gorilla* by James Taylor, *Young Americans* by David Bowie, *Born to Run* by Bruce Springsteen, *Gaucho* by Steely Dan, and *Living in the USA* by Linda Ronstadt. His ubiquity made him one of the most imitated alto sounds in pop and jazz; his use of the altissimo register, although not new in jazz, became his trademark and was widely adopted by most fusion saxophonists.

However, it wasn't until his early thirties that Sanborn recorded under his own name. His association with Warner Brothers records produced an almost unbroken run of successful albums from the late 1970s through the 1980s, with *Voyeur* winning a Grammy in 1981 for "Best Rhythm and Blues Instrumental" and *Straight to the Heart* a 1985 Grammy for "Best Fusion Record of the Year," further enhancing his career in crossover music. In 1992 he observed, "I've made about fifteen or sixteen albums now and I like them. I don't want to sound pretentious, but I want them to say something, more than just a chronicle of the moment in time. For example, on *Backstreet* I did a tune called 'A Tear for Crystal,' more interesting changes than a straight-ahead vamp. But in order to fit the album I had to compromise some of the ideas that would have naturally evolved in developing a tune like that so it would fit the context of the album."[28]

Compromises are, of course, a part of crossover music; the question is, how many and how far do they go? Sanborn, who was always at pains to emphasize he was not a jazz musician, nevertheless was a soloist who was almost always engaging and imbued with the spirit of jazz—as his solos for Gil Evans albums such as *Svengali, Priestess,* and *Live at the Festival Hall 1978* attest. During the 1980s he worked extensively with Marcus Miller, and his albums were derived from the pop end of R&B and funk. "I would say that 75% of the time I was playing to some kind of metric, some kind of click," Sanborn said. "I just got

tired of the process, it started getting clinical to me. In terms of production values I found myself sliding into that area and it felt very uncomfortable, like musical necrophilia, doing all the work and getting nothing back."[29] Then followed an
acoustic outing in 1992 with *Another Hand*, which did not fare well at the hands
of the critics. Sanborn's answer was his best-selling album *Upfront*. Back in the
FM electric crossover field, he appeared as one of the finest performers within
the genre.

Perhaps the biggest-selling crossover artist was the saxophonist Kenny
Gorelick, who debuted on the Arista label in 1982 with *Kenny G*, followed by *G
Force*, which sold over 200,000 copies. An uncomplicated R&B-based fusion
aimed at FM airplay, both albums and the subsequent *Gravity* were not served
well by the inclusion of vocal tracks. With *Duotones*, the vocals were dropped
and, with the success of the single taken from the album, "Songbird," Kenny G
hit the big time. Subsequent best-selling albums and sellout tours seemed to suggest that an awful lot of people enjoyed his middle-of-the-road, no-surprises,
easy-listening style, which had become omnipresent on FM radio.

With the success of artists like Sanborn and Kenny G in the 1980s, Chick
Corea, one of the most popular crossover artists of the 1970s, decided to reenter
the field. Corea had returned to acoustic jazz at the end of the 1970s and reaffirmed his status as one of the most accomplished pianists of his generation,
alongside Herbie Hancock, who similarly undertook acoustic endeavors, and
Keith Jarrett, who remained unflinchingly acoustic post-Miles. But in 1986, after
a period of diverse musical activities from playing Mozart with the pianists
Fredrich Gulda and Keith Jarrett to experimenting with freeform playing and
accompanying spoken word, he nailed his colors to the fusion mast with a new
outfit, The Chick Corea Elektric Band, which took its name from the poem
"Elektric City."

Formed around two precocious young musicians, John Patitucci on acoustic
and electric basses and Dave Weckl on drums, its alter ego was his Grammy-
winning trio, the Akoustic Band. *The Chick Corea Elektric Band* was basically an
electric trio set recorded live at Iowa State University in 1986 with the guitar
whizz Scott Henderson guesting on one track. From the start, this band took off
from where RTF had left off in the 1970s with its dedication to the exposition of
chops with rhythmically and melodically complex themes, tight ensemble passages, and colorful writing with plenty of hooks. But as with RTF, great technical skills are no guarantee of great music and, despite the mechanical expertise
on display, nothing of genuine substance seemed to be on offer. Indeed,
Corea's stated intention for their second album, *Light Years*, with Eric
Marienthal on tenor sax and the Australian guitarist Frank Gambale added to
the basic Elektric trio, was to get radio airplay with all the compromises this
entailed. A musician as talented and experienced as Corea knew all the right
moves, and the album entered the *Billboard* chart at 15 and won a Grammy in
1987. In 1990 the band made the more ambitious *Inside Out*, which Patitucci
amusingly dubbed "Chick and Bartok meet the Elektric Band."[30] It featured
complex, angular, and virtuosic playing not normally associated with fusion

recordings. Weckl's and Patitucci's last recording together with the Elektric Band was on *Beneath the Mask* (1991). This was perhaps the best of the Elektric Band's albums, but despite the faultless techniques of the participants, the music remained glossy and emotionally distancing. In 1993, Corea introduced the Chick Corea Elektric Band II, with Corea on keyboards, Marienthal on saxes, Mike Miller on guitar, Jimmy Earl on bass, and Gary Novak on drums. Their debut album, *Paint the World,* was dominated by high-tech confectionery. "[Corea's] warmed over fusion licks and bluesy clichés sound plodding and stale," said *Downbeat,* awarding the album two and one-half stars.[31]

Both Weckl and Patitucci developed their own careers on records with the GRP label and both brought high-powered guests into the studios, including Corea, Mike Brecker, Vinnie Colaiuta, Anthony Jackson, and each other—Patitucci on Weckl's *Sketchbook* (1990), *Another World* (1993), and *Mistura Fina* (1995), Weckl on Patitucci's *Master Plan* (1990), *Heads Up* (1992), and *Hard Wired* (1994). They were albums of contemporary-sounding, melodic music, slickly played with precise technical skills, but after a while it all becomes a blur. The triplets, the breathtaking unison lines, the double stops wedded to a predominance of major-key tonalities and catchy, predictable hooks meant that this music could function equally well as both background and undemanding foreground music. In short it was music designed for the millions of listeners who tuned in to commercial FM stations.

This roturierian music proliferated in the 1980s and 1990s, with musicians framing their product to compete in a marketplace of playlists, formatting, and the *Billboard* charts. The GRP label signed a whole stable of artists to function in this musical environment, including Lee Ritenour, Larry Carlton, Tom Scott, Dave Benoit, George Howard, Nelson Rangell, and Eric Marienthal and the groups Spyro Gyra, the Yellowjackets, and the Rippingtons. Spyro Gyra, with the demise of Weather Report, became the longest-established of the regular touring fusion bands, featuring the easy virtuosity of saxophonist Jay Beckstein and vibraphonist Dave Samuels. Originally members of the Buffalo Jazz Ensemble, they put themselves on the map with a single, "The Shaker Song," taken from their album *Spyro Gyra,* in 1978. The following year they had a monster hit with the title track off *Morning Dance,* which established them as a solid, middle-of-the-road fusion band with soft Latin leanings. They were far more convincing in concert than their run of somewhat bland albums, which often sacrificed a true group identity by importing countless studio guests.

The Yellowjackets began with the British blues guitarist Robben Ford in their midst, but he left after appearing on the group's first two albums, *Yellowjackets* (1981) and the Grammy-nominated *Mirage à Trois* (1983). Founded by the bassist Jimmy Haslip and the pianist Russell Ferrante, the group became FM radio-play certainties with a run of sure-footed but unsensational instrumental pop through the 1980s and into the 1990s. Often employing synthesizers orchestrally in a manner reminiscent of Weather Report, such as in "Out of Town" on their 1987 album *Four Corners,* their accessible brand of fusion enjoyed a wide following in the 1980s, winning them a Grammy for "Best Fusion Album of the

Russ Freeman: His band the Rippingtons was the band jazz fans loved to hate. His retort: "The kind of instrumental electric music we play I'm sure helps people to find a way into jazz. I can understand some of the criticism of fusion, and I believe that jazz is a great art form and should be preserved. But I also find merit in some of the newer electric forms too—it's time some of the die-hards started checking it out!" (Photograph by Stuart Nicholson.)

Year" with *Politics* in 1988. By the 1990s Bob Mintzer had joined the band in place of Marc Russo on saxophones.

In this highly competitive field of radio-play-oriented fusion, guitarist Russ Freeman's creation, The Rippingtons, were among the most popular and perhaps the best crafted of the FM bands, largely because of Freeman's songwriting and arranging skills. Their albums, featuring Bill Mayer's distinctive (and humorous) cover art, sold consistently well, carried by Freeman's ingenious hooks that were often written into quite sophisticated songforms. Freeman, a studio musician, was catapulted into band leading when *Moonlighting,* recorded in July 1986 for a small independent label, leapt onto the *Billboard* chart. More albums followed, and the Rippingtons, initially an ad hoc gathering of studio musicians, evolved into a regular band through the popularity of their albums. By 1989, they began venturing onto the touring circuits for about eighty or ninety concerts a year. Freeman forged a distinctive group sound—airplay-friendly to be sure—but mediated by a thoroughgoing understanding of the popular songwriter's and arranger's crafts. "Compositionally, I have tried to get away from the usual pop song format," said Freeman. "I've worked hard at that. Off the *Moonlighting* album there was 'Angela' for example, and the *Kilimanjaro* album had 'Morocco' which the band like to play live. And a composition from *Tourist in Paradise*—one of my favorite songs—was 'Long Summers Night in Brazil' that has a pretty expansive bridge that develops. I gauge these compositions like, 'Is this still fun to play after 500 times!'"[32]

The position of the Rippingtons in the marketplace was helped by the rise of "smooth jazz"—airplay-friendly instrumental pop-jazz that used slick production values and musical hooks from contemporary popular music. Radio KTWV in Los Angeles came up with the formula in 1987 and became the city's most popular radio station among the 25–52 age group. "Smooth jazz" soon became the fastest growing radio format of the 1990s, with the revenue growth of radio stations featuring the music rising to a phenomenal 75.7 percent between January 1993 to December 1995, compared to 54.2 percent for alternative music, 37.1 percent for adult contemporary, 20.4 percent for country, and only 15.2 percent for rock.[33]

There was no doubt that the "smooth jazz" format had become a potent commercial force in the 1990s, with musicians writing tunes to coincide with the requirements of rigid formatting. "Unless our music follows certain pre-established formulas," said Spyro Gyra's Jorge Strunz, "stations won't touch us with a ten foot pole."[34] As one New York music station manager put it, "Primarily we are looking for bright tempos and melodies that are recognizable. . . . We want melodic strength that the casual listener or non-aficionado can pick up on."[35] The essence of the music was to get onto playlists that were constructed with the lowest common denominator in mind to appeal to the broadest possible constituency. The music was unadventurous, nonchallenging, and unthreatening because it had to be, programmed to attract audiences and thus advertisers. "It's a money decision," said Guy Napoleon, national program director for the twelve-station Nationwide Communications. "In the radio business, the 25–55 age group is called 'the money demographic.'"[36] It just so happened that in the 1990s "smooth jazz" appealed to the "money demographic," the demographic with the biggest proportion of net disposable income. Increasingly, it seemed, the "smooth jazz" phenomenon appeared to be transforming an art form back into a commodity by responding to commercial logic.

Notes

1. *American Popular Music Business in the 20th Century,* by Russell Sanjek and David Sanjeck (Oxford University Press, New York, 1991), p. 212.
2. Freddie Hubbard's *A Soul Experiment,* Illinois Jacquet's *Soul Explosion,* Cedar Walton's *Soul Cycle,* Clifford Jordan's *Soul Fountain,* The Three Sounds' *A Soul Symphony,* Leo Wright's *Soul Talk,* Idris Muhammad's *Power of Soul,* Sonny Stitt's *Soul Girl,* and Dizzy Gillespie's *Souled Out,* to name a few, all appeared at this time.
3. *Music '71* (Maher Publications, Chicago, 1970), p. 10.
4. Columbia trade advertisement, fall 1974.
5. "A Year of Selling Out," by Leonard Feather, *Music '71* (Maher Publications, Chicago, 1970), p. 10.

6. Selmer trade advertisement for the Varitone, winter 1968. Stitt recorded the somewhat bizarrely titled *Parallel-a-Stitt: Sonny Stitt on the Varitone,* and Terry weighed in with *It's What's Happenin': The Varitone Sound of Clark Terry.*

7. *New York Times,* November 9, 1996.

8. With albums like *One, Two, Three, BJ4, Heads, Touchdown, Lucky Seven, Hands Down,* and *Foxie.*

9. *Black Music,* December 1973, p. 40.

10. Heard on the live album *In Performance at the Playboy Jazz Festival* (Elektra Musician 60298–1).

11. *Downbeat,* September 11, 1975, p. 45.

12. Laws continued to record through the eighties for a variety of labels; after a long hiatus from recording, he signed with The Right Stuff label in 1996 and put out *Natural Laws,* which was as glossy as anything he had ever done.

13. *Talking Jazz,* by Ben Sidran (Pomegranate Artbooks, San Francisco, 1992), p. 156.

14. *African Rhythm and African Sensibility,* by John Miller Chernoff (University of Chicago Press, Chicago, 1979), p. 60.

15. *Downbeat,* June 21, 1973, p. 20.

16. Ibid., June 17, 1976, pp. 40–41.

17. Ibid. The Crusaders' work is anthologized on Blue Thumb (BTD-4-700), a four-CD set, which includes their work from the Jazz Crusaders days of *The Young Rabbits* to the overtly commercial *Street Life.*

18. Ibid., July 1981, p. 30.

19. Mitchell, a bona fide pop music great, always had a strong affinity for jazz musicians. Her 1979 *Shadows and Light* tour and subsequent album, for example, included a strong lineup of Mike Brecker, Pat Metheny, and Jaco Pastorius; and *Mingus,* her tribute to Charles Mingus from 1979, although unsuccessful, was originally slated as a collaboration.

20. *Downbeat,* May 23, 1974, p. 18.

21. Ibid., March 1994, p. 32.

22. Ibid., March 1994, p. 31.

23. Others who composed soundtrack music for films and TV in a jazz-fusion style include Lalo Schifrin (most notably on *Bullitt* and *Dirty Harry*), Quincy Jones, Michael Legrand, Dave Grusin, and James William Guerio.

24. *Downbeat,* February 28, 1974, p. 20.

25. All of these are represented on a 1996 anthology, *The Best of Black Jazz Records* (Universal Sound USCD2).

26. Quoted in *The Jazz Book,* by Joachim E. Berendt (Palladin, London, 1984), p. 47.

27. Interview with the author, published in *Jazz Express,* June 1992, p. 16.

28. Ibid.

29. Ibid.

30. Liner notes, *Chick Corea: Music Forever & Beyond* (GRP GRD 5 9819), p. 23.

31. *Downbeat,* October 1993, p. 34.

32. Interview with the author, July 11, 1992.

33. Quoted in *Newsweek,* May 20, 1996, p. 76.

34. *Downbeat,* August 9, 1979, p. 23.

35. Ibid., p. 22.

36. *USA Today,* provenance unknown, "Adult Top 40 Makes Waves in Radio."

CHAPTER 12

Is What It Is

When George Wein announced that Miles Davis was to play Avery Fisher Hall in Lincoln Center on July 5, 1981, after a long period of inactivity by the trumpeter, it became the most publicized event in jazz history. Virtually every newspaper in the world made some reference to the event, even though Davis's first postfurlough public appearance had been a month before at a relatively unknown Boston club called Kix. Jazz, at the end of the 1970s, by general agreement, appeared to have lost direction, and Davis, who more than once had influenced the course of jazz history, was widely anticipated to reassert his role as musical pathfinder.

But it wasn't only jazz that had lost direction during the final years of the 1970s. Davis himself had pursued what can only be described as an unsavory lifestyle, a mixture of sex and cocaine.[1] Music had played a small part in his life since he retired from the business in 1975, although in 1978 his friend Elena Steinberg invited him to stay at her Connecticut home along with house guests Larry and Julie Coryell, who persuaded him to record some new music he had recently composed at the piano. Davis went into the studio with Coryell on guitar, Masabumi Kikuchi and George Paulis on keyboards, T. M. Stevens on electric bass, and Al Foster on drums, with some horn parts sketched out by Bobby Scott. Davis played little trumpet, if any at all, concentrating on keyboards, but he was not entirely happy with the results and he gave the tapes to Coryell as a gift. But the exercise stimulated his interest in music and with the help of Cicely Tyson he reduced his intake of drugs, alcohol, and tobacco. Gradually he began playing the trumpet more and more. He also began taking an active interest in a rock band that his nephew Vincent Wilburn, a graduate of the Chicago Conservatory of Music, had put together. Despite learning that he was suffering from diabetes, Davis, with the encouragement of his manager Mark Rothbaum, felt ready to talk seriously about a comeback and phoned George Butler of Columbia with his news in 1980. Butler's response was to send Davis a Yamaha grand piano to his house on West 77th Street as a "welcome back" present.

In April 1981 Davis's nephew brought his band to New York and after some twelve weeks of rehearsal, during which time saxophonist Bill Evans was added to the lineup, they went into the recording studio to cut *The Man With the Horn*, the least successful album in Davis's discography. "This record—parts of it—is pleasant. That's all. No more. But one expects more than pleasantries from Miles Davis," said *Downbeat*.[2] And here lay the problem: Davis's long and distinguished past meant that his achievements weighed heavily on present aspirations. It mattered not that the critics who had lambasted him for "going electric" in the 1970s had now come to see great merit in much of that work; the problem lay in what his work *was not*—it was not *Walkin'*, it was not *Porgy and Bess,* it was not *Kind of Blue,* it was not *Jack Johnson*—and not what it *was.* Even so, *The Man With the Horn* was an anticlimax in a way that his return to the touring circuits was not.

Touring with a lineup of Bill Evans on tenor saxophone, Mike Stern on guitar, Marcus Miller on bass, Al Foster on drums, and Mino Cinelu on percussion, Davis's "comeback" concerts at Boston and Avery Fisher were recorded, along with a performance from Tokyo the following October, and released in the late summer of 1982 as *We Want Miles.* It was far more cogent, despite its imperfections, than *The Man With The Horn,* and it gave a far better idea of how Davis envisaged his music. While his pre-1975 bands were engaged in collective improvisation and abstraction, Davis had returned to a theme-solos-theme format, albeit themes that were childlike in their simplicity, such as "Jean Pierre." Perhaps more for past achievements than present accomplishments, it was awarded a Grammy in 1982, and Davis was nominated "Musician of the Year" by *Jazz Forum.*

As soon as he returned to the concert stage, Davis became *the* major draw in jazz, a superstar the like of which had never been known in the jazz firmament. For his four nights at Boston's Kix Club he got $60,000, for his Avery Fisher appearance $90,000, while his eight-show tour through Japan in October brought him $700,000. And audiences came in droves; box offices could have sold out three and four times over. The reason was simple; audiences wanted to consume the aura of the physical presence of one of the great and enduring legends of twentieth-century music and to acknowledge a musical legend during his lifetime. In many ways the music, paradoxically, was less important than the event.

On Thanksgiving Day 1981, Davis married Cicely Tyson at Bill Cosby's Massachusetts home. It was his fourth marriage. His round of concert appearances continued, without even a break for a honeymoon, but his health had became a cause of concern as his unrelenting schedule continued into 1982. In February, after a tour of Japan and an appearance on the *Saturday Night Live* show, Davis woke to find his right hand immobile; he had suffered a stroke. After a modest recuperation, he attended therapy at New York Hospital four times a week to regain the use of his fingers. Remarkably he felt able to return to the touring circuit in April, and for the next eight weeks toured Sweden, Denmark, Germany, England, Italy, Holland, France, and Belgium. "Although I was looking very sick I was, in fact, feeling stronger than I had felt in a long, long time," said Davis. "My health wasn't good but we were able to keep stories of my stroke out of the newspapers and away from the media . . . [until] we had completed our European tour."[3]

Miles Davis and John Scofield: The three albums on which Scofield appeared are widely acknowledged to be the best of Davis's postfurlough discography. (Photograph by Stuart Nicholson.)

In November 1982 Davis began work on *Star People,* collaborating with Gil Evans on the cut "Star on Cicely," although, privately, Davis's relationship with Cicely Tyson had begun to deteriorate. He also added the guitarist John Scofield to his lineup, and Scofield's powerful, disciplined improvisations created tension between Stern's often garrulous flights. Davis appeared more comfortable with Scofield's style and was encouraged to introduce more blues-based originals to the repertoire, including the title track and "It Gets Better," prompting him to cast aside the limping lyricism of the previous two albums and to play his best solos on record since emerging from retirement. As he finished *Star People,* Marcus Miller departed the group and was replaced by Tom Barney, who toured with the band in the spring of 1983 through France, Italy, Belgium, and England. As Davis notes in his autobiography, critical reaction to his music was mixed: "[He] was sad, at times boring, even ugly," said London's *Sunday Times.* "Miles Davis is back on the high seas and in front of the fleet again," enthused its sister paper, the *Times.*[4] As always, the critics' reaction to his music left Davis deeply unimpressed. "[They did] the same thing to Bird," he said, "[and they] criticized Trane and Philly Joe when they were in my band. I hadn't listened to them then, and I wasn't about to listen to them now."[5]

On their return to the U.S., Barney was replaced by Darryl Jones, a friend of Davis's nephew from Chicago, and in the autumn the band toured Japan. However, after that tour, Davis was forced to let Stern go, because of his increasing use of drugs and alcohol. "I was getting too high and he said so," Stern confessed. "He said to cool out. And when Miles Davis tells you that you gotta realize that something must be wrong."[6] Davis began work on a new album, *Decoy,* with the addition of Robert Irving III on synthesizer and Branford Marsalis on soprano sax. With the addition of synthesizers, Davis drew on the experience of Gil Evans, who was credited for his contribution on "That's Right," but was on hand as "a consultant" for much of the recording. The album was a mix of two live numbers recorded at the Festival International de Jazz at Montréal on July 7 and studio sessions from August and September. The music was functional rather than challenging, validated by Davis's presence. The critics seemed perplexed: was this music as it appeared, fairly bland vamps relieved by the strength of the improvising talent on hand—Davis himself, Scofield, and Branford Marsalis—or would some deep message be revealed in later years and the music be hailed as a triumph? Certainly the Davis enigma allowed him a critical latitude unavailable to a lesser artist. The album won a Grammy. "Miles Davis's music often projects mystery and menace, but the mystery of *Decoy* is: . . . whose ideas are these anyway?"[7] pondered *Downbeat,* who awarded the album four and one-half stars.

On November 6, 1983, the music business feted Davis as the true star he was. "Miles Ahead: A Tribute to an American Music Legend," a four-hour retrospective, even impressed the phlegmatic Davis. "It was a beautiful night and I was happy they honored me the way they did," he said later.[8] Shortly afterwards, Fisk University awarded him an honorary doctorate, but almost immediately he was hospitalized for a hip operation that was followed by a bought of pneumonia, preventing him from performing for six months. *Decoy* was released in May 1984, complete with a four-minute music video, to coincide with his return to live performance at a concert in Los Angeles on June 2 with tenor saxophonist Bob Berg standing in for Bill Evans. The band launched on an extensive European tour; *Jazz Journal* was on hand for their London concert, observing somewhat inscrutably, "Miles Davis might not be the giant he was in 1958 but, in the 100 minutes he spent on stage, he proved himself still to be a very good one."[9]

At the end of 1984, Miles began recording *You're Under Arrest,* appropriating three tunes from popular culture, D Train's "Something's On Your Mind," Cyndi Lauper's "Time After Time," and Michael Jackson's "Human Nature." Lauper's "Time After Time" was transformed into Davis's own personal lament, and the 12-inch single version is among his most engaging recordings of his comeback. Jackson's "Human Nature" became a kind of Davis anthem used to open his concerts, with Irving following Jackson's original arrangement on keyboards and allowing Davis to play a haunting meditation on the melody. In taking these tunes, Davis inhabited them as if they were his own, and they became staples of his live performances; without them a Miles Davis concert was not complete. For a new generation of Davis fans, it was these tunes that they associated with him, rather than those from a *Porgy and Bess* or a *Kind of Blue*.

The album revealed a new interest in recorded sound, with a change in instrumental balance that was more characteristic of a rock recording; the bass drum, for example, is given a very prominent position in the mix. Davis himself overdubbed trumpet punches and synthesized lines were added doubling several of his trumpet parts. Instruments were given digital reverb to enhance their sound and then combined with analogue reverb in the final mix. "One Phone Call/Street Scenes" had a strong resonance with Davis's past as much as with the inner-city life it was meant to portray; it opens with the sound of someone "sniffing," a car pulls up, the police hustle Davis. Is it for drugs? For being with a white woman? For driving a sports car? The background music to this illustrative scene came from *Jack Johnson,* the Police-man's voice from Sting. This rigorously fundamental programmatic approach is repeated on the final track "And Then There Were None": the sequence of audio events includes a kid's theme ("Jean Pierre"), happy baby sounds, countdown, rockets, and explosion. Certainly the album was uneven, but it seemed to define Davis in the 1980s as *Bitches Brew* had done in the 1970s or *My Funny Valentine* in the 1960s.

During the course of making the album, musical differences between Al Foster and Davis came to a head, forcing a parting of the ways. "I asked him over and over again to play that funky backbeat but he just wouldn't play it,"[10] said Davis, but anyone who saw the band live might raise their eyebrows at this assertion. Foster appeared on four tracks before making way for Davis's nephew to join the band on a full-time basis. In November 1984, Davis was awarded the Sonning Music Award, Denmark's highest honor, for a lifetime's achievement in the arts. He was the first jazz musician and the first black person to be so honored, a source of some pride to Davis, since previously it had been given to composers and soloists from the European tradition: Copland, Bernstein, Messiaen, Stravinsky, and Isaac Stern. In December he travelled to Denmark to rehearse *Aura,* a two-album statement written for Davis by Palle Mikkelborg, to mark the event.

Aura was recorded in January and February 1985 and was Davis's first recording with a large orchestra since his memorable collaborations with Gil Evans in the 1950s and early 1960s. Not released until 1989, when it won a Grammy, Davis considered it his latter-day masterpiece. The large orchestra consisted of musicians from the Danish Radio Big Band and included the bassist Niels-Henning Orsted Pedersen plus guests John McLaughlin on guitar, Vince Wilburn, Jr. on drums, and Marilyn Mazur on percussion. Full of symbolism that evoked his remarkable musical past, *Aura* contained a riff reminiscent of "So What" from *Kind of Blue,* a bass and piano section that had resonances of *Miles in the Sky,* and allusions to Davis's orchestral collaborations with Gil Evans, albeit at a bleak and unsentimental remove. His finest album of the 1980s, Columbia reputedly withheld funding for it when it was only half completed, and Davis was forced to seek a grant from the National Endowment for the Arts to finish the project, which signalled the beginning of the end of his long relationship with Columbia.

In August, John Scofield left the band and was replaced by Mike Stern. The following month Davis took a small acting role in an episode of the popular cops-and-robbers series *Miami Vice* and then did a Honda commercial, which along with regular appearances on prime-time TV shows such as *Saturday Night Live* (his first appearance was almost as soon as he made his comeback in 1981) and popular morning and late-night talk shows were all moves calculated to bring his name before an ever-increasing public. However, as he launched out on a European tour in October, he was beginning to suspect that Columbia was more interested in the careers of younger performers like Wynton Marsalis than in his own. It was a cause of tension that he resolved by moving to Warner Bros in 1986. The dramatic Irving Penn photograph on the cover of *Tutu* announced his new label affiliation. A collaboration with his former bassist Marcus Miller, the album was built up through patient multitracking using compositions by Miller, arrangements by Miller and George Duke, with Adam Holzman and Bernard Wright on synthesizers, Steve Reid and Paulinho da Costa on percussion, Omar Hakim on drums, Michael Urbaniak on electric violin, and Miller on bass and a variety of instruments. Dedicated to the South African bishop, *Tutu* ended Wynton Marsalis's three-year reign as the Grammy-winning Top Instrumental Jazz Soloist. The synthesized orchestral effects had echoes of Gil Evans, and its powerful title track featured a slow, loping bass-line figure that would become a hallmark of Davis's music.

Although the album did not include any of his current band—which now featured Robben Ford on guitar—they reproduced "Tutu" in live performance, often to powerful effect with heavily synthesized orchestrations that allowed Davis's Harmon-muted trumpet license to embellish its glossy surfaces. However, Ford, an accomplished blues guitarist, did not stay for long. "When I first joined [the tunes] were loose and extended," he recalled, "but then he started going more and more toward the *Tutu* record, and he wanted to play it just like the record. I've always had a hard time with that. I just don't enjoy playing the same shit every night. I couldn't hang with that."[11] He was replaced by Garth Webber.

Miller received joint billing for Davis's 1987 album *Siesta*, which paid homage to *Sketches of Spain* in its conscious evocation of Andalusia for the soundtrack of the Lorimar film of the same name. In effect, Davis became a "featured soloist" on his own album, his trumpet laments one of several elements Miller drew upon, including guitarists John Scofield and Earl Klugh, flautist James Walker, and Miller himself, once again revealing his multi-instrumental dexterity. "*Siesta* and *Tutu* were projects," explained Miller. "They were not representative of how he usually made his music. . . . I would never contend that what we did could compete with what Miles did in the '50s, but it served a purpose in his career."[12] Since his return to active performance, Davis's star had been in the ascendance to a degree unmatched at any time in his career. He was no longer simply "a jazz musician," but a media superstar who in early 1987 dined with President Ronald Reagan and Secretary of State George Schultz.

However, there were many changes in Davis's touring band that year. Davis fired his nephew Vince Wilburn because he felt he was letting "the time drop"

and replaced him with Ricky Wellman. Bob Berg left when Davis added Gary
Thomas on tenor, but the latter bluntly refused to play funk-licks and left, so
Davis turned to Art Blakey's Jazz Messengers for alto saxophonist/flautist Kenny
Garrett. Other personnel changes included hiring Joseph Foley McCreary on
"lead" bass, a four-string piccolo bass. "The band I had in 1987 was a motherfucker, man," recalled Davis. "My band was right and my health was right and so
was everything else in life."[13]

On New Year's Eve, Davis brought in the New Year with Prince, joining him
on the bandstand for one number that was taped. He would again venture into
the realm of pop music by recording with the group Scritti Politti, remaining
defiantly Harmon-muted and unmistakably Miles Davis. His round of touring
continued unabated through 1988, including a performance at the Montreux
Jazz Festival.[14] He was back in the recording studios at the end of the year to
record *Amandla,* again midwifed by Marcus Miller, and dedicated it to Gil
Evans, who had died on March 20 of that year. "I envisioned *Amandla* as closer
to the sound of his band, with Ricky Wellman on drums, Foley on guitar and
Kenny Garrett playing alto," explained Miller.[15] Somewhat overproduced, the
overall impression is of monotony of tone, not helped by short solos and emphasis on studio-generated ensemble textures. In general it was well received—
Downbeat awarded it four stars, for example[16]—but although Davis's art maintained its mysterious allure, he and Garrett were left to decorate a series of
glittering surfaces manufactured by Miller.

On November 13, Miles was inducted into The Grand Knights of Malta; this
ceremony coincided with an attack of pneumonia that forced him to cancel his
early 1989 touring plans, reputedly a loss of a million dollars. However, he
returned to the touring circuits in April playing Italy and France, and made the
summer round of festivals with Rick Margitza on tenor replacing Garrett.[17]
Garrett returned in August to play Hawaii and Europe in October and November. Since 1988 Warner Bros had occasionally been dispatching a remote recording unit to Davis gigs. The album *Live Around the World* presented the trumpeter
as a visiting sultan bestowing pearls on New York, Italy, France, Austria, Los
Angeles, Japan, and the 1990 Montreux Jazz Festival, and on the occasion of his
final appearance with his band. But, as Robben Ford noted, Davis had moved
towards highly arranged, stylized structures to frame his broken-wing improvisations rather than the looser jams of his bands with Stern and Scofield. Consequently, live recordings of his later bands, such as *Live Miles Davis* from his last
concert in Avignon, add little to our understanding of his music.

In 1989 *Miles: The Autobiography* was published. Never was a jazz musician's
story more eagerly awaited. It was proof, if proof were needed, that it is impossible to discern the mind's construction through music. Davis was candid, probably
as candid as he could have been in print, and stood revealed as an icon with
imperfections which many found shocking. "It is full of stories that take the
reader down into the sewers of Davis's musical, emotional and musical decline,"
opined Stanley Crouch. "We are left aghast at a man of monumental insecurity
who for all his protests about white power is often controlled by his fear of it."[18]

Pearl Cleage had the unsettling experience of discovering the man she admired for so long confessing to physically abusing his women.[19] In many ways these responses echoed those expressed about *Lady Sings the Blues,* a similar "warts and all" autobiography of another jazz great, Billie Holiday, written more than thirty years before. Then, many observers wished she had never written it, failing to realize that her music was her principal testimony.

From the latter half of 1989 through summer 1991, Davis staged four very successful European tours. Audiences could not get enough of him; huge crowds lionized him. "Nobody else could do big long tours every summer and fall and sell out stadiums all over Europe," said John Scofield. "And these people were not jazz snobs, they just dug Miles. He could make a believer out of a non-jazz person with the beauty of his sound and his rhythm and his notes. That's pretty heavy."[20]

In New York in early 1991, Davis, who was working on some tapes with Prince, began work on an album quite unlike anything he had ever undertaken previously. Intrigued by the sounds of the street, hip-hop, he contacted Russell Simmons, who ran Def Jam records, for help. Simmons sent him producer/DJ Easy Mo Bee. Work started in the studios as Easy Mo Bee put together a track of samples and, whenever Davis liked what he heard, he improvised over the top. "He just amazed me," said the hip-hopper. "I'd get on the drum sampler and he'd fall right in with it. That tripped me out. To him it was an art form!"[21] Six tracks were completed, and the trumpet solos from tapes Davis had been experimenting with in the late 1980s with what he called his "Rubber Band" formed the basis of two more tracks on *Doo-Bop.*

Here was undeniable evidence that Davis never stood still, that change was the leitmotif of his career, even if his regular band had become more gesture than substance. Yet while it was closer to the street than *On the Corner,* these tracks did not seem too far removed from "Splatch" or "Full Nelson" on *Tutu*— indeed, they would not have sounded out of place on *Doo-Bop* and vice versa. Ultimately, however, jazz and hip-hop could never be anything more than an uncomfortable liaison between man and machine. Never part of the music's internal construction, the collage of beats and samples assumed an independent existence as a rhythmic, rather than musical, medium, thus musical considerations in hip-hop were subservient to the message. The jazz musician, robbed of his storytelling privilege, remained apart, an outsider never central to the performance (the machine), his role that of an occasional participant with a solo here, a solo there, or an obbligato, ingredients of decoration rather than an integral part of music's overall construction. Nevertheless, *Doo-Bop* won a Grammy had and had sold almost 300,000 units within two years of release.

On July 8, 1991, Davis was persuaded by Quincy Jones to confront his distinguished past on the occasion of the Montreux Jazz Festival's 25th anniversary and perform the original arrangements of *Sketches of Spain, Birth of the Cool, Miles Ahead,* and *Porgy and Bess.* Billed simply as "L'Evenement" (The Event), the Gil Evans Orchestra and the George Grunz Concert Band were conducted by Jones, the festival's musical director. It was a concert that set up a buzz of anticipation around the world: could Davis cut it in the same way as he did in the 1950s? Would he even turn up? He didn't attend the New York rehearsals where the two orchestras met to prepare for the event, heightening the tension. But at the final rehearsal the day before in Montreux he suddenly appeared, as if on cue. "Quincy showed up at 2 P.M., that was the first time we had actually met face to face," said keyboard player Gil Goldstein. "By 11 P.M. Miles showed up. It was unbelievable, just the perfect entry for Miles Davis. We were rehearsing 'Boplicity' and he just kind of walked in on the first phrase, sat down and took out his horn."[22]

The following evening Davis received an incredible ovation as he made his way to the stage. *Miles Davis & Quincy Jones Live at Montreux* records a historic night that no one thought would ever happen. Davis gradually warmed to his task and played with an assurance and poise in a musical idiom he had left behind thirty years before. To one side, trumpeter Wallace Roney was on hand to spell him if the need arose, shadowing Davis on some parts, and engaging in open horn dialogue on "Blues For Pablo." "I was never supposed to play the concert," said Roney. "But when they rehearsed the orchestra they needed someone to play Miles's part. We rehearsed a couple of hours and then Miles came in . . . next thing I know he and I were playing together. The next day he gave me more stuff to play. By the time it got to the concert we were sharing everything. . . . On top of that we hung. He was telling me everything he could think of about music, like he was trying to cram 45 years of music into three days. I didn't know he was ill, I didn't think he was going to die, but maybe he did."[23]

On July 10, Davis appeared in Paris with a variety of groups that represented certain phases of his musical odyssey through jazz, including Jackie McLean, John McLaughlin, Chick Corea, Herbie Hancock, Wayne Shorter, Dave Holland, Joe Zawinul, and Steve Grossman. It was as if he was saying his good-byes.[24] On July 18, the French government bestowed on him their highest honor, making him a Chevalier in the Legion of Honor.[25] On August 25, Miles played his final concert at the Hollywood Bowl. "The last number he played I knew he was tired," said Wayne Shorter, who was in the audience as Davis's guest. "I noticed he was much more fragile than six weeks before, in Paris. . . . It was the first time I ever heard that kind of fatigue coming from him. Now I know, it was the illness. But even when he was tired, his tone had a solidness and fullness."[26] On September 28, 1991, Miles Dewy Davis III died at St. Johns Hospital and Health Center in Santa Monica, California, from pneumonia, respiratory failure, and a stroke. He was laid to rest with one of his trumpets near the Duke Ellington family site in Woodlawn Cemetery in the Bronx.

Davis's return to public performance in 1981 focused much welcome media attention on jazz, which by the end of the 1970s was in desperate need of revital-ization. He quickly assumed the mantle of a genuine superstar, the major draw at jazz festivals around the world. If he failed to reassert his role as musical pathfinder in the way that he had done in the past, then at the very least he could claim was that his comeback reignited a flagging scene. While in the late 1970s fusion had become widely discredited through commercial excess, Davis's active engagement in electric jazz-rock once again suggested that the artistic potential of the music was far from exhausted. Gradually jazz-rock fusion crept back onto the musical agenda as several former jazz-rock stars of the 1970s began putting together new bands for the 1980s.

As the old arguments were rehearsed about jazz-rock representing a sellout to commercial aspirations, former Davis guitarist John Scofield formed a touring group in 1986 that would begin his path towards recognition as one of the major

Miles Davis: When Davis returned to active performance in 1981 he became *the* major draw in jazz. The reason was simple—audiences wanted to consume the aura and physical presence of one of the great and enduring legends of twentieth-century music before it was too late. In many ways his music, paradoxically, was less important than the event. (Photograph by Stuart Nicholson.)

instrumentalists to emerge in the decade. Scofield was a graduate of the Berklee College of Music in Boston and had already established a solid reputation in jazz by the time he joined Davis in 1982. His recording debut was as a last-minute replacement for Mike Goodrick at the 1974 Carnegie Hall reunion of Gerry Mulligan and Chet Baker. Two weeks later he was a member of the Billy Cobham/George Duke band, where he remained for two years prior to joining the Gary Burton Quartet. A profusion of gigs around New York City followed, including recording with Charles Mingus and as a member of the Dave Liebman band. In 1979 he formed his own trio with Steve Swallow on bass and Adam Nussbaum; their albums *Bar Talk, Shinola,* and *Out Like a Light* reveal him exploring his Jim Hall–oriented roots.

When in 1982 Scofield was invited to join Miles Davis, it caused something of a stir, because it was widely believed the guitarist had returned to bop-oriented jazz after his 1970s fusion adventures. Scofield's impact on the Davis band was considerable; indeed, the three albums on which he appeared are widely acknowledged to be the best of Davis's postfurlough output. His solo in the ten-minute slow blues "It Gets Better" from *Star People* encouraged Davis to intro-duce more blues-based material into his performing repertoire, while his solo in "Speak" from the same album provided a melodic motif that became the basis for "That's What Happened" on *Decoy.* By the time Davis cut *Decoy,* Scofield's influence on the band was palpable. There was another long, slow blues, "That's Right," which features him prominently, and he shares composer honors on "What It Is." On his final album with Davis, *You're Under Arrest,* Scofield even adds Nile Rogers-like fills to "Time After Time" and "Human Nature."

In 1984 Scofield signed as a solo artist with Gramavision, and his first album for the label was *Electric Outlet.* "[That] was an overdubbed record," he said. "I was working with Miles and I had just gotten one of those four-track home demo set-ups. So I put down the bass parts, laid in the drum machine and said, 'This is the way to do it!' I was really into the process."[27] Using guests Dave Sanborn on alto and Ray Anderson on trombone, it was a tribute to the great blues guitarists like B. B. King and Albert King. *Still Warm* from 1985 was made with another pickup group, this time with Daryl Jones on bass and Omar Hakim on drums, that pointed the direction in which his music would follow over the next couple of years, pursued by a strong touring group with Marc Cohen on keyboards, Gary Grainger on bass, and Rick Sebastian on drums. By now, Scofield's playing had developed in leaps and bounds since his trio recordings earlier in the 1980s. Rhythmically secure, he had developed a readily identifiable use of unusual intervals and rhythmic sequences and fluid, polytonal harmonies.

When Dennis Chambers replaced Sebastian, Scofield had one of the great bands of the 1980s, something they demonstrated on their first album together, *Blue Matter,* released in 1987. On it the ex-Pockets bassist Sebastian and the for-mer P-Funk drummer Chambers combine with astonishing cohesion. The title track, with its sinister, Miles Davis-like bass-line, the soaring "Heaven Hill," and a lesson in laying down the funk in "The Nag," were among the album highlights that the band featured during their extensive touring schedule. "[*Blue Matter*] is

Miles to the max," said Scofield. "It's the sort of thing Miles would like to play on. . . . It's true, I do emulate Miles's horn. He's my man, you know?"[28] Two more strong albums followed—*Pick Hits,* a live album recorded at the Hitomi Memorial Hall, Tokyo, in October 1987, with Robert Aires now on keyboards, which included impressive versions of "Blue Matter" and "Heaven Hill," and *Loud Jazz,* recorded in December 1987, which demonstrated through solid creative musicianship of integrity and depth that jazz-rock did not have to be cop-out, sellout, or crossover. However, after three years of almost constant touring, Scofield abruptly decided to disband. "We had a serious following all over the world," said Dennis Chambers. "It just ended too soon. I honestly believe that John got uptight with notoriety the band were getting. . . . When you saw and heard it live, it was energy: total raw energy. We'd go out and play until we dropped, that was the vibe. Gary and I were coming from the funk thing, we gave it the groove and the flavor, John was coming from like a New Orleans jazz thing. It was those mixtures that made it what it was, which was great. It gave jazz-fusion a shot in the arm."[29]

In 1989 Scofield signed with the reactivated Blue Note label and released *Time On My Hands*—with Joe Lovano on tenor, Charlie Haden on bass, and Jack DeJohnette on drums—which marked a new direction for his imaginative vision of electric jazz. This lean, keyboardless sound forged a remarkable alchemy between Scofield and Lovano, who formed a regular band with Anthony Cox on bass and John Riley on drums. The group was subsequently enhanced by the addition of the up-and-coming drum star Bill Stewart, who replaced Riley in 1990; Stewart's New Orleansian second-line grooves became an important feature of the group's sound. Scofield and Lovano remained together through 1993, producing an excellent run of albums.[30] After Lovano left the group, Scofield cut *Hand Jive* with Eddie Harris on tenor. However, Harris was unable to duplicate the strong solo voice that Lovano had provided to compliment Scofield's playing, although the band—and Scofield—clearly enjoyed the session, which was a kind of revival of 1960s soul jazz, 1990s style. With *Groove Elation* from 1995, Scofield was back on course, with the regulars Larry Goldings on keyboards and Dennis Irwin on bass, but now with the robust Idris Muhammad on drums, who kept the energy level high.

Scofield's *Blue Matter* band and his quartet with Joe Lovano were two important ensembles in 1980s and early 1990s jazz. In both instances, Scofield created effective contexts for his playing that allowed him to explore jazz-rock from two perspectives, an uncompromising jazz-funk viewpoint and a more free-wheeling, fluid mutation of post-bop that showed how jazz-rock could be absorbed into the jazz mainstream to produce something new and fresh.

Scofield's predecessor in the Miles Davis band, Mike Stern, was an accomplished guitarist in his own right. His talents were not well displayed with Davis, with whom he made three albums, becoming the guitarist critics loved to hate for his heavy-handed, heavy-metal excursions. Although strongly influenced by Wes Montgomery and Jim Hall, he was told by Davis to "play some Hendrix, turn it up or turn it off!" However, during his stay with Davis he fell prey to drug and alcohol abuse, forcing Davis to let him go in order to clean up his life. However, he joined a band led by the bassist Jaco Pastorius, whose tales of alcohol and drug excess were legendary, hardly helping his plight.

When Stern formed his own ensembles, he was less successful than Scofield in developing a suitable context for his playing. In 1986, Stern debuted as a leader with *Upside, Downside,* sharing the front line with the tenor saxophonist Bob Berg, then still a member of Davis's ensemble. Full of high-tech runs and a heavy backbeat, this was genial, high-energy, foot-tapping stuff with an emphasis on slickness at the expense of depth. This musical give-and-take extended over several albums of flashy but ultimately wearing fusion that did not allow either Berg or Stern the opportunity to reveal their true potential as soloists. Stern's best playing was to be found elsewhere, on bassist Harvie Swartz's *Urban Earth* and *Smart Moves* from 1986 and *In a Different Light* from 1990. On the latter he stretched out on "Alone Together," "Softly As in a Morning Sunrise," and "Sonnymoon for Two," songs from the Real Book that he had been exploring in the relative anonymity of the 55 Club on Grand Street in Greenwich Village, not too far from the Village Vanguard. There, late into the night, he would jam on standards revealing a player of harmonic subtlety and invention, as far removed from his head-banging image with Miles Davis as is possible to imagine. *Standards (and Other Songs)* from 1992 revealed more of the inner man, yet he seemed unable to reconcile the diverse elements that made up his style, as *Between the Lines* (1996) revealed.

Equally, Bob Berg also seemed unable to create a context to give his post-bop playing full reign within the jazz-rock environment. After five albums in the fusion vein under his own name and after touring with the hard-hitting Stern-Berg band, featuring Lincoln Goines on bass and Dennis Chambers on drums, he returned to post-bop with *Enter the Spirit* in 1993. "I'm planning to pursue this type of music for a while," he explained. "At this stage of my life, I feel like, for me, it's the truest mirror of my spirit. . . . On some of my other records, I felt I was a little removed from who I was."[31] Who he was, of course, was a fine post-bop saxophonist, and an uncomfortable fusion journeyman.

Berg's predecessor in the Miles Davis band, saxophonist Bill Evans, was another musician who seemed unable to define himself on record. It was fair to say that Evans never truly impressed Davis, who would cut off his solos with a peremptory blast of his trumpet, and his debut as a leader on *Living In the Crest of a Wave,* made while still with Davis, did nothing to rectify the image of Miles's "Man Who Never Was." Evans joined John McLaughlin's relaunched Maha-vishnu Orchestra in 1983, but any expectations aroused by the memory of one of the great jazz-rock bands of all time were soon dashed by the group's albums *Mahavishnu* and *Adventures in Radioland.* Evans was also a member of Herbie Hancock's Headhunters II, reformed to tour the festival circuits after Miles Davis's successes, and a group coled by former Pat Metheny sidemen Danny Gottlieb and Mark Egan called Elements. However this later group's New Age fusion was surprisingly bland, despite the talent brought to bear.

Evans's search for identity continued into the early nineties, with mixed results. Finally, he formed a new fusion group, Push, in 1993, which gained a large audience on the continent of Europe who remembered him from his tours there with Davis in the early 1980s. "What's a mindblower is that you've just finished playing 2,000-seat halls to packed audiences in Spain . . . and clubowners in the States don't want to take a chance on filling a 200-seat club," he said.[32] *Bill Evans & Push Live in Europe* (1994) featured the former Defunkt rhythm tandem of Scooter Warner on drums with Ron Jenkins on bass plus a lineup that included rapper KC Flight. The result was a version of hip-hop–fusion that sweated towards predictable climaxes. *Escape* (1996) offered a more refined version of the band's sound, but still the feeling persists of an artist yet to emerge from Miles Davis's shadows.

When Davis hit the comeback trail in 1981, he was not the only musician the jazz community was looking to with high hopes for the future. At the end of that year, bassist Jaco Pastorius left Weather Report, and expectations were that the electric bass virtuoso might finally exert a defining role in the music. Yet in the early evening of September 21, 1987, Pastorius's life ended after a blood vessel burst in his brain, terminating the life of a brilliant, but ultimately doomed, self-destructive talent. His end was hastened by drugs, alcohol, and fast living that had echoes of other great tragic jazz heroes, like Charlie Parker and Billie Holiday—not to mention rock heroes like Jimi Hendrix, to whom he was often compared. Nine days before, at 4 A.M. on September 12, Pastorius had been beaten into a comatose state outside the Midnight Bottle Club in Fort Lauderdale. He was just thirty-five years old.

Yet, the 1980s had begun so full of promise. Warner Bros. had made him a lucrative offer following his debut album *Jaco Pastorius,* stealing him from under the noses of Columbia. "There was a big buzz about him," said Ricky Schultz of Warners. "He was special, he was creative, he was innovative, he was making news. He definitely seemed to be the element that had pushed Weather Report to a new level of public awareness, their record sales had doubled after Jaco joined the group. So the expectation was that Jaco was going to create some great contemporary jazz."[33]

While he was working on his debut album for Warner, Pastorius put together a quintet of friends to play an engagement at Seventh Avenue South, the jazz club in which the Brecker brothers had a financial interest. Using Mike Brecker and Bob Mintzer on tenor saxophone, Peter Erskine on drums, Don Alias on percussion, and, in a couple of numbers, Othello Molineaux on steel drums, Pastorius discovered that his name could not be used to advertise the engagement because of his commitment to Weather Report. As it turned out, the place was packed, the news of the gig spreading by word of mouth, which gave Pastorius the title for his upcoming album and the name for his band. "[When the] gig was set up at Seventh Avenue South, we got together for a rehearsal," said Bob Mintzer. "Jaco had given me a cassette of the recently completed *Word of Mouth* album. Based on this I figured there would be elaborate arrangements on several of the tunes from the record. Instead we found very little in the way of written down music. What happened was Jaco sang us the parts we were to play and in some cases left it up to us to find our own parts based on our individual interpretations of the music to hand. What I noticed immediately was the color-fulness and openness of Jaco's music. Without a chord instrument there was lots of room for improvisation in terms of playing the tunes and playing behind the soloists."[34]

Word of Mouth was released in the summer of 1981 after a delay of four months because of a contractual tussle between Columbia and Warner Brothers, the former claiming that Pastorius still owed them an album. When the dust set-tled, the album won Japan's coveted Golden Disc Award. *Downbeat,* however, was more cautious, awarding the album three and one-half stars. "The question of whether Pastorius is an artist with a vision and a new music or simply a skilled sideman and instrumentalist has persisted," it pointed out.[35] It was a question that remains moot today.

On December 1, 1981, Pastorius threw a monster birthday bash for himself at Mr. Pip's, a nightclub near Deerfield Beach, Florida. For the event, his friend Peter Graves arranged for the performance of a big band of favored friends from various periods of Pastorius's musical life, from the bands of Joni Mitchell, Wayne Cochran & the C. C. Riders, Blood, Sweat & Tears, the Peter Graves Orchestra, Las Olas Brass, Weather Report, and the Miami Concert Jazz Band. The lineup included Randy Brecker, Ken Faulk, and Ron Tooley on trumpets; Jim Pugh and Dave Taylor on trombones; Peter Gordon on French horn; Dave Bargeron on tuba; Mike Brecker, Bob Mintzer, and Randy Emerick on saxo-phones; Peter Erskine on drums; Don Alias on percussion; and Othello Molineaux on steel drums. It was, in effect, the debut of the Word of Mouth big band, which Pastorius would periodically gather for appearances across America and Japan. Preparation was minimal, and this was the first time much of Pastorius's music had been presented in such a manner, including "The Chicken," "Continuum," "Invitation," "Three Views of a Secret," "Liberty City," "Punk Jazz," "Reza," "Domingo," and Pastorius's tribute to Jimi Hendrix, "Amerika." Overall, it was an eclectic mixture of World beat, rhythm and blues, and jazz. *Jaco Pastorius: The Birthday Concert* documents this lively debut, with Mike Brecker's playing and that of Pastorius album highlights.

The New York debut of the Word of Mouth big band took place on January 15, 1982 at the Savoy Theater with a cast of twenty New York musicians. It took Pastorius's audience, who were not quite sure what to expect, by surprise, mark-ing an impressive debut and the beginning of his post-Weather Report career. Gigs followed in Chicago, Los Angeles, Miami, and New York's Birdland and Lone Star Café, but gradually Pastorius's temperamental unsuitability to being a leader began to manifest itself. During this period he was living with Mike Stern, then with Miles Davis, and both were into drugs. In September, Pastorius and the Word of Mouth big band toured Japan. It comprised some of New York's finest musicians, but Pastorius's behavior was nothing short of bizarre. "That's when Jaco really started getting out of hand," said Peter Erskine. "It was a great band, with some of the best players in New York but Jaco was sabotaging our efforts."[36] Even so, *Twins I* and *Twins II* (so named because Pastorius's wife was about to give birth to twins) documented the band's appearances in Tokyo,

Osaka, and Yokohama and included solid performances using the *Birthday* charts, plus "Okonkole Y Trompa," "Giant Steps," "Elegant People," "Pac-Man Blues (Fannie Mae)," "Eleven," and "Sophisticated Lady." Taken in their totality, Pastorius's charts were by no means great—they were more functional structures that allowed for plenty of latitude for solos, which often led to indulgence. Rhythmically, however, the band was vital and exciting, but even this was not sufficient to sustain interest across two albums.

On his return, Pastorius formed a smaller version of Word of Mouth that included Delmar Brown on keyboards, saxophonist Alex Foster, and drummer Kenwood Dennard, who would remain regulars for the next couple of years. A tour of Italy at the end of 1982 again revealed his personality problems when he stormed off the stage after the first number in Milan and refused to go on, causing crowd unrest, as a result of which the police fired tear gas into the audience. In the summer of 1983, Mike Stern joined the band, and they embarked on a European tour followed by an American tour that was marked by an outrageous partying spirit, on and off stage. To compound Pastorius's problems, Warner Brothers dropped him from the label based on poor sales and his increasingly erratic behavior, exemplified by his being pulled off-stage during the 1983 Playboy Jazz Festival. Finally after months of excess, Stern checked himself into a rehabilitation center to kick drugs and alcohol, but Pastorius's lifestyle continued unchecked. He toured Japan as a guest with the Gil Evans orchestra in May 1984, but his bizarre antics were making him almost unemployable. In December, he and Rashid Ali traveled to Guadeloupe to give clinics and concerts. *Blackbird* captures their duets broadcast on French radio, and reveals the bassist playing as strongly as ever, despite his personal problems.

By now, Pastorius was known as "the bad boy of jazz," and despite his great talent, work was becoming hard to find. In the spring of 1985, he toured Europe with drummer Brian Melvin, and returned to a semi-regular engagement at New York's Lone Star Café, but by the summer he was homeless and penniless. *Jaco Pastorius in New York*, featuring a trio called Pretty Damn Bad, comprising Hiram Bullock on guitar, Kenwood Dennard on drums, and a Word of Mouth octet, charted this period of his life. Loose and sprawling, the results were surprisingly bland. In September, Pastorius was arrested and agreed to accept medical help, and lithium was prescribed to control his enormous mood swings. When he celebrated his birthday on December 1, 1985, he was heard to exclaim, "I can't believe I'm still alive."

In March 1986, Pastorius briefly toured Europe with Bireli Lagrene, but dropped out in Germany; *Bireli Lagrene & Jaco Pastorius: Stuttgart Aria* revealed Pastorius's virtuosity in a less than riveting context. Attempts to rehabilitate his fast unraveling career by the music critic and journalist (and subsequently Pastorius's biographer) Bill Milkowski, sadly came to nothing. By now Pastorius was living in a van near West Fourth Street, and a promising career had disappeared from under him. In July he was admitted to Bellevue Hospital and was diagnosed as a manic-depressive. After seven weeks, Pastorius was released and returned to work, including a second European tour with Lagrene. But the endgame was in sight and was slowly and sadly being played out. The drummer Peter Erskine spoke for many in the jazz community when he said, "In a lot of ways I feel I haven't done enough to help a dear friend. But it's tough when a guy sets out to join the ranks of jazz legends who completely fucked up their lives."[37] Erskine, together with Bob Mintzer on saxes and EWI (Electric Wind Instrument), Michael Formanek on keyboards, and Jeff Andrews on bass, cooperated on a heartfelt tribute, *I Remember Jaco* (1991); the track "What Might Have Been," a Mintzer original, said everything that needed to be said.

Pastorius had been the key element in guitarist Pat Metheny's debut as a leader on record with *Bright Size Life* (1976). An impressive statement, it documented a trio that Metheny had assembled for performances in the Boston area. However, drummer Bob Moses did not think the album documented the performance highs they achieved. "I don't listen to that album," he said. "A lot of people love it, but for me it doesn't capture what we were doing and it makes me really sad that this is the only representation of that band. Live it was like a power trio. It was like Cream, but with a lot of sixteenth-notes and a million chord changes, because Metheny's music was really complex . . . but the ECM [the label that signed Metheny] vibe kind of squelched all that energy. They didn't want it to be too ballsy and grooving."[38]

Metheny was a child prodigy, teaching guitar at the University of Miami at seventeen and joining the faculty of Berklee College of Music at nineteen. He joined the Gary Burton Quartet in 1974, and *Bright Size Life* was recorded while he was still playing with Burton. Metheny left Burton, and Berklee, in 1976 to form The Pat Metheny Group with Lyle Mays on keyboards, Mark Egan on bass, and Danny Gottlieb on drums. At the time he was virtually unknown outside the Boston area. But by tireless low-budget barnstorming, piling into a cramped van and traveling hundreds of miles between gigs, he built the group into a national attraction. The success of their 1978 album, *The Pat Metheny Group,* helped build their reputation, with its nonthreatening, romantic, almost Brahmsian soundscapes interpolated with breezy, sometimes intricate, sometimes folksy good humor firmly based on a high standard of musicianship and group interplay.

Metheny's career in the eighties was a balancing act of populist tendencies versus serious jazz offerings. Even his popular work, however, was mediated by good taste. *American Garage* was dedicated to embryonic groups getting it together in the family garage. The title track was thus intentionally biased in favor of simple rock patterns, but "The Epic" purposefully strode into blowing territory, even if the cadences were a little cute. The album *80/81,* recorded in 1980, was an excellent collaboration with saxophonists Dewey Redman and Mike Brecker, bassist Charlie Haden, and Jack DeJohnette on drums. Again, Metheny offered bright and breezy FM-radio favorites—like "Every Day" and "Goin' Ahead"—balanced with tracks that revealed Metheny's love of Ornette Coleman, directly through the Coleman composition "Turnaround," and obliquely through Metheny's "The Bat" and "Pretty Scattered." "To me Ornette is one of the most melodic musicians ever," he said. "It's not the same kind of melodies that you would find from somebody like Chet Baker or Wes

Pat Metheny and Ornette Coleman: None of Coleman's electric albums had the coruscating edge of *Song X*, his 1985 collaboration with Metheny. (Photograph: Andy Freeburg/ Geffen Records.)

Montgomery or something, and it doesn't fall in the usual cadences, but what kills me about Ornette is that he can't play anything that isn't melodic."[39]

Intentionally evocative, full of pastel moods and atmospheric episodes, *As Falls Wichita, So Falls Wichita Falls* (1981) achieved New Age symbolism at a time when the Windham Hill label was taking off, although Metheny rejected the handle being put on the album. "We wanted to try something where the improvisation happened not so much in a linear sense as a textural sense," he explained.[40] The Grammy-winning *Offramp* from October 1981 introduced bassist Steve Rodby and Metheny's first use on disc of the Roland GR300 series guitar synthesizer and the Synclavier. His best-selling album, its diversity of material satisfied his more temperate listeners, while the title track managed to rattle the bars of a few cages of those dismayed by his more commercial cadences. Metheny's winning way with audiences was documented on the Grammy-winning *Travels*, which presented concert versions of his popular favorites. Free from sharp edges and strong on lilting melodies, it was what the crowds paid to hear. In contrast was *Rejoicing* from November 1983, a trio session with Haden and Billy Higgins on drums that included three Ornette Coleman tunes that recalled his debut album (which had two Coleman originals on it).

The Grammy-winning *First Circle* (1984) demonstrated how Metheny's music was constantly being refined and moved forward, its compositional design remaining accessible while providing an effective context in which to focus his playing. Metheny had previously provided the soundtrack for a low-budget movie, *Little Sister,* when in 1985 he and Lyle Mays combined with David Bowie, a boys' choir, and the National Philharmonic to provide the music for the John Schlesinger film *The Falcon and the Snowman,* which included Bowie's Top-20 hit "This Is Not America." Despite the smoothly accessible veneer of Metheny's music, an album like *Song X* was always on the cards, given his love of Ornette Coleman's music. A collaboration from December 1985 with Ornette Coleman, Charlie Haden, Jack DeJohnette, and Deonardo Coleman, it voyaged into Coleman's harmolodic electronic tone colors and pumping body rhythms which had first been revealed to the world on Coleman's 1976 album *Dancing in Your Head.* Yet while *Song X* was only the fourth representation of Coleman's revolutionary method on record, none of his electronic albums had, or would have, the same coruscating edge, the same sense of danger or drama as his meeting with Metheny, who together with Haden and DeJohnette brought to Coleman's music the skills, reflexes, technique, and imagination of virtuosos. "It was a fantastic experience," said Metheny, "making the record and especially the tour afterwards."[41] Powerful, uncompromising, and raw, it left some of his audience shell-shocked and others crying for more. "One of the events of the 1980s," enthused *The Illustrated Encyclopedia of Jazz.* "Practically unlistenable," grouched *The Times* (London).

The Grammy-winning *Still Life Talking* (1987) continued Metheny's ability to mix electronic and acoustic instruments and come up with a homogenized whole that set the tone for a romantic series of albums into the 1990s that had range and color if not surprise. As with *Letter from Home* (1989), it mixed wordless vocals that were further testament to Metheny's ability to create a suave musical compromise that appealed to a worldwide audience. *Secret Story* from 1992 came from two pieces that were originally written for the Montréal Ballet in 1988— one a convoluted melody with odd chord movements called "Antonia," the other a many-layered New Age-sounding piece called "The Truth Will Always Be." A musical autobiography, it included Lyle Mays, Nana Vasconcelos, Toots Thielmans, and the London conductor and orchestrator Jeremy Lubbock with a string section. It mixed familiar Metheny cadences with some typically well-executed guitar playing. "I wouldn't call it a jazz record," claimed Metheny, "but ironically it's got some of my best improvising ever on record."[42] With *We Live Here* (1995), the great dichotomy of Metheny's music came into sharper focus. His obvious technical mastery of the guitar versus his inclination to portray himself as the hurt romantic brought to mind Anthony Blanche's observation in *Brideshead Revisited* that "charm can be fatal to works of art."

Along with the Pat Metheny Group, the group Steps offered tangible evidence in the late 1970s that jazz-rock fusion was far from exhausted. Formed in 1979 as the Mike Mainieri Quintet to fulfill a run of gigs at Seventh Avenue South, the band comprised Mainieri on vibes, Mike Brecker on tenor, Don Grolnick on keyboards, Eddie Gomez on bass, and Steve Gadd on drums. The group attracted considerable underground interest—their performances were never advertised—including two Japanese record company executives who offered them a contract to record in Japan. Assuming the name Steps, they recorded *Step by Step* in Tokyo on December 8–10, 1980 and *Smokin' in the Pit,* a live double album at Roppongi Pit Inn four days later. At the time they were largely playing straight-ahead jazz—Mainieri called them a "contemporary bebop band"—but Steve Gadd's drumming sometimes moved close to square rhythm patterns that suggested rock. But above all the band were exciting, their musicianly handling of tension and release leading to moments of genuine creative drama; right from the beginning, the band served notice they had the potential to become a major force in the 1980s jazz scene.

Four months after returning from Japan, Steps returned to Seventh Avenue South and after another successful run they were invited to cut another album and tour Japan. Gadd, unable to tour, was replaced by Peter Erskine, who had just emerged from the revolving rhythm-section door of Weather Report. *Paradox,* recorded live at Seventh Avenue South in 1981, had fewer highs than their previous albums, and more of an emphasis on ensemble dynamics, structure, and form. Grolnick's atmospheric Prophet synthesizer added color to "Four Chords." While in Japan to promote the album, the band decided to stay together on a permanent basis, and arranged dates to take them back to New York via Hawaii, the West Coast, and the Middle West. When they returned, they enlarged their repertoire and completed further tours, including their first appearance in Europe. After the European venture, Grolnick left, tired of the road. A transitory version of Steps with Bob Mintzer in for Brecker, Omar Hakim in for Erskine, and Warren Bernhardt on keyboards is documented on the CD *Live at Seventh Avenue South,* recorded in late 1981, which presents stirring versions of "Tee Bag," "Song for Seth," and "Sarah's Touch" from *Smokin' in the Pit,* and "Bullet Train" from *Step by Step.*

In 1982, Brazilian pianist Elianne Elias joined the band when they finally secured a U.S. recording contract. However, they discovered that a bar-room band in the deep South had registered the name Steps, so they became Steps Ahead. Released in 1983, *Steps Ahead* was a meticulously recorded studio representation of their sound, with some outstanding compositions including "Islands," "Both Sides of the Coin," and "Pools," the latter later arranged by John Fedchock for the Woody Herman band. Critically acclaimed in Europe, if not the U.S.—*Downbeat* only awarded it three and one-half stars[43]—the band was hailed as the "Band of the 1980s"; sophisticated and progressive critics dubbed their music "the new acoustic fusion." "We were all refugees from fusion at that time—well, not from fusion maybe, but from more electronic settings," said Mike Brecker. "We brought that approach to the way we played. Different rhythmic approaches, the interaction of the bass line and the drums, the function of the melody, the development of texture . . . slowly the lean began toward the compositional elements and as that happened the freedom in the playing diminished. I don't mind that at all if other things are working, and I really liked the compositions we were playing and the way we were delivering them."[44]

Much of the material on *Steps Ahead* was featured on their 1983 tour across Europe, yet despite the acclaim the album received, they continued to experience difficulty in obtaining work in the U.S. "They didn't think we were serious," said Mainieri. "There'd been dozens of 'all star' albums by studio musicians who refuse to go out on the road, then the media was pretty apathetic, nothing in the *New York Times* or the *Village Voice*. They just couldn't work out what we were doing. One critic said 'It would be great to hear them play the blues, that would help,' but I've played the blues for thirty years, who wants to keep playing the blues; we were trying to come up with new music. We were just problems, Mike Brecker for example. If he was black and playing the same thing the critics would call him the new genius. But musicians know. That's why Herbie Hancock, McCoy Tyner, Chick Corea, the greats—that's why everyone wants him on their sessions."[45]

In 1983, Elias became pregnant—she was married to Randy Brecker—and was replaced by Warren Bernhardt. By now the band was increasingly being booked alongside electric jazz groups, including a fall concert alongside Weather Report at the Hollywood Bowl. "Since Peter Erskine had left Weather Report

Steps Ahead: *Left to right:* Eddie Gomez, Mike Mainieri, Peter Erskine, Mike Brecker, Don Grolnick (off-camera). Steps Ahead, in their acoustic phase, emerged as one of the important bands of the early 1980s. (Photograph by Stuart Nicholson.)

and played with us, they thought we were a fusion group," said Mainieri, "but we were still a largely acoustic contemporary bebop band and alongside Weather Report with all their amplifiers and speakers I said, 'Oh my God, we sound just like a High School band.' Everybody just got up and took an intermission, they couldn't hear us, it was awful! We were increasingly being faced with the advances in the electronic revolution so we said, 'We've got no choice, we're not an electric band, we better pump it up a little! We're going to have to go electric.' Brecker was beginning to experiment with the EWI (Electric Wind Instrument), Warren had come in with synthesizers and things and it seemed like the way to go. So that's what was going on when we did *Modern Times.*"[46]

Recorded in January–February 1984, *Modern Times* sacrificed their unique acoustic poise for an electric sound that almost immediately solved the band's identity problem. Now that the band was plainly labelled, the album became a bestseller! In repositioning themselves, Gomez decided to leave. "[He] left because he felt he couldn't contribute as much as we needed," said Mainieri. "That was his point of view not ours. We were working with synthesizers a little more and our music was headed in a new direction. I got into the computer and sequencers and stuff like that and I wanted the new technology on the album, so Michael and I started working on some new material."[47] In 1985 they composed, arranged, and performed all the music for Jane Fonda's *Prime Time Workout* album and video, bringing their music to a broader audience.

By the time they went out on the touring circuits in the summer, Warren Bernhardt had left to pursue his career on acoustic piano, and the lineup was Mainieri and Brecker, Chuck Loeb on guitar (who had appeared on *Modern Times*), Victor Bailey on bass, and Peter Erskine on drums. In early 1986, they recorded *Magnetic,* which confirmed their transformation into a powerful electric band. Mainieri was featured on synthi-vibes and Brecker on his Steiner EWI, but the group were in transition; Victor Bailey only appeared on couple of numbers, and for the rest the bass sounds were generated on a synth with Warren Bernhardt guesting on one track. When the band went out on the touring circuits later in the year, the lineup was Mainieri and Brecker plus Mike Stern on guitar, Daryl Jones on bass, and Steve Smith on drums. Their *Live in Tokyo 1986* drew on material from *Modern Times* and *Magnetic* and included moments of energy and power with arresting solos from Brecker, Mainieri, and Stern, but unfortunately also moments of indulgence. Nevertheless, this version of the band appeared to have much potential and seemed poised to take over the mantle of fusion respectability after the demise of Weather Report, but by 1987 they had gone their separate ways.

In 1989, Mainieri revived Steps Ahead, this time not as a cooperative but with himself as leader with Bendik Hofseth on tenor sax, Steve Kahn on guitar, ex-King Crimson bassist Tony Levin, and Steve Smith on drums. *NYC* reveals a more thoughtful version of the band, leaning towards a World music–jazz-rock viewpoint. Clearly the band was not seeking to compete with the tremendous energy and charisma that earlier versions of the group with Mike Brecker projected; here were considered arrangements and solos that gave a new personality to the group. When they went out on tour, Smith and Hofseth remained with Rachel Nicalazzo (Rachel Z) on keyboards, Jimi Tunnell on guitar, and Victor Bailey on bass. In 1992 they produced *Ying Yang,* with guest appearances by the likes of Steve Khan, Rick Margitza, Victor Bailey, and Wayne Krantz. Yet this and *Vibe* (1995) were perhaps too scrupulously planned and executed with daunting yet predictable precision. Even so, Mainieri was pushing the envelope of fusion, utilizing the latest technology, and the brightest young musicians— Tim Hagans, Clarence Penn, James Genus, Michael Cain—while taking account of the latest trends. Reflecting the state of serious fusion music in the mid-nineties, Mainieri was forced to distribute his product and that of others through his own record company because of major-label indifference.

Steps Ahead was a victim of its inability to slot neatly into a marketing category. Too electric to be played on jazz radio and too jazzy for "smooth jazz"—"They told us, more than half of the tracks have to have an acoustic bass before we'll play your record on jazz radio and the commercial stations won't play it because it's too edgy," said Mainieri[48]—nevertheless, the group demonstrated how jazz-rock fusion continued to show potential for further exploration. Another band that mocked the limpness of FM radio programming was Tribal Tech, formed by guitar whiz Scott Henderson. An alumnus of the Guitar Institute of Technology, Henderson drew on ten years of experience playing rock and blues in bar bands from the age of sixteen. A product of the rock and roll generation, his early rock influences would stay with him through his career. "I think the stuff you grew up listening to is the stuff that never really leaves you," he said, "so no matter what kind of music I play, there's going to be that love of heavy metal."[49] He was introduced to jazz through the Mahavishnu Orchestra, later discovering Joe Pass and bebop, Miles Davis and Weather Report. In 1986 he took over from Wayne Shorter when Joe Zawinul went on the road with Weather Update, subsequently appearing on the Zawinul Syndicate's *The Immigrants* from 1988 and *Black Water* from 1989. He then joined Chick Corea's Elektric Band.

Concurrent with his work with Corea and Zawinul, Henderson formed his own band, Tribal Tech, in 1986, a collaboration with bassist Gary Willis, whose compositions increasingly came to define the band. Debuting with *Spears,* Henderson quickly made a reputation for gasket-blowing fusion that seldom let up. His legato, flowing, blues-based lines evoked the playing of his friend Allan Holdsworth, whose style as well as his bilateral affinity to rock (Jimmy Page and Jeff Beck) and jazz (Weather Report) was a particular source of inspiration to him. A series of albums—*Dr. Hee* (1987), *Nomad* (1990), *Tribal Tech* (1991), *Illicit* (1993), and *Reality Check* (1995)—made these influences plain as well as reinforcing Henderson's reputation as one of the "bad boys" of fusion with an aggressive, hard-core approach. Henderson challenged the fusion orthodoxy with irreverent disdain; *Illicit* featured a warning sticker: "Contains explicit melodies, suggestive harmony, graphic rhythm." Indeed, "Riot" and "Aftermath" were group improvisations made during and after the Los Angeles riots. "Even

Scott Henderson: His band Tribal Tech mocked the limpness of FM programming. (Photograph by Stuart Nicholson.)

though we're primarily known as a jazz group . . . I still think that a lot of young heavy metal cats out there, whose primary listening is Eddie Van Halen, could come and enjoy this group," Henderson said.[50]

In the early nineties, Henderson also appeared on record with former Santana keyboard player Tom Coster, who shared a similar hard-core approach to fusion. Using a nucleus of players that included Henderson, Bob Berg, Alphonso Johnson, Jeff Andrews, Paul Rekow, and Dennis Chambers, *Let's Set the Record Straight* (1993), *The Forbidden Zone* (1994), and *Up From the Street* (1996) were described by Jon Newey as "out to butcher the creeping ogre of radio targeted fuzak."[51] Both Henderson and Coster suggested a general rule of thumb that became progressively more clear as the 1980s drew to a close: the more unlikely a jazz-rock fusion recording was to be heard on FM radio, the more satisfying that record was likely to be.

Mick Goodrick, the highly respected guitar guru at Berklee College of Music, made few albums under his own name, but returned to the touring circuits in the late 1980s as a member of Jack DeJohnette's Special Edition. *Biorhythms* (1990), with Harvie Swartz on bass and Gary Chafee on drums, was an album of high executive skill, great taste, and lucid imagination and an example of jazz-rock fusion at its best. The opening track, "In Praise of Bass Desires," was a tribute to one of the important bands of the 1980s.

Flim and the BBs provided undercover work for tenor saxophonist Dick Oatts, moonlighting from the Village Vanguard's Monday Night Orchestra. An underground fusion story, the band initially found a national following among CD audiophiles before being discovered by a wider audience. *Vintage BBs* is a good representation of their style. Drummer Steve Smith's group Vital Information had been around in various guises since 1983, when the leader was playing in the group Pockets. By the late 1980s, the group had consolidated around Larry Schneider on sax, Frank Gambale on guitar, Tom Coster on keyboards, and for the live *Vitalive!* (1989) had acoustic bassist Larry Grenadier. Considering the talent brought to bear, the band promised much but oscillated between solid bop-influenced blowing and plain, boring, multi-note fusion. Better by far was Wayne Krantz's musical odyssey: *Signals* from 1990 revealed a solid guitarist and composer who by 1995's *2 Drink Minimum,* recorded live at the 55 Bar in New York—Mike Stern's home through much of the 1980s—avoided the fusion trap of dissolving into speed and power clichés. Instead, he created a solid unpretentious jazz-rock album with Lincoln Goines on bass and Zach Danziger on drums. Krantz was a frequent collaborator with guitarist Lennie Stern, she appearing on his *Signals,* he appearing on her *Closer to Light* (1990). They recorded several albums on the German Enja label, *Separate Cages* (1997) representative of their unpretentious ambitions.

Although the house style of the German ECM label was of pastoral moods, subdued rhythmic and linear events, and a serene, often minimalistic-inspired approach to jazz that favored chamber group-like ensembles, label chief Manfred Eicher signed a wide variety of artists, despite his very specific preferences. Norwegian Terje Rypdal, originally a rock guitarist, studied with George Russell, and his albums (fifteen for the label by 1995) all had a certain muted eeriness punctured by spiky guitar shapes. *Whenever I Seem Far Away,* his third album for the label, featured John Abercrombie, who became influenced by Rypdal's "nice guy–nasty guy" approach to improvisation, contributing to the dreamy textures. His Chasers[52] period of the mid-1980s saw his work become more rock-oriented, but in his recent work he has returned to his initial style, with a studied use of space that makes his occasionally jarring pronouncements appear profound.

Rypdal was also an influence on the American guitarist Bill Frisell, who took over from him in saxophonist Jan Garbarek's group in the early 1980s. Garbarek's impressionistic séances often placed his rigorous and disciplined saxophone in opposition to the more unruly elements in has band; *Paths Prints* (1981) brought together frequent collaborator Eberhard Weber on bass with Frisell and Jon Christensen on drums. Weber was a major ECM artist in his own right and performed in a variety of contexts for the label, from playing with the Oslo Philharmonic to solo adventures. His *Yellow Fields* and *Silent Feet,* both with Charlie Mariano on soprano sax, were examples of an aesthetically satisfying European version of fusion.

Garbarek brought in David Torn on guitar for his album *It's OK to Listen to the Grey Voice* (1985). Torn had drunk at the well of Jimi Hendrix, and his radical reordering of blues, rock, and jazz would see him voted "Best Experimental Guitarist" in *Guitar Player* magazine's readers' poll for 1994. As a member of the Everyman Band with Don Cherry in 1979 he came to the notice of ECM, and his subsequent album for the label, *Best Laid Plans* (1985), introduced his work to Jan Garbarek. Torn's second ECM album, *Cloud About Mercury* (1987), with Mick Karn, Bill Bruford, and Mark Isham, reached 13 on the *Billboard* jazz charts in 1987. Torn survived a potentially fatal brain tumor in 1992, and when he returned to recording it was with the German CMP label, which gave him even greater sonic license. *Tripping Over God* (1994) and *What Means Solid Traveller* (1995) were recorded in his home studio. "The proceedings are roughly split between strangulated fuzzgrunge and cumulative meditational floatation," observed *Q* Magazine.[53]

More orthodox were albums by the former Frank Zappa drummer Chad Wackerman and the former Santana drummer Michael Shrieve. Wackerman's work with Zappa included *You Can't Do That On Stage Any More, Vol IV* with the notoriously difficult chart in "The Back Page," *Guitar*, the rock equivalent of the Coltrane-Elvin Jones exchanges, and *Make a Jazz Noise Here*, a collection of instrumental and improvised music from Zappa's 1988 tour. A tumultuous drummer of ferocity and power, Wackerman began drumming at thirteen at a Stan Kenton big-band clinic and had played bebop since high school. He attended a Zappa audition in 1981 and subsequently played on four tours. He also worked extensively with the British guitarist Allan Holdsworth in the 1980s; on Wackerman's *Forty Reasons* from June 1991, they are joined by Jim Cox on keyboards and Jimmy Johnson on bass to combine straight-ahead fusion with five tracks of collective improvisation that suggested Last Exit–meets–Frank Zappa. *In View* from June 1993 continued their mixture of nerve-jangling outré dialogues and pile-driver fusion, less impressive compositionally but with some interesting cuts, particularly when trumpeter Walt Fowler joins the fray. Holdsworth shines: a guitarist's guitarist who never quite succeeded in finding an audience, probably because his playing was so free from cliché it was virtually uncategorizable—he didn't consider himself a jazz player yet his music could only just be called rock—his association with Wackerman yielded a more compelling legacy than his association with Tony Williams in the 1970s.

Michael Shrieve was the original drummer with Santana, with whom he played from 1969 to 1976, during which time he was credited by the guitarist as having turned him on to jazz and the music of Miles Davis and John Coltrane. In 1994 he debuted on the CMP label with *Fascination* with the guitarist Bill Frisell and the organist Wayne Horvitz. The territory they explored was originally opened up by Tony Williams's Lifetime, with ambient, faintly noirish jazzscapes and compelling improvisational interplay. Their dialogue was continued on one CD of *Two Doors* (1995), a double-CD set; the second CD had Shrieve with Shaun Lake on guitar and Jonas Hellborg on bass performing music influenced by the Pakistani singer Nusrat Fateh Ali Khan.

Another group who drew on Lifetime as a source of inspiration was Let's Be Generous. Their eponymously titled album from 1991, with Joachim Kühn on keyboards, Miroslav Tardic on guitar, Tony Newton on bass, and Mark Nauseef on drums and percussion, was a coruscating experience, exploiting noise, grunge, and free abandon in almost equal quantities. "Mark called me and said, 'Why don't we do a crazy record, something totally uncompromising . . . take it to a higher level than the typical mediocre jazz-rock, something a bit freer and wilder,'" said Kühn. "I kind of liked this idea so I checked out some new keyboards. . . . The new stuff all sounded too clean, too cold. So I used a Jupiter 4 with a Big Muff pedal, the sort Jimi Hendrix used. And I played it through a Marshall amp, which gave me the kind of overtones and feedback I liked. That and a Fender Rhodes with a wah-wah pedal were the my only instruments on that session. And to me it's kind of nostalgic sound. It reminds me of the early days of fusion when the music was really adventurous."[54]

Equally not for the squeamish or lyrical minded, guitarist Marc Ribot upended standard practice with jagged-edge, odd-time takes that marked him out as one of the instrument's radical rethinkers. Debuting with his group Rootless Cosmopolitans in 1990, *Rootless Cosmopolitans* and *Requiem for What's His Name* (1992) were not so much jazz-rock as jazz-mayhem, but serious mayhem that was inventive and witty and, more importantly, original.

These deconstructionist urges served only to highlight how fusion had become limited by the conventions of the idiom as much as the sound. The music had become self-referential, the same as happened to hard bop and the big bands in previous eras of jazz. Indeed, there were more than a few echoes of history repeating itself when it came to fusion and the big bands, both areas of jazz that were increasingly tailored to the demands of consumerism. As Hsio Wen Shih pointed out in *Jazz*, "There is a terrifying record, an anthology called *The Great Swing Bands*. . . . If [it is] played without consulting notes or label, it is impossible to distinguish one [band] from another."[55] The same thing had become true of fusion, whose perspectives, like those of the big bands, were shaped by commercial expectations. Yet while fusion had ceased to evolve and had become a commodity, a Scofield, a Rypdal, or a Ribot were reminders that the experimenters were always there, with scant regard for musical boundaries. Futurist manifestos do not concern themselves with limits, and it was the zealous reformers, often out of sight of the comfortably accessible mainstream, to whom the future ultimately belonged.

Notes

1. *Miles: The Autobiography,* by Miles Davis with Quincy Troupe (Macmillan, London, 1990), ch. 16.
2. *Downbeat,* November 1981, p. 33.
3. *Miles: The Autobiography,* by Miles Davis with Quincy Troupe (Macmillan, London, 1990), pp. 340–341.
4. *Sunday Times* review by Derek Jewell; *Times* review by Miles Kington following Davis's concert at the Hammersmith Odeon, London, April 27, 1983.

5. *Miles: The Autobiography,* by Miles Davis with Quincy Troupe (Macmillan, London, 1990), p. 346.
6. *Downbeat,* August 1987, p. 29.
7. Ibid., August 1984, p. 33.
8. *Miles: The Autobiography,* by Miles Davis with Quincy Troupe (Macmillan, London, 1990), p. 348.
9. *Jazz Journal,* September 1984, p. 14.
10. *Miles: The Autobiography,* by Miles Davis with Quincy Troupe (Macmillan, London, 1990), p. 349.
11. *Downbeat,* January 1993, p. 31.
12. Ibid., December 1991, p. 20.
13. *Miles: The Autobiography,* by Miles Davis with Quincy Troupe (Macmillan, London, 1990), p. 374.
14. Festival organizer Claude Nobs put together a time capsule to be opened in two thousand years. Asked what message he wished to leave for civilization in the year 3988, Davis's response was "Catch you next time."
15. *Downbeat,* December 1991, p. 20.
16. Ibid., October 1989, p. 29.
17. Their Montreux performance from July 21 appeared on a bootleg CD as *Miles in Montreux* and included an appearance of vocalist Chaka Khan on "Human Nature" that is to be avoided at all costs.
18. *On the Corner: The Sellout of Miles Davis,* by Stanley Crouch, republished in *Reading Jazz: A Gathering of Autobiography, Reportage and Criticism from 1919 to Now,* edited by Robert Gottlieb (Pantheon, New York, 1996), pp. 909–910.
19. *Mad at Miles,* by Pearl Cleage, republished in *The Miles Davis Reader,* edited by Gary Carner (Schirmer Books, New York, 1996), p. 210.
20. *Musician,* December 1991, p. 48.
21. *Downbeat,* February 1993, p. 33.
22. Ibid., October 1991, p. 26.
23. *Musician,* December 1991, p. 45.
24. The issuing of the recording of the event, however, was delayed because of the immense undertaking of obtaining artists' clearances from their respective recording companies.
25. Minister of Culture Jacques Lang called him the "Picasso of jazz" and continued, "France has a very special kind of love for you. . . . Miles Davis, you are in a constant musical adventure . . . able to cross all the eras while staying eternally avant garde." *The Miles Davis Reader,* edited by Gary Carner (Schirmer Books, New York, 1996), p. 218.
26. *Musician,* December 1991, p. 50.
27. *Wire,* July 1988, p. 32.
28. *Downbeat,* January 1987, p. 17.
29. *Rhythm,* October 1991, p. 46.
30. These included *Meant to Be* (Blue Note CDP 7 954792) from 1991 and *What We Do* (Blue Note CDP 99586-2) from 1993.
31. *Downbeat,* November 1993, p. 30.
32. *Jazz Times,* May 1995, p. 40.
33. *Jaco: The Extraordinary and Tragic Life of Jaco Pastorius,* by Bill Milkowski (Miller Freeman Books, San Francisco, 1995), p. 98.
34. Liner notes, *I Remember Jaco,* by Bob Mintzer (RCA Novus PD 90618), p. 2.
35. *Downbeat,* December 1981, p. 54.
36. *Jaco: The Extraordinary and Tragic Life of Jaco Pastorius,* by Bill Milkowski (Miller Freeman Books, San Francisco, 1995), p. 118.
37. Ibid., p. 184.
38. Ibid., p. 67.
39. Interview in *Q Magazine* with David Sinclair

40. *Wire,* August 1992, p. 15.
41. Ibid.
42. Ibid., p. 14.
43. *Downbeat,* August 1983, p. 26.
44. *Wire,* November 1987, p. 33.
45. Interview with the author, January 14, 1997.
46. Ibid.
47. *Jazz Journal,* December 1984, p. 11.
48. Interview with the author, January 14, 1997.
49. *Guitar Extra!,* spring 1991, p. 42.
50. Ibid., p. 45.
51. *Jazz Magazine,* Spring 1994, p. 28.
52. His guitar-heavy power trio with Bjorn Kjellymyr on bass and Andun Kleive on drums. See *Blue* (ECM 1346).
53. *Q Magazine,* June 1995.
54. *Downbeat,* February 1993, p. 28.
55. *Jazz,* edited by Nat Hentoff and Albert J. McCarthy (Jazz Book Club, London, 1962), p. 187.

CHAPTER 13

Make a Jazz Noise Here

If jazz-rock fusion held out the promise of larger markets and expanded musical vocabularies, it also confronted the dichotomy between artistic and commercial motivation. As we have seen, the whole history of jazz-rock has been about the tension between these two apparently irreconcilable opposites. When the latter was overruled in favor of the former, the artistic possibilities of fusion seemed to diminish in direct proportion to commercial motivation. However, the aesthetic potential suggested by the eclecticism inherent in jazz-rock has always offered a set of possibilities that continued to warrant serious exploration, something that was attractive to musicians from jazz as much as rock.

But in attempting to chart the musical potential presented by the different stylistic configurations to be found within jazz-rock, it becomes apparent that the term jazz-rock, or even fusion, excludes as much as it includes since genres actually keep out as much as they keep in. Generic categories tend to be an after-the-fact rationalization to define music in its market used by the music industry to organize the sales process and thus target potential consumers. They are not determined by musical style—fusion, for example, soon ceased to be a "fusion" of styles—but by the audience's perception of that style, and they are as much about selling as they are about organizing our musical expectations. "Without calling it something, record companies don't know how to market music or even what it is," asserted the bassist and guerrilla producer Bill Laswell.[1]

Laswell's music existed in several zones simultaneously and evolved from an experimental group he formed in 1979 with the synthesizer player Michael Beinhorn. They began recording in 1979 with their group Material, which moved into the sonic spaces opened up by the first wave of jazz-rock innovators such as Jimi Hendrix, the Tony Williams Lifetime, the Mahavishnu Orchestra, and prefurlough Miles Davis. "They were reference points of things that I was trying to do, which became a bit more minimal when mixed with other influences such as certain English bands like Henry Cow, Hadfield and the North, ambient references to Brian Eno, and German stuff like Kraftwerk and Cluster," explained Laswell.[2]

Bill Laswell: His tough-minded connoisseurship of music past and present juxtaposed traditions and created a true "fusion" of styles that existed in several zones simultaneously. (Photograph by Stuart Nicholson.)

Their first album, *Temporary Music*, was a compilation of three EPs made for Philadelphia's Red Records label, and was followed by the impressive *Memory Serves* in 1982. "That was just a product of intuitively jumping into stuff quickly, without a whole lot of preparation, and mixing it with Ornette Coleman's Prime Time influence of the moment," said Laswell.[3] Included was a tape collage—"Unauthorized"—and a grouping of some of New York's finest improvisers, including trumpeter Olu Dara, trombonist George Lewis, violinist Billy Bang, Henry Threadgill on alto, and the then-neglected Sonny Sharrock on guitar. In 1983 came *One Down*, which for much the same sort of inscrutable reasons as *On the Corner*, contained no musician listing on its original vinyl issue.

At the time, "punk-jazz," "jazz-funk," and "new fusion" were all terms whistled up to try and describe this highly original music. Expertly assembled and carefully manipulated in the recording studio by Laswell, whose arsenal of effects included tape loops, white noise, electronic drones, industrial noise, and some inspired improvisation, his reputation as a production auteur began to grow. His first notable commercial success came with Herbie Hancock's pop album *Future Shock,* and the subsequent monster success of "Rock-It," the street-beat-scratch single taken from it.

"I had just finished doing a series of hip-hop records and I was very tired," recalled Laswell. "I wanted to do something crazy and experimental. I had met this guy who was working with Herbie [Hancock], helping him put his records together, and he asked me to work with him. So I got a DJ—I'll never forget this—he came via a car service and we cut the track really quickly, 45 minutes, while his driver waited on a couch! We put the track together, went to California, played it to Herbie and I don't think he had a clue what it was! So I just said, 'Play this,' 'Do this,' 'Say this,' and it was like an hour. We mixed it down—an hour and a half—and I had a cassette. I wanted new speakers and . . . I went into this shop, told them to play this cassette as I wanted to check out the bottom end. [The salesman] put the tape in and for a few weird seconds there was a feeling in the room like something was happening. I turned around and there was literally like a hundred kids going, 'What was *that*?' At that moment we realized what we had done. And then it just blew up."[4] From then on Laswell was in demand—Mick Jagger, Yoko Ono, Laurie Anderson, Fela Kuti, Public Image Ltd., and Manu Dibango all drew on his production skills.

Amid albums under his own name such as *Praxis* (1982), *Baselines* (1985) with Ronald Shannon Jackson, and *Hear No Evil* (1988)—the latter a dark, trance-inducing pan-ethnic album with L. Shankar on violin, Nicky Skopelitis on guitar, and Zakir Hussain, Daniel Ponce, and Aiyb Dieng on percussion—Material's albums were fascinating post-modern soundscapes that confronted diverse musical traditions amid the swirling energy inspired by early jazz-rock. The musicians Laswell chose to work with were all strong and possibly eccentric individuals. "These are the characters who stand for something," he explained. "Those are the kinds of people I work with. Those people that don't stand for something I avoid. Around this time I was working with an exceptional nucleus of people, all like-minded, who together were creating a sound to take the music in a new direction. I had been experimenting with mixing people and from this period a number of instrumental albums emerged through collaborations with Indian and African musicians."[5] Albums that emerged from this highly productive period—from around 1988–1989—included *Horses and Trees, Next To Nothing, Seven Souls* with readings by William Burroughs, and Material's *Third Power.* The latter was an extraordinary gathering of innovative pioneers of black music from the preceding three decades, including Bootsy Collins, Bernie Worell, Maceo Parker, various James Brown and P-Funk alumni, Sly & Robbie, Herbie Hancock, and Henry Threadgill.

Even more intriguing was Material's release *Hallucination Engine* (1994), claimed to be "The Ultimate Ambient and Jazz Funk and Dub Light in Extension." Such record company hyperbole often makes the artists themselves cringe, but in this case it was difficult to think of any other album that could compete for such a claim—indeed, it stands as an excellent example of Laswell's work. Including Wayne Shorter on soprano and tenor saxes, Shankar on violin, Nicky Skopelitis on guitar, Bernie Worrell on keyboards, Bootsy Collins on bass, Sly Dunbar on drums, Trilok Gurtu and Zakir Hussain on tablas, this World-music slant on fusion prefigured the late 1990s "drum 'n' bass" craze while reaching back to touch base with early Weather Report grooves—a hypnotic version of "Cucumber Slumber" is included—and the electric Miles, without sacrificing its avowed modernistic stance (sampling the voice of William S. Burroughs, on "Words of Advice for Young People"). Shorter's role was that of elliptic melodist and epigrammatic embellisher on "Black Light," in which he rises from a matrix of industrial noise to enunciate the insistent theme.[6]

In 1995 he recorded *South Delta Space Age* with a group called Third Rail, comprising James "Blood" Ulmer on guitar, Amina Claudine Myers and Bernie Worell on Hammond B-3 organs, and former Meters drummer Joseph "Ziggy" Modeliste. It was a shrewd blend of blues, gospel, and harmolodic-influenced jazz. Laswell explained, "The idea was to remind people that playing simple stuff or the blues was all about creating a feel. Everyone is in such a hurry to play stuff. This is laid-back, doesn't worry about getting on to the next thing and a lot of things that 'Blood' and Amina do have a kind of spirituality, a sanctified quality, which is really not available in music these days."[7]

This kind of tough-minded connoisseurship of music past and present juxtaposed disparate traditions to intriguing ends and struck at the very heart of the aesthetic failure of commercial fusion by avoiding technical excess and predictability by seeking out the unorthodox. Laswell was a conceptualist who realized the endless possibilities of combining jazz improvisation, rock, and black music, cloaking them all in mystery to form his own dark, deep, nonlinear (and often ambient) creations. His manifesto was simple: "It's very much the responsibility of the underground to offer an alternative to all the homogenized shit you hear on the radio, overcome resistance to new ideas and find record companies to get your music and ideas out to people who are interested."[8]

Laswell's mixture of the obscure and the obvious had strong resonance in the work of producer/situationist Kip Hanrahan, for whom he had played bass on Hanrahan's debut album, *Coup de Tête*. But where Laswell liked to peer into the darker waters that surround the recondite, Hanrahan brushed alongside the exotic. His projects included Astor Piazzolla's Nuevo Tango Band, his own Conjure albums that wedded Ishmael Reed's poems to an unlikely combination of soul, New Orleans, R&B, harmolodic funk, and Latin percussion, and genre crossover albums under his own name. On the latter albums he fashioned an original style with elements that were simultaneously argumentative and supportive. Mixing stylistically diverse musicians while burdening them with impossibly wordy titles like "The September Dawn Shows Itself to Elizabeth and Her

Lover on East 18th Street in Manhattan," Hanrahan worked like a film direc- tor—he came up with a script, cast the parts, and let his players feel their way into their roles until the basic template around which his ideas had been gath- ered was superseded, its ultimate shape defined by the musicians themselves.

Describing his musical background, he said, "I grew up as a Jew among a lot of Latinos in the Bronx and it was the music I learned earlier than anything else. I can't say it's my music, but it is the music I learned myself through, learned myself against."[9] Combining this knowledge of Latin music—absorbed it seems through a process of osmosis—with rock, he called the result "the soundtrack to everybody's life, whether they know it or not,"[10] to which were added "the man- nerisms of defiance and rebellion that everyone appropriates from jazz."[11] Hanrahan's albums up to *A Thousand Nights and a Night* (1996) tended towards conceptual pieces about the struggles for power. Early albums such as *Desire Develops an Edge, Vertical's Currency,* and *Tenderness* dealt with sexual politics; *Exotica* attempted to be "relaxed and conversational about politics"; and *All Roads Are Made of Flesh,* a series of live tracks made by various editions of his bands from 1985 to 1994, was a testament to the emotional intensity that the instrumental combinations he assembled could generate.

From *Desire Develops an Edge,* the former Cream bassist Jack Bruce estab- lished himself as a Hanrahan regular. He had met Bruce when he played percus- sion for Carla Bley's Big Band, later asking him to record some vocals when he knew he could not do justice to them himself. "I was taken by the intensity of Jack," he said. "When he enters the room the walls vibrate. He could do the vocal things backwards and then tell me how you could take it so much further. He got the intimacy and asymmetricality of the lyrics exactly and immediately. I was stunned. He and [Don] Pullen formed the nucleus of the band, and when they found a chord everyone would follow them."[12]

In 1987, the pianist-organist Don Pullen joined the entourage. A veteran of the Charles Mingus groups of the 1970s and the Don Pullen/George Adams Quartet of the 1980s, he brought along his partner George Adams on tenor sax— also a fellow Mingus alumnus—who became another Hanrahan regular. Other Hanrahan inductees from time to time included guitarist Leo Nocentelli of the Meters, saxophonists Charles Neville of the Neville Brothers and Chico Freeman, vocalist Carmen Lundy, and some of New York's finest percussion players such as Jerry Gonzalez from the Fort Apache Band, JT Lewis, Milton Cardona, Anthony Carillo, and Richie Flores. Other musicians who drifted through Hanrahan's extravaganzas included New Orleans legend Allen Toussaint, bassist Steve Swallow, Wolfgang Pusching on alto sax, drummers Ralph Peterson Jr., Cindy Blackman, and Marvin "Smitty" Smith, pianist Mike Cain, guitarist Brandon Ross, and Henry Threadgill on flute.

These extraordinary gatherings of talent could be wholly compelling, but the instrumental potential was often overwhelmed by the libretto. Hanrahan's vocal parts were often no more than animated *Sprechstimme* over static or simple har- monies, posing the question of whether the auteur should relax his vision to allow more light to shine on his cast of instrumentalists. *A Thousand Nights and a Night* (1996), was the first part of a proposed nine-album cycle based on the stories of *Scheherazade,* partly inspired by the cinematographic interpretation of Pier Paolo Pasolini and by Hanrahan's own first-hand experiences in the Middle East. It included some of the last recorded work of Don Pullen and was a blend of cutting-edge jazz (David Murray, Steve Coleman), rock, African and Asian rhythms, and vocals that reflected the uncertain provenance of much Arabian folklore.

But while Hanrahan's and Laswell's music suggested a literal application of the meaning of the word fusion, "a union or blending . . . together of different elements" to extend the original premise of jazz-rock in highly original ways, such a prospect was equally appealing to several rock musicians from the late 1960s on. Yet their work has often been overlooked by jazz audiences since their music was not marketed within the generic category of either "jazz" or "jazz-rock" but within the larger forum of rock music. The reason for this was simple: the rock market held out the prospect of better sales and besides, in the late 1960s and 1970s jazz was seen as distinctly unhip and an impediment to selling records. Even so, among rock artists who experimented with the jazz-rock concept was Frank Zappa, whose album *Hot Rats* from 1969 numbers among the classic early jazz-rock albums.

Zappa began his working musical career as a rock 'n' roll band guitarist, forming the Mothers of Invention in 1964, when he met a group of musicians who were willing to experiment with his original compositions. "I figured the only way I was going to get [my music] played was to put my own band together and write for that band," he said. "Then I found out it was not easy to find people who could read what I was doing, so I wound up doing things that were not exactly complicated but at least it was mine."[13] The Mothers were fired from countless venues because of their refusal to perform cover versions of then-current hits. One day, Tom Wilson from MGM happened into the Whisky A Go Go Club in Los Angeles at the moment the band was playing a blues number and signed them on the surmise that he had discovered a white blues group.[14] This is not as far-fetched as it sounds. Zappa was an accomplished, gutsy, blues-based player; Johnny "Guitar" Watson was an early influence, occasional recording companion, and lifelong friend. However, speaking in a 1978 interview, Zappa also claimed to have been influenced as much by Eastern music as the blues, citing Greek, Turkish, Bulgarian, and Indian sources. He added, "If there's anything from the composers I like that's incorporated in my playing, it's Stravinsky's idea of economy of means, because I'll take just a few notes and change the rhythm."[15] He maintained a strong sense of thematic development in his solos, which made them appear as compositional entities in themselves, obeying their own compositional logic, as Zappa's biographer Neil Slaven pointed out: "[He regarded his guitar solos] as compositions in themselves, expositions of a unique playing style that matched form and content with bravura control of effects and amplification. . . . Beneath all the harsh angular phrasing was a gift for creating starkly beautiful melodies that remain in the mind long after their conclusion."[16]

In 1966 Zappa's dazzling debut *Freak Out* was released, the first rock double album and one of the first concept albums that was an acknowledged influence on the Beatles' *Sgt. Pepper's Lonely Hearts Club Band.* It made *Billboard*'s Top 200 album chart, establishing the Mothers as an "underground" rock act and setting the tone for Zappa's early musical direction—musically eclectic and weighted towards political debate and satire with songs like "Who Are the Brain Police?" A mixture of good melodies, blasting satire, political contempt, parody, and experimentation with black and sometimes immature humor, it established a somewhat confusing reputation for the band, who were sometimes reviewed as a comedy act rather than a musical one.

Being forced to accept the need for a music accessible to hippie audiences was a source of frustration to Zappa: "You're not selling to a bunch of jazz aesthetes in Europe. You're selling to Americans, who really hate music and love entertainment," he said. "So the closer your product is to mindless entertainment material, the better off you're going to be."[17] Nevertheless, selling was a task he undertook with vigor, and while maintaining high musical standards, he set about adding to the vocabulary of rock and contemporary music. "The first bunch of Mothers could not read and they didn't have any concept of time signatures above and beyond 4/4, and 3/4 was sometimes difficult but we managed to squeeze in a couple of 6/8 bars here and there," said Zappa. "They didn't have any concept of what was going on in contemporary music. They'd never heard of Stravinsky; they liked rock 'n' roll. So it was very difficult to teach them how to play the things I wanted to have played."[18]

In 1967 Zappa and the Mothers decamped to New York City to play a six-month residency in the Garrick Theater, above the Café au Go Go, that helped, Zappa would later claim, establish an experimental arts scene in the city. Performances would vary nightly. "I was playing with Jeremy and the Satyrs downstairs at the time," said Mike Mainieri. "We were there on and off for almost a year. Zappa was upstairs with his band. A lot of people are not familiar with Zappa's classical work. He would have workshops and whoever showed up, showed up. He was exploring the more classical approach to composition, written structures. Zappa, myself, Don Preston who played piano for Zappa, and Joe Beck and a few others organized some small chamber ensembles and we would write some weird shit to perform for our own entertainment. That's why there's a string group on my album *Journey Thru an Electric Tube,* which was recorded around then."[19] Despite what Mainieri called "the wildness" of these sessions, Zappa often sat in with the jazz musicians, sowing the seeds of what would subsequently produce a new color in his music that would surface intermittently through his career. With his own band Zappa was developing a reputation as a hard musical taskmaster, rehearsing his band during their New York stopover for long periods as a way of achieving the more complex results he was after.

As successive iterations of the Mothers unfolded, so the level of musicianship within the band became more accomplished. By 1969, there were four reading musicians and the band had increased to a ten-piece group, with horns and two

drummers. While this allowed Zappa to increase the sophistication of the voicings in the band's arrangements, it needed a clean break to develop further, so in
1969, after releasing seven albums, Zappa disbanded, saying, "George Wein,
impresario of the Newport Jazz festival put us in a package tour with Rahsaan
Roland Kirk, Duke Ellington and Gary Burton. Before I went on I saw Duke
Ellington begging—pleading—for a ten dollar advance. It was really depressing.
I told the guys: 'That's it—we're breaking the band up.'"[20]

   In September 1969, Zappa was to be found sitting in with Jean-Luc Ponty and
the George Duke trio at The Experience in San Francisco, a rock club. Duke and
Ponty were playing an early version of jazz-rock, straight-ahead jazz improvisation over a rock beat. During 1969 Zappa produced *Burnt Weeny Sandwich,* a
proto-jazz-rock album, and *Uncle Meat,* which anticipated progressive rock. He
also recorded *Hot Rats,* a mainly instrumental jazz-rock album of original compositions and arrangements that showcased his guitar playing, and which had Ponty
guesting on the track "I Must Be a Comet." *Hot Rats* was accessible, sophisticated, and unencumbered with disruptive parody, satire, and Zappa's apparently
insatiable need to sneer at and ridicule the establishment (even the words of
"Willie the Pimp," sung by Captain Beefheart, are in context with the gutsy low-
down drive of the arrangement). Ironically the album flopped in the U.S., probably confirming Zappa's worst fears about the tastes of American audiences, but
charted in Europe, appearing in the Top-10 listings for both Britain and Holland.

   The album highlights are "Peaches en Regalia" and "Son of Mr. Green
Genes." "Peaches" contains no soloing or improvisation as such, but related
orchestrated variations of the theme. It starts with an eight-bar intro, then moves
to the first of eight themes or variations on themes, building all the while. In 4/4
time, it contained uneven theme lengths:

> A theme (8 bars) + B (10 bars, also including a cycle of key changes) + C
> (8 bars) + D (4 bars) + E (5 bars) + F (8 bars) + G (5 bars) + H (8 bars) +
> A (8 bars) + A (8 bars) + A (8 bars)

Such was the affection among jazz musicians for this track that it later inspired
"A New Regalia," composed by Vince Mendoza, on Peter Erskine's 1988 album
Motion Poet. "Mr. Green Genes" is a sixteen-bar tune consisting of two eight-bar
melodies and is shorn of the inane lyrics of the original version that had previously appeared on *Uncle Meat.* It derived a lot of its momentum from the interplay between the soloist, Zappa, the drumming, and the textures of the intricate
backing figures. Within the texture of the tight, attractive, and unusual voicings
for the instruments lay an original approach to fusion. Zappa was particularly
proud of the quality and quantity of overdubbing work undertaken on the
album: "The real reason for *Hot Rats* was to do the overdubbing, because I don't
think there'd been anything outside the early experiments of Les Paul where
there was that much overdubbage applied to a piece of tape. We were using a
primitive, maybe even prototype sixteen track recorder for that. So it was the
first time that we could really pile on the tracks," he said later.[21] It also gave full

reign to Zappa's imagination, allowing him to score for highly unusual combinations of instruments, including keyboards and saxophones (Ian Underwood), violins ("Sugar Cane" Harris or Jean-Luc Ponty), bass (Max Bennett or Shuggy Otis), and drums (John Guerin, Paul Humphrey, or Ron Selico).

Although *Weasels Ripped My Flesh* was released in 1970, it was essentially outtakes from the previous three years, albeit containing an interesting tribute to the late Eric Dolphy. When Zappa reformed the Mothers of Invention in 1970, the new band was increasingly obvious in its style, and despite Zappa's protestations to the contrary, included more and more ribald and coarse material. But as ever with Zappa's output, there is the juxtaposition of styles, genres, and targets for his satire and wit.

With *Waka/Jawaka* and *The Grand Wazoo,* both from 1972, Zappa produced two ambitious jazz-rock albums. The lineup included George Duke on keyboards, Sal Marquez on trumpet, Mike Altschul on saxophones, and Bill Byers on trombone. The first track of *Waka/Jawaka* is the extended "Big Swifty." The emphasis is rhythmic, with the original, complex theme—incorporating several meter changes—fading into a modal, bluesy blowing section in 3/4. The original theme is not repeated later, but played at half tempo, then speeding up and paraphrased over a constant tempo. The improvisers then return hinting at the theme to fade out. "Waka/Jawaka" avoids repeating the original theme, the arrangement building through complex waves of overdubs and, during the final five minutes, introduces elaborate arranged variations of the main theme complete with tubular bells on the last chorus, displaying a unique voice paralleling the richness associated with Gil Evans. Indeed, Robert Christgau has suggested, on the basis of the presence of the trumpeter Marquez, that Zappa had been listening to a lot of Miles Davis.[22]

Grand Wazoo, recorded with his regular group augmented to big band proportions by an array of Hollywood studio musicians, had a distinctly jazzy feel throughout. The form of title track is intro, theme, solos, and theme. However, the theme is 87 bars in length with key, rhythm, and theme shifts with a blowing section that has carefully marshalled background figures ebbing and flowing throughout against an intriguing rock-swing feel generated by the rhythm section. "Cleetus Awreetus" starts with a jaunty light classical feel to it, moving into parody, while "Eat that Question" is in a minor key, with a strident eight-bar riff. The soloists build to a dramatic entry by Zappa and a beefed-up recapitulation of the theme to close and fade. How "Blessed Relief," performed here as a wistful ballad, has not become a jazz standard is a mystery. The musical success of these sessions tempted Zappa into a limited tour with a twenty-piece band, debuting at Hollywood Bowl on September 10, 1972. These sessions alone would have landed a less outrageous artist in the pages of jazz-rock history. But Zappa's music as a whole was too broad and diverse to be limited by conventional categorization.

In 1973 Zappa reformed the Mothers with a strong lineup that included Tom and Bruce Fowler, Ian and Ruth Underwood, George Duke, and Jean-Luc Ponty, but *Overnight Sensation* did little justice to the team of virtuoso musicians he had assembled. However, *Roxy and Elsewhere,* a live set from 1974, did capture the impressive élan of the group with strong jazz solos and little-big-band attack. The track "Be-Bop Tango (Of the Old Jazzmen's Church)" prompted Zappa's immortal line, "Jazz is not dead, it just smells funny!" The following year Zappa sounded decidedly jazz-rock-ish on *One Size Fits All,* amid vocals that "gave up on mere scatology and extended Zappa's private mythology to new extremes of obscurity."[23]

Zappa employed a number of jazz musicians in his bands in the seventies and eighties, including Jean-Luc Ponty and George Duke, Bruce, Walt and Tom Fowler (sons of the musicologist Dr. William Fowler), Ian Underwood (ex-Don Ellis; he had played bebop with Steve Swallow, Sugar Cane Harris, and Glen Ferris), Don Preston (a former Herbie Mann sideman who had worked with Paul Bley and Charlie Haden in the 1950s), and the brothers Bunk and Buzz Gardner. "For me it was always more interesting to encounter a musician who had a unique ability," Zappa said. "Find a way to showcase that, and build that unusual skill into the composition . . . so [it] would be stamped with the personality of the person who was there when the composition was created."[24] His later bands always employed excellent drummers and percussionists who possessed an admirable ability to play and read in a wide breadth of styles. Art Tripp had been percussionist with the Cincinnati Orchestra, and the percussionist Ruth Komanoff was a Juilliard graduate; Zappa's drummers included Terry Bozzio, Chad Wackerman, Chester Thompson, and Paul Humphrey. Later Wackerman spoke of his time with Zappa: "He pushed everyone who worked for him. He'd ask me to play something incredibly complex. When I couldn't do it, he'd get more specific and ask me to play something even more difficult. I couldn't do that either, but as I would try, then I'd realize I was playing what he had originally asked me to play."[25]

In the 1970s Zappa-as-composer started to broaden the musical contexts in which he worked, and the true extent of his imagination started to unfold. As well as the live band and his more popular rock albums, he recorded in a diverse range of contexts. In 1970 he collaborated with Jean-Luc Ponty on Ponty's *King Kong,* subtitled "Jean-Luc Ponty plays the music of Frank Zappa." It was a mixture of absorbing and not-so-absorbing fusion compositions, but the nineteen-minute "Music for Electric Violin and Low Budget Orchestra" sustained interest and momentum through imaginative and resourceful writing. The orchestral Zappa—inspired largely by Edgard Varèse but also by Krystof Penderecki, Pierre Boulez, and Elliot Carter—emerged in 1971 with *200 Motels,* the atonal soundtrack music for the film of the same name. *Orchestral Favorites* (1975) was a truly awful orchestral album conducted by Michael Zearott that used electric bass and drums. *Joe's Garage* (1979) was a rock opera. *The London Symphony Orchestra Vols. 1, 2, 3* was described in 1991 as "a luxuriant swamp of quintessential Zappa,"[26] while in 1984 came *Boulez Conducts Zappa: The Perfect Stranger,* which awaits posterity's verdict—was it important modern music, or, as Zappa claimed, "preposterously non-modern" music? Other albums included an eerie but uproarious night at the opera, *Thing Fish* (1984); *Francesco Zappa*, an album of Synclavier-generated string trios based on 200-year-old manuscripts; and the Grammy-winning *Jazz From Hell* (1988), an album of original compositions for the Synclavier, the computer-to-digital interface used by, among others, Miles Davis on *Tutu*. On release it contained a warning against offensive lyrics; it was an instrumental album.

Zappa gave up running road bands in 1988 after recording *Make A Jazz Noise Here, The Best Band You Never Heard in Your Life,* and *Broadway the Hard Way.* His group, augmented by an agile horn section, acquitted themselves with precision and showed what a fertile musical imagination could achieve using the "horns plus rock" formula that was quickly exhausted by bands operating in the Blood, Sweat & Tears and Chicago nexus. After sinking a good deal of money into the group, he finally called it quits mid-tour.

Zappa's ability to claim the musical low ground as well as scaling the high ground meant that he was easy meat for critics, who were unable to pigeonhole his music and selected, or were deflected by, the slapstick elements of his band's performances. Hereby lies the conundrum, and the need to dig into his recorded repertoire to discover the good material, with the aid of the judicious use of the fast forward button. As one reviewer noted, "The constant temptation is to say that Zappa is a genius (which he is) and consequently to rank highly all his offerings."[27] Yet all his work is littered with good examples of his guitar playing, the only real constant in his musical output. From early solos like "Willie The Pimp" *(Hot Rats)* to later examples like "Fire and Chain" *(Make a Jazz Noise Here)* and "Watermelon in Easter Hay" *(Guitar),* Zappa showed a preference for minor moods, spinning sensuously intense lines within his own unique context and musical vocabulary. *Shut Up 'n' Play Yer Guitar* (recorded between 1977 and 1980) was a collection of guitar solos, largely from the jazzy "Inca Roads," while another collection, *Guitar* (from 1978–1984) contained powerful playing with Chad Wackerman on drums and Scott Thunes on bass. Zappa was not the only guitarist to be heard on his sessions; guitar monster Steve Vai was a memorable guest on his later work, such as his mind-boggling vocalized melodic guitar solo on "The Jazz Discharge Party Hats" in *The Man from Utopia*.

Zappa continued composing and conducting up to his death from cancer in December 1993. "What kept me and so many other people percolating to Zappa's music for the last 27 years was the thrill of hitching a ride with a critical mind that was always pushing into uncharted territory," said *The New Yorker*.[28] Nominated for at least seven Grammy awards, in September 1994 he became the second rock musician (after Jimi Hendrix) to enter the *Downbeat* Critic's Hall of Fame and in January 1995 he was inducted into the "Rock & Roll Hall of Fame."

Zappa made a significant contribution on an inside-outside basis to the rock mainstream; indeed the whole of his music is underpinned by influences outside the normal experiences of the rock world, of which jazz was just one element among many. He disdained success, opting instead for "bad taste" and its attendant lack of air play, although *Apostrophe (')* was eventually certified gold, making 10 on the *Billboard* chart, and the single from it, "Don't Eat the Yellow Snow," was Zappa's first in *Billboard*'s Hot 100 (albeit at number 86). Zappa fulfilled the criteria for a genuinely creative artist, concerned with exploring and extending the rock form, which inevitably brought him into contact with jazz as a means to this end. Yet while he combined jazz and rock in a particularly individual way, producing at least one classic jazz-rock album and several others of great interest in the genre, jazz-rock per se was never central to Zappa's musical thinking, but more a musical challenge among many to be confronted and surmounted, another musical flavor in a miscellany of musical genres that comprised his music.

Captain Beefheart—alias Don Van Vliet—was a classmate of Zappa's when he attended high school in Lancaster, California, a relationship that was destined to alter both their lives. Both had outrageous and bizarre senses of humor, and both claim to have influenced the other. Beefheart always said most of the ideas that Zappa first became known for were taken from an eleven-and-a-half-hour, stream-of-consciousness home tape he and Zappa made in the early 1960s. Beefheart and Zappa planned to form a band called Soots together and make a movie called *Captain Beefheart Meets the Grunt People.* Nothing came of these projects, although they subsequently worked together—most notably on Zappa's jazz-rock classic *Hot Rats*—and for a while their careers remained inextricably linked: Zappa's sidemen worked with Beefheart and it was Zappa who produced the album by which Beefheart is remembered today, *Trout Mask Replica* (1969). Beefheart's musical creations have often been compared to post-Ornette Coleman free jazz and were as amazing as the paintings and drawings of his subsequent career as an artist. His songs were crammed full of incident and extraordinary lyrics and remained simultaneously jarring and unnerving. A revolt against what he called "Mamma Heartbeat," a steady and unvarying rhythmic pulse, and against the tempered scale, Beefheart's music is not what rock is supposed be. In fact a live late-1970s tape contained long improvised Beefheart sax solos over a slippery rock beat that was some distance from *Trout Mask.*

In his late teens Van Vliet listened intensively to two kinds of music— Mississippi Delta blues and avant-garde jazz of John Coltrane, Ornette Coleman, and Cecil Taylor. These influences are clear in his music, but it is the way the influences are ordered to produce something striking and original that remains the hallmark of his music. In 1964 Beefheart entered into the first of a long series of disastrous agreements with record producers. He released a single for A&M records called "Diddy Wah Diddy," but a subsequent album was turned down by label boss Jerry Moss (Herb Alpert and Jerry Moss combined to form A&M) as "too negative." His second break came when Bob Krasnow of Kama Sutra Records agreed to release the material rejected by A&M, and *Safe as Milk* became, in the eyes of many, one of the forgotten classics of rock. It featured blues and bottleneck guitar, that became a Beefheart trademark, and a theremin, the precursor to the electronic synthesizer ubiquitous by the mid-1970s. Sharp practice and misunderstanding surrounded Krasnow's release of

Strictly Personal, which revealed considerable progress in Beefheart's adventur-
ousness, although it was marred by poor recording quality and a "psychedelic"
mix. In stepped Zappa, who considered Beefheart something akin to a genius,
and offered to record anything Beefheart wanted to do. *Trout Mask Replica*
clearly has its roots in avant-garde jazz and in the Delta Blues. The glass finger-
guitar of Zoot Horn Rollo, the steel guitar of Jimmy Semens, a fluid approach to
rhythm, Beefheart's stark vocals, and his post–Ornette Coleman saxophone combine to create a classic recording that anticipated the "New Wave" of the 1980s
by almost a decade. Today it stands as an unnerving document showing how
close the avant-garde in rock and jazz had become.

In 1970 came *Lick My Decals Off, Baby,* which maintained the manic energy
level of *Trout Mask* with a harder edge. Subsequent albums for the Warner/
Reprise label had their recondite edge blunted by commercial concessions,
although *The Spotlight Kid* was his definitive blues statement even if *Clear Spot*
turned out to be avant-rock for the dance floor. Even so, Beefheart *always*
sounded forbidding (that was part of his charm). He then signed with the
Mercury label "because of those little wings on the bottom of my feet,"[29] and
released *Unconditionally Guaranteed* and *Blue Jeans and Moon Beams,* which
were frankly poor. It was not until he teamed up with Zappa again in 1975 for a
tour, after appearing as "Bloodshot Rollin' Red" on Zappa's *One Size Fits All*
and *Bongo Fury,* that the next Beefheart album was completed, although *Shiny
Beast (Bat Chain Puller)* for Warner Brothers was not released until 1978. Here
he managed, at last, to recapture the intensity of *Trout Mask.*

Since the 1960s, Beefheart's compositions were always taught note by note,
beat by beat, to his Magic Bands. His late-1970s pianist, Eric Drew Feldman,
said that once each musician was given his part, it had to stay that way. "He was
the most strict person in that way," he recalled. "It would be an insult to him
otherwise. I never had a problem with that. I felt like I was getting parts dictated
to me by one of the best, especially when they were designed for me. You just
feel like a model in a fashion show wearing a really nice dress, I guess."[30]
However, caught up in the record industry slump of 1979, Beefheart was
dropped from the Warner Brothers label just as *Shiny Beast* appeared to be
achieving some degree of popularity. He went on the road with a new band in
1980, promoting *Doc at the Radar Station,* recorded for the British Virgin label
and distributed in the U.S. by Atlantic. "This album may be the most successful
utilization of the harmolodic ideas articulated by Ornette Coleman," said
Downbeat.[31] Within weeks of the album's release, however, the distribution deal
fell through and the album was left in limbo. Painting, however, had long
become his main source of income, and after recording *Crow,* Captain Beefheart
once again became Don Van Vliet and continued his pursuit of the avant-garde
by ocular means.

If analogy, the critic's most efficient tool, can get nowhere near the heart of
Zappa's and Beefheart's subcutaneous conflations of jazz within rock, the career
of Carlos Santana, leading one of the last of the important San Francisco bands to
emerge at the end of the 1960s, was more transparent in his application of influ-

Carlos Santana: Although he catered to the expectations of rock audiences, his work—encompassing the big (Latin) beat, the blues, and jazz—was often jazz-rock in spirit, if not in name. (Photograph by Stuart Nicholson.)

ences. Santana crossed over into jazz from rock so often during his career that at his best, who was able to say whether he was playing rock-jazz or jazz-rock? Carlos Devadip Santana arrived in the U.S.A. from Tijuana in 1966. At the time he was into blues players like B. B. King, Albert King, and Mike Bloomfield. He formed The Santana Blues band with fellow guitarist Tom Frazier and auditioned successfully for Bill Graham, who started him off as an opening act at the Fillmore on June 16, 1968. He was soon headlining the bill, the first—and only— unrecorded artist to have done so. When Graham was asked to lend his name, experience, and expertise to the Woodstock Festival, he did so on the understand- ing that the still unrecorded Santana be given a choice spot in the lineup. Alongside bands like Jimi Hendrix Experience, Sly & the Family Stone, Jefferson Airplane, The Grateful Dead, Crosby Stills & Nash, and The Who, Santana showed the world what he could do on August 16, 1969. "Soul Sacrifice" earned the band a standing ovation and a prominence in the festival's film documentary. "Woodstock was the biggest door we ever had the pleasure of walking through," he would say later.[32] After an appearance on the *Ed Sullivan Show* he was signed by Columbia. *Santana* was released in October 1969 and remained on the *Billboard* chart for over two years, selling nearly four million albums.

Santana may have come out of the acid rock scene, but as *Rolling Stone* point- ed out, his music "was braced by jazz and Latin influences,"[33] to the extent that there were no pigeonholes that comfortably fitted the band or its leader. He evolved a style that embraced true improvisation rather than embellishing a melody or rotating a collection of stock blues phrases. The first major jazz influence on his playing came from the guitarist Gabor Szabo, for whom he would write the composition "Gardenia" in 1980. His early drummer Michael Shrieve introduced him to the music of John Coltrane and Miles Davis and by the time he was recording his second album, *Abraxis,* released in October 1970 and named after a deity in Herman Hesse's 1919 novel *Demian,* Davis himself was sitting in the front row every night at Fillmore East checking out Santana's playing and calling into the recording studio to listen to the band at work. "When Miles used to come and hear us every night I began to realise that maybe—just maybe—we had something important to say," he reflected in 1981.[34] *Abraxis* yielded two hit singles, Tito Puente's "Oye Como Va" and a cover of Fleetwood Mac's "Black Magic Woman." Another side of Santana's musical personality was his sensitive ballad playing, and "Samba Pa Ti," based on a major-7 to minor-7 (I–ii) progression, revealed his jazz influences while still reaching out to the blues. "We were listening to Eddie Harris, Horace Silver, Albert Collins, Mongo Santamaria," explained Santana. "We were getting more and more popular."[35]

In the summer of 1970, he toured the United States with Miles Davis as his opening act. "Through Miles Davis I learned about the use of space between phrases," Santana explained. "Silence gives people time to absorb the music. Otherwise you sound like a machine gun."[36] His subsequent fusion outing *Caravanserai* (1972) reflected the influence of Davis on his playing, particularly on the track "Waves Within," something that surfaced even more overtly on *Fillmore—The Last Days* with a convincing version of "In a Silent Way" taken from the Miles Davis album of the same name. "I was under a spell . . . like everybody was with Miles Davis," he said. "This song was a very close part of my psyche. We used it when they closed the Fillmore."[37] *Lotus,* recorded live in 1973 but released in December 1975, was inspired by Miles Davis's *Bitches Brew.* It was an expansive jazz-rock jam, with numbers like "A-1 Funk" and "Every Step of the Way" that actually anticipated the sound of the Miles Davis band of 1974–1975. Also from 1973 came the explosive jazz-rock album *Love, Devotion, Surrender,* an impressive meeting with John McLaughlin, organist Larry Young, and drummer Billy Cobham in a series of ecstatic jams that included a moving version of Coltrane's "Naima" and a powerful interpretation of the saxophonist's "A Love Supreme" that actually sparked interest among rock audiences for Coltrane's original 1964 album.

The choice of "Welcome" as the title track for Santana's next album, released in November 1973, came from Coltrane's 1965 album *Kulu Se Mama* and continued Santana's devotion to the musical substance of the Coltrane legacy. Featuring John McLaughlin and ex-Gabor Szabo pianist Tom Coster, Santana revealed a resourceful adaptation of the flutter-tonguing technique used by Coltrane on soprano sax. Coltrane's memory was further evoked by pianist Alice Coltrane's arrangement of "Going Home" that ran straight into a vocal version of "Love Devotion Surrender." When pianist Coster joined the band he was impressed by the musical climate created by his leader. "I was very surprised at the music the new Santana band was playing," said Coster. "It was highly jazz oriented but unfortunately it might have been a little over the heads of the kids. So the *Borboletta* album [released October 1974 with Airto and Flora Purim] was much more commercial than *Welcome* was."[38]

On *Illuminations* (1974) with Alice Coltrane, Dave Holland, and Jack DeJohnette, the accent was on creating moods. "It isn't a matter of coming and playing your part," continued Coster. "It's a matter of feeling those moods . . . that's what the music on *Illuminations* is all about."[39] These new and challenging directions culminated in *Swing of Delight,* from 1980, which admitted ex-Miles men Wayne Shorter, Herbie Hancock, Ron Carter, and Tony Williams into his musical world.

Santana's evolving ability as a soloist and conceptualist in the mid-1970s coincided with his spiritual awakening through his guru Sri Chinmoy, who figures prominently on the sleeve of *Love, Devotion, Surrender,* but as he strayed from his Latin roots the sometimes esoteric direction of his music, in rock terms at least, was not selling in the sort of numbers that please major labels. In 1976 he and his manager Bill Graham had a long talk; Graham, a long-time salsa freak, urged him to return to his roots. His subsequent album, *Amigos* (1976), was his first album to reach the *Billboard* Top 10 since *Santana III.* When the band opened in London later in the year, *Melody Maker* hailed them the "best in the world."[40] Santana was re-signed by Columbia for a five-year, seven-album contract guaranteeing him more than $400,000 an album. Hot on the heels of *Amigos* came a string of albums that reestablished his regular band as the ideal forum to express his talent; *Festival* (1976), *Moonflower* (1977), and *Inner Secrets* (1978) were tastefully and energetically intended to reach a mass audience.

Yet much of Santana's music stands equally well as a highly effective fusion of Latin-blues-jazz-and-rock that hit people at a gutsy street level. On *Moonflower,* for example, there is a blazing fusion workout on "Zulu" and, on a remake of the Zombies 1965 hit "She's Not There," his guitar was so beefed up by electrical effects that it seemed about to explode. An updated version of "Soul Sacrifice" exceeds the band's earlier version at Woodstock, while his highly melodic ballad playing is featured on the band's signature tune "Europa," Santana's own personal blues. Yet, as he shows almost four minutes into this track, his improvisations could be complex, virile, and even ferocious.

Santana occupies an unusual position in the emergence of jazz-rock fusion. Hugely popular with rock audiences and able to sell out stadiums throughout the world, his music is not readily associated with jazz-rock, yet his band had an honesty and integrity that was not apparent in the work of many jazz-rock musicians who by the mid-1970s had moved lemming-like towards the slick and vacuous. In contrast, Santana continued to stretch himself as a musician, his technique keeping pace with a vivid imagination. His appearance on McCoy Tyner's 1982 album *Looking Out* and on Weather Report's 1986 album *This Is This,* and his 1988 tour with saxophonist Wayne Shorter, frequently took him into the province of pure jazz improvisation. On his 1992 *Milagro,* both Miles Davis and John Coltrane made an appearance—courtesy of sampling—in a tribute to Davis and Bill

Graham. Although he has always catered to the expectations of rock audiences, his work encompassing the big (Latin) beat, his blues-and-jazz was often jazz-rock in spirit, if not in name.

Like Carlos Santana, the group Steely Dan wore their love of jazz on their sleeves. A fusion of rock and roll, jazz, R&B, and Tin Pan Alley pop, they virtually forged a new genre in the 1970s. The group became a favorite of both jazz musicians and jazz fans right from the start of their career with the release in 1972 of *Can't Buy A Thrill*. Here was a group that was consciously returning to the popular song form and wrestling with its complexities, instead of extended instrumental jamming or head arrangements worked up in the studio or on the job that tended to ignore popular song conventions like choruses, bridges, and harmonic ingenuity. In compositions like "Kings," "Fire in the Hole," and "Change of the Guard" there was a distinctiveness in their approach to harmony, form, and structure plus a quirky lyric content that appeared in opposition to the boy-meets-girl-falls-in-love-gets-married pop tradition. The big hit from the album, "Do It Again," had a mysterious narrative line and a brooding groove and was quickly picked up by other bands, including Eumir Deodato.[41]

Guitarist-bassist Walter Becker and keyboard player Donald Fagen were New Yorkers who met in 1967 while attending Bard College. While Becker dropped out, Fagen, an English major, transferred to music and back again to English before graduating, which goes some way to explaining the literary aspirations of his lyrics. By 1969 Becker and Fagen had become a songwriting team and began their career with an obscure Zalman King film, *You Gotta Walk It Like You Talk It (Or Lose That Beat)*. They got a job in the Brill Building writing pop songs and ended up working for the production company that handled Jay and the Americans. It was during this period that they met musicians Denny Dias and Jeff "Skunk" Baxter and the independent producer Gary Katz. Katz took them on as staff writers for ABC/Dunhill, a Los Angeles-based record label, but encouraged them to form a band to showcase their material. Borrowing the name of the steam-powered dildo from William Burroughs's novel *Naked Lunch*, Steely Dan was born, comprising Becker on keyboards and Fagen on bass with Baxter and Dias on guitars and Jim Hodder on drums and with vocals by David Palmer.

Although Dan's debut *Can't Buy a Thrill* went gold, it was far from the kind of perfection they sought. While Baxter and Dias were ideally qualified to interpret Steely Dan music—Dias was a student of the bebop guitarist Billy Bauer and was rooted in jazz influences from Charlie Parker to Miles Davis, while Baxter was inspired as much by Jimi Hendrix as by Howard Roberts—a certain unevenness in several songs and obscure lyrics meant that in artistic terms at least, this was their least successful album. Even so there was an excellent Dias solo on sitar in "Do It Again" and a widely admired guitar solo from Elliot Randall that won the band considerable attention in "Reelin' In the Years." With *Countdown to Ecstasy* (1973) Fagen had taken over as lead vocalist and the basic unit became a quintet. Again Dan created some gems of jazz-rock-R&B-pop fusion: an intriguing arrangement of "My Old School" for sax ensemble that included Lanny Morgan, Ernie Watts, Bill Perkins, and John Rotella, with an arresting Baxter solo on guitar, and "Bodhisattva," a modal boogie with a well-constructed Dias solo (Dias would later work with pianist Hampton Hawes). Bassist Ray Brown guested in the ballady "Razor Boy," and Victor Feldman was in evidence throughout on vibes, marimba, and percussion.

By the time of *Pretzel Logic* (1974), the band were using the resources of the studio with confidence, and the music included nods of approbation in the direction of Becker and Fagen's jazz heroes; the bass introduction from "Rikki Don't Lose That Number" came from Horace Silver's "Song For My Father," "Parker's Band" is, of course, a tribute to Charlie Parker, and "East St. Louis Toodle-oo" is a transcription of Ellington's original signature tune, with wah-wah guitar emulating Bubber Miley's trumpet and a pedal steel guitar taking off "Tricky" Sam Nanton's trombone.

After *Pretzel Logic,* Becker and Fagen announced that henceforth the band would exist only in the studio, metamorphosing into what Fagen described as "a concept more than a band." Now effectively a duo, they were aided in the studio by a roster of top-notch session musicians including Jeff Porcaro on drums, Michael McDonald on keyboards, and Elliot Randall, Rick Derringer, and Denny Dias on guitars. *Katy Lied,* from 1975, was the first in a series of studio-conceived and -crafted releases. Larry Carlton, who was building a tremendous reputation with the Crusaders, came in "Your Gold Teeth," and Becker switched to guitar in "Black Friday," a role he would increasingly perform on the group's albums following *Katy Lied.* "Friday" is a blues with unexpected chord changes, odd structural elements, and typically inscrutable lyrics, in which Becker contributes a burning solo halfway between Chicago blues and post-bebop jazz. *The Royal Scam* (1976) was to all intents and purposes dominated by Larry Carlton's playing, the glue that held the ensembles together and the prominent solo voice in cuts such as "Don't Take Me Alive," "Everything You Did," and "Kid Charlemange." In the latter he contributed a particularly effective solo making use of extended substitutions rather than scales and licks. The instrumental break in "Green Earrings," played by a horn section that included West Coast studio veteran Plas Johnson, was as arresting as it was audacious.

Becker and Fagen went a step further with the ambitious, jazz-oriented *Aja* (1977). An industry benchmark, it presents in the minds of many the quintessential Steely Dan sound. "One of the things we were looking for was clarity," said Fagen, "making sure you could hear all the instruments. And not too much reverberation or echo to muddy up the actual sound of the instruments. And if there's any model, I would say a lot of jazz records Rudy Van Gelder recorded in the late 1950s. They have a very dry, live sound which, I guess Walter and I loved as kids."[42] Guitarists Larry Carlton, Steve Khan, and Lee Ritenour provided sympathetic backings for Becker's blues- and jazz-based solos on "Josie" and "Home at Last." On the title track, Wayne Shorter contributes a memorable solo, weaving around the tune's structural symmetry with notable support from Steve Gadd on drums. By now Steely Dan sessions were legendary for reducing renowned musicians to jelly as a result of the meticulous care the two leaders brought to their work. A case in point was the solo in the quirky thirteen-bar blues number "Peg." After a number of abortive attempts by Steely Dan "satellite musicians"—including Elliot Randall, Dennis Budimir, Robben Ford, Rick Derringer, Tom Scott on saxophone—and even Becker himself failed to yield what the leaders had in mind, ace studio guitarist Jay Graydon got the call. It took four hours to record the solo, but three hours were spent, under the close direction of Becker and Fagen, searching for the opening phrase. Nothing was left to chance in their meticulously crafted music.

Steely Dan went on to record just one more album before winding up in 1981. *Gaucho,* more R&B- than jazz-influenced, was memorable for "The Glamour Profession," which included Michael Brecker on tenor, Tom Scott on lyricon, Steve Khan on guitar, Anthony Jackson on bass, Steve Gadd on drums, and Ralph McDonald on percussion. It became a favorite of many jazz musicians and represented one of Steely Dan's finest cuts. "Third World Man" featured a Larry Carlton solo from several years before, while Hugh McCracken was featured on "Hey Nineteen" and Mark Knopfler on "Time Out of Mind."

Steely Dan had created a style and musical personality that they could claim as their own. Their compositions, with quirky changes and often unusual forms, found several takers in jazz, not least Woody Herman, who devoted an album side to their numbers, and the Hoops McCann Band, whose album-length statement *Plays the Music of Steely Dan* showed Becker and Fagen in a new light. Nothing was heard from the band until the end of 1989, when Fagen began playing sixties soul classics with a group of friends at the Roadhouse on New York's 52nd Street. Over the ensuing months, the lineup evolved into what became the New York Rock and Soul Revue, culminating in two sold-out shows at the Beacon Theater in 1991. In 1992, Walter Becker joined his old partner to re-ignite Steely Dan at Long Island's Jones Beach Arena as the New York Rock and Soul Revue became the Steely Dan reunion tour of 1992. In 1993 they started touring again as a "band"—or orchestra—and in 1995 came *Alive In America,* when audiences marvelled at a pristine renewal of the Steely Dan myth.

It was not just in America where jazz influences were being drawn into the rock mainstream. In Britain, Gordon Summer began his playing career at fifteen doing Dixieland gigs before moving on to the Newcastle Big Band. His tastes, however, went far beyond the acoustic mainstream, taking in the Beatles, Jimi Hendrix, and Cream, as well as the Miles Davis classics *Kind of Blue* and *Bitches Brew.* While in Newcastle, he played with Eric Burdon of Animals fame, Zoot Money, and Kevin Ayers before moving on to the London circuit. There he joined a nascent punk group which, after a few false starts and a couple of changes in the lineup, emerged in 1978 as The Police, with Summer as its lead singer-bassist now calling himself Sting. Disowned by the punks (the group were musically too sophisticated for them), they quickly graduated to wide pop acceptance with their good looks, ingenious songs, and "white reggae." In what was universally agreed to be a pretty boring music scene, The Police stood head and shoulders above all around them, and the rest was pop history.

By 1985, however, Sting wanted to return to his roots. He formed a "superband" that ensured the breakup of the Wynton Marsalis quintet when Wynton's brother Branford on saxes and pianist Kenny Kirkland threw in their lot to join Sting in a group that also included Darryl Jones on bass and Omar Hakim on drums. Sting's intention was to bring jazz-influenced music into the rock mainstream, and in this he was largely successful. "I picked who I considered the best young jazz musicians in the world—on the understanding they weren't going to play jazz," he said. "What I wanted was a flavor, I didn't want to go off and give Branford 120 bars to explore a theme; I was going to say, 'You're going to have sixteen bars and you're going to *burn* from the first bar.'"[43] Conceptually the project worked, and in 1985 they recorded *The Dream of the Blue Turtles.* "To my horror and embarrassment [it] was nominated for a Grammy in the Jazz category. Thankfully and rightfully the award went to Branford's brother Wynton—the first time I've been relieved not to receive an award," said Sting later.[44]

Bring On the Night, a live album from 1986, yielded an extended version of the title track that segued into "When the World is Running Down," which amid the "yeah, yeahs" and "whoa, whoas" contained a solo executed *ex animo* by. Kirkland with a brief flurry from Marsalis. Musically it suggested that Sting's compositions could stand up to a more searching examination than they had thus far received within the forum of pop. Marsalis contributed a strong Coltrane-esque solo in "Children's Crusade," while the reggae groove for which Sting was famed was sustained with deferential intensity by Jones and Hakim in "One World," which segued into "Seventh Wave." Neither jazz nor rock, but an engaging, if lightweight, halfway house, Sting's compositions were no strangers to the ii–V–I progression, but then so were so many vehicles for improvisation used in jazz. There was a melodic strength in his writing that used set progressions, more than vamps, and the songs were usually well constructed, not afraid of the slightly more complex forms such as ABC or AAB that lifted them out of the usual run-of-the-mill pop song of the period.

When Sting got to meet Gil Evans, he was pleased, flattered even, that Evans had heard of him and liked his work. After sitting in with the Evans band at the Sweet Basil, Evans agreed to participate on Sting's *Nothing Like the Sun* album from 1987, even making a cameo appearance with his band playing "Little Wing." With the assistance of Maria Schneider, Evans orchestrated some numbers for an appearance with Sting in Europe. After Evans's death, the arranger Bob Belden, a graduate of the North Texas State jazz program, decided to take the idea a stage further and arrange a whole album of Sting tunes for his own ensemble. Belden had debuted as a leader on record with a sixteen-piece big band on *Treasure Island* (1989), the title track a six-part suite, with the rest of the album an appreciation of the composers Joe Zawinul, Wayne Shorter, and Bobby Watson plus three originals and an arrangement of Spencer Williams's "Basin Street Blues" based on the Miles Davis version on *Seven Steps to Heaven.* Belden's Sting project was recorded in 1989 and 1990 with his "Treasure Island" band plus several ringers signed to the Blue Note label, who bankrolled the deal. *Straight To My Heart: The Music of Sting* was uneven. Belden admitted he was looking for the album to surface in *Billboard*'s Contemporary Jazz Chart as well as the Adult Contemporary Chart,[45] but concessions to the latter excepted—

Dianne Reeve's vocal in "Wrapped around Your Finger," Mark Ledford's vocal in "Every Breath You Take," and R&B singer Phil Perry's "Sister Moon"—some pieces work well. "Roxanne" is almost pure Gil Evans–Miles Davis, featuring Tim Hagans in the Davis role as Sting's love song to a prostitute becomes transformed into a substantial piece of music. "Straight To My Heart" and "Dream of Blue Turtles" are genial if somewhat functional, Belden unable to capture the gravitas of "Roxanne," but they do contain interesting solos that sustain the interest. "They Dance Alone," "Shadows in the Rain," and "Children's Crusade" succeed through a combination of deft writing and absorbing solos. As with *The Gil Evans Orchestra Plays the Music of Jimi Hendrix* and *The Hoops McCann Band Plays the Music of Steely Dan,* the most successful cuts are when the arrangers take liberties with the original compositions and, while respecting the composer's intentions, show the pieces in a new light. Belden took succor from the Davis-Evans collaborations, John Coltrane, Weather Report, and Oliver Nelson. In his arrangement of "Roxanne," for example, he uses just enough of the tune to be effective, while in "Straight to My Heart" he changes the meter from 7/4 to 6/4 to produce a jazz-waltz feel.

The issue here was authenticity—the extent to which a popular song could be disentangled from a single, specific recording of it without surrendering the dimensions that made it compelling in the first place. The answer lay in deconstructing the original, stripping the song of the elements that gave it autonomy over chord progression and melody that made it appear the "possession" of one artist. The whole point was not to "cover" the tune but to reinvent it in another guise, a jazz guise. Belden seemed to sense the potential in what he had achieved with several numbers from the Sting songbook, turning his attention to Puccini's *Turandot* in 1993. Again the patron saints of his inspiration were Miles Davis and Gil Evans, who, incidentally, had had both talked in principle about doing Puccini's *Tosca* in 1979. Here Belden emerged with a more distinct writing personality, with a cast that included Joe Lovano and Dave Liebman on reeds, Wallace Roney and Tim Hagans on trumpet, Geoff Keezer and Joey Calderazzo on keyboards, Gary Peacock and Ira Coleman on bass, and the drummers Tony Williams, Bobby Previte, and Joe Chambers.

Traditionally, one of the weaknesses within jazz (a few notables excepted) was its original compositions, which were often no more than functional structures to present improvisation. The potential suggested in Belden's writing on *Straight To My Heart* and *Turnadot* again raised the possibilities of jazz turning to popular culture in the way it had turned to Tin Pan Alley in the 1920s through the 1940s. However, when Belden approached the music of Prince the wheel seemed to have abruptly turned full circle, back to such unsuccessful projects such as Count Basie covering Beatles hits, with apparently nothing much learned in the meantime. All the subtleties of deconstruction, all the nuance of substitute voicings, new rhythms, and meter—indeed, all the room given to soloists—went out of the window on the pop-oriented *When Doves Cry,* recorded in May 1993. Apparently aimed more at *Billboard*'s Adult Contemporary Chart than the Jazz Chart, it paid the price for commercially overreaching itself. Far better was the instrumental *Princejazz* with Manhattan Rhythm Club, which included good solos from trumpeters Tim Hagans and Wallace Roney, the pianist Jacky Terrasson, and the guitarist Mike Stern.

On *The New Standard* by Herbie Hancock (1996), Belden was responsible for arranging a selection of contemporary pop tunes by Kurt Cobain, Prince, Paul Simon and Art Garfunkel, Stevie Wonder, Peter Gabriel, John Lennon and Paul McCartney, Don Henley, Donald "Babyface" Edmonds, Sade, and Donald Fagen and Walter Becker. For the first time since *Quartet* with Wynton Marsalis, from 1982, Hancock recorded in an acoustic environment under his own name, this time with Mike Brecker on tenor sax, John Scofield on guitar, Dave Holland on bass, Jack DeJohnette on drums, and Don Alias on percussion. The project was conceived by Verve vice-president and producer Guy Eckstine, whose idea of taking pop songs and restructuring them to sound as if they were originally written to be jazz tunes was passed to Belden, since Hancock did not have time to do the arrangements himself. Belden, by now well known for his love of Miles Davis and Gil Evans, was also familiar with Hancock's acoustic work. "I tried to think like [Herbie] in a way that would allow him to come to the music and change it, personalize it, which he did," he explained.[46] In the studio, Hancock adapted the arrangements to suit his own ideas. One of the most arresting interpretations is of Don Henley's ballad "New York Minute," which is played up-tempo and stands as an excellent example of post-bop jazz in the 1990s with exemplary solos from Hancock, Brecker, and Scofield and consistently inventive accompaniment from Hancock, Holland, and DeJohnette that provides a benchmark of excellence for aspiring young musicians. The album is not wholly successful, however, surrendering to the temptations of gloss (there are a couple of sweet-shocks as strings and brass pop-up in four selections) and arrangements that do not go the whole distance to transform but merely reiterate the original. Nevertheless, enough had been done to suggest that some songs from contemporary pop contained sufficient wit and melodic wisdom to enliven a jazz repertoire that had turned in on itself with dour, frequently humorless original compositions.

Notes

1. Interview with the author, July 12, 1997.
2. Ibid.
3. Ibid.
4. Ibid.
5. Conversation with the author, August 5, 1997.
6. Curiously, Shorter sounds more effective against Laswell's ominous sonic backdrop than on his own Grammy-winning but disappointing *High Life* (Verve 529 224–2) from 1996, where he appears to be trying to create a similar ambience acoustically, with desks of violins, violas, English horns, bassoons, and other chamber orchestra trappings that fail to evoke the aura of mystery that Laswell achieves electronically. At one point, his own "At the Fair" even seemed to evoke "Black Light" in mood and paraphrase.
7. Interview with the author, July 12, 1997.
8. Ibid.
9. *Wire*, June 1995, p. 10.

10. Ibid.
11. Ibid.
12. *Independent,* September 29, 1995.
13. *Downbeat,* September 13, 1973, p. 15.
14. BBC TV interview, Zappa documentary.
15. *Downbeat,* May 18, 1978, p. 44.
16. *Electric Don Quixote: The Story of Frank Zappa,* by Neil Slaven (Omnibus Press, London, 1996).
17. *Downbeat,* October 30, 1969, p. 14.
18. Ibid., September 13, 1973, p. 15.
19. Interview with the author, January 14, 1997.
20. Quoted in *Wire,* September 1991, p. 69.
21. *Electric Don Quixote: The Story of Frank Zappa,* by Neil Slaven (Omnibus Press, London, 1996), p. 122.
22. Quoted in *Wire,* August 1991, p. 26.
23. *Wire,* August 1991, p. 29.
24. BBC TV interview, Frank Zappa documentary.
25. *Downbeat,* March 1994, p. 22.
26. *Wire,* September 1991, p. 17.
27. *Downbeat,* September 1994.
28. *Electric Don Quixote: The Story of Frank Zappa,* by Neil Slaven (Omnibus Press, London, 1996).
29. *Rolling Stone,* June 6, 1974, p. 14.
30. *Wire,* December 1996, p. 18.
31. *Downbeat,* January 1981, p. 36.
32. Liner notes to *Dance of the Rainbow Serpent* (Columbia C3K 64605), p. 15.
33. *The Rolling Stone Illustrated History of Rock & Roll,* edited by Jim Miller (Picador, London 1981), p. 271.
34. *Downbeat,* January 1981, p. 15.
35. *Musician,* December 1990, p. 76.
36. *Downbeat,* January 1981, p. 15.
37. Liner notes to *Dance of the Rainbow Serpent* (Columbia C3K 64605), p. 19.
38. *Downbeat,* January 30, 1975, p. 28.
39. Ibid., January 30, 1975, p. 28.
40. *Melody Maker,* November 24, 1974, p. 26.
41. Deodato recorded the number in 1973 on *In Concert: Live at Felt Forum* (CBS Associated ZK 45221).
42. *Talking Jazz,* by Ben Sidran (Pomegranate Artbooks, San Francisco, 1992), p. 191.
43. Liner notes to *Bring On the Night* (A&M Bring 1).
44. Ibid.
45. *Downbeat,* October 1991, p. 14.
46. Ibid., April 1996, p. 23.

CHAPTER 14

Thundering Herds

f, by the end of the 1950s, the Swing Era was beginning to seem remote, big bands were by no means obsolete. While musical tastes had changed dramatically since the thirties and forties, the big bands that had once dominated the music scene then could count on a considerable following, and not only from the middle-aged bobby-soxers who once danced to their music. In 1959 bandleader Stan Kenton had established the first of his university "jazz clinics" at Indiana and Michigan State Universities, giving momentum to the "stage band" movement then taking root in high schools, colleges, and universities throughout the country. Young musicians cut their teeth on arrangements once played by name bands, and when a Kenton, a Woody Herman, or a Count Basie came to town, they could count on support from student musicians. "When we play universities," said Basie, "[the kids] ask us to play certain charts they play because they want to see if they sound anything like us."[1]

By the 1960s, all the major big bands who had survived the Swing Era were now something akin to institutions, largely sticking to the sound and style that had made them famous some twenty years before. But on February 7, 1964, the Beatles touched down at Kennedy Airport, and immediately the first tremors of the seismic shift about to be felt in popular music began reverberating across the United States. In jazz, the big bands were the first to feel those tremors because of their close proximity to the dance floor. No bandleader, whether it was a Count Basie or the leader of a hotel band, could ignore the currents of fashion now running through popular music. They always carried a few current pops in their library to accede to the inevitable requests from younger dancers, whether at a college prom or a swanky hotel. "You've got to bend a little their way," continued Basie, "meet them halfway at least—give a little of their flavor . . . just to let them know that we know they're alive."[2]

In responding to the challenges posed by the dominant popular culture of the 1960s, big bands were among the first jazz ensembles to grapple with the idiomatic problems of combining jazz and rock. However, rock was a new language that took time for the tried-and-tested structure of a big band to absorb. The bands initially tried to solve the problem through modifying their repertoire, by playing jazz versions of popular hits, which sometimes worked and sometimes didn't. This prompted a tendency to dismiss the big band's involvement in com-

276

bining jazz and rock as a commercial aberration and their performances of "cover versions" of popular songs as exploitative and feeble. After all, one only had to look to Pat Boone's version of "Tutti Frutti"—the nearest thing in popular music history to a consensual bad record—to believe that it was impossible for musicians outside of the rock 'n' roll culture to cover a rock song.

Yet big bands could exploit volume, an important element of rock music. They could also offer greater musical color than the guitar-based music of rock, and they could hit a groove that in their own way could be just as satisfying as a guitar-based jam. The big bands were no strangers to the backbeat, which can be demonstrated as early as 1938 on Benny Goodman's aircheck of "St. Louis Blues," where Gene Krupa's single-accented rim-shot on the 2 and 4 was the earliest, loudest, and clearest precursor of a rock beat.[3] In the 1940s, Lionel Hampton had come up with an early version of jazz-rock by drenching his repertoire in R&B. With Billy Mackel's loud, amplified guitar and the introduction of a Fender electric bass in the 1950s, Hampton was all but offering a big-band version of rock 'n' roll. Also in the 1950s Sun Ra was bringing electronic tone colors into the forum of the big band, anticipating the trend by almost two decades. Among his huge, variegated repertoire actually lie examples of jazz-rock (and doo-wop and fusion).[4]

Clearly, then, the cards were not totally stacked against the big bands, yet from the moment the Beatles arrived, the question of repertoire was crucial. In the beginning, arrangers, however distinguished—a Shorty Rogers, a Bill Holman, or an Oliver Nelson—believed that pop music could be approached in the same way as arranging a standard by George Gershwin or Richard Rogers. But it soon became obvious that the tune had to have certain characteristics to work as big-band jazz-rock, and that there had to be some element whereby the big bands could actually add to the dimensions of the original, introducing a subversive or compelling element that was denied to a guitar-based band. Gradually some notable successes emerged that produced aesthetically pleasing variants of big-band jazz-rock. Others, however, tied to the weight of their past, had such specific musical identities that change of any sort, never mind trying to adapt to rock, sat uncomfortably with their style.

In 1963 Count Basie recorded *Hits of the '50s & '60s,* an album of popular songs arranged by Quincy Jones that adapted well to Basie's sound, including "This Could Be the Start of Something Big," "One Mint Julep," "I Can't Stop Loving You," and "Nice 'n' Easy." It was an effective way of appearing *au courant* without sacrificing the band's integrity—indeed, the album was widely regarded as another great Basie album. However, *Pop Goes the Basie* (1964) was an artistic disaster. Covers of pop songs such as the Everley Brothers' "Bye, Bye Love" and the New Christy Minstrels' "Walk Right In" did not suit Basie's style at all. The same was true of *Basie's Beatle Bag,* arranged by Arturo "Chico" O'Farrill and recorded in 1966. Here, both O'Farrill and the Basie band found it impossible to disentangle the songs from the singular, specific recordings made by the Beatles, a problem that they would encounter again in 1969 with a second Beatles album, *Basie on the Beatles.* Yet Basie was far from alone in trying to appropriate the Beatles' songbook; among others in the 1960s, were Ella Fitzgerald, Sarah Vaughan, and Duke Ellington, but none had quite the conviction that Ray Charles was able to bring to "Yesterday" and "Eleanor Rigby," investing new meaning in the songs that the composers never imagined.

Generally during the 1960s Basie yielded a less-than-fascinating batch of recordings made for recording companies who felt the inclusion of pop material represented a safe investment for their outlay. What is striking about this period of his career is that hardly any pops were incorporated into his regular repertoire, reflecting how both leader and band felt about the material. Live, Basie was performing to a script written years before, with solid versions of his 1950s classics by Neal Hefti and Quincy Jones, with Basie providing the "plinks" in between the *treble forte* "blats" of familiar material.

While Basie's response to the rock explosion was one of reluctance, an it-pays-the-rent approach that yielded little of artistic merit, Duke Ellington lightly kissed rock on both cheeks before following his own muse. In September 1964, he recorded an album-length adaptation of songs from the then-popular Disney film *Mary Poppins* that stemmed less from his affection for the Sherman brothers' score than from a policy decision by Reprise Records.[5] Ellington, however, imposed his own distinctive imprimatur on the material, which responded remarkably well to the "Ellington effect." In contrast to earlier arrangements of non-Ellington pop songs recorded for *Ellington '65,* including "Hello Dolly," "Blowin' in the Wind," "Stranger on the Shore," and the Beatles tunes he cut for *Ellington '66,* several Poppins numbers found their way into the band's regular repertoire. In concerts, Ellington was equally inscrutable, bringing on his long-serving vocalist Tony Watkins to perform a kind of boogaloo-twist-dance-vocal routine over a multipurpose Ellington blues that remained his token gesture to pop culture.

During the 1950s, Basie's most successful arrangers were Neal Hefti and Quincy Jones, and it came as no surprise in 1959 when Jones decided to form his own big band for the touring company of a new blues opera by Harold Arlen called *Free and Easy.* After the show finished in Paris in February 1960, the band toured Europe before becoming stranded. Severely out of pocket, Jones returned to New York in 1961 and became the head of A&R for Mercury Records. There he produced a series of albums by studio big bands of soul jazz hits featuring a stellar cast of sidemen including Clark Terry, a regularly featured soloist. On albums such as *Bossa Nova, Quincy Jones Plays Hip Hits, Quincy's Got a Brand New Bag, Quincy Plays for Pussycats,* and *Golden Boy,* Jones's work varies from straightforward hack jobs to the occasionally inspired arrangements. His fun versions of "Soul Bossa Nova," "Boogie Stop Shuffle," and "Comin' Home Baby," for example, are very much of their time, but effective for all that, as are several other tracks he made prior to 1966, when composing music for films[6] took over his career.

In 1969 Jones signed to the A&M label, where he produced his first big-band album in three years, the Grammy-winning *Walking In Space.* It featured a memorable version of Benny Golson's "Killer Joe" that had impressive solos from Freddie Hubbard on trumpet and Hubert Laws on flute. Using Bob James's electric piano and Grady Tate's unequivocal backbeat to provide a haunting but powerful vamp, an arresting feature was the appearance of a female vocal quartet in the coda. Overall the feeling was one of spaciousness that, together with the other singular elements of the arrangement, contributed to a memorable performance. The title track, an ambitious extended piece with solos from Hubert Laws, Jimmy Cleveland, and Freddie Hubbard and a wonderful, tumbling effort from Roland Kirk is a free-flowing composition that alternated rock rhythms and straight-ahead swing.

Jones's next album was the overlooked *Gula Matari,* recorded in March and May 1970. The title track, an extended composition of some thirteen minutes, stands the test of time somewhat better than the cover of "Bridge Over Troubled Water." The Nat Adderley composition "Hummin'" featured the composer's cornet solo from Cannonball's *74 Miles Away* transcribed for the entire trumpet section; all is going well until Jones indulges in three of his foibles: a bowed-bass-and-vocal-unison from Major Holley, a guitar-and-unison-whistle solo from Toots Thielemans, and Thielemans's wearying harmonica blowing. In fact, Jones had arranged "Hummin'" with Jimi Hendrix in mind. "That was originally written for Jimi Hendrix. Hendrix wanted to solo over that and I wrote it for him," said Jones. "He was saying, 'Let's do the thing. I'll meet you out in Jersey [at Rudy Van Gelder's studio].' He was supposed to be featured on that tune, but he got hung up or got too high."[7]

The Thielemans-Holley aberrations crop up through *Smackwater Jack* from 1971 and *You've Got It Bad Girl* from 1973, which nevertheless share moments of excellent, if orthodox, big-band writing with solos to match. While subsequent albums reflected Jones's highly successful odyssey into popular music, by then he had done enough to demonstrate that it was possible for jazz and rock to comfortably coexist within the big-band context, even achieving some success in integrating voices with ensemble passages in numbers like "Gula Matari" and "Killer Joe." Certainly his rhythmic approach was often authentic, helped by musicians like Carol Kaye, the Motown and session bassist, guitarists Eric Gayle and Joe Beck, and the experienced session drummer Grady Tate.

While Jones came from a black perspective, with his roots in soul-jazz and Basie-style big-band writing, Stan Kenton often evoked Richard Wagner in his love of a grand, theatrical climax. Kenton quickly identified the one thing he had in common with rock, the decibel level, the rise of rock encouraging him to beef up his rhythm section with Ramon Lopez on percussion and John "Baron" Von Ohlen on drums. Von Ohlen was well versed in what rock was all about, and his show-stopping style was the key to Kenton's approach on new charts like "Chiapas." On *Live at Redlands University* (1970) and *Live at Brigham Young University* (1971), Kenton mixed favorites from his 1940s and 1950s bands with numbers like "Hey Jude," "MacArthur Park," and "Didn't We." Certainly young college audiences appeared to identify with the power and volume of Kenton's band as much as Von Ohlen's extroverted drumming. Kenton's presentation of pieces like the ambitious four-part "Macumba Suite" to rock audiences left them stunned. "[Kenton] has us blowing so loud we couldn't believe it," said Von

Ohlen. "There are times, like on 'Macumba Suite,' where I feel the world's coming to an end. . . . There's nothing in the business like it."[8] This band remained
largely intact through 1972, when the ensemble cohesion combined with the
polyrhythmic intensity of his rhythm section helped make *Stan Kenton Today:
Live In London* one of Kenton's best albums in years.

Von Ohlen's role in Kenton's success was immense, but at the end of 1972
he left to form his own quartet in the Indiana area. His debut album, *Baron,*
failed to capitalize on the great promise he showed with Kenton. His successor
was an eighteen-year-old who had been playing with the Steel Pier Orchestra,
Club Harlem, and the Ice Capades while studying at Indiana University. Peter
Erskine quickly revealed that he was one of the great drummers in jazz, appearing first on Kenton's *Birthday in Britain,* recorded during the band's 1973
European tour. By now Kenton had returned to a less complex, straight-ahead
approach. In 1974 Erskine was featured in Hank Levy's "Pete Is a Four Letter
Word" on *Fire, Fury and Fun,* but this and subsequent albums, like *Journey to the
Capricorn* (1976), lacked the truly distinctive arrangements of Kenton's better
ensembles. Kenton died on August 25, 1979, having begun the 1970s seemingly
rejuvenated, but his recordings progressively seemed less to be a reflection of
his powerful ensembles and more concerned with "concepts" that might sell
records, such as an album of national anthems prompted by the response given
to his special arrangement of "God Save the Queen" for his tour of England in
1972. By then, however, Kenton seemed to be breeding not so much great jazz
soloists as great jazz educators.

If Ellington, Basie, and Kenton regarded any accommodation with rock as an
irritant to the main thrust of their bands' distinctive personalities, others
embraced the opportunity to explore new territory. Woody Herman, whose
whole career seemed to be one of constant renewal, reinvented his band time
and again, from the "Band that Plays the Blues" in the 1930s to his "Swingin'
Young Herd" of the mid-1960s.[9] In 1968, Herman signed with Cadet, a subsidiary of the Chicago-based Chess label. Since the band had been taking more
and more bookings at colleges and high schools, where they had shared the bill
with rock groups, the idea was to include numbers from pop culture. Chess
house arranger Richard Evans—bassist, arranger, composer, leader of Soulful
Strings, and the man responsible for the Ramsey Lewis hit "Wade in the Water"
in 1966—was given the job of retaining the power and fire of the Herman Herd
tradition, but framing it with a contemporary context.

Light My Fire was recorded at the Ter Mar Studios in Chicago in October
1968, and while not wholly successful in its objectives, it did produce some interesting tracks that are worth revisiting today. "Pontieo" and "I Say a Little
Prayer" are neat and lively, while the title track has a dark, brooding power that
adds a compelling element to the dimensions of the original. "MacArthur Park,"
the first and best of many big-band versions of the tune, made effective use of
the contrasting sections, a slow exposition of the theme with solos from Herman
and trombonist Bob Burgess, and the fast "vamp" section featuring Steve
Lederer on tenor, John Hicks on piano, and a trumpet spectacular performed by

the entire section. The impact these numbers had in live performance was startling. "MacArthur Park" was used to climax Herman's concerts, with four trumpeters discreetly going out into the audience during the sax and piano solos and exploding into life from the corners of the concert hall, improvising while walking back to the stand. It was good theater and brought the house down, but more importantly it helped reestablish Herman, whose fortunes had begun to flag in 1967, as a major force in big-band music. "Herman's 'Fire' Lights Way to Young Market," announced *Billboard*. "Woody Herman's first album for Cadet, *Light My Fire,* has introduced the veteran bandleader to young people . . . [and] opens up a new market [for the band]." [10]

Their next album, *Heavy Exposure,* did not fare so well. Once again Evans had control over the session in terms of repertoire and arranging, but his ambitions became somewhat overextended, importing a mélange of electronic effects and included "hip" spoken introductions to each side of the album. Nevertheless, Herman's mixture of jazz-rock charts and established repertoire went down well live, as a bootleg *Light My Fire*—a complete concert recorded live at Tampa, Florida on March 17, 1970—reveals. "The Herd has taken on a promising new dimension and by all indications, has attracted a whole new generation of listeners," said *Downbeat.* [11] On May 29, Herman made his debut at Fillmore East for three days, followed by three days at Fillmore West on June 17, opening for The Who.

Woody, from October, 1970 proved to be a somewhat controversial representation of the band at this time. Although it was produced by Richard Evans, Herman decided to go with material arranged "in-house" by members of the band. New Zealander Alan Broadbent, the band's twenty-three-year-old pianist, provided five-sixths of the charts, including a four-movement production of the old Herman hit from the early 1940s, "Blues in the Night," and "Smiling Phases." "The hot group at the time was Blood, Sweat & Tears, which featured jazz soloing," recalled Broadbent. "I did a chart . . . and the kids went wild. . . . Woody was kind of intrigued by 'Smiling Phases' and all this Blood, Sweat & Tears stuff. He said, 'Why don't you do something on "Blues in the Night."' When I had pieced it together we rehearsed it. Woody just loved it." [12]

Downbeat assistant editor Jim Szantor was in the recording studio preparing a feature "Recording with Woody" and was shocked when *Woody* was finally released. "Little did I suspect that the product of this session would [be] improperly mixed and thus [bear] no resemblance to the music put down in the studio," he said. [13] Even so, the recording could not conceal the trumpeter-flügelhornist Tom Harrell's beautiful solo in "A Time for Love."

In 1971, Herman signed with Fantasy, and although *Brand New,* his first album for the label, got a four-star rating from *Downbeat,* [14] it seemed more for past achievement than present aspiration. A collaboration with guitarist Mike Bloomfield, it failed to do either the guitarist or Herman justice. However, things were back on course with *The Raven Speaks* from the following year, Herman's best since *Light My Fire.* With strong solos from Greg Herbert on tenor, Bobby Burgess on trombone, and Bill Stapleton on trumpet, the choice of

numbers sat far more comfortably with the band, while the straight-ahead material was right out of the "Herd" tradition, exemplified by Alan Broadbent's
"Reunion at Newport 1972."

Artistically, Herman's jazz-rock-influenced albums to this point had been
curate's eggs. While they were good in parts, they reflected the impetus for experimentation coming from within the band. For a while, Herman seemed a hostage
to fortune, recording good material and not-so-good material as he tried to establish a new, contemporary direction. The feeling that the band had turned a corner
came with *Giant Steps,* recorded in April 1973. Although Broadbent had left the
fold by then, he continued to contribute charts and, together with Tony Klakta
and Bill Stapleton, helped shaped an album whose highlights included impressive
performances of Chick Corea's "La Fiesta," "Freedom Jazz Dance," "Giant
Steps," and "Be-bop and Roses." The album was released to universal acclaim
and won a Grammy later in the year. Herman's move into jazz-rock territory was
vindicated at last, and as if to emphasize this, *Thundering Herd,* from the following year, also picked up a Grammy. Again, the material was tailor-made for the
band, an eclectic mix of John Coltrane, Frank Zappa, Carole King, and Michael
Legrand numbers sympathetically arranged by Broadbent, Stapleton, and Klatka.
The Herd's solo strength was as strong as it had been for years with the exemplary
Greg Herbert and Gary Anderson on tenor saxophones, trombonist Jim Pugh,
Andy Laverne on keyboards, and Stapleton and Klatka on trumpets.

After two Grammy awards, Herman's stock increased considerably, but in
spring 1974, Klatka, a sound soloist and important writing talent for the band, left
to join Blood, Sweat & Tears. On July 6, Herman played the Montreux Jazz
Festival, documented on *Herd at Montreux,* which featured a mixture of contem-
porary material including the then-current Emerson, Lake & Palmer hit "Fanfare
for the Common Man" by Aaron Copland, which was adapted for the band by
Gary Anderson, and "Crosswind" from former the Mahavishnu drummer Billy
Cobham's album of the same name. Later in the year the Herman toured with
Frank Sinatra, although Sinatra's material swallowed the band's identity:
Sinatra—The Main Event, Live.

While touring with Sinatra, the band took four days off at the end of October
to perform and record Broadbent's ambitious "The Children of Lima" and
"Variations on a Scene" with the Houston Symphony Orchestra. Seven years
later Herman would record a piece called "Theme in Search of a Movie," which
is how these pieces come across today. Recorded at a time when pomp-rock was
at its height, they at least reflect Herman's open-minded attitude. When
Children of Lima was released in spring 1975, it was filled out by four additional
tunes, including Chicago's "25 or 6 to 4." In January 1975, Herman recorded
King Cobra, including a powerful version of Carole King's "Jazzman" and a well-
executed Gary Anderson arrangement of Chick Corea's "Spain." "[Woody's] not
a writer," commented Anderson, "but he knows what he wants to hear. He is
very exacting in wanting to maintain . . . 'The Woody Herman Sound.'" [15]

The success of *Giant Steps* in 1973 and Herman's sympathetic treatment of
Chick Corea's "La Fiesta" inspired a dialogue between bandleader and compos-

er about Corea contributing a major work for the band. Corea agreed and in January 1978 Herman recorded "Suite for Hot Band" in three movements. Since Corea somewhat whimsically described it as "Stravinsky meets Sousa," the portents appeared extremely unpromising, but after the staccato opening movement reminiscent of the *allegro moderato* section of Stravinsky's "Ebony Concerto," it opens up into good old down-home Herman. However, it detracted somewhat from Herman's adaptation of five Steely Dan numbers that made up the balance of the album. In fact, Alan Broadbent's arrangement of "Aja" actually succeeds in adding a compelling new dimension to the original, with Frank Tiberi's tenor taking Wayne Shorter's role in the original. Tiberi also makes a telling contribution to "Kid Charlemagne" from Dan's *Royal Scam* album, while ringer Tom Scott's tenor and lyricon were impressive on "I Got the News," another composition from Dan's best-selling *Aja*. Had the "Chick" element been left out of *Chick, Donald, Walter & Woodrow* in favor of more Donald Fagen and Walter Becker numbers, Herman could well have had his most successful recording of the 1970s.

In 1978 Herman turned 65, a time in his life when he could not unreasonably have been contemplating retirement, but tax problems brought on by a band manager with a gambling habit forced him to keep working to pay off back taxes. In the face of great adversity that included the death of his wife from cancer and an attempted eviction from his longtime Hollywood home by the U.S. Internal Revenue Service, Herman maintained his enthusiasm and high standards until his death on October 29, 1987. Ever responsive to contemporary trends, his 1982 album *World Class* included Chick Corea's "Crystal Silence" and his 50th Anniversary Tour in 1986 included a John Fedchock arrangement of "Pools" from Steps Ahead's eponymously titled album. And, as had been the case throughout his career, his band remained a finishing school for some of the greatest musicians in jazz.

When the swing era came to an end sometime in the latter half of the 1940s, maintaining a regular road-band year after year seemed only possible if your name was Ellington, Basie, Herman, or Kenton. But in 1957 a new entrant emerged in the form of the high-note trumpeter Maynard Ferguson, who, with the promise of steady employment in New York's Birdland jazz club and $3,500 in cash from his wife's insurance settlement, moved to New York to form a regular, working band. Paring down his ensemble from behemoths of up to nine brass and five saxes, Ferguson slimmed down to a three-trumpet, two-trombone, four-sax lineup, plus rhythm, which he considered better able to survive the vicissitudes of financial fortune. The portents looked good, attracting young, highly able musicians. Mike Zwerin was in the band at the time, and he recalled: "In 1959 Maynard Ferguson had the hottest big band a white musician could hope to play with. There was still Woody Herman, true, but Maynard was zappier, integrated and younger. Forte was as quiet as it got and allegro was a slow tempo . . . [and] his music accused you of being a sissy for not liking it."[16]

The band's exuberant period with the Roulette label between 1958 and 1962 helped provide the inspiration behind the horns-and-rock concept of Blood,

Sweat & Tears.[17] But in 1967 one of his five children contracted an illness, and Ferguson relocated to England where suitable specialist treatment could be found. He promptly formed a British version of the Maynard Ferguson Orchestra, described by *Downbeat* as "a plain, straight-ahead British big band."[18] A recording contract with Columbia led to a number of albums that revealed an increasing accomodation with pop, rather than rock culture. First came the Grammy-nominated *M. F. Horn* from 1971, which had a somewhat elongated "MacArthur Park" and several lukewarm jazz-rocky numbers. *M. F. Horn 2* and *M. F. Horn 3* dipped a cautious toe a bit deeper into contemporary culture, but none registered higher than three and one-half stars on the *Downbeat* scale. In 1973, Ferguson returned to the States, having sojourned in India and reformed his group with a mixture of British and American musicians. *M. F. Horn 4 & 5*, recorded live July 10, 1973 at Jimmy's on West 52nd Street in New York, is an unsubtle but pulsating set with plenty of solo space for the New Zealand baritone saxophonist Bruce Johnstone, who would later leave to form his own jazz-rock group, New York Mary. By now Ferguson had become expert at finding a variety of ways of demonstrating more or less the same three qualities: stamina, power, and technical fireworks.

In 1974, under pressure for greater sales from Columbia, Ferguson delved deeper into projecting a specific jazz-rock identity. The band enjoyed a boost in 1976 when the drummer Peter Erskine joined from Stan Kenton and immediately made his presence felt in "Airegin" from *New Vintage* (1977), which was more representative of the band in live performance. In 1978 Jay Chattaway's arrangement of Bill Conti's "Gonna Fly Now," the theme song of the hit movie *Rocky*, put Ferguson's album *Conquistador* on the best-seller charts and his band among the major draws in jazz, pulling audiences of up to 20,000 in live appearances. *Carnival*, from May 1978, was Erskine's last recording with the band before he joined Weather Report—coincidentally, Ferguson had just covered WR's hit "Birdland" on the album. A transparently calculated effort at satisfying the tremendous audience he had found through the walloping trombone of "Gonna Fly Now," the jazz quotient in Ferguson's offerings was becoming smaller and smaller, exemplified by *Hot* from a year later, another heavily produced album, and like the rest professional, mechanized, and overtly populist in its appeal.

Ferguson's eighties output was equally predictable. In 1983 he made his first live album in ten years; nothing of any great artistic merit was on offer, but the rhythm section with Gregg and Matt Bissonette cooked. The brothers later enjoyed a career in rock, combining with power-guitarist Joe Satriani. Ferguson continued into the 1990s, with a big band he called Big Bop Nouveau, that appeared to satisfy his somewhat limited artistic aspirations which continued to place a premium on flash at the expense of content.

If the late 1950s had seemed an unpromising time for Ferguson to launch his new big band, then 1966, the height of the rock boom, seemed not only unpromising, but economic suicide. However, very few people told Buddy Rich what to do or what not to do. In early April 1966, he left the financial security of the Harry James band (where he was widely believed to be the highest paid side-

The Buddy Rich Band: When Rich connected with popular culture, his version of "Norwegian Wood" became what "Four Brothers" was to Woody Herman, or "April in Paris" to Count Basie. (Photograph by Stuart Nicholson.)

man in the history of big-bandom) and headed to the Alladin Hotel in Las Vegas, where he had arranged financial backing to form his own band. He hired Oliver Nelson to write and arrange several charts and paid for him to spend a week in Las Vegas rehearsing the band. The rest of his book was filled out by arrangements from Bill Holman, Phil Wilson, Bill Reddie, and his tenor saxophonist, Jay Corre. A new band was born.

Rich's big band made their debut on Richard Bock's Pacific Jazz (later World Pacific) label with *Swingin' New Band,* recorded live in the fall of 1966 at the Chez Club on Santa Monica Boulevard, Hollywood. It reveals just why Rich was rated one of the great drummers in jazz; the drive, lift, and élan he brought to his ensemble made a competent, professional big band sound special. Concessions were made to contemporary culture in song selection—"Up Tight," "More Soul," "What'd I Say"—but the writing showed little grasp of handling the modern idiom. They fare much better on "Critic's Choice" from Nelson's *More Blues and the Abstract Truth,* smoothing the contours of Nelson's "rock" writing for saxophones and realizing an effective performance. This was a time when jazz musicians, particularly Rich, thought rock simplistic and sought to compensate for its perceived shortcomings by performing over-busy and complicated arrangements, missing the point by a mile. Yet on *Big Swing Face* from February 1967, again recorded at the Chez, the Bill Holman arrangement of

"Norwegian Wood" gave him one of his most enduring and popular numbers, which together with the Pete Meyers arrangement of "Love for Sale" became to Rich what "Four Brothers" was to Woody Herman or "April in Paris" was to Count Basie.

Rich's band was probably the only big band to rise to national prominence through television exposure. In 1966–1967 they appeared on *The Ed Sullivan Show, The Mike Douglas Show, Hollywood Palace, The Garry Moore Show,* and the show that would regularly bring them before an audience of millions, *The Tonight Show Starring Johnny Carson.* Rich's quick wit and virtuoso drumming was a natural for TV, but while skeptics acknowledged that Rich was off to a flying start, they all thought he would find it impossible to survive on the road. Rich proved them wrong. They embarked on their first European tour on March 31, 1967 and on their return were the summer replacement for the house band on Jackie Gleason's *Away We Go Show,* giving them more welcome TV exposure. In June the band began recording their third album, *Take It Away!* The opening track was the "Away We Go" theme of the Gleason show; "The Rotten Kid" came from the pen of Buddy Greco, who cohosted the Gleason show with Rich during the host's absence.

After an appearance at the Newport Jazz Festival on July 1, 1967, the band went on tour backing Frank Sinatra. In the winter, they were the first jazz attraction to appear at Chicago's major rock venue, the Kinetic Playground, where, in keeping with the times, the clientele sat on the floor. Looking slightly incongruous in suits and bow ties, the band scored a major hit, and his management began looking to place the band in more rock venues.[19] On August 1, 1968, the cost of running his band was brought home to him when he was forced to declare personal bankruptcy. However, Rich's financial problems did not directly affect the future of his band, who had opened at Caesar's Palace in July. Gone were the bow ties: the band now sported more contemporary garb, with Rich adorned with heavy Indian necklaces. The "psychedelic" cover art of *Mercy, Mercy, Mercy*—recorded live, but after hours, on July 7, 1968—said it all.

By now, the band's repertoire had undergone a contemporary update. Where he once included an occasional jazz-rock number as a change of pace, he now made jazz-rock central to his repertoire. The band was probably one of his strongest ever, yet its potential could only be said to be partially realized. Some of the arrangements—such as Don Sebesky's "Big Mama Cass"—handled the rock phrasing awkwardly, and Rich was by no means an effective rock drummer. However, while pieces in 4/4 sounded over-busy and strained, Rich was exceptional in his handling of pieces in a driving 3/4 or 6/8, such as "Preach and Teach," "Goodbye Yesterday," and "Ode to Billy Joe," which were better representations of the tremendous drive his band could generate. By now, Rich had played Fillmore West, opening for Ten Years After. "As I was making the introduction, people were screaming 'ALVIN! TEN YEARS AFTER! ROCK AND ROLL,'" recalled Bill Graham. "The brass section stood up . . . and Buddy took off. . . . The entire room swerved. All the kids getting something to eat turned around and looked at the stage. Buddy fucking wailed . . . the room was mesmerised . . . they could not believe how good it was. They were just glued to the stage. He held that room for more than an hour and he was great. He went off and the kids went wild, 'MORE, MORE, BUDDY!'" [20]

Rich, despite his misgivings about rock in general and rock drummers in particular (the mere mention of Ginger Baker was enough to set off a lengthy tirade), continued to reposition his music with a more unequivocal approach to jazz-rock. As a drummer, his shortcomings are again apparent on *Buddy and Soul,* probably the least successful of his jazz-rock albums.[21]

After playing to 15,000 rock fans over three days at Fillmore West in February 1970, Rich recorded the live album *Keep the Customer Satisfied* during a brief residency at the Tropicana in Las Vegas. It includes some of his best jazz-rock material. Although Bill Holman's arrangement of the title track sticks closely to the Simon & Garfunkel orchestration, soloists Richie Cole and Jim Mosher provide sparks, and Rich sticks to an uncomplicated backbeat and lets the arrangement do the work. Don Piestrup, an especially sympathetic arranger for the Rich band, contributed "Long Days Journey," a blues with a suspended rhythmic feel, and "Celebration," which is brought alive by a beautifully introspective trumpet solo, a rare thing indeed in Rich's band, by George Zonce. Shortly after the Tropicana date, World Pacific dropped Rich from their label, and nothing further was heard from him on record for fifteen months.

A move from the West Coast to New York City in mid-1970 led to an inevitable turnover of personnel. When the dust settled, Rich was heading another fine version of his band, and in June 1971 he signed with the RCA label, beginning a stormy relationship in which he always maintained he had to fight for artistic control over his own band. His first album for the label, *A Different Drummer,* recorded in July 1971, saw the beginning of the band retreating into formula. On December 6–8, 1971, the band recorded live at Ronnie Scott's club in London, producing the best album they made for RCA.[22] Subsequently, Rich's output on record became variable, and recording dates few and far between. *Stick It,* from August 1972, was the last to be heard from Rich for some while on record, because his contract with RCA expired shortly afterwards. In 1973, he signed with the fledgling Groove Merchant label, commissioning Manny Albam and Ernie Wilkins to provide some rock-oriented charts for his debut album, *The Roar of '74.*

However, on March 18, 1974 Rich disbanded, saying he would form a small group to work his own club, "Buddy's Place," which opened on April 10. The club only lasted until November 23, however, Rich continued working with a small group until April 1975, when he had trumpeter Lloyd Michels contract a new band; among the new personnel was former Count's Rock Band alumnus Steve Marcus on tenor and soprano sax who would later inherit the mantle of the band's straw boss. They opened on April 28, 1975, at a second "Buddy's Place," this time at Marty's Bum Steer at 133 West 33rd Street, to a packed house. This version of the club lasted until December. Two days after opening, they were in the recording studios for a final album before Groove Merchant folded. *Big Band Machine* was dominated by a suite from the rock opera *Tommy.* Now called

Buddy Rich and his Big Band Machine, they were capable of impressing the most seasoned observers. "One of the most exciting sets I've ever witnessed anywhere," said John McDonough eleven weeks later. "Yet if this band has a weakness it would seem to be the quality of its writing. . . . Too often what lifts the audience out of its seats sounds like brassy bluster on records."[23] It was an observation that generally held true for the Rich band in subsequent years.

Without a record label, Rich contracted again with RCA, and in February 1976 he made one of his worst albums by allowing himself to be talked into responding to the disco craze. "I did [*Speak No Evil*] at the request of the record company," he explained later. "It's not what we do best but at least I was open minded enough to give it a shot."[24] A February 1977 session produced *Buddy Rich Plays and Plays and Plays,* which served to emphasize the gulf between his crisp and energetic live performances (captured on the bootleg *Europe '77*) and a tendency to record new material for new material's sake. In October 1977, the band cut *Class of '78,* which included Weather Report's "Birdland," a workman-like arrangement from Mike Abene featuring Steve Marcus on soprano saxophone that became a staple in live performance. During this period, tenor saxophonist Bob Mintzer was in the band, and began contributing arrangements which were featured on both *Plays and Plays* and *Class of '78.* His grounding with Rich led him to form his own rehearsal band in the 1980s, featuring his tenor playing and arrangements that often incorporated rock rhythms. His albums *Incredible Journey, Camouflage, Spectrum,* and *Urban Contours* are all good representations of the band.

As the 1980s loomed, road-bands were becoming an endangered species. Rich continued to tour until three months before his death on April 2, 1987, yet he was unable produce a worthwhile album after *Class of '78,* with the exception of the cheering retrospective *Mr. Drums—Live on King Street, San Francisco* (1985). Rich had kept going by building up an international audience by constant touring and insisting, and getting, the highest standards of musicianship, even if it meant, according to Rich's biographer Mel Tormé, those close to him fearing for his life, such was the level of "creative stress" he imposed on his band.[25] He had responded to the changing times by adapting to rock, yet overall the band lacked consistency in handling the idiom, even if his discography does include several examples of his well-executed, aesthetically pleasing brand of big-band jazz-rock. In 1994 the drummer-producer Neil Peart reassembled the Rich band in conjunction with Rich's estate and, using the original arrangements, had a succession of drummers sit in with the band for one track each. Among those paying tribute to Rich on *Burning for Buddy* were Steve Gadd, Billy Cobham, Dave Weckl, Steve Smith, Bill Bruford, Omar Hakim, Ed Shaughnessy, Kenny Aronoff, Joe Morello, and—unusually—Matt Sorum from Guns 'n' Roses. Several charts stood the test of time, including "Beulah Witch," "Machine," "Nutville," the timeless "Love for Sale," and "Dancing Men." Of all the guest drummers, Marvin "Smitty" Smith best captured the essence of Rich's style on "Ya Gotta Try."

In general, Rich's best jazz-rock charts tended to be numbers that were not written in 4/4, a time signature that he habitually overcomplicated when employ-

Don Ellis: "Live the band was electric and electrifying," said jazz photographer David Redfern. "It was a big band in tune with the spirit of the 1960s." (Photograph by David Redfern/Redferns.)

ing square rhythm patterns. Jazz drummers usually shared this tendency, apparently keen to demonstrate their technical superiority over their rock counterparts. The use of nonstandard time signatures was something trumpeter Don Ellis made a hallmark of his style. An early proponent of the avant garde, by 1966 he had decided freedom was degenerating into "musical incoherence" and saw a future for jazz based on "a new rhythmic complexity."[26] In 1962 Ellis had been feeling his way towards rhythmic sophistication in a group he co-led with Hari Har Rao, a former pupil of Ravi Shankar, while pursuing graduate studies at UCLA's music department. Called the Hindustani Jazz Sextet, Ellis was the first Western musician to play with an Indian musician over an extended period. From this association, Ellis gained a considerable understanding of Indian music, ragas, and of unconventional meters, which he began to integrate into jazz.

In 1966, Ellis formed a rehearsal band at the Club Havana on Sunset Strip in Los Angeles that was notable for the number of drummers and bassists in its ranks. His first album, *"Live" at Monterey,*[27] revealed a Kentonesque grandeur and a penchant for outré time signatures that was as audacious as it was exciting, earning him one of the longest standing ovations in the history of the festival.

"33 222 1 222" was a piece in 19/4, "New Nine," in 9/4, and "Concerto for Trumpet" in a modest 5/4. "Ellis's amendment to the traditional constitution of jazz is yet another test of the music's accommodating nature, as well as a tribute to his inventiveness," said *Downbeat,* awarding the album four stars.[28]

When the Club Havana was closed down, Ellis found a home for the band at a club named Bonesville in West Los Angeles. With his wife on the door taking tickets and selling "Where's Don Ellis?" bumper stickers, word of the band spread, helped by Kenton himself. Ellis's second album, *Live in $3\frac{2}{3}/4$ Time,* using three tracks from the Monterey performance plus three recorded at Shelly's Manne Hole in 1967, again fearlessly trod in rhythmic territory where only Dave Brubeck had ventured previously, including "Freedom Jazz Dance" in 7/4, "Orientation" in 16/8, and "Upstart," which used the exotic signature in the album's title, in effect 11/8. "[This band] go through 'odd' time signatures, the current Ellis trademark, with seemingly no effort," said *Downbeat,* but they remained concerned about the novelty of it all, awarding the album just three stars.[29] Yet what was remarkable was that, despite the heavy head count—drummers bashing, bassists sawing, and additional percussion walloping away—the band actually swung, succeeding in presenting something new and fresh.

On both these albums, it is easy to understand why Ellis was being tagged as the "new Kenton." While on the one hand the band could justifiably claim to have brought some of the most complex time signatures to jazz—Charlie Haden was once said to have quipped, "The only thing Don Ellis plays in 4/4 is 'Take Five'"—on the other there was a certain brassy splendor that placed the band in the shadow of Kenton's ensembles. This was exacerbated by using charts such as "Pasacaglia and Fuge" (featured on the *Monterey* album) from the pen of Hank Levy, who contributed extensively to Kenton's book. After an impressive appearance at the 1967 Newport Jazz Festival, where the band appeared attired in "Prince Valiant" uniforms, John Hammond arranged for the band to be signed by the Columbia label. By the time they came to record *Electric Bath* in September, they had developed a much more individual personality. Coincidental to the band's emergence was the rise of rock music and the blooming of the San Francisco sound. Suddenly psychedelic tone colors and the sound of the sitar had become all the rage.

The composition that brings together these diverse strands is "Indian Lady," a piece that would become something of a showstopper in live performance, and which Ellis would subsequently record twice more for Columbia in somewhat fragmented live versions.[30] The original version is the best, opening with a drone and a rubato statement of the five-note and four-note phrases on which the theme is based. Ellis responds with an obbligato, manipulating quarter tones, using a four-valve trumpet he had specially customized for the purpose. The overall tonality strongly suggests Indian music until the band enter a tempo in a brisk 5/4. The initial exposition is straightforward:

(rubato intro—band plus Ellis) + (a tempo—8 bars tbn riffs) + A (8 bars) + A (8 bars) + A[1] (8 bars) + (9-bar interlude—stop time) + A (8 bars) +(4 bars tbn riffs to solos)

This is a modal piece whose basic form is modified as the performance progresses, the A sections appearing in rondo form between solo interludes and also in variation. Ellis takes the first solo, and for a modernist he has a surprisingly broad tone. He had a very precise technique that allowed him to construct a solo of beguiling intricacy that embraces quarter tones while retaining its focused intensity, an impression that remains even after repeated listenings. The ensemble begins generating a powerful groove under Ellis's high notes, and Lang enters to contribute a clavinet solo that sustains the swirling momentum of the ensemble passages. Then, Ron Myers emerges on trombone with a solo based on motifs and variations of the "Indian Lady" theme. As the band recapitulate and embellish the "A" theme, Ron Starr on tenor contributes what can only be described as a booting solo in character with the shouting brass from which he is catapulted. Steve Bohannon's inspired drums provide a link to the treble forte brass finale of rousing intensity.[31] The tongue-in-cheek false ending presages a grandstand finish whose underlying humor provides the perfect release to the intensity of the performance, one of the more memorable post–Swing Era performances by a big band and a superbly realized meeting of jazz and popular culture, numbering among the great performances of classic jazz-rock. "I've never been a miniaturist," explained Ellis. "I like the grandiose sweep. I want my music to be thrilling."[32] Despite its uneven quality, *Electric Bath* earnt a five-star rating from *Downbeat*[33] and came first in their 1968 "Reader's Poll" ahead of Miles Davis's *Miles in the Sky* (4th) and *Nefertiti* (6th), which, although representing miscarriage of justice in aesthetic terms, does reveal how quickly Ellis reacted to popular culture.

Ellis was one of the first in jazz to embrace the new technology of rock, seeing it as having the potential to broaden the scope of his music. He realized that volume was a vital component of rock's appeal, applied this principle to jazz, "electrifying" his band with Cohn Multividers through banks of speakers, and began appearing at rock venues such as the Cheetah, the Kaleidoscope, and the Carousel.

Hard on the heels of *Electric Bath* came *Shock Treatment,* the first truly psychedelic jazz album in terms of cover art and musical content. Not only were Simon and Garfunkel present at the recording session, but the whole album was produced with rock audiences in mind. A certain degree of controversy surrounded the release of the album; Ellis mixed and edited it in California and sent the finished product to New York. However, only when the album was released did he discover that the final pressing contained rejected masters, unapproved edits, and wrong tunes. The result was so bad that *Downbeat* took the unusual step of refusing to rate it. Eventually the album as Ellis intended it found its way into the shops, but the damage had been done. Today the album fails to capitalize on the promise shown on "Indian Lady"; there are moments in "A New Kind of Country" and "Beat Me Daddy, Seven to the Bar"—both in 7/4—that convey the infectious spirit of the band, but the group too often opt for Kentonesque "halls of brass" that repel rather than attract.

With John Hammond finding producing Ellis's albums frustrating, he handed over the task to former BS&T keyboard man Al Kooper. *Autumn* includes a

1968 live date at Stanford University in Palo Alto, California, that produced "K. C. Blues" and another version of "Indian Lady." Here the tremendous impact of the band in live performance is captured; "K. C. Blues" uses the Charlie Parker improvisation as a sax solo, with impressive solos from Frank Strozier on alto and John Klemmer on tenor. "Lady" loses momentum during a showcase "electronic" trumpet solo by Ellis but is revived by a memorable climax. The remaining tracks were recorded in the studio, and again are marred by inconsistency and a love of the grand gesture.

Following the less-than-successful *Don Ellis Goes Underground*,[34] two live albums were issued—*At Fillmore*, recorded at the Fillmore West in 1969, and *Tears of Joy*, recorded during his 1971 U.S. tour. Columbia's public-relations machine urged, "Turn up the volume, sit down between the speakers and good luck. It is difficult to predict which will be destroyed first; your speakers, your ears or your mind."[35] Perhaps it would be kinder to view Ellis's mixture of avant-garde showmanship, big-band power-play, burlesque, and humor as serious fun; certainly these sprawling albums are a product of the times. The band was now heavily into electronic experimentation, yet when one cuts through the rallentandos, epic cadenzas, blistering instrumental soli, and electronic gallimaufry, little had changed in the basic orchestral concept of Ellis's band since the Swing era. Nevertheless, *At Fillmore* has some absorbing moments, such as "Final Analysis" and "Great Divide." *Tears of Joy* offered no significant advance on Ellis's basic plan, despite the addition of a woodwind quartet and a string quartet. Grandiose though it might have been—has there ever been anything more pompous in jazz than the opening of Ellis's "5/4 Getaway"?—it is impossible to escape the feeling of fun that permeates Ellis's music, conveyed in "Blues in Elf" in 11/4 and "How's This for Openers?" in 25/4 with a bridge in 27/4 that the band handle faultlessly.

Brash and of its time, it was the band's ability to handle unorthodox time signatures with ease, and to present improvisations that were stylistically satisfying in a complex rhythmic context (Sam Falzone on tenor deserves credit)—such as 19/4 counted 3 + 3 + 2 + 2 + 2 + 1 + 2 + 2 + 2—that remind us today that this area of jazz has still not been explored to the full. Arguably, by 1970 Ellis had suggested greater conceptual possibilities within jazz-rock than had Miles Davis. "I've developed odd meters further than anybody else," he was able to claim. "I've developed electronics for a big band further than anybody else, and then there was the emphasis on R&B and rock. I've done all these things."[36]

Ellis's music, with its flair for the dramatic, had a natural resonance with Hollywood, and in 1973 he earned a Grammy award for the soundtrack music of *The French Connection*. Even so, he continued to perform regularly, capable of attracting a crowd of 28,000 for an outdoor concert in San Francisco in 1974. Although many of his later recordings failed to capture the band's excitement as a live outfit, jazz was much the poorer for the loss of his engaging eccentricities when he died on December 17, 1978. Sadly, his ideas to enrich jazz with a broader range of time, meter, and new tone colors seemed to have died with him.

In the pall of conformity that descended over jazz in the 1980s and 1990s, when major recording companies studiously avoided adventurous ideas and new concepts, the sheer range and variety of ideas that were triggered by the rock explosion in the late 1960s and 1970s could not be better illustrated by contrasting Ellis's brash excitement with flügelhornist Chuck Mangione's romantic excursions into peace and love. On the recommendation of Dizzy Gillespie, Art Blakey invited Mangione to join his Jazz Messengers in 1966, where he stayed for three years. When he left, Mangione devised an orchestral project with the Rochester Philharmonic that led to his first album, the multistylistic *Friends and Love* (1970), which included a tune called "Hill Where the Lord Hides" that was nominated for a Grammy, helping establish a solo career. The subsequent *Alive* with Gerry Niewood on saxes, Tony Levin on bass guitar (later replaced by Alphonso Johnson), and Steve Gadd (later replaced by Joe LaBarbera), contained some articulate improvisation from Mangione and Niewood. However, it was quickly overshadowed by the double Grammy-nominated *Land of Make Believe,* a collaboration with vocalist Esther Satterfield. Subsequently, Mangione became synonymous with jeans, a T-shirt, and a flat-brimmed hat, his image and easily accessible music an anathema to jazz critics—"a suburbanite housewife's dream of a white Miles Davis," said one.[37]

While this was lightweight stuff, there was nevertheless an ingenious, innocent charm about Mangione's early albums—indeed, when Esther Satterfield intones "that's what we call integration" on *Land of Make Believe,* a significant social point is made with profound modesty. Today these albums serve to illustrate just one aspect of a remarkable range of ideas that resulted in jazz's collision with popular culture at this time. It is impossible to think of music like this being recorded in Reagan's 1980s or the gray 1990s, and maybe if *Land of Make Believe* existed alone, it would be regarded with more affection as an interesting period piece. It doesn't. Subsequent albums beat to death the idea of a large-scale, pop-jazz extravaganza and, by the time of *Eyes of the Veiled Temptress* (1988), nothing of interest was on view. It had all ended up sounding glib and unrewarding, despite Mangione's gift for musical hooks, acceding to the commercial maxim that says if you have a good idea, stick with it. While he enjoyed considerable success with the title track of *Feels So Good,* the initial charm of "Land of Make Believe" had already become impossible to sustain.

While Mangione represented the lighter side of the 1970s music scene, Gil Evans, long recognized as one of the music's giants, was about to enter his most prolific period of touring and recording in his life. "I started having the idea of having a band. All my life I'd been sitting in front of that piano trying to figure another way to voice a minor seventh chord," he said. "It was such a lonesome thing that I decided that I needed adventure and the only way to get adventure was to get a band together."[38] Although in the past he had formed a band for specific engagements or recording sessions, this would be the first time he tried to sustain a regular working unit. Impressed with the music of Jimi Hendrix, he was keen to import electronic tone colors into his writing after experiencing Hendrix's playing at first hand. "I heard Jimi Hendrix in the studio," he recalled. "I was mixing our Ampex album [*Gil Evans* (1971)] and he was rehearsing in the same studio with Buddy Miles."[39] Some months later, he saw Robert Moog

Gil Evans embraced electronic tone colors and rock rhythms, and with *Svengali* (1973) he created a classic. (Photograph by Stuart Nicholson.)

demonstrate his Moog Synthesizer at Columbia University and realized that here was a way of introducing electronic sounds into his band. While it is often thought that *Gil Evans* (1971)[40] used a synthesizer, it didn't—it was Evans's imaginative writing for an electric piano and Joe Beck's guitar with percussion combinations, and unusual mikings, that made it seem that way. Nevertheless, it was enough for the sleeve note annotator, Ralph J. Gleason, to predict that Evans's experimentation was headed in the direction of electronics.[41]

Evans's first album using a synthesizer was *Where Flamingos Fly*, recorded in 1971 but not released until a decade later. With former Mothers of Invention keyboard player Don Preston providing the new tone colors to Evans's rich musical palette, the album included two numbers that Evans would use time and again with his band in performance—"Jelly Rolls," which came from a collaboration with Miles Davis for a play called *Time of the Barracuda,* and "Zee Zee," a blues in 5/4. Evans, whose brooding art had already managed to coax new and eerie sounds from acoustic-instrumental combinations, was yet to fully realize the potential that electronics offered, but clearly his ensembles were never again going to sound like those on the albums *Out of the Cool* or *The Individualism of Gil Evans,* his two 1960s classics. The first time he used electronics at an engagement was at Slug's in New York City in January 1972, where Dave Horowitz played synthesizer from lead sheets. It was the first time the Gil Evans Orchestra had appeared in a New York club since a few memorable weeks at the Jazz Gallery in 1960.

In July, Evans visited Japan with a just a few key personnel, filling the band out with Japanese musicians for a two-week tour that took in TV and recordings. On his return, work around New York began picking up, with the band subbing for the Mel Lewis–Thad Jones Jazz Orchestra at the Village Vanguard and spending most of October at the Bitter End. *Svengali,* a live 1973 recording from a concert at Manhattan's Trinity Church plus one track from a Philharmonic (now Avery Fisher) Hall concert, was made possible by the painter Ken Noland financing the recording at his own expense—$30,000—and eventually selling the tapes to Atlantic. By now the synthesizer had been integrated into Evans's ensemble to better effect, giving an air of mystery to the brass phrases in "Thoroughbred" and providing the ghostly chimes in "Zee Zee." It was one of his finest albums; Evans's Lorca-esque settings for tenor saxophonist Billy Harper in "Cry of Hunger" and alto saxophonist Dave Sanborn on George Russell's "Blues in Orbit" were highlights. What is striking is how the band slipped easily between freeform passages and the written arrangement. "Quintessential Gil Evans," said *Downbeat,* awarding *Svengali* five stars.[42]

Evans's music had taken on a decidedly contemporary rhythmic orientation. "Those chunks or clusters that you hold for a long time, from the audience you can hardly tell whether its three French horns or an electronic instrument doing it," he observed, "and rock rhythms . . . you can superimpose anything over them."[43] On July 7, 1974 he appeared at the Montreux Jazz Festival, and the resulting live album included a side-long "Waltz," a slowly evolving freeform piece, which by indirection found its direction, providing tracts of acreage for his soloists to roam in.

That the band was heading towards a freeform jazz-rock approach was not immediately obvious from *The Gil Evans Orchestra Plays the Music of Jimi Hendrix,* recorded in June 1974.[44] Evans arranged only two and a half pieces on the original vinyl release;[45] the rest of the band members contributed the balance of the tracks. "Once Gil established the standard of excellence we all tried to write up to that," said percussionist Warren Smith, "and it pulled us outside of ourselves. He shaped the band and the interpretations so his personality always showed through."[46] Naturally, without Hendrix, the album was doomed to be a series of speculative "what-ifs," perhaps the most tantalizing of which was speculation on how Hendrix and Evans might have shaped the ultimate destiny of jazz-rock. It was not meant to be. The recording engineer was reluctant to allow distortion in case people "thought he was no good at his job," immediately creating something of a disadvantage for the guitarist Ryo Kawasaki, who, try as he might, cannot bring the visceral power that Hendrix might have used to pull the project together. Even so, "1983 . . . A Merman I Should Turn To Be" works well, the staccato brass passages with former BS&T trumpeter Lew Soloff's lead etching itself into the memory. Subsequently, Evans would always perform at least one Hendrix composition in his live concerts, most often "Little Wing," which was added to the CD compilation from another session.

In March and April 1975, Evans was in the studio to cut *There Comes a Time.* The original vinyl issue and the subsequent CD issue vary substantially.[47] However, whichever version is considered, it is among the best of Evans's discography. In scope it ranges from tense abstract blues to a swinging revival of a Jelly Roll Morton standard, interpreted with audible glee by an impressive assembly of young musicians including Tony Williams, Dave Sanborn, George Adams, Howard Johnson, Lew Soloff, Bob Stewart, Billy Harper, Tom Malone, and Hannibal Marvin Peterson.

Although Evans's albums suggested otherwise, increasingly the emphasis was moving from the meticulous orchestrations of the 1960s to sympathetic interaction on the bandstand to reshape his compositions into new orchestral tapestries, making a core of sympathetic musicians familiar with his methods vital. Although work was intermittent in the late 1970s, he continued to accept occasional engagements and festivals, drawing on a circle of close musical friends including Lew Soloff, George Adams, John Clark, Sue Evans, Pete Levin, Dave Sanborn, Bob Stewart, Hanibal Peterson, and Ernie Royal, who tried to make themselves available for his engagements.

This move towards looser forms becomes clear on *Priestess,* recorded live at the St. George Church in New York on May 13, 1977, and *Gil Evans Live at the Festival Hall London 1978* and *The Rest of Gil Evans Live at the Festival Hall 1978,* both from February 25, 1978. Except for one or two extra faces, the personnel are drawn from his regular stock company, who collectively move from the written to the improvised and back again with hypnotic precision, blurring the distinctions between the two. The balance between the juxtaposition of ideas freely expressed and Evans's writing allowed the music to create its own time and space, a work in progress that the bandleader and arranger Angel Rangelow, who studied with Evans, once described as "like hearing birds in a forest: you don't know how it started or where its going to end."[48] There is no doubt that Evans's albums were coming to reflect this high-risk policy of public experimentation. *Little Wing,* a concert in West Germany from October 1978, has long versions of the title track and "The Meaning of the Blues" that slowly unwind mixing dense throbbing electronic sounds and unhurried solos from Gerry Niewood (formerly with Chuck Mangione's groups) on alto and soprano and Soloff on trumpet. *Live at the Public Theatre Vols. 1 & 2,* from February 1980, equally contains moments of inspiration and aimless drift. With a stellar cast of musicians including Arthur Blythe, Billy Cobham, Hamiet Bluiett, and George Lewis alongside the regular faces, the band was now using more sophisticated synthesizers played by Pete Levin and

Masabumi Kikuchi that haloed the performances with swathes of electronic tone colors like rings around Jupiter. Evans toured England in 1983 with his son Miles and a band of British musicians including John Surman, John Taylor, and Chris Hunter—who later joined him in New York—on alto. *Gil Evans—The British Orchestra* includes restrained but successful versions of "Hotel Me" and "Friday the 13th" with highly sympathetic solos from Surman on baritone and synthesizer.

A chance meeting between James Browne, a disc jockey at WBGO-FM (a Newark, N.J.–based public radio station devoted to jazz), and Evans in a Greenwich Village supermarket set in motion a chain of events that resulted in Evans picking up a regular Monday night spot in the Sweet Basil at 88 Seventh Avenue South in Greenwich Village. Representative of this period are *Gil Evans and the Monday Night Orchestra Live at Sweet Basil Vols. 1 & 2* from August 1984 and the 1988 Grammy winner *Gil Evans and the Monday Night Orchestra Live at Sweet Basil: Bud and Bird.* There were new faces in the band—Bill Evans, Hiram Bullock, Mark Egan, Gil Goldstein, and Danny Gotlieb—and the overall effect is that of a spontaneous, freewheeling, musical workshop running the knife edge between success and failure. With his regular appearances at Sweet Basil, Evans the septuagenarian was bemused to find himself in vogue. In 1985 he arranged and conducted the soundtrack for the British pop movie *Absolute Beginners* and, later, *The Color of Money.* In 1987 his band appeared in Europe with the pop singer Sting. Later in the year they collaborated on Sting's album *Nothing Like the Sun,* which included a number by the Evans band, "Little Wing." However, in 1988 Evans underwent surgery and left New York for Cuernavaca, Mexico, to recuperate; on March 20 he died of peritonitis.

Using a suave mix of rock rhythms and electronic and acoustic tone colors, Evans's music, at its finest, represented an aesthetically satisfying variation of big-band jazz-rock. Although he did nothing particularly innovative within the idiom, his use of electronics washed his music with contemporary tone colors that gave his music a timeless quality. If his earlier orchestrations for Miles Davis on *Miles Ahead, Porgy and Bess,* and *Sketches of Spain,* or his two 1960s masterworks *Out of the Cool* and *The Individualism of Gil Evans,* sounded ten years ahead of their time, then his writing on *Svengali* and parts of *There Comes a Time* sounded like a twenty-first-century big band.

When Evans first started working out his ideas in a basement room on 55th Street, at the height of the bop revolution, his modest apartment became a meeting place for all forward thinkers in jazz, among them Charlie Parker, John Lewis, Miles Davis, Gerry Mulligan—and George Russell. Russell's greatest contribution to jazz would emerge with his theoretical study "The Lydian Chromatic Concept of Tonal Organization," something of a work in progress as he kept expanding and redefining his concepts. It came as no surprise to anyone that academia claimed him in 1969, with his appointment to the New England Conservatory of Music's faculty.

Russell's first attempt to confront the new electronic technology came in 1968 with *Othello Ballet Suite* and *Electric Organ Sonata No. 1.* In 1969 his *Electronic Sonata for Souls Loved by Nature* was meant to "suggest that man, in the face of encroaching technology, must confront technology and attempt to humanize it."⁴⁹ An ambitious piece that combined a pan-stylistic tape composed of many fragments of musical styles—including rock, avant garde, blues, serial music, and more—it was only partially successful in its realisation, but it was clear from the opening "Event" that Russell favored the explicit rhythmic pulse of rock rhythms.

Although Russell ceased to compose for a while in the 1970s to complete his "Lydian Chromatic Concept," he began performing and recording again in 1976 with *Vertical Form VI*, an exercise in reconciling his brilliant and sometimes abstract concepts with the logical order suggested by his theories. "I can't imagine any piece based on African music that didn't reflect Vertical Form because Africans were innovators," he explained. "In a drum choir one drummer is the rhythmic gravity while others gradually layer on sophisticated rhythms on top of the tonal center. The whole isn't really evolving in a horizontal way. . . . It's vertical and it's getting higher and higher."⁵⁰

New York Big Band (1978) mixes Russell's abstract sensibilities with a more unequivocal approach to rock rhythms. "Living Time, Event V," for example, alternates rock patterns with episodes of straight-ahead swing and some strong solos from Stanley Cowell on piano, Cameron Brown on bass, John Clark on French horn, Gary Valente on trombone, and saxophonist Roger Rosenberg. However, *Live in American Time Spiral* from 1982, the seventh of Russell's "Vertical Forms," is surprisingly ordinary, despite a strong cast of players. His two live albums for the Blue Note label in 1983, *African Game* and *So What*, used a band made up primarily of New England Conservatory students who were not always up to the task of performing his music. However, a standout is an excellent version of "So What" from the latter album, which eschews the familiar theme from *Kind of Blue* in favor of the classic Miles Davis solo. It was scored for the whole band by Gotz Tangerding and works well, Davis's improvised line sounding remarkably effective over raunchy rock rhythms, inspiring Mike Peipman on trumpet and Dave Mann to rise above the workaday. In 1989, Russell toured Europe with a British version of his Living Time Orchestra, and the resulting *The London Concert* is a solid representation of old and new compositions that respond to Russell's belief that "jazz is a language that speaks simultaneously to the intellect and the body." With some strong solos by Andy Sheppard on tenor and Ian Carr on trumpet, Russell's long-form compositions with their powerful rock rhythms contain moments that are positively uplifting, just as their composer intended.

Carla Bley once studied with George Russell, and formed what would become a semipermanent big band in 1976. In the 1960s her compositions had been featured by Gary Burton, including her "Genuine Tong Funeral," and by Charlie Haden's Liberation Music Orchestra. Between 1968 and 1971, she gradually pieced together her most substantial work, the eclectic "jazz opera" *Escalator Over the Hill*, which combined opera singers with singing tuba players, Linda Ronstadt and a singing bassist, and mixed members of Ornette Coleman's band with Jack Bruce and John McLaughlin. In her big-band work, Bley sought not so much to break the mold of the big band, but to subvert and reassess the values it had come to represent. Bley regarded rock as a means to this end but not as an end in itself. Her band albums reflect her diverse approaches to try to find a new style for the traditional band setting. *European Tour 1977* mixes her unpredictable, zany, clever, and crude compositions with large chunks of theatrical parody and humor. At her best she could be affecting, moving, and eventually triumphant. On *Dinner Music* (1977) she imported the Stuff rhythm section for a good-humored blow, but the minimalistic *Social Studies* was rather more introverted. *Live* from a 1981 concert at the Great American Music Hall is a solid representation of her music that underlined the importance of rock in her thinking. However, *Heavy Heart* suffered from an apparent desire to secure FM airplay.

Mike Gibbs: Between 1970 and 1972 Gibbs recorded three albums with his British big band that include some of the best crafted and emotionally serious compositions to reflect the influence of rock on big-band jazz. (Photograph by Stuart Nicholson.)

Subsequent albums, including *The Very Big Carla Bley Band* (1990) and *Goes to Church* (1996), showed her continued subversion of the big-band vocabulary.

Like Carla Bley, trombonist Mike Gibbs had the distinction of hearing his compositions performed and recorded by the Gary Burton quartet, and, in 1967 he provided the title track for Stan Getz's album *Sweet Rain*. A Rhodesian by birth, Gibbs left Africa to study at the Berklee College of Music in 1959, graduating in 1962 and winning a scholarship to study at the Lennox School of Jazz. In 1963 he graduated from the Boston Conservatory and subsequently studied at Tanglewood Summer School with Aaron Copeland, Iannis Xenakis, Gunther Schuller, and Lukas Foss. In 1965 he settled in Britain, working with the Graham Collier and Johnny Dankworth bands, forming his own big band in 1969. *Michael Gibbs* (1970) assembled an impressive array of British jazz talent, including Kenny Wheeler and Henry Lowther on trumpets, Bobby Lambe and Ray Premru on trombones, John Surman and Alan Skidmore on saxes, Jack Bruce on bass, and John Marshall and Tony Oxley on drums, to perform some of the best-crafted and emotionally serious compositions to reflect the influence of rock on a big band in jazz.

Where the Woody Herman and Buddy Rich bands had struggled to find an authentic voice when performing rock-influenced numbers, Gibbs succeeded by completely rethinking his approach to the idiom, aware that the arrangers for Herman and Rich had simply applied traditional methods of arranging to rock material, utilizing devices that had changed little since the Swing era, combined with complex, often idiomatically inappropriate lines that owed more to bebop than rock. Gibbs applied a radically simplified approach in terms of composition and structure. His writing, revealing a debt to Gil Evans on his early albums, emphasized rich, slow-moving melodies that left room for expressive embellishment by his band. Interestingly, Gibbs did not confront volume or feature driving, repetitive rhythmic patterns, instead contrasting the rock and session guitarist Chris Spedding's overdriven guitar solos with acoustic solos to telling effect.

The result was a series of elegantly crafted originals, such as "And on the Third Day" (previously recorded by Gary Burton on *Country Roads and Other Places*), "Throb" (the title track of Burton's 1969 album), "Sweet Rain" (recorded by Stan Getz), and "Family Joy, Oh Boy!" (written for the birth of Burton's daughter Nicola). *Tanglewood '63*, recorded in November and December 1970, almost aspires to the high standards of his outstanding debut. While the "hip" cover was somewhat misleading—the music was anything but psychedelic—it does include a strong title track and an interesting "Canticle," commissioned by the Dean & Chapter of Canterbury Cathedral and written with Cathedral echo in mind. The live album *Just Ahead* (1972) includes a version of "So Long Gone" that encapsulates Gibbs's writing style. Gibbs uses the familiar twelve-bar blues form in a new and interesting way by stretching the form and making a fifteen-minute performance of just two choruses. Each chord of blues is played for several bars so that the chord cycle moves so slowly as to be almost unrecognizable. As the composition unfolds, the listener responds with intuitive familiarity to the

I–VI–I–V–I progression, sensing what is coming next without quite knowing why. The album's other highlights were "Grow Your Own" by Gibbs and Gary Burton's "Country Roads," which in their contrasting use of rock rhythms succeed in broadening the scope of big-band music with their compelling originality and sympathetic interpretation.

It's impossible not to think that the languid, laid-back feel of Gibbs's first three albums was very much a British thing. Certainly with *In the Public Interest,* a collaboration with Gary Burton from 1973, the American approach to big-band music, specifically fire and aggression, is readily apparent, particularly when comparing the new version of "Family Joy, Oh Boy!" with Gibbs's 1970 original. However, with Gibbs's career developing in a multitude of directions, his big band fell by the wayside. He provided the score for John McLaughlin's *Apocalypse* (1974) conducted by Michael Tilson Thomas, and between stints in academia he worked in a wide variety of musical contexts including films, television, ballet, symphony, jazz, and pop, with artists as varied as Joni Mitchell, Peter Gabriel, Jaco Pastorius, Sister Sledge, Whitney Houston, and Kevin Eubanks—for whom he also acted as producer. His returns to the big-band idiom were sporadic—*The Only Chrome Waterfall* (1975) and the forthright *Big Music* (1988), although critically well received, sacrificed the subtle elements that made his early recordings so timeless.

Like Mike Gibbs, Maria Schneider developed a highly individual voice that, while taking account of Gil Evans's methods, was not subservient to them.[51] Her composition "Wrgly" from *Evanescence,* for example, begins in a manner reminiscent of Neal Hefti's "Cute" but quickly transforms into a darker, brooding performance through several deft changes of meter. Gradually, Schneider intensifies the rhythmic activity behind each succeeding soloist so that, by John Fedchock's trombone solo, there are strong allusions to rock rhythms. What is at issue is not that the band is now playing "rock rhythms," but how this transformation from such humble rhythmic origins as brushes and a high hat at the outset of the composition had been achieved. When Ben Moder enters at the climax, his overdriven guitar is straight out of the Jimi Hendrix textbook, yet this non-acoustic sound is totally subservient to the needs of the composition, which demanded an impressive climax. Here, both the sound and volume of the electrified guitar take the composition into another dimension, a dimension where acoustic instruments could not go. Yet the climax is made in an impressive yet subtle way, as Monder holds a chord for one bar while the rest of the band drop out. The point here is so obvious that it is perhaps surprising it has to be made at all: rock elements, in the right hands, have the potential to broaden the expressionism of jazz.

Clearly rock rhythms and technology could be integrated into a big band without compromising the authenticity of the finished product—the music. By reconceptualising traditional concepts, the performances actually expanded the range of the big band, moving it forward in terms of both tonal color and rhythmic variety in a way that had not happened in any significant way since the Swing era. By the 1990s, the extent to which the colors and rhythms of rock had any place in the forum of the big bands had ceased to become a contentious issue. By then it presented the resourceful arranger with additional elements that could be called upon alongside the more traditional devices that, if used with originality, enhanced the musical status quo.

Notes

1. *The Big Bands,* by George T. Simon (Schirmer Books, New York, 1981), p. 523.
2. Ibid.
3. *Benny Goodman Jazz Concert No. 2,* reissued with additional tracks as *Benny Goodman On the Air 1937–38* (Columbia Legacy C2K 48836).
4. Ra's life is dealt with in commendable detail in *Space Is the Place* by John F. Swed (Pantheon Books, New York, 1977), that also separates the variegated musical legacy of this neglected giant.
5. Its release in October 1964 coincided with two other Mary Poppins sets from the label by Keely Smith and Dean Martin.
6. At the time, his credits included *The Pawnbroker, Walk Don't Run, In Cold Blood, In the Heat of the Night, For the Love of Ivy, Bob and Carol and Ted and Alice,* and *Brother John,* among many others.
7. *Downbeat,* January 1990, p. 20.
8. Ibid., March 16, 1972, p. 19.
9. A memorable batch of albums from the "Swingin' Young Herd" include *Woody Herman 1963, Woody Herman: Encore 63, Woody Herman 1964,* and *Woody's Winners.*
10. *Billboard,* March 26, 1969.
11. *Downbeat,* April 16, 1970, p. 30.
12. *Woodchopper's Ball: The Autobiography of Woody Herman,* by Woody Herman and Stuart Troup (Limelight Editions, New York, 1994), p. 119.
13. *Downbeat Yearbook 1971,* p. 34.
14. *Downbeat,* December 23, 1971, p. 29.
15. *Woody Herman: Chronicles of the Herds,* by William D. Clancy with Audree Coke Kenton (Schirmer Books, New York, 1995), p. 297.
16. *Close Enough for Jazz,* by Mike Zwerin (Quartet, London, 1983), pp. 35, 37.
17. *The Complete Roulette Recordings of the Maynard Ferguson Orchestra* (Mosaic MD10–156) amply represents this period on record.
18. *Downbeat,* December 29, 1971, p. 28.
19. With the interest in Eastern music and religion during the 1960s, Ravi Shankar, who recorded for the same label as Rich, had become one of the label's best selling artists. As an interesting aside, on February 5, 1968 Rich sat in on dhoiak opposite Alla Rhaka on tabla and Shamim Ahmed on sitar in a session arranged and conducted by Shankar, few ever suspecting the presence of an American drummer in the Indian ensemble.
20. *Bill Graham Presents: My Life inside Rock and Out,* by Bill Graham and Robert Greenfield (Delta, New York, 1993), p. 314.
21. Mostly recorded live at the Whisky A Go-Go in Hollywood on June 21, 1969; the recording quality is poor.
22. Issued as a double-LP set in Britain; only an edited-down single LP version appeared in the United States, much to Rich's annoyance.
23. *Downbeat,* November 6, 1975, pp. 36–37.
24. *We Don't Play Requests,* by Doug Meriwether, Jr. (Creative Communications Corp., Maryland, 1984), p. 53.
25. *Traps the Drum Wonder: The Life of Buddy Rich,* by Mel Tormé (Mainstream Publishing, Edinburgh, 1991).

26. *Downbeat,* June 30, 1966, p. 21.
27. Recorded at the Monterey Jazz Festival on September 18, 1966; also recorded that year at the same festival was Charles Lloyd's *Forest Flower.*
28. *Downbeat,* April 20, 1967, p. 36.
29. Ibid., p. 29.
30. *Autumn* (Columbia 472622–2) and *Live at Fillmore West.*
31. An equally able pianist, Bohannon created something of a stir by playing his gigs barefoot, but he was to die shortly after the session in a car crash.
32. *Downbeat,* April 16, 1970, p. 16.
33. Ibid., August 3, 1968, p. 23.
34. His pianist Peter Robinson observed, "The more the A&R people got to Don, the more he started getting pressured into this star identity . . . the Don Ellis Underground album in which he had to do rock . . . and he can't write rock. Right after that I left" (*Downbeat,* April 29, 1971, p. 26).
35. Columbia trade advertisement, winter 1970.
36. *Downbeat,* April 16, 1970, p. 17.
37. Quoted in *Downbeat,* May 8, 1975, p. 13.
38. Liner notes, *Where Flamingos Fly* (A&M CD 0831).
39. Liner notes, *The Rest of Gil Evans Live at the Royal Festival Hall* (Mole 3).
40. Later rereleased as Enja 3069.
41. Liner notes, *Gil Evans* (Ampex A10102).
42. *Downbeat,* February 14, 1974, p. 18.
43. Ibid., May 23, 1974, p. 13.
44. See chapter 6 for the details surrounding this album.
45. Which, incidentally, has better sound than the remixed CD.
46. Liner notes, *Gil Evans Plays the Music of Jimi Hendrix,* CD issue (RCA ND88409).
47. The CD issue loses "Little Wing" to the CD version of *Plays Jimi Hendrix;* "Aftermath, the Fourth Movement Children of Fire" is deleted; short portions of the title track were edited out; "The Meaning of the Blues," on vinyl just under six minutes, flowers to over twenty minutes; and three previously unreleased tracks, "Joy Spring," "So Long," and "Buzzard Variation," are added.
48. *Downbeat,* October 1988, p. 26.
49. Liner notes for *Electronic Sonata for Souls Loved by Nature* (Soul Note 121034–2).
50. *Blue Notes,* by Mort Goode, no. 1UU6.
51. During the last three years of Gil Evans's life, Schneider worked on several challenging projects with Evans, including the film score for Martin Scorcese's *The Color of Money* (1986) and arrangements for Sting's European Concert with the Gil Evans Orchestra at the Umbria Jazz Festival. In June 1993 she was invited to conduct the Gil Evans Orchestra Spoleto Festival in a performance of selections from *Miles Ahead, Porgy and Bess, Sketches of Spain* and *Quiet Nights.* In June 1986 she conducted her own band during the first half of a concert at New York's Florence Gould Hall and the Gil Evans Orchestra during the second. Her second album *Coming About* (ENJA ENJ 9069-2) lived up to the promise of her debut album.

CHAPTER 15

On the Edge
of Tomorrow

If the premise on which jazz-rock was originally founded was based on risk, then by the mid-1970s it had been overshadowed by a commercially commodified variant known as "fusion" which favored rampant virtuosity, the cute cadences of pop music, and nonthreatening electronics. "In order to match that marketing concept of what people think of as 'Fusion,'" observed Frank Zappa, "it has to sound 'fusion.' This has little to do with whether you're fusing anything together. It means that the keyboard player has to sound like Jan Hammer, the guitar player, the drummer, the bass player all have to play in a certain vein."[1] Yet it was inevitable that recording companies would ultimately set about the commodification of jazz-rock, because rock music itself became systematically exploited as the 1960s progressed.

When rock first broke, its great appeal was its apparent rebelliousness. It didn't come out of the Brill building, where songwriters wrote what they thought audiences wanted to hear. It came from the life experiences of artists who interacted with an audience who were roughly their own age and who shared the same rebellious fantasies as the stars. But that rebellious spontaneity and creativity quickly became analyzed and exploited. "Pop isn't rebellious," concluded David Rimmer in 1985. "It embraces the star system. It conflates art, business and entertainment. It cares more about sales and royalties and the strength of the dollar than anything else and to make matters worse, it isn't the least bit guilty about it."[2] Equally, commercial fusion owed its position in the marketplace to obedience to the laws of commerce rather than to the tenets of aesthetics, such that FM airplay leveraged album sales and albums sales leveraged airplay in an incestuous cycle governed by radio formatting. By the 1990s there were not enough elevators in the world to accommodate all the elevator music marketed under the guise of "fusion," which had become a depository for the worst elements of adulthood—safety, conformity, and lack of imagination.

Yet, through it all, the risk-takers were always there, often out of sight of a disenchanted jazz mainstream who saw jazz-rock claimed by commerce in the 1970s and who welcomed the emergence of a somewhat self-righteous acoustic mainstream in the 1980s who played in the adopted voices of jazz's older and sometimes posthumous heroes. These young neoconservatives and their advocates were outspoken in their hostility to electric instruments in general and post-1969 Miles Davis in particular. "It's like records like *Jack Johnson* and *Bitches Brew* don't exist," commented John McLaughlin, "or *Super Nova* from Wayne Shorter—that period. The new boppers all stop in '68, then jump to '83."[3] A schism had formed in jazz during the 1980s and 1990s: the past seemed to be more important than the future. Jazz, once a music representing a flight *from* the status quo, became characterized by a flight *back to* the status quo. The battle lines were drawn, with the more adventurous musicians viewing the jazz tradition as a tradition for change, for moving the music forward; "Jazz is not about wearing an Armani suit and regurgitating somebody else's music as if you invented it," said Greg Osby.[4] Yet through active major recording-company promotion and unprecedented media attention, jazz was artificially re-centered around virtuosic recapitulation as young musicians retreated into the hard-bop certainties of the early 1960s. The neoconservatives defined themselves by what they excluded; thus outsiders, anyone not prepared to accept their version of what jazz was about, ipso facto could not be playing jazz, which was in itself a shrewd marketing ploy. Their list of outsiders was a long one. C. S. Lewis, the writer and moralist, warned of the perils of the "Inner Ring" that exists in every workplace and every social setting. "There would be no fun if there were no outsiders," he said. "The invisible line would have no meaning unless most people were on the wrong side of it." And, from the mid-1970s, a lot of people would be on the "wrong side" of the line, because that was where the action was.

In December 1962, Ornette Coleman staged a remarkable concert at New York's Town Hall. After programming a poor string quartet, Coleman capped the evening by bringing on an R&B group with a technically complex drummer and a virtuoso bass player. On the one hand he was returning to his rhythm and blues upbringing in road bands in Texas, but on the other he was seeking an allegory of the past, present, and future of jazz. It was concept that he did not forget. Around 1974–1975 he was exploring ways of advancing his music while performing with a guitar-based ensemble.[5] Coleman's concept of free jazz-rock was introduced to the world on the 1977 album *Dancing in Your Head,* which combined two sessions with the master musicians of Joujouka, Morocco recorded in January 1973 and included a single track recorded in Paris in 1976 with an electronic group he called Prime Time, which collapsed the melody of "The Good Life," a bluesy theme from his puzzling symphony *Skies of America,* into a near nursery-rhyme chant renamed "Theme from a Symphony." Significantly, Coleman's saxophone dominated the ensemble. The simple blues-based head from "Theme from a Symphony" was repeated over and over and was followed by a solo of convoluted intensity that perhaps more than any other revealed his close links with the blues in its earthy realism and emotional force. As ever, Coleman refused to play en règle; the backdrop against which he was now performing, a squabble of competing electronic voices in different keys and meters, was dominated by funky rhythm section patterns. Yet today the very vitality and vigor of Coleman's electronic music—not to mention good humor—is in con-

Ornette Coleman: The *vox populi* of free jazz, his Prime Time ensemble communicated beyond his usual following. (Photograph by Stuart Nicholson.)

trast to Miles Davis's ambient prefurlough albums such as *Pangaea* and *Agharta* of around the same time period, which reflected the trumpeter's progressive disenchantment with jazz. Coleman, it seemed, was close to realizing his earlier dream of creating a music of the past, present, and future. *Body Meta,* recorded at the same time as *Dancing in Your Head,* lacked the former's jarring focus, sounding perhaps more like a work-in-progress though exploring more moods.

Although these two albums appeared at the time as a radical departure from Coleman's acoustic work, he had brought an electric guitar across his acoustic threshold in the early 1970s in the person of Jim Hall on the album *Broken Dreams,* although this was not released until 1982. Consequently, the radical realignment of his music with electric sounds appeared without precedent when these albums were originally released in the 1970s. Yet Coleman's approach to improvising had changed little; indeed, the explicit rhythmic pulse in his music could even be traced back to "T&T" (1961). Although much has been made of his harmolodic theories that underwrote this music, when Coleman himself attempted to explain these principles[6] it was impossible to decipher what he meant. Like harmolodic music itself, total understanding and comprehension remained tantalizingly beyond one's grasp. But what these albums made clear was the primacy of melody (Coleman's saxophone) over rhythm. Any system of cadences was abandoned in favor of polymodality; several simultaneous tonal centers allowed Coleman's melodic brief to roam free on the impulse of the moment, the rhythm section converging around him like a drum choir with each instrument acting rhythmically in a way that forsook traditional harmonic thinking.

Of Human Feelings, recorded on April 25, 1979 but not released until 1982, presented a far more cogent statement than was realized on either *Dancing in Your Head* or *Body Meta.* Using essentially the same personnel as the earlier albums, Charlie Ellerbee and Bernie Nix (a Berklee graduate who, until Coleman intervened, was on the verge of becoming a security guard) on guitars and the virtuoso bassist Jamaaladeen Tacuma, the only change was bringing Calvin Weston in for Shannon Jackson on drums. It was this stability of personnel that made such a radical shift in ensemble conventions appear so cohesive. Here was a visceral intensity that was just as focused as any of his acoustic recordings and seemed to establish a connection between punk-rock and jazz, even though Coleman's harmolodics—which indeed sounded "punk"—had none of punk's hallmarks such as feedback guitars, snarled vocals, and brevity. In fact it seemed to be Coleman's rhythmic impatience and delight in discord (the jazz equivalent to punk noise) that made his music "sound" punk. It was Coleman's claim that anyone in the band was free to solo or play rhythm at any time, and this took the form of free collective improvisation. As early as 1960, in the liner notes to *Free Jazz,* Coleman had said, "The most important thing was for us to play together all at the same time, without getting in each other's way and also have enough room for each player to ad-lib alone." After almost twenty years this principle remained the same; the only thing different was that now the musicians congregated around a funky backbeat. Coleman, the major soloist and voice of reason within the ensemble, now had a band whose music communicated beyond the perimeter of free jazz.

"Love Words" made it clear that no limitations were imposed on the use of polymodality, the heart of harmolodics. Coleman, having set mood and tempo, launches out on an extended improvisation that appears free of predetermined harmonic relationships against a backdrop suggesting West African rhythmic complexity in its dense textures and a collective spirit of improvisation that could be traced back to New Orleans jazz. "Sleep Talk" seemed to have been derived from the opening bassoon solo in Stravinsky's *The Rite of Spring* and emerges as a genial excursion that can be returned to time and again. Early Coleman laments such as "Lonely Woman" or "Sadness" are echoed in the first section of "What Is the Name of That Song?" before being claimed by a contrasting funky section. "Times Square" is an atonal strut, a surreal excursion into a twenty-second-century dance music, a testament to Coleman's race to keep one step ahead of history. Yet, as always in Coleman's playing, the blues remained at the heart of his music: "Jump Street" is a blues with a bridge.

In 1986 Coleman collaborated with the guitarist Pat Metheny on *Song X*. It revealed a steely edge to the guitarist's playing that left his more temperate fans somewhat shell-shocked. When the album was released, it created instant controversy, but, despite an ambivalent critical response, it sold some 200,000 copies in the first year of its release, quite astonishing sales for an avant-garde album, and won the *Downbeat* readers' poll as "Jazz Album of the Year." It suggested that Coleman might be the vox populi of free jazz—indeed, since his Five Spot debut in 1959 he quite probably always had been.

In 1987–1988, Prime Time was invited by the Grateful Dead to open their concerts for them. "There were moments that were truly magical," said Peter Apfelbaum. "The Dead really understood what Ornette was doing. He probably played for about forty minutes without stopping, and then when they did their own tunes Bob Weir would sing and then he'd step back for Ornette to play. At the end it was more interesting. Because rather than the Dead improvising and taking it out in deference to Ornette, here was Ornette superimposed on top of the Dead, playing on their music, which was really way out. That was where the magic was to me—having Ornette superimposed over just a simple rock song. It was incredible, really free, yet really lyrical."[7]

Coleman's association with the Dead lead to an invitation to Jerry Garcia to guest on Prime Time's upcoming record date, *Virgin Beauty* (1987). "He had a beautiful tone and a fantastic ear," said Coleman later. "When he played with us, I just told him, 'Play yourself.' I showed him some things I'd been working on. He took his guitar and started, and that's what he did. He played really well. We tried to get him to do a tour with us, but he was so busy with his own band and the Dead. But he said, 'Yeah, I'm going to do it, I'm going to do it.' Because lots of rock musicians welcome ways of going out and doing something different, to change. I know I'm trying to get my band more visibility without being compared to any other music. It's hard."[8]

Coleman's work in both acoustic and electric settings has continued into the nineties, exploring the fringes of jazz and jazz-rock music. *Tone Dialling* (1995), described as "one of his sunniest albums,"[9] revealed Coleman at sixty-six as electrifying as ever. *Sound Museum–Hidden Man* and *Sound Museum–Three Women* (both 1996) were by his acoustic group, The New Quartet—with Geri Allen on piano, Charnett Moffett on bass, and his son Deonardo on drums. When promo copies of the album were sent out, included was a jigsaw that read, "Remove the caste system from sound."

Coleman's concepts were adapted by some of the graduates from his electric ensembles. Ronald Shannon Jackson had been the drummer on Coleman's first two Prime Time releases and had his vision further sharpened working in the band of the guitarist James Blood Ulmer. He then formed his own ensemble, The Decoding Society, an octet that became a forum for his hyperactive rhythmic intensity, mixing electronic and acoustic instruments, rock rhythms and freedom, gritty textures and tightly arranged lines that brought a sense of party to the harmolodic rainbow. Playing his own compositions, he created a slashing rhythmic undertow that fell somewhere between funk, rock, and avant-garde coloration. *Eye On You* (1980), introduced the group, heralding a series of exuberant albums through the eighties: *Barbeque Dog,* which traded control and adventure in equal measures; *De-Code Yourself,* which contained the first non-Jackson composition recorded by the band, a version of Dizzy Gillespie's "Be-bop" that said all you needed to know about the band in 49 coruscating seconds; *Pulse,* which, like so many of Jackson's albums, appears inexplicable at first, the leader's shamanic drumming the focal point of his idiomatically oblique ensemble image; and *Texas,* possibly his finest album since *Barbeque Dog.* From *Raven Roc* (1992) forward, Jackson performed with a slimmed-down personnel of two guitars, bass, and drums, presenting a metal perspective on harmolodics.

Jackson's message is that there are many ways to swing, march, shamble, or hip-hop, and that the classifications that were pinned on him in the 1980s—No-Wave, funk-jazz, punk-jazz—were only part of a hyphenated maze of possible pigeonholes to slot his music into. But Jackson's groups, for all their initial angularity and on-the-edge ensemble work, were overreliant on his powerful rhythmic personality. Even Vernon Reid on guitar and Melvin Gibbs on bass, who both appeared on Jackson's earlier albums, seemed unable to command attention in the way their leader did, something that even the most tightly knit ensemble playing could not compensate for. Even so, after early fusion's pilgrimage through mysticism, European romanticism, and the infinities of space—with the Mahavishnu Orchestra, Chick Corea, and Herbie Hancock, respectively—Coleman and Jackson represented a return to and reinvestigation of urban black sensibilities, bringing the music back to the inner city, with occasional trips to Africa, just as Sly Stone, Stevie Wonder, and Marvin Gaye had done in pop music during the early 1970s.

The headlong march of Jackson's drums was also the energizing factor behind Last Exit and Power Tools, a quartet and trio that respectively pared down the dizzying multilayered textures of Prime Time and the Decoding Society to establish a more elemental, one-to-one expressionism. But it was Last Exit that represented perhaps the most exciting merger of the crude and the complex in jazz. Guitarist Sonny Sharrock, German saxophonist Peter Brötzmann, bassist and producer Bill Laswell, and Jackson took the raw energy of Jimi Hendrix and expanded it onto a broader canvas. Sharrock, who debuted on records on Pharoah Sanders's 1967 *Tahid,* made an uncredited appearance on Miles Davis's *Jack Johnson* and at various times between 1967 and 1974 was a disruptive element in flautist Herbie Mann's otherwise lightweight jazz combo. After constant knocking for being too far out, he quit music to work with the emotionally disturbed until producer Bill Laswell introduced him to New York's Downtown experimenters in the early 1980s, enabling him to enjoy a career renaissance until his death in 1994.[10]

With Last Exit, Sharrock's "shards of splintered glass," Brötzmann's energy and Jackson's cavalry charges gave shape to a modernist vision of angst as meaning and ugliness as an aspect of authenticity. The collage of the past and the present presented in the mini-suite "Straw Dog/You Got Me Rockin'/Take Cover/Ma Rainey/Crack Butter" from *The Noise of Trouble* (1986) took the lis-

Last Exit: The dynamic, disruptive elements of a memorable ensemble of 1980s jazz, Peter Brötzmann and Sonny Sharrock. Bill Laswell and Ronald Shannon Jackson do not appear in this photograph. (Photograph by Stuart Nicholson.)

tener from Jimmy Reed to Ma Rainey, from heavy metal to Delta blues, from avant-garde jazz to punk-rock in the shadow of Hendrix's more deconstructionist urges. These reference points speed by in a dizzying fury of sound; there is joy and terror in Sharrock's guitar—he once said "I've been trying to find a way for the terror and the beauty to live together in one song"[11]—and his is a central force amid this interweaving of diverse musical elements. Sharrock's guitar is focused; his blistering speed combined with his use of raw noise has both the openness of jazz and the power of rock. "What we were trying to do was explore higher levels of intensity which meant overlooking the traditional systems of music. What is often overlooked is the rhythmic interaction between me and Shannon. He came out of the blues while I came out of Country music, so you had this confluence of American musics," said Laswell.[12] Perhaps here was a continuum of the Pandora's box opened up by Tony Williams's Lifetime.

Yet Last Exit, by rejecting traditional and historically acquired values, were paradoxically limited by them. Their emotional focus was narrow, appealing to one aspect of the human psyche: the "Godzilla Principle," the attraction of the strong and the ugly. In abandoning the system of cadences built around the well-tempered scale, they were limited to degrees of light or shade; to become more or less ugly, to become more or less loud, to favor more or less abstraction, to become more or less implicit rhythmically. The search for instantaneous impact was ultimately marked by a parallel search for depth, acknowledging impact has no sustaining power over a period of time.

Jackson was equally creative on *Strange Meeting* (1987), recorded with the trio Power Tools (Bill Frisell and Melvin Gibbs); Frisell and Jackson stepped back to allow each other space to breathe, a musical standoff that allowed their mutual creativity to grow in stature. "Playing with Frisell—who has a spacious sense—allows rhythmic ideas I'm already working on to work," Jackson explained, "[so I can] play with the energy and expressionism the drums are capable of."[13]

Like Jackson, guitarist James "Blood" Ulmer was drawn into Coleman's orbit in the mid-1970s, moving into Coleman's Manhattan loft for a year to study the harmolodic theory. They played the 1974 Ann Arbor Jazz and Blues Festival and the 1977 Newport Jazz Festival together and made a lot of rehearsal tapes that culminated in Ulmer's first album, *Tales of Captain Black* (1978). Alongside Jamaaladeen Tacuma on bass, Deonardo Coleman on drums, and Coleman himself on alto, Ulmer sounded like the return of a cutting-edge Jimi Hendrix, full of tonal distortions and savage riffing. His sound was not entirely unrelated to what was going on in rock music, with punk the then-current craze. In fact,

James "Blood" Ulmer: A spacey conceptualist and post-Hendrix funkster, in the early 1980s there were elements of his style that had much in common with punk's dissolution of rock's certainties. (Photograph by Stuart Nicholson.)

Ulmer's group played the Manhattan punk joints as well as other ultra-hip venues, and certainly there were elements of his style that had much in common with punk's dissolution of rock's certainties. *Are You Glad To Be in America?* followed with Jackson on drums, bassist Amin Ali, and a front line of the saxophonists Oliver Lake and David Murray and the trumpeter Olu Dara. One reviewer quipped that they sounded like the Bar-Kays gone berserk.

With fusion bottoming out at the end of the 1970s, Columbia began showing interest in the jazz avant-garde who, after almost a decade of bloodletting, playing to an audience that consisted mainly of fellow musicians, a realization was dawning that total freedom in itself could be limiting. Gradually, musicians adept at playing outside the changes began creeping back inside them. One of the first to benefit from this new rationalization was the alto saxophonist Arthur Blythe, who in 1979 was signed by Columbia. His debut for the label, *Lennox Avenue Breakdown,* was strongly rhythmical, and had what Blythe described as "that body thang."[14] Ulmer's appearance on the album brought his playing to the attention of Columbia, who saw the guitarist as a strong influence in what appeared to be a new music breaking. "His oblique and eccentric stylings are so new and so right for these times. . . . When the music has stagnated someone has always come along to rejuvenate the scene. [Ulmer] has that aura," said *Downbeat.*[15] He was signed to the label in 1981, and his label debut, *Free Lancing,* saw Ulmer as both spacey conceptualist and post-Hendrix funkster. Having expressed populist ambitions in the music press prior to the album, it came as no surprise that three tracks were supported by female backup vocalists. Even so, it was a refreshing blast in the face of what fusion had become; clearly Blood's vision embraced a new idiom that attempted to subsume jazz, rock, and soul in one transcendendant unity, something new, nerve-jangling, and raw. *Black Rock* (1982) in essence continued the search for an avant-garde fusion by tacking harmolodics onto a backbeat. More successful was *Odyssey* (1983), a trio with Ulmer, Charles Burnham on violin, and Warren Benbow on drums that returned to the format Ulmer often used live, mixing his Hendrixesque guitar with Hendrixesque vocals that retraced his Southern roots—"Little Red House," "Love Dance," and "Swing & Thing"—and reexamined his original composition "Are You Glad to Be in America?," a number he was convinced would eventually be some kind of hit recording.

With Wynton Marsalis achieving the success predicted for Ulmer and Blythe, Columbia dropped Ulmer's contract. In any event, his more satisfying work was already to be found on a series of independent labels. He continued to record through the eighties, briefly resurfacing on a major record label, this time for the reconstituted Blue Note records, in 1987 with *America—Do You Remember the Love?* Featuring Bill Laswell on bass and Shannon Jackson on drums, this album was both subdued and ironic in the title track and "I Belong in the U.S.A." Post-Blue Note, Ulmer's recorded work appeared on the Japanese DIW label, featuring three groups he formed to reveal separate aspects of his performing personality: Phalanx, the Quartette Indigo—a string quartet—and Music Revelation Ensemble. "Before I tried to do everything at once," he said in 1994. "But now I want to separate the styles of my music, I don't want to play all mixed up. . . . Now I don't do but three things, I do records of songs, I have the Music Revelation Society which plays harmolodic music in instrumental form and I write music such as the string quartet music with guitar."[16] However, as the 1980s drew to a close, Ulmer's radical guitar had begun to sound out of place amid the pall of neoconservative conformity that had descended over jazz. "I'd like to play in America again, like I did in '81, '82, '83, '84—but something happened," he observed ruefully, having to travel to Europe and Japan for most of his work.[17]

Like Ulmer, Jean-Paul Bourelly was another guitarist who fell under the influence of Hendrix's playing, but he did little to extend its parameters, despite the debt his playing owed to the late guitar hero (and to Ulmer himself). By the time he had debuted as a leader in 1988 with *Jungle Cowboy,* Bourelly had worked with Elvin Jones, who had taken him under his wing when he was a teenager. Although he appeared on Miles Davis's *Amandla* in 1989, his style became associated with loud, Hendrix-like intemperance. With his group the BluWave Bandits, he found his voice, specializing in out musicianship and outright funk. On his albums, such as *Live! Fade to Cacophony* (1995), he created music that was a perfect antidote to middle-of-the-road "smooth jazz." "I'm interested in playing through the changes with a real psychedelic rock sensibility," he said. "I've had a lot of problems dealing with your typical jazz mentality. . . . To be real in art you gotta bring all your experiences to the table. I can't play Miles from '58 to '65 and have that be my zone. I mean, I grew up with Aretha and Led Zeppelin and Hendrix. That shit is real, man. And you gotta bring all of that in there or else you're just playing half your self, half of what you feel. . . . I'm not playing for a cat who's trying to have a glass of chablis on a white tablecloth and wants conversation. I'm really doing it for people who want to get a cathartic experience."[18] On *Tribute to Jimi,* also from 1995, Bourelly set out to show there was a political message in Hendrix's lyrics; while his playing avoided flash it often offered gritty, street level belligerence.

During periods when Prime Time was off the road, Coleman's bassist Jamaaladeen Tacuma almost succeeded in the theoretically impossible, creating a glossy version of the avant-garde. Tacuma was recruited by Coleman while still in high school, and after his playing on *Of Human Feelings* he was widely regarded as one of the most distinctive bassists to arrive in jazz since Jaco Pastorius. He had studied with Tyrone Brown (Grover Washington's former bassist) and Eligio Rossi of the Philadelphia Orchestra and had already acquired a formidable technique by the time he linked up with Coleman when he was eighteen years old. With his own band largely made up of musicians from his home town of Philadelphia, he retained the complex vertical structures of Prime Time but framed them within commercially accessible melodies with engaging hooks.

Tacuma's debut album as a leader, *Showstopper* (1983), covered several bases—chamber music, R&B, harmoldics, etc.—that all appeared a little glib. His response was that "the moment you're connected to only one style you're through."[19] On following albums, Tacuma presented compositions for string quartet, disco-fied jazz, and multitracked musings. By the decade's end, it was

clear that, in Tacuma's case, eclectic scope also meant lack of focus. Although
Jukebox (1988) at last showed some direction, by then his career had taken off in
a myriad of directions including production work for Harold Melvin and the
Bluenotes, Taj Mahal, and Grace Jones.

While Coleman's harmolodic credo appeared flexible enough to survive
Tacuma's glossy spin, it crashed down to earth at the hands of Joseph Bowie's
Defunkt. More determinedly ragged than Prime Time, Blood Ulmer, or
Shannon Jackson's avant-garde fusion of the 1980s, Bowie emphasized the funk,
drawing heavily on James Brown and George Clinton's P-Funkadelic, but was at
heart inspired by the electric Miles Davis. "Miles was a great idol of mine," said
Bowie, "mainly because of his fusion with rock 'n' roll music and jazz—I just
wanted to take that a step further and include the voice."[20] Bowie played body
music that penetrated the escapist glamour of black dance music to reveal the
bleak inner-city realities of life.

Joseph and his saxophone-playing brother Byron were at the heart of
Defunkt. The younger brothers of Lester Bowie of the Art Ensemble of Chicago
fame, they had formerly been proponents of "outside" music. Defunkt came
about after Joseph played with James Chance's Contortions and Blood Ulmer
on the No Wave circuit in the late 1970s. James Chance—given name James
Siegfried—and his Contortions appeared on Brian Eno's 1978 compilation *No
New York* and achieved a kind of notoriety among the arty SoHo audiences, with
Chance leaping into their midst and fighting them for "not dancing." The music
was a cocktail of jazz sarcasm, nihilist funk, and punk nuisance. Chance, never
predictable, renamed the group James White and the Blacks with a horn section
now led by Joseph Bowie. The Blacks' horn section, under Bowie's stewardship,
then mutated into Defunkt, a band that made conventional mainstream jazz curl
at the edges.

Their debut album, *Defunkt* (1980), included the Ulmer-influenced guitar-
man Kelvyn Bell, Melvin Gibbs on bass, Byron on sax, Ronnie Burrage on
drums, and Ted Daniel on trumpet. Bowie's in-your-face vocals anticipated rap
by over five years, but the joy of the band lay in its sheer visceral power in numbers like "Make Them Dance," "Strangling Me With Your Love," and
"Thermonuclear Sweat." This last piece became the title of their second album,
from 1982, Bowie's sardonic edge growing in confidence, lending rage to the
O'Jays antimaterialistic message on "For the Love of Money." While guitars carried the music over the funk-locked bass line, the front line splashed their solos
over the rhythmic stew, none more convincingly than the leader, particularly on
The Razor's Edge (1983).

After almost five years of inactivity after a lapse into substance abuse, Bowie
returned to performing in 1987. "Right now I'm concentrating on clarity," he
said, outlining his credo: "High energy is really important, we still uses elements
of avant garde jazz. I'm interested in getting a big clean sound. I want relevant,
sometimes ambiguous, but pertinent lyricism used, I want a lot of rhythm used
and I want it stated very clearly."[21] The band's defining characteristic, a potent
combination of rock, funk, jazz, and soul, was influential in the music of bands

like Living Color (Vernon Reid was a member of Defunkt in the early 1980s), Fishbone, and rock-funk-rappers The Red Hot Chili Peppers ("Really nice guys, they're quick to acknowledge we made an influence," Bowie said).[22] The band continued to make albums, and although their work was never especially well recorded, the dance floor remained the best place to experience them.

By the mid-1980s, Kelvyn Bell had left Defunkt to form his own band Kelvynator, but he was also hanging out and performing with a Brooklyn cooperative of like-minded musicians including the trumpeter Graham Haynes, the drummers Marvin "Smitty" Smith and Mark Johnson, the alto saxophonist Greg Osby, the vocalist Cassandra Wilson, the trombonist Robin Eubanks, and the guitarist Jean-Paul Bourelly. This loose coalition of rebels gathered around the aegis of alto saxophonist Steve Coleman, perhaps the most original and talented musician of his generation. Coleman built on the funky ostinatos of Defunkt, sharply refining and sophisticating their instrumental and rhythmic approach, mixing the influence of James Brown with the jazz tradition to create a music he called M-Base, an equal and opposite reaction to the 1980s regression into hard bop. The name M-Base was decided partly as a preemptive strike so that the artists could retain control over their music, rather than have the critics pigeonhole it under "crossover," "fusion," or "jazz-funk," and partly to emphasize that what was on offer was something "new," something marketable. "I like to have certain elements in my music," Coleman said, "something for people who want to dance, something for people who are intellectual and want to find some abstract meaning and something for people who just want to forget their troubles."[23] As a marketing strategy it worked; the jazz world, like the worlds of pop, rock, and classical, are always vulnerable to the record company claim of something "new," and jazz writers seized upon M-Base as the coming thing.

Coleman called his group Five Elements, which, like Red Nichols's Five Pennies sixty years before, had no relationship to the headcount. They debuted with *Motherland Pulse,* which included an excellent vocal by Cassandra Wilson in "No Good Time Fairies" that effectively launched her solo career. At the core of the music were chattering funk rhythms. "[It's] not a pop band," asserted Coleman. "There's so much improvisation in what we do you have to call it jazz."[24] The albums *On the Edge of Tomorrow, World Expansion,* and *Sine Die* followed, polyrhythmic and polytonal, giving an overall impression of a rococo jazz funk despite the rhythmic subtleties that were a feature of Coleman's compositions. More rewarding was his work in tandem with the altoist Greg Osby with Strata Institute; Coleman called it "a dialect of the M-Base language." *Cipher Syntax,* recorded in March–April 1988, fulfilled Coleman's intention to keep M-Base in touch with the dance floor while relying on the inventiveness of the musicians to communicate. The more expansive *Transmigration,* recorded in January 1991 with guest Von Freeman on tenor sax, introduced some nonoriginal material for the first time: Henry Mancini's "Mr. Lucky," Tadd Dameron's "If You Could See Me Now," and Eddie "Lockjaw" Davis's "Jimdog" to accommodate Freeman. The straight-ahead rhythms appear as a shaft of light, bringing

Steve Coleman: An inclusive vision of jazz that touched base with the polyrhythmic complexity of James Brown. (Photograph by Stuart Nicholson.)

a touch of humanity to a band that appeared to be adhering too scrupulously to a rulebook that was in danger of excluding rather more than it included.

In 1990 Coleman signed with BMG/Novus and debuted on the label with *Rhythm People,* which brought a tighter focus to his music. The title track paid homage to James Brown's "Cold Sweat," which says a lot about the source of Coleman's inspiration for polyrhythmic complexity—as in Brown's music, everyone is a drummer in M-Base. But while the band's rhythmic home might have been with the J.B.'s—"I think the music that we grew up with stays with you throughout your life," he explained in 1997[25]—his vista extended from the virtuosity of Charlie Parker to the polytonality of Ornette Coleman through to Public Enemy, with some arcane rapping by the leader in "Dangerous" and "No Conscience." While the 1980s had produced what appeared to be a series of interesting works in progress, here Coleman seemed to be getting closer to the finished article. However, his nineties output continued to be variable, with perhaps his best work occuring with the "Hot Brass" trilogy, recorded live during a weeklong stint in Paris in March 1995: *Curves of Life* (with guest David Murray on two tracks) with the Five Elements, *Myths Modes and Means* with the Mystic Rhythm Society, and *The Way of the Cipher* with the Metrics.

Greg Osby's career remained rooted in M-Base thinking for his own projects, as well as performing in an impressive array of groups with musicians such as Andrew Hill, Jack DeJohnette, Cecil Brooks III, Michelle Rosewoman, and Jon Faddis. "My development is more accelerated than it would be if I played with my peers," he explained. "Being under the apprenticeship of someone who's done more than you is really important to growing as an artist."[26] After graduating from Berklee College of Music his music constantly remained open to new ideas, although his albums sometimes seemed anticlimactic, considering the talent he brought to bear to interpret his work. "During the late 1980s and early 1990s, the saxophonist Greg Osby seemed ready to make a contribution to jazz," said the *New York Times*. "He had a distinct sound and improvisational approach, knotty and complex. But he moved out of New York . . . and he's been a shadowy presence ever since, experimenting with a blend of hip-hop and jazz improvisation that hasn't always worked."[27] After cutting an uneven series of albums in the late eighties, he signed with Blue Note records in 1990; his label debut, *Man-Talk for Moderns Vol. X,* was Osby's personal take on M-Base; it included guests Steve Coleman and Gary Thomas. *3-D Lifestyles* (1993), took on rap but was a flop. His third album for Blue Note, *Black Book* (1995), like Steve Coleman's *Def Trance Beat (Modalities of Rhythm)* from the same year, continued to experiment with off-center, hip-hop beats with ensemble passages meant (more or less) to duplicate the functions of a sampling machine. Osby's was the more jazz-flavored disc of the two, with heavy doses of beat poetry commenting on the current scene. *Art Forum,* from the following year, saw him moving back to straight-ahead jazz. Perhaps it was there, rather than following in his close friend Steve Coleman's footsteps, that he could best realize his undeniable talent.

When cornetist Graham Haynes recorded his second album in 1994, *The Griot's Footsteps,* the music was anything but M-Base. Instead, he was looking to the distant horizons of World music, in particular African, Arabic, and Indian musics, to blend with funk and jazz. In the liner notes, he thanks everyone from Alfred Hitchcock to Brian Eno for their "Inspiration, Insight and Influence," underlining that this generation of jazz musicians were brought up against a background of sixties and seventies pop culture, so why shouldn't the music of Jimi Hendrix, Sly Stone, Donny Hathaway, and James Brown be reflected in their music along with that of John Coltrane, Woody Shaw, and Booker Little? Haynes, an accomplished cornet player, mixed his influences so much that the album is in danger of losing focus. But good solos from the leader and the British sax whiz Steve Williamson largely compensate, although the sitar-heavy "Enlightenment" wanders on for an interminable twenty-seven minutes.

Transition (1995), returns to urban New York, with samples and scratching that seize the street beat as Miles Davis did with *On the Corner, Tutu,* and *Doo-Bop,* but had nothing significant to add.

If by the mid-1990s both Haynes and Osby appeared coming greats yet to arrive, then so too did saxophonist Gary Thomas. Making his debut with *Seventh Quadrant* in 1987, he impressed with *Code Violations* the following year, and with echoes of the Varitone from twenty years before, the saxophonist employed an IVL Pitchrider tracked by a MIDI synthesizer. "Instead of having the synthesizer play parallel notes," Thomas explained, "I assigned a different harmony note to each note I play on the saxophone; I set it up the way I prefer to hear notes run together. It's mixed low. I wasn't going to put the synthesizer up front—I mean, I still play the saxophone."[28] His already rugged tenor saxophone sound at once achieved more depth with a ghostly halo of sound made possible by the new technology. In both ensemble and solos, it added a new dimension to the tenor that was as attractive as the Varitone was repellent. His compositions, all originals, were in general well thought out and were more flexible than straightforward funk grooves, allowing for harmonic and rhythmic interaction from the rhythm section. His 1990 album *By Any Means Necessary* presented a clear vision of his musical range, with a strong lineup that included John Scofield and Mick Goodrick on guitars, Greg Osby on alto, Gery Allen on keyboards, Anthony Cox on bass, and Dennis Chambers on drums. Conceptually, Thomas seemed to have struck a darker, deeper side to jazz-funk than Coleman and Osby, winning a Bronze Award from Japan's *Swing Journal.* The following year, *While the Gate is Open* took the Gold Award. It was an album that featured an impressive reading of standards, with Renee Rosnes on piano, sometime M-Base member Kevin Eubanks on guitar, Dave Holland on bass, and Dennis Chambers on drums. "[The success of *While the Gate Is Open*] tells me people aren't ready to hear original compositions," said Thomas, "They're in this standards groove perpetuated by this new wave of young players . . . but the tradition is ultimately about creating something new."[29]

Exile's Gate (1993) continued his bold uncompromising essays in electronic jazz-rock-funk that were not getting the exposure they deserved in the retro climate of the 1990s, dominated by a comfortably accessible acoustic mainstream. His response to this conservatism was the ghetto-blast *Overkill* (1995), which came with a record company warning: "This Compact Disc contains language that may cause offense." Nihilistic lyrics were the name of the game in Thomas's no joke–no hope scenario using hardcore rappers who exploded with frustrated, furious gangsta-style messages like "I don't give a fuck about how you feel, I just want you to feel the steel, poundin' at your fuckin' head." Approaching themes of racism, sexism, AIDS, drugs, black-on-black violence, and moral depravity certainly had social relevance, but musically it was a limited meeting of two musical forms, the lyrics edging Thomas to the margins as an occasional participant on his own album with obbligatos and short solos. But of all the jazz-rap experimenters, from Donald Byrd to Slim Gaillard, Thomas could at least claim the distinction of grappling with the idiom in an authentic manner.

In 1986 Thomas had begun an association with drummer Jack DeJohnette's Special Edition. Formed in 1979, Special Edition's eponymously titled debut album was a swinging reconciliation of inside-outside expressionism. One of the key ensembles of the 1980s, their continually evolving conceptualism created two memorable acoustic albums—*Tin Can Alley* (1980) and *Inflation Blues* (1982)—before looking to expand their horizons with rock and World beats and electric instrumentation.

With *Album Album* (1984) DeJohnette incorporated the new technology, rock rhythm patterns and a front line of three first-rate improvisers in David Murray, John Purcell, and Howard Johnson to produce one of the finest albums of the 1980s. "New Orleans Strut" and "Third World Anthem" showed how his inclusive vision could move jazz forward in an emotionally and aesthetically convincing way in the 1980s. When Thomas and Greg Osby joined the band, they added an M-Base flavor to *Irresistible Forces* (1987) and *Audio Visual Landscapes* (1988), although DeJohnette's personality continued to shape the music.

DeJohnette could also be heard on several key albums by the guitarist John Abercrombie, appearing on the memorable and impetuously driven *Gateway* (1975) with the addition of Dave Holland on bass. "I always think meeting Jack was one of the big turning points," said Abercrombie in 1994. "Just being able to play different kinds of music within one band and not being stuck into the fusion

Gateway: *Left to right:* Dave Holland, Jack DeJohnette, John Abercrombie. Memorable and impetuously driven. (Photograph by Stuart Nicholson.)

bag . . . 'multi dimensional' music as Jack would call it . . . being able to play very abstract jazz music, but still play standard songs, write our own material, improvise and delve into more abstracted rock-type fields."[30] This freeform approach to improvisation was wholly absorbing in the hands of such accomplished musicians, and in 1978 the group reconvened to record *Gateway 2.* Yet it was not for another seventeen years that the project was resurrected with *Homecoming* (1995) and *In the Moment* (1996).

In the interim, Abercrombie had appeared in a variety of contexts for the ECM label, often in the hushed surroundings of a trio with Marc Johnson and Peter Erskine that evoked memories of the late Bill Evans's trio. However, from 1987 they were joined from time to time by Mike Brecker.[31] Abercrombie's debut on the ECM label had been with *Timeless* in 1974, with a trio including Jan Hammer on keyboards and Jack DeJohnette, which at the time appeared as a highly creative abstraction of jazz-rock. Ten years later the group was reassembled with the addition of Mike Brecker for *Night,* one of the latter-day classics of jazz-rock. This was tight, dramatic, and creative music-making of the highest order. In 1993 Abercrombie formed a trio with the organist Dan Wall and the drummer Adam Nussbaum that once again set about expanding the tradition through untraditional means: *While We're Young, Speak of the Devil,* and *Tactics.*

Both Marc Johnson and Peter Erskine were key elements in the group Bass Desires, an occasional quartet that paired the guitarists Bill Frisell and John Scofield to create one of the most critically acclaimed ensembles of the 1980s. The group was convened by Johnson, an accomplished bassist who had distinguished himself with Woody Herman and the pianist Bill Evans. *Bass Desires* (1985) marked the debut of a strikingly original and exciting group. Among the album's highlights was a Johnson original, "Samurai Hee-Haw," which contrasted the styles of Frisell and Scofield, two of the most-admired musicians to emerge during the 1980s, in shimmering ensemble colors and solos. "I'm just the leader in quotation marks," said Johnson. "I see myself as co-ordinator, just getting everybody together and coming up with a few tunes."[32] Bass Desires was only made possible by juggling the busy schedules of the in-demand participants for a short tour for a few weeks each year. Their follow-up album, *Second Sight* (1987), continued the group's high level of conception and execution. Scofield's "Twister" was a subtle and affectionate parody of the Beatles' "Twist and Shout," while his robust "Thrill Seekers" was in contrast to the album's more reflective atmosphere epitomized by Erskine's original "Sweet Soul," a model of disciplined ensemble playing that later became the title track of the drummer's own album from 1991.

Bass Desires' elusive style resisted convenient pigeonholing, existing in that nebulous area halfway between post-bop and jazz-rock, much like the groups led by drummer Paul Motian, who had gained international recognition for his work in the hushed surrounds of the pianist Bill Evans's trio between 1959 and 1964. In 1980 he formed a forthright quintet with Joe Lovano and Jim Pepper on tenor saxophones, Bill Frisell on guitar, and Ed Schuller on bass, with Lovano and

Bill Frisell and Marc Johnson: Here performing together as part of Bass Desires, one of the most critically acclaimed groups of the 1980s. (Photograph by Stuart Nicholson.)

Frisell the standouts on the group's recordings. With *One Time Out* (1987), Motian began using just Lovano and Frisell, inaugurating a run of some of the most creative and aesthetically satisfying jazz to be heard in the late 1980s and early 1990s.

The distinctive sound of the trio was mediated by Bill Frisell's revolutionary approach to the guitar by pulling the apparently opposing poles of Jim Hall and Jimi Hendrix under one roof. His style was unique, his imagination broad, and the result was the most individual guitar style heard in years. "Every few years a guitarist appears who manages to wring something new out of the most played instrument in the world," said the *New York Times*.[33] Motian's sparse trio of tenor saxophone, guitar, and drums left the musicians nowhere to hide, and they consistently responded with a high level of creativity. In 1994, with increasing demands on the accelerating careers of both Frisell and Lovano, Motian formed his Electric Bebop Band with Kurt Rosenwinkel and Wofgang Muthspiel on guitars, Chris Potter and Chris Cheek on saxophones, Steve Swallow on bass, and Don Alias on percussion; *The Electric Bebop Band* (1993) and *Reincarnation of a Love Bird* (1990).

Frisell's career as a leader in his own right had begun on the ECM label as early as 1982, but it wasn't until 1988 that he had a regular group of his own with Hank Roberts on cello, Kermitt Driscoll on bass, and Joey Baron on drums. By then Frisell had moved some distance from the eerie originals of his ECM output to embrace the more robust thinking of saxophonist John Zorn, with whom he frequently performed and who produced Frisell's 1989 album *Before We Were Born.* Frisell's 1990s albums documented the artistic growth of an important, original jazz voice. *Live* (1995) is an excellent representative album of his highly creative trio. "What we do comes out of jazz," explained Frisell. "I think it has a lot of the kind of stuff that attracted me to jazz in the first place, but we don't confine ourselves to a certain era or a certain style. We use everything we know, everything that's around us. As a matter of fact, that's what all the great players always did, isn't it?"[34]

In 1996, Frisell tried a new approach with Ron Miles on trumpet, Eyvind Kang on violin, and Curtis Fowlkes on trombone, creating a rather self-conscious evocation of a chamber group that appeared rather precious. Ron Miles, however, proved to be an original thinker on his own albums, *My Cruel Heart* (1996) and *Woman's Day* (1997), again showing the importance of an inclusive rather than an exclusive viewpoint as a basis of finding a voice in jazz. What is especially interesting is "You Taste," from the latter album, where he uses a slow, floating Wayne Shorter-esque theme of sustained tones played with Miles Davis-like delicacy over a rhythmically turbulent, heavy-metal backdrop. In this track, Ron Miles achieves a corollary with electric instruments to what Miles Davis did in his acoustic quartet of 1965–1968 by shifting the burden of complexity from the front line to the rhythm section. The result is startling when one realizes that Davis himself did not employ this approach when he went electric, preferring, instead, free-form collectivism; Ron Miles succeeds in suggesting that this might have been a logical path for Davis to have pursued into jazz-rock—even down to the distortion-laden Hendrix guitar.

Frisell was a part of what has become known as the "Downtown" scene in New York, a vibrant and vigorous experimental forum dedicated to stretching the generic word "jazz" to accommodate what the *New York Times* called "music that flew past the pigeonholes."[35] Many of these experimenters made regular appearances at Michael Dorf's Knitting Factory, originally a four-story walkup at 47 East Houston Street that was formerly an Avon products office. The club became a magnet for talent, open seven nights a week. "The New York music scene, from jazz to rock, was desperate at this time for a new venue," said Dorf. "The 'jazz' clubs—The Blue Note, Sweet Basil, The Village Vanguard, Carlos I, The Angry Squire and so on—were all in line with the George Wein's [Newport, Kool, and JVC Jazz Festivals] definition of jazz."[36] Within eighteen months the club had established a whole new experimental music scene. "The Knitting Factory is at the center of an international music movement," said the *Wall Street Journal,* "acclaimed for having single handedly invigorated, if not created, an eclectic post-punk jazz-rock scene."[37]

The first jazz artist to play the club was the keyboard player Wayne Horvitz. *This New Generation* (1987) by his group, The President, combined jazz (phrases rather than solos), gamelan music, and electronically generated sounds that evoked a computer-like soundscape where the composer was firmly in control. Solos came and went as part of the music's overall architecture. "One of the best discs representing the lively East Village scene," said the *New York Times*.[38] *Bring Yr Camera* (1988) brought the group into sharper focus with more pronounced rock rhythms laid down by drummer Bobby Previte. With *Miracle Mile* (1992), Horvitz produced a wholly compelling album of wit and originality that was in sharp contrast to the more fashionable, but predictable, offerings elsewhere in jazz. Horvitz was a restless experimenter: his other group Pig Pen was dedicated to more recondite impulses and sampling, while the New York Composers Orchestra, a project he ran jointly with his wife, the composer and pianist Robin Holcomb, performed works by them both, as well as Anthony Braxton, Marty Ehrlich, Bobby Previte, Lenny Pickett, and others.[39]

Alto saxophonist, iconoclast, and arch conceptualist John Zorn was responsible for the first line outside the Knitting Factory when he premiered his group Hu Die, featuring two guitars and a narration in Korean. Zorn's imagination never stood still, from his coruscating *Spy vs. Spy* with Tim Berne, dedicated to impacting as many Ornette Coleman tunes onto the head of a pin as possible, to his group Masada, that played music with a Hebraic tinge. His group Naked City, comprising Zorn, Horvitz on keyboards, Bill Frisell on guitar, Fred Frith on bass, and Joey Baron on drums, was unquestionably the most startling band in contemporary jazz. The group came together to produce a series of rehearsal-concerts at the Knitting Factory in 1989. "The five days and nights Naked City

John Zorn and Naked City: *Left to right:* Wayne Horvitz, Zorn, Fred Frith. (Joey Baron not shown.) The best band of its kind in the world, because it was the only band of its kind, with a fluency in all musical languages and a breathtaking ability to speak them all at once. (Photograph by Stuart Nicholson.)

played and rehearsed were amazing," said Michael Dorf. "John came in at 10 A.M. and passed out a booklet of songs he had prepared for everyone. By the 8 P.M. showtime, the group had learnt 25 songs and played them for a standing-room only crowd in our new [performance] space. The next morning, the band came in, John gave them 15 new songs and by showtime they had those down and played some of the old material. This went on each day. In five days they had a whole repertory and went on a European tour as if they had been together for years."[40]

The concept of Naked City had grown out of two album-length statements, *The Big Gundown* (1985), dedicated to the music of Ennio Morricone, and *Spillane* (1987), a celebration of the film noir in general and the Mike Hammer character in particular. The latter, a largely programmatic piece with powerful, compulsively changing imagery relentlessly aroused the listener's curiosity by defying expectations; the title track, for example, charges through sixty sections in twenty-five minutes. These abrupt changes of musical direction that seemed to turn on a dime were dubbed "jump-cuts," something Zorn, a compulsive TV addict always searching for old movies, likened to channel-zapping. Zorn's jump-cuts reflected his interest in the cartoon music of Carl W. Stalling, of whom he wrote, "[Stalling followed] the visual logic of screen action rather than the tradi-tional rules of musical form," thus creating "a radical compositional arc unprece-dented in the history of music."[41] Other musical references swimming through Zorn's music included the music of the Black Artists Group in St. Louis, Stravinsky, Stockhausen, Varèse, the whole jazz tradition, and heavy metal thrash bands like Napalm Death and the speed-metal group Blind Idiot God.

With *Naked City* (1990) Zorn pared his sweeping extravaganzas *The Big Gundown* and *Spillane* down to their essence. The album is dotted with eight musical fragments of ferocious ear slaughter (between eight and thirty-two sec-onds at a time) that rub shoulders with Morricone's "The Sicilian Clan," Henry Mancini's "Shot in the Dark," "Batman" (a Zorn original), and Monty Norman's (not John Barry's) "The James Bond Theme," which attest to Zorn the movie freak; all were produced with great affection for the genre. Ornette Coleman's "Lonely Woman" is equipped with a Peter Gunn-like bass line and closes with a flourish from Coleman's "Dancing In Your Head," while "The Latin Quarter" is full of abruptly changing programmatic imagery, literally a stroll past the bars and cafés in Zorn's imagination. Overall, the album juxtaposed sound bites, shuffles, and overlapping sequences of thrash jazz, heavy metal melodrama, cocktail jazz, country boogie, Led Zeppelin, and surf music. Zorn's music sur-prised, startled, and delighted; part of the fun was hanging on for dear life through some thirty seconds of numbers like "Snagglepuss" to see what was on the other side. It was no exaggeration to say that Naked City was the best band of its kind in the world because it was the only band of its kind with a fluency in all musical languages and a breathtaking ability to speak them all at once.

Both *The Big Gundown* and *Spillane* featured Bobby Previte playing drums, who like Zorn, was more than an accomplished instrumentalist; he was a conceptualizer of great imagination and one of the foremost composers in jazz of his generation, described by the *New York Times* as one of the smartest composers to come of age in the 1980s.[42] He has written for film, video, television, theater, and dance, and for the Moscow State Circus, and he has contributed to the repertoire of the String Trio of New York. In 1990 he won *Downbeat* magazine's "Composer Deserving Wider Recognition," and in 1991 *Rolling Stone*'s "Hot Jazz Artist of the Year" awards. He made his debut as a leader with an acoustic band in 1985, but with his third album, *Claude's Late Morning* (1988), he began using electric tone colors including Bill Frisell's guitar and Josh Dubin on pedal steel guitar, plus a harp and accordion. It revealed Previte's growing maturity as a composer and produced one of the best albums of the 1980s. At this point, Previte decided to separate his acoustic and electric writing, forming the group Weather Clear, Track Fast to perform his acoustic compositions and Empty Suits for his electric ones.

In October 1990, *Empty Suits* was released, featuring his new band of the same name. Here rhythm became central to his ideas, around which the compositional structures were erected. His soloists slot their ideas within the parameters he set up, so that the written and improvised flow into each other naturally, rather than the head–solos–head disjunction of hard-bop. Although the rhythms are implicit and the tone colors electric, this was not simply jazz-rock, but something more expansive that embraced World music (specifically the Afropop juju of Sunny Ade), a Duane Eddyish twang that first appeared on Claude's *Late Morning,* mid-Eastern microtones in "Break the Cups," and minimalism in "Great Wall," plus a myriad of imaginative—and subtle—sonic juxtapositions. This is music that was of a whole, yet constructed from diverse influences that probably would never have existed without jazz-rock, the starting point for mixing diverse musical traditions to produce something quite new. Previte extended the boundaries with post-modernistic zeal, creating a unified musical vision that made its own space beyond jazz-rock and the mainstream. "Now that adherence to a museum curator's idea of authenticity has become the rallying cry, Previte's music argues for divergence and the freedom to ransack traditions however you choose," said *Downbeat,* awarding the album five stars.[43] It was followed by *Slay the Suitors,* released in Japan in May 1994, which spread his ideas over a broader canvas, allowing his musicians greater breathing space to inhabit and define his compositions with their own musical statements. Away from the comfortably accessible mainstream, Previte was moving jazz forward and redefining it in the process.

In May and June 1991, Previte had toured Europe with the Irish guitarist Christy Doran, tenor saxophonist Gary Thomas, and Mark Helias on bass. While Previte was dismissive of the resultant *Corporate Art* ("It's just a producer's idea of a band"), the drummer brings life and energy to what would otherwise be some so-so compositions: "You've got to make some concessions to make things work sometimes," he said.[44] While one suspects he would have liked to exert more control over the music rather than to paper over the cracks with some exceptionally inventive drumming, the result was a loose, rugged, contemporary jazz-rock jam that was light-years ahead of contemporary fusion. In 1996, Previte released *Close to the Pole* by Weather Clear, Track Fast, which actually seemed to evoke the electronic imagery of Empty Suits by acoustic means. Shortly after its release he said: "I have actually been experimenting with Weather Clear, Track Fast with two guitars instead of saxophones, so there you go, they're conflating, becoming Empty Track or maybe even Weather Suits!"[45] In January 1997, Previte formed the electric quartet Latin for Travellers and began playing Monday nights at the Knitting Factory with an eleven-piece ensemble, The Horse They Rode On, which celebrated the groundbreaking sounds of early jazz-rock.

Fellow downtowners Medeski, Martin, and Wood attacked their career more like a rock band than a jazz group, breaking out of the downtown scene to unprecedented cult status for a jazz group. Organist John Medeski studied at the New England Conservatory before moving to New York's downtown scene. Drummer Billy Martin studied drums with Joe Morello and Michael Carvin, and Latin percussion with Frankie Malabe, while bassist Chris Wood's resumé included studying at the New England Conservatory before moving onto the downtown scene.

Medeski Martin and Wood came together as a group in 1991, with *Notes From the Underground* following a year later. This had Medeski on piano plus fellow Downtowners Thomas Chapin, Doug Yates, Steve Bernstein, and others who responded to the trio's imaginative heads with audible passion. It was an impressive debut, ranging from Wayne Shorter to New Orleans in the typically eclectic fashion of Downtown bands, but there was also solid musicianship on show—"cocky bass line, nasty piano and rolling funk drums," said *Downbeat,* who awarded it four stars.

For the next two years, the trio traversed America, sleeping in campsites in their cramped RV, hauling their equipment behind them, and playing coffee-houses, discos, rock, and blues joints. And while this was not uncommon for rock acts it was highly unusual for a conservatory-trained jazz group. There was no great marketing plan at work other than to find enough work to keep the band together and develop as musicians. "We drove 500 miles between gigs and would be fired by the time we did our soundcheck," said Wood.[46] Adopted by Grateful Dead fans and the rock group Phish—who played MM&W tapes between their sets—they gradually began to build a following by reconnecting jazz to the dance floor with imaginative rhythmic jams that mixed blues, rock, and African rhythms with solid improvisation. Their second album, *It's a Jungle In Here* (1993), had Medeski on organ for most tracks. Wide-ranging in its imagination, its inspirations drew on the *Tutu*-era Miles Davis, King Sunny Ade, Sly Stone, and John Coltrane. In one imaginative sweep, they segued Monk's "Bemsha Swing" with Bob Marley's "Lively Up Yourself." In an album cast in the light of the band's main influences—soul-jazz of the late 1950s and early 1960s, New Orleans barrelhouse, early 1970s funk (James Brown, George Clinton), Sun Ra, Larry Young, and Booker T and the MGs—with a sense of fun (the ending of "Where's Sly?") the result stands as the trio's most imaginative recording.

In 1994, John Medeski combined with the guitarist David Fiuczynski on *Lunar Crush,* an album of power vamps and syncopated shuffles that reinvestigated the roots of jazz-rock, 1990s style. A mix of explosive solos and dense, eerie atmospheres, its charm lay in the over-the-top abandon of the participants. Its potential was left unexplored, however, as both musicians were committed to their own projects, Fiuczynski with Screaming Headless Torsos and Medeski with Martin and Wood. MM&W continued a run of critically acclaimed albums with *Friday Afternoon in the Universe* (1995) and *Shack Man* (1996), which concentrated on Hammond B-3 "grooves" that, as the *New York Times* observed, "did not forgo the pleasures of the backbeat."[47] Irresistible and to the point, their understanding of a wide range of music gave their eclecticism a contemporary edge, prompting the *The Boston Phoenix* to observe that there was "still hope for creative jazz fusion."[48]

The music of Medeski Martin and Wood was frequently referred to as "acid jazz," which as the end of the 1990s approached had become a catchall phrase for music that mixed contemporary dance rhythms with jazz themes and improvisations. The term "acid jazz" was coined in the late 1980s by Giles Peterson, a British disc jockey who used the term to describe his musical mix for the evening, a mixture of soul jazz, 1970s soul classics, jazz-funk, and almost anything that comfortably sat alongside these sounds. It reached New York in 1990 at a jazz-meets-hop club called the Giant Step, set in the small, tidy, marble-pillared basement of Metropolis Café at 31 Union Square West, run by Maurice Bernstein, a Briton, and Jonathan Rudnick, a South African. As DJs Smash and Jazzy Nice spun jazz, funk, and hip-hop records, a loose collective of musicians and rappers took turns improvising. With the success of Digable Planets, who debuted their single "Rebirth of Slick" at the club in 1992, things took off. Giant Step quickly grew into big business, spawning a management agency, a record company, and the Groove Academy, which presented Thursday night dances at the club. One of the bands they nurtured was Groove Collective, ten musicians linked by the common goal of playing improvised but danceable music. "When we step up to the mike," said trombonist Josh Roseman, "we're trying to summon the type of energy a rapper might have. We happily lean towards the classicism of trombone, saxophone, and trumpet, because it connects us to great dance music of the past like Count Basie and Duke Ellington."[49]

In 1992 the band became a regular Friday night attraction at a Soho club called Sybarie.[50] Three months later they cut *Groove Collective* live at the Giant Step, with Gordon "Nappy G" Clay on percussion and rap vocals, Fabio Morgera on trumpet, Josh Roseman on trombone, Jay Rodriguez and Richard Worth on saxophones, Bill Ware on vibraphone, Itaal Schuur on keyboards, Jonathan Maron on bass, Genji Siraisi on drums, and Chris Therberge on percussion. Here were bebop-sounding charts with a big beat, featuring solid solos from Morgera, Rodriguez, and Ware—the latter impressive on "Whatchugot"—that never let the temperature dip. *We the People* (1996) was a little sweet in parts, but when the band locked on to a groove they sounded as if they could play into the night, which indeed they did as a fixture on New York's music scene in the middle and late 1990s. "The whole thing about Groove Collective and Giant Step was learning how to spontaneously arrange on the stage so the groove is consistent," said Ital Schuur. "The audience plays an important part. . . . If they start dancing and get into the groove that's when it really locks up."[51] The Collective's "I Am" is a good of example of the band, although "Everybody (We the People)" veered a little close to 1970s disco, a common problem among the acid-jazz crowd.

Indeed, other acid-jazz bands produced a variety of musical styles that hark back to some of the excesses and empty pop sounds of the seventies. The Brand New Heavies' "Dream on Dreamer" and Jamiroquai's "Blow Your Mind" are lite-funk, while Incognito's "Sunburn" is lite-jazz, yet all came under the acid-jazz catchall. British guitarist Ronny Jordan was more convincing; his "new-jazz-swing" album *The Antidote* (1992) sped up *Billboard*'s chart, spending five weeks in the top five listings and selling over 200,000 copies thanks to his funked-up cover of Miles Davis's "So What." "Charlie Christian played the pop music of his day," he rationalized. "Wes Montgomery played Beatles songs and George Benson did soul-funk fusion. So I was trying to do a jazz guitar album for today. A lot of people see my music as acid jazz but I'm a musician, not a deejay."[52]

This funky dance-floor music was often vocal (and rap) laden, the voice being the most personal and communicative link between bandstand and dance floor; bands like Digable Planets, Guru, Raw Stylus, The Brand New Heavies, A Tribe Called Quest, and Diana Brown and Barrie K Sharp usually had mildly tooting saxophones or flutes lurking somewhere in the mix, but it was the words and vocal gymnastics that counted, carrying more weight than the music, for the most part monochrome vamps and the dead hand of the synthidrum. However, Jazzstarr's "Jazzthing," a scratch-sample-rap of the history of jazz, had some novelty value, as did the work of US3, whose hit version of Herbie Hancock's "Cantaloop Island (Flip Fantasia)" (with an inventive solo by the British trumpeter Gerard Prescencer) from *Hand on the Torch* thrust hip-hop into mainstream consciousness.[53]

Comprising rappers Shabaam Sahdeeq and KCB with keyboardist Tim Vine plus producer Geoff Wilkinson, US3 emerged out of the jazz dance scene in London playing 1960s Art Blakey, Horace Silver, and Lee Morgan at a time when most of the sampling in America was 1970s funk tracks rather than hard bop. With *Broadway and 52nd* (1997), they stuck to the formula that put them on the map with "Cantaloupe Island": sampled '50s and '60s jazz tracks, raps, some brief jazz soloing—this time by Steve Williamson on tenor—aimed at the young dancers. But this is not music of substance, it is déjà-vu jazz with a backbeat; take out the scratching and the rapping and we seem to be on terra firma not far from the ivory tower Wynton Marsalis inhabits.

To cash in on this fad, in 1996 EMI instituted "The Blue Note Remix Project," an if-you-can't-beat-them-join-them album project inspired by the success of US3 and based on the premise that because hip-hop and rap have sampled so much of the original Blue Note albums of the 1950s and 1960s, EMI may as well get a slice of the action (very few samples resulted in any sort of payment—even chart hits). Guru, DJ Smash, Easy Mo Bee, and Spearhead's Michael Franti remixed tracks by Cannonball Adderley, Donald Byrd, Ronnie Foster, Grant Green, Gene Harris, Bobby Hutcherson, Ronnie Laws, Horace Silver, Lonnie Smith, and others; all of these tracks had a synthi-drum backbeat added for the paying customers on the dance floor. "Seriously Funky" claimed Blue Note in their publicity, but the real spinoff was the interesting series of reissues the genre spawned. US3 in particular helped make a case for reissuing 1960s hard-bop classics, opening up an audience for soul-jazz and prompting the launch of the Blue Note "Rare Groove Series," which sold between 10,000 and 25,000 an album and even sparked a couple of comeback careers. "There's a lot of fine material that wasn't considered re-issuable until it became popular with DJ's," said Blue Note producer Michael Cuscuna. "It's great since John Patton and Reuben Wilson are out there playing."[54]

As the end of the 1990s approached, acid jazz had spread to most of the major U.S. cities. In California there was a thriving scene, with The Grassy Knoll, art-school graduate Bob Green's creation, producing dark, murky music with a trumpet-sax-clarinet front-line backed by drums, tablas, and turntables that bordered on monotony. San Francisco boasted its own record labels specializing in its acid-jazz scene—such as Ubiquity and Mammoth/Prawn Song—and venues like the Up and Down Club, the pioneering jazz venue owned by J. J. Morgan in the SoMa district. Out of this scene emerged the Charlie Hunter Trio, whose music appealed to a young audience while also working from within the jazz tradition. Hunter also ran a guitar-heavy quartet called T. J. Kirk (with guitarists Will Bernard and John Scott, and Scott Amendola on drums), which specialized in funk/hip-hop versions of classics by Thelonious Monk, James Brown, and Roland Kirk (hence the name). Their eponymous 1995 album was clever without being a clever-clever pastiche of influences.

With his trio, however, Hunter tried to move away from the acid-jazz movement with which he had been lumped, towards more complex voicings and ensemble interplay and claiming that what he played was "antacid jazz." Hunter developed a style that was uniquely his own on a custom-built eight-string guitar made by Ralph Novak, with three bass strings (E, A, D) and five regular guitar strings (A, D, G, B, E). He played bass and guitar simultaneously and with startling fluency, bringing to his playing a thorough understanding of jazz guitar old (Christian, Montgomery) and new (Scofield, Frisell, Tuck Andress, and Pat Martino). Frequently, he processed the guitar signals to sound like a Hammond B-3 using a Leslie speaker that attested to his love of organ aces Larry Young and Big John Patton. "Organic is the sound I'm going for," he said. "I keep the rotating-speaker Leslie sound mostly for comping. I also like the plain guitar tone—plain and full-bodied, like Wes [Montgomery] would use."[55] As a teenager, Hunter took lessons from the rock virtuoso Joe Satriani, and he was brought up on a broad diet of music. "Growing up in Berkeley we were exposed to all kinds of music, from the Dead Kennedys and Parliament Funkadelic to Art Blakey," he said. "In the Bay Area you have so many different cultures living together. It all gets semi-assimilated into a non-

The Charlie Hunter Quartet: *Left to right:* Calder Spanier, Scott Amendola, Hunter. (Saxophonist Kenny Brooks appears behind Spanier.) A unique guitarist, Hunter's eight-string guitar comprised three bass strings and five regular guitar strings. Hunter was no novelty act—he could play! (Photograph by Stuart Nicholson.)

polarized type of existence where hybridization of the music is possible. There are so many genres to work with."[56]

Hunter gigged with various bar bands that played reggae, rockabilly, and Motown covers before he joined Michael Franti and Rono Tse's Disposable Heroes of Hiphoprisy. The band was constantly on the road, leading Hunter to quit to form his own jazz trio in the San Francisco Bay Area. He linked up with tenor saxophonist David Ellis, to whom he had turned for jazz lessons, and drummer Jay Lane. Ellis had previously held down the first tenor chair in the Berkeley High School Jazz Orchestra, which over the years had schooled David Murray, Benny Green, and Joshua Redman. *The Charlie Hunter Trio* (1993) was an album of originals (save for Charles Mingus's "Fables of Faubus"), that included intriguing titles like "Dance of the Jazz Fascists" and "20, 30, 40, 50, 60, Dead." Sprung with ingenious rhythms and earnest improvising, it suggested great potential. In 1995, he was signed to Blue Note records, and his label debut, *Bing, Bing, Bing!* was awarded four stars by *Downbeat*, who called it "unaffected, unpretentious, inviting."[57]

By now the group had developed a greater empathy, and both Hunter and Ellis played with and off each other to greater effect, while Hunter's mastery of integrating bass and guitar lines was virtually seamless. On a couple of tracks, Hunter augmented the band with the addition of clarinet and trombone and in 1996 he decided to move into new musical territory afforded by a larger ensemble. Adding Calder Spanier on alto, he explained, "I had done the trio thing long enough. I needed to take the next step. I either wanted to add a trumpet or an alto sax guy. When Calder came to town I knew he'd be perfect."[58] Hunter had met Spanier in Montréal and later reconnected with him on the streets of Europe, where both gigged for spare change in the late 1980s.

With Scott Amendola moving across from T. J. Kirk in place of Jay Lane, Hunter recorded *Ready . . . Set . . . Shango!* in 1996. As a conscious effort to move away from the acid-jazz moniker, he invented a dance with no steps which he called the Shango, and composed an album of songs to "dance" the Shango to. If this did not exactly set the record straight—a jazz album for a cultural dance movement that was a figment of his imagination—it did at least succeed in getting the message across that his music was for the mind as much as for the body. "The groove is there, but it's much more jazz-oriented this time," said Hunter. "It has a much looser feeling than anything we've recorded so far. For this album we wanted to emulate the stuff Cannonball Adderley, Big John Patton, and Eddie Harris were doing back in the 1960s, but update it with a modern twist."[59] Shortly after the album was recorded, Ellis left the band and was replaced by Kenny Brooks from Alphabet Soup, the hip-hop-bop San Francisco band.

This revised lineup appears on *Natty Dread* (1997), Hunter's jazz take on the Bob Marley album from 1974 (the first Marley album after the Peter Tosh/Bunny Wailer split) adapted by the band to produce their most accomplished statement to date. It was an absorbing lesson in how songs from popular culture could be adapted by jazz as a basis for improvisation; sometimes the whole mood of a song was changed by dramatically altering the tempo, rhythm, and harmonic characteristics, including a "gospel speed metal romp" version of "Down Low," a Ry Cooder-esque solo in "No Woman, No Cry" (Cooder is a Hunter favorite), and imaginative recastings of "Them Belly Full" and "Revolution." "We're seeing young people have a whole new attitude toward jazz," he said. "That's why the [neotraditional] movement is such a scary thing. It's a bizarre Trappist monk mindset where there's no connection to the outside world and an unwillingness to converse with modern culture."[60]

Saxophonist Kenny Brook's previous band Alphabet Soup was an active member of the West Coast jazz-rap movement, their *Layin' Low in the Cut* (1995) full of snappy grooves, biting lyrics, and Fender Rhodes figures. Broun Fellini's *Aphrokubist Improvisations Vol. 9* has Black Edgar Kenyatta soloing over rap grooves, while *Up and Down Club Sessions Vols. 1 & 2* chronicles live sets from these and other bands like Hueman Flavor and the Josh Jones Latin Ensemble from the club at the center of the West Coast acid jazz scene of the 1990s. Drummer/percussionist Josh Jones was a key member of Peter Apfelbaum's Hieroglyphics Ensemble, conceptually and musically one of the finest ensembles to have appeared in jazz during the 1990s. Apfelbaum was the prime mover in the Bay Area's youth-driven jazz scene, from his days at

Berkeley High School in the late 1970s through much of the 1980s. When he was ten, he was playing drums professionally, and by the time he was fourteen he was playing regularly as a jazz saxophonist. At sixteen he formed the Hieroglyphics Ensemble as a forum to try out his original compositions. The day after he left high school, Apfelbaum moved to New York City to try his luck, playing with Eddie Jefferson, Carla Bley's punk band Burning Sensations (where he played keyboards), and Karl Berger, where he met trumpeter Don Cherry. But unable to get his own music played, he moved back to California in 1982. The Hieroglyphics Ensemble was only reunited occasionally, but after some rave reviews and recognition by Grateful Dead bassist Phil Lesh, the ensemble opened for the Dead's 1987 New Year's Eve show and was awarded the Rex Foundation Award for Creative Excellence. In 1988 Apfelbaum received a commission from the San Francisco Jazz Festival to compose a suite for the Hieroglyphics Ensemble, and as a result he invited Don Cherry to appear as guest soloist. Cherry was deeply impressed with Apfelbaum's music and hired a small band from within the Hieroglyphics Ensemble as his Multikulti group for tours of Europe and Japan. Later Cherry invited the Hieroglyphics Ensemble en masse to appear on his album *Multikulti*. Recorded in late 1989 and early 1990, Apfelbaum appears as a guest in "Dedication to Thomas Mapfumo," and he and his ensemble play in three impressive tracks, "Until the Rain Comes," "Divinity Tree," and "Rhumba Multikulti."

In 1990, Apfelbaum finally got a record contract of his own; his debut, *Signs of Life,* shows why Phil Elwood of the San Francisco Examiner was moved to write, "Those who have followed Apfelbaum's career came to realize long ago that he is a genius."[61] The album opens with the Grammy-nominated mini-suite "Candles and Stones." The composition begins with an a-cappella call on twin soprano saxophones that is in the style of Yoruba praise-singing. The rhythm instruments enter with guitar and bass using a repeated phrase built on a scale found in Gnawa music of Morocco and Bambara music of Mali over an organ drone. A horn riff at the end of the section is a literal adaptation of the rhythm "Rumba Obatala" of Afro-Cuban origin traditionally played on bata drums. The horn section that follows utilizes what Apfelbaum calls his "rhythm-block" method, a technique he developed where each of the wind instruments plays a separate melodic line in "rhythmic unison." The third section, in 6/8, revolves around a central phrase produced by three guitars and bass each accenting a different place with a two-bar section. The three percussionists each have their own patterns but also accent the guitar rhythms. The bridge sections are in a brisk 5/8 and are harmonically more varied, with cycles of changing chords in contrast to the static harmony of the preceding sections. These contrasting "movements" flow together without a break, with Peck Allmond's trumpet rising from the ensemble with poise and authority. The ensemble passages were learned by the band so that they could be played with the fluency and freedom of a jazz improvisation while the rhythmic underpinning relied on the sympathetic interaction of three electric guitars, a bass, two drummers (one of whom alternates on percussion), and a percussionist. It produced music of extraordinary depth and fluidity. There is always

Peter Apfelbaum: *Left to right:* John Shifflett, Josh Jones, Will Bernard, Apfelbaum, Jeff Cressman, Deszon Claiborne. Music of depth, fluidity, and rhythmic imagination; there was always more to Apfelbaum's music than initially caught the ear. (Photograph by Jason Langer/Gramavision.)

more to Apfelbaum's music than initially catches the ear; indeed, it seems to exist in a series of interacting layers of rhythmic complexity. So tightly woven are the individual rhythmic strands, often in contrasting meters, that it is difficult to discern what time Apfelbaum has written certain pieces in; at one European jazz festival, trumpeter Kenny Wheeler enquired what time-signature a particular composition was in and was astonished to learn it was in 4/4.[62]

"Walk to the Mountain (And Tell the Story of Love's Thunderclapping Eyes)" is, like "Candles and Stones," built up through the African "rhythm tapestry" approach. It uses the big beat—but not of rock, rather of African Music. It features Jai Uttal on harmonium followed by Apfelbaum on tenor saxophone, imperiously melodic and using his trademark alternate fingering to emphasize certain notes; there is an intensity to his playing that even on the most benign phrases lifts them out of the ordinary. "The Last Door" is in 7/8 and begins with sitar sounds from Jai Uttal's MIDI guitar setup accompanying James Harvey's straight-muted trombone. As the composition unfolds there is a wordless vocal by Uttal with, at two points, Apfelbaum on a police-style electric bullhorn commanding "Take the last door to get out." Will Bernard's overdriven guitar touches base with Hendrix, yet is careful to operate within the mood of the piece, growing organically from it rather than being a simple solo statement.

"Forwarding, Parts 1 & 2" was originally part of a longer suite entitled "Notes from the Rosetta Stone" commissioned by the San Francisco Jazz Festival and performed with guest Don Cherry. "Forwarding" comes from the Rastafarian concept that one goes "forward" in an "upfull" and enlightened existence, never "backward." "Part 1" thus uses a reggae rhythm while "Part 2," which directly segues on, is the only piece Apfelbaum has recorded to date that uses a "walking" bass line. Yet even here, the rhythmic complexity that is "layered" above it makes it quite unlike a straight-ahead jazz piece. The tenor solo is taken by Tony Jones, and it raises the intensity level up a few notches. The arrangement again features Apfelbaum's exhilarating "rhythm block" writing.[63]

Recorded in early 1992, Apfelbaum's next album, *Jodoji Brightness,* is a more disparate statement than its predecessor, because several tracks rely on free improvisation, with the effect of setting the clock back thirty years. For all their accomplishment, there was a feeling of déjà vu much like what the resurgence of hard bop generated in the 1980s. Yet there were again impressive ensemble statements, if fewer of them, that confirmed Apfelbaum as one of the most important musicians of his generation, as a conceptualist, instrumentalist, arranger, and composer—the track "Gypsies," for example, was a part of a suite commissioned by the Kronos Quartet in 1990.

However, Apfelbaum's recording company Antilles was bought by Polygram shortly after *Jodoji Brightness* was released, and the parent company promptly downsized its roster. Despite high praise for both albums—in 1991 Apfelbaum was voted top big band in the "Talent Deserving of Wider Recognition" section of the *Downbeat* Critic's Poll, for example—he found himself without a record contract just as his career was beginning to get into gear. Without new recorded product in front of the critics, the jazz press, and the public, his career lost momentum. Since 1992 the Hieroglyphics Ensemble played fewer and fewer gigs and several members began to develop their own careers. Josh Jones formed two bands, Hueman Flavor and the Josh Jones Latin Ensemble, and worked with David Murray and Steve Coleman. Drummer Deszon X. Claiborne became a regular in the blues singer Charles Brown's band. Guitarist Will Bernard formed two ensembles, his funk-jazz-rock band Pothole and a jazz quartet, and also became a member of Charlie Hunter's jazz-rock group T. J. Kirk. Jai Uttal formed the Pagan Love Orchestra and was signed to the Triloka label, releasing *Footprints* and *Monkey,* both with Apfelbaum in the ensemble and soloing. The latter album was somewhat over-reliant on vocals, yet on the title track produced an intriguing fusion of Indian music, jazz, and rock.

Less subtle than Uttal's conscious ethnic authenticity, the work of the European-based Trilock Gurtu aimed for a more forthright fusion of Indian music, World music, and jazz-fusion. His albums on the German CMP label included guests Don Cherry, L. Shankar, Ralph Towner, Jan Garbarek, and, on *Crazy Saints* (1993), Pat Metheny and Joe Zawinul. Born in Bombay to a prominent musical family, Gurtu's training in Indian classical music began when he was five and was followed by an interest in jazz and rock as a teenager that was very much in the spirit of the 1960s but with a difference—when jazz and popular music were looking to India for inspiration, Gurtu was going in the opposite direction. His travel through the United States brought him into contact with Don Cherry and Colin Walcott, and he replaced Walcott in the jazz-fusion band Oregon in the 1980s. In 1988 he became associated with John McLaughlin, cutting two albums and touring with the guitarist.

In the 1990s, Gurtu formed his group Crazy Saints with keyboardist Dabiel Goyone, bassist Chris Minh Doky (who had performed with Mike Stern, the Brecker Brothers, and George Benson), and guitarist David Gilmore, whose playing experience included stints with Steve Coleman. Voted "Best Percussionist" in Downbeat's 1994 and 1995 Critic's Polls, Gurtu's fifth release for CMP, Bad Habits Die Hard (1996), essayed his "East meets West" fusion. "I want to cross fertilize jazz and Eastern music," he said. "It's not about saying, 'Oh, let's bring in a Japanese guy,' it doesn't work. There has to be understanding, a feeling for the thing."[64]

With fewer and fewer gigs for his Hieroglyphics Ensemble, Apfelbaum devoted himself to teaching, work on sax with vocalist Ann Dyer, work as a drummer with bassist Lisle Ellis, and playing in the horn section of the rock group Phish. "I got to the point where I realized I couldn't be putting all my eggs in one basket anymore," he rationalized. "In order to work more I had to put together a smaller band. So I developed a sextet, I found a combination of musicians who are incredibly strong as improvisers and interpreters."[65] Finally he secured a record deal, and Luminous Charms was released in 1996. A powerful statement by a wholly original band, here was a kind of Afro-fusion, using polymetric grooves, dark tone colors (Apfelbaum's tenor and Jeff Cressman's trombone), menacing ostinatos, and drummer Claiborne's muscular funk in odd meters. Apfelbaum's playing was given more exposure, his lean intensity more focused as was the level of intrigue and logic of his compositions. "At no point in the process of writing these compositions was there a decision to incorporate specific cultural elements, I just write and build and adjust the shape of these pieces as I go," he explained. "My vocabulary reflects the fact I started life as a drummer, was trained in jazz theory, blues and gospel music as a teenager, was inundated with African, Latin and jazz, became involved in group improvisation, listened a lot to twentieth-century classical music, worked in R&B, reggae, blues, Latin, African, Jazz, funk, Middle Eastern and Indian bands, and for as long as I can remember, I've been fascinated how all these sounds can be fitted together."[66] Despite the album's obvious originality of concept, Downbeat awarded it only two stars.[67]

It is impossible not to think of Apfelbaum's music existing in the precise form it did without the historical precedent of jazz having reached out to use aspects of rock and other dance forms such as funk to broaden its expressionism. Although the Hieroglyphics ensemble were by no means a jazz-rock group or a product of jazz-rock, they nevertheless emerged as the most exciting ensemble exploring contemporary groove-oriented eclecticism in the 1990s. "I think what I share with others of my generation, like Graham Haynes, Charlie Hunter, T. J. Kirk and Medeski Martin and Wood, is that we see the dance music of our time (or 'groove music,' as Medeski Martin and Wood call it) as having potential for creative development," Apfelbaum explained. "I also align myself with the 'restructuralists' (Braxton's word) like Henry Threadgill, Roscoe Mitchell, Anthony Braxton, Steve Coleman, Dave Douglas, Karl Berger, Tim Berne, Carla Bley, Julius Hemphill, Bob Moses, John Zorn, and others who, in the explosion of musical structure in the 1990s, are putting the pieces back together in different ways, as it were."[68]

Perhaps the true legacy of jazz-rock within the jazz pantheon is that the evolution of the music did not stop with rock. Initially rock offered a new rhythmic backdrop whose cohesion offered a new basis for jazz improvisation, not least because in bop the cymbals carried the basic rhythmic pulse, while in rock it went back to the drums because, at rock's high volume levels, cymbals allowed little definition to subdivisions of the beat, dissolving into a blanket of sound. Once this rhythmic Rubicon had been crossed it opened the way in quick succession to funk, World music, and a whole lot else. The rhythmic unit that had served jazz since its beginnings at the turn of the twentieth century when it was a provincial Southern music was threatened by a new rhythmic complexity opened up by James Brown. By the early 1970s it had flowed into the jazz-rock mainstream—everybody is a drum—and almost at once began mutating through African, Latin, and World beats enacted out against the backdrop of the new electric tone colors ushered in by the rock age.

As in the past, any sea change in jazz has been accompanied by a rhythmic revolution, but this time the rhythmic revolution became a work in progress. Jazz was at last released from the straight-ahead four that had boxed-in its aspirations for so long, a limitation Jelly Roll Morton had cautioned against back in the 1920s when he insisted that jazz should have a "Spanish tinge." Jazz-rock set in sway a hunt for new, interesting rhythmic combinations to invigorate compositional forms. And while much jazz-rock was based on simple musical structures such as vamps, ostinatos, and modes, musicians such as Wayne Shorter and Joe Zawinul explored compositional forms of considerable sophistication. Ultimately, jazz-rock realigned jazz alongside popular culture, a position jazz itself had historically occupied and strayed from at its peril. It seemed as soon as jazz began to desert its vernacular roots it was in danger of taking itself too seriously. Jazz-rock set a new musical agenda for change as free jazz floundered on the discovery that total freedom was in itself ultimately limiting. Yet from the beginning jazz-rock was never a static genre with clearly defined boundaries but a genre in constant flux, often through the impact of what was happening in neighboring genres. "We must acknowledge the fact that jazz music has always borrowed from other sources and changed the rules as it expanded and moved on," said Jack DeJohnette in 1993.[69] By then it was clear that jazz-rock had become something else, something more inclusive. Rock had never been enough.

Notes

1. *Downbeat,* May 18, 1978, p. 46
2. *Like Punk Never Happened: Culture Club and the New Pop,* by David Rimmer (Faber & Faber, London, 1985), p. 13.

3. *Guitar Player,* April 1996, p. 97.
4. *Downbeat,* February 1993, p. 33.
5. That Coleman's concept of free jazz could coexist alongside rock had previously been suggested by Captain Beefheart and by Lou Reed's guitar solo on "I Heard Her Call My Name" on the Velvet Underground's *White Light/White Heat,* from 1968.
6. *Downbeat,* March 1984, p. 54.
7. Interview with the author, December 20, 1996.
8. *Jazziz,* January–February 1996, p. 53.
9. *Downbeat,* February 1996, p. 23.
10. He appeared with Laswell's experimental avant-jazz-rock ensemble Material on the 1982 album *Memory Serves,* and Laswell produced Sharrock's albums, including *Guitar, Seize the Rainbow,* and *Highlife,* which had the openness of jazz and the rawness of rock, and his *Ask the Ages,* which combined Pharoah Sanders, Elvin Jones, and Charnett Moffett to blast the spirit of John Coltrane into the future positive.
11. *New York Times,* May 31, 1994.
12. Conversation with the author, August 5, 1997.
13. Quoted in *Jazz: The 1980s Resurgence,* by Stuart Nicholson (Da Capo, New York, 1995), p. 117.
14. Liner notes, *Lennox Avenue Breakdown* (CBS 83350).
15. *Downbeat,* May 1980, p. 32.
16. Ibid., April 1994, p. 25.
17. Ibid.
18. *Jazz Times,* May 1997, p. 26.
19. *Downbeat,* January 1985, p. 32.
20. *Wire,* July 1992, p. 12.
21. Ibid., p. 10.
22. Ibid., p. 12.
23. Quoted in *Jazz: The 1980s Resurgence,* by Stuart Nicholson (Da Capo, New York, 1995), p. 258.
24. Ibid., p. 260.
25. Interview with the author, May 21, 1997.
26. Interview with the author, April 1992, published in *Jazz Express,* June 1992, pp. 12–13.
27. *New York Times,* July 3, 1995.
28. Liner notes, *Code Violations* (Enja LP 5085 1).
29. *Downbeat,* July 1991, p. 26.
30. Ibid., November 1994, p. 32.
31. Abercrombie's *Getting There* (ECM 833 494-2) from 1988 has Brecker guesting impressively on two tracks, "Sidekicks" and "Furs on Ice." Their collaboration also appeared on video.
32. Quoted in *Jazz: The 1980s Resurgence,* by Stuart Nicholson (Da Capo, New York, 1995), p. 203.
33. Ibid., p. 272.
34. *The Wire,* February 1993, p. 28.
35. *New York Times,* December 4, 1988.
36. *Knitting Music,* by Michael Dorf (Knitting Factory Works, New York, 1992), p. 10.
37. Quoted in *Knitting Music,* by Michael Dorf (Knitting Factory Works, New York 1992) on the backflap.
38. Quoted in *Jazz: The 1980s Resurgence,* by Stuart Nicholson (Da Capo, New York, 1995), p. 269.
39. *The New York Composers Orchestra* (New World NW 397-2) from 1990 and *First Program in Standard Time* (New World 80418-2) from 1992.
40. *Knitting Music,* by Michael Dorf (Knitting Factory Works, New York, 1992), p. 45.
41. Liner notes by John Zorn, *The Carl Stalling Project: Music for Warner Bros. Cartoons 1936–'58* (Warner Bros. 2–26027).
42. *New York Times,* July 1, 1994.

43. *Downbeat,* February 1991, p. 31.
44. Conversation with the author, June 1994.
45. Interview with the author, December 21, 1996.
46. *Jazz Times,* December 1966, p. 68.
47. *New York Times,* September 26, 1996.
48. *Boston Phoenix,* November 26, 1994.
49. *Who's Who at the North Sea Festival,* p. 35.
50. Their residence ended in March 1993 when angry neighbors had the club shut down.
51. *Downbeat,* February 1993, p. 35.
52. Ibid., p. 34.
53. It was the Blue Note label's best-selling record of all time to that date, with over two million copies sold worldwide, overtaking Donald Byrd and Ronnie Jordan.
54. *Downbeat,* April 1997, p. 19.
55. *The Guitar Magazine,* vol. 7, no. 7, p. 44.
56. Blue Note press release, May 1996.
57. *Downbeat,* September 1995, p. 38.
58. Blue Note press release, May 1996.
59. Ibid.
60. *Downbeat,* June 1994, p. 14.
61. *San Francisco Examiner,* circa 1986, repeated by Elwood in its pages on May 17, 1996. "About a decade ago I noted Apfelbaum's genius in print and found that as usual those who knew of his work agreed and those who didn't questioned my use of the term. . . . I see no reason to retract my 'genius' appraisal." Apfelbaum's album was nominated in a detailed discussion of the five hundred best jazz albums of the twentieth century in *The Essential Jazz Records Vol. II (Bop to Postmodernism),* by Max Harrison, Stuart Nicholson, and Eric Thacker (Mansell, London, 1998).
62. Interview with the author, December 20, 1996.
63. Also featured in "Divinity Tree" on Don Cherry's *Multikulti* and "Chant #9" on Apfelbaum's second album, *Jodoji Brightness.*
64. *Top Magazine,* November 1993, p. 12.
65. *Express,* December 1996, p. 26.
66. Interview with the author, December 20, 1996.
67. *Downbeat,* October 1996, p. 57.
68. Interview with the author, December 20, 1996.
69. *Downbeat,* February 1993, p. 26.

A Jazz-Rock Fusion Discography

Jon Newey

In his celebrated book *The Old Straight Track,* 1920s visionary and naturalist Alfred Watkins first revealed how key elements in the landscape were connected to each other in continuous straight lines known as leys, whose origin and significance predates modern history. In jazz history you'll find few straight lines, but everything connects, especially through the key elements. This discography is fundamentally about connections.

My aim is to present a comprehensive compendium of music that relates to the evolution of jazz-rock fusion, and hopefully will embellish the tale from its beginnings in the mid-1960s up to the present day. Conceivably it will offer a map of exploration to the interested reader, a shopping list for the brave-hearted or another earnest timetable for the dear old trainspotter, of which the music attracts more than its fair share.

Beginning at chapter 2 (chapter 1 acts as a scene-setting prologue), the discography is laid out to interact with the content of each chapter, following the flow and flavor of the text and spinning out in a web of associated releases that, however obscure or odd the choice may seem, either influenced the development of jazz-rock or were noticeably affected by it. Each is worthy, at the very least, of a cursory listen. Yesterday's ugly ducklings increasingly prove to be today's prize swans. Just remember the critical lambasting that Miles Davis's now lauded *Agharta* received at the time of its release. This discography is studded with hundreds more similar cases.

As well as the artist and album title, I have listed both the vinyl and CD labels and the original date of release. One glance at the discography, unfortunately, reveals the surprising number of long-deleted vinyl releases which have yet to gain compact-disc status—in sharp contrast, it would seem, to the rock marketplace, where, in most instances, every last burp and squeak has now been enshrined in the digital format. Interest in jazz-rock, particularly its explosive early years, is currently undergoing a feverish renaissance, especially among today's generation of dance, techno, and rare groove fans, while prices in the vinyl collectors' market are rapidly approaching minor mortgage levels. My advice is to write, pester, or petition the reluctant record labels until the tape-vault doors are finally prized open.

Where prominent artists figure in more than one chapter, as is the case with Miles Davis, their discographical details are split and tailored to the chronological flow of that particular phase. Artists outside of the book's remit, such as John Coltrane and Sun Ra, who had a significant influence on the coming electric zeitgeist, have been included with a selected grouping of pertinent works. However, for some recording artists working around the fusion idiom, most notably during the 1980s, who chose to channel and in some instances "dumb down" the genre to a level of sub-easy listening, I have included only token entries.

With certain artists the temptation to go beyond the usual label parameters proved irresistible. Whatever your standpoint, the rights and wrongs of bootleg recordings are not a matter for debate in this book. Jazz, however, is fundamentally a live music and, even though unofficial releases might prove undesirable to major record labels, all the live bootleg releases featured here show important facets of the artist's development unavailable elsewhere. To differentiate between official released recordings, I have listed the bootlegs in italics. Of course, I have absolutely no idea where these recordings can be obtained.

Needless to say, the phrases "too many albums" and "not enough time" became an unrelenting mantra during the course of writing this discography. Both refused to abate until their limits had been thoroughly abused. For this I take full blame, but hey, once you start, it's knowing how to stop. Maybe, as Miles once suggested to John Coltrane, I should have just tried taking the damn thing out of my mouth.

Extra special thanks go to Steve Sanderson and Kerstan Mackness at New Note, Adam Sieff and Sharon Kelly at Sony Jazz UK, Richard Cook and Becky Stevenson at Verve UK, Wendy Furness at Blue Note UK, Trevor Mainwaring at Harmonia Mundi, Mike Gott at BGO, Amadu Sowe and Gaylene Martin at Coalition, Brent Keefe, Gareth Jones, Colin Schofield, and especially Jill, Candy, and Charlie for the lost weekend. And then some.

Jon Newey
LONDON, AUTUMN 1997

CHAPTER 2

Wheels of Fire

Artist's Name	Album Title	LP Record Label	CD Label	Original Release
ALEXIS KORNER	R&B at the Marquee	Ace of Clubs	n/a	1962
	Blues Incorporated	Ace of Clubs	n/a	1965
	Bootleg Him!	Castle Classics	n/a	1992
GRAHAM BOND	The Sound of '65	EMI Columbia	n/a	1966
	There's a Bond between Us	EMI Columbia	n/a	1966
	Love Is the Law	Pulsar	n/a	1968
	Solid Bond	Warner Bros.	n/a	1970
	Holy Magick	Veritigo	n/a	1971
	We Put Our Magic on You	Vertigo	n/a	1971
	Beginnings of Jazz-Rock	Charley	n/a	1977
JOHN MAYALL	Blues Breakers	Decca	London	1966
	Crusade	Decca	London	1967
	Bare Wires	Decca	London	1968
	Jazz Blues Fusion	Polydor	Polydor	1972
	Primal Solos	Polydor	Polydor	1985
CREAM	Fresh Cream	Reaction	Polydor	1966
	Disraeli Gears	Reaction	Polydor	1967
	Wheels of Fire	Polydor	Polydor	1968
	Cream Live	Polydor	Polydor	1969
	Cream Live Two	Polydor	Polydor	1972
	Royal Albert Hall 1968	WRMB	n/a	1969
CREAM	Those Were the Days (4 CD Box Set)	n/a	Polydor	1997
JACK BRUCE	Songs for a Tailor	Polydor	Polydor	1969
	Things We Like	Polydor	n/a	1970

Artist's Name	Album Title	LP Record Label	CD Label	Original Release
JACK BRUCE	Harmony Row	polydor	n/a	1971
GINGER BAKER'S AIRFORCE	Airforce	Polydor	n/a	1970
	Airforce 2	Polydor	n/a	1972
COLOSSEUM	Those Who Are About to Die Salute You	Fontana	Sequel	1969
	Valentyne Suite	Vertigo	Sequel	1969
	Daughter of Time	Vertigo	Sequel	1970
	Colosseum Live	Bronze	Sequel	1971
	Collectors Colosseum	Bronze	Sequel	1971
COLOSSEUM II	Strange New Flesh	Bronze	n/a	1976
	Electric Savage	MCA	One Way	1977
	War Dance	MCA	One Way	1978
PINK FLOYD	London 66–67	n/a	See for Miles	1995
	Live at the Oude-Ahoy Hallen Rotterdam 1967	n/a	Living Legends	1989
	Stoned Alone—Live in Copenhagen 1967	n/a	Gold Standard	1993
SOFT MACHINE	The Soft Machine	Probe	One Way	1968
	Volume 2	Probe	One Way	1969
	Third	CBS	Columbia	1970
	Fourth	CBS	One Way	1971
	Fifth	CBS	One Way	1972
	Six	CBS	Columbia Holland	1973
	Seven	CBS	One Way	1973
	Bundles	Harvest	See for Miles	1975
	Triple Echo Compilation	Harvest	n/a	1977
	Live at the Proms 1970	Reckless	Reckless	1988
	The Peel Sessions	n/a	Strange Fruit	1991
	Spaced	n/a	Cuneiform	1996
	Live at the Paradiso 1969	n/a	Voiceprint	1996

Discographer's Note: Soft Machine's subsequent albums did little to enhance their earlier adventurous reputation, drifting further towards polite progressive rock.

Artist's Name	Album Title	LP Record Label	CD Label	Original Release
SOFT HEAD	Rogue Element	Ogun	Ogun	1979
SOFT HEAP	Soft Heap	Charly	n/a	1979
NATIONAL HEALTH	National Health	Affinity	Decal	1977
	Of Ques and Cures	Affinity	Decal	1978
	D S al Coda	Lounging	n/a	1983
BRIAN AUGER	Open	Marmalade	n/a	1967
	Definitely What	Marmalade	n/a	1968
	Streetnoise	Marmalade	n/a	1968
	Befour	RCA	One Way	1970
	Oblivion Express	RCA	One Way	1971
	A Better Land	Polydor	One Way	1971
	Augerization—The Best of Brian Auger	n/a	Tongue and Groove	1995
	The Best of Brian Auger's Oblivion Express	n/a	Polygram Chronicles	1996

Discographer's Note: Despite achieving retro appeal status among 1990s Acid Jazzers, the steam largely went out of Auger's Oblivion Express from the mid-70s onwards.

Artist's Name	Album Title	LP Record Label	CD Label	Original Release
TEN YEARS AFTER	Undead	Deram	Deram	1968
JETHRO TULL	This Was	Chrysalis	Chrysalis	1968
BLODWYN PIG	Ahead Rings Out	Chrysalis	BGO	1969
	Getting to This	Chrysalis	BGO	1970
PETE BROWN & HIS BATTERED ORNAMENTS	A Meal You Can Shake Hands With in the Dark	Harvest	n/a	1969
AQUILA	Aquila	RCA	n/a	1970
MOGUL THRASH	Mogul Thrash	RCA	n/a	1971
KEEF HARTLEY	Halfbreed	Deram	Deram	1969
	The Battle of NW6	Deram	Deram	1970
	Overdog	Deram	n/a	1970
	Little Big Band	Deram	n/a	1971
LOL COXHILL	Ear of the Beholder	Dandelion	n/a	1971
	Troverbal Suite	Mushroom	n/a	1972

Artist's Name	Album Title	LP Record Label	CD Label	Original Release
LOL COXHILL	Coxhill Miller	Caroline	See for Miles	1973
	Lol Coxhill and the Welfare State	Caroline	n/a	1975
	Fleas in the Custard	Caroline	n/a	1975
	Diverse	Ogun	n/a	1976
KEITH TIPPETT	You Are Here, I Am There	Polydor	n/a	1970
	Dedicated to You but You Weren't Listening	Vertigo	Repertoire	1971
	Blue Print	RCA	n/a	1972
CENTIPEDE	Septober Energy	RCA	n/a	1971
OVARY LODGE	Ovary Lodge	RCA	n/a	1973
	Ovary Lodge	Ogun	n/a	1976
RAY RUSSELL	Turn Circle	CBS	n/a	1968
	Dragon Hill	CBS	n/a	1969
	Rites & Rituals	CBS	n/a	1971
GONG	Magick Brother, Mystic Sister	Charley	Decal	1970
	Camembert Electrique	Charley	Decal	1971
	Continental Circus	Philips	Giacomo	1971
	The Flying Teapot	Virgin	Decal	1973
	Angel Eggs	Virgin	Decal	1973
	You	Virgin	Decal	1974
	Shamal	Virgin	Virgin	1975
	Gazeuse	Virgin	Virgin	1976
	Live Etc.	Virgin	Virgin	1977
	Expresso II	Virgin	Virgin	1978
	Gong Est Mort Vive Gong	Tapioca	n/a	1979
PIERRE MOERLEN'S GONG	Downwind	Arista	Great Expectations	1979
	Time Is the Key	Arista	Great Expectations	1979
	Live	Arista	Great Expectations	1980
	Leave It Open	Arista	n/a	1981
ASSAGAI	Assagai	Vertigo	n/a	1971

Artist's Name	Album Title	LP Record Label	CD Label	Original Release
	Afrorock	Sounds Superb	n/a	1971
	Zimbabwe	Vertigo	n/a	1972
OSIBISA	Osibisa	MCA	Sequel	1971
	Woyoya	MCA	Sequel	1971
	Heads	MCA	Sequel	1972
KING CRIMSON	In the Court of the Crimson King	Island	Island	1969
	In the Wake of Poseidon	Island	EG	1970
	Epitaph	n/a	DGM	1997
	Lizards	Island	EG	1970
	Islands	Island	EG	1971
	Earthbound	Island	EG	1972
	Lark's Tongue in Aspic	Island	EG	1973
	Starless and Bible Black	Island	EG	1974
	Red	Island	EG	1974
	Discipline	EG	EG	1981
	The Great Deceiver (4 CD box)	n/a	Discipline	1995
BURNING RED IVANHOE	Burnin Red Ivanhoe	Warner Brothers	n/a	1970
CAN	Tago Mago	UA	Blast First	1971
	Ege Bamyasi	UA	Blast First	1972
	Soon Over Babaluma	UA	Blast First	1974
HENRY COW	Legends	Virgin	n/a	1973
	Unrest	Virgin	n/a	1974
GORDON BECK	Experiments with Pops	Major Minor	n/a	1968
	Conversation Piece	Vinyl Records	n/a	1977
	Sunbird	JMS	JMS	1979
	The Things You See	JMS	JMS	1980
	With a Heart in My Song	JMS	JMS	1989
MATCHING MOLE	Matching Mole	CBS	BGO	1972
	Matching Mole's Little Red Record	CBS	BGO	1973

Artist's Name	Album Title	LP Record Label	CD Label	Original Release
QUIET SUN	Mainstream	Island	n/a	1974
COSMIC EYE	Dream Sequence	Regal Zonophone	n/a	1972
BROTHERHOOD OF BREATH	Brotherhood of Breath	Neon	n/a	1971
	Brotherhood	RCA	n/a	1972
	Live at Willisau	Ogun	n/a	1974
	Progression	Ogun	n/a	1978
NUCLEUS	Elastic Rock	Vertigo	BGO	1970
	We'll Talk About It Later	Vertigo	BGO	1970
	Solar Plexus	Vertigo	n/a	1971
	Labyrinth	Vertigo	n/a	1973
	Under the Sun	Vertigo	n/a	1973
	Snake Hips Etcetera	Vertigo	n/a	1975
	Alley Cat	Vertigo	n/a	1975
	Direct Hits	Vertigo	n/a	1976
	Awakening	Mood	n/a	1980
IAN CARR	Belladonna	Vertigo	n/a	1972
	Inflagrante Delcite	Capitol	n/a	1977
	Out of the Long Dark	Capitol	n/a	1978
MIKE CARR	Bebop from the East Coast	n/a	Birdland	1996
IF	IF	Island	n/a	1970
	IF 2	Island	n/a	1970
	IF 3	UA	n/a	1971
	IF 4	UA	n/a	1972
	Not Just a Bunch of Pretty Faces	Gull	n/a	1974
	Tea Break Is Over	Gull	n/a	1975
	Forgotten Roads—The Best of IF	n/a	Sequel	1995
	Live in Europe 1972	n/a	Repertoire	1997
ISOTOPE	Isotope	Gull	See for Miles	1974
	Illusion	Gull	See for Miles	1974

Artist's Name	Album Title	LP Record Label	CD Label	Original Release
MAJOR SURGERY	Deep End	Gull	n/a	1976
PAZ	The First Cut	Next	n/a	1977
	Kandeen Love Song	Spotlite	n/a	1977
	Look Inside	Paladin	n/a	1983
	Paz Are Back	Spotlite	n/a	1983
	The Best of Paz	n/a	Spotlite	1996
PACIFIC EARDRUM	Pacific Eardrum	Charisma	n/a	1977
	Beyond Panic	Charisma	n/a	1978
BRAND X	Unorthodox Behaviour	Charisma	Virgin	1976
	Moroccan Roll	Charisma	Virgin	1977
	Livestock	Charisma	Virgin	1977
	Masques	Charisma	Virgin	1978
	Product	Charisma	Virgin	1979
	Do They Hurt	Charisma	Virgin	1980
	Communication	n/a	Ozone	1992
	Is There Anything About	CBS	Sony	1982
	Live at the Roxy 1979	n/a	Zok	1996
BARBARA THOMPSON	Paraphernalia	MCA	n/a	1978
	Jubiaba	MCA	n/a	1978
	Wilde Tales	MCA	n/a	1979
	Live in Concert	MCA	n/a	1980
	Mother Earth	Temple Music	n/a	1983
MORRISSEY MULLEN	Up	Embryo	n/a	1977
	Cape Wrath	Harvest	n/a	1979
	Badness	Beggar's Banquet	Beggars Banquet	1981
	Life on the Wire	Beggar's Banquet	Beggars Banquet	1982
	It's About Time	Beggar's Banquet	Beggars Banquet	1983
	After Dark	Beggar's Banquet	Beggars Banquet	1983
	This Must Be the Place	Beggar's Banquet	Beggars Banquet	1984
	Happy Hour	Beggar's Banquet	Beggars Banquet	1988

Artist's Name	Album Title	LP Record Label	CD Label	Original Release
BILL BRUFORD	Feels Good to Me	Polydor	n/a	1978
	One of a Kind	Polydor	n/a	1979
	The Bruford Tapes	Polydor	n/a	1980
	Gradually Going Tornado	Polydor	n/a	1980
BILL BRUFORD'S EARTHWORKS	Earthworks	Editions EG	Editions EG	1986
	Dig	Editions EG	Editions EG	1988
	All Heaven Broke Loose	n/a	Editions EG	1991

Chapter 3
Free Spirits

Artist's Name	Album Title	LP Record Label	CD Label	Original Release
THE FREE SPIRITS LARRY CORYELL	Out of Sight and Sound	ABC	n/a	1967
	Lady Coryell	Vanguard	n/a	1969
	Coryell	Vanguard	n/a	1969
	Spaces	Vanguard	Vanguard	1970
	Fairyland	Flying Dutchman	n/a	1971
	At the Village Gate	Musidisc	n/a	1971
	Barefoot Boy	Flying Dutchman	n/a	1972
	Offering	Vanguard	n/a	1972
	The Real Great escape	Vanguard	n/a	1973
	Introducing the 11th House	Vanguard	Vanguard	1974
	Planet End	Vanguard	Vanguard	1976
	Level One	Arista	n/a	1976
	Aspects	Arista	n/a	1976
	Lion and the Ram	Arista	n/a	1976
	Back Together Again	Atlantic	n/a	1977
	At Montreux 1974	Vanguard	n/a	1978

Artist's Name	Album Title	LP Record Label	CD Label	Original Release
	European Impressions	Arista	n/a	1978
	Differences	Egg	n/a	1978
	Standing Ovation	Mood	n/a	1978
	Return	Vanguard	n/a	1979
	Live from Bahia	n/a	CTI	1992
	Fallen Angel	n/a	CTI	1993
	Spaces Revisited	n/a	Shanachie	1997
STEVE MARCUS	Tomorrow Never Knows	Vortex	n/a	1968
	Count's Rock Band	Vortex	n/a	1969
	The Lords Prayer	Vortex	n/a	1969
	Steve Marcus	Kinetic	n/a	1970
	Green Line	STV	n/a	1970
COMPOST	Compost	CBS	n/a	1971
	Take Off Your Body	CBS	n/a	1972
	Life Is Round	CBS	n/a	1973
GARY BURTON	Tennessee Firebird	RCA	n/a	1966
	Duster	RCA	n/a	1967
	Lofty Flake Anagram	RCA	n/a	1967
	A Genuine Tong Funeral	RCA	n/a	1968
	Gary Burton in Concert	RCA	n/a	1968
	Throb	Atlantic	Atlantic	1969
	Good Vibes	Atlantic	n/a	1969
	Gary Burton and Keith Jarrett	Atlantic	Atlantic	1971
DAVE PIKE SET	Noisy Silence	MPS	n/a	1969
	Four reasons	MPS	n/a	1969
	Live at the Philarmonie	MPS	n/a	1970
	Infra Red	MPS	n/a	1970
	Album	MPS	n/a	1971
	Masterpieces	n/a	MPS	1996

Artist's Name	Album Title	LP Record Label	CD Label	Original Release
SPECTRUM	Spectrum	MPS	n/a	1972
	Spectrum—Live at Heidelberg Jazz Festival	MPS	n/a	1973
VOLGER KREIGEL	Inside Missing Link	MPS	n/a	1972
	Volger Kreigel Quintet	MPS	n/a	1972
	Lift	MPS	n/a	1973
	Mild Maniac	MPS	n/a	1974
	Tropical harvest	MPS	n/a	1976
	Octember Variations	MPS	n/a	1977
	Elastic Menu	MPS	n/a	1978
	Houseboat	MPS	n/a	1978
	Live in Bayern	MPS	n/a	1981
THE UNITED JAZZ & ROCK ENSEMBLE	Live in Schutzenhaus	Mood	n/a	1977
	Teamwork	Mood	n/a	1978
	Break Even Point	Mood	n/a	1979
	Live in Berlin	Mood	n/a	1981
	United Live Opus Sechs	Mood	n/a	1984
WOLFGANG DAUNER	Free Action	MPS	n/a	1967
	Fur	Calig	n/a	1969
	The Oimels	MPS	n/a	1970
	Music Zounds	MPS	n/a	1970
	Output	ECM	n/a	1970
WOLFGANG DAUNER'S ET CETERA	Knirsch	MPS	n/a	1972
	Live	MPS	n/a	1973
WOLFGANG DAUNER	Changes	Mood	n/a	1978
	Get Up and Dauner	n/a	MPS	1996
VARIOUS ARTISTS	Piano Conclave—Palais Anthology	MPS	n/a	1975
JASPER VAN'T HOF	Eyeball	Keytone	Limetree	1974
JASPER VAN'T HOF'S PORK PIE	Transitory	MPS	n/a	1974

ARTIST'S NAME	ALBUM TITLE	LP RECORD LABEL	CD LABEL	ORIGINAL RELEASE
	The Door Is Open	MPS	n/a	1975
JASPER VAN'T HOF	The Selfkicker	Delta	n/a	1976
	However	MPS	n/a	1977
	Fairytale	MPS	n/a	1978
	Live in Montreux	MPS	n/a	1979
	Eyeball	CMP	n/a	1980
CHRIS HINZE COMBINATION	Chris Hinze Combination	CBS	n/a	1970
	Stoned Flute	CBS	n/a	1970
	Live at Montreux	CBS	n/a	1971
	Mission Suite	CBS	n/a	1973
JOHN LEE GERRY BROWN	Infinite Jones (Bamboo Madness)	Keytone	Limetree	1973
	Mango Sunrise	Blue Note	n/a	1975
	Still Can't Say Enough	Blue Note	n/a	1977
	Brothers	Mood	n/a	1980
PASSPORT	Passport	Atlantic	n/a	1971
	Second	Atlantic	n/a	1972
	Handmade	Atlantic	n/a	1973

Discographer's Note: Passport somehow managed to produce a further fourteen albums of ever decreasing interest without being dropped by their record company. Surely a world record for a jazz-rock act on a major label.

ARTIST'S NAME	ALBUM TITLE	LP RECORD LABEL	CD LABEL	ORIGINAL RELEASE
MICHAL URBANIAK	Constellation	Muza	Power Bros.	1973
	Paratyphus B	Speigelei	n/a	1975
	Inactin	Speigelei	n/a	1975
	Fusion	Columbia	n/a	1975
URBANATOR	Urbanator I	n/a	Hip Bop	1993
	Urbanator II	n/a	Hip Bop	1996
URSZULA DUDZIAK	Newborn Light	Cameo	n/a	1973
	Urszula	Arista	n/a	1976
	Future Talk	Inner City	n/a	1979
	Sorrow Is Not Forever . . . but Love Is	Keytone	n/a	1983

Artist's Name	Album Title	LP Record Label	CD Label	Original Release
JEREMY STEIG	Flute Fever	CBS	n/a	1963
	Jeremy and the Satyrs	Reprise	n/a	1967
	Legwork	Solid State	n/a	1968
	This Is Jeremy Steig	Solid State	n/a	1969
	Fusion	Groove Merchant	n/a	1970
	Something Else	n/a	Denon	1970
	Elephant Hump	n/a	MusiDisc	1970
	Monium	CBS	n/a	1974
	Firefly	CTI	CTI Japan	1977
	Lend Me Your Ears	CMP	n/a	1978
	Rainforest	CMP	n/a	1980
	Jigsaw	n/a	Triloka	1992
MIKE MAINIERI	Journey thru an Electric Tube	United Artists	n/a	1969
	Love Play	Arista	Arista	1977
	White Elephant Vol. 1	n/a	NYC	1994
	White Elephant Vol. 2	n/a	NYC	1994
	Wanderlust	Warner Bros.	NYC	1980
Mike Mainieri continues in ch. 12				
STUFF	Stuff	Warner Bros.	n/a	1977
	More Stuff	Warner Bros.	n/a	1977
	Stuff It	Warner Bros.	n/a	1978
	Live in Japan	Warner Bros.	n/a	1979
	Live in New York	Warner Bros.	Warner Bros.	1980
STEVE GADD	Gaddabout	King	Projazz	1980
	The Gadd Gang	Columbia	n/a	1986
	Here and Now	Columbia	n/a	1988
DREAMS	Dreams	CBS	Columbia	1970
STARDRIVE	Imagine My Surprise	CBS	Arista Japan	1971
	Intergalactic Trot	Elektra	n/a	1973

Artist's Name	Album Title	LP Record Label	CD Label	Original Release
BRECKER BROTHERS	The Brecker Brothers	Arista	One Way	1975
	Back to Back	Arista	One Way	1976
	Don't Stop the Music	Arista	One Way	1977
	Heavy Metal Be Bop	Arista	One Way	1978
	Détente	Arista	One Way	1980
	Straphangin'	Arista	One Way	1981
	Collection Vol. 1	n/a	BMG/Novus	1990
	Collection Vol. 2	n/a	BMG/Novus	1991
	Return of the Brecker Bros.	n/a	GRP	1992
	Out of the Loop	n/a	GRP	1994
	Brecker Brothers Live	*n/a*	*Jazz Door*	*1994*
RANDY BRECKER	Score	Blue Note	Blue Note	1969
	Amanda	Passport	Passport	1985
MICHAEL BRECKER	Cityscape	Warner Bros.	Warner Bros.	1982
	Michael Brecker	Impulse	Impulse	1987
	Don't Try This at Home	impulse	Impulse	1988
	Now You See It . . . Now You Don't	n/a	GRP	1990
	The Michael Brecker Band Live	*n/a*	*Jazz Door*	*1993*
	The Cost of Living (Live)	*n/a*	*Jazz Door*	*1994*
	Tales from the Hudson	n/a	Impulse	1996
DON GROLNICK	Hearts and Numbers	Hip Pocket	Hip Pocket	1985

Chapter 4
Spinning Wheels

Artist's Name	Album Title	LP Record Label	CD Label	Original Release
WES MONTGOMERY	Fusion	Riverside	OJC	1963
	Movin' Wes	Verve	Verve	1964
	Goin' Out of My Head	Verve	Verve	1965
	Tequila	Verve	Verve	1966
	California Dreamin'	Verve	Verve	1967
	Down Here on the Ground	A&M	A&M	1967
	A Day in the Life	A&M	A&M	1967
	Talkin' Verve: Roots of Acid Jazz	n/a	Verve	1996
PAUL BUTTERFIELD BLUES BAND	East West	Elektra	Elektra	1966
	Resurrection of Pigboy Crabshaw	Elektra	Elektra	1967
ELECTRIC FLAG	The Trip	Sidewalk	n/a	1967
	A Long Time Comin'	CBS	BGO	1968
	Old Glory: The Best Of	n/a	Columbia	1996
BLUES PROJECT	Live at the Café a Go Go	Verve	n/a	1966
	Projections	Verve	n/a	1967
	Live at the Town Hall	Verve	One Way	1967
BUDDY MILES	Express Way to Your Skull	Mercury	n/a	1968
	Electric Church	Mercury	n/a	1969
	Them Changes	Mercury	n/a	1970
	We Got to Live Together	Mercury	n/a	1970
	Message to the People	Mercury	n/a	1971
	Live	Mercury	n/a	1971
KOOPER, STILLS & BLOOMFIELD	Super Session	CBS	Columbia	1968
BLOOD, SWEAT & TEARS	Child Is Father to the Man	CBS	Columbia	1968
	Blood, Sweat and Tears	CBS	BGO	1969

Artist's Name	Album Title	LP Record Label	CD Label	Original Release
	Three	CBS	n/a	1970
	Four	CBS	n/a	1971
	New Blood	CBS	n/a	1972
CHICAGO TRANSIT AUTHORITY	Chicago Transit Authority	CBS	Columbia	1968
CHICAGO	Chicago	CBS	n/a	1969
	Live at Carnegie Hall	Columbia	Columbia	1971
FLOCK	Flock	CBS	Columbia	1969
	Best of	n/a	Columbia	1993
	Dinosaur Swamps	CBS	n/a	1970
LIGHTHOUSE	Lighthouse	RCA	n/a	1969
	Peacing It All Together	RCA	n/a	1970
	Suite Feeling	RCA	n/a	1970
GAS MASK	Gas Mask	Tonsil	n/a	1970
DALLAS COUNTY	Dallas County	Enterprise	n/a	1970
SONS OF CHAMPLIN	Loosen Up Naturally	Capital	See for Miles	1969
	The Sons	Capital	n/a	1969
AMBERGRIS	Ambergris	Paramount	n/a	1970
JOHN D'ANDREA & THE YOUNG GYANTS	Live at the Chez	Parkway	n/a	1967
ILLUSTRATION	Illustration	Janus	n/a	1970
IDES OF MARCH	Vehicle	Warner Bros.	n/a	1970
	Common Bond	Warner Bros.	n/a	1971
	World Woven	RCA	n/a	1972
TEN WHEEL DRIVE	Construction No 1	Polydor	n/a	1969
	Brief Replies	Polydor	n/a	1970
	Peculiar Friends	Polydor	n/a	1971
COLD BLOOD	First Blood	San Francisco	n/a	1970
	Sisyphus	San Francisco	n/a	1971

Artist's Name	Album Title	LP Record Label	CD Label	Original Release
TOWER OF POWER	East Bay Grease	San Francisco	Warner Bros.	1970
	Bump City	Warner Bros.	Warner Bros.	1972
	Tower of Power	Warner Bros.	Warner Bros.	1974
	Back to Oakland	Warner Bros.	Warner Bros.	1974
	In the Slot	Warner Bros.	Warner Bros.	1975
	Urban Renewal	Warner Bros.	Warner Bros.	1975
	Live and in Living Colour	Warner Bros.	Warner Bros.	1976
	Ain't Nothin' Stoppin' Us Now	Columbia	Columbia	1976
	We Came to Play	Columbia	Columbia	1978

Discographer's Note: Subsequent Tower of Power albums merely re-ran the formula without the weight or thrust the name once implied.

CHASE	Chase	Epic	n/a	1971
	Ennea	Epic	n/a	1972
	Pure Music	Epic	n/a	1974
HERBIE MANN	Impressions of the Middle East	Atlantic	n/a	1967
	Beat Goes On	Atlantic	n/a	1967
	Wailing Dervishes	Atlantic	n/a	1968
	Memphis Underground	Atlantic	Atlantic	1969
	Live at the Whisky	Atlantic	Atlantic	1969
	Stone Flute	Atlantic	n/a	1970
	Muscle Shoals Nitty Gritty	Atlantic	n/a	1971
	Evolution of Mann	Atlantic	n/a	1972

Chapter 5

Sorcerer

MILES DAVIS	ESP	CBS	Columbia	1965
	Four and More	CBS	Columbia	1966
	Miles Smiles	CBS	Columbia	1967
	The Sorcerer	CBS	Columbia	1967

Artist's Name	Album Title	LP Record Label	CD Label	Original Release
	Nefertiti	CBS	Columbia	1968
	Miles in the Sky	CBS	Columbia	1968
	Complete Live at the Plugged Nickel (7 CD set)	n/a	Columbia	1995
Miles Davis continues in ch. 7				
CHICO HAMILTON	Drumfusion	Columbia	n/a	1962
	Passin' Thru	Impulse	n/a	1962
GABOR SZAZBO	The Dealer	MCA	MCA	1966
	Gypsy '66	Impulse	n/a	1966
	Spellbinder	Impulse	n/a	1966
	Jazz Raga	Impulse	n/a	1966
	Simpatico	Impulse	n/a	1967
	The Sorceror	Impulse	n/a	1967
	Wind, Sky and Diamonds	Impulse	n/a	1968
	At Monterey	Impulse	n/a	1968
	More Sorcery	Impulse	n/a	1968
PHIL WOODS	Greek Cooking	Impulse	Impulse Japan	1967
CHARLES LLOYD	Discovery	Columbia	n/a	1964
	Of Course, Of Course	Columbia	n/a	1965
	Dream Weaver	Atlantic	n/a	1966
	Forest Flower	Atlantic	Rhino	1966
	In Europe	Atlantic	n/a	1966
	Love In	Atlantic	n/a	1967
	Journey Within	Atlantic	n/a	1967
	Soundtrack	Atlantic	Rhino	1968
	The Flowering	Atlantic	n/a	1970
	Forest Flower—Live in Europe 1967	*n/a*	*J-Bop*	*1994*
GRATEFUL DEAD	Grateful Dead	Warner Bros.	Warner Bros.	1967
	Anthem of the Sun	Warner Bros.	Warner Bros.	1968
	Aoxomoxoa	Warner Bros.	Warner Bros.	1969

Artist's Name	Album Title	LP Record Label	CD Label	Original Release
GRATEFUL DEAD	Live Dead	Warner Bros.	Warner Bros.	1970
	Two from the Vaults	n/a	Line	1992
	Infrared Roses	n/a	GDC	1992
JOE GALLANT	Blues for Allah	n/a	Knitting Factory	1997
DAVID MURRAY	Dark Star	n/a	Astor Place	1996
JERRY GARCIA	Garcia	Warner Bros.	Grateful Dead Recs	1972
	Hooteroll	Warner Bros.	Rykodisc	1972
	Live at the Keystone	Fantasy	n/a	1973
JEFFERSON AIRPLANE	Surrealistic Pillow	RCA	RCA	1967
	After Bathing at Baxter's	RCA	RCA	1968
	Bless Its Pointed Little Head	RCA	RCA	1969
THE DOORS	The Doors	Elektra	Elektra	1967
	The Soft Parade	Elektra	Elektra	1969
QUICKSILVER MESSENGER SERVICE	Happy Trails	Capitol	Capitol	1969
	Maiden of the Cancer Moon	Psycho	n/a	1983
THE DAILY FLASH	I Flash Daily	Psycho	n/a	1983
LOADING ZONE	Loading Zone	RCA	n/a	1968
THE CORPORATION	The Corporation	Capitol	Repertoire	1969
BIG BROTHER & THE HOLDING COMPANY	Cheap Thrills	CBS	Columbia	1968
EDEN'S CHILDREN	Eden's Children	ABC	n/a	1969
IT'S A BEAUTIFUL DAY	It's a Beautiful Day	CBS	Columbia	1969
VARIOUS ARTISTS	Last Days of the Fillmore	Fillmore/Atlantic	n/a	1972
ALLMAN BROTHERS	Live at Fillmore East	Atlantic	Polydor	1971
JOHN COLTRANE	My Favourite Things	Atlantic	Atlantic	1960
	Impressions	Impulse	Impulse	1963
	A Love Supreme	Impulse	Impulse	1964
	Transition	Impulse	Impulse	1965

Artist's Name	Album Title	LP Record Label	CD Label	Original Release
	Kulu Se Mama	Impulse	Impulse	1965
	New Thing at Newport	Impulse	Impulse	1966
	Sun Ship	Impulse	Impulse	1966
	OM	Impulse	Impulse	1966
	Meditations	Impulse	Impulse	1966
PHAROAH SANDERS	Tauhid	Impulse	Impulse	1966
	Izipho Zam	Strata East	Strata East	1969
	Karma	Impulse	Impulse	1969
	Thembi	Impulse	n/a	1971
	Black Unity	Impulse	Impulse	1971
	Live at the East	Impulse	n/a	1971
JOHN HANDY	Live at the Monterey Jazz Festival	CBS	Koch	1965
	The Second John Handy Album	CBS	n/a	1966
	John Handy	CBS	n/a	1966
	New View	CBS	n/a	1967
	Projections	CBS	n/a	1968
	Karuna Supreme	MPS	MPS	1975
	Hard Work	Impulse	n/a	1976
	Live at Yoshi's	n/a	Boulevard	1995
JERRY HAHN	Ara-Be-In	Arhoolie	n/a	1967
FOURTH WAY	The Fourth Way	Capitol	n/a	1969
	The Sun and Moon Have Come Together	Harvest	Jazz View	1970
	Werewolf	Harvest	n/a	1971
MICHAEL WHITE	Spirit Dance	Impulse	n/a	1972
	The Land of Spirit and Light	Impulse	n/a	1973
	Music, Mother Dance	Impulse	n/a	1974
	Go with the Flow	Impulse	n/a	1974
ALMANAC	Almanac	Improvising Artists	Improvising Artists	1967

CHAPTER 6

Voodoo Child

ARTIST'S NAME	ALBUM TITLE	LP RECORD LABEL	CD LABEL	ORIGINAL RELEASE
JIMI HENDRIX	Are You Experienced?	Track	Universal	1967
	Axis Bold as Love	Track	Universal	1967
	Electric Ladyland	Track	Universal	1968
	Live at Monterey	Reprise	Polydor	1970
	Band of Gypsies	Track	Polydor	1970
	Cry of Love	Polydor	Polydor	1971
	Rainbow Bridge	Reprise	n/a	1971
	Experience Soundtrack (Albert Hall 1969)	Ember	n/a	1971
	More Experience (Albert Hall 1969)	Ember	n/a	1972
	Isle of Wight	Polydor	Polydor	1971
	In the West	Polydor	Polydor	1972
	War Heroes	Polydor	Polydor	1973
	Loose Ends	Polydor	n/a	1973
	Crash Landing	Polydor	Polydor	1975
	Midnight Lightning	Polydor	Polydor	1976
	Nine to the Universe	Polydor	n/a	1980
	Concerts	CBS	Castle	1985
	Live at Winterland	Polydor	Polydor	1987
	Radio One	Castle	Castle	1989
	Live and Unreleased	n/a	Castle	1989
	Stages (4 CD live set)	n/a	Polydor	1991
	Blues	n/a	Polydor	1994
	Voodoo Soup	n/a	Polydor	1995
	The First Rays of the New Rising Sun	n/a	Universal	1997
	Hells Session	*BGR*	*BGR*	*1988*
	Live at Woodstock	*n/a*	*ITM*	*1992*

Artist's Name	Album Title	LP Record Label	CD Label	Original Release
GIL EVANS	Plays the Music of Jimi Hendrix	RCA	RCA	1974
CHRISTY DORAN	Plays the Music of Jimi Hendrix	n/a	Call It Anything	1994
VARIOUS ARTISTS inc				
McLaughlin, Williams, Clarke	In from the Storm	n/a	BMG	1995
VARIOUS ARTISTS	Woodstock Soundtrack	Atlantic	Atlantic	1970

CHAPTER 7
Dark Magus

Artist's Name	Album Title	LP Record Label	CD Label	Original Release
MILES DAVIS	Water Babies	CBS	Columbia Japan	1977
	Filles de Kilimanjaro	CBS	Columbia	1968
	In a Silent Way	CBS	Columbia	1969
	Circle in the Round	CBS	Columbia	1979
	Directions	CBS	Sony Japan	1980
	1969 Miles—Festiva De Juan Pins	n/a	Sony Japan	1995
	Double Image	n/a	Moon	1989
	Paraphernalia	n/a	JMY	1992
	Voodoo Down	n/a	Moon	1995
	Bitches Brew	CBS	Columbia	1970
	Bitches Brew Live	n/a	Golden Age of Jazz	1992
	Live—Evil	CBS	Columbia	1970
	Tribute to Jack Johnson	CBS	Columbia	1970
	At the Fillmore	CBS	Columbia	1970
	Black Beauty	CBS	Columbia	1974
	What I'd Say Vol. 1	n/a	JMY	1994
	What I'd Say Vol. 2	n/a	JMY	1994
	Miles Davis Live 1970–1973 3 CD set	n/a	Minotauro	1994
	Miles Davis and Keith Jarrett Live	n/a	Golden Age of Jazz	1992

Artist's Name	Album Title	LP Record Label	CD Label	Original Release
MILES DAVIS	*Another Bitches Brew*	*n/a*	*Jazz Door*	*1995*
	Two Miles Live 1971	*n/a*	*Discurios*	*1990*
	On the Corner	CBS	Columbia	1973
	In Concert	CBS	Columbia	1973
	En Concert avec Europe 1—11 Juillet 1973	*n/a*	*Europe 1*	*1994*
	Call It What It Is	*n/a*	*JMY*	*1995*
	Big Fun	CBS	Sony Japan	1974
	Dark Magus	Sony Japan	Columbia	1977
	Get up with It	CBS	Columbia	1974
	Agharta	CBS	Columbia	1975
	Agharta—Master Sound (w/ 10 mins. extra music)	n/a	Sony Japan	1996
	Pangea	CBS	Columbia	1975
VARIOUS ARTISTS inc				
Miles Davis	The First Great Rock Festivals of the Seventies	CBS	n/a	1972
VARIOUS ARTISTS inc				
Miles Davis	Message to Love Isle of Wight 1970	n/a	Castle	1996
Miles Davis continues in ch. 12				
DAVE LIEBMAN	Lookout Farm	ECM	n/a	1973
	Drum Ode	ECM	n/a	1974
	Live at Onkel Po's	Polydor Germany	n/a	1975
	Sweet Hands	Horizon	n/a	1975
	Light'n Up Please	Horizon	n/a	1976
	What It Is	Columbia	n/a	1980

CHAPTER 8

The Inner Mounting Flame

Artist's Name	Album Title	LP Record Label	CD Label	Original Release
TONY WILLIAMS	Lifetime	Blue Note	Blue Note	1965
	Spring	Blue Note	Blue Note Japan	1966
	Emergency	Polydor	Verve	1969
	Turn It Over	Polydor	Verve	1970
	Ego	Polydor	n/a	1971
	The Old Bum's Rush	Polydor	n/a	1971
	Spectrum: The Anthology	n/a	Verve	1997
	Believe It	CBS	n/a	1975
	Million Dollar Legs	CBS	n/a	1976
	The Collection (w/ Believe It & Million Dollar Legs)	n/a	Columbia	1992
	The Joy of Flying	CBS	Columbia Japan	1979
	Wilderness	n/a	Ark21	1996
ARCANA	The Last Wave	n/a	DIW	1996
	Arc of the Testimony	n/a	DIW	1997
STAN GETZ	Captain Marvel	CBS	Columbia	1972
LARRY YOUNG	Into Something	Blue Note	Blue Note Japan	1964
	Unity	Blue Note	Blue Note Japan	1965
	Of Love and Peace	Blue Note	n/a	1966
	Contrasts	Blue Note	n/a	1967
	Heaven on Earth	Blue Note	n/a	1968
	Mother Ship	Blue Note	n/a	1969
	Lawrence of Newark	Perception	n/a	1973
	Spaceball	Arista	n/a	1975
	Fuel	Arista	n/a	1975
	Complete Blue Note Recordings	Mosaic	Mosaic	1993

Artist's Name	Album Title	LP Record Label	CD Label	Original Release
NICHOLAS & GALLIVAN & YOUNG	Love Cry Want	n/a	Nicom	1997
JOHN McLAUGHLIN	Extrapolation	Polydor	Polydor	1969
	Devotion	Douglas	Celluoid	1970
	My Goals Beyond	Douglas	Rykodisc	1970
	Where Fortune Smiles	Dawn	BGO	1972
	Electric Guitarist	Columbia	Columbia	1978
	Electric Dreams	Columbia	Columbia	1979
	Belo Horizonte	Warner Bros.	Warner Bros.	1981
	Music Spoken Here	Warner Bros.	n/a	1983
JOHN McLAUGHLIN w/ Al DiMeola & Paco De Lucia	Passion Grace and Fire	Columbia	Columbia	1984
	Friday Night in San Francisco	Columbia	Columbia	1985
JOHN McLAUGHLIN	Adventures in Radioland	n/a	Verve	1987
	Live at the Royal Festival Hall	JMT	JMT	1990
	Que Alegria	n/a	Verve	1992
JOHN McLAUGHLIN & FREE SPIRITS	Tokyo Live	n/a	Verve	1994
JOHN McLAUGHLIN	After the Rain	n/a	Verve	1994
	The Promise	n/a	Verve	1996
MAHAVISHNU ORCHESTRA	Inner Mounting Flame	CBS	Columbia	1971
	Birds of Fire	CBS	Columbia	1972
	Between Nothingness and Eternity	CBS	Columbia	1974
	Apocalypse	CBS	Columbia	1974
	Visions of the Emerald Beyond	CBS	Columbia	1975
	Inner Worlds	CBS	Columbia	1976
	Mahavishnu	Warner Bros.	n/a	1984
	Live 1971	n/a	*Oh Boy*	1990
	The Inner Flaming Axe—Syracruse Uni 1972	n/a	*Minotauro*	1994
	Bundled Sunspray Demise	*TARKL*	n/a	1973

Artist's Name	Album Title	LP Record Label	CD Label	Original Release
JAN HAMMER	*Dance of the Maya*	*Phonygraf*	*n/a*	*1974*
	Make Love	MPS	n/a	1976
	The Early Years	Nemperor	n/a	1975
	The First Seven Days	Nemperor	n/a	1975
	Oh Yeah	Nemperor	n/a	1976
	Live with Jeff Beck	CBS	Epic	1977
	Melodies	Epic	n/a	1979
	Black Sheep	Asylum	n/a	1979
DAVID EARLE JOHNSON	The Midweek Blues	Plug	n/a	1974
	Route Two	Landslide	n/a	1975
	Time Is Free	Vanguard	n/a	1977
	Skin Deep	JDE	n/a	1978
	Hip Address	CMP	n/a	1980
JEFF BECK	Blow by Blow	Epic	Epic	1975
	Wired	Epic	Epic	1976
	Live with the Jan Hammer Group	Epic	Epic	1977
JERRY GOODMAN	Like Children	Nemperor	n/a	1974
	It's Alive	Private	Private	1989
BILLY COBHAM	Spectrum	Atlantic	n/a	1973
	Crosswinds	Atlantic	n/a	1974
	Total Eclipse	Atlantic	n/a	1975
	Shabazz	Atlantic	n/a	1975
	A Funky Thide of Sings	Atlantic	n/a	1975
	Life and Times	Atlantic	n/a	1976
BILLY COBHAM/ GEORGE DUKE	Live on Tour in Europe	Atlantic	n/a	1976
BILLY COBHAM	Inner Conflicts	Atlantic	n/a	1978
	Best Of	Atlantic	Atlantic	1980
	Magic	CBS	n/a	1977

Artist's Name	Album Title	LP Record Label	CD Label	Original Release
BILLY COBHAM	Alivemutherforya	CBS	n/a	1977
	Simplicity of Expression	CBS	n/a	1978
	BC	CBS	n/a	1979
	Flight Time	Inak	Inak	1981
	Stratus	Inak	Inak	1981
	Observations	Elektra	n/a	1982
	Smokin'	Elektra	n/a	1983
	Warning	GRP	GRP	1985
	Powerplay	GRP	GRP	1986
	Picture This	GRP	GRP	1987
	By Design	n/a	FNAC	1992
	Traveler	n/a	Evidence	1993
	Paradox	n/a	Tiptoe	1996
NARADA MICHAEL WALDEN	Garden of Love Light	Atlantic	n/a	1976
	I Cry, I Smile	Atlantic	n/a	1977
JEAN-LUC PONTY	Electric Connection	Pacific Jazz	n/a	1969
	King Kong: Ponty Plays Zappa	World Pacific	World Pacific	1969
	Canteloupe Island	Blue Note	n/a	1969
	Experience	Pacific Jazz	n/a	1969
	Live at Dontes	Blue Note	Blue Note	1970
	Open Strings	BASF	n/a	1971
	Upon the Wings of Music	Atlantic	Atlantic	1975
	Aurora	Atlantic	Atlantic	1975
	Imaginary Voyage	Atlantic	Atlantic	1976
	Enigmatic Ocean	Atlantic	Atlantic	1977
	Cosmic Messenger	Atlantic	Atlantic	1978
	A Taste Foe Passion	Atlantic	n/a	1979
	Live	Atlantic	n/a	1979
	Civilized Evil	Atlantic	n/a	1980

Artist's Name	Album Title	LP Record Label	CD Label	Original Release
	Mystical Adventures	Atlantic	n/a	1981
	Individual Choice	Atlantic	n/a	1983
	Open Mind	Atlantic	n/a	1984
	Fables	Atlantic	n/a	1985
	The Gift of Time	Columbia	Columbia	1987
	Storytelling	Columbia	Columbia	1989
	Tchokola	n/a	Epic	1991
	No Absolute Time	n/a	Fnac	1993
	Le Voyage: Anthology	n/a	Rhino	1996
JOE HARRIOTT & JOHN MAYER DOUBLE QUINTET	Indo Jazz Fusions Vol. 1	EMI	n/a	1966
	Indo Jazz Fusions Vol. 2	EMI	n/a	1967
SHAKTI	Shakti with John McLaughlin	CBS	Columbia	1976
	Handful of Beauty	CBS	Columbia	1977
	Natural Elements	CBS	Columbia	1978
L SHANKAR	Touch Me There	ZAPPA	ZAPPA	1979
	Vision	ECM	ECM	1984
	Song for Everyone	ECM	ECM	1985
	M.R.C.S.	n/a	ECM	1991
	Soul Searcher	n/a	Axiom	1990
ZAKIR HUSSAIN	Making Music	ECM	ECM	1987

CHAPTER 9

The Mysterious Travellers

ARTIST'S NAME	ALBUM TITLE	LP RECORD LABEL	CD LABEL	ORIGINAL RELEASE
CANNONBALL ADDERLEY	Mercy, Mercy, Mercy	Capitol	Capitol	1966
	Why Am I Treated So Bad	Capitol	n/a	1966
	Live in Japan	Capitol	Capitol	1966
	74 Miles Away	Capitol	n/a	1967
	Accent on Africa	Capitol	n/a	1969
	Country Preacher	Capitol	Capitol	1969
	Black Messiah	Capitol	n/a	1970
	The Price You Got to Pay to Be Free	Capitol	n/a	1970
	Inside Straight	Fantasy	Fantasy	1973
	Pyramid	Fantasy	n/a	1974
CANNONBALL ADDERLEY	Phenix	Fantasy	n/a	1975
	Lovers	Fantasy	n/a	1975
RAMSEY LEWIS	At the Bohemian Caverns	Argo	n/a	1965
	The In Crowd	Chess	n/a	1965
	Sun Goddess	CBS	n/a	1974
	Routes	CBS	n/a	1980

Discographer's Note: "Wade in the Water," Lewis's big 1966 hit was originally released as a single. Subsequently it has appeared on various compilations such as:

RAMSEY LEWIS	The Greatest Hits of	n/a	MCA	1987
JOE ZAWINUL	The Beginning	n/a	Fresh Sounds	1996
	Money in the Pocket	Atlantic	Rhino/Atlantic	1966
	The Rise and Fall of the Third Stream	Atlantic	Rhino/Atlantic	1967
	Concerto Retitled	Atlantic	n/a	1970
	Zawinul	Atlantic	Atlantic	1971
	Dialects	CBS	Sony Japan	1986

Artist's Name	Album Title	LP Record Label	CD Label	Original Release
	Stories of the Danube	n/a	Phillips	1995
	My People	n/a	Escapade	1996
WAYNE SHORTER	Super Nova	Blue Note	Blue Note	1969
	Moto Grosso Feio	Blue Note	One Way	1970
	Odyssey of Iska	Blue Note	Blue Note	1970
	Native Dancer	Blue Note	Columbia	1974
	Atlantis	CBS	Columbia	1985
	Phantom Navigator	CBS	Columbia	1987
	Joy Rider	CBS	Columbia	1987
	High Life	n/a	Verve	1995
MIROSLAV VITOUS	Infinite Search (Mountain in the Clouds)	Embryo	Atlantic Japan	1969
	Purple	Epic	n/a	1970
	Magic Shepherd	Warner Bros.	n/a	1976
	Majesty Music	Arista	n/a	1977
	Guardian Angels	Evidence	n/a	1979
WEATHER REPORT	Weather Report	CBS	Columbia	1971
	I Sing the Body Electric	CBS	Columbia	1972
	Live in Tokyo (2 CD)	CBS	Sony Japan	1972
	Sweetnighter	CBS	Columbia	1973
	Mysterious Traveller	CBS	Columbia	1974
	Mysterious Traveller—Mastersound (w/ extra track)	n/a	Sony Japan	1997
	Tail Spinnin'	CBS	Columbia	1975
	Black Market	CBS	Columbia	1976
	Heavy Weather	CBS	Columbia	1977
	Mr. Gone	CBS	Columbia	1978
	8.30	CBS	Columbia	1979
	Night Passage	CBS	Columbia	1980
	Weather Report	CBS	Columbia	1982
	Procession	CBS	Columbia	1983

Artist's Name	Album Title	LP Record Label	CD Label	Original Release
WEATHER REPORT	Domino Theory	CBS	Columbia	1984
	Sportin' Life	CBS	Columbia	1984
	This Is This	CBS	Columbia	1985
	Solarizations—Live	*Allied*	*All of Us*	*1974*
	Montreux '76	*n/a*	*Four Aces*	*1994*
	Italian Weather—Live	*n/a*	*All of Us*	*1994*
	Live Weather	*n/a*	*Showco*	*1996*
VARIOUS ARTISTS	Havana Jam Vol. I featuring Weather Report	CBS	Sony Japan	1979
	Havana Jam Vol. II featuring Weather Report	CBS	Sony Japan	1979
	In Performance at the Playboy Jazz Festival	Elektra	n/a	1982
ZAWINUL SYNDICATE	The Immigrants	CBS	Columbia	1988
	Black Water	CBS	Columbia	1989
	Lost Tribes	CBS	Columbia	1992
THE MANHATTAN PROJECT	The Manhattan Project	n/a	Blue Note	1990
ALPHONSO JOHNSON	Moonshadows	Epic	n/a	1976
	Yesterday's Dreams	Epic	n/a	1976
	Spellbound	Epic	n/a	1978
DOM UM ROMAO	Dom Um Romao	Muse	Muse	1974
PETER ERSKINE	Peter Erskine	Fantasy	Fantasy	1982
	Transition	n/a	Denon	1986
	Big Theatre	n/a	Ah Um	1986
	Motion Poet	n/a	Denon	1988
	Sweet Soul	n/a	Novus	1991

CHAPTER 10
Light as a Feather

ARTIST'S NAME	ALBUM TITLE	LP RECORD LABEL	CD LABEL	ORIGINAL RELEASE
HERBIE HANCOCK	Empyrean Isles	Blue Note	Blue Note	1964
	Maiden Voyage	Blue Note	Blue Note	1965
	Blow Up Soundtrack	Capitol	Capitol	1966
	Speak Like a Child	Blue Note	Blue Note	1968
	The Prisoner	Blue Note	Blue Note	1969
	Fat Albert Rotunda	Warner Bros.	n/a	1969
	Mwandishi	Warner Bros.	n/a	1971
	Crossings	Warner Bros.	n/a	1972
	Mwandishi: The Complete Warner Bros. Recordings	n/a	Warner Bros.	1995
	Sextant	CBS	Columbia	1972
	Headhunters	CBS	Columbia	1974
	Thrust	CBS	Columbia	1974
	Death Wish Soundtrack	CBS	n/a	1975
	Man Child	CBS	Columbia	1975
	Secrets	CBS	Columbia	1976
	Flood	CBS-Sony	Sony Japan	1977
	VSOP	CBS	Columbia	1977
	Sunlight	CBS	Columbia	1978
	Feet's Don't Fail Me Know	CBS	Columbia	1979
	Tempest in the Colosseum	CBS-Sony	Columbia Holland	1978
	Direct Step	CBS-Sony	Sony Japan	1979
	Monster	CBS	Columbia	1980
	Mr. Hands	CBS	Columbia	1980

Discographer's Note: Caution, Hancock's dalliance with disco-funk produced Feet's Don't Fail Me Know, Monster, Magic Windows, and Lite Me Up. Headhunters they most certainly aren't.

Artist's Name	Album Title	LP Record Label	CD Label	Original Release
HERBIE HANCOCK	Magic Windows	CBS	Columbia	1981
	Lite Me Up	CBS	Columbia	1982
	Future Shock	CBS	Columbia	1983
	Sound System	CBS	Columbia	1984
	Village Life	CBS	Columbia	1985
	Perfect Machine	CBS	Columbia	1988
	The Herbie Hancock Quartet Live 1992	*n/a*	*Jazz Door*	*1996*
	Dis Is Da Drum	n/a	Verve	1994
	The New Standard	n/a	Verve	1996
EDDIE HENDERSON	Realization	Capricorn	n/a	1973
	Inside Out	Capricorn	n/a	1973
	Sunburst	Blue Note	n/a	1975
	Heritage	Blue Note	n/a	1975
	Comin' Through	Capitol	n/a	1977
	Mahal	Capitol	n/a	1978
HARVEY MASON	Marching in the Street	Arista	n/a	1975
	Funk in a Mason Jar	Arista	n/a	1976
	Most Valuable Player	Arista	n/a	1981
BERNIE MAUPIN	The Jewel in the Lotus	ECM	n/a	1974
	Slow Traffic to the Right	Mercury	n/a	1977
THE HEADHUNTERS	Survival of the Fittest	Arista	Arista Japan	1975
	Straight from the Gate	Arista	Arista Japan	1977
MIKE CLARK & PAUL JACKSON	The Funk Stops here	n/a	TipToe	1992
SLY & THE FAMILY STONE	Dance to the Music	Epic	Epic	1968
	Life	Epic	Epic	1968
	Stand	Epic	Epic	1969
	There's a Riot Going On	Epic	Epic	1971
	Fresh	Epic	Epic	1973
JAMES BROWN	Cold Sweat	Polydor	Polydor	1967
	Say It Loud, I'm Black and I'm Proud	Polydor	Polydor	1969

Artist's Name	Album Title	LP Record Label	CD Label	Original Release
	It's a New Day—So Let a Man Come In	Polydor	Polydor	1970
	Sex Machine	Polydor	Polydor	1970
	Super Bad	Polydor	Polydor	1971
GRAHAM CENTRAL STATION	Graham Central Station	Warner Bros.	Warner Bros.	1974
	Release Yourself	Warner Bros.	Warner Bros.	1974
	Ain't No Bout Adout It	Warner Bros.	Warner Bros.	1975
PARLIAMENT	Up for the Down Stroke	Casablanca	Polygram	1974
	Mothership Connection	Casablanca	Polygram	1976
FUNKADELIC	Free Your Mind and Your Ass Will Follow	Westbound	Westbound	1970
	Maggot Brain	Westbound	Westbound	1971
	America Eats Its Young	Westbound	Westbound	1972
EARTH WIND & FIRE	Earth Wind and Fire	Warner Bros.	Warner Bros.	1971
	Last Days and Time	Columbia	Columbia	1973
	Gratitude	Columbia	Columbia	1975
STEVIE WONDER	Music of My Mind	Motown	Motown	1972
	Talking Book	Motown	Motown	1972
	Innervisions	Motown	Motown	1973
	Fulfillingness First Finale	Motown	Motown	1974
	Songs in the Key of Life	Motown	Motown	1976
MARVIN GAYE	What's Going On	Motown	Motown	1971
	Trouble Man	Motown	Motown	1972
ISSAC HAYES	Hot Buttered Soul	Stax	Stax	1969
	Issac Hayes Movement	Stax	Stax	1970
	Shaft	Stax	Stax	1971
	Black Moses	Stax	Stax	1972
VARIOUS ARTISTS	Wattstax Soundtrack	Stax	Charly	1972
DONNY HATHAWAY	Donny Hathaway	Atco	n/a	1972
	Live	Atco	WEA	1972
	Extensions of a Man	Atco	WEA	1973
	In Performance	Atco	WEA	1980

Artist's Name	Album Title	LP Record Label	CD Label	Original Release
KING CURTIS	Live at Fillmore West	Atlantic	n/a	1971
CURTIS MAYFIELD	Curtis	Buddah	Charly	1974
	Superfly	Buddah	Charly	1974
	Back to the World	Buddah	Charly	1974
	Live	Buddah	Charly	1974
DONALD BYRD	Up with Donald Byrd	Verve	n/a	1964
	Fancy Free	Blue Note	Blue Note	1969
	Kofi	n/a	Blue Note	1994
	Electric Byrd	Blue Note	Blue Note	1970
	Ethiopian Nights	Blue Note	Blue Note Japan	1971
	Street Lady	Blue Note	Blue Note	1973
	Stepping Into Tomorrow	Blue Note	n/a	1974
	Black Byrd	Blue Note	Blue Note	1974
	Places and Spaces	Blue Note	Blue Note	1975
	Caricatures	Blue Note	Blue Note	1976
	Thank You for F.U.M.L.	Elektra	n/a	1978
	Love Byrd: Donald Byrd and 125th St. NYC	Elektra	Elektra	1981
	Words, Sounds, Colours and Shapes	Elektra	n/a	1982
LONNIE SMITH	Think	Blue Note	Blue Note	1968
	Move Your Hand	Blue Note	Blue Note	1969
	Turning Point	Blue Note	n/a	1969
	Drives	Blue Note	Blue Note	1970
BOBBY HUTCHERSON	San Francisco	Blue Note	Blue Note	1970
GRANT GREEN	His Majesty King Funk	Verve	Verve	1965
	Carryin' On	Blue Note	Blue Note	1969
	Alive!	Blue Note	Blue Note	1970
JIMMY McGRIFF	Electric Funk	Blue Note	Blue Note	1969
JOE HENDERSON	Power to the People	Milestone	n/a	1969
	If You're Not Part of the Problem . . .	Milestone	n/a	1971
	In Pursuit of Blackness	Milestone	n/a	1971

Artist's Name	Album Title	LP Record Label	CD Label	Original Release
	Black Is the Colour	Milestone	n/a	1972
	Multiple	Milestone	n/a	1973
	The Elements	Milestone	OJC	1974
	Canyon Lady	Milestone	n/a	1974
	Black Narcissus	Milestone	n/a	1975
	Black Miracle	Milestone	n/a	1976
	The Milestone Years (8 CD Box set)	n/a	Milestone	1994
ERIC KLOSS	To Hear Is to See	Prestige	n/a	1969
	Consciousness	Prestige	n/a	1970
STAN GETZ	Captain Marvel	Columbia	n/a	1972
	Stan Getz at Montreux	Polydor	n/a	1972
CHICK COREA	Return to Forever	ECM	ECM	1972
	Light as a Feather	ECM	ECM	1972
	The Leprechaun	Polydor	Polydor	1975
	My Spanish Heart	Polydor	Polydor	1976
	The Mad Hatter	Polydor	Polydor	1978
	Friends	Polydor	Polydor	1978
	Secret Agent	Polydor	n/a	1978
	Tap Step	Warner Bros.	Stretch	1980
	Touchstone	n/a	Stretch	1982
	Again and Again	Elektra	Elektra	1982
Chick Corea continues in ch. 11				
RETURN TO FOREVER	Hymn of the Seventh Galaxy	Polydor	Polydor	1973
	Where Have I Known You Before	Polydor	Polydor	1974
	No Mystery	Polydor	Polydor	1975
	Romantic Warrior	CBS	Columbia	1976
	Music Magic	CBS	Columbia	1977
	Return to Forever Live	CBS	Columbia	1977
	Return to the 7th Galaxy—The Anthology	n/a	Verve	1996

Artist's Name	Album Title	LP Record Label	CD Label	Original Release
BILL CONNORS	Theme to the Guardian	ECM	ECM	1975
	Of Mist and Melting	ECM	ECM	1977
	Swimming with a Hole in My Body	ECM	ECM	1979
	Step It	Line	Line	1984
	Double-Up	Line	Line	1986
	Assembler	Line	Line	1987
AL DIMEOLA	Land of the Midnight Sun	CBS	Columbia	1976
	Elegant Gypsy	CBS	Columbia	1976
	Casino	CBS	Columbia	1977
	Spendido Hotel	CBS	Columbia	1979
	Electric Rendezvous	CBS	Columbia	1981
	Tour De Force Live	CBS	Columbia	1982
	Scenario	CBS	Columbia	1983
	Soaring through a Dream	EMI	n/a	1984
	Cielo El Terra	EMI	n/a	1985
	Tirami Su	EMI	EMI	1987
	World Sinfonia	n/a	Tomato	1990
	The Collection	n/a	Castle	1991
	Kiss My Axe	n/a	Tomato	1991
	Orange and Blue	n/a	Tomato	1994
STANLEY CLARKE	Children of Forever	Polydor	One Way	1972
	Stanley Clarke	Epic	Epic	1974
	Journey to Love	Epic	Epic	1975
	School Days	Epic	Epic	1976
	Live	Epic	Epic	1977
	I Wanna Play for You	Epic	Epic	1977
	Modern Man	Epic	Epic	1978
	Rocks, Pebbles and Sand	Epic	Epic	1980
	The Clarke/Duke Project Vol. 1	Epic	Epic	1981

Artist's Name	Album Title	LP Record Label	CD Label	Original Release
	Let Me Know You	Epic	Epic	1982
	The Clarke/Duke Project Vol. 2	Epic	Epic	1983

Discographer's Note: Later Clarke albums drifted off in a variety of forgettable directions, including disco and electro-funk.

Artist's Name	Album Title	LP Record Label	CD Label	Original Release
LENNY WHITE	Venusian Summer	Nemperor	n/a	1975
	Big City	Nemperor	n/a	1976
	The Adventures of Astral Pirates	Nemperor	n/a	1977
	Streamline	Elektra	n/a	1978
	Attitude	Elektra	n/a	1982
	Present Tense	n/a	Hip Bop	1995
	Renderers of Spirit	n/a	Hip Bop	1997
DAVID SANCIOUS	Forest of Feeling	Epic	Epic	1975
	Transformation	Epic	n/a	1976
	Dance of the Age of Enlightenment	Arista	n/a	1977
	True Stories	Arista	n/a	1978
	Just as I Thought	Arista	n/a	1980
	Bridge	Elektra	n/a	1981
GEORGE DUKE	Save the Country	Liberty	n/a	1970
	The Inner Source	MPS	n/a	1971
	Feel	MPS	n/a	1974
	Faces in Reflections	MPS	n/a	1974
	I Love the Blues/She Heard Me Cry	MPS	n/a	1976
	Liberated Fantasies	MPS	n/a	1976
	The Aura Will Prevail	MPS	n/a	1976
ALPHONSE MOUZON	The Essence of Mystery	Blue Note	n/a	1975
	Funky Snakefoot	Blue Note	RPM	1975
	Mind Transplant	Blue Note	RPM	1975
	The Man Incognito	Blue Note	RPM	1976
	Back Together Again	Atlantic	n/a	1977
	Virtue	MPS	n/a	1976

Artist's Name	Album Title	LP Record Label	CD Label	Original Release
	In Search of a Dream	MPS	n/a	1977
	Star Edition	MPS	n/a	1978
	By All Means	MPS	n/a	1980
	Step Into the Funk	Polydor	n/a	1982

CHAPTER 11
Chain Reaction

Artist's Name	Album Title	LP Record Label	CD Label	Original Release
EDDIE HARRIS	The Electrifying Eddie Harris	Atlantic	Rhino	1967
	Plug Me In	Atlantic	Rhino	1968
	Silver Cycles	Atlantic	n/a	1968
	High Voltage	Atlantic	n/a	1969
	Swiss Movement	Atlantic	Rhino	1969
	Free Speech	Atlantic	n/a	1969
	Come on Down	Atlantic	n/a	1970
	Live at Newport	Atlantic	n/a	1970
	Instant Death	Atlantic	n/a	1971
	Second Movement	Atlantic	n/a	1971
	Sings the Blues	Atlantic	n/a	1972
	Eddie Harris in the UK	Atlantic	n/a	1973
	Is It In	Atlantic	n/a	1974
	I Need Some Money	Atlantic	n/a	1975
	That Is Why You're Overweight	Atlantic	n/a	1975
	Tale of Two Cities	Night	n/a	1975
	Artists Choice Box Set	n/a	Rhino	1994
GROVER WASHINGTON, JR.	Inner City Blues	Kudu	n/a	1972
	All the Kings Horses	Kudu	n/a	1973
	Mister Magic	Kudu	n/a	1975

Artist's Name	Album Title	LP Record Label	CD Label	Original Release
	Feels So Good	Kudu	n/a	1975
	A Secret Place	Kudu	n/a	1976
	Live at the Bijou	Kudu	n/a	1978
	Reed Seed	Motown	n/a	1978
	Paradise	Elektra	Elektra	1979
BOB JAMES	One	CTI	Castle	1974
	Two	CTI	Castle	1975
	Three	CTI	Castle	1976
	BJ4	CTI	Castle	1977
	Heads	CBS	Castle	1977
MARK COLBY	One Good Turn	Tappan Zee	n/a	1979
VARIOUS ARTISTS	The Best of Tappan Zee	n/a	Castle	1997
JOE BECK	Nature Boy	Verve Forecast	n/a	1969
	Beck and Sanborn	Kudu	Epic	1975
	Friends	DMP	DMP	1984
GEORGE BENSON	Beyond the Blue Horizon	CTI	CTI	1972
	White Rabbit	CTI	Epic	1972
	In Concert at Carnegie Hall	CTI	Epic	1975
	Good King Bad	CTI	n/a	1975
	Breezin'	Warner Bros.	Warner Bros.	1976
	In Flight	Warner Bros.	Warner Bros.	1977
FREDDIE HUBBARD	Red Clay	CTI	Epic	1970
	Straight Life	CTI	Epic	1971
	First Light	CTI	Epic	1971
	Sky Dive	CTI	n/a	1972
	In Concert Vols. I & II	CTI	Epic	1973
	Keep Your Soul Together	CTI	n/a	1973
	High Energy	CBS	n/a	1974
JOE FARRELL	Song of the Wind	CTI	n/a	1970

Artist's Name	Album Title	LP Record Label	CD Label	Original Release
JOE FARRELL	Outback	CTI	n/a	1971
	Moon Germs	CTI	n/a	1972
	Penny Arcade	CTI	n/a	1973
	Upon This Rock	CTI	n/a	1974
	Canned Funk	CTI	n/a	1974
RON CARTER	Blues Farm	CTI	Epic	1973
	All Blues	CTI	n/a	1973
DEODATO	Prelude	CTI	Epic	1973
RONNIE LAWS	Pressure Sensitive	Blue Note	Blue Note	1975
	Friends and Strangers	Blue Note	n/a	1977
JAZZ CRUSADERS	Freedom Sound	Pacific Jazz	n/a	1961
	Looking Ahead	Pacific Jazz	n/a	1962
	At the Lighthouse	Pacific Jazz	n/a	1963
	Thought Talk	Pacific Jazz	n/a	1963
	Heat Wave	Pacific Jazz	n/a	1965
	Chile Con Soul	Pacific Jazz	n/a	1966
	Lighthouse 66	Pacific Jazz	n/a	1966
	Talk That Jazz	Pacific Jazz	n/a	1966
	Festival Jazz	Pacific Jazz	n/a	1967
	Lighthouse 68	Pacific Jazz	n/a	1968
	Uh Huh	Pacific Jazz	n/a	1968
	Powerhouse	Pacific Jazz	n/a	1969
	Lighthouse 69	Pacific Jazz	n/a	1969
	Give Peace a Chance	Liberty	n/a	1970
	Young Rabbits	Blue Note	n/a	1976
	Old Sox New Shoes	Rare Earth	n/a	1971
	Pass the Plate	Chisa	n/a	1972
	Holly wood	Mowest	n/a	1973
CRUSADERS	Crusaders I	ABC	n/a	1971

Artist's Name	Album Title	LP Record Label	CD Label	Original Release
	Second Crusade	ABC	n/a	1972
	Unsung Heroes	ABC	n/a	1973
	Scratch	ABC	MCA	1975
	Southern Comfort	ABC	MCA	1975
	Chain Reaction	ABC	MCA	1975
	Those Southern Nights	ABC	MCA	1976
	Free as the Wind	ABC	MCA	1977
	Images	ABC	MCA	1978
	Street Life	MCA	MCA	1979
	Rhapsody & Blues	MCA	MCA	1980
	Live in Japan	n/a	GRP	1992

Discographer's Note: The Crusaders' later releases had little of the true spirit of earlier albums as they headed off towards FM radio's easy listening zone.

Artist's Name	Album Title	LP Record Label	CD Label	Original Release
JONI MITCHELL	Court and Spark	Asylum	Asylum	1974
	Miles of Aisles	Asylum	Asylum	1974
	Hissing of Summer Lawns	Asylum	Asylum	1975
	Hejira	Asylum	Asylum	1976
	Don Juan's Reckless Daughter	Asylum	Asylum	1977
	Mingus	Asylum	Asylum	1979
TOM SCOTT	HoneySuckle Breeze	Impulse	n/a	1968
	Rural Still Life	Impulse	Impulse Japan	1970
	Hair to Jazz	Flying Dutchman	n/a	1970
	Great Scott	A&M	n/a	1971
	Tom Scott and the LA Express	Epic	Epic	1974
	Tom Cat	Epic	Epic	1975
	New York Connection	Epic	Epic	1975
	Blow It Out	Epic	Epic	1977
	Apple Juice	Columbia	n/a	1981
DOUG CARN	Infant Eyes	Black Jazz	n/a	1971

Artist's Name	Album Title	LP Record Label	CD Label	Original Release
DOUG CARN	Spirit of the New Land	Black Jazz	n/a	1972
	Revelation	Black Jazz	n/a	1973
	The Best of Doug Karn	n/a	Universal Sound	1996
THE AWAKENING	Hear, Sense and Feel	Black Jazz	n/a	1972
	Mirage	Black Jazz	n/a	1973
CALVIN KEYS	Shawn-Neeq	Black Jazz	n/a	1971
	Proceed with Caution	Black Jazz	n/a	1974
KELLEE PATTERSON	Maiden Voyage	Black Jazz	n/a	1973
RUDOLPH JOHNSON	Spring Rain	Black Jazz	n/a	1971
	The Second Coming	Black Jazz	n/a	1973
HENRY FRANKLIN	The Skipper	Black Jazz	n/a	1972
	The Skipper at Home	Black Jazz	n/a	1974
ROLAND HAYNES	Roland Haynes	Black Jazz	n/a	1975
WALTER BISHOP JR.	Coral Keys	Black Jazz	n/a	1971
	Keeper of My Soul	Black Jazz	n/a	1973
CHESTER THOMPSON	Powerhouse	Black Jazz	n/a	1971
VARIOUS ARTISTS	The Best of Black Jazz	n/a	Universal Sound	1996
	Soul Jazz Loves Strata East	n/a	Soul Jazz	1994
	Strata-2-East	n/a	Universal Sound	1997
	Universal Sounds of America	n/a	Soul Jazz	1994
	Message from the Tribe—An Anthology 1972–1977	n/a	Universal Sound	1996
CATALYST	Perception	Muse	n/a	1972
	Unity	Muse	n/a	1974
	Catalyst	Muse	n/a	1974
	A Tear and a Smile	Muse	n/a	1975
NATHAN DAVIS	Makatuka	Segue	n/a	1971
	If	Tomorrow	n/a	1976
SHAMEK FARRAH	First Impressions	Strata East	n/a	1975

Artist's Name	Album Title	LP Record Label	CD Label	Original Release
WELDON IRVINE	La Dee La La	RA	n/a	1978
	Time Capsule	Nodlew	P-Vine	1973
	In Harmony	Strata-East	n/a	1974
	Cosmic Vortex	RCA	n/a	1974
	Spirit Man	RCA	RCA Japan	1975
SONNY FORTUNE	Long Before Our Mothers Cried	Strata-East	n/a	1974
	Waves of Dreams	A&M	n/a	1976
	Serengeti Minstrel	Atlantic	n/a	1977
	Infinity Is	Atlantic	n/a	1978
STANLEY COWELL	New World	Galaxy	n/a	1978
CARLOS GARNETT	Black Love	Muse	Muse	1974
GARY BARTZ NTU TROOP	Harlem Bush Music: Taifa	Milestone	Milestone	1970
	Harlem Bush Music: Uhuru	Milestone	Milestone	1971
	Juju Street Songs	Prestige	Prestige	1972
	Follow the Medicine Man	Prestige	n/a	1972
	I've Known Rivers and Other bodies	Prestige	n/a	1973
	Singerella/A Ghetto Fairy Tale	Prestige	n/a	1974
GARY BARTZ	The Shadow Do	Prestige	n/a	1975
	Music is My Sanctuary	Capitol	n/a	1975
	Bartz	Arista	n/a	
NORMAN CONNERS	Dance of Magic	Buddah	Sequel	1972
	Dark of Light	Buddah	Sequel	1973
	Love from the Sun	Buddah	n/a	1973
	Slewfoot	Buddah	n/a	1974
GIL SCOTT-HERON	Small Talk at 125th and Lennox	Flying Dutchman	Flying Dutchman	1972
	Free Will	Flying Dutchman	Flying Dutchman	1972
	Pieces of a Man	Flying Dutchman	Flying Dutchman	1973
	Winter in America	Strata East	Strata East	1975
	The Revolution Will Not Be Televised	Flying Dutchman	Flying Dutchman	1975

Artist's Name	Album Title	LP Record Label	CD Label	Original Release
GIL SCOTT-HERON	First Minute of a New Day	Arista	Arista Japan	1975
	From South Africa to South Carolina	Arista	Arista Japan	1976
	It's Your World	Arista	Arista Japan	1976
	Bridges	Arista	Arista Japan	1977
	Secrets	Arista	Arista Japan	1978
	Real Eyes	Arista	Arista Japan	1980
	Reflections	Arista	Arista	1981
	Movin' Targets	Arista	Arista	1982
	Tales of Gil Scott-Heron	Arista	Arista	1990
	Old Glory (Anthology)	Arista	Arista	1990
LONNIE LISTON SMITH	Astral Travelling	Flying Dutchman	Flying Dutchman	1973
	Expansions	Flying Dutchman	Flying Dutchman	1974
	Cosmic Funk	Flying Dutchman	Flying Dutchman	1974
	Reflections of a Golden Dream	Flying Dutchman	Flying Dutchman	1976
	Live	RCA	n/a	1977
	Loveland	Columbia	n/a	1978
	Dreams of Tomorrow	Doctor Jazz	n/a	1979
	Visions of a New World	RCA	n/a	1980
	Renaissance	RCA	n/a	1980
	Silhouettes	Doctor Jazz	n/a	1984
	Rejuvenation	Doctor Jazz	n/a	1985
SUN RA	Horizon	Saturn	n/a	1971
	Nidhamu	Saturn	n/a	1971
	Astro-Black	Impulse	n/a	1972
	Space is the Place	Blue Thumb	n/a	1972
CHARLES EARLAND	Black Talk	Prestige	OJC	1970
	Black Drops	Prestige	n/a	1970
	Living Black	Prestige	n/a	1970
	Leaving This Planet	Prestige	Prestige	1974

Artist's Name	Album Title	LP Record Label	CD Label	Original Release
	Smokin'	Muse	n/a	1977
	Pleasant Afternoon	Muse	n/a	1978
	Infant Eyes	Muse	n/a	1978
	Coming to You Live	Columbia	n/a	1979
	Front Burner	Milestone	Milestone	1988
	Third Degree Burn	Milestone	Milestone	1989
ROY AYERS	Virgo Vibes	Atlantic	n/a	1967
	Daddy Bug and Friend	Atco	n/a	1969
	Ubiquity	Polydor	Polydor	1970
	He's Coming	Polydor	n/a	1971
	Ubiquity Live at Montreux	Polydor Japan	Verve	1973
	Mystic Voyage	Polydor	n/a	1975
	Red Black and Green	Polydor	n/a	1976
	Vibrations	Polydor	n/a	1977
	Evolution	n/a	Polydor Chronicles	1995
LEE RITENOUR	First Course	Epic	Epic	1976
	Captain Fingers	Epic	Epic	1977
LEE RITENOUR	Feel the Night	Elektra	Elektra	1979
	Wes Bound	n/a	GRP	1992
	Larry and Lee	n/a	GRP	1995
	Live in LA	n/a	GRP	1997
LARRY CARLTON	Larry Carlton	Warner Bros.	Warner Bros.	1978
	Live in Japan	Warner Bros.	Warner Bros.	1979
	Sleepwalk	MCA	n/a	1981
	Friends	MCA	n/a	1982
JEFF LORBER	Fusion	Inner City	n/a	1977
	Soft Space	Inner City	n/a	1978
	Water Sign	Arista	n/a	1979
JOHN KLEMMER	All the Children Cried	Cadet	n/a	1969

Artist's Name	Album Title	LP Record Label	CD Label	Original Release
JOHN KLEMMER	Eruptions	Cadet	n/a	1970
	Constant Throb	Impulse	n/a	1971
	Waterfalls	Impulse	n/a	1972
	Intensity	Impulse	n/a	1973
	Magic and Movement	Impulse	n/a	1973
	Touch	Impulse	n/a	1976
DAVID SANBORN	Taking Off	Warner Bros.	Warner Bros.	1975
	Sanborn	Warner Bros.	Warner Bros.	1976
	Heart to Heart	Warner Bros.	Warner Bros.	1978
	Hideaway	Warner Bros.	Warner Bros.	1979
	Voyeur	Warner Bros.	Warner Bros.	1980
	As We Speak	Warner Bros.	Warner Bros.	1981
	Backstreet	Warner Bros.	Warner Bros.	1982
	Straight to the Heart	Warner Bros.	Warner Bros.	1984
	Double Vision	Warner Bros.	Warner Bros.	1986
	A Change of Heart	Warner Bros.	Warner Bros.	1987
	Close Up	Warner Bros.	Warner Bros.	1988
	Another Hand	Warner Bros.	Warner Bros.	1991
	Upfront	Warner Bros.	Warner Bros.	1992
	Hearsay	Warner Bros.	Warner Bros.	1994
KENNY G	Duotones	Arista	Arista	1986

Discographer's Note: Many would argue that even one Kenny G. entry is highly questionable. I would not disagree. As it's mentioned in the text, though, a certain obligation prevails.

Artist's Name	Album Title	LP Record Label	CD Label	Original Release
CHICK COREA ELEKTRIC BAND	The Elektric Band	GRP	GRP	1986
	Light Years	GRP	GRP	1987
	Eye of the Beholder	n/a	GRP	1988
	Inside Out	n/a	GRP	1990

Artist's Name	Album Title	LP Record Label	CD Label	Original Release
CHICK COREA ELEKTRIC BAND II	Paint the World	n/a	GRP	1993
	Live at Elario's	n/a	Stretch Japan	1997
VARIOUS ARTISTS	GRP Super Live in Concert	GRP	GRP	1988
JOHN PATITUCCI	John Patitucci	GRP	GRP	1987
	On the Corner	n/a	GRP	1989
	Sketchbook	n/a	GRP	1990
	Heart of the Bass	n/a	GRP	1991
	Another World	n/a	GRP	1993
	Mistura Fina	n/a	GRP	1994
	One More Angel	n/a	Stretch	1997
ERIC MARIENTHAL	Voices of the Heart	GRP	GRP	1988
	Round Trip	n/a	GRP	1989
	Crossroads	n/a	GRP	1990
	Oasis	n/a	GRP	1991
	One Touch	n/a	GRP	1993
	Street Dance	n/a	GRP	1994
	Easy Street	n/a	i.e. Music	1997
DAVE WECKL	Masterplan	n/a	GRP	1990
	Heads Up	n/a	GRP	1992
	Hard Wired	n/a	GRP	1994
JIMMY EARL	Jimmy Earl	n/a	Legato	1994
JOHN BEASLEY	Cauldron	n/a	Windham Hill	1992
	A Change of Heart	n/a	Windham Hill	1993
JEFF BEAL	Liberation	Antilles	Antilles	1988
	Perpetual Motion	Antilles	Antilles	1989
	Objects in the Mirror	n/a	Triloka	1991
	Three Graces	n/a	Triloka	1993
	Contemplations	n/a	Triloka	1994

Artist's Name	Album Title	LP Record Label	CD Label	Original Release
STEVE TAVAGLIONE	Blue Tav	n/a	MIDI	1994
MICHAEL LANDAU	Tales from the Bulge	n/a	Smashed Hits	1994
LOS LOBOTOMYS	Los Lobotomys	n/a	Maxus	1989
VINNIE COLAIUTA	Vinnie Colaiuta	n/a	Stretch	1995
BILL MEYERS	Images	Spindletop	Spindletop	1986
BARNABY FINCH	Digital Madness	Alfa	Alfa	1989
FIRE MERCHANTS	Fire Merchants	Medusa	Medusa	1989
	Landlords of Atlantis	n/a	Renaissance	1994
JIMI TUNNEL	Trilateral Commission	n/a	Glasshouse	1992
JON HERRINGTON	The Complete Rhyming Dictionary	n/a	Glasshouse	1993
BILLY CHILDS	Take for Example This	Windham Hill	Windham Hill	1988
	Twilight Is upon Us	Windham Hill	Windham Hill	1989
	His April Touch	Windham Hill	Windham Hill	1991
	Portrait of a Player	Windham Hill	Windham Hill	1993
	I've Known Rivers	n/a	Stretch	1995
WISHFUL THINKING	Wishful Thinking	Pausa	Pausa	1985
	Think Again	Pausa	Pausa	1986
	Way Down West	Soundwings	Soundwings	1988
	That Was Then	n/a	Intima	1990
MICHEL COLOMBIER	Michel Colombier	Chrysalis	Arista	1979
BRANDON FIELDS	The Other Side of the Story	Nova	Nova	1986
	The Traveller	Nova	Nova	1988
	Other Places	n/a	Nova	1989
	Everybody's Business	n/a	Nova	1991
	Brandon Fields	n/a	Positive	1995
MITCH FORMAN	Train of Thought	Magenta	Magenta	1985
BOB MALACH	Mood Swing	n/a	Go Jazz	1991
STANLEY JORDAN	Magic Touch	Blue Note	Blue Note	1995
	Flying Home	n/a	EMI	1988
	Street Talk	n/a	EMI	1990

Artist's Name	Album Title	LP Record Label	CD Label	Original Release
SPYRO GYRA	Stolen Moments	n/a	Blue Note	1991
	Spyro Gyra	MCA	MCA	1976
	Morning Dance	MCA	MCA	1979
	Catching the Sun	MCA	MCA	1980
	Carnival	MCA	MCA	1980
	Freetime	MCA	MCA	1981
	Incognito	MCA	MCA	1982
	City Kids	MCA	MCA	1983
	Access All Areas	MCA	MCA	1984
	Alternating Currents	MCA	MCA	1985
	Breakout	MCA	MCA	1986

Discographer's Note: Subsequent Spyro Grya albums slipped even deeper into an MOR format with uncanny ease. Live, though, they are still capable of occasional fireworks.

Artist's Name	Album Title	LP Record Label	CD Label	Original Release
YELLOWJACKETS	20/20	n/a	GRP	1997
	Yellowjackets	Warner Bros.	Warner Bros.	1981
	Samurai Samba	Warner Bros.	Warner Bros.	1984
	Four Corners	MCA	MCA	1987
	Politics	MCA	MCA	1988
	Green House	n/a	GRP	1991
	Live Wires	n/a	GRP	1992
	Like a River	n/a	GRP	1992
	Run for Your Life	n/a	GRP	1993
VARIOUS ARTISTS	GRP Live at the North Sea Jazz Festival	n/a	GRP	1995
JIMMY HASLIP	Arc	n/a	GRP	1993
THE RIPPINGTONS	Moonlighting	GRP	GRP	1986
	Kilimanjaro	GRP	GRP	1988
	Tourist in Paradise	GRP	GRP	1989

Discographer's Note: See remarks after Kenny G. entry.

Artist's Name	Album Title	LP Record Label	CD Label	Original Release
NELSON RANGELL	Playing for Keeps	GRP	GRP	1989

CHAPTER 12

Is What It Is

Artist's Name	Album Title	LP Record Label	CD Label	Original Release
MILES DAVIS	The Man with the Horn	Columbia	Columbia	1981
	We Want Miles	Columbia	Columbia	1982
	Live in Japan 1981	n/a	Sony Japan	1992
	Spring (Live in Rome 1982)	n/a	Jazz Rarities	1992
	Forum New York 1982	n/a	Jazz Masters	1992
	Star People	Columbia	Columbia	1983
	In the West (Live in Japan 1983)	n/a	Jazz Masters	1993
	Decoy	Columbia	Columbia	1983
	You're Under Arrest	Columbia	Columbia	1985
	Aura	Columbia	Columbia	1990
	Human Nature	n/a	Jazz File	1993
	Pacific Express: Japan (Live 1985)	n/a	Jazz Masters	1992
	Unissued '85: Live in Kopenhagen	n/a	On Stage	1993
	Tutu	Warner Bros.	Warner Bros.	1986
	The Scarlet Letter Act 2 (Live in Germany 1986)	n/a	Prime of Rarities	1994
	Social Music (Live in New York 1986)	n/a	Tiki	1993
	King of Priests (Live USA 1986)	n/a	Tiki	1995
	Time after Time (Live in Montreux 1986)	n/a	Tiki	1993
	Music from Siesta	Warner Bros.	Warner Bros.	1987
	Greek Theatre '88	n/a	Jazz Masters	1991
	Last Concert in Avignon 1988	n/a	Laserlight	1995
	The Scarlet Letter Act 1 (Live 1988)	n/a	Prime of Rarities	1994
	Grosse Freiheit 36 (w/ Prince)	n/a	Sabotage	1993
	Amandla	Warner Bros.	Warner Bros.	1989
	Time after Time (Live in Milan 1989)	n/a	Jazz Door	1992
	Live Tutu (Perugia 1989)	n/a	Golden Age of Jazz	1992

Artist's Name	Album Title	LP Record Label	CD Label	Original Release
	Miles in Montreux 1989	n/a	Jazz Door	1993
	The Gate of Heaven (Live in Paris 1989)	n/a	Back Stage	1993
	Dingo	Warner Bros.	Warner Bros.	1990
	King of Trumpets (Live in Toronto 1990)	n/a	Flashback	1995
	The Hot Spot	Antilles	Antilles	1990
	Doo-Bop	n/a	Warner Bros.	1991
	Live at Montreux	n/a	Warner Bros.	1993
	Black Devil (Live Paris 1991)	n/a	Beech Marten	1993
	Live Around the World	n/a	Warner Bros.	1996
	Panthalassa: The Music of Miles Davis 1969–1974. Reconstruction and Mix Translation by Bill Laswell	n/a	Columbia	1998
MARCUS MILLER	The Sun Don't Lie	n/a	Dreyfus	1993
	Tales	n/a	Dreyfus	1994
	Live and More	n/a	Dreyfus	1996
PAOLO RUSTICHELLI	Mystic Jazz	n/a	Polydor	1991
JOHN SCOFIELD	East Meets West	Blackhawk	n/a	1977
	John Scofield Live	Enja	Enja	1977
	Rough House	Enja	Enja	1978
	Bar Talk	Novus	Novus	1979
	Shinola	Enja	Enja	1981
	Out Like a Light	Enja	Enja	1981
	Electric Outlet	Gramavision	Gramavision	1984
	Still Warm	Gramavision	Gramavision	1986
	Blue Matter	Gramavision	Gramavision	1986
	Pick Hits Live	Gramavision	Gramavision	1987
	Loud Jazz	Gramavision	Gramavision	1988
	Flat Out	Gramavision	Gramavision	1989
	Time on My Hands	n/a	Blue Note	1990

Artist's Name	Album Title	LP Record Label	CD Label	Original Release
JOHN SCOFIELD	Meant to Be	n/a	Blue Note	1991
	Grace Under Pressure	n/a	Blue Note	1992
	What We Do	n/a	Blue Note	1992
	Hand Jive	n/a	Blue Note	1993
	Plays Live	*n/a*	*Jazz Door*	*1993*
JOHN SCOFIELD & PAT METHENY	I Can See Your House from Here	n/a	Blue Note	1994
JOHN SCOFIELD	Groove Elation	n/a	Blue Note	1995
DENNIS CHAMBERS	Big City	n/a	Pearl Audiophile	1991
	Getting Even	n/a	Pioneer	1992
BIRELI LAGRENE	Inferno	Blue Note	Blue Note	1988
	Foreign Affairs	Blue Note	Blue Note	1988
STEVE KHAN	Tightrope	Columbia	n/a	1977
	The Blue Man	Columbia	n/a	1978
	Arrows	Columbia	n/a	1979
	Evidence	Novus	n/a	1980
	Eyewitness	Antilles	Antilles	1982
	Blades	Passport	Passport	1983
	Casa Loco	Antilles	Antilles	1983
	Local Colour	Denon	Denon	1987
	Public Access	n/a	GRP	1989
	Let's Call This	n/a	Bluemoon	1991
	Headline	n/a	Bluemoon	1992
	Crossings	n/a	Verve	1994
JIM BEARD	Song of the Sun	n/a	CTI	1991
CHROMA	Music on the Edge	n/a	CTI	1991
GRAFFITI	Good Groove	n/a	Lipstick	1991
MIKE STERN	Upside Downside	Atlantic	Atlantic	1986
	Time in Place	Atlantic	Atlantic	1987

Artist's Name	Album Title	LP Record Label	CD Label	Original Release
	Jigsaw	Atlantic	Atlantic	1989
	Odds and Evens	n/a	Atlantic	1991
	Standards (and other Love Songs)	n/a	Atlantic	1992
	Is What It Is	n/a	Atlantic	1993
	Between the Lines	n/a	Atlantic	1995
BOB BERG	Short Stories	n/a	Denon	1987
	Cycles	n/a	Denon	1988
	Back Roads	n/a	Denon	1990
	In the Shadows	n/a	Denon	1990
	Virtual Reality	n/a	Denon	1992
	Enter the Spirit	n/a	Stretch	1993
	Riddles	n/a	Stretch	1994
BOB BERG & MIKE STERN	Games—Live 1990	n/a	Jazz Door	1994
ADAM HOLZMAN	In a Loud Way	n/a	Manhattan	1992
	Overdrive	n/a	Lipstick	1994
	Manifesto	n/a	Lipstick	1995
	The Big Picture	n/a	Escapade	1997
HARVIE SWARTZ	Underneath It All	Gramavision	Gramavision	1980
	Urban Earth	Gramavision	Gramavision	1985
	Smart Moves	Gramavision	Gramavision	1986
	Full Moon Dancer	n/a	Blue Moon	1989
	In a Different Light	n/a	Blue Moon	1990
	Arrival	n/a	Novus	1991
BILL EVANS	Living in the Crest of a Wave	Elektra	n/a	1983
	Alternative Man	Blue Note	Blue Note	1985
	Let the Juice Loose	n/a	Jazz City	1990
	Summertime	n/a	Jazz City	1991
	The Gambler	n/a	Jazz City	1991
	Petit Blonde	n/a	Lipstick	1992

Artist's Name	Album Title	LP Record Label	CD Label	Original Release
BILL EVANS	Push	n/a	Lipstick	1993
	Live in Europe	n/a	Lipstick	1994
	Escape	n/a	Escapade	1996
ELEMENTS	Elements	Antilles	n/a	1982
	Forward Motion	Antilles	Antilles	1983
	Blown Away	Blue Moon	Blue Moon	1985
	Illuminations	RCA Novus	RCA Novus	1989
	Liberal Arts	RCA Novus	RCA Novus	1989
	Spirit River	RCA Novus	RCA Novus	1990
	Far East	n/a	Lipstick	1993
PASTORIUS, METHENY, DITMAS, BLEY / JACO PASTORIUS	Pastorius, Metheny, Ditmas, Bley	Improvising Artists	Improvising Artists	1974
	Jaco Pastorius	Epic	Epic	1976
	Word of Mouth	Warner Bros.	Warner Bros.	1981
	Twins I	Warner Bros.	n/a	1982
	Twins II	Warner Bros.	n/a	1982
	Invitation	Warner Bros.	Warner Bros.	1983
	Birthday Concert	n/a	Warner Bros.	1995
	Holiday for Pans	Sound Hills	Sound Hills	1982
	Blackbird Timeless	ALCR	n/a	1984
	Last Flight—Essence	DIW	DIW	1984
	Natural	DIW	DIW	1988
	Honestly	n/a	JIM	1990
	Live in Italy	n/a	Jazzpoint	1991
	Stuttgart Aria	n/a	Jazzpoint	1992
	Heavy 'n' Jazz	n/a	Jazzpoint	1992
	Live in New York, Vols. 1, 2, and 3	n/a	Jazz Door	1993
	Golden Roads	n/a	Soundhill	1997
PAT METHENY	Bright Size Life	ECM	ECM	1975
	Watercolors	ECM	ECM	1977

Artist's Name	Album Title	LP Record Label	CD Label	Original Release
	Pat Metheny Group	ECM	ECM	1978
	New Chautauqua	ECM	ECM	1979
	American Garage	ECM	ECM	1979
	80/81	ECM	ECM	1980
	As Falls Wichita So Falls Wichita Falls	ECM	ECM	1980
	Offramp	ECM	ECM	1981
	Travels	ECM	ECM	1982
	Rejoicing	ECM	ECM	1983
	First Circle	ECM	ECM	1984
	The Falcon and the Snowman	ECM	ECM	1984
	Song X	Geffen	Geffen	1985
	Still Life (Talking)	Geffen	Geffen	1987
	Letter from Home	n/a	Geffen	1989
	Question and Answer	n/a	Geffen	1989
	Blue Asphalt	*n/a*	*Jazz Door*	*1991*
	Secret Story	n/a	Geffen	1992
	Zero Tolerance for Silence	n/a	Geffen	1992
	In Concert	*n/a*	*Jazz Door*	*1993*
	Unity Village	*n/a*	*Jazz Door*	*1993*
	Road to You—Live in Europe	n/a	Geffen	1993
	This World	*n/a*	*Octopus*	*1994*
	We Live Here	n/a	Geffen	1994
	Quartet	n/a	Geffen	1996
	Autumn Leaves	*n/a*	*Oxygen*	*1996*
	Sign of Four	n/a	Knitting Factory	1997
	Imaginary Day	n/a	Warner Bros.	1997
STEPS	Step by Step	Denon	Denon	1981
	Smokin' in the Pit: Live	Denon	Denon	1981
	Paradox	Denon	Denon	1982

Artist's Name	Album Title	LP Record Label	CD Label	Original Release
STEPS AHEAD	Steps Ahead	Elektra	Elektra	1983
	Modern Times	Elektra	Elektra	1985
	Magnetic	Elektra	Elektra	1986
	Live in Tokyo	n/a	NYC	1986
STEPS AHEAD	NYC	n/a	NYC	1989
	Yin-Yang	n/a	NYC	1992
	Vibe	n/a	NYC	1994
MIKE MAINIERI	Live at Seventh Avenue South	n/a	NYC	1996
	An American Diary	n/a	NYC	1996
	An American Diary: The Dreamings	n/a	NYC	1997
SCOTT HENDERSON & TRIBAL TECH	Spears	Passport	Passport	1985
	Dr. Hee	Relativity	Relativity	1987
	Nomad	Relativity	Relativity	1988
TRIBAL TECH	Tribal Tech	n/a	Relativity	1990
	Illicit	n/a	Blue Moon	1992
	Face First	n/a	Blue Moon	1993
	Reality Check	n/a	Blue Moon	1995
SCOTT HENDERSON	Dog Party	n/a	Blue Moon	1994
	Tore Down House	n/a	Bluemoon	1997
GARY WILLIS	No Sweat	n/a	Alchemy	1996
TOM COSTER	TC	Fantasy	n/a	1981
	Ivory Expedition	Fantasy	n/a	1983
	Did Jah Miss Me	Headfirst	n/a	1989
	From Me to You	Headfirst	n/a	1990
	Gotcha	n/a	JVC	1991
	Let's Set the Record Straight	n/a	JVC	1993
	The Forbidden Zone	n/a	JVC	1994
	Back to the Streets	n/a	JVC	1995

Artist's Name	Album Title	LP Record Label	CD Label	Original Release
STEVE SMITH'S VITAL INFORMATION	Vital Information	Columbia	n/a	1983
	Orion	Columbia	n/a	1984
	Global Beat	Columbia	n/a	1988
	Fiafiaga	Columbia	Columbia	1988
	Vitalive!	n/a	Verabra	1990
	Easier Said Than Done	n/a	Manhattan	1992
	Ray of Hope	n/a	Verabra	1996
FRANK GAMBALE	Live	n/a	Legato	1989
	Thunder from Down Under	n/a	JVC	1990
	Note worker	n/a	JVC	1991
	The Great Explorers	n/a	JVC	1993
	Passages	n/a	JVC	1994
	Thinking Out Loud	n/a	JVC	1995
MVP—FRANK GAMBALE/ ALAN HOLDSWORTH	Truth in Shredding	n/a	Legato	1991
MVP	Centrifugal Funk	n/a	Legato	1992
ALAN HOLDSWORTH	Velvet Darkness	Columbia	n/a	1977
	Road Games	Warner Bros.	Cream	1983
	Metal Fatigue	Enigma	Cream	1985
	I.O.U.	Enigma	Cream	1985
	Atavachron	Enigma	Cream	1986
	Sand	Restless	Cream	1987
	Secrets	Intima	Cream	1989
	Live in Japan 1985	n/a	Four Aces	1990
	Wardenclyffe Tower	n/a	Cream	1992
	Live Secrets	n/a	All of Us	1993
	Hard Hat Area	n/a	Cream	1993
	Alien Hand	n/a	Worthless	1996
	None Too Soon	n/a	Cream	1996

Artist's Name	Album Title	LP Record Label	CD Label	Original Release
JOHANNSEN, JOHANNSEN & HOLDSWORTH				
GONGZILLA	Heavy Machinery	n/a	Heptagon	1996
	Suffer	n/a	USG	1995
	Thrive	n/a	USG	1997
ANDREA MARCELLI	Oneness	n/a	Lipstick	1993
CHAD WACKERMAN	Forty Reasons	n/a	CMP	1991
	In View	n/a	CMP	1993
MICHAEL SHRIEVE	Fascination	n/a	CMP	1994
	Two Doors	n/a	CMP	1995
MICK GOODRICK	Biorhythms	n/a	CMP	1990
FLIM & THE BB'S	Tricycle	DMP	DMP	1983
KENWOOD DENNARD	Just Advance	n/a	DMP	1992
WAYNE KRANTZ	Signals	n/a	Enja	1990
	Long to Be Loose	n/a	Enja	1993
	Two Drink Minimum	n/a	Enja	1995
MITCH WATKINS	Underneath it All	n/a	Enja	1989
	Curves	n/a	Enja	1990
	Strings with Wings	n/a	Enja	1992
	Humhead	n/a	Dos	1995
BARBARA DENNERLEIN	Straight Ahead	n/a	Enja	1988
	Hot Stuff	n/a	Enja	1990
	That's Me	n/a	Blue moon	1992
	Take Off!	n/a	Verve	1995
	Junkanoo	n/a	Verve	1997
LENNIE STERN	Clairvoyant	Passport	Passport	1986
	The Next Day	Passport	Passport	1987
	Secrets	n/a	Enja	1989
	Closer to the Light	n/a	Enja	1990
	Ten Songs	n/a	Lipstick	1992

Artist's Name	Album Title	LP Record Label	CD Label	Original Release
	Like One	n/a	Lipstick	1993
	Words	n/a	Lipstick	1995
TERJE RYPDAL	Whenever I Seem to Be Far Away	ECM	ECM	1974
	Odyssey	ECM	ECM	1975
	After the Rain	ECM	ECM	1976
	Waves	ECM	ECM	1977
	Rypdal, Vitous, DeJohnette	ECM	ECM	1978
	Descendre	ECM	ECM	1979
	To Be Continued	ECM	ECM	1981
	Eos	ECM	ECM	1983
	Chaser	ECM	ECM	1985
	Blue	ECM	ECM	1986
	The Singles Collection	ECM	ECM	1988
	If Mountains Could Sing	n/a	ECM	1995
	Skywards	n/a	ECM	1997
JAN GARBAREK	The Esoteric Circle	Flying Dutchman	n/a	1969
	Sart	ECM	ECM	1971
	Photo with Blue Sky	ECM	ECM	1978
	Eventyr	ECM	ECM	1980
	Paths Prints	ECM	ECM	1981
	Wayfarer	ECM	ECM	1983
	It's Okay to Listen to the Grey Voices	ECM	ECM	1984
DAVID TORN	Best Laid Plans	ECM	ECM	1985
	Cloud About Mercury	ECM	ECM	1987
	Tripping Over God	n/a	CMP	1994
	What Means Solid Traveller	n/a	CMP	1995
EBERHARD WEBER	Yellow Fields	ECM	ECM	1975
	Silent Feet	ECM	ECM	1977
KAZUMI WATANABE	Mermaid Boulevard	Inner City	n/a	1978

Artist's Name	Album Title	LP Record Label	CD Label	Original Release
KAZUMI WATANABE	Mobo Vol. 1	Gramavision	Gramavision	1983
	Mobo Vol. 2	Gramavision	Gramavision	1984
	To Chi Ka	Denon	Denon	1984
	Mobo Splash	Gramavision	Gramavision	1985
	Spice of Life	Gramavision	Gramavision	1987
	Spice of Life Too	Gramavision	Gramavision	1988
	Kilowatt	Gramavision	Gramavision	1989
	Pandora	n/a	Gramavision	1992
NGUYEN LE	Miracles	n/a	Musidisc	1990
	Zanzibar	n/a	Musidisc	1992
	Million Waves	n/a	ACT	1995
	Tales from Vietnam	n/a	ACT	1995
	Three Trios	n/a	ACT	1997
KOINONIA	Pilgrim's Progression	n/a	Maxus	1991
UZEB	Fast Emotion	Cream	Cream	1982
	You Be Easy	Cream	Cream	1983
	Live in Bracknell	Cream	Cream	1984
	Between the Lines	Cream	Cream	1985
	Absolutely Live	Cream	Cream	1986
	Live in Europe	Cream	Cream	1988
	Noisy Nights	Cream	Cream	1988
	Club	Cream	Cream	1989
	World Tour '90	n/a	Cream	1991
ALAIN CARON	Le Band	n/a	Cream	1993
	Rhythm 'n Jazz	n/a	Cream	1995
SIXUN	Live	n/a	Bleu Citron	1989
	L'Eau de La	n/a	Bleu Citron	1990
	Nomads' Land	n/a	Emarcy	1993
LOUIS WINSBERG	Appassionata	n/a	Kid	1989

Artist's Name	Album Title	LP Record Label	CD Label	Original Release
	Camino	n/a	Bleu Citron	1990
MICHEL CUSSON	Wild Unit 2	n/a	JMS	1994
J.K. SPECIAL	J.K. Special	n/a	Lipstick	1992
LET'S BE GENEROUS	Let's Be Generous	n/a	CMP	1991
MARC RIBOT	Rootless Compositions	n/a	Disques du Crepuscule	1990
	Requiem for What's His Name	n/a	Disques du Crepuscule	1992d

CHAPTER 13

Make a Jazz Noise Here

Artist's Name	Album Title	LP Record Label	CD Label	Original Release
MATERIAL	Temporary Music	Red	n/a	1980
	Discourse/Slow Murder	Red	n/a	1980
	Memory Serves	Celluloid	Celluloid	1981
	Temporary Music 2	Red	n/a	1981
	One Down	Elektra	Restless	1982
	Seven Souls	Virgin	Virgin	1989
	The Third power	n/a	Axiom	1991
	Live at Soundscape	n/a	DIW	1991
	Temporary music 1979–1981	n/a	Restless	1992
	Mantra	n/a	Axiom	1993
	Live in Japan	n/a	Restless	1993
	Hallucination Engine	n/a	Axiom	1994
BILL LASWELL	Baselines	Celluloid	Celluloid	1984
	Material and Friends	Celluloid	Celluloid	1984
BILL LASWELL & PETER BROTZMAN	Lowlife	Celluloid	Celluloid	1987
BILL LASWELL	Hear No Evil	n/a	Virgin Venture	1988
	Deconstruction	n/a	Restless	1993
	Oscillations	n/a	Sub Rosa	1996

Artist's Name	Album Title	LP Record Label	CD Label	Original Release
MASSACRE	Killing Time	Celluloid	Recommended (Swiss)	1982
DEADLINE	Down by Law	n/a	Celluloid	1985
BERNIE WORRELL	Funk of Ages	n/a	Gramavision	1990
	Blacktronic Science	n/a	Gramavision	1994
	Pieces of Woo	n/a	CMP	1994
SONNY SHARROCK	Guitar	Enemy	Enemy	1986
SONNY SHARROCK & NICKY SKOPELITIS	Faith Moves	n/a	CMP	1991
SONNY SHARROCK	Ask the Ages	n/a	Axiom	1991
	Into Another Life	n/a	Enemy	1996
PRAXIS	Transmutation	n/a	Axiom	1992
	Sacrifist	n/a	Subharmonic	1994
	Metatron	n/a	Subharmonic	1994
BAHIA BLACK	Ritual Beating System	n/a	Axiom	1992
ANTON FIER	Dreamspeed	n/a	Axiom	1993
NICKY SKOPELITIS	Ekstasis	n/a	Axiom	1993
PAINKILLER	Rituals Live in Japan	n/a	Toy's Factory (Japan)	1993
	Execution Ground	n/a	Toy's Factory (Japan)	1994
AUTOMATON	Points of Order	n/a	Strata	1995
THIRD RAIL	South Delta Space Age	n/a	Antilles	1995
KIP HANRAHAN	Coup De Tête	American Clave	American Clave	1980
	Desire Develops an Edge	American Clave	American Clave	1982
	Conjure	American Clave	American Clave	1983
	Vertical's Currency	American Clave	American Clave	1984
	Days and Nights of Blue Luck Inverted	American Clave	American Clave	1987
	Cab Calloway Stands In for the Moon	American Clave	American Clave	1988
	Tenderness	n/a	American Clave	1990
	Exotica	n/a	American Clave	1992
	A Thousand Nights and a Night	n/a	American Clave	1996

Artist's Name	Album Title	LP Record Label	CD Label	Original Release
THE MOTHERS OF INVENTION	Freak Out	Verve	Rykodisc	1966
	Absolutely Free	Verve	Rykodisc	1967
	We're Only in It for the Money	Verve	Rykodisc	1968
FRANK ZAPPA	Lumpy Gravy	Verve	Rykodisc	1968
THE MOTHERS OF INVENTION	Uncle Meat	Bizarre	Rykodisc	1969
FRANK ZAPPA	Hot Rats	Bizarre	Rykodisc	1969
THE MOTHERS OF INVENTION	Burnt Weeny Sandwich	Bizarre	Rykodisc	1969
	Weasels Ripped My Flesh	Bizarre	Rykodisc	1970
	Chunga's Revenge	Bizarre	Rykodisc	1970
	Fillmore East 1971	Bizarre	Rykodisc	1971
	Just Another Band from LA	Bizarre	Rykodisc	1972
FRANK ZAPPA	Waka/Jawaka	Bizarre	Rykodisc	1972
	The Grand Wazoo	DiscReet	Rykodisc	1972
	Over-Nite Sensation	DiscReet	Rykodisc	1973
	Apostrophe	DiscReet	Rykodisc	1974
	Roxy and Elsewhere	DiscReet	Rykodisc	1974
	One Size Fits All	DiscReet	Rykodisc	1975
	Bongo Fury	DiscReet	Rykodisc	1975
	Zoot Allures	Warner Bros.	Rykodisc	1976
	Zappa in New York	DiscReet	Rykodisc	1978
	Studio Tan	DiscReet	Rykodisc	1978
	Sleep Dirt	DiscReet	Rykodisc	1978
	Sheik Yerbouti	Zappa	Rykodisc	1979
	Joe's Garage Acts I, II & III	Barking Pumpkin	Rykodisc	1979
	Tinsel Town Rebellion	Barking Pumpkin	Rykodisc	1979
	Shut Up 'n' Play Yer Guitar	Barking Pumpkin	Rykodisc	1981
	You Are What You Is	Barking Pumpkin	Rykodisc	1981
	Ship Arriving Too Late to Save a Drowning Man	Barking Pumpkin	Rykodisc	1982
	The Man from Utopia	Barking Pumpkin	Rykodisc	1983

Artist's Name	Album Title	LP Record Label	CD Label	Original Release
FRANK ZAPPA	Baby Snakes	Barking Pumpkin	Rykodisc	1983
	Them Or Us	Barking Pumpkin	Rykodisc	1984
	Thing Fish	Barking Pumpkin	Rykodisc	1984
	Frank Zappa Meets the Mothers of Prevention	Barking Pumpkin	Rykodisc	1985
	Does Humor Belong in Music?	EMI	Rykodisc	1986
	Jazz from Hell	Barking Pumpkin	Rykodisc	1987
	Guitar	Barking Pumpkin	Rykodisc	1988
	Broadway the Hard Way	Barking Pumpkin	Rykodisc	1988
	The Best Band You Never Heard in Your Life	n/a	Rykodisc	1991
	Make a Jazz Noise Here	n/a	Rykodisc	1991
	Playground Psychotics	n/a	Rykodisc	1992
	Ahead of Their Time	n/a	Rykodisc	1993
	You Can't Do That on Stage Anymore Vol. 1	n/a	Rykodisc	1988
	You Can't Do That on Stage Anymore Vol. 2	n/a	Rykodisc	1988
	You Can't Do That on Stage Anymore Vol. 3	n/a	Rykodisc	1989
	You Can't Do That on Stage Anymore Vol. 4	n/a	Rykodisc	1991
	You Can't Do That on Stage Anymore Vol. 5	n/a	Rykodisc	1992
	You Can't Do That on Stage Anymore Vol. 6	n/a	Rykodisc	1992
	Lost Episodes	n/a	Rykodisc	1996
	Lather	n/a	Rykodisc	1996

Author's Note: The following album reached me too late to include in the text, but represents a persuasive argument for presenting Zappa's compositions in a jazz context.

ED PALERMO BIG BAND	Play the Music of Frank Zappa	n/a	Astor Place	1997
CAPTAIN BEEFHEART	Trout Mask Replica	Bizarre	Reprise	1969
	Lick My Decals Off Baby	Straight	Warner Bros.	1970
SANTANA	Santana	CBS	Columbia	1969
	Abraxas	CBS	Columbia	1970
	Santana with Buddy Miles Live	CBS	Castle	1971
	Santana 3	CBS	Columbia	1972

Artist's Name	Album Title	LP Record Label	CD Label	Original Release
	Caravanserai	CBS	Columbia	1972
	Welcome	CBS	Castle	1974
	Lotus	CBS	Columbia	1975
	Borboletta	CBS	Columbia	1974
	Viva Santana	CBS	Columbia	1988
	Milagro	n/a	Polydor	1992
	Dance of the Rainbow Spirit (3 CD set)	n/a	Columbia	1996
CARLOS SANTANA & JOHN McLAUGHLIN	Love Devotion and Surrender	CBS	Columbia	1973
CARLOS SANTANA WITH ALICE COLTRANE	Illuminations	CBS	Columbia	1974
CARLOS SANTANA	Oneness	CBS	n/a	1979
	Golden Reality	CBS	n/a	1979
	Swing of Delight	CBS	Columbia	1980
	Havana Moon	CBS	n/a	1983
	Blues for Salvador	CBS	Columbia	1987
	Brothers	n/a	Polydor	1994
LOUIS GASCA	For Those Who Chant	Blue Thumb	n/a	1972
MALO	Malo	Warner Bros.	n/a	1972
	Dos	Warner Bros.	n/a	1972
	Evolution	Warner Bros.	n/a	1973
	Ascension	Warner Bros.	n/a	1974
CALDERA	Caldera	Capitol	n/a	1976
	Sky Islands	Capitol	n/a	1977
	Time and Chance	Capitol	n/a	1978
	Dreamer	Capitol	n/a	1979
WAR	War	United Artists	Rhino	1971
	All Day Music	United Artists	Rhino	1972
	The World Is a Ghetto	United Artists	Rhino	1973

Artist's Name	Album Title	LP Record Label	CD Label	Original Release
WAR	Deliver the World	United Artists	Rhino	1973
	Live	United Artists	Rhino	1974
	Platinum Jazz	MCA	n/a	1979
AZYMUTH	Depart	ECM	n/a	1980
	Light as a Feather	Milestone	n/a	1980
	Outbro	Milestone	n/a	1980
	Carnival	n/a	Far Out	1996
AZTECA	Azteca	CBS	n/a	1972
	Pyramid of the Sun	CBS	n/a	1973
IRAKERE	Irakere	CBS	n/a	1978
	Irakere II	CBS	n/a	1979
	Live at Ronnie Scott's 1991	n/a	World Pacific	1993
AIRTO MOREIRA	Free	CTI	n/a	1972
	Fingers	CTI	n/a	1973
	Virgin Land	CTI	n/a	1974
	Identity	Arista	n/a	1975
	Promises of the Sun	Arista	n/a	1976
	I'm Fine	Warner Bros.	n/a	1977
	Three Way Mirror	Reference	n/a	1985
	The Other Side of This	n/a	Rykodisc	1992
FOURTH WORLD	Fourth World	n/a	Jazz House	1992
	Fourth World	n/a	B&W	1993
	Encounters of the Fourth World	n/a	B&W	1995
	Live in South Africa	n/a	B&W	1996
RALPH MacDONALD	The Sound of a Drum	Marlin	n/a	1978
	The Path	Marlin	n/a	1979
VARIOUS ARTISTS	New Yorica	n/a	Soul Jazz	1996
MICHEL CAMILO	Why Not	Evidence	Evidence	1985
	Suntan	Evidence	Evidence	1986

Artist's Name	Album Title	LP Record Label	CD Label	Original Release
	Michel Camilo	Portrait	Portrait	1988
	On Fire	Epic	Epic	1989
	On the Other hand	Epic	Epic	1990
	Rendezvous	Columbia	Columbia	1993
	One More Once	Columbia	Columbia	1994
STEELY DAN	Can't Buy a Thrill	ABC	ABC	1972
	Countdown to Ecstasy	ABC	ABC	1973
	Reeling through the Years—Live 1974	*n/a*	*Living Legend*	*1974*
	Pretzel Logic	ABC	ABC	1974
	Katy Lied	ABC	ABC	1975
	The Royal Scam	ABC	ABC	1976
	Aja	ABC	ABC	1977
	Gaucho	ABC	ABC	1980
	Alive in America	n/a	Giant	1995
	Doing It Live 1993	*n/a*	*Kiss the Stone*	*1996*
DONALD FAGEN	The Nightfly	Warner Bros.	Warner Bros.	1982
	Kamikiriad	n/a	Reprise	1995
HOOPS MCANN BAND	Plays the Music of Steely Dan	n/a	MCA	1991
MICHAEL FRANKS	The Art of Tea	Reprise	Warner Bros.	1976
	Sleeping Gypsy	Reprise	Warner Bros.	1977
	Burchfield Nines	Warner Bros.	Warner Bros.	1977
	Tiger in the rain	Warner Bros.	Warner Bros.	1979
	One Bad Habit	Warner Bros.	Warner Bros.	1980
STING	Dream of the Blue Turtles	A&M	A&M	1985
	Bring on the Night	A&M	A&M	1986
	Nothing like the Sun	A&M	A&M	1987
	The Soul Cages	A&M	A&M	1991
	Ten Summoners' Tales	n/a	A&M	1993
	Mercury Falling	n/a	A&M	1996

Artist's Name	Album Title	LP Record Label	CD Label	Original Release
BOB BELDEN	Treasure Island	Sunnyside	Sunnyside	1989
	Straight to My Heart: The Music of Sting	n/a	Blue Note	1991
	When Doves Cry: The Music of Prince	n/a	Blue Note	1993
	Turandot	n/a	Blue Note Japan	1993
	Prince Jazz	n/a	Blue Note Japan	1996

CHAPTER 14
Thundering Herds

Artist's Name	Album Title	LP Record Label	CD Label	Original Release
QUINCY JONES	Walking in Space	A&M	A&M	1969
	Gula Matari	A&M	A&M	1970
	Smackwaterjack	A&M	A&M	1971
	Mellow Madness	A&M	A&M	1972
	You've Got It Bad, Girl	A&M	A&M	1973
	Body Heat	A&M	A&M	1974
	The Dude	A&M	A&M	1976
	Back on the Block	n/a	Warner Bros.	1990
	Q's Juke Joint	n/a	Warner Bros.	1995
STAN KENTON	Live at Redlands University	Creative World	n/a	1970
	Live at Brigham Young University	Creative World	n/a	1971
	Birthday in Britain	Creative World	n/a	1972
	Stan Kenton Today: Live in London	Creative World	n/a	1972
	Journey Into Capricorn	Creative World	n/a	1976
WOODY HERMAN	Light My Fire	Cadet	n/a	1968
	Heavy Exposure	Cadet	n/a	1969
	Woody	Cadet	n/a	1970
	Brand New	Fantasy	n/a	1971
	The Raven Speaks	Fantasy	OJC	1972

Artist's Name	Album Title	LP Record Label	CD Label	Original Release
	Giant Steps	Fantasy	n/a	1973
	Thundering Herd	Fantasy	n/a	1974
	Herd at Montreux	Fantasy	n/a	1974
	King Cobra	Fantasy	n/a	1975
	Road Father	Century	n/a	1978
	Chick, Donald, Walter & Woodrow	Century	n/a	1978
	Light My Fire (Live 1970)	n/a	Moon	1993
MAYNARD FERGUSON	MF Horn	Columbia	n/a	1970
	MF Horn 2	Columbia	n/a	1972
	MF Horn 3	Columbia	n/a	1973
	MF Horn 4 & 5	Columbia	n/a	1973
	Chameleon	Columbia	n/a	1974
	Primal Scream	Columbia	n/a	1976
	New Vintage	Columbia	n/a	1977
	Conquistador	Columbia	n/a	1978
	Carnival	Columbia	n/a	1978
	Hot	Columbia	n/a	1979
	Storm	Palo Alto	Status	1982
	Live from San Francisco	Palo Alto	Status	1983
BUDDY RICH	Swingin' New Big Band	Pacific Jazz	Pacific Jazz	1966
	Big Swing Face	Pacific Jazz	Pacific Jazz	1967
	Mercy, Mercy, Mercy	Pacific Jazz	Pacific Jazz	1968
	Take It Away!	Pacific Jazz	Pacific Jazz	1968
	Buddy and Soul	Pacific Jazz	BGO	1969
	Keep the Customer Satisfied	Pacific Jazz	BGO	1970
	Different Drummer	RCA	n/a	1971
	Live in London	RCA	n/a	1972
	Stick It!	RCA	n/a	1972
	The Roar of '74	Groove Merchant	n/a	1974

Artist's Name	Album Title	LP Record Label	CD Label	Original Release
BUDDY RICH	Very Live at Buddy's Place	Groove merchant	n/a	1974
	Big Band Machine	Groove Merchant	n/a	1975
	Plays and Plays and Plays	RCA	n/a	1977
	Class of '78	Gt. American Gramophone Co.	n/a	1977
	The Man From Jazz	PRT	n/a	1981
	Live on King Street	Cafe Records	n/a	1985
	Europe '77	n/a	Magic	1992
VARIOUS ARTISTS				
BOB MINTZER	Burnin' for Buddy	n/a	Warner Bros.	1995
	Incredible Journey	DMP	DMP	1985
	Camouflage	DMP	DMP	1986
	Spectrum	DMP	DMP	1988
	Urban Contours	DMP	DMP	1989
	I Remember Jaco	n/a	Novus	1991
	Departure	n/a	DMP	1991
	One Music	n/a	DMP	1992
	Only in New York	n/a	DMP	1994
DON ELLIS	Live at Monterey	Pacific Jazz	n/a	1966
	Live in 3 $\frac{2}{4}$ Time	Liberty	n/a	1967
	Electric Bath	Columbia	Columbia	1967
	Shock Treatment	Columbia	n/a	1968
	Autumn	Columbia	Columbia	1968
	Don Ellis Goes Underground	Columbia	n/a	1969
	Don Ellis at Fillmore	Columbia	n/a	1970
	Tears of Joy	Columbia	n/a	1971
	Connection	Columbia	n/a	1972
	Haiku	BASF	n/a	1973
	Soaring	BASF	n/a	1974
	Live at Montreux	Atlantic	n/a	1977

Artist's Name	Album Title	LP Record Label	CD Label	Original Release
CHUCK MANGIONE	Music from Other Galaxies and Planets	Atlantic	n/a	1977
	Alive!	Mercury	n/a	1972
	Land of Make Believe	Mercury	n/a	1973
	Bellavia	A&M	n/a	1975
	Chase the Clouds Away	A&M	n/a	1975
	Main Squeeze	A&M	n/a	1976
	Feels So Good	A&M	A&M	1977
	An Evening of Magic Live at the Hollywood Bowl	A&M	n/a	1978
	Children of Sanchez	A&M	n/a	1978
	Fun and Games	A&M	n/a	1979
	Tarantella	A&M	n/a	1980
	Eyes of the Veiled Temptress	CBS	Columbia	1988
GIL EVANS	Out of the Cool	Impulse	Impulse	1961
	The Individualism of	Verve	Verve	1961
	Gil Evans	Ampex	n/a	1971
	Where Flamingos Fly	Artists House	A&M	1971
	Svengali	Atlantic	ACT	1973
	Plays the Music of Jimi Hendrix	Bluebird	Bluebird	1974
	There Comes a Time	Bluebird	Bluebird	1975
	Priestess	Antilles	n/a	1977
	Little Wing	Inner City	DIW	1978
	Live at the Festival Hall 1978	RCA	n/a	1978
	Live at the Public Theatre in New York Vol. 1	Blackhawk	n/a	1980
	Live at the Public Theatre in New York Vol. 2	Blackhawk	n/a	1980
	The Rest of Gil Evans Live Festival Hall 1978	Mole	n/a	1981
	Live at Sweet Basil Vol. 1	Evidence	n/a	1984
	Live at Sweet Basil Vol. 2	Evidence	n/a	1984
	Farewell—Sweet Basil	Evidence	n/a	1985
	Bud and Bird	King Record Co.	King	1987

Artist's Name	Album Title	LP Record Label	CD Label	Original Release
GEORGE RUSSELL	Othello Ballet Suite/Electronic Organ Sonata No. 1	Flying Dutchman	Soul Note	1967
	Electronic Sonata for Souls Loved by Nature	Flying Dutchman	Soul Note	1969
	Trip to Prillargui	Soul Note	n/a	1970
	Listen to the Silence	Concept	n/a	1971
	Vertical Form V1	Soul Note	Soul Note	1976
	New York Big Band	Soul Note	Soul Note	1978
	Electronic Sonata for Souls Loved by Nature 1980	Strata East	n/a	1980
	Live in an American Time Spiral	Soul Note	Soul Note	1982
	African Game	Blue Note	n/a	1983
	So What	Blue Note	Blue Note	1987
	London Concert Vols. 1 & 2	Stash	Stash	1989
CARLA BLEY	Escalator Over the Hill	ECM	ECM	1971
	Tropic Appetites	Watt	Watt	1974
	Dinner Music	Watt	Watt	1976
	European Tour 1977	Watt	Watt	1977
	Social Studies	Watt	Watt	1980
	I Hate to Sing	Watt	Watt	1981
	Live!	Watt	Watt	1981
	Heavy heart	Watt	Watt	1983
	Night Glo	Watt	Watt	1985
	Sextet	Watt	Watt	1987
CARLA BLEY	Fleur Carnivore	Watt	Watt	1988
	The Very Big Carla Bley Big Band	Watt	Watt	1990
	Big Band Theory	Watt	Watt	1993
MICHAEL GIBBS	Michael Gibbs	Deram	n/a	1970
	Tanglewood 63	Deram	n/a	1971
	Just Ahead	Polydor	n/a	1972
	In the Public Interest	Polydor	n/a	1974

Artist's Name	Album Title	LP Record Label	CD Label	Original Release
	The Only Chrome Waterfall Orchestra	Island	Ah Um	1975
	Big Music	n/a	Venture	1988
MARIA SCHNEIDER	Evanescence	n/a	Enja	1992
	Coming About	n/a	Enja	1996
VARIOUS ARTISTS	Montreux Summit Vol. 1	Columbia	Columbia	1977
VARIOUS ARTISTS	Montreux Summit Vol. 2	Columbia	n/a	1977
VARIOUS ARTISTS	The Atlantic Family Live at Montreux	Atlantic	n/a	1978
McNEELEY/SCOFIELD/ NUSSBAUM & THE WDR BIG BAND	East Coast Blow Out	n/a	Lipstick	1991
VARIOUS ARTISTS	Rhythmstick	n/a	Castle	1991
GEORGE GRUNTZ CONCERT JAZZ BAND	Blues 'n' Dues Et Cetera	n/a	Enja	1991
	GRP All Star Big Band	n/a	GRP	1992
GRP ALL STAR BIG BAND	All Blues	n/a	GRP	1995

CHAPTER 15

On the Edge of Tomorrow

Artist's Name	Album Title	LP Record Label	CD Label	Original Release
ORNETTE COLEMAN & PRIME TIME	Dancing in Your Head	A&M	A&M	1976
	Body Meta	Artists House	Artists House	1976
ORNETTE COLEMAN	Of Human Feelings	Antilles	n/a	1979
	Opening the Caravan of Dreams	Caravan of Dreams	Caravan of Dreams	1985
	Prime Design Time Design	Caravan of Dreams	Caravan of Dreams	1985
	In All Languages	Caravan of Dreams	Caravan of Dreams	1987
	Virgin Beauty	Portrait	Portrait	1988
	Tone Dialing	n/a	Verve	1995

Artist's Name	Album Title	LP Record Label	CD Label	Original Release
RONALD SHANNON JACKSON	Eye on You	About Time	n/a	1980
	Nasty	Moers	n/a	1981
	Street Priest	Moers	n/a	1981
	Mandance	Antilles	n/a	1982
	Barbecue Dog	Antilles	n/a	1983
	Pulse	Celluloid	n/a	1984
	Decode Yourself	Island	n/a	1985
	When Colors Play	Caravan of Dreams	n/a	1986
	Texas	Caravan of Dreams	n/a	1986
	Red Warrior	Axiom	Axiom	1990
	Taboo	Venture	Venture	1990
	Ask the Ages	Axiom	Axiom	1991
	Raven Roc	n/a	DIW	1992
	What Spirit Say	n/a	DIW	1994
LAST EXIT	Last Exit	Enemy	Enemy	1986
	The Noise of Trouble	Enemy	Enemy	1986
POWER TOOLS	Strange Meeting	Antilles	n/a	1987
JAMES BLOOD ULMER	Tales of Capt. Black	Artists House	n/a	1978
	Are You Glad to Be in America?	Rough Trade	n/a	1980
	Freelancing	Columbia	n/a	1981
	Black Rock	Columbia	n/a	1982
	Odyssey	Columbia	Columbia	1983
	Part Time	Rough Trade	n/a	1984
	Got Something Good for You	Moers	Moers	1985
	America: Do You Remember the Love	Blue Note	n/a	1986
	Live at the Caravan of Dreams	Caravan of Dreams	n/a	1986
	In Touch	DIW	DIW	1988
	Blues All Night	DIW	DIW	1989
JEAN-PAUL BOURELLY	Jungle Cowboy	n/a	JMT	1991

Artist's Name	Album Title	LP Record Label	CD Label	Original Release
	Saint and Sinners	n/a	DIW	1994
	Freestyle	n/a	DIW	1994
	Tribute to Jimi	n/a	DIW	1995
	Live Fade to Cacophony	n/a	Evidence	1997
JAMALDEEN TACUMA	Show Stopper	Gramavision	Gramavision	1983
	Renaissance Man	Gramavision	Gramavision	1984
	So Tranquilizin'	Gramavision	Gramavision	1985
	Music World	Gramavision	Gramavision	1986
	Jukebox	Gramavision	Gramavision	1988
	Boss of the Bass	n/a	Gramavision	1993
	Dreamscape	n/a	DIW	1995
DEFUNKT	Defunkt	Hannibal	n/a	1980
	Thermonuclear Sweat	Hannibal	n/a	1982
	A Defunkt Anthology	Hannibal	Hannibal	1988
	Avoid the Funk	Hannibal	n/a	1988
	In America	Antilles	Antilles	1988
	Heroes	DIW	DIW	1990
	Live at the Knitting Factory	Knitting Factory Works	Knitting Factory Works	1990
	Crisis	Enemy	Enemy	1992
KELVYNATOR	Refunkanation	n/a	Enemy	1992
STEVE COLEMAN	Motherland Pulse	JMT	JMT	1985
	On the Edge of Tomorrow	JMT	JMT	1986
	World Expansion	JMT	JMT	1986
	Sine Die	Pangea	Pangea	1988
	Rhythm People	n/a	RCA Novus	1990
	Black Science	n/a	RCA Novus	1991
	Phase Space	n/a	DIW	1991
	Rhythm in Mind	n/a	RCA Novus	1991

Artist's Name	Album Title	LP Record Label	CD Label	Original Release
STEVE COLEMAN	Drop Kick	n/a	RCA Novus	1992
	The Tao of Mad Phat	n/a	RCA Novus	1993
	Def Trance beat	n/a	RCA Novus	1994
	Curves of Life	n/a	RCA	1996
	The Way of the Cipher	n/a	RCA	1996
	Myths, Modes and Means	n/a	RCA	1996
	The Sign and the Seal	n/a	RCA	1997
STRATA INSTITUTE	Cypher Syntax	n/a	JMT	1989
	Transmigration	n/a	DIW	1991
VARIOUS ARTISTS	Flashback on M-Base	n/a	JMT	1993
M-BASE COLLECTIVE	Anatomy of a Groove	n/a	DIW	1992
GREG OSBY	Greg Osby and the Sound Theatre	JMT	JMT	1987
	Mind Games	JMT	JMT	1988
	Season of Renewal	JMT	JMT	1989
	Man Talk for Moderns	n/a	Blue Note	1990
	3-D Lifestyles	n/a	Blue Note	1992
	Black Book	n/a	Blue Note	1994
GARY THOMAS	Seventh Quadrant	Enja	Enja	1987
	Code Violations	Enja	Enja	1988
	By Any Means Necessary	n/a	JMT	1989
	While the Gate Is Open	n/a	JMT	1990
	The Kold Kage	n/a	JMT	1991
	Till We Have Faces	n/a	JMT	1992
	Exiles gate	n/a	JMT	1993
	Overkill	n/a	JMT	1995
KEVIN EUBANKS	Guitarist	Elektra	Discovery	1983
	Sundance	GRP	GRP	1984
	Opening Night	GRP	GRP	1985
	Face to Face	n/a	GRP	1986

Artist's Name	Album Title	LP Record Label	CD Label	Original Release
KEVIN EUBANKS	The Heat of Heat	n/a	GRP	1987
	Shadow Prophets	n/a	GRP	1988
	The Searcher	n/a	GRP	1988
	Promise of Tomorrow	n/a	GRP	1989
	Turning Point	n/a	Blue Note	1992
	Spirit Talk	n/a	Blue Note	1993
	Spirit Talk 2	n/a	Blue Note	1994
	Karma	n/a	JMT	1990
ROBIN EUBANK	My Heart	n/a	Bellaphon	1990
GRAHAM HAYNES	The Griot's Footsteps	n/a	JMT	1994
	Transition	n/a	Verve	1995
LOST TRIBE	Lost Tribe	n/a	Windham Hill	1993
	Soulfish	n/a	High Street	1994
LONNIE PLAXICO	Plaxico	n/a	Muse	1990
CHICO FREEMAN & BRAINSTORM	The Mystical dreamer	n/a	In and Out	1989
	Sweet Explosion	n/a	In and Out	1990
	Threshold	n/a	In and Out	1993
SANTI DEBRIANO	Soldiers of Fortune	n/a	Freelance	1989
	Panamaniacs	n/a	Freelance	1993
JACK WALRATH	Neohippus	Blue Note	Blue Note	1988
	Serious Hang	n/a	Muse	1992
	Hipgnosis	n/a	TCB	1995
DAVID MURRAY	The Tip	n/a	DIW	1994
	Jug-A-Lug	n/a	DIW	1995
JACK DeJOHNETTE	The DeJohnette Complex	Prestige	OJC	1969
	Have You Heard	Epic	n/a	1970
	Sorcery	Prestige	OJC	1974
	Cosmic Chicken	Prestige	n/a	1975

Artist's Name	Album Title	LP Record Label	CD Label	Original Release
JACK DeJOHNETTE	Pictures	ECM	ECM	1976
	New Rags	ECM	ECM	1977
	New Directions	ECM	ECM	1978
	Special Edition	ECM	ECM	1979
	New Directions in Europe	ECM	ECM	1980
	Tin Can Alley	ECM	ECM	1981
	Inflation Blues	ECM	ECM	1982
	Album, Album	ECM	ECM	1984
	Zebra	MCA	MCA	1985
	Irresistible Forces	MCA	MCA	1987
	Audio-Visualscapes	MCA	MCA	1988
	Parallel Realities	n/a	MCA	1990
	Parallel Realities Live	*n/a*	*Jazz Door*	*1993*
	Earthwalk	n/a	Blue Note	1991
	Music for the Fifth World	n/a	Blue Note	1992
JOHN ABERCROMBIE	Friends	Oblivion	n/a	1971
	Timeless	ECM	ECM	1974
	Gateway	ECM	ECM	1975
	Pilgrim and the Stars	ECM	ECM	1976
	Untitled	ECM	ECM	1976
	Sargasso Sea	ECM	ECM	1976
	Cloud Dance	ECM	ECM	1976
	Gateway 2	ECM	ECM	1977
	Pictures	ECM	ECM	1977
	Characters	ECM	ECM	1978
	Arcade	ECM	ECM	1979
	Straight Flight	ECM	ECM	1979
	Abercrombie Quartet	ECM	ECM	1980
	M	ECM	ECM	1981

Artist's Name	Album Title	LP Record Label	CD Label	Original Release
	Five Years Later	ECM	ECM	1981
	Solar	Palo Alto	n/a	1982
	Drum Strum	Arch	n/a	1983
	Night	ECM	ECM	1984
	Current Events	ECM	ECM	1986
	Witchcraft	Justin Time	n/a	1986
	Getting There	ECM	ECM	1987
	John Abercrombie, Marc Johnson & Peter Erskine	ECM	ECM	1988
	Animato	ECM	ECM	1990
	While We're Young	ECM	ECM	1992
	November	ECM	ECM	1993
	Speak of the Devil	ECM	ECM	1993
	Gateway: Homecoming	ECM	ECM	1995
	Tactics	ECM	ECM	1997
BASS DESIRES	Bass Desires	ECM	ECM	1985
	Second Sight	ECM	ECM	1987
MARC JOHNSON	Right Brain Patrol	n/a	JMT	1992
THE PAUL MOTIAN TRIO	Monk in Motian	JMT	JMT	1988
	On Broadway, Vol. 1	JMT	JMT	1989
	On Broadway, Vol. 2	JMT	JMT	1990
	Bill Evans	JMT	JMT	1990
	In Tokyo	JMT	JMT	1991
	On Broadway, Vol. 3	JMT	JMT	1992
	Trioism	JMT	JMT	1994
	At the Village Vanguard	JMT	JMT	1995
PAUL MOTIAN	Paul Motian and the Electric Bebop Band	n/a	JMT	1992
	Reincarnation of a Love Bird	n/a	JMT	1994
BILL FRISELL	In Line	ECM	ECM	1982

Artist's Name	Album Title	LP Record Label	CD Label	Original Release
BILL FRISELL	Smash and Scatteration	Minor Music	Minor Music	1985
	Lookout for Hope	ECM	ECM	1988
	Before We Were Born	Elektra Musician	Elektra Musician	1989
	Is That You	Elektra Musician	Elektra Musician	1989
	Where in the World	Elektra Nonesuch	Elektra Nonesuch	1991
	Works	ECM	ECM	1991
	This Land	Elektra Nonesuch	Elektra Nonesuch	1992
	Have a Little Faith	Elektra Nonesuch	Elektra Nonesuch	1993
	Live	Gramavision	Gramavision	1994
	Go West: Music from the Films of Buster Keaton	Elektra Nonesuch	Elektra Nonesuch	1995
RON MILES	My Cruel Heart	n/a	Gramavision	1996
	Woman's Day	n/a	Gramavision	1997
WAYNE HORVITZ	Some Order, Long Understood	Black Saint	Black Saint	1982
	The New Generation	Elektra Nonesuch	Elektra Nonesuch	1985
	Nine Below Zero	Sound Aspects	Sound Aspects	1986
	Todos Santos	Sound Aspects	Sound Aspects	1988
	Miracle Mile	n/a	Elektra Nonesuch	1991
NEW YORK COMPOSERS ORCHESTRA	New York Composers Orchestra	n/a	New World	1990
	First Program in Standard Time	n/a	New World	1992
PIGPEN	V as in Victory	n/a	Avant	1993
NAKED CITY	Naked City	Nonesuch	Elektra Nonesuch	1991
	Heretic: Jeux Des Dames Cruelles	n/a	Avant	1991
	Grand Guignol	n/a	Avant	1992
	Radio	n/a	Avant	1993
	Absinthe	n/a	Avant	1993
JOHN ZORN	The Big Gundown	Elektra Nonesuch	Elektra Nonesuch	1985
	Cobra	Hat Art	hat art	1986
	Spillane	Elektra Nonesuch	Elektra Nonesuch	1987

Artist's Name	Album Title	LP Record Label	CD Label	Original Release
BOBBY PREVITE	Spy vs. Spy	Elektra Nonesuch	Elektra Nonesuch	1988
	Weather Clear, Track Fast	n/a	Enja	1991
	Claude's Late Morning	Gramavision	Gramavision	1988
	Empty Suits	n/a	Gramavision	1990
	Slay the Suitors	n/a	DIW	1996
	Close to the Pole	n/a	Enja	1996
CHRISTY DORAN	Corporate Art	n/a	JMT	1992
	What a Band	n/a	hat art	1992
BOUD DEON	Fiction and Several Days	n/a	EHP	1995
	Astronomy Made Easy	n/a	Cunieform	1997
JOHN MEDESKI AND DAVID FIUCZYNSKI	Lunar Crash	n/a	Gramavision	1994
MEDESKI, MARTIN & WOOD	Notes from the Underground	n/a	Gramavision	1992
	Its a Jungle in Here	n/a	Gramavision	1993
	Friday Afternoon in the Universe	n/a	Gramavision	1995
	Shack Man	n/a	Gramavision	1996
GROOVE COLLECTIVE	Groove Collective	n/a	Giant Step	1993
	We the People	n/a	Impulse	1996
DIRECTIONS IN GROOVE	Dig	n/a	Verve Forecast	1994
	Speakeasy	n/a	Verve Forecast	1995
RONNY JORDAN	The Antidote	n/a	Antilles	1992
US3	Hand on the Torch	n/a	Blue Note	1993
	Broadway and 52nd	n/a	Blue Note	1996
STEVE WILLIAMSON	A Waltz for Grace	n/a	Verve	1990
	Journey to Truth	n/a	Verve Forecast	1995
COURTNEY PINE	Modern Day Jazz Stories	n/a	Antilles	1995
ANDY SHEPPARD	Andy Sheppard	Antilles	Antilles	1987
	Introductions in the Dark	n/a	Antilles	1989
	Soft on the Inside	n/a	Antilles	1990
	In Co-Motion	n/a	Antilles	1991

Artist's Name	Album Title	LP Record Label	CD Label	Original Release
ANDY SHEPPARD	Rhythm Method	n/a	Blue Note	1993
	Delivery Suite	n/a	Blue Note	1994
	Moving Image	n/a	Verve	1996
JASON ROBELLO	A Clearer View	n/a	Novus	1991
ORPHY ROBINSON	When Tomorrow Comes	n/a	Blue Note	1992
	The Vibe Describes	n/a	Blue Note	1994
TONY REMY	Boof	n/a	GRP	1994
	Metamorfollow-G	n/a	New Note	1997
JEAN TOUISSANT	Life I Want	n/a	New Note	1995
JIM MULLEN	Into the 90s	n/a	SAP	1990
	Thumbs Up	Beggar's Banquet	Beggars Banquet	1983
	Soundbites	n/a	EFZ	1993
MORNINGTON LOCKETT	Mornington Lockett	n/a	EFZ	1994
LAURENCE COTTLE	Five Seasons	n/a	Cream	1993
	Live	n/a	Jazzizit	1995
HUBBARD'S CUPBOARD	Hubbard's Cupboard	Coda	Coda	1983
	Nip It in the Bud	Coda	Coda	1985
JOE HUBBARD	Vanishing Point	n/a	Music Maker	1991
ROADSIDE PICNIC	Roadside Picnic	n/a	Novus	1990
	For Madmen Only	n/a	Novus	1991
	La Famille	n/a	B&W	1995
SIMON PHILLIPS	Protocol	n/a	Food for Thought	1988
	Protocol Force Majeure	n/a	B&W	1993
GROON	Symbiosis	n/a	Lipstick	1995
CONGLOMERATE	Refusal to Comply	n/a	Dissenter	1994
	Precisely the Opposite of What We Now Know to Be True	n/a	Dissenter	1994
VARIOUS ARTISTS	Atlantic Jazz-Fusion	Atlantic	Atlantic	1986
	The Real Birth of Fusion	n/a	Columbia	1996

Artist's Name	Album Title	LP Record Label	CD Label	Original Release
	The Real Birth of Fusion 2	n/a	Columbia	1998
	Stolen Moments: Red Hot and Cool	n/a	GRP	1994
	Jazz Satellites—Electrification	n/a	Virgin	1996
	The Blue Note Remix Project	n/a	Blue Note	1996
	Blue Break Beats	n/a	Blue Note	1992
	Blue Break Beats Vol. 2	n/a	Blue Note	1993
	Blue Break Beats Vol. 3	n/a	Blue Note	1996
	Blue Note Rare Grooves	n/a	Blue Note	1996
	The Lost Grooves	n/a	Blue Note	1995
	Move to Groove: Best of 1970s Jazz Funk	n/a	Verve	1995
	Talkin' Verve: The Roots of Acid Jazz	n/a	Verve	1995
	Diggin' Deeper: The Roots of Acid Jazz	n/a	Columbia	1996
	Diggin' Deeper 2: The Roots of Acid Jazz	n/a	Columbia	1997

Discographer's Note: The DJ/media-coined genre "Acid Jazz" is little more than a glossy handle for 1990s retro funk, which, because of its close affinity with the dance floor, is a potpourri of James Brown, 1970s disco, soul, rap, easy listening, and very New Heavies, Ronnie Jordan, US3, Guru, Digable Planets, Jamiroquai, etc.

Artist's Name	Album Title	LP Record Label	CD Label	Original Release
	100% Acid Jazz	n/a	Telstar	1994
	100% Acid Jazz, Vol. 2	n/a	Telstar	1995
THE GRASSY KNOLL	The Grassy Knoll	n/a	Verve	1994
	Positive	n/a	Verve	1997
THE INTERGALACTIC MAIDEN BALLET	Gulf	n/a	Tip Toe	1994
TRANCE GROOVE	Solid Gold Easy Action	n/a	Call It Anything	1994
	Paramount	n/a	Call It Anything	1996
CHARLIE HUNTER	The Charlie Hunter Trio	n/a	Mammoth	1993
	Bing, Bing, Bing!	n/a	Blue Note	1995
	Ready Set Shango!	n/a	Blue Note	1996
	Natty Dread	n/a	Blue Note	1997
ALPHABET SOUP	Layin' Low in the Cut	n/a	Mammoth	1995

Artist's Name	Album Title	LP Record Label	CD Label	Original Release
BROUN FELLINIS	Aphrokubist Improvisations Vol. 9	n/a	Moonshine	1995
VARIOUS ARTISTS	Up and Down Club Sessions Vol. 1	n/a	Mammoth	1995
	Up and Down Club Sessions Vol. 2	n/a	Mammoth	1995
DON CHERRY	Multikulti	n/a	A&M	1990
PETER APFELBAUM'S				
HIEROGLYPHICS ENSEMBLE	Signs of Life	n/a	Antilles	1990
	Jodoji Brightness	n/a	Antilles	1992
	Luminous Charms	n/a	Gramavision	1996
JAI UTTAL	Footprints	n/a	Triloka	1993
	Monkey	n/a	Triloka	1994
TRILOK GURTU	Usfret	CMP	CMP	1989
	Living Magic	n/a	CMP	1991
	Crazy Saints	n/a	CMP	1993
	Believe	n/a	CMP	1994
	Old Habits Die Hard	n/a	CMP	1996
	The Glimpse	n/a	CMP	1997

Index to Personal Names

Index to Subjects
and Group Names

439

Index to Albums and Works

ALBUMS

WORKS